Managerial Paper P1

MANAGEMENT ACCOUNTING
PERFORMANCE EVALUATION

For exams in May 2005

Study Text

In this July 2004 new edition

- A new **user-friendly format** for easy navigation

- **Targeted topic coverage**, directly linked to CIMA's new learning outcomes and syllabus content

- Regular **fast forward** summaries emphasising the key points in each chapter

- **Exam focus points** showing you what the examiner will want you to do

- **Questions** and **quick quizzes** to test your understanding

- **Exam question bank** containing exam standard questions with answers

- A full index

BPP's **MCQ cards** and **i-Learn** and **i-Pass** products also support this paper.

FOR EXAMS IN MAY 2005

Multiple choice question cards

Multiple choice questions form a large part of the exam. To give you further practice in this style of question, we have produced a bank of **150 multiple choice question cards**, covering the syllabus. This bank contains exam style questions in a format to help you **revise on the move**.

Computer-based learning products from BPP

If you want to reinforce your studies by **interactive** learning, try BPP's **i-Learn** product, covering major syllabus areas in an interactive format. For **self-testing**, try **i-Pass,** which offers a large number of **objective test questions**, particularly useful where objective test questions form part of the exam.

See the order form at the back of this text for details of these innovative learning tools.

Virtual Campus

The Virtual Campus uses BPP's wealth of teaching experience to produce a fully **interactive** e-learning resource **delivered via the Internet**. The site offers comprehensive **tutor support** and features areas such as **study, practice, email service, revision** and **useful resources**.

Visit our website www.bpp.com/virtualcampus/cima to sample aspects of the campus free of charge.

Learning to Learn Accountancy

BPP's ground-breaking **Learning to Learn Accountancy** book is designed to be used both at the outset of your CIMA studies and throughout the process of learning accountancy. It challenges you to consider how you study and gives you helpful hints about how to approach the various types of paper which you will encounter. It can help you **get your studies both subject and exam focused**, enabling you to **acquire knowledge, practise and revise efficiently and effectively**.

The BPP Study Text

Aims of this Study Text

> To provide you with the knowledge and understanding, skills and application techniques that you need if you are to be successful in your exams

This Study Text has been written around the **Management Accounting Performance Evaluation** syllabus.

- It is **comprehensive**. It covers the syllabus content. No more, no less.

- It is written at the **right level**. Each chapter is written with CIMA's precise learning outcomes in mind.

- It is targeted to the **exam**. We have taken account of the pilot paper, guidance the examiner has given and the assessment methodology.

> To allow you to study in the way that best suits your learning style and the time you have available, by following your personal Study Plan (see page (viiii))

You may be studying at home on your own until the date of the exam, or you may be attending a full-time course. You may like to (and have time to) read every word, or you may prefer to (or only have time to) skim-read and devote the remainder of your time to question practice. Wherever you fall in the spectrum, you will find the BPP Study Text meets your needs in designing and following your personal Study Plan.

> To tie in with the other components of the BPP Effective Study Package to ensure you have the best possible chance of passing the exam (see page (vi))

Recommended period of use	Elements of the BPP Effective Study Package
From the outset and throughout	**Learning to Learn Accountancy** Read this invaluable book as you begin your studies and refer to it as you work through the various elements of the BPP Effective Study Package. It will help you to acquire knowledge, practice and revise, efficiently and effectively.
Three to twelve months before the exam	**Study Text and i-Learn** Use the Study Text to acquire knowledge, understanding, skills and the ability to apply techniques. Use BPP's **i-Learn** product to reinforce your learning.
Throughout	**Virtual Campus** Study, practise, revise and take advantage of other useful resources with BPP's fully interactive e-learning site with comprehensive tutor support.
Throughout	**Big Picture Posters** Display these posters where you're studying and give yourself a feel for the overall shape of the paper and the connections between syllabus areas. Examiners have stressed that you will need to be able to link up different areas when you take the exam. The visual stimulation the posters provide will help you remember the key areas of the syllabus.
Throughout	**MCQ cards and i-Pass** Revise your knowledge and ability to apply techniques, as well as practising this key exam question format, with 150 multiple choice questions. **i-Pass**, our computer-based testing package, provides objective test questions in a variety of formats and is ideal for self-assessment.
One to six months before the exam	**Practice & Revision Kit** Try the numerous examination-format questions, for which there are realistic suggested solutions prepared by BPP's own authors. Then attempt the two mock exams.
From three months before the exam until the last minute	**Passcards** Work through these short, memorable notes which are focused on what is most likely to come up in the exam you will be sitting.
One to six months before the exam	**Success CDs** The CDs cover the vital elements of your syllabus in less than 90 minutes per subject. They also contain exam hints to help you fine tune your strategy.

Help yourself study for your CIMA exams

Exams for professional bodies such as CIMA are very different from those you have taken at college or university. You will be under **greater time pressure before** the exam — as you may be combining your study with work. There are many different ways of learning and so the BPP Study Text offers you a number of different tools to help you through. Here are some hints and tips: they are not plucked out of the air, but **based on research and experience**. (You don't need to know that long-term memory is in the same part of the brain as emotions and feelings - but it's a fact anyway.)

The right approach

1 The right attitude

Believe in yourself	Yes, there is a lot to learn. Yes, it is a challenge. But thousands have succeeded before and you can too.
Remember why you're doing it	Studying might seem a grind at times, but you are doing it for a reason: to advance your career.

2 The right focus

Read through the Syllabus and learning outcomes	These tell you what you are expected to know and are supplemented by Exam focus points in the text.
Study the Exam Paper section	The pilot paper is likely to be a reasonable guide to what you should expect in the exam.

3 The right method

The whole picture	You need to grasp the detail - but keeping in mind how everything fits into the whole picture will help you understand better. • The **Introduction** of each chapter puts the material in context. • The **Syllabus content, Learning outcomes** and **Exam focus points** show you what you need to **grasp**. BPP's Big Picture Posters will help you see the links here.
In your own words	To absorb the information (and to practise your written communication skills), it helps to **put it into your own words**. • **Take notes.** • Answer the **questions** in each chapter. You will practise your written communication skills, which become increasingly important as you progress through your CIMA exams. • Draw **mindmaps**. • Try **'teaching' a subject** to a colleague or friend.
Give yourself cues to jog your memory	The BPP Study Text uses **bold** to **highlight key points**. • Try **colour coding** with a highlighter pen. • Write **key points** on cards.

4   **The right review**

Review, review, review	It is a **fact** that regularly reviewing a topic in summary form can **fix it in your memory**. Because **review** is so important, the BPP Study Text helps you to do so in many ways.
	• **Chapter roundups** summarise the 'fast forward' key points in each chapter. Use them to recap each study session.
	• The **Quick quiz** is another review technique you can use to ensure that you have grasped the essentials.
	• Go through the **Examples** in each chapter a second or third time.

Developing your personal Study Plan

BPP's **Learning to Learn Accountancy** book emphasises the need to prepare (and use) a study plan. Planning and sticking to the plan are key elements of learning success.
There are four steps you should work through.

Step 1   **How do you learn?**

First you need to be aware of your style of learning. The BPP **Learning to Learn Accountancy** book commits a chapter to this **self-discovery**. What types of intelligence do you display when learning? You might be advised to brush up on certain study skills before launching into this Study Text.

BPP's **Learning to Learn Accountancy** book helps you to identify what intelligences you show more strongly and then details how you can tailor your study process to your preferences. It also includes handy hints on how to develop intelligences you exhibit less strongly, but which might be needed as you study accountancy.

Are you a **theorist** or are you more **practical**? If you would rather get to grips with a theory before trying to apply it in practice, you should follow the study sequence on page (ix). If the reverse is true (you like to know why you are learning theory before you do so), you might be advised to flick through Study Text chapters and look at examples, case studies and questions (Steps 8, 9 and 10 in the **suggested study sequence**) before reading through the detailed theory.

Step 2   **How much time do you have?**

Work out the time you have available per week, given the following.

- The standard you have set yourself
- The time you need to set aside later for work on the Practice & Revision Kit and Passcards
- The other exam(s) you are sitting
- Very importantly, practical matters such as work, travel, exercise, sleep and social life

Hours

Note your time available in box A.   A [   ]

BPP)))
PROFESSIONAL EDUCATION

Step 3   **Allocate your time**

- Take the time you have available per week for this Study Text shown in box A, multiply it by the number of weeks available and insert the result in box B.   B [   ]

- Divide the figure in box B by the number of chapters in this text and insert the result in box C.   C [   ]

Remember that this is only a rough guide. Some of the chapters in this book are longer and more complicated than others, and you will find some subjects easier to understand than others.

Step 4   **Implement**

Set about studying each chapter in the time shown in box C, following the key study steps in the order suggested by your particular learning style.

This is your personal **Study Plan**. You should try and combine it with the study sequence outlined below. You may want to modify the sequence a little (as has been suggested above) to adapt it to your **personal style**.

BPP's **Learning to Learn Accountancy** gives further guidance on developing a study plan, and deciding where and when to study.

Suggested study sequence

It is likely that the best way to approach this Study Text is to tackle the chapters in the order in which you find them. Taking into account your individual learning style, you could follow this sequence.

Key study steps	Activity
Step 1 **Topic list**	Each numbered topic is a numbered section in the chapter.
Step 2 **Introduction**	This gives you the big picture in terms of the context of the chapter, the content you will cover, and the learning outcomes the chapter assesses. In other words, it sets your objectives for study.
Step 3 **Knowledge brought forward boxes**	In these we highlight information and techniques that it is assumed you have 'brought forward' with you from your earlier studies. If there are topics which have changed recently due to legislation for example, these topics are explained in more detail.
Step 4 **Fast forward**	Fast forward boxes give you a quick summary of the content of each of the main chapter sections. They are listed together in the roundup at the end of each chapter to provide you with an overview of the contents of the whole chapter.
Step 5 **Explanations**	Proceed methodically through the chapter, reading each section thoroughly and making sure you understand.
Step 6 **Key terms and Exam focus points**	• Key terms can often earn you *easy marks* if you state them clearly and correctly in an appropriate exam answer (and they are highlighted in the index at the back of the text). • Exam focus points give you a good idea of how we think the examiner intends to examine certain topics.
Step 7 **Note taking**	Take brief notes, if you wish. Avoid the temptation to copy out too much. Remember that being able to put something into your own words is a sign of being able to understand it. If you find you cannot explain something you have read, read it again before you make the notes.

ix

Key study steps	Activity
Step 8 **Examples**	Follow each through to its solution very carefully.
Step 9 **Case studies**	Study each one, and try to add flesh to them from your own experience. They are designed to show how the topics you are studying come alive (and often come unstuck) in the real world.
Step 10 **Questions**	Make a very good attempt at each one.
Step 11 **Answers**	Check yours against ours, and make sure you understand any discrepancies.
Step 12 **Chapter roundup**	Work through it carefully, to make sure you have grasped the significance of all the fast forward points.
Step 13 **Quick quiz**	When you are happy that you have covered the chapter, use the Quick quiz to check how much you have remembered of the topics covered and to practise questions in a variety of formats.
Step 14 **Question(s) in the Exam question bank**	Either at this point, or later when you are thinking about revising, make a full attempt at the Question(s) suggested at the very end of the chapter. You can find these at the end of the Study Text, along with the Answers so you can see how you did. We highlight those that are introductory, and those which are of the standard you would expect to find in an exam.
Step 15 **Objective test questions**	Use the bank of OTs at the back of this Study Text to practise, and to determine how much of the Study Text you have absorbed. If you have bought the MCQ cards or i-Pass, use these too.

Short of time: Skim study technique?

You may find you simply do not have the time available to follow all the key study steps for each chapter, however you adapt them for your particular learning style. If this is the case, follow the **skim study** technique below (the icons in the Study Text will help you to do this).

- Study the chapters in the order you find them in the Study Text.
- For each chapter:

    - Follow the key study steps 1-3

    - Skim-read through step 5, looking out for the points highlighted in the fast forward boxes (step 4)

    - Jump to step 12

    - Go back to step 6

    - Follow through steps 8 and 9

    - Prepare outline answers to questions (steps 10/11)

    - Try the Quick quiz (step 13), following up any items you can't answer

    - Do a plan for the Question (step 14), comparing it against our answers

    - You should probably still follow step 7 (note-taking), although you may decide simply to rely on the BPP Passcards for this.

Moving on...

However you study, when you are ready to embark on the practice and revision phase of the BPP Effective Study Package, you should still refer back to this Study Text, both as a source of **reference** (you should find the index particularly helpful for this) and as a way to **review** (the Fast forwards, Chapter roundups and Quick quizzes help you here).

And remember to keep careful hold of this Study Text – you will find it invaluable in your work.

More advice on Study Skills can be found in BPP's **Learning to Learn Accountancy** book.

Syllabus and learning outcomes

The syllabus comprises:

Topic and Study Weighting

A	Cost Accounting Systems	25%
B	Standard Costing	25%
C	Budgeting	30%
D	Control and Performance Measurement of Responsibility Centres	20%

Learning aims

Students should be able to:

- Apply both traditional and contemporary approaches to cost accounting in a variety of contexts and evaluate the impact of "modern" data processing and processing technologies such as MRP, ERP and JIT;

- Explain and apply the principles of standard costing, calculate variances in a variety of contexts and critically evaluate the worth of standard costing in the light of contemporary criticisms;

- Develop budgets using both traditional and contemporary techniques, evaluate both interactive and diagnostic uses of budgets in a variety of contexts and discuss the issues raised by those that advocate techniques 'beyond budgeting';

- Prepare appropriate financial statements for cost, profit and investment center managers, calculate appropriate financial performance indicators, assess the impact of alternative transfer pricing policies and discuss the behavioural consequences of management control systems based on responsibility accounting, decentralisation and delegation.

Learning outcomes and Syllabus content

A – Cost Accounting systems – 25%

Learning outcomes

On completion of their studies students should be able to:

(i) compare and contrast marginal and absorption costing methods in respect of profit reporting and stock valuation;

(ii) apply marginal and absorption costing approaches in job, batch and process environments;

(iii) prepare ledger accounts according to context: marginal or absorption based in job, batch or process environments, including work-in-progress and related accounts such as production overhead control account and abnormal loss account;

(iv) explain the origins of throughput accounting as 'super variable costing' and its application as a variant of marginal or variable cost accounting;

(v) apply standard costing methods within costing systems and demonstrate the reconciliation of budgeted and actual profit margins;

(vi)   compare activity-based costing with traditional marginal and absorption costing methods and evaluate its potential as a system of cost accounting;

(vii)   explain the role of MRP and ERP systems in supporting standard costing systems, calculating variances and facilitating the posting of ledger entries;

(viii) evaluate the impact of just-in-time manufacturing methods on cost accounting and the use of 'back-flush accounting' when work-in-progress stock is minimal.

Syllabus content

(1)   Marginal (or variable) costing as a system of profit reporting and stock valuation.

(2)   Absorption costing as a system of profit reporting and stock valuation.

(3)   Throughput accounting as a system of profit reporting and stock valuation.

(4)   Activity-based costing as a potential system of profit reporting and stock valuation.

(5)   The integration of standard costing with marginal cost accounting, absorption cost accounting and throughput accounting.

(6)   Process accounting including establishment of equivalent units in stock, work-in-progress and abnormal loss accounts and the use of first-in-first-out, average cost and standard cost methods of stock valuation.

(7)   MRP and ERP systems for resource planning and the integration of accounting functions with other systems, such as purchase ordering and production planning.

(8)   Back-flush accounting in just-in-time production environments. The benefits of just-in-time production, total quality management and theory of constraints and the possible impacts of these methods on cost accounting and performance measurement.

B – Standard costing – 25 %

Learning outcomes

On completion of their studies students should be able to:

(i)   explain why and how standards are set in manufacturing and in service industries with particular reference to the maximisation of efficiency and minimisation of waste.

(ii)   calculate and interpret material, labour, variable overhead, fixed overhead and sales variances;

(iii)   prepare and discuss a report which reconciles budget and actual profit using absorption and/or marginal costing principles;

(iv)   calculate and explain planning and operational variances;

(v)   prepare reports using a range of internal and external benchmarks and interpret the results;

(vi)   discuss the behavioural implications of setting standard costs.

Syllabus content

(1)   Manufacturing standards for material, labour, variable overhead and fixed overhead.

(2)   Price/rate and usage/efficiency variances for materials, labour and variable overhead. Further subdivision of total usage/efficiency variances into mix and yield components. (Note: The calculation of mix variances on both individual and average valuation bases is required.)

(3)   Fixed overhead expenditure and volume variances. (Note: the subdivision of fixed overhead volume variance into capacity and efficiency elements will not be examined.)

(4)   Planning and operational variances.

(5) Standards and variances in service industries, (including the phenomenon of "McDonaldization"), public services (e.g. Health), (including the use of "diagnostic related" or "reference" groups), and the professions (e.g. labour mix variances in audit work). Criticisms of standard costing in general and in advanced manufacturing environments in particular.

(6) Sales price and sales revenue/margin volume variances (calculation of the latter on a unit basis related to revenue, gross margin and contribution margin). Application of these variances to all sectors, including professional services and retail analysis.

(7) Interpretation of variances: interrelationship, significance.

(8) Benchmarking.

(9) Behavioural implications of setting standard costs.

C –Budgeting – 30%

Learning outcomes

On completion of their studies students should be able to:

(i) explain why organisations prepare forecasts and plans;

(ii) calculate projected product/service volumes employing appropriate forecasting techniques;

(iii) calculate projected revenues and costs based on product/service volumes, pricing strategies and cost structures;

(iv) evaluate projected performance by calculating key metrics including profitability, liquidity and asset turnover ratios;

(v) describe and explain the possible purposes of budgets, including planning, communication, co-ordination, motivation, authorisation, control and evaluation;

(vi) evaluate and apply alternative approaches to budgeting;

(vii) calculate the consequences of "what if" scenarios and evaluate their impact on master profit and loss account and balance sheet;

(viii) explain the concept of responsibility accounting and its importance in the construction of functional budgets that support the overall master budget;

(ix) identify controllable and uncontrollable costs in the context of responsibility accounting and explain why "uncontrollable" costs may or may not be allocated to responsibility centres;

(x) explain the ideas of feedback and feed-forward control and their application in the use of budgets for control;

(xi) evaluate performance using fixed and flexible budget reports;

(xii) discuss the role of non-financial performance indicators and compare and contrast traditional approaches to budgeting with recommendations based on the 'balanced scorecard';

(xiii) evaluate the impact of budgetary control systems on human behaviour;

(xiv) evaluate the criticisms of budgeting particularly from the advocates of techniques that are 'beyond budgeting'.

Syllabus content

(1) Time series analysis including moving totals and averages, treatment of seasonality, trend analysis using regression analysis and the application of these techniques in forecasting product and service volumes.

(2) Fixed, variable, semi-variable and activity-based categorisations of cost and their application in projecting financial results.

(3) What-if analysis based on alternate projections of volumes, prices and cost structures and the use of spreadsheets in facilitating these analyses.

(4) The purposes of budgets and conflicts that can arise (e.g. between budgets for realistic planning and budgets based on 'hard to achieve' targets for motivation).

(5) The creation of budgets including incremental approaches, zero-based budgeting and activity-based budgets.

(6) The use of budgets in planning: 'rolling budgets' for adaptive planning.

(7) The use of budgets for control: controllable costs and variances based on 'fixed' and 'flexed' budgets. The conceptual link between standard costing and budget flexing.

(8) Behavioural issues in budgeting: participation in budgeting and its possible beneficial consequences for ownership and motivation; participation in budgeting and its possible adverse consequences for 'budget padding' and manipulation; setting budget targets for motivation etc.

(9) Criticisms of budgeting and the recommendations of the advocates of the balanced scorecard and 'beyond budgeting'.

D – Control and Performance Measurement of Responsibility Centres – 20%

Learning outcomes

On completion of their studies students should be able to:

(i) discuss the use of cost, revenue, profit and investment centres in devising organisation structure and in management control;

(ii) prepare cost information in appropriate formats for cost centre managers, taking due account of controllable/uncontrollable costs and the importance of budget flexing;

(iii) prepare revenue and cost information in appropriate formats for profit and investment centre managers, taking due account of cost variability, attributable costs, controllable costs and identification of appropriate measures of profit centre 'contribution';

(iv) calculate and apply measures of performance for investment centres (often 'strategic business units' or divisions of larger groups);

(v) discuss the likely behavioural consequences of the use of performance metrics in managing cost, profit and investment centres;

(vi) explain the typical consequences of a divisional structure for performance measurement as divisions compete or trade with each other;

(vii) identify the likely consequences of different approaches to transfer pricing for divisional decision making, divisional and group profitability, the motivation of divisional management and the autonomy of individual divisions.

Syllabus content

(1) Organisation structure and its implications for responsibility accounting.

(2) Presentation of financial information including issues of controllable/uncontrollable costs, variable/fixed costs and tracing revenues and costs to particular cost objects.

(3) Return on investment and its deficiencies; the emergence of residual income and economic value added to address these.

(4)   Behavioural issues in the application of performance measures in cost, profit and investment centres.

(5)   The theory of transfer pricing, including perfect, imperfect and no market for the intermediate good.

(6)   Use of negotiated, market, cost-plus and variable cost based transfer prices. 'Dual' transfer prices and lump sum payments as means of addressing some of the issues that arise.

(7)   The interaction of transfer pricing and tax liabilities in international operations and implications for currency management and possible distortion of internal company operations in order to comply with Tax Authority directives.

The exam paper

Format of the paper

		Number of marks
Section A:	Around 20 multiple choice and other objective test questions, 2-4 marks each	50
Section B:	6 compulsory questions, 5 marks each	30
Section C:	1 out of 2 questions, 20 marks each	20
		100

Time allowed: 3 hours

Section A will always contain some multiple choice questions but will not consist solely of multiple choice questions. Section A may contain types of objective test question that are different from those included in the pilot paper.

Further guidance on objective test questions and multiple choice questions is included on pages (xix) and (xx)

Section B questions will be mainly written discussion, although some calculations may be included. This section will require breadth of syllabus knowledge and also good time management skills.

Section C questions will be in various different styles including more complex calculations and analysis of data. Most questions will require calculation and written evaluation. Questions may include issues from a number of areas of the syllabus. Careful planning of answers will be essential.

Pilot paper

Section A

1   Nineteen objective test questions covering the whole syllabus.

Section B

2   A compulsory section comprising six short answer questions on the following topics

       (a)   Feedback control and feedback loop
       (b)   Total Quality Management (TQM) in a Just-in-Time (JIT) production environment
       (c)   Setting budgets
       (d)   EVA and RI compared
       (e)   Controllability principle
       (f)   Transfer prices in an international context

Section C

3   Performance assessment, interpretation of variances and report to the Operations Director

4   Preparation of process account

What the examiner means

The table below has been prepared by CIMA to help you interpret exam questions.

Learning objective	Verbs used	Definition
1 Knowledge What you are expected to know	• List • State • Define	• Make a list of • Express, fully or clearly, the details of/facts of • Give the exact meaning of
2 Comprehension What you are expected to understand	• Describe • Distinguish • Explain • Identify • Illustrate	• Communicate the key features of • Highlight the differences between • Make clear or intelligible/state the meaning of • Recognise, establish or select after consideration • Use an example to describe or explain something
3 Application How you are expected to apply your knowledge	• Apply • Calculate/ compute • Demonstrate • Prepare • Reconcile • Solve • Tabulate	• To put to practical use • To ascertain or reckon mathematically • To prove with certainty or to exhibit by practical means • To make or get ready for use • To make or prove consistent/compatible • Find an answer to • Arrange in a table
4 Analysis How you are expected to analyse the detail of what you have learned	• Analyse • Categorise • Compare and contrast • Construct • Discuss • Interpret • Produce	• Examine in detail the structure of • Place into a defined class or division • Show the similarities and/or differences between • To build up or compile • To examine in detail by argument • To translate into intelligible or familiar terms • To create or bring into existence
5 Evaluation How you are expected to use your learning to evaluate, make decisions or recommendations	• Advise • Evaluate • Recommend	• To counsel, inform or notify • To appraise or assess the value of • To advise on a course of action

Tackling objective test questions

Of the total marks available for the paper, objective test questions (OTs) comprise 20/50 per cent.
Questions will be worth between 2 to 4 marks.

What is an objective test question?

An **OT** is made up of some form of **stimulus**, usually a question, and a **requirement** to do something.

(a)   Multiple choice questions

(b)   Filling in blanks or completing a sentence

(c)   Listing items, in any order or a specified order such as rank order

(d)   Stating a definition

(e)   Identifying a key issue, term, figure or item

(f)   Calculating a specific figure

(g)   Completing gaps in a set of data where the relevant numbers can be calculated from the
         information given

(h)   Identifying points/zones/ranges/areas on graphs or diagrams, labelling graphs or filling in lines on
         a graph

(i)   Matching items or statements

(j)   Stating whether statements are true or false

(k)   Writing brief (in a specified number of words) explanations

(l)   Deleting incorrect items

(m)   Choosing right words from a number of options

(n)   Complete an equation, or define what the symbols used in an equation mean

OT questions in CIMA exams

CIMA has offered the following **guidance** about OT questions in the exam.

●   Credit may be given for **workings** where you are asked to calculate a specific figure.

●   If you **exceed a specified limit on the number of words** you can use in an answer, you will **not be
       awarded any marks**.

●   If you make **more than one attempt** at a question, clearly **cross through** any answers that you do
       not want to submit. If you don't do this, only your first answer will be marked.

Examples of OTs are included within each chapter, in the **quick quizzes** at the end of each chapter and in
the **objective test question bank**.

> BPP's i-Pass for this paper provides you with plenty of opportunity for further practice of OTs.

Tackling multiple choice questions

In a multiple choice question on your paper, you are given how many **incorrect** options?

A   Two
B   Three
C   Four
D   Five

The correct answer is B.

The MCQs in your exam contain four possible answers. You have to **choose the option that best answers the question**. The three incorrect options are called distracters. There is a skill in answering MCQs quickly and correctly. By practising MCQs you can develop this skill, giving you a better chance of passing the exam.

You may wish to follow the approach outlined below, or you may prefer to adapt it.

Step 1   **Skim read** all the MCQs and **identify** what appear to be the easier questions.

Step 2   Attempt each question – **starting with the easier questions** identified in Step 1. Read the question thoroughly. You may prefer to work out the answer before looking at the options, or you may prefer to look at the options at the beginning. Adopt the method that works best for you.

Step 3   Read the four options and see if one matches your own answer. **Be careful with numerical questions**, as the distracters are designed to match answers that incorporate common errors. Check that your calculation is correct. Have you followed the requirement exactly? Have you included every stage of the calculation?

Step 4   You may **find that none of the options matches your answer**.

- Re-read the question to ensure that you understand it and are answering the requirement.

- Eliminate any obviously wrong answers.

- Consider which of the remaining answers is the most likely to be correct and select the option.

Step 5   If you are still **unsure** make a note **and continue to the next question**.

Step 6   **Revisit unanswered** questions. When you come back to a question after a break you often find you are able to answer it correctly straight away. If you are still unsure have a guess. You are not penalised for incorrect answers, so **never leave a question unanswered!**

Exam focus. After extensive practice and revision of MCQs, you may find that you recognise a question when you sit the exam. Be aware that the detail and/or requirement may be different. If the question seems familiar read the requirement and options carefully – do not assume that it is identical.

> BPP's MCQ cards and i-Pass for this paper provide you with plenty of opportunity for further practice of MCQs.

Part A
Cost accounting systems

Marginal costing and Absorption costing

Introduction

The main principles underlying the content of this chapter should be familiar to you from your earlier studies. You should already be able to apply a system of **marginal costing** and understand how it differs from **absorption costing.**

Whereas absorption costing recognises fixed costs (usually fixed production costs) as part of the cost of a unit of output and hence as **product costs**, marginal costing treats all fixed costs as **period costs**.

The emphasis in your *Management Accounting Performance Evaluation* syllabus is on a comparison between the two systems and their effect on reported profit and inventory valuation, and on their application in different learning environments.

Topic list	Learning outcomes	Syllabus references	Ability required
1 The principles of marginal costing	A(i)	A 1	Analysis
2 The principles of absorption costing	A(i)	A 2	Analysis
3 The effect of marginal costing and absorption costing on reported profit and inventory valuation	A(i)	A 1, 2	Analysis
4 Marginal and absorption costing compared	A(i)	A 1, 2	Analysis
5 Job costing and batch costing	A(ii)	A 1, 2	Application

Knowledge brought forward from earlier studies

Terminology

- **Absorption costing** is a method of costing that, in addition to direct costs, assigns all, or a proportion of, product overhead costs to cost units by means of one or a number of overhead absorption rates.

- **Marginal costing** is an alternative method of costing to absorption costing. In marginal costing, only variable costs are charged as a cost of sale and a contribution is calculated which is sales revenue minus the variable cost of sales. Closing inventories of work in progress or finished goods are valued at marginal (variable) production cost. Fixed costs are treated as a period cost, and are charged in full to the income statement of the part of the accounting period in which they are incurred.

- **Marginal cost** is 'The part of the cost of one unit of product or service which would be avoided if that unit were not produced, or which would increase if one extra unit were produced'.

- **Contribution** is 'Sales value less variable cost of sales'.

CIMA *Official Terminology*

1 The principles of marginal costing

The principles of marginal costing (also known as variable costing) are as follows.

(a) Period fixed costs are the same, for any volume of sales and production (provided that the level of activity is within the 'relevant range'). Therefore, by selling an extra item of product or service the following will happen.

- Revenue will increase by the sales value of the item sold.
- Costs will increase by the variable cost per unit.
- Profit will increase by the amount of contribution earned from the extra item.

(b) Similarly, if the volume of sales falls by one item, the profit will fall by the amount of contribution earned from the item.

FAST FORWARD

The marginal costing philosophy is that profit measurement should be based on an analysis of total contribution.

(c) Since fixed costs relate to a period of time, and do not change with increases or decreases in sales volume, it is misleading to charge units of sale with a share of fixed costs. Absorption costing is therefore misleading, and it is more appropriate to deduct fixed costs from total contribution for the period to derive a profit figure.

(d) When a unit of product is made, the extra costs incurred in its manufacture are the **variable production costs**. Fixed costs are unaffected, and no extra fixed costs are incurred when output is increased.

FAST FORWARD

Supporters of marginal costing argue that the valuation of closing inventories should be at variable production cost (direct materials, direct labour, direct expenses (if any) and variable production overhead) because these are the only costs properly attributable to the product.

Before reviewing marginal costing principles any further, it will be helpful to remind yourself of the basics by looking at a numerical example.

1.1 Example: marginal costing

Water and Sons makes a product, the Splash, which has a variable production cost of £6 per unit and a sales price of £10 per unit. At the beginning of September 20X0, there were no opening inventories and production during the month was 20,000 units. Fixed costs for the month were £30,000 for production and £15,000 for administration, sales and distribution). There were no variable marketing costs.

Required

Calculate the contribution and profit for September, using marginal costing principles, if sales were as follows.

- (a) 10,000 Splashes
- (b) 15,000 Splashes
- (c) 20,000 Splashes

Solution

The first stage in the profit calculation must be to identify the variable costs, and then the contribution. Fixed costs are deducted from the total contribution to derive the profit. All closing inventories are valued at marginal production cost (£6 per unit). Production during the month in all three cases is 20,000 units.

	10,000 Splashes		15,000 Splashes		20,000 Splashes	
	£	£	£	£	£	£
Sales (at £10)		100,000		150,000		200,000
Opening inventory	0		0		0	
Variable production cost	120,000		120,000		120,000	
	120,000		120,000		120,000	
Less value of closing inventory (at marginal cost)	60,000		30,000		0	
Variable cost of sales		60,000		90,000		120,000
Contribution		40,000		60,000		80,000
Less fixed costs		45,000		45,000		45,000
Profit/(loss)		(5,000)		15,000		35,000
Profit/(loss) per unit		£(0.50)		£1		£1.75
Contribution per unit		£4		£4		£4

The conclusions which may be drawn from this example are as follows.

- (a) The **profit per unit varies** at differing levels of sales, because the average fixed overhead cost per unit changes with the volume of output and sales.

- (b) The **contribution per unit is constant** at all levels of output and sales. Total contribution, which is the contribution per unit multiplied by the number of units sold, increases in direct proportion to the volume of sales.

- (c) Since the **contribution per unit does not change**, the most effective way of calculating the expected profit at any level of output and sales would be as follows.

    - (i) First calculate the total contribution.

    - (ii) Then deduct fixed costs as a period charge in order to find the profit.

- (d) In our example the expected profit from the sale of 17,000 Splashes would be as follows.

	£
Total contribution (17,000 × £4)	68,000
Less fixed costs	45,000
Profit	23,000

2 The principles of absorption costing

The principles of absorption costing are as follows.

(a)   Fixed production costs are an integral part of the production cost of an item and so should be absorbed into product costs.

FAST FORWARD

With absorption costing, fixed production costs are absorbed into product unit costs using a predetermined overhead absorption rate, based on the normal level of production for the period.

(b)   Inventories are valued at their full production cost including absorbed fixed production costs.

FAST FORWARD

If the actual production is different from the normal level there will be an under or over absorption of fixed production costs for the period. This amount is written off against the absorption costing profit for the period.

2.1 Example: absorption costing

Using the earlier example of Water and Sons, assume that the normal level of activity is 15,000 Splashes per month and that budgeted fixed production costs were £30,000 for the month.

Required

Prepare profit statements for September, using absorption costing, for the three sales levels given.

Solution

The fixed production cost per unit, based on the normal level of activity, is £30,000/15,000 = £2 per unit.

The full production cost per unit = £6 + £2 = £8 per unit

With production of 20,000 Splashes the fixed overhead will be over-absorbed.

	£
Fixed production costs absorbed (20,000 units × £2)	40,000
Fixed production costs incurred	30,000
Over- absorbed fixed production cost	10,000

	10,000 Splashes		15,000 Splashes		20,000 Splashes	
	£	£	£	£	£	£
Sales		100,000		150,000		200,000
Opening inventory	0		0		0	
Full production costs	160,000		160,000		160,000	
	160,000		160,000		160,000	
Less closing inventory						
(at full production cost)	80,000		40,000		0	
Full production of sales	80,000		120,000		160,000	
Adjustment for over-						
absorbed overhead	10,000		10,000		10,000	
Full production costs		70,000		110,000		150,000
Gross profit		30,000		40,000		50,000
Administration, sales and						
distribution costs		15,000		15,000		15,000
Net profit		15,000		25,000		35,000

3 The effect of marginal costing and absorption costing on reported profit and inventory valuation

The results of the last two examples can be compared as follows.

	Sales volume (Splashes)		
	10,000	15,000	20,000
Marginal costing profit/(loss)	£(5,000)	£15,000	£35,000
Absorption costing profit	£15,000	£25,000	£35,000
Increase in inventory units	10,000	5,000	0

An important conclusion can be drawn from these results.

FAST FORWARD

> If there are changes in inventories during a period, marginal costing and absorption costing systems will report different profit figures.

In this example the inventory levels increased with the two lower sales volume figures and the reported profit figure was higher with absorption costing than with marginal costing.

FAST FORWARD

> If inventory levels increase, absorption costing will report a higher profit than marginal costing.

This is because some of the fixed production overhead incurred during the period will be carried forward in closing inventory (which reduces cost of sales) to be set against sales revenue in the following period instead of being written off in full against profit in the period concerned.

FAST FORWARD

> If inventory levels decrease, absorption costing will report the lower profit.

This is because as well as the fixed overhead incurred, fixed production overhead which had been brought forward in opening inventory is released and is included in cost of sales.

In our example the two reported profit figures were the same when sales volume was 20,000 Splashes, ie when production and sales volumes were equal and there was no change in inventory.

FAST FORWARD

> If the opening and closing inventory volumes and values are the same, marginal costing and absorption costing will report the same profit figure.

It is important to appreciate that the differences in reported profits occur only in the short run, ie in reporting the profit of individual accounting periods.

FAST FORWARD

> In the long run, the total reported profit will be the same whether marginal or absorption costing is used.

This is because in the long run, total costs will be the same by either method of accounting. Short term differences are the result of changes in the level of inventory.

3.1 Calculating the difference in reported profit

The difference in the profit reported by the two systems therefore results from the fixed production overhead that is carried forward in inventory in an absorption costing system.

FAST FORWARD

> The difference in reported profit is equal to the change in inventory volume multiplied by the fixed production overhead rate per unit.

In our example the profit figures can be reconciled as follows.

		Sales volume (Splashes)		
		10,000		20,000
		£		£
Marginal costing profit/(loss)		(5,000)		15,000
Increase in inventory units @ £2 per unit	(10,000 × £2)	20,000	(5,000 × £2)	10,000
Absorption costing profit		15,000		5,000

In both cases the absorption costing profit was higher because the inventory level increased and fixed production overhead was carried forward to next month in the absorption costing valuation.

Exam focus point

The calculation of the difference between the reported profit in the two costing systems is a subject that lends itself well to an objective testing question format.

Question

Marginal versus Absorption costing – effect on profit

Learning outcome: A(i)

The overhead absorption rate for product X is £10 per machine hour. Each unit of product X requires five machine hours. Inventory of product X on 1 January was 150 units and on 31 December it was 100 units. What is the difference in profit between results reported using absorption costing and results reported using marginal costing?

A   The absorption costing profit would be £2,500 less
B   The absorption costing profit would be £2,500 greater
C   The absorption costing profit would be £5,000 less
D   The absorption costing profit would be £5,000 greater

Answer

Difference in profit = **change** in inventory levels × fixed overhead absorption per unit = (150 – 100) × £10 × 5 = £2,500 **lower** profit, because stock levels **decreased**. The correct answer is therefore option A. The key is the change in the volume of inventory. Inventory levels have **decreased** therefore absorption costing will report a **lower** profit. This eliminates options B and D.

Option C is incorrect because it is based on the closing inventory only (100 units × £10 × 5 hours).

4 Marginal costing and absorption costing compared

FAST FORWARD

There are arguments in favour of each costing method.

4.1 Arguments in favour of absorption costing

Arguments in favour of absorption costing are as follows.

(a) Fixed production costs are incurred in order to make output; it is therefore 'fair' to charge all output with a share of these costs.

(b) Closing Inventory values, by including a share of fixed production overhead, will be valued on the principle required for the financial accounting valuation of inventories as specified by the international accounting standard governing the valuation of inventories (IAS 2).

(c) A problem with calculating the contribution of various products made by an enterprise is that it may not be clear whether the contribution earned by each product is enough to cover fixed costs, whereas by charging fixed overhead to a product it is possible to ascertain whether it is profitable or not.

4.2 Arguments in favour of marginal costing

Arguments in favour of marginal costing are as follows.

(a) It is simple to operate.

(b) There are no apportionments, which are frequently done on an arbitrary basis, of fixed costs. Many costs, such as the marketing director's salary, are indivisible by nature.

(c) Fixed costs will be the same regardless of the volume of output, because they are period costs. It makes sense, therefore, to charge them in full as a cost to the period.

(d) The cost to produce an extra unit is the variable production cost. It is realistic to value closing inventory items at this directly attributable cost.

(e) Under or over absorption of overheads is avoided.

(f) Marginal costing information can be used for decision making but, absorption costing information is not suitable for decision making.

(g) Fixed costs (such as depreciation, rent and salaries) relate to a period of time and should be charged against the revenues of the period in which they are incurred.

(h) Absorption costing may encourage over-production since reported profits can be increased by increasing inventory levels.

4.3 Example: absorption costing encouraging over-production

To demonstrate the last argument in favour of marginal costing, consider an organisation that produces a product that sells for £60 per unit.

Variable production costs are £35 per unit and the fixed production costs of £30,000 per period are absorbed on the basis of the normal capacity of 5,000 units per period.

Fixed administration, selling and distribution overheads are £19,000 per period. There was no opening inventory for the latest period.

Required

Calculate the profit reported for sales of 5,000 units last period for production volumes of 5,000 units, 6,000 units and 7,000 units, using:

(a) Absorption costing
(b) Marginal costing

9

5.2 Example: the effect of the overhead absorption base in job costing

Fixit uses the job costing method and currently absorbs fixed production overhead into job costs using a pre-determined rate per labour hour. The general manager is considering changing the absorption base to a pre-determined rate per machine hour.

Information for the latest period is as follows.

	$
Budgeted fixed production overhead	350,000
Budgeted machine hours	70,000
Budgeted labour hours	87,500

Extracts from data concerning two jobs completed during the period are as follows.

	Job 876	Job 890
Direct labour hours	24	9
Machine hours	11	15

Required

Calculate the fixed production overhead to be absorbed by each job using:

(a)   A direct labour hour rate of overhead absorption
(b)   A machine hour rate of overhead absorption

Solution

Direct labour hour rate = $350,000/87,500 = $4 per direct labour hour
Machine hour rate = $350,000/70,000 = $5 per machine hour

Fixed production overhead absorbed:

			Job 876		Job 890
			$		$
(a)	Direct labour hour rate	($4 x 24)	96	($4 x 9)	36
(b)	Machine hour rate	($5 x 11)	55	($5 x 15)	75

The alteration in overhead absorption basis would thus have a significant impact on the amount of production overhead absorbed by each of these jobs. If Fixit uses **cost plus pricing** this could lead to under or over pricing of the jobs to the customer.

5.3 Activity based costing in a job costing environment

A costing method that might be used to ensure that each job absorbs an amount of fixed overhead that more accurately reflects the incidence of overhead costs is **activity based costing (ABC).** We will return later in this text to learn more about the application of ABC.

5.4 Absorption costing in a batch environment

The same principles apply to absorption costing in a batch environment as in a job environment. Once the total production cost of each batch has been determined the total cost is divided by the number of units in the batch to ascertain the total production cost of each unit in the batch.

5.5 Marginal costing in a job and batch environment

If marginal costing is applied in a job or batch environment then each job or batch would be valued at its variable or direct cost. Fixed production overhead costs would not be absorbed into the cost of individual jobs or batches. Instead the total fixed production overhead cost for the period would be deducted from the contribution earned by all jobs or batches, to determine the profit for the period.

The use of marginal costing in a **cost plus pricing** system within a job or batch environment can create real dangers of under pricing of jobs or batches. In this situation it is extremely important for managers to ensure that the profit mark-up is sufficient to cover fixed costs as well as leave sufficient profit for the organisation.

Question	Absorption costing and inventory valuation

Learning outcome: A(ii)

P uses an absorption costing system and absorbs fixed production overheads as a percentage of direct labour cost.

Three jobs were worked on last period, details of which are as follows.

	Job X		Job Y		Job Z	
	€	€	€	€	€	€
Opening work in progress:						
materials	4,200		800			
labour	1,900		600			
production overhead	3,325		1,050			
		9,425		2,450		0
Costs incurred in period:						
materials		540		120		545
labour		860		380		220

Job X was completed during the period.

What was the value of the work in progress inventory at the end of the period? (2 marks)

Answer

Production overhead absorption rate = €3,325/ €1,900
= 175% of the labour cost

Jobs Y ad Z are still in progress at the end of the period.

The value of work in progress can now be calculated.

	Job Y		Job Z		Total
	€		€		€
Opening work in progress	2,450		0		2,450
Costs incurred in period	500		765		1,265
Production overhead absorbed	665	(220 × 175%)	385		1,050
	(380 × 175%)				
Total value of closing work in progress	3,615		1,150		4,765

Chapter Roundup

- The marginal costing philosophy is that profit measurement should be based on an analysis of total contribution

- Supporters of marginal costing argue that the valuation of closing inventories should be at variable production cost (direct materials, direct labour, direct expenses (if any) and variable production overhead) because these are the only costs properly attributable to the product.

- With absorption costing, fixed production costs are absorbed into product unit costs using a predetermined overhead absorption rate, based on the normal level of production for the period.

- If the actual production is different from the normal level there will be an under or over absorption of fixed production costs for the period. This amount is written off against the absorption costing profit for the period.

- If there are changes in inventories during a period, marginal costing and absorption costing systems will report different profit figures.

- If inventory levels increase, absorption costing will report a higher profit than marginal costing.

- If inventory levels decrease, absorption costing will report the lower profit.

- If the opening and closing inventory volumes and values are the same, marginal costing and absorption costing will report the same profit figure.

- In the long run, the total reported profit will be the same whether marginal or absorption costing is used.

- The difference in reported profit is equal to the change in inventory volume multiplied by the fixed production overhead rate per unit.

- There are arguments in favour of each costing method.

- For a given level of sales, marginal costing will report the same level of profit whatever the level of production. In contrast, absorption costing will report higher levels of profit for the same level of sales, if production levels are higher.

- Marginal and absorption costing approaches can also be applied in job and batch environments.

Quick Quiz

1   Marginal costing and absorption costing are different techniques for assessing profit in a period. If there are changes in inventory during a period, marginal costing and absorption costing give different results for profit obtained.

Which of the following statements are true?

I   If inventory levels increase, marginal costing will report the higher profit.

II   If inventory levels decrease, marginal costing will report the lower profit.

III   If inventory levels decrease, marginal costing will report the higher profit.

IV   If the opening and closing inventory volumes are the same, marginal costing and absorption costing will give the same profit figure.

A   All of the above
B   I, II and IV
C   I and IV
D   III and IV

2 Identify which of the following relate to either

A = Absorption costing
M = Marginal costing

		A or M
(a)	Closing inventories valued at marginal production cost	
(b)	Closing inventories valued at full production cost	
(c)	Cost of sales include some fixed overhead incurred in previous period in opening inventory values	
(d)	Fixed costs are charged in full against profit for the period	

3 Which of the following are arguments in favour of marginal costing?

(a) Closing inventory is valued in accordance with international accounting standards.
(b) It is simple to operate.
(c) There is no under or over absorption of overheads.
(d) Fixed costs are the same regardless of activity levels.
(e) The information from this costing method may be used for decision making.

4 When opening inventories were 8,500 litres and closing stocks 6,750 litres, a firm had a profit of $62,100 using marginal costing.

Assuming that the fixed overhead absorption rate was $3 per litre, what would be the profit using absorption costing?

5 When sales fluctuate but production is constant, absorption costing smooths out fluctuations in profit.

(delete as appropriate) **True/false**

Answers to Quick Quiz

1 D

2

		A or M
(a)	Closing inventories valued at marginal production cost	M
(b)	Closing inventories valued at full production cost	A
(c)	Cost of sales include some fixed overhead incurred in previous period in opening inventory values	A
(d)	Fixed costs are charged in full against profit for the period	M

3 (b), (c), (d), (e)

4 Difference in profit = (8,500 − 6,750) × $3 = $5,250

Since inventory levels reduced, the absorption costing profit will be lower than the marginal costing profit.

Absorption costing profit = $62,100 − $5,250 = $56,850

5 True. Absorption costing caries fixed production overheads forward in inventory values to be matched against sales as they arise.

Now try the question below from the Exam Question Bank			
Number	**Level**	**Marks**	**Time**
Q1	Introductory	20	36 mins

Cost bookkeeping

Introduction

As with Chapter 1, much of the material in this chapter will be familiar to you from your earlier studies. You should already have a good understanding of the principal ledger accounts in a **cost bookkeeping system** and how the most common transactions are recorded in the double entry system.

Your *Management Accounting Performance Evaluation* syllabus requires you to be able to **prepare ledger accounts according to context**: marginal or absorption costing based in job, batch or process environments.

In this chapter you will study ledger accounts and in particular how they are maintained in a **job or batch environment**. In the next chapter you will go on to apply the same basic double entry principles in a process environment.

Topic list	Learning outcomes	Syllabus references	Ability required
1 Integrated systems	A(iii)	A 1,2	Application
2 Interlocking systems	A(iii)	A 1,2	Application
3 Ledger accounts in job or batch environments	A(iii)	A 1,2	Application

> **Knowledge brought forward from earlier studies**

Terminology

- **Interlocking accounts**. 'A system in which the cost accounts are distinct from the financial accounts, the two sets of accounts being kept continuously in agreement by the use of control accounts or reconciled by other means'.

- **Integrated accounts**. 'A set of accounting records which provides both financial and cost accounts using a common input of data for all accounting purposes'

CIMA *Official Terminology*

Interlocking and integrated accounts

- The cost accounts in interlocking systems use the same basic data (purchases, wages and so on) as the financial accounts, but frequently adopt different bases for matters such as depreciation and inventory valuation.

- With integrated accounts the same basis for items such as inventory valuation and depreciation will be used and there is **no need for a reconciliation** between cost profit and financial profit. Financial profit will simply be the cost profit adjusted by non-cost items such as income from investments and charitable donations.

1 Integrated systems

1.1 The principal accounts in a system of integrated accounts

FAST FORWARD

There are four main groups of accounts in an integrated system

- The resources accounts
- Accounts which record the cost of production items from the start of production work through to cost of sales
- Sales account
- Income statement

   (a)   **The resources accounts**

- Materials control account or stores control account
- Wages (and salaries) control account
- Production overhead control account
- Administration overhead control account
- Selling and distribution overhead control account

   (b)   **Accounts which record the cost of production items from the start of production work through to cost of sales**

- Work in progress control account
- Finished goods control account
- Cost of sales control account

   (c)   Sales account

   (d)   Income statement

1.2 Accounting entries in an integrated system

The accounting entries in an integrated system can be confusing and it is important to keep in mind some general principles.

(a) When **expenditure** is incurred on materials, wages or overheads, the actual amounts paid or payable are debited to the appropriate **resources accounts**. The credit entries are made in the cash or payables accounts.

(b) When production begins, **resources are allocated to work in progress**. This is recorded by crediting the resources accounts and debiting the work in progress account. In the case of production overheads in an absorption costing system, the amount credited to the overhead account and debited to work in progress should be the amount of overhead absorbed. If this differs from the amount of overhead incurred, there will be a difference on the overhead control account; this should be written off to an under-/over-absorbed overhead account. (One other point to remember is that when **indirect** materials and labour are allocated to production, the entries are to credit the materials and wages accounts and debit **production overhead account**.)

(c) As **finished goods** are produced, work in progress is reduced. This is recorded by debiting the finished goods control account and crediting the work in progress control account.

(d) At the end of the period, the cost of goods sold is transferred from the finished goods account to the cost of sales account, and from there to the income statement.

(e) The balances on the administration overhead control account and the selling and distribution overhead control account are usually transferred direct to the income statement at the period end.

(f) **Sales** are debited to the receivables control account and credited to the sales account.

(g) **Profit** is established by transferring to the income statement the balances on the sales account, cost of sales account and under-/over-absorbed overhead account.

1.3 Accounting entries in absorption costing and marginal costing systems

The two diagrams on the following pages will remind you of the principal entries in the operation of integrated systems using absorption costing and marginal costing. Follow the entries through the various control accounts and notice the main differences between the two diagrams.

- The marginal costing system **analyses separately the fixed overhead and the variable overhead**. The flowchart shows separate accounts for fixed overhead and variable overhead. Alternatively the total overhead may first be collected in a single overhead control account pending subsequent analysis into fixed overhead and variable overhead

- The absorption costing system collects all production overheads in a single control account and then **absorbs production overheads into the cost of work in progress**. Transfers between work in progress and finished goods inventory, and between finished goods and the income statement, are **valued at full production cost**. Inventories of work in progress and finished goods are **valued at full production cost, including absorbed overhead**

- In the marginal costing system only the **variable production overheads are absorbed into the cost of work in progress**. Transfers between work in progress and finished goods inventory, and between finished goods and the income statement, are **valued at marginal cost**. Inventories of work in progress and finished goods are valued at marginal cost

- In the marginal costing system the fixed overheads are collected in a fixed overhead control account and then **transferred in full to the income statement at the end of the period**. There is **no need to account for under- or over-absorbed overheads**

1.4 Example: integrated accounts

Using the information given below for October, you are required to prepare the following accounts in an absorption costing system.

- Raw materials control
- Work in progress control
- Finished goods control
- Production overhead control
- Wages and salaries control
- Selling and administration overhead control
- Cost of sales
- Income statement

Balances as at 1 October

	£'000
Raw materials control	10
Work in progress control	15
Finished goods control	18

Transactions for October

	£'000
Materials received from suppliers on credit	50
Materials issued to production	42
Materials issued to production service departments	5
Direct wages incurred	30
Production indirect wages incurred	13
Selling and administration salaries incurred	12
Production expenses paid as incurred	8
Selling and administration expenses paid as incurred	9
Provision for depreciation: production equipment	3
selling and administration equipment	2
Wages and salaries paid: direct wages	28
production indirect wages	13
selling and administration salaries	12
Production completed and transferred to finished goods store	90
Production cost of goods sold	97
Sales on credit	145

Production overhead is absorbed at the rate of 80 per cent of direct wages incurred.

PROFESSIONAL EDUCATION

Cost accounting using absorption costing

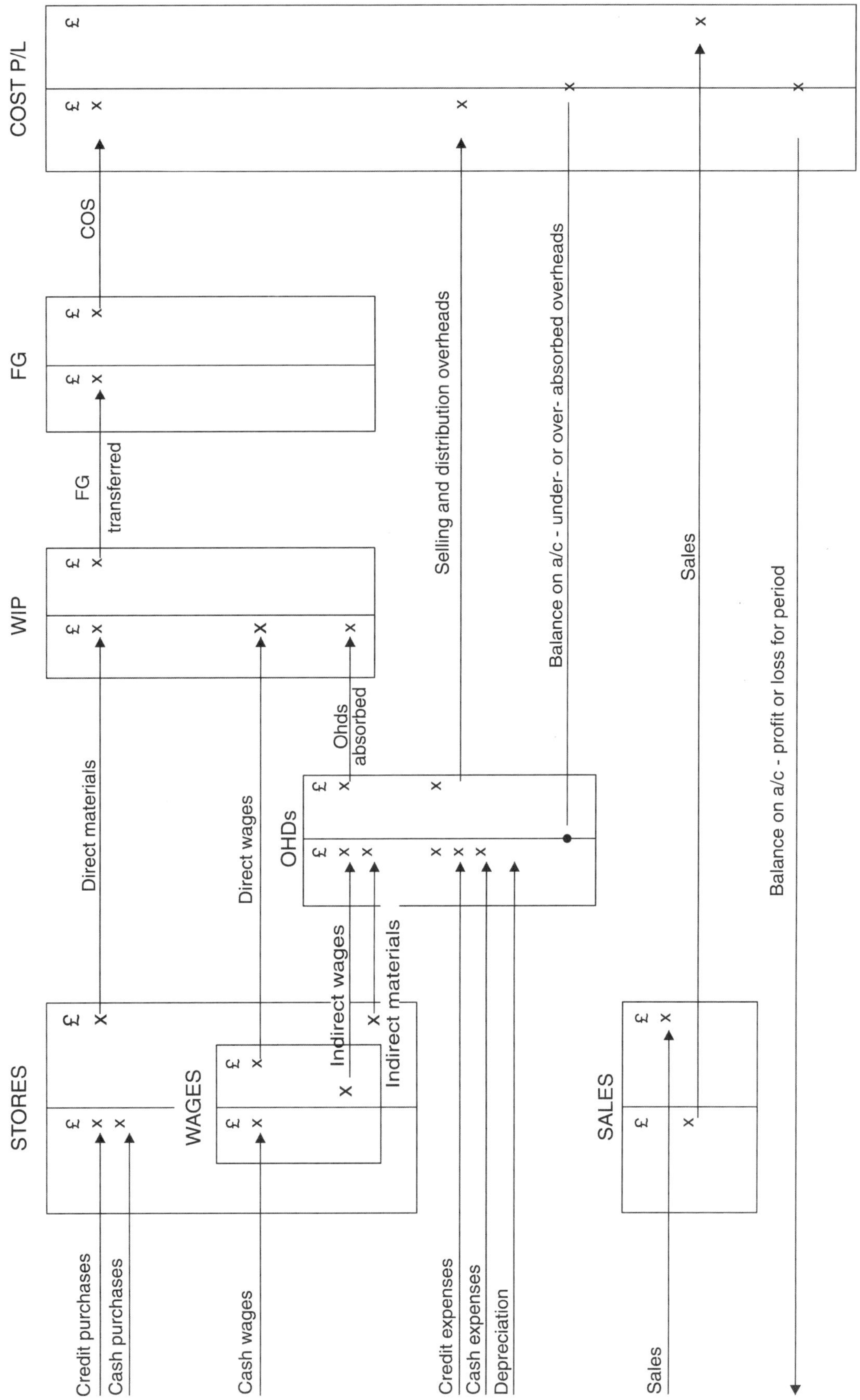

COST P/L

FG

COS

WIP

FG
transferred

OHDs

Ohds
absorbed

STORES

WAGES

SALES

£ £ £

Direct materials

Direct wages

Indirect wages

Indirect materials

Selling and distribution overheads

Balance on a/c - under- or over- absorbed overheads

Sales

Balance on a/c - profit or loss for period

Credit purchases
Cash purchases

Cash wages

Credit expenses
Cash expenses
Depreciation

Sales

Cost accounting using marginal costing

Solution

The figures in brackets refer to the explanations which follow after the ledger accounts.

RAW MATERIALS CONTROL

	£'000		£'000
Balance b/d	10	Work in progress (1)	42
Creditors	50	Production overhead control (1)	5
		Balance c/d	13
	60		60
Balance b/d	13		

WORK IN PROGRESS CONTROL

	£'000		£'000
Balance b/d	15	Finished goods control (4)	90
Raw materials control (1)	42	Balance c/d (4)	21
Wages and salaries control (2)	30		
Production overhead control (3)	24		
	111		111
Balance b/d	21		

FINISHED GOODS CONTROL

	£'000		£'000
Balance b/d	18	Cost of sales (5)	97
Work in progress control (4)	90	Balance c/d (5)	11
	108		108
Balance b/d	11		

PRODUCTION OVERHEAD CONTROL

	£'000		£'000
Raw materials control (1)	5	Work in progress control (3)	24
Wages and salaries control (2)	13	Under absorption to income	
Bank (6)	8	statement	5
Provision for depreciation (6)	3		
	29		29

WAGES AND SALARIES CONTROL

	£'000		£'000
Bank (7)	53	Work in progress control (2)	30
Balance c/d (7)	2	Production overhead control (2)	13
		Selling and admin o/h control (2)	12
	55		55
		Balance b/d	2

SELLING AND ADMINISTRATION OVERHEAD CONTROL

	£'000		£'000
Bank (6)	9	Income statement	23
Wages and salaries control (2)	12		
Provision for depreciation (6)	2		
	23		23

COST OF SALES

	£'000		£'000
Finished goods control (5)	97	Income statement	97

INCOME STATEMENT

	£'000		£'000
Cost of sales (5)	97	Sales – receivables	145
Gross profit c/d	48		
	145		145
Under-absorbed overhead (8)	5	Gross profit b/d	48
Selling and admin o/h	23		
Net profit for October	20		
	48		48

Notes

1   The materials issued to production are charged as **direct materials** to work in progress. The materials issued to production service departments are **indirect materials**. The cost of indirect materials is 'collected' in the production overhead control account, pending its later absorption, along with all the other production overheads, into the value of work in progress.

2   The wages and salaries **incurred** are debited to the relevant control accounts:

- direct wages to work in progress
- indirect wages to production overhead control
- selling and administration salaries to selling and administration overhead control

The credit entry for wages **incurred** is made in the wages and salaries control account.

3   Once the direct material and direct wages have been debited to work in progress, the next step is to **absorb production overheads**, using the predetermined overhead absorption rate. The work in progress account is charged with 80 per cent of wages incurred: £30,000 × 80% = £24,000.

4   Now that all of the elements of production cost have been charged to work in progress, the **production cost of goods completed** can be transferred to the finished goods control account. The balance on the work in progress account represents the inventory at the end of October.

5   The **production cost of goods sold** is transferred from the finished goods account to the cost of sales account. The balance on the finished goods account represents the inventory at the end of October.

6   The production expenses incurred and the depreciation on production machinery are debited in the production overhead control account. Thus they are 'collected' with the other production overheads, for later **absorption into work in progress**.

7   The total amount of wages **paid** (£28,000 + £13,000 + £12,000) is debited to the wages and salaries control account. The balance remaining on the account is the difference between the wages paid and the wages incurred. This represents a £2,000 accrual for wages, which is carried down into next month's accounts.

8   The balance remaining on the production overhead control account is the difference between the production overhead incurred, and the amount absorbed into work in progress. On this occasion the overhead is **underabsorbed** and is transferred as a debit in the income statement.

Question   Raw materials inventory control account

Learning outcome: A(iii)

The following information relates to E for March.

Opening balance of raw materials	£12,000
Raw materials purchased on credit	£80,000
Raw materials issued: to production	£73,000
to production maintenance	£8,000
Raw materials returned to supplier	£2,000

Required

Complete the raw materials inventory control account for March.

Answer

RAW MATERIALS INVENTORY CONTROL

	£		£
Balance b/d	12,000	Work in progress	73,000
Payables	80,000	Production overhead control	8,000
		Payables	2,000
		Balance c/d	9,000
	92,000		92,000
Balance b/d	9,000		

Question   Production overhead control account

Learning outcome: A(iii)

The following information relates to Jamboree.

Production overheads incurred	$50,000
Labour hours worked	5,000
Production overhead absorption rate	$11 per labour hour

Required

Complete the production overhead control account for the period.

Answer

PRODUCTION OVERHEAD CONTROL ACCOUNT

	$		$
Cash/payables	50,000	Work in progress control	
Over-absorbed overhead to income		(5,000 hr × $11)	55,000
statement	5,000		
	55,000		55,000

Question
Integrated system

Learning outcome: A(iii)

At the end of a period, in an integrated cost and financial accounting system, the accounting entries for £18,000 overheads under-absorbed would be

A	Debit work-in-progress control account	Credit overhead control account
B	Debit income statement	Credit work-in-progress control account
C	Debit income statement	Credit overhead control account
D	Debit overhead control account	Credit income statement

Answer

Eliminate the incorrect options first. The only overhead charge made to work in progress (WIP) is the overhead absorbed into production based on the predetermined rate. Under or over absorption does not affect WIP. This eliminates A and B. Under-absorbed overhead means that overhead charges have been too low therefore there must be a further debit to the income statement. This eliminates D, and the correct answer is C.

2 Interlocking systems

2.1 How an interlocking system works

An **interlocking system** features two separate ledgers.

(a)   The **financial ledger** contains asset, liability, revenue, expense and appropriation (eg dividend) accounts. The trial balance of an enterprise is prepared from the financial ledger.

(b)   The **cost ledger** is where cost information such as the build-up of work in progress is analysed in more detail.

2.2 The cost ledger control account

Certain items of cost or revenue are of no interest to the cost accountant because they are **financial accounting items**. These include the following.

- Interest or dividends received
- Dividends paid
- Discounts allowed, or received for prompt payment of invoices

Some financial accounting items are related to costs and profits (and hence they interest the cost accountant), although accounts for these items are not included in the separate cost accounting books. The most important of these items are cash, payables, receivables and accumulated profits.

FAST FORWARD

> To overcome the need to have accounts for cash, payables and so on in the cost books in an interlocking system, a **cost ledger control account** is used. It represents all the accounts in the financial accounting books which are not included in the corresponding cost accounting books.

Question

Learning outcome: A(iii)

M uses an interlocking marginal costing bookkeeping system. The following data has been extracted from M's records for March.

	€
Work in progress inventory opening	8,040
closing	2,100
Production overhead expenditure incurred on credit	41,300
Direct material issued to production	21,800
Materials issued to production maintenance department	3,930
Direct labour cost incurred	29,100
Indirect labour cost incurred	7,200
Depreciation of production machinery	10,000

Thirty per cent of all production overhead costs are deemed to be variable.

Required

Prepare the following ledger accounts for March

(a)   Production overhead control account
(b)   work in progress control account

Answer

(a)   PRODUCTION OVERHEAD CONTROL ACCOUNT

	€		€
Cost ledger control	41,300	Work in progress (variable	
Material stores control	3,930	overhead 30% × €62,430)	18,729
Wages control	7,200	Income statement – fixed	
Cost ledger control	10,000	overhead	43,701
	62,430		62,430

(b)   WORK IN PROGRESS CONTROL ACCOUNT

	€		€
Balance b/d	8,040	Finished goods control	75,649
Material stores control	21,880	Balance b/d	2,100
Wages control	29,100		
Production overhead control	18,729		
	77,749		77,749
Balance b/d	2,100		

3 Ledger accounts in job or batch environments

The ledger accounts in a job or batch environment use exactly the same principles that we have demonstrated so far in this chapter. The difference is that **a separate work in progress account is maintained for each individual job or batch.**

FAST FORWARD

The work in progress control account in a job or batch environment contains the summary totals of the entries in the individual job or batch accounts.

Another difference is a job costing environment is that **goods are not produced for inventory, but for individual customers' requirements.**

In a job costing environment, the cost of completed production is transferred direct from work in progress control to the cost of sales account. There is unlikely to be a ledger account for finished goods inventory.

3.1 Example: ledger accounts in a job environment

This example demonstrates the ledger accounts in an absorption costing system. If a marginal costing system was used instead, **only the variable production overhead cost would be added to job costs work in progress**. The fixed production overhead would be charged direct to the income statement and **there would be no account for under-/over-absorbed overheads**.

A jobbing company operates an absorption costing system. On 1 June 20X2, there was one uncompleted job in the factory. The job card for this work is summarised as follows.

Job Card, Job No 6832

Costs to date	£
Direct materials	630
Direct labour (120 hours)	840
Factory overhead (£2 per direct labour hour)	240
Factory cost to date	1,710

During June, three new jobs were started in the factory, and costs of production were as follows.

Direct materials		£
Issued to:	Job 6832	2,390
	Job 6833	1,680
	Job 6834	3,950
	Job 6835	4,420
Damaged inventory written off from stores		2,300

Material transfers	£
Job 6834 to Job 6833	250
Job 6832 to Job 6834	620

Materials returned to store	£
From Job 6832	870
From Job 6835	170

Direct labour hours recorded	
Job 6832	430 hrs
Job 6833	650 hrs
Job 6834	280 hrs
Job 6835	410 hrs

The cost of labour hours during June 20X2 was £8 per hour, and production overhead is absorbed at the rate of £2 per direct labour hour. Production overheads incurred during the month amounted to £3,800. Completed jobs were delivered to customers as soon as they were completed, and the invoiced amounts were as follows.

Job 6832	£8,500
Job 6834	£9,000
Job 6835	£9,500

Administration and marketing overheads are added to the cost of sales at the rate of 20% of factory cost. Actual costs incurred during June 20X2 amounted to £4,418.

Required

(a)   Prepare the job accounts for each individual job during June 20X2; (the accounts should only show the cost of production, and not the full cost of sale).

(b)   Prepare the summarised job cost cards for each job, and calculate the profit on each completed job.

(c)   Show how the costs would be shown in the company's cost control accounts.

Solution

(a)   **Job accounts**

JOB 6832

	£		£
Balance b/f	1,710	Job 6834 a/c	620
Materials (stores a/c)	2,390	(materials transfer)	
Labour (wages a/c)	3,440	Stores a/c (materials returned)	870
Production overhead (o'hd a/c)	860	Cost of sales a/c (balance)	6,910
	8,400		8,400

JOB 6833

	£		£
Materials (stores a/c)	1,680	Balance c/f	8,430
Labour (wages a/c)	5,200		
Production overhead (o'hd a/c)	1,300		
Job 6834 a/c (materials transfer)	250		
	8,430		8,430

JOB 6834

	£		£
Materials (stores a/c)	3,950	Job 6833 a/c (materials transfer)	250
Labour (wages a/c)	2,240		
Production overhead (o'hd a/c)	560	Cost of sales a/c (balance)	7,120
Job 6832 a/c (materials transfer)	620		
	7,370		7,370

JOB 6835

	£		£
Materials (stores a/c)	4,420	Stores a/c (materials returned)	170
Labour (wages a/c)	3,280		
Production overhead (o'hd a/c)	820	Cost of sales a/c (balance)	8,350
	8,520		8,520

(b)   **Job cards, summarised**

	Job 6832	Job 6833	Job 6834	Job 6835
	£	£	£	£
Materials	1,530*	1,930	4,320 **	4,250
Labour	4,280	5,200	2,240	3,280
Production overhead	1,100	1,300	560	820
Factory cost	6,910	(c/f) 8,430	7,120	8,350
Admin & marketing o'hd (20%)	1,382		1,424	1,670
Cost of sale	8,292		8,544	10,020
Invoice value	8,500		9,000	9,500
Profit/(loss) on job	208		456	(520)

* £(630 + 2,390 − 620 − 870)   ** £(3,950 + 620 − 250)

(c)   **Control accounts**

STORES CONTROL (incomplete)

	£		£
WIP a/c (returns)	1,040	WIP a/c	
		(2,390 + 1,680 + 3,950 + 4,420)	12,440
		Income statement:	
		inventory written off	2,300

WORK IN PROGRESS CONTROL

	£		£
Balance b/f	1,710	Stores control a/c (returns)	1,040
Stores control a/c	12,440	Cost of sales a/c	
Wages control a/c	*14,160	(6,910 + 7,120 + 8,350)	22,380
Production o'hd control a/c	**3,540	Balance c/f (Job No 6833)	8,430
	31,850		31,850

* 1,770 hours at £8 per hour
** 1,770 hours at £2 per hour

COST OF SALES CONTROL

	£		£
WIP control a/c	22,380	Income statement	26,856
Admin & marketing o'hd a/c			
(1,382 + 1,424 + 1,670)	4,476		
	26,856		26,856

SALES

	£		£
Income statement	27,000	Receivables	27,000
		(8,500 + 9,000 + 9,500)	
	27,000		27,000

PRODUCTION OVERHEAD CONTROL

	£		£
Overhead incurred – payables	3,800	WIP a/c	3,540
		Under-absorbed o'hd a/c	260
	3,800		3,800

UNDER-/OVER-ABSORBED OVERHEADS

	£		£
Production o'hd control a/c	260	Admin & marketing o'hd a/c	58
		Income statement	202
	260		260

ADMIN & MARKETING OVERHEAD CONTROL

	£		£
Overhead incurred – payables	4,418	Cost of sales a/c	4,476
Over absorbed o'hd a/c	58		
	4,476		4,476

INCOME STATEMENT

	£		£
Cost of sales a/c	26,856	Sales a/c	27,000
Stores a/c (inventory written off)	2,300		
Under-absorbed overhead a/c	202	Loss	2,358
	29,358		29,358

The loss of £2,358 is the sum of the profits/losses on each completed job £(208 + 456 – 520) = £144, minus the total of under-absorbed overhead (£202) and the inventory write-off (£2,300).

Chapter Roundup

- There are four main groups of accounts in an integrated system

    - The resources accounts

    - Accounts which record the cost of production items from the start of production work through to cost of sales

    - Sales account

    - Income statement

- To overcome the need to have accounts for cash, payables and so on in the cost books in an interlocking system, a **cost ledger control account** is used. It represents all the accounts in the financial accounting books which are not included in the corresponding cost accounting books.

- The work in progress control account in a job or batch environment contains the summary totals of the entries in the individual job or batch accounts.

- In a job costing environment, the cost of completed production is transferred direct from work in progress control to the cost of sales account. There is unlikely to be a ledger account for finished goods inventory.

Quick Quiz

1   What is the double entry for the following in an integrated accounts absorption costing system?

(a)   Production overhead absorbed in the cost of production
(b)   Completed work transferred from the production process to inventory

2   GF bought £100,000 worth of materials and issued £75,000 to production. Which of the following entries represents the correct bookkeeping treatment? (Select three options.)

I	Dr	Raw materials	£75,000
II	Dr	Raw materials	£100,000
III	Dr	Work-in-progress	£75,000
IV	Cr	Raw materials	£75,000
V	Cr	Raw materials	£100,000
VI	Dr	Work-in-progress	£75,000
VII	Dr	Work-in-progress	£100,000

3 The production overhead control account for October looks like this.

PRODUCTION OVERHEAD CONTROL ACCOUNT

	$		$
Raw materials control	1,840	Work in progress	55,400
Wages control	7,900	Under-/over-absorbed overhead	1,520
Payables control	47,180		
	56,920		56,920

Indicate whether the following statements are true or false.

		True	False
I	Indirect materials issued during October were $1,840	☐	☐
II	Direct wages incurred during October were $7,900	☐	☐
III	Production overhead incurred during October was $55,400	☐	☐
IV	Production overhead for October was over-absorbed	☐	☐

4 Rocky Landscapes undertakes small landscaping jobs on customers' premises.

Three jobs were worked on last period. Details are as follows.

	Job P €	Job Q €	Job R €	Total €
Opening work in progress	1,405	-	-	1,450
Direct materials added in period	240	1,640	1,230	3,110
Direct wages incurred in period	920	984	610	2,514
Overhead absorbed	390	370	420	1,180
	3,000	2,994	2,260	8,254

Job R was the only incomplete job at the end of the period.

Which of the following ledger entries is correct?

	Debit		Credit	
A	Work in progress	€2,260	Cost of sales	€2,260
B	Cost of sales	€2,260	Work in progress	€2,260
C	Finished goods	€5,994	Work in progress	€5,994
D	Cost of sales	€5,994	Work in progress	€5,994

5 IN a batch costing system, a separate work in progress account is maintained for each unit in the batch.

True ☐

False ☐

Answers to Quick Quiz

1   (a)   Dr   Work in progress control account
            Cr   Production overhead account

    (b)   Dr   Finished goods control account
            Cr   Work in progress control account

2   II
    IV
    VI

Costs incurred are debited to the materials account, and those issued as direct materials to production are credited to the materials account and subsequently debited to the work-in-progress account.

3   I   True. Issues of indirect materials are charged to the production overhead control account

    II   False. *Indirect* wages incurred were $7,900

    III   False. Production overhead *absorbed* was $55,400

    IV   False. Production overhead for October was *under-absorbed* because overhead incurred ($56,920) was greater than overhead absorbed ($55,400)

4   D.   The completed cost of jobs P and Q is transferred from work in progress to cost of sales. No finished goods inventory is held therefore C is not correct.

5   False.   A separate work in progress is maintained for each *batch*, as well as a work in progress control account which summarises the costs of all batches in progress.

Now try the questions below from the Exam Question Bank

Number	Level	Marks	Time
Q2	Examination	5	9 mins
Q3	Examination	5	9 mins

Process costing

3

Introduction

You will already be familiar with the principles of process costing from your earlier studies. However, many students feel daunted by process costing so we are going to **start from basics again** and in **Section 1** we will provide you with **four steps** that you can **use as a framework to answer any process costing question**.

In this chapter we will be revising what you know already, such as **losses** in **Section 2**, dealing with **closing work in progress** in **Section 3** and the **weighted average cost method** of valuing opening work in progress in **Section 4**, building on that knowledge and considering some more complex applications.

Your *Management Accounting Performance Evaluation* syllabus also requires you to be able to **apply marginal and absorption approaches in process environments** so we will be spending some time reviewing the difference between the two approaches within a process environment.

This is quite a **long chapter** but don't worry because you have **covered lots of it already**.

Topic list	Learning outcomes	Syllabus references	Ability required
1 A framework for dealing with process costing questions	A(iii)	A 4	Application
2 Losses in process	A(iii)	A 4	Application
3 Dealing with closing work in progress	A(iii)	A 4	Application
4 Dealing with opening work in progress – weighted average cost method	A(iii)	A 4	Application
5 Dealing with opening work in progress – FIFO method	A(iii)	A 4	Application
6 Selecting the method of valuing work in progress	A(iii)	A 6	Application
7 Changes in WIP levels and losses	A(iii)	A 4	Application
8 Losses/gains at different stages	A(iii)	A 4	Application
9 Marginal or absorption costing in a process environment	A(ii)	A 1, 2, 6	Application
10 Joint products and by-products	A(iii)	A 4	Application
11 Valuing joint products	A(iii)	A 4	Application
12 Valuing by-products	A(iii)	A 4	Application

Key term

Process costing is 'The costing method applicable where goods or services result from a sequence of continuous or repetitive operations or processes. Costs are averaged over the units produced during the period, being initially charged to the operation or process'.   (CIMA *Official Terminology*)

Knowledge brought forward from earlier studies

Process costing

- It is common (but not essential) to **identify process costing with continuous production** such as oil refining, or the manufacture of soap, paint, textiles, paper, foods and drinks, many chemicals and so on. Process costing may also be associated with the continuous production of large volumes of low-cost items, such as cans or tins and with mass production industries such as car manufacturing.

- The **features** of process costing which make it different from job or batch costing are as follows.

  - The continuous nature of production in many processes means that there will usually be **opening and closing work in progress which must be valued**. In process costing it is not possible to build up cost records of the cost per unit of output or the cost per unit of closing stock because **production in progress is an indistinguishable homogeneous mass.**

  - There is often a **loss in process** due to spoilage, wastage, evaporation and so on.

  - Output from production may be a single product, but there may also be a **by-product** (or by-products) and/or **joint products**.

- The basic idea behind process costing is that, where a series of separate processes is required to manufacture the finished product, **the output of one process becomes the input to the next** until the final output is made in the final process. For example, if two processes are required the accounts would look like this.

PROCESS 1 ACCOUNT

	Units	£		Units	£
Direct materials	1,000	50,000	Output to process 2	1,000	90,000
Direct labour		20,000			
Production overhead		20,000			
	1,000	90,000		1,000	90,000

PROCESS 2 ACCOUNT

	Units	£		Units	£
Materials from process 1	1,000	90,000	Output to finished goods	1,500	150,000
Added materials	500	30,000			
Direct labour		15,000			
Production overhead		15,000			
	1,500	150,000		1,500	150,000

  - Direct labour and production overhead may be treated together in an examination question as **'conversion cost'**.

  - Added materials, labour and overhead in process 2 are added gradually throughout the process. Materials from process 1, in contrast, will be introduced in full at the start of process 2.

  - The 'units' columns in the process accounts are for memorandum purposes only and help you to ensure that you do not miss out any entries.

1 A Framework for dealing with process costing questions

Process costing is centred around four key steps.

| Step 1 | Determine output and losses. |

- Determine expected output.
- Calculate normal loss and abnormal loss and gain.
- Calculate equivalent units if there is closing or opening work in progress.

| Step 2 | Calculate cost per unit of output, losses and WIP. |

- Calculate cost per unit or cost per equivalent unit.

| Step 3 | Calculate total cost of output, losses and WIP. |

- In some examples this will be straightforward

- If there is closing and/or opening work-in-progress a **statement of evaluation** will have to be prepared.

| Step 4 | Complete accounts. |

- Complete the process account.
- Write up the other accounts required such as abnormal loss/gain accounts.

Exam focus point

This framework should be familiar to you from your earlier studies. The exact work done at each step will depend on whether there are losses, opening stock, closing stock and so on, but this four-step approach can be adopted in any question. It would be a good idea to commit the layout to memory since the pilot paper awarded three marks for presentation in a process costing question.

2 Losses in process

Losses during processing can happen through evaporation of liquids, wastage, or rejected units, and so the quantity of materials output from a process might be less than the quantities input. How would any losses be costed?

2.1 Three different ways of costing losses

One way of costing output is to say that the **cost per unit should be based on actual units produced (output), so that any lost units have no cost at all**. This would mean that the cost varies according to the actual loss in the period. If some loss in process is unavoidable, and if the amount of loss varies a little from period to period, this approach to costing will result in fluctuations in unit costs.

It might be more satisfactory to take a longer-term view of loss, and calculate average unit costs on the basis of average loss over a longer period of time. This would give greater stability and consistency to unit costs of production between one period and the next.

A second way of costing the output is to say that **lost units have a cost, which should be charged to the income statement whenever they occur**. The cost per unit would then be **based on units of *input* rather than units of output.**

The main drawback to this method of costing is that **if some loss in processing is unavoidable** and to be expected, there would be **some cost of production unavoidably written off to the income statement** in every period, and this is an unsatisfactory method of costing.

The third method of costing loss (described below and covered in your earlier studies) is a **compromise system**, which is based on the following view.

- **If some loss is to be expected, it should not be given a cost.**
- **If there is some loss that 'shouldn't happen', it ought to be given a cost.**

2.2 Normal loss and abnormal loss/gain

Key terms

- **Normal loss** is the loss expected in the normal course of operations for unavoidable reasons.

- **Abnormal loss** is the loss resulting when actual loss is greater than the normal or expected loss.

- **Abnormal gain** is the gain resulting when actual loss is less than the normal or expected loss.

As alternatives, here are the *Official Terminology* definitions.

Normal loss is 'An expected loss, allowed for in the budget, and normally calculated as a percentage of the good output from a process during a period of time'.

Abnormal loss/gain are 'Any losses which exceed the normal loss allowance (abnormal loss) or reduction in the volume of process loss below that set by the normal loss allowance (abnormal gain).

FAST FORWARD

Losses and gains may arise in a process

- Normal loss is not given a cost.

- Abnormal loss is given a cost.

- Abnormal gain is given a 'cost', which is debited rather than credited to the process cost account: it is a 'negative' cost and so an item of gain.

Question

Losses

Learning outcome: A(iii)

3,000 units of material are input to a process. Process costs are as follows.

Material	$11,700
Conversion costs	$6,300

Output is 2,000 units. Normal loss is 20% of input.

What value will abnormal loss and normal loss have in the process account?

	Normal loss	Abnormal loss
A	$4,500	$3,000
B	$4,500	$nil
C	$nil	$3,000
D	$nil	$nil

The correct answer is C.

Step 1   **Determine output and losses**

We are told that output is 2,000 units.
Normal loss = 20% × 3,000 = 600 units
Abnormal loss = (3,000 − 600) − 2,000 = 400 units

Step 2   **Calculate cost per unit of output and losses**

$$\text{Cost per unit} = \frac{\$(11,700 + 6,300)}{2,400} = \$7.50$$

Step 3   **Calculate total cost of output and losses**

		$
Output	(2,000 × $7.50)	15,000
Normal loss		0
Abnormal loss	(400 × $7.50)	3,000
		18,000

Step 4   **Complete accounts**

PROCESS ACCOUNT

	Units	$		Units	$
Material	3,000	11,700	Output	2,000	15,000
Conversion costs		6,300	Normal loss	600	
			Abnormal loss	400	3,000
	3,000	18,000		3,000	18,000

Normal loss will have a zero value and so **options A and B** must be incorrect. Abnormal losses are valued at the full cost per unit so **options B and D** must be incorrect.

2.3 Scrap

Scrap is 'Discarded material having some value'.   (CIMA *Official Terminology*)

Loss or spoilage may be scrap.

> • **The scrap value of normal loss is usually deducted from the cost of materials.**
>
> • **The scrap value of abnormal loss (or abnormal gain) is usually set off against its cost, in an abnormal loss (abnormal gain) account.**

As the questions that follow will show, the three steps to remember are these.

Firstly   Separate the scrap value of normal loss from the scrap value of abnormal loss or gain.

Secondly   In effect, subtract the scrap value of normal loss from the cost of the process, by crediting it to the process account (as a 'value' for normal loss).

Thirdly   *Either* subtract the value of abnormal loss scrap from the cost of abnormal loss, by crediting the abnormal loss account.

        or subtract the cost of the abnormal gain scrap from the value of abnormal gain, by debiting the abnormal gain account.

Question

Learning outcome: A(iii)

Look back at the previous question. Suppose the units of loss could be sold for $1 each. Prepare appropriate accounts.

Answer

Step 1   **Determine output and losses**

Actual output	2,000 units
Abnormal loss	400 units
Expected output	2,400 units

Step 2   **Calculate cost per unit of output and losses**

	$
Scrap value of normal loss	600
Scrap value of abnormal loss	400
Total scrap (1,000 units × $1)	1,000

Step 3   **Calculate total cost of output and losses**

		$
Output	(2,000 × $7.25)	14,500
Normal loss	(600 × $1.00)	600
Abnormal loss	(400 × $7.25)	2,900
		18,000

$$\text{Cost per expected unit} = \frac{\$((11,700 - 600) + 6,300)}{2,400} = \$7.25$$

Step 4   Complete accounts

PROCESS ACCOUNT

	Units	$		Units	$
Material	3,000	11,700	Output	2,000	14,500
Conversion costs		6,300	Normal loss	600	600
			Abnormal loss	400	2,900
	3,000	18,000		3,000	18,000

ABNORMAL LOSS ACCOUNT

	$		$
Process a/c	2,900	Scrap a/c	400
		P&L a/c	2,500
	2,900		2,900

SCRAP ACCOUNT

	$		$
Normal loss	600	Cash	1,000
Abnormal loss	400		
	1,000		1,000

 Question   Two processes, losses and scrap

Learning outcome: A(iii)

JJ has a factory which operates two production processes, cutting and pasting. Normal loss in each process is 10%. Scrapped units out of the cutting process sell for £3 per unit whereas scrapped units out of the pasting process sell for £5. Output from the cutting process is transferred to the pasting process: output from the pasting process is finished output ready for sale.

Relevant information about costs for control period 7 are as follows.

	Cutting process		Pasting process	
	Units	£	Units	£
Input materials	18,000	54,000		
Transferred to pasting process	16,000			
Materials from cutting process			16,000	
Added materials			14,000	70,000
Labour and overheads		32,400		135,000
Output to finished goods			28,000	

Required

Prepare accounts for the cutting process, the pasting process, abnormal loss, abnormal gain and scrap.

Answer

(a)   *Cutting process*

Step 1   Determine output and losses

The normal loss is 10% of 18,000 units = 1,800 units, and the actual loss is (18,000 − 16,000) = 2,000 units. This means that there is abnormal loss of 200 units.

Actual output	16,000 units
Abnormal loss	200 units
Expected output (90% of 18,000)	16,200 units

Step 2   Calculate cost per unit of output and losses

(i)   The total value of scrap is 2,000 units at £3 per unit = £6,000. We must split this between the scrap value of normal loss and the scrap value of abnormal loss.

	£
Normal loss (1,800 × £3)	5,400
Abnormal loss (200 × £3)	600
Total scrap (2,000 units × £3)	6,000

(ii)   The scrap value of normal loss is first deducted from the materials cost in the process, in order to calculate the output cost per unit and then credited to the process account as a 'value' for normal loss. The cost per unit in the cutting process is calculated as follows.

	Total cost		Cost per expected unit of output
	£		£
Materials	54,000		
Less normal loss scrap value*	5,400		
	48,600	(÷ 16,200)	3.00
Labour and overhead	32,400	(÷ 16,200)	2.00
Total	81,000	(÷ 16,200)	5.00

* It is usual to set this scrap value of normal loss against the cost of materials.

Step 3   Calculate total cost of output and losses

		£
Output	(16,000 units × £5)	80,000
Normal loss	(1,800 units × £3)	5,400
Abnormal loss	(200 units × £5)	1,000
		86,400

Step 4   Complete accounts

PROCESS 1 ACCOUNT

	Units	£		Units	£
Materials	18,000	54,000	Output to pasting process *	16,000	80,000
Labour and			Normal loss (scrap a/c)	1,800	5,400
overhead		32,400	Abnormal loss a/c	200	1,000
	18,000	86,400		18,000	86,400

* At £5 per unit

(b)   *Pasting process*

Step 1   Determine output and losses

The normal loss is 10% of the units processed = 10% of (16,000 + 14,000) = 3,000 units. The actual loss is (30,000 − 28,000) = 2,000 units, so that there is abnormal gain of 1,000 units. These are *deducted* from actual output to determine expected output.

	Units
Actual output	28,000
Abnormal gain	(1,000)
Expected output (90% of 30,000)	27,000

Step 2   Calculate cost per unit of output and losses

(i)   The total value of scrap is 2,000 units at £5 per unit = £10,000. We must split this between the scrap value of normal loss and the scrap value of abnormal gain. Abnormal gain's scrap value is 'negative'.

		£
Normal loss scrap value	3,000 units × £5	15,000
Abnormal gain scrap value	1,000 units × £5	(5,000)
Scrap value of actual loss	2,000 units × £5	10,000

(ii)   The scrap value of normal loss is first deducted from the cost of materials in the process, in order to calculate a cost per unit of output, and then credited to the process account as a 'value' for normal loss. The cost per unit in the pasting process is calculated as follows.

	Total cost £		Cost per expected unit of output £
Materials:			
Transfer from cutting process	80,000		
Added in pasting process	70,000		
	150,000		
Less scrap value of normal loss	15,000		
	135,000	(÷ 27,000)	5
Labour and overhead	135,000	(÷ 27,000)	5
	270,000	(÷ 27,000)	10

Step 3   Calculate total cost of output and losses

		£
Output	(28,000 units × £10)	280,000
Normal loss	(3,000 units × £5)	15,000
		295,000
Abnormal gain	(1,000 units × £10)	(10,000)
		285,000

Step 4   Complete accounts

PASTING PROCESS ACCOUNT

	Units	£		Units	£
From cutting process	16,000	80,000	Finished output *	28,000	280,000
Added materials	14,000	70,000			
Labour and overhead		135,000	Normal loss	3,000	15,000
	30,000	285,000	(scrap a/c)		
Abnormal gain a/c	1,000*	10,000			
	31,000	295,000		31,000	295,000

* At £10 per unit

(c) and (d)

Abnormal loss and abnormal gain accounts

For each process, one or the other of these accounts will record three items.

(i)   The cost/value of the abnormal loss/gain (corresponding entry to that in the process account).

(ii)   The scrap value of the abnormal loss or gain, to set off against it.

(iii)   A balancing figure, which is written to the income statement as an adjustment to the profit figure.

ABNORMAL LOSS ACCOUNT

	Units	£		£
Cutting process	200	1,000	Scrap a/c (scrap value of ab. loss)	600
			Income statement (balance)	400
		1,000		1,000

ABNORMAL GAIN ACCOUNT

	£		Units	£
Scrap a/c (scrap value of abnormal gain units)	5,000	Pasting process	1,000	10,000
Income statement (balance)	5,000			
	10,000			10,000

(e)   **Scrap account**

This is credited with the cash value of actual units scrapped. The other entries in the account should all be identifiable as corresponding entries to those in the process accounts, and abnormal loss and abnormal gain accounts.

SCRAP ACCOUNT

	£		£
Normal loss:		Cash:	
Cutting process (1,800 × £3)	5,400	Sale of cutting process scrap (2,000 × £3)	6,000
Pasting process (3,000 × £5)	15,000	Sale of pasting process scrap (2,000 × £5)	10,000
Abnormal loss a/c	600	Abnormal gain a/c	5,000
	21,000		21,000

FAST FORWARD   Abnormal losses and gains never affect the cost of good units of production. The scrap value of abnormal losses is not credited to the process account, and abnormal loss and gain units carry the same full cost as a good unit of production.

2.4 Losses with a disposal cost

The **basic calculations required** in such circumstances are as follows.

(a) Increase the process costs by the cost of disposing of the units of normal loss and use the resulting cost per unit to value good output and abnormal loss/gain.

(b) The normal loss is given no value in the process account.

(c) Include the disposal costs of normal loss on the debit side of the process account.

(d) Include the disposal costs of abnormal loss in the abnormal loss account and hence in the transfer of the cost of abnormal loss to the profit and loss account.

Suppose that input to a process was 1,000 units at a cost of £4,500. Normal loss is 10% and there are no opening and closing stocks. Actual output was 860 units and loss units had to be disposed of at a cost of £0.90 per unit.

Normal loss = 10% × 1,000 = 100 units and so abnormal loss = 900 − 860 = 40 units

Cost per unit = (£4,500 + (100 × £0.90))/900 = £5.10

The relevant accounts would be as follows.

PROCESS ACCOUNT

	Units	£		Units	£
Cost of input	1,000	4,500	Output	860	4,386
Disposal cost of			Normal loss	100	-
normal loss		90	Abnormal loss	40	204
	1,000	4,590		1,000	4,590

ABNORMAL LOSS ACCOUNT

	£		£
Process a/c	204	Income statement	240
Disposal cost (40 × £0.90)	36		
	240		240

3 Dealing with closing work in progress

In the examples we have looked at so far we have assumed that opening and closing work in progress has been nil. We must now look at more realistic examples and consider how to allocate the costs incurred in a period between completed output (that is, finished units) and partly completed closing inventory.

> **Attention!**
>
> You covered this in Paper 2 but the following examples illustrate the problem and remind you of the technique used to share out (apportion) costs between finished output and work in progress inventory.

3.1 Example: dealing with closing work in progress

Suds is a manufacturer of soap. In control period 7, in one process, there was no opening work in progress, but 15,000 units of input were introduced to the process during the month, at the following cost.

	€
Direct materials	49,680
Direct labour	22,080
Production overhead	16,560
	88,320

Of the 15,000 units introduced, 12,000 were completely finished during the month and transferred to the next process. Closing work in progress of 3,000 units was only 60% complete with respect to materials and conversion costs.

The problem in this example is to **divide the costs of production** (€88,320) **between the finished output** of 12,000 units **and** the **closing work in progress** of 3,000 units. It is argued, with good reason, that a division of costs in proportion to the number of units of each (12,000:3,000) would not be 'fair' because the work in progress has not been completed, and has not yet 'received' its full amount of materials and conversion costs, but only 60% of the full amount. The 3,000 units of closing work in progress, being only 60% complete, are the equivalent of 1,800 fully worked units.

FAST FORWARD

To apportion costs fairly and proportionately when there is work in progress, **units of production must be converted into** the equivalent of completed units, that is, into **equivalent units of production**. Equivalent units then provide a basis for apportioning costs.

Key term

Equivalent units are 'Notional whole units representing uncompleted work'.

(CIMA *Official Terminology*)

Let's continue with our four-step approach.

Step 1   **Determine output and losses.**

In this case output is in terms of equivalent units.

	Total units	Completion	Equivalent units
Fully worked units	12,000	100%	12,000
Closing WIP	3,000	60%	1,800
	15,000		13,800

Step 2   **Calculate cost per unit of output, losses and WIP.**

Equivalent units are the basis for apportioning costs and so we need a 'cost per equivalent unit' as follows.

$$\frac{\text{Total cost}}{\text{Equivalent units}} = \frac{€88,320}{13,800}$$

Cost per equivalent unit   = €6.40

Step 3   **Calculate total cost of output, losses and WIP.**

A statement of evaluation may now be prepared, to show how the costs should be apportioned between finished output and closing WIP.

Item	Equivalent units	Cost per equivalent unit	Valuation €
Fully worked units	12,000	€6.40	76,800
Closing WIP	1,800	€6.40	11,520
	13,800		88,320

Step 4 Complete accounts.

The process account (work in progress, or work in process account) would be shown as follows.

PROCESS ACCOUNT

		Units	€		Units	€
(Stores a/c)	Direct materials	15,000	49,680	Output to next process	12,000	76,800
(Wages a/c)	Direct labour		22,080			
(O'hd a/c)	Production o'hd		16,560	Closing WIP c/f	3,000	11,520
		15,000	88,320		15,000	88,320

When preparing a process 'T' account, it might help to make the entries as follows.

(a) Enter the units first. The units columns are simply memorandum columns, but they help you to make sure that there are no units unaccounted for (for example as loss).

(b) Enter the costs of materials, labour and overheads next (and the value of opening WIP, if any). These should be given to you.

(c) Enter your valuation of finished output and closing WIP next. The value of the credit entries should, of course, equal the value of the debit entries.

3.2 Different rates of input

In many industries, materials, labour and overhead may be **added at different rates** during the course of production.

(a) **Output from a previous process** (for example the output from process 1 to process 2) may be introduced into the subsequent process all at once, so that **closing WIP is 100% complete** in respect of these materials.

(b) **Further materials may be added gradually** during the process, so that **closing WIP is only partially complete** in respect of these added materials.

(c) **Labour and overhead may be 'added' at yet another different rate**. When production overhead is absorbed on a labour hour basis, however, we should expect the degree of completion on overhead to be the same as the degree of completion on labour.

When this situation occurs, **equivalent units**, and a **cost per equivalent unit**, should be **calculated separately for each type of material, and also for conversion costs**.

3.3 Example: closing WIP and different degrees of completion

Suppose that we have the following process account for Process A for period 13.

PROCESS ACCOUNT

	Units	£		Units	£
Materials	1,000	6,200	Finished goods	800	?
Labour and overhead		2,850	Closing WIP	200	?
	1,000	9,050		1,000	9,050

47

Required

Closing WIP is 100% complete for materials and 25% complete for labour and overhead. Calculate a value for finished goods and closing WIP.

Solution: the four-step approach

Step 1   **Determine output and losses.**

		Materials		Labour and overhead	
	Total units	Degree of completion	Equivalent units	Degree of completion	Equivalent units
Finished output	800	100%	800	100%	800
Closing WIP	200	100%	200	25%	50
	1,000		1,000		850

Step 2   **Calculate cost per unit of output, losses and WIP.**

	Materials	Labour and overhead
Costs incurred in the period	£6,200	£2,850
Equivalent units of work done	1,000	850
Cost per equivalent unit (approx)	£6.20	£3.3529

Step 3   **Calculate total cost of output, losses and WIP.**

	Materials			Labour and overheads			
Item	Equivalent units	Cost per equivalent unit	Cost	Equivalent units	Cost per equivalent unit	Cost	Total cost
			£		£	£	£
Finished output	800	6.2	4,960	800	3.3529	2,682	7,642
Closing WIP	200	6.2	1,240	50	3.3529	168	1,408
	1,000		6,200	850		2,850	9,050

Step 4   **Complete accounts.**

PROCESS ACCOUNT

	Units	£		Units	£
Materials	1,000	6,200	Finished goods	800	7,642
Labour overhead		2,850	Closing WIP	200	1,408
	1,000	9,050		1,000	9,050

4 Dealing with opening work in progress – weighted average cost method

4.1 Valuing opening work in progress

FAST FORWARD

Work in progress can be valued using either the weighted average cost method or the FIFO method.

The weighted average cost method, which you covered in your earlier studies, is dealt with in this section. The FIFO method is considered in the next.

4.2 Weighted average cost method

The work required to complete units of opening stock is 100% minus the work in progress done in the previous period. For example, if 100 units of opening WIP are 70% complete at the beginning of June 20X2, the equivalent units of production would be as follows.

Equivalent units in previous period	(May 20X2) (70%)	=	70
Equivalent units to complete work in current period	(June 20X2) (30%)	=	30
Total work done			100

The weighted average cost method of valuation involves calculating a **weighted average cost of units produced from both opening WIP and units introduced in the current period**.

FAST FORWARD

When opening WIP is valued on a weighed average loss:

- **No distinction** is made between **units of opening WIP** and **new units introduced** to the process during the current period.

- The **cost of opening WIP** Is **added** to **costs incurred during the period**.

- **Completed units of opening WIP** are each given a **value of one full equivalent unit** of production.

4.3 Example: weighted average cost method

Suppose that we have the following process account for period 13.

PROCESS ACCOUNT

	Units	£		Units	£
Opening WIP	300	800			
Materials	700	5,400	Finished goods	800	?
Labour and overhead		2,850	Closing WIP	200	?
	1,000	9,050		1,000	9,050

Let's suppose that in the example above the degree of completion is as follows.

(a) **Direct materials**. These are added in full at the start of processing, and so any opening WIP or closing WIP have 100% of their direct material content. (This is not always the case. Materials might be added gradually throughout the process, in which case opening WIP will only be a certain percentage complete as to material content.)

(b) **Direct labour and production overhead**. These are usually assumed to be incurred at an even rate through the production process, so that when we refer to a unit that is 50% complete, we mean that it is half complete for labour and overhead, although it might be 100% complete for materials.

Continuing with the example, let us also make the following suppositions.

(a) The opening WIP is 100% complete for materials, and one-third complete for labour and overhead.

(b) The opening WIP's total cost of £800 consists of £550 direct materials and £250 labour and overhead.

(c) The closing WIP is 100% complete for materials and 25% complete for labour and overhead.

Solution: the four-step approach

If we use weighted average costing to value closing WIP, our four-step approach would be as follows.

Step 1   **Determine output and losses**

| | | Equivalent units | |
	Total units	Materials	Labour and overhead
Finished output	800	800	800
Closing WIP	200	200	50
Total	1,000	1,000	850

Step 2   **Calculate cost per unit of output, losses and WIP**

	Materials	Labour and overhead
Costs incurred in the period	£5,950*	£3,100**
Equivalent units of work done	1,000	850
Cost per equivalent unit (approx)	£5.95	£3.647

* £(550 + 5,400)   **£(250 + 2,850)

Step 3   **Calculate total cost of output, losses and WIP**

	Units	Materials £	Labour and overheads £	Total £
Finished output	800	4,760 (W1)	2,918 (W2)	7,678
Closing WIP	200	1,190 (W3)	182 (W4)	1,372
	1,000	5,950	3,100	9,050

Workings

1   800 × £5.95
2   800 × £3.647
3   200 × £5.95
4   50 × £3.647

Step 4   **Complete accounts**

PROCESS ACCOUNT

	£		£
Opening WIP	800	Finished output	7,678
Materials	5,400		
Labour and overhead	2,850	Closing WIP	1,372
	9,050		9,050

5 Dealing with opening work in progress – FIFO method

FAST FORWARD

When opening WIP is valued on a FIFO basis:

- Total output is divided between opening WIP and units started and completed in the period
- Cost of opening WIP is not added to costs incurred during the period
- Opening WIP completed is valued on an equivalent units basis

5.1 Example: FIFO method

With **FIFO**, we take the following view.

(a) **Opening WIP is finished first**. It is part-costed at the start of the period (in our example, at £800). We must therefore calculate how much it has cost to complete the units during the current period. The total cost to completion of these units of opening WIP is the sum of the cost brought forward as opening WIP value plus the cost in the current period to complete the units.

(b) **Some units are started and finished in the period**, and so are 100% produced during the period. In our example, the total finished output in the period is 800 units, of which 300 units were opening WIP, finished first, and so 500 units must have been started and finished in the period.

(c) **Some units are started and only part-completed**. These are the units of closing WIP.

Solution: the four-step approach

Step 1   **Determine output and losses**. We know what the output is and there are no losses, but we need to calculate equivalent units.

	Total units	Materials		Labour and overhead	
		Equivalent units of work in the current period			
Opening WIP	300	0	(note (a))	200	(note (b))
Units started and finished in the period	500	500	(note (c))	500	(note (c))
Total finished output	800				
Closing WIP	200	200	(note (d))	50	(note (e))
	1,000	700		750	

Notes

(a) Opening WIP already 100% complete for materials, so no more cost to add

(b) Opening WIP one-third complete at the start of the period, and so two-thirds of work (labour and overhead) needed to complete in this period. Equivalent units = $^2/_3 \times 300$ = 200

(c) Units started and completed in this period are one equivalent unit each

(d) Closing WIP: 100% complete for materials

(e) Closing WIP: equivalent units of labour and overhead = 25% of 200 = 50

Step 2   **Calculate cost per unit of output, losses and WIP**. We can now calculate an average cost per equivalent unit.

	Materials	Labour and overhead
Costs incurred in the period	£5,400	£2,850
Equivalent units of work done	700	750
Cost per equivalent unit (approx)	£7.715	£3.80

Step 3 **Calculate total cost of output, losses and WIP.** These costs per equivalent unit can now be used to build up the total costs of finished output and closing WIP.

	Units	Materials	£	Labour and overhead Units	£	Total cost £
Opening WIP cost b/f			550		250	800
Cost to complete			-	200 × £3.80	760	760
Total	300		550		1,010	1,560
Other finished units	500	× £7.715	3,857	500 × £3.80	1,900	5,757
Total finished output	800		4,407		2,910	7,317
Closing WIP	200	× £7.715	1,543	50 × £3.80	190	1,733
	1,000		5,950		3,100	9,050

Step 4 **Complete accounts**

PROCESS ACCOUNT

	£		£
Opening WIP	800	Finished goods	7,317
Materials	5,400		
Labour and overhead	2,850	Closing WIP	1,733
	9,050		9,050

5.2 Previous process costs

A common mistake made by students is to forget to include the costs of the previous process as an input cost in a subsequent process when dealing with production that passes through a number of processes (such as in the example in the 'knowledge brought forward' box at the beginning of the chapter).

Note that the **costs of the previous process** (Process 1 in the aforementioned box) are **combined together into a single cost of input in Process 2** and that we always **assume that the transfers into Process 2 are 100% complete with respect to Process 1 costs.** The cost of any additional materials added in Process 2 is treated separately from Process 1 costs.

Let's have a look at another example of the FIFO method as it's new to you.

5.3 Example: WIP and FIFO

Morrisey produces product Ash in a two-stage production process. Information relating to process 1 is as follows, for March 20X1.

Opening WIP 500 units:	degree of completion	60%
	cost to date	$2,800
Costs incurred in March 20X1		$
Direct materials (2,500 units introduced)		13,200
Direct labour		6,600
Production overhead		6,600
		26,400
Closing WIP 300 units: degree of completion		80%

There was no loss in the process.

Required

Prepare the process 1 account for March 20X1.

Solution

As the term implies, first in, first out means that in March 20X1 the first units completed were the units of opening WIP.

Opening WIP:	work done to date =	60%
	plus work done in March 20X1 =	40%

The cost of the work done up to 1 March 20X1 is known to be $2,800, so that the cost of the units completed will be $2,800 plus the cost of completing the final 40% of the work on the units in March 20X1.

Once the opening WIP has been completed, all other finished output in March 20X1 will be work started as well as finished in the month.

	Units
Total output in March 20X1*	2,700
Less opening WIP, completed first	500
Work started and finished in March 20X1	2,200

(* Opening WIP plus units introduced minus closing stock = 500 + 2,500 − 300)

What we are doing here is taking the **total output** of 2,700 units, and saying that we must **divide it into two parts** as follows.

(a)   The **opening WIP**, which was first in and so must be first out.

(b)   The **rest of the unit**s, which were 100% worked in the period.

Dividing finished output into two parts in this way is a necessary feature of the FIFO valuation method.

Continuing the example, closing WIP of 300 units will be started in March 20X1, but not yet completed.

The total cost of output to process 2 during March 20X1 will be as follows.

	$
Opening stock cost brought forward	2,800 (60%)
plus cost incurred during March 20X1,	
to complete	x (40%)
	2,800 + x
Fully worked 2,200 units	y
Total cost of output to process 2, FIFO basis	2,800 + x + y

Equivalent units will again be used as the basis for apportioning *costs incurred during March 20X1*. Be sure that you understand the treatment of 'opening WIP units completed', and can relate the calculations to the principles of FIFO valuation.

Step 1   **Determine output and losses.**

	Total units		Equivalent units of production in March 20X1
Opening stock units completed	500	(40%)	200
Fully worked units	2,200	(100%)	2,200
Output to process 2	2,700		2,400
Closing stock	300	(80%)	240
	3,000		2,640

Step 2   **Calculate cost per unit of output, losses and WIP.**

The cost per equivalent unit in March 20X1 can now be calculated.

$$\frac{\text{Cost incurred}}{\text{Equivalent units}} = \frac{\$26,400}{2,640}$$

Cost per equivalent unit = $10

Note that costs do *not* include the costs brought forward in opening WIP.

Step 3   Calculate total cost of output, losses and WIP.

	Equivalent units	Valuation $
Opening WIP, work done in March 20X1	200	2,000
Fully worked units	2,200	22,000
Closing WIP	240	2,400
	2,640	26,400

The total value of the completed opening WIP will be $2,800 (brought forward) plus $2,000 added in March before completion = $4,800.

Step 4   Complete accounts.

PROCESS 1 ACCOUNT

	Units	$		Units	$
Opening stock	500	2,800	Output to process 2:		
Direct materials	2,500	13,200	Opening stock completed	500	4,800
Direct labour		6,600	Fully worked units	2,200	22,000
Production o'hd		6,600		2,700	26,800
			Closing WIP	300	2,400
	3,000	29,200		3,000	29,200

We now know that the value of x is $(4,800 − 2,800) = $2,000 and the value of y is $22,000.

Question

Learning outcome: A(iii)

MacDonalds manufacture carbonated drinks. One particular drink, Sweet and Sickly, is produced in a three-stage production process.

The following information relates to the final process (colouring) for control period 2.

Opening WIP

30,000 litres complete as to:		Yen
materials from process 2 (stirring)	100%	4,400
added materials	90%	1,150
labour	80%	540
production overhead	80%	810
		6,900

In control period 2, a further 180,000 litres were transferred from process 2 at a valuation of Yen 27,000. Added materials amounted to Yen 6,600 and direct labour to Yen 3,270. Production overhead is absorbed at the rate of 150% of direct labour cost. Closing WIP at the end of control period 2 amounted to 45,000 litres, complete as to:

process 2 materials	100%
added materials	60%
labour and overhead	50%

Required

Prepare the colouring account for control period 2 using FIFO valuation principles.

Answer

Step 1 — Determine output and losses

	Total litres	Process 2 materials		Added materials		Conversion costs	
Opening WIP	30,000	0	(10%)	3,000	(20%)	6,000	
Fully worked units *	135,000	135,000		135,000		135,000	
Output to finished goods	165,000	135,000		138,000		141,000	
Closing WIP	45,000	45,000	(60%)	27,000	(50%)	22,500	
	210,000	180,000		165,000		163,500	

* Transfers from process 2, minus closing WIP.

Step 2 — Determine cost per unit of output, losses and WIP

	Total cost Yen	Equivalent units	Cost per equivalent unit Y
Process 2 materials	27,000	180,000	0.15
Added materials	6,600	165,000	0.04
Direct labour	3,270	163,500	0.02
Production overhead (150% of Yen 3,270)	4,905	163,500	0.03
			0.24

Step 3 — Determine total cost of output, losses and WIP

	Process 2 materials Yen		Additional materials Yen		Labour Yen		Overhead Yen		Total Yen
Opening WIP cost b/f	4,400		1,150		540		810		6,900
Added in period	-	(W1)	120	(W2)	120	(W3)	180		420
	4,400		1,270		660		990		7,320
Fully worked units	20,250		5,400		2,700		4,050		32,400
Output to finished goods	24,650		6,670		3,360		5,040		39,720
Closing WIP									
(45,000 × Yen 0.15)	6,750	(W4)	1,080	(W5)	450	(W6)	675		8,955
	31,400		7,750		3,810		5,715		48,675

Working

1	3,000 × Yen 0.04	4	27,000 × Yen 0.04
2	6,000 × Yen 0.02	5	22,500 × Yen 0.02
3	6,000 × Yen 0.03	6	22,500 × Yen 0.03

Step 4 — Complete account

COLOURING ACCOUNT

	Units	Yen		Units	Yen
Opening stock b/f	30,000	6,900	Finished goods a/c	165,000	39,720
Process 2 a/c	180,000	27,000			
Stores a/c		6,600			
Wages a/c		3,270			
Production o'hd a/c		4,905	Closing WIP c/f	45,000	8,955
	210,000	48,675		210,000	48,675

6 Selecting the method of valuing work in progress

The valuation of work in progress will usually affect the reported unit costs for the period.

In practice, if it is important for managers to be able to **compare unit costs** from one period to the next, **FIFO** might be the best method to use as the costs for each period will be analysed separately and no averaging takes place. If **costs fluctuate** dramatically from one period to the next, however, managers may wish to even out the effect of these fluctuations and so the **weighted average** method should be used.

In some circumstances the FIFO method will give very similar results to the weighted average method, including the following.

- When unit costs are relatively constant from one period to the next. In this circumstance the separate analysis of each period's costs using FIFO would produce a similar result to the averaging process

- When the conversion cost value of the closing WIP at the end of the period is relatively low compared with the total conversion costs incurred during the period. In this circumstance, even if costs fluctuate dramatically from one period to the next, the costing treatment of the relatively small amount of conversion cost brought forward in opening WIP would not have a significant effect on the final unit cost

- When the degree of completion of work in progress is relatively constant between periods. In this circumstance the amount of work done on the opening and closing WIP is relatively constant each period.

Exam focus point

The **FIFO method of valuation is more common than the weighted average method, and should be used in an exam unless an indication is given to the contrary**. You may find that you are presented with limited information about the opening WIP, however.

- If you are **told the degree of completion of each element in opening WIP**, but not the value of each cost element, then you must use the **FIFO method**.

- If you are not given the degree of completion of each cost element in opening WIP, but you are **given the value of each cost element**, then you must use the **weighted average method**.

7 Changes in WIP levels and losses

The previous paragraphs have dealt separately with the following.

- The treatment of loss and scrap

- The use of equivalent units as a basis for apportioning costs between units of output and units of closing WIP

We must now look at a situation where **both problems** occur together. We shall begin with an example where loss has no scrap value.

The rules are as follows.

(a)   **Costs** should be **divided between finished output, closing WIP and abnormal loss/gain** using **equivalent units** as a basis of apportionment.

(b)   **Units of abnormal loss/gain** are often taken to be **one full equivalent unit each**, and are valued on this basis, ie they carry their full 'share' of the process costs.

(c)   **Abnormal loss units are an addition** to the total equivalent units produced but **abnormal gain units are subtracted** in arriving at the total number of equivalent units produced.

(d)   Units of **normal loss are valued at zero equivalent units**, ie they do not carry any of the process costs.

7.1 Example: changes in WIP level and losses

Consider the following information for a process.

	Units	Degree of completion Materials	Degree of completion Conversion cost	Cost €
Opening WIP	700 units	100%	30%	6,400
Closing WIP	300 units	100%	40%	
Costs of input:				
direct materials	4,000 units			€30,400
conversion costs				€16,440

Normal loss: 5% of input during the period
Output to next process: 4,300 units

Required

Prepare the process account for the period, using the FIFO method of valuation.

Solution: The four-step approach

Step 1   **Determine output and losses**

(a)   Total loss   = opening WIP plus input minus (output plus closing WIP)
                       = 700 + 4,000 − (4,300 + 300)
                       = 100 units

    Normal loss   =   200 units (5% of 4,000)

    Abnormal gain =   100 units (200 −100)

Units of abnormal gain are subtracted in arriving at the total of equivalent units of production in the period.

(b)

	Total units		Materials		Equivalent units Conversion costs
Opening WIP completed	700	(0%)	0	(70%)	490
Fully worked units	3,600		3,600		3,600
Output to next process	4,300		3,600		4,090
Normal loss	200		0		0
Closing WIP	300	(100%)	300	(40%)	120
	4,800		3,900		4,210
Abnormal gain	(100)		(100)		(100)
Equivalent units	4,700		3,800		4,110

Step 2   Calculate cost per unit of output, losses and WIP

	Materials	Conversion costs
Costs incurred during the period	€30,400	€16,440
Equivalent units of production	3,800 units	4,110 units
Cost per equivalent unit	€8	€4

Step 3   Calculate total cost of output, losses and WIP

	Materials		Conversion costs		Total
	Units	€	Units	€	€
Opening WIP b/f					6,400
Work this period	0	0	490	1,960	1,960
					8,360
Fully worked units	3,600	28,800	3,600	14,400	43,200
Closing WIP	300	2,400	120	480	2,880
Abnormal gain	(100)	(800)	(100)	(400)	(1,200)
	3,800	30,400	4,110	16,440	53,240

Step 4   Complete accounts

PROCESS ACCOUNT

	Units	€		Units	€
Opening WIP	700	6,400	Normal loss	200	0
Direct materials	4,000	30,400	Output to next process:		
Conversion costs		16,440	Opening WIP completed	700	8,360
	4,700	53,240	Fully worked units	3,600	43,200
Abnormal gain	100	1,200	Closing WIP	300	2,880
	4,800	54,440		4,800	54,440

7.2 Changes in work in progress levels, loss and scrap

When loss has a scrap value, the accounting procedures are the same as those previously described, and changes in WIP levels during a period do not affect these procedures in any way. However, if the **equivalent units are a different percentage** (of the total units) for **materials, labour and overhead,** it is a convention that the **scrap value of normal loss is deducted from the cost of materials before a cost per equivalent unit is calculated.** This point will be illustrated in the following example.

7.3 Example: WIP, loss and scrap

The following information relates to process 2 of a three-stage production process for period 8.

Material input from process 1 5,000   units at £1.85 per unit
Material added   £2,245
Labour   £4,320
Overhead   £3,090
Number of units scrapped   800   units

Opening WIP was 600 units, complete as to:

		£
material from process 1	100%, cost	945
material added	60%, cost	180
labour	30%, cost	405
overhead	30%, cost	135
		1,665

Work in progress at period end   1,000 units

Complete as to:
material from process 1	100%
material added	75%
labour	40%
overhead	20%

Normal loss is taken as 10% of input during the period. Scrap value of any loss is 50p per unit.

Required

Prepare the process account and the abnormal loss account.

Solution: the four-step approach

Normal loss is 10% of 5,000 units = 500 units. The normal loss on the opening stock of 600 units was accounted for in the previous period, period 7, and should not be calculated a second time in period 8.

Step 1   **Determine output and losses**

(a)	*Input*	Units	Units
	Opening WIP		600
	Input materials		5,000
			5,600
	Output		
	Opening WIP completed	600	
	Normal loss	500	
	Abnormal loss (800 – 500)	300	
	Closing WIP	1,000	
			2,400
	Units started and finished in period 8		3,200

(b)

	Total units	Process 1 material	Added material	Labour	Overhead
			Equivalent units		
Normal loss	500	0	0	0	0
Abnormal loss	300	300	300	300	300
Opening WIP completed	600	0	240	420	420
Fully worked units	3,200	3,200	3,200	3,200	3,200
Closing WIP	1,000	1,000	750	400	200
	5,600	4,500	4,490	4,320	4,120

Step 2   **Calculate cost per unit of output, losses and WIP**

	Total £	Equivalent units	Cost per equivalent unit £
Material from process 1	* 9,000	4,500	2.00
Added material	2,245	4,490	0.50
Labour	4,320	4,320	1.00
Overhead	3,090	4,120	0.75

* (5,000 units × £1.85 less scrap value of normal loss = £9,250 – £250 = £9,000)

It is a convention that the scrap value of normal loss should be deducted from the cost of materials and more specifically, where appropriate, from the cost of materials input from the previous process.

59

Step 3   Calculate the total cost of output, losses and WIP

	Opening WIP completed £	Fully worked units £	Abnormal loss £	Closing stock £
Material from process 1 (at £2)	0	6,400	600	2,000
Added material (at £0.50)	120	1,600	150	375
Labour (at £1)	420	3,200	300	400
Overhead (at £0.75)	315	2,400	225	150
	855	13,600	1,275	2,925

The cost of work to complete the opening WIP was £855 in period 8. Period 7 costs were £1,665. Total costs of these units were therefore £(855 + 1,665) = £2,520.

Step 4   Complete accounts

(a)   PROCESS 2 ACCOUNT - PERIOD 8

	Units	£		Units	£
Opening WIP	600	1,665	Normal loss (scrap a/c)	500	250
Material from process 1	5,000	9,250	Abnormal loss a/c	300	1,275
Added materials		2,245	Process 3:		
Labour		4,320	Opening WIP finished	600	2,520
Overhead		3,090	Other units	3,200	13,600
			Closing WIP c/d	1,000	2,925
	5,600	20,570		5,600	20,570

(b)   ABNORMAL LOSS ACCOUNT

	£		£
Process 2 a/c	1,275	Scrap a/c (300 units × 50p)	150
		Income statement	1,125
	1,275		1,275

7.4 Using the weighted average basis

Where inventories are valued, not on a FIFO basis, but on a **weighted average basis**, the value of opening WIP is added to the costs in period 8, and completed units of opening WIP are each given a value of one full equivalent unit of production.

In the previous example, the cost per equivalent unit would have been as follows.

	Process 1 material £	Added material £	Labour £	Overhead £
Period 8 costs	9,000 (net)	2,245	4,320	3,090
Value of opening WIP	945	180	405	135
	9,945	2,425	4,725	3,225
Equivalent units: as before	4,500	4,490	4,320	4,120
Opening WIP	600	360	180	180
	5,100	4,850	4,500	4,300
Costs per equivalent unit	£1.95	£0.50	£1.05	£0.75

Total cost per equivalent unit = £4.25

Evaluation would be as follows.

			£
(a)	Output to Process 3	3,800 units × £4.25	16,150
(b)	Abnormal loss	300 units × £4.25	1,275
(c)	Closing WIP	(1,000 × £1.95 plus 750 × £0.50 plus 400 × £1.05 plus 200 × £0.75)	2,895
			20,320

Question
Weighted average method

Learning outcome: A(iii)

Use the statement of evaluation above to re-state the process account using the weighted average basis of stock valuation.

Answer

PROCESS 2 ACCOUNT - PERIOD 8
(using weighted average basis)

	Units	£		Units	£
Opening stock	600	1,665	Normal loss (scrap a/c)	500	250
Material from Process 1	5,000	9,250	Abnormal loss	300	1,275
Added materials		2,245	Process 3	3,800	16,150
Labour		4,320	Closing stock c/d	1,000	2,895
Overhead		3,090			
	5,600	20,570		5,600	20,570

8 Losses/gains at different stages

In our previous examples, we have assumed that loss **occurs at the completion of processing,** so that **units of abnormal loss or abnormal gain** count as a **full equivalent unit of production.** It may be, however, that **units are rejected as scrap or 'loss' at an inspection stage before the completion of processing.**

FAST FORWARD

If units are rejected before the completion of processing, **units of abnormal loss should count as a proportion of an equivalent unit**, according to the volume of work done and materials added up to the point of inspection.

An example may help as an illustration.

8.1 Example: incomplete rejected items

Koffee is a manufacturer of processed goods, and the following information relates to process 2 during September 20X2.

During the month 1,600 units were transferred from process 1, at a valuation of £10,000. Other costs in process 2 were as follows.

Added materials	£4,650
Labour and overhead	£2,920

Units are inspected in process 2 when added materials are 50% complete and conversion cost 30% complete. No losses are normally expected, but during September 20X2, actual loss at the inspection stage was 200 units, which were sold as scrap for £2 each.

The company uses a FIFO method of inventory valuation.

Required

Prepare the process 2 account and abnormal loss account for September 20X2.

Solution: The four-step approach

Step 1 **Determine output and losses**

		Equivalent units		
Item	Total units	Process 1 material	Added material	Conversion costs
Units from process 1	1,600			
Abnormal loss	(200)	200	(50%) 100	(30%) 60
Fully worked units, Sept 20X2	1,400	1,400	1,400	1,400
		1,600	1,500	1,460

Step 2 **Calculate cost per unit of output and losses**

Costs incurred, Sept 20X2	£10,000	£4,650	£2,920
Equivalent units	1,600	1,500	1,460
Cost per equivalent unit	£6.25	£3.10	£2

Step 3 **Calculate the total cost of output and losses**

	Process 1 material £	Added material £	Conversion cost £	Total £
Fully worked units	8,750	4,340	2,800	15,890
Abnormal loss	1,250	310	120	1,680
	10,000	4,650	2,920	17,570

The only difference between this example and earlier examples is that abnormal loss has been valued at less than one equivalent unit, for added materials and conversion costs.

Step 4 **Complete accounts**

PROCESS 2 ACCOUNT

	Units	£		Units	£
Process 1	1,600	10,000	Good units	1,400	15,890
Added materials	-	4,650	Abnormal loss	200	1,680
Labour and overhead	-	2,920			
	1,600	17,570		1,600	17,570

ABNORMAL LOSS ACCOUNT

	£		£
Process 2 account	1,680	Cash (sale of scrap)	400
		Income statement	1,280
	1,680		1,680

8.2 Losses in process: gradual loss

When the loss during process occurs continuously the calculation of equivalent units is a little more tricky if we want the apportionment of the process costs to be as 'fair' as possible.

If it is possible physically to distinguish opening work in progress from material input in a period, and to distinguish output from closing work in progress, then these **items can be treated separately in the equivalent units calculations**.

(a)   For example, in a continuous process (such as a chemical process) a loss may be the result of evaporation, so that work in progress may be of a significantly higher concentration than input (and kept in different tanks).

(b)   Alternatively, if a large number of small objects (like confectionery) are produced in a process, objects at the end of the process may be more advanced (for example if chocolate has been moulded or shaped) than at the beginning.

The fact that loss is continuous does not therefore mean that work in progress at the beginning of a period, and materials input during the period need to be aggregated either physically, or in the calculation of equivalent units.

9 Marginal or absorption costing in a process environment

In all of the examples so far in this chapter it has been implied that an absorption costing system is in use. The total overhead has been added to or absorbed into process costs and then included in the calculation of the total production cost per unit or per equivalent unit.

The process accounts operate as a part of the double entry ledger system in the same way as the work in progress accounts that we saw in the last chapter. A production overhead control account is used to collect the overheads prior to their absorption into process costs.

9.1 Example: absorption costing in a process environment

Fletcher operates an absorption costing system in a process environment. The following extracts were taken from the trial balance of Fletcher at the beginning of May.

	£	£
Process 1 work in progress:		
direct materials	2,300	
direct labour	2,800	
production overhead	5,600	
		10,700
Process 2 work in progress:		
direct materials	1,400	
direct labour	1,300	
production overhead	1,950	
		4,650

Transactions for May included:

	£
Direct labour cost incurred:	
Process 1	14,500
Process 2	22,100
Production overhead incurred	58,400
Material issued:	
Process 1	21,200
Process 2	16,780
Abnormal loss in process 1	3,400
Abnormal gain in process 2	1,290
Total production cost of output transferred:	
From process 1 to process 2	63,800
From process 2 to finished goods	136,320

Required

Complete the following ledger accounts for May:

(a)   Production overhead control account
(b)   Process 1 work in progress account
(c)   Process 2 work in progress account

Solution: Ledger accounts in a process environment

The first step is to use the information available to determine the production overhead absorption base. This can be deduced from the value of the cost elements in the opening work in progress.

Process 1

Production overhead rate $= \dfrac{£5{,}600}{£2{,}800} \times 100\% = 200\%$ of direct labour cost

Process 2

Production overhead rate $= \dfrac{£1{,}950}{£1{,}300} \times 100\% = 150\%$ of direct labour cost

Now we can produce the required amounts.

PRODUCTION OVERHEAD CONTROL ACCOUNT

	£		£
Overhead incurred	58,400	Overhead absorbed:	
Over absorbed overhead to income		process 1 £14,500 × 200%	29,000
statement	3,750	process 2 £22,100 × 150%	33,150
	62,150		62,150

PROCESS 1 WORK IN PROGRESS ACCOUNT

	£		£
Balance b/d	10,700	Abnormal loss	3,400
Wages control	14,500	Process 2	63,800
Stores control	21,200		
Production overhead control	29,000	Balance b/d	8.200
	75,400		75,400

PROCESS 2 WORK IN PROGRESS ACCOUNT

	£		£
Balance b/d	4,650	Finished goods	136,320
Process 1 transfer	63,800		
Wages control	22,100		
Stores control	16,780		
Production overhead control	33,150		
Abnormal gain	1,290	Balance b/d	5,450
	141,770		141,770

9.2 Marginal costing in a process environment

If a marginal costing system is in use then **only the variable production overhead is debited to the process account**. The fixed production overhead is charged in full to the income statement for the period, ie the fixed production overhead is treated as a **period cost**. There will be no need to account for any under or over absorption of fixed production overhead.

10 Joint products and by-products

> **Key term**
>
> **Joint products** are 'Two or more products produced by the same process and separated in processing, each having a sufficiently high saleable value to merit recognition as a main product'.
>
> (CIMA *Official Terminology*)

FAST FORWARD

> **Features of joint products**
>
> - Produced in the same process
> - Indistinguishable from each other until the separation point
> - Each have a substantial sales value (after further processing, if necessary)
> - May require further processing after the separation point

For example, in the oil refining process the following joint products all arise from the same process.

- Diesel fuel
- Petrol
- Paraffin
- Lubricants

10.1 By-products

> **Key term**
>
> A **by-product** is 'Output of some value produced incidentally in manufacturing something else (main product)'.
>
> (CIMA *Official Terminology*)

The distinguishing feature of a **by-product** is its **relatively low sales value** in comparison to the main product.

In the timber industry, for example, by-products include sawdust, small off-cuts and bark.

10.2 Valuing joint products and by-products

(a) A **joint product** is regarded as an important saleable item, and so it should be **separately valued**. The profitability of each joint product should be assessed in the cost accounts.

(b) A **by-product** is not important as a saleable item, and whatever revenue it earns is a 'bonus' for the organisation. Because of their relative insignificance, by-products are **not separately valued**. It is therefore equally irrelevant to consider a by-product's profitability. The only question is how to account for the 'bonus' net revenue that a by-product earns.

11 Valuing joint products

Joint products are not separately identifiable until a certain stage is reached in the processing operations. This stage is the **'split-off point'**, sometimes referred to as the **separation point**. In the following sketched example, there are two different split-off points.

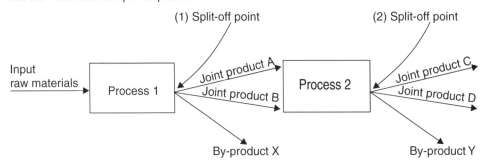

The problem of valuing joint products concerns **common costs** (or **joint costs**), that is those common processing costs shared between the units of eventual output up to their 'split-off point'.

Key term

A **joint cost** is 'The cost of a process which results in more than one main product'.

(CIMA *Official Terminology*)

Some method needs to be devised for sharing the common costs between the individual joint products.

Here are some examples of the common costs problem.

- How to spread the common costs of oil refining between the joint products made (petrol, naphtha, kerosene and so on).

- How to spread the common costs of running the telephone network between telephone calls in peak rate times and cheap rate times, or between local calls and long distance calls.

11.1 Methods of valuing joint products

Methods that might be used to establish a basis for apportioning or allocating common costs to each joint product.

- **Physical measurement**
- **Sales value at split-off point**
- **Sales value of end product less further processing costs after split-off point**
- **Weighting**

11.2 The physical measurement basis

With physical measurement, the common cost is apportioned to the joint products on the basis of the proportion that the output of each product bears by weight or volume to the total output. An example of this would be the case where two products, product A and product B, incur common costs to the point of separation of £6,000 and the output of each product is 1,200 tonnes and 2,400 tonnes respectively.

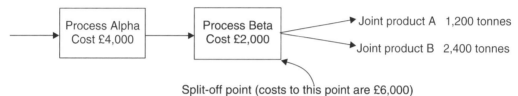

Split-off point (costs to this point are £6,000)

Product A sells for £4 per tonne and product B for £2 per tonne.

The division of the common costs (£6,000) between product A and product B could be based on the tonnage of output.

	Product A	Product B	Total
Output	1,200 tonnes	+ 2,400 tonnes	3,600 tonnes
Proportion of common cost	$\dfrac{1,200}{3,600}$	$+\dfrac{2,400}{3,600}$	
	£	£	£
Apportioned cost	2,000	4,000	6,000
Sales	4,800	4,800	9,600
Profit	2,800	800	3,600
Profit/sales ratio	58.3%	16.7%	37.5%

Physical measurement has the following limitations.

- Where the products separate during the processes into different states, for example where one product is a gas and another is a liquid, this method is unsuitable.

- This method does not take into account the relative income-earning potentials of the individual products, with the result that one product might appear very profitable and another appear to be incurring losses.

11.3 The sales value at split-off point basis

With this method, **the cost is allocated according to the product's ability to produce income**. This method is most widely used because the assumption that some profit margin should be attained for all products under normal marketing conditions is satisfied. The common cost is apportioned to each product in the proportion that the sales (market) value of that product bears to the sales value of the total output from the particular processes concerned. Using the previous example where the sales price per tonne is £4 for product A and £2 for product B.

(a) Common costs of processes to split-off point   £6,000
(b) Sales value of product A at £4 per tonne   £4,800
(c) Sales value of product B at £2 per tonne   £4,800

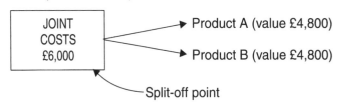

	Product A	Product B	Total
Sales	£4,800	£4,800	£9,600
Proportion of common cost apportioned	$\left(\dfrac{4,800}{9,600}\right)$	$\left(\dfrac{4,800}{9,600}\right)$	
	£	£	£
Apportioned cost	3,000	3,000	6,000
Sales	4,800	4,800	9,600
Profit	1,800	1,800	3,600
Profit/sales ratio	37.5%	37.5%	37.5%

A comparison of the gross profit margin resulting from the application of the above methods for allocating common costs will illustrate the greater acceptability of the relative sales value apportionment method. Physical measurement gives a higher profit margin to product A, not necessarily because product A is highly profitable, but because it has been given a smaller share of common costs.

Question   Joint products

Learning outcome: A(iii)

Three products are produced from a single process. During one period in which the process costs are expected to be £200,000, the following outputs are expected.

	Output	Selling price
Product A	8,000 tonnes	£5 per tonne
Product B	20,000 tonnes	£5 per tonne
Product C	25,000 tonnes	£10 per tonne

Required

(a) Calculate the apportionment of joint costs using the physical measurement method
(b) Calculate the apportionment using the relative sales value apportionment method.
(c) Why might the sales value method be considered fairer of the two?

Answer

(a) **Physical measurement**

Product	A	B	C	Total
Output (tonnes)	8,000	20,000	25,000	53,000
Proportion of joint cost allocated	$8/53$	$20/53$	$25/53$	
Joint costs	£30,188	£75,472	£94,340	

(b)   **Relative sales value apportionment**

Product	A	B	C	Total
Sales value	(8,000 × £5) £40,000	(20,000 × £5) £100,000	(25,000 × £10) £250,000	£390,000
Proportion of joint cost allocated	4/39	10/39	25/39	
Joint costs	£20,513	£51,282	£128,205	

(c)   A comparison of the gross profit margins illustrates that the relative sales value apportionment method could be regarded as the 'fairer' of the two, by ensuring that each joint product makes the same gross profit margin after deducting the product's share of the common costs. In contrast, the physical measurement basis of apportionment could result in high gross profits for some joint products and low gross profits - even losses - for others.

11.4 The sales value minus further processing costs basis

Joint products may have no known market value at the point of separation, because they need further separate processing to make them ready for sale. The allocation of common product costs should be done as follows.

(a)   Ideally, by determining a **relative sales value at the split-off point** for each product.

(b)   If a relative sales value cannot be found, by taking the **final sales value of the joint products, deducting further processing costs** of each product from its sales value, and **using the resulting residual sales value as a basis for allocation**. This residual sales value is sometimes referred to as the notional or proxy sales value of a joint product.

11.5 Example: sales value minus further processing costs

LM has a factory where four products are originated in a common process.

During period 2, the costs of the common process were $16,000. Output was as follows.

	Units made	Sales value Units sold	per unit
Product L1	600		
Product U1	400		
Product C	500	400	$7
Product Y	600	450	$10

Products L1 and U1 are further processed, separately, to make end-products L2 and U2.

	Units processed	Units sold	Cost of further processing	Sales value per unit
Product L1/L2	600	600	$1,000	$10 (L2)
Product U1/U2	400	300	$2,500	$20 (U2)

Required

Calculate the costs of each joint product and the profit from each of them in period 2. There were no opening stocks.

Solution

(a)   It is helpful to begin a solution to joint product problems with a diagram of the process.

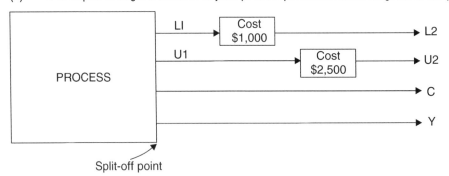

Split-off point

(b)   Next we calculate the assumed sales values of L1 and U1.

	L2 $	U2 $
Sales value of production	6,000	8,000
Less further processing costs	1,000	2,500
Assumed sales value, L1, U1	5,000 (L1)	5,500 (U1)

(c)   Now we can apply sales values to apportion common costs.

Joint product	Sales value of production $	%	Apportionment of common costs $
L1	5,000	25	4,000
U1	5,500	27 $1/2$	4,400
C	3,500	17 $1/2$	2,800
Y	6,000	30	4,800
	20,000	100	16,000

(d)   We can now draw up the profit statement.

	L1/2 $	U1/2 $	C $	Y $	Total $
Common costs	4,000	4,400	2,800	4,800	16,000
Further processing	1,000	2,500	-	-	3,500
Cost of production	5,000	6,900	2,800	4,800	19,500
Less closing inventory (W)	0	1,725	560	1,200	3,485
Cost of sales	5,000	5,175	2,240	3,600	16,015
Sales	6,000	6,000	2,800	4,500	19,300
Profit	1,000	825	560	900	3,285
Profit/sales ratio	17%	14%	20%	20%	17%

Working

Production cost per unit

L1/2	$5,000/600 =	$8.33
U1/2	$6,900/400 =	$17.25
C	$2,800/500 =	$5.60
Y	$4,800/600 =	$8.00

Value of closing inventory

L1/2	$8.33 × 0 =	$0
U1/2	$17.25 × (400 – 300) =	$1,725
C	$5.60 × (500 – 400) =	$560
Y	$8.00 × £(600 – 450) =	$1,200

Question

Learning outcome: A(iii)

Calculate the profit for the period and the value of closing stocks if common costs are apportioned using the units method in the example above.

Answer

Joint product

	Units produced	%	Apportionment of common costs $
L1	600	28.6	4,576
U1	400	19.0	3,040
C	500	23.8	3,808
Y	600	28.6	4,576
	2,100	100.0	16,000

Profit statement

	L1/2 $	U1/2 $	C $	Y $	Total $
Common costs of production	4,576	3,040	3,808	4,576	16,000
Further processing	1,000	2,500	-	-	3,500
Cost of production	5,576	5,540	3,808	4,576	19,500
Less closing stock	0	1,385	762	1,144	3,291
Cost of sales	5,576	4,155	3,046	3,432	16,209
Sales	6,000	6,000	2,800	4,500	19,300
Profit/(loss)	424	1,845	(246)	1,068	3,091
Profit/sales ratio	7%	31%	-	24%	16%

11.6 The weighting basis

The weighting method of common cost apportionment is a development of the units method of apportionment. Since units of joint product may not be comparable in physical resemblance or physical weight (they may be gases, liquids or solids) units of **each joint product may be multiplied by a weighting factor, and 'weighted units' would provide a basis for apportioning the common costs.**

11.7 Example: weighting

MG manufactures four products which emerge from a joint processing operation. In April 20X3, the costs of the joint production process were as follows.

	£
Direct materials	24,000
Direct labour	2,000
	26,000

Production overheads are added using an absorption rate of 400% of direct labour costs. Output from the process during April 20X3 was as follows.

Joint product	Output
D	600 litres
W	400 litres
F	400 kilograms
G	500 kilograms

Units of output of D, W, F and G and to be given weightings of 3, 5, 8 and 3 respectively for apportioning common costs.

Required

Apportion the joint costs.

Solution

Total costs are £26,000 for direct cost plus £8,000 overhead. The costs would be £34,000, apportioned as follows.

Joint product	Output Units	Weighting	Weighted units
D	600	3	1,800
E	400	5	2,000
F	400	8	3,200
G	500	3	1,500
			8,500

The costs are therefore apportioned at a rate of £34,000/8,500 = £4 per weighted unit.

Joint product	Apportionment of common cost £
D	7,200
E	8,000
F	12,800
G	6,000
	34,000

Question   Joint cost apportionment

Learning outcome: A(iii)

Describe briefly TWO methods of apportioning common costs to joint products and state the advantages and disadvantages of each.   (5 marks)

Answer

Two methods of apportioning common costs to joint products are the physical measurement method and the sales value apportionment method.

The physical measurement method uses the weight or volume of output at the split off point as the basis of apportionment. The main advantages of this method are its simplicity and ease of understanding. The disadvantages are as follows.

- Its use may be impossible in situations where the outputs of joint products are not in the same form, for example a liquid, a gas and a solid might be the three joint products

- The resulting profit margin for each product could be very different, leading to the erroneous impression that one joint product is more or less profitable than another

The sales value apportionment method uses the relative sales value of each joint product at the split off point as the basis of apportionment. The main advantage of this method is that each joint product will earn the same profit margin percentage after deducting the product's share of the common costs. The main disadvantage is that some products might not be saleable at the split off point and more detailed calculations will be necessary, taking into account costs incurred after the split off point, to determine each product's net realisable value as a proxy measure.

11.8 Joint products in process accounts

The following example will illustrate how joint products are incorporated into process accounts.

11.9 Example: joint products and process accounts

Three joint products are manufactured in a common process, which consists of two consecutive stages. Output from process 1 is transferred to process 2, and output from process 2 consists of the three joint products, Alpha, Beta and Gamma. All joint products are sold as soon as they are produced.

Process 2 data for period 2 are as follows.

Opening and closing work in progress	None
Input from process 1	26,000 units valued at £130,000
Conversion costs	£221,000
Normal loss	10% of input
Output	10,000 units of Alpha
	7,000 units of Beta
	6,000 units of Gamma

Selling prices are £18 per unit of Alpha, £20 per unit of Beta and £30 per unit of Gamma.

Required

(a) Prepare the Process 2 account using the sales value method of apportionment.
(b) Prepare a profit statement for the joint products.

Solution: the four-step process

(a) **Step 1**   **Determine output and losses.**

	Units
Units of Alpha produced	10,000
Units of Beta produced	7,000
Units of Gamma produced	6,000
Normal loss (10% of 26,000)	2,600
Abnormal loss (balance)	400
	26,000

$$\therefore \text{Expected output} = 26,000 - 2,600$$
$$= 23,400$$

Step 2 Calculate cost per unit of output and losses.

	£
Material costs - from process 1	130,000
Conversion costs	221,000
	351,000

$$\text{Cost per unit} = \frac{£351,000}{\text{Expected output}} = \frac{£351,000}{23,400} = £15$$

Step 3 Calculate total cost of output and losses.

Cost of good output (10,000 + 7,000 + 6,000) = 23,000 units × £15 = £345,000

The sales value of joint products, and the apportionment of the output costs of £345,000, is as follows.

	Sales value		Costs (process 2)
	£	%	£
Alpha (10,000 × £18)	180,000	36	124,200
Beta (7,000 × £20)	140,000	28	96,600
Gamma (6,000 × £30)	180,000	36	124,200
	500,000	100	345,000

Cost of abnormal loss = 400 × £15 = £6,000

Step 4 Prepare accounts

PROCESS 2 ACCOUNT

	£		£
Process 1 materials	130,000	Finished goods accounts	
Conversion costs	221,000	- Alpha	124,200
		- Beta	96,600
		- Gamma	124,200
		Normal loss	-
		Abnormal loss a/c	6,000
	351,000		351,000

(b) PROFIT STATEMENT

	Alpha	Beta	Gamma
	£'000	£'000	£'000
Sales	180.0	140.0	180.0
Costs	124.2	96.6	124.2
Profit	55.8	43.4	55.8
Profit/ sales ratio	31%	31%	31%

 Question   Process accounts and joint products

Learning outcome: A(iii)

Prepare the Process 2 account and a profit statement for the joint products in the above example, using the units basis of apportionment.

PROCESS 2 ACCOUNT

	£		£
Process 1 materials	130,000	Finished goods accounts	
Conversion costs	221,000	- Alpha (10,000 × £15)	150,000
		- Beta (7,000 × £15)	105,000
		- Gamma (6,000 × £15)	90,000
		Normal loss	-
		Abnormal loss a/c (400 × £15)	6,000
	351,000		351,000

PROFIT STATEMENT

	Alpha	Beta	Gamma
	£'000	£'000	£'000
Sales	180	140	180
Costs	150	105	90
Profit	30	35	90
Profit/ sales ratio	16.7%	25%	50%

12 Valuing by-products

The by-product has some commercial value. Income earned by the by-product can be treated in a number of ways.

Treatment of by-product income	Detail
Added to sales of the main product	This increases sales turnover for the period.
Treated as a separate, incidental source of income	The revenue would be recorded in the income statement as 'other income'.
Deducted from the cost of production or cost of sales of the main product	
Net realisable value of the by-product may be deducted from the cost of production of the main product	The net realisable value is the final saleable value of the by-product minus any post-separation costs. Any closing inventory valuation of the main product or joint products would therefore be reduced.

The choice of method will be influenced by the circumstances of production and ease of calculation, as much as by conceptual correctness.

The method you are **most likely to come across** in examinations is **the last**. This method was used to value a by-product question in the pilot paper.

An example will help to clarify the distinction between the different methods.

FAST FORWARD

The most common method of accounting for by-products is to deduct the net realisable value of the by-product from the cost of the main products.

12.1 Example: methods of accounting for by-products

During November, Splatter recorded the following results.

Opening inventory	main product P, nil
	by-product Z, nil
Cost of production	£120,000

Sales of the main product amounted to 90% of output during the period, and 10% of production was held as closing inventory at 30 November.

Sales revenue from the main product during November was £150,000.

A by-product Z is produced, and output had a net sales value of £1,000. Of this output, £700 was sold during the month, and £300 was still in inventory at 30 November.

Required

Calculate the profit for November using the four methods of accounting for by-products.

Solution

The four methods of accounting for by-products are shown below.

(a)   **Income from by-product added to sales of the main product**

	£	£
Sales of main product (£150,000 + £700)		150,700
Opening inventory	0	
Cost of production	120,000	
	120,000	
Less closing inventory (10%)	12,000	
Cost of sales		108,000
Profit, main product		42,700

The closing inventory of the by-product has no recorded value in the cost accounts.

(b)   **By-product income treated as a separate source of income**

	£	£
Sales, main product		150,000
Opening inventory	0	
Cost of production	120,000	
	120,000	
Closing inventory (10%)	12,000	
Cost of sales, main product		108,000
Profit, main product		42,000
Other income		700
Total profit		42,700

The closing inventory of the by-product again has no value in the cost accounts.

(c)   **Sales income of the by-product deducted from the cost of production in the period**

	£	£
Sales, main product		150,000
Opening inventory	0	
Cost of production (120,000 – 700)	119,300	
	119,300	
Less closing inventory (10%)	11,930	
Cost of sales		107,370
Profit, main product		42,630

Although the profit is different from the figure in (a) and (b), the by-product closing inventory again has no value.

(d) **Net realisable value of the by-product deducted from the cost of production in the period**

	£	£
Sales, main product		150,000
Opening inventory	0	
Cost of production (120,000 − 1,000)	119,000	
	119,000	
Less closing inventory (10%)	11,900	
Cost of sales		107,100
Profit, main product		42,900

As with the other three methods, closing inventory of the by-product has no value in the books of accounting, but the value of the closing inventory (£300) has been used to reduce the cost of production, and in this respect it has been allowed for in deriving the cost of sales and the profit for the period.

Exam focus point

When given no clear guidance in a question on how to account for a by-product, follow approach (d) above. In the question on the pilot paper no guidance was given about the valuation of the by-product and approach (d) was used in the solution.

Question

By-product

Learning outcome: A(iii)

Randolph manufactures two joint products, J and K, in a common process. A by-product X is also produced. Data for the month of December were as follows.

Opening inventories		nil	
Costs of processing	direct materials		£25,500
	direct labour		£10,000

Production overheads are absorbed at the rate of 300% of direct labour costs.

		Production Units	Sales Units
Output and sales consisted of:	product J	8,000	7,000
	product K	8,000	6,000
	by-product X	1,000	1,000

The sales value per unit of J, K and X is £4, £6 and £0.50 respectively. The saleable value of the by-product is deducted from process costs before apportioning costs to each joint product. Costs of the common processing are apportioned between product J and product K on the basis of sales value of production.

Required

Calculate the profit for December. Analyse this profit by individual products.

Answer

The sales value of production was £80,000.

	£
Product J (8,000 × £4)	32,000 (40%)
Product K (8,000 × £6)	48,000 (60%)
	80,000

The costs of production were as follows.	£
Direct materials	25,500
Direct labour	10,000
Overhead (300% of £10,000)	30,000
	65,500
Less sales value of by-product (1,000 × 50p)	500
Net production costs	65,000

The profit statement would appear as follows (nil opening stocks).

		Product J £		Product K £	Total £
Production costs	(40%)	26,000	(60%)	39,000	65,000
Less closing stock	(1,000 units)	3,250	(2,000 units)	9,750	13,000
Cost of sales		22,750		29,250	52,000
Sales	(7,000 units)	28,000	(6,000 units)	36,000	64,000
Profit		5,250		6,750	12,000

12.2 By-products and process costing statements

The following example illustrates how to incorporate by-product information into process costing statements.

12.3 Example: waste and losses

The relevant data for process 3 of the manufacturing operations of Kie, a chemical company, in period 6 are as follows.

Opening and closing inventories	Nil
Materials transferred from process 2	20,000 litres at £5 per litre
Conversion costs	£67,000

Output

Finished production	12,500 litres
By-product	3,000 litres
Waste	2,500 litres

Wasted units are the same chemical as finished output, except that they have been polluted during the process. They must be disposed of at a cost of £2 per litre.

The by-product is packed at a further cost of £2 per litre. Its selling price is £3 per litre. The net realisable value of the by-product produced in a period is credited to the process 3 account during that period. During period 6, 2,000 litres of by-product were sold.

The normal output from the process per 1,000 litres of input is as follows.

Finished production	700 litres
By-product	150 litres
Waste	100 litres
Loss through evaporation	50 litres

Required

Prepare the process 3 account, the by-product account, the waste account and the abnormal loss/gain account for period 6.

Solution: the four-step approach

There are two types of loss in this example: evaporation and waste. In each case it is necessary to distinguish between normal waste loss and normal evaporation loss on the one hand, and abnormal loss or gain on the other.

Another point to note about normal waste is that instead of having a scrap value to be credited to the process account, it has a disposal cost. The disposal cost of normal waste is **debited** to the process account.

Step 1   Determine output and losses

	Litres	Equivalent units
Finished output	12,500	12,500
By-product	3,000	0
Normal waste (20 × 100)	2,000	0
Abnormal waste (2,500 – 2,000)	500	500
Normal loss through evaporation (20 × 50)	1,000	0
Abnormal loss (balance)-evaporation	1,000	1,000
Total input units	20,000	14,000

Step 2   Calculate cost per unit of output and losses

	£
Materials from process 2	100,000
Conversion costs	67,000
Normal waste: disposal costs (2,000 × £2)	4,000
	171,000
Less net realisable value of by-product *(3,000 litres × £1)	3,000
	168,000

* Units sold are irrelevant, given the wording of the question.

Cost per equivalent unit = £168,000 ÷ 14,000 = £12

Steps 3 and 4 Calculate total cost of output and losses and complete accounts

PROCESS 3 ACCOUNT

	£		£
Process 2 materials	100,000	By-product: net realisable value	3,000
Conversion costs	67,000	Finished production	
Normal waste disposal costs	4,000	(12,500 × £12)	150,000
		Abnormal loss - evaporation	
		(1,000 × £12)	12,000
		Abnormal loss - waste	
		(500 × £12)	6,000
	171,000		171,000

BY - PRODUCT ACCOUNT

	£		£
Cash		Cash	
(packing costs, 2,000 × £2)	4,000	(sales of 2,000 litres)	6,000
Process account		Closing inventory (1,000 litres)	
(3,000 litres × £1)	3,000	(balancing figure)	1,000
	7,000		7,000

It is assumed that the unsold by-product has not yet been packed. (The closing inventory, if not yet packed, is valued at its net realisable value.)

NORMAL WASTE ACCOUNT

	£		£
Cash		Process 3 account	
(Disposal costs paid for)	4,000	(Disposal cost of normal waste)	4,000

Normal waste disposal costs are 2,000 litres × £2

ABNORMAL LOSS (WASTE) ACCOUNT

	£		£
Cash		Income statement	7,000
(Disposal costs 500 litres × £2)	1,000		
Process a/c (abnormal loss of			
waste)	6,000		
	7,000		7,000

ABNORMAL LOSS (EVAPORATION) ACCOUNT

	£		£
Process account (1,000 × £12)	12,000	Income statement	12,000

Chapter Roundup

- Process costing is centred around four key steps.

    - **Step 1**   **Determine output and losses.**
    - **Step 2**   **Calculate cost per unit of output, losses and WIP.**
    - **Step 3**   **Calculate total cost of output, losses and WIP.**
    - **Step 4**   **Complete accounts.**

- Losses and gains may arise in a process

    - Normal loss is not given a cost.

    - Abnormal loss is given a cost.

    - Abnormal gain is given a 'cost', which is debited rather than credited to the process cost account: it is a 'negative' cost and so an item of gain.

- **The scrap value of normal loss is usually deducted from the cost of materials.**

- **The scrap value of abnormal loss (or abnormal gain) is usually set off against its cost, in an abnormal loss (abnormal gain) account.**

- Abnormal losses and gains never affect the cost of good units of production. The scrap value of abnormal losses is not credited to the process account, and abnormal loss and gain units carry the same full cost as a good unit of production.

- To apportion costs fairly and proportionately when there is work in progress, **units of production must be converted into** the equivalent of completed units, that is, into **equivalent units of production**. Equivalent units then provide a basis for apportioning costs.

- Work in progress can be valued using either average cost method or the FIFO method.

- When opening WIP is valued on a weighed average loss:

    - **No distinction** is made between **units of opening WIP** and **new units introduced** to the process during the current period.

    - The **cost of opening WIP** is **added** to **costs incurred during the period**.

    - **Completed units of opening WIP** are each given a **value of one full equivalent unit** of production.

- When opening WIP is valued on a FIFO basis:

    - Total output is divided between opening WIP and units started and completed in the period
    - Cost of opening WIP is not added to costs incurred during the period
    - Opening WIP completed is valued on an equivalent units basis

- If units are rejected before the completion of processing **units of abnormal loss should count as a proportion of an equivalent unit**, according to the volume of work done and materials added up to the point of inspection.

- **Features of joint products**

    - Produced in the same process
    - Indistinguishable from each other until the separation point
    - Each have a substantial sales value (after further processing, if necessary)
    - May require further processing after the separation point

Chapter Roundup cont'd

- The distinguishing feature of a **by-product** is its **relatively low sales value** in comparison to the main product.

- Methods that might be used to establish a basis for apportioning or allocating common costs to each joint product.

  - **Physical measurement**
  - **Sales value at split-off point**
  - **Sales value of end product less further processing costs after split-off point**
  - **Weighting**

- The most common method of accounting for by-products is to deduct the net realisable value of the by-product from the cost of the main products.

Quick Quiz

1   Fill in the blanks in the four steps to dealing with process costing questions using some of the words from the list below and then put the steps in the correct order.

Steps

(a)   Complete ....

(b)   Determine .... and ....

(c)   Calculate .... of output, losses and WIP

(d)   Calculate .... of output losses and WIP

Possible missing words

abnormal loss	losses
accounts	output
cost per unit	total cost
normal loss	abnormal gain
WIP	

2   What is the correct way to record the scrap value of normal loss?

   A   DR   Scrap a/c
         CR   Process a/c ('value' for normal loss)

   B   DR   Normal loss a/c
         CR   Scrap a/c

   C   DR   Process a/c ('value' for normal loss)
         CR   Scrap a/c

   D   DR   Scrap a/c
         CR   Cash a/c

3 *Record the following entries correctly in the appropriate accounts below.*

Entries

Materials	Finished output
Labour and overhead	Scrap value of normal loss
Abnormal loss	Income statement
Abnormal gain	Scrap value of abnormal gain
Income statement	Abnormal gain
Scrap value of normal loss	Scrap value of abnormal loss
Abnormal loss	Scrap value of abnormal gain
Scrap value of abnormal loss	Cash

PROCESS A/C

£   £

ABNORMAL LOSS A/C

£   £

ABNORMAL GAIN A/C

£   £

SCRAP A/C

£   £

4   Consider the following process account.

PROCESS A

	Units		Units
Opening WIP	25	Finished goods	70
Materials	100	Closing WIP	55
	125		125

Opening WIP is 20% complete for labour and overhead, 100% complete for material. Closing WIP is 20% complete for labour and overhead, 100% complete for material.

Calculate the equivalent units for material and for labour and overhead using both FIFO and weighted average.

5   *Match the correct statement to the appropriate method of valuing joint products.*

Statement 1

Widely used because the assumption that some profit margin should be attained for all products under normal marketing conditions is satisfied

Statement 2

Unsuitable where the products separate during processing into different states

Statement 3

Useful if the units of joint product are not comparable in physical resemblance or physical weight

Statement 4

Suitable if products require further processing after the point of separation.

Valuation methods

(a)   Physical measurement
(b)   Sales value at split-off point
(c)   Sales value minus further processing costs
(d)   Weighted average

6   *Fill in the blanks in the following statements covering the rules for dealing with changes in work in progress levels and losses.*

(a)   Costs should be divided between ...., ... and .... using equivalent units as a basis of apportionment.

(b)   Units of abnormal loss/gain are valued on the basis of .... each.

(c)   In arriving at the total number of equivalent units produced, abnormal loss units are .... to the total equivalent units produced, abnormal gain units are ....

(d)   Units of normal loss are valued at ....

7   If units are rejected as scrap or 'loss' at an inspection stage before the completion of processing, units of normal loss should count as a proportion of an equivalent unit. *True or false?*

8   *List four key features of joint products.*

(a)   ....

(b)   ....

(c)   ....

(d)   ....

9   How does the most common treatment of by-product income affect the valuation of the main product/joint products?

A   Increases it
B   Reduces it
C   Has no effect
D   Can increase or decrease it depending on the level of income

Answers to Quick Quiz

1   Determine output and losses.

   Calculate total cost of output, losses and WIP.
   Calculate cost per unit of output, losses and WIP.
   Complete accounts.

2   A

3   PROCESS A/C

	£		£
Materials		Finished output	
Labour and o/hd		Abnormal loss	
Abnormal gain		Scrap value of normal loss	

                                        ABNORMAL LOSS A/C

	£		£
Abnormal loss		Scrap value of abnormal loss	
		Income statement	

                                        ABNORMAL GAIN A/C

	£		£
Scrap value of abnormal gain		Abnormal gain	
Profit/loss			

                                        SCRAP A/C

	£		£
Scrap value of normal loss		Cash	
Scrap value of abnormal loss		Scrap value of abnormal gain	

4   **FIFO**

	Total	Materials	Labour & o/hd
Opening WIP	25	0	20
Units started/finished	45	45	45
Total finished	70	45	65
Closing WIP	55	55	11
	125	100	76

   Weighted average

	Total	Materials	Labour & o/hd
Finished output	70	70	70
Closing WIP	55	55	11
	125	125	81

5   *Statement   Method*

   1   (b)
   2   (a)
   3   (d)
   4   (c)

6   (a)   finished output, closing work in progress, units of abnormal loss/gain
   (b)   one full equivalent unit
   (c)   added, subtracted
   (d)   zero equivalent units

7   *False.* It is units of abnormal loss that are dealt with in this way.

8   •   Produced in the same process
     •   Indistinguishable from each other until the separation point
     •   Each has a substantial sales value (after further processing, if necessary)
     •   May require further processing after the separation point

9   B

Now try the questions below from the Exam Question Bank

Number	Level	Marks	Time
Q4	Examination	20	36 mins
Q5	Examination	5	9 mins
Q6	Examination	5	9 mins

The modern business environment

Introduction

In recent years there have been **significant changes in the business environment** in which both manufacturing and service organisations operate

We look at these **changes** in some detail in **Section 1**.

Organisations have therefore adopted new **management approaches (Sections 6 and 7)**, have changed their **manufacturing systems (Sections 3 to 5 and 8)** and have invested in **new technology (Section 2)**, and it is these changes that we will be looking at in this chapter.

These changes do mean that **traditional management accounting methods may no longer be appropriate** and in the chapters which follow we look at **alternative systems of management accounting** that have been developed which are claimed to be more suitable for the modern business environment.

Topic list	Learning outcomes	Syllabus references	Ability required
1 The changing business environment	A(vii)(viii)	A 7,8	Comp/evaluation
2 Advanced manufacturing technology	A(vii)(viii)	A 7,8	Comp/evaluation
3 Production management strategies	A(vii)	A 7	Comprehension
4 Just-in-time (JIT) systems	A (viii)	A 8	Comp/evaluation
5 Synchronous manufacturing	A(vii)(viii)	A 7,8	Comp/evaluation
6 Total quality management (TQM)	A(vii)(viii)	A 7,8	Comp/evaluation
7 Costs of quality and cost of quality reports	A(vii)(viii)	A 7,8	Comp/evaluation
8 World class manufacturing (WCM)	A(vii)(viii)	A 7,8	Comp/evaluation

1 The changing business environment

Changes to the **competitive environment**, **product life cycles** and **customer requirements** have had a significant impact on the modern business environment.

1.1 The changing competitive environment for manufacturing organisations

Before the 1970s, **barriers of communication** and **geographical distance** limited the extent to which overseas organisations could compete in domestic markets. Cost increases could often be passed on to customers and so there were **few efforts to maximise efficiency and improve management practices**, or to reduce costs. **During the 1970s**, however, **overseas competitors** gained access to domestic markets by **establishing global networks for acquiring raw materials and distributing high-quality, low-priced goods**. To succeed, organisations had to compete against the best companies in the world.

1.2 The changing competitive environment for service organisations

Prior to the 1980s, many service organisations (such as the utilities, the financial services and airlines industries) were either **government-owned monopolies** or were **protected by a highly-regulated, non-competitive environment**. **Improvements in quality and efficiency** of operations or levels of profitability were not expected, and costs increases were often covered by increasing service prices. Cost systems to measure costs and profitability of individual services were not deemed necessary.

The competitive environment for service organisations changed radically in the **1980s**, however, following **privatisation** of government-owned monopolies and **deregulation**. The resulting intense competition and increasing product range has led to the **requirement for cost management and management accounting information systems** which allow service organisations to assess the costs and profitability of services, customers and markets.

1.3 Changing product life cycles

Today's **competitive environment**, along with high levels of **technological innovation** and **increasingly discriminating and sophisticated customer demands**, constantly **threaten a product's life cycle**.

Product life cycle is 'The period which begins with the initial product specification, and ends with the withdrawal from the market of both the product and its support. It is characterised by defined stages including research, development, introduction, maturity, decline and abandonment'.

(CIMA *Official Terminology*)

Organisations can no longer rely on years of high demand for products and so, to compete effectively, they need to continually **redesign their products** and to **shorten the time it takes to get them to the market place**.

In many organisations today, **up to 90% of a product's life cycle cost is determined by decisions made** early within the cycle, **at the design stage. Management accounting systems that monitor spending and commitment to spend during the early stages of a product's life cycle** are therefore becoming **increasingly important**.

1.4 Changing customer requirements

Successful organisations in today's competitive environment make **customer satisfaction** their **priority** and concentrate on the following **key success factors**.

Key success factor	Detail
Cost efficiency	
Quality	Focusing on total quality management (TQM), covered in Section 6
Time	Providing a speedier response to customer requests, ensuring 100% on-time delivery and reducing the time taken to develop and bring new products to market
Innovation	Developing a steady stream of innovative new products and having the flexibility to respond to customer requirements

They are also taking on board **new management approaches**.

Approach	Detail
Continuous improvement	A facet of TQM, being a continuous search to reduce costs, eliminate waste and improve the quality and performance of activities that increase customer satisfaction or value
Employee empowerment	Providing employees with the information to enable them to make continuous improvements without authorisation from superiors
Total value-chain analysis	Ensuring that all the factors which add value to an organisation's products - the value chain of research and development, design, production, marketing, distribution and customer service - are coordinated within the overall organisational framework

1.5 Changing manufacturing systems

FAST FORWARD

Different approaches for **organising a manufacturing process** include **jobbing industries**, **batch processing** and **mass production**.

Traditionally, manufacturing industries have fallen into a few broad groups according to the **nature of the production process** and **materials flow**.

Type of production	Description
Jobbing industries	Industries in which **items are produced individually**, often for a specific customer order, as a 'job'. Such a business requires versatile equipment and highly skilled workers to give it the flexibility to turn its hand to a variety of jobs. The jobbing factory is typically laid out on a **functional** basis with, say, a milling department, a cutting department, finishing, assembly and so on.
Batch processing	Involves the manufacture of **standard goods in batches**. 'Batch production is often carried out using **functional** layouts but with a greater number of more **specialised machines**. With a functional layout batches move by different and complex routes through various specialised departments travelling over much of the factory floor before they are completed.' (Drury, *Management and Cost Accounting*)

Type of production	Description
Mass or flow production	Involves the **continuous production of standard items** from a sequence of continuous or repetitive operations. This sort of production often uses a **product-based** layout whereby product A moves from a milling machine to a cutting machine to a paint-spraying machine, product B moves from a sawing machine to a milling machine to an oven and then to finishing and so on.
	The point is that there is no separate 'milling department' or 'assembly department' to which all products must be sent to await their turn on the machines: each product has its own dedicated machine.

In recent years, however, a new type of manufacturing system known as **group technology** (or **repetitive manufacturing**) has emerged. The system involves a **flexible or cellular arrangement of machines** which **manufacture groups of products having similar manufacturing requirements.** By grouping together facilities required to produce similar products, some of the **benefits associated with flow production systems** (lower throughput times, easier scheduling, reduced set-up times and reduced work in progress) are possible to achieve. Moreover, the increase in **customer demand for product diversity can be satisfied** by such a manufacturing system.

1.5.1 Dedicated cell layout

The modern development in this sphere is to merge the flexibility of the functional layout with the speed and productivity of the product layout. **Cellular** manufacturing involves a **U-shaped flow** along which are arranged a number of different machines that are used to make products with similar machining requirements.

The machines are operated by workers who are **multi-skilled** (can operate each machine within the cell rather than being limited to one operation such as 'lathe-operator', 'grinder', or whatever) and are able to perform routine preventative maintenance on the cell machines. The aim is to facilitate **just-in-time** production (see Section 4) and obtain the associated improvements in **quality** and reductions in **costs**.

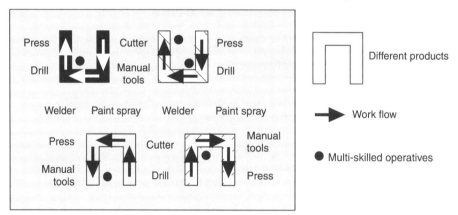

BPP
PROFESSIONAL EDUCATION

In January 1994 the *Financial Times* carried a good example of this approach in an article about the Paddy Hopkirk car accessory factory in Bedfordshire.

One morning the factory was just an untidy sprawl of production lines surrounded by piles of crates holding semi-finished components. Two days later, when the workforce came to work (after Christmas), the machines has been brought together in tightly grouped 'cells'. The piles of components had disappeared, and the newly cleared floor space was neatly marked with colour-coded lines mapping out the flow of materials.

Overnight there were dramatic differences. In the first full day, productivity on some lines increased by up to 30%, the space needed for some processes had been halved, and work in progress had been cut considerably. The improved layout had allowed some jobs to be combined, freeing up operators for development elsewhere in the factory.

As we saw earlier, **to compete effectively** organisations need to **redesign continually their products** and to **shorten the time it takes to get them to the market place**. **Manufacturing processes** must therefore be **sufficiently flexible** both to accommodate new product design rapidly and to satisfy the demand for greater product diversity.

2 Advanced manufacturing technology (AMT)

Organisations need to be able to compete in today's fast-moving, sophisticated world markets. As noted above, they need to be innovative and flexible and be able to deal with short product life cycles. They need to be able to offer greater product variety whilst maintaining or reducing their costs. They may want to reduce set-up times and inventories and have the greatest possible manufacturing flexibility. AMT helps them to do this.

FAST FORWARD

> **Advanced manufacturing technology (AMT)** is a general expression encompassing **computer-aided design (CAD), computer-aided manufacturing (CAM), flexible manufacturing systems (FMS)** and a wide array of innovative computer equipment.

2.1 Computer-aided design (CAD)

Computer-aided design allows new products to be designed (and old ones modified) on a computer screen.

(a) The effects of **changing product specifications** (for example to test stress and find weaknesses or to optimise usage of materials) can be explored.

(b) **Designs can be assessed in terms of cost and simplicity**. A simple design is likely to produce a more reliable product and a simple product is easier to manufacture, thereby reducing the possibility of production errors. Quality and cost reduction can therefore be incorporated into a product at the design stage.

(c) **Databases can be used** to match part requirements of the new design with existing product parts, thereby allowing a reduction in product parts required and a minimisation of inventories.

2.2 Computer-aided manufacturing (CAM)

Computer-aided manufacturing refers to the control of the physical production process by computers.

Feature	Detail
Robots	Typically comprise computer controlled arms and attachments that can perform tasks like welding, bolting parts together and moving them about.
Computer numerically controlled (CNC) machines	Programmable machine tools for punching holes, cutting and so on. Manufacturing configurations and set-up instructions are stored on computer programs and so can be changed almost immediately via a keyboard. Flexibility and a reduction in set-up times are thus major advantages of CAM. Moreover, computers can repeat the same operation in an identical manner time and time again, without tiring or error, unlike human operators, with obvious advantages for both quality control and production control.
Automated guided vehicles (AGV)	Used for materials handling, often in place of the traditional conveyor belt approach.

The **ultimate aim** of CAM is a **set-up time of zero**. Although this may not be achievable (in the near future at least), CAM has provided, and still is providing, the **possibility** of economic **production in smaller and smaller batch sizes** with the result that the production schedule is becoming more and more driven by customer requirements.

2.3 Flexible manufacturing systems (FMS)

Key term

A **flexible manufacturing system** (**FMS**) is 'An integrated, computer-controlled production system which is capable of producing any of a range of parts, and of switching quickly and economically between them'.

(CIMA *Official Terminology*)

A flexible manufacturing system (FMS) is a **highly-automated manufacturing system**, which is computer controlled and capable of producing a broad 'family' of parts in a flexible manner. **It is characterised by small batch production, the ability to change quickly from one job to another and very fast response times**, so that output can be produced quickly in response to specific orders that come in.

The sophistication of flexible manufacturing systems varies from one system to another, but **features** can include the following.

- A **JIT system** (discussed later in this chapter)
- Full **computer-integrated manufacturing (CIM)** (the integration of many or all of the elements of AMT into one coherent system) or perhaps just **islands of automation (IAs)** (a series of automated sub-systems within the factory)
- **Computerised materials handling systems (MHS)**
- **Automated storage and retrieval systems (ASRS)** for raw materials and parts

2.4 Electronic data interchange (EDI)

It is not simply within the manufacturing functions of an organisation that technology has made an impact. Electronic data interchange facilitates communication between an organisation and its customers and suppliers by the electronic transfer of information.

3 Production management strategies

The **production management strategies** linked to AMT are materials requirement planning (MRPI), manufacturing resource planning (MRPII), enterprise resource planning (ERP), optimised production technology (OPT) and just-in-time (JIT).

In Section 1 we looked at the various methods of organising the production process. In this section and the next we shall now look at **various production management strategies** and **resource planning systems** that are used to **manage the production process**.

3.1 Traditional approach

The traditional approach to **determining materials requirements** is **to monitor the level of inventories** constantly so that once they fall to a preset level they can be reordered. The problem with this approach is that **relationships between different inventory lines** are **ignored** whereas, in reality, the demand for a particular item of inventory is interdependent on the assemblies and subassemblies of which it forms a part. The computer techniques we will look at below overcome this problem by integrating interrelationships into the inventory ordering process.

3.2 Material requirements planning (MRP I)

Key term

Material requirements planning (MRPI) is 'A system that converts a production schedule into a listing of the materials and components required to meet that schedule, so that adequate stock levels are maintained and items are available when needed'.

(CIMA *Official Terminology*)

MRP I is a computerised information, planning and control system that can be used in a traditional manufacturing environment as well as with AMT. MRP I uses information from a master production schedule which details how many finished goods items are needed, and when, and works back from this to determine the requirements for parts and materials in the earlier stages of the production process. MRP I systems are chiefly used in a batch manufacturing environment.

3.3 The aims of MRP I

- Minimising inventory levels
- Avoiding the high costs of rush orders
- Minimum disruption to production

MRP I is therefore concerned with **maximising efficiency in the timing of orders for raw materials or parts that are placed with external suppliers** and **efficient scheduling of the manufacturing and assembly of the end product**.

3.4 Manufacturing resource planning (MRP II)

Key term

Manufacturing resource planning (MRPII) is 'An expansion of material requirements planning (MRPI) to give a broader approach than MRPI to the planning and scheduling of resources, embracing areas such as finance, logistics, engineering and marketing'.

(CIMA *Official Terminology*)

MRP I evolved into MRP II. MRP II **plans production jobs and also calculates resource needs such as labour and machine hours**. It therefore attempts to integrate materials requirement planning, factory capacity planning, shopfloor control, management accounting, purchasing and even marketing into a **single complete (and computerised) manufacturing control system**. Most MRP II systems are a collection of computer programs that permit the sharing of information with and between departments in an organisation.

MRP II is used by many companies for manufacturing planning, but with the advent of JIT manufacturing (see Section 4) it has been **criticised** as a planning system.

> 'The primary criticism of the MRP II approach is that **by modelling the reality of manufacturing plant, it builds in all the bad habits**. It takes account of long leadtimes, shopfloor queues, large batch sizes, scrap and quality problems. Instead of accommodating these things, it should be driving towards their elimination. Poor productivity is built into MRPII and planned into the production process.'
>
> (Brian Maskell, *Management Accounting*, January 1989 (with BPP's emphasis))

Many world class manufacturers in Japan have therefore taken an alternative approach to dealing with complex production scheduling and purchasing by attempting to simplify their production processes.

Even so, MRP II has advantages as a system for planning and controlling manufacturing systems, especially when JIT methods are unsuitable.

3.5 Enterprise resource planning (ERP)

Key term

Enterprise resource planning (ERP) systems are accounting-orientated information systems for identifying and planning the enterprise-wide resources needed to take, make, distribute and account for customer orders.

(*S Shankarnarayanan* 'ERP Systems - Using IT to gain competitive advantage')

The *Official Terminology* definition is 'A software system which is designed to support and automate the business processes of medium and large enterprises. ERP systems are accounting orientated information systems which aid in identifying and planning the enterprise wide resources needed to resource, make, account for and deliver customer orders. Initially developed from MRPII systems, ERP tends to incorporate a number of software developments ...'.

ERP has been described as an umbrella term for integrated business software systems that power a corporate information structure, thus helping companies to control their inventory, purchasing, manufacturing, finance and personnel operations.

Originally, ERP systems were simple extensions of MRP II systems, but their scope has now widened. They allow an organisation to automate and integrate most of its business processes, share common data and practices across the whole enterprise and produce and access information in a real-time environment. ERP may also incorporate transactions with an organisation's suppliers.

They help large national and multinational companies in particular to manage geographically dispersed and complex operations. For example, an organisation's UK sales office may be responsible for marketing, selling and servicing a product assembled in the US using parts manufactured in France and Hong Kong. ERP enables the organisation to understand and manage the demand placed on the plant in France.

3.6 Customer relationship management (CRM) systems

Customer relationship management (CRM) systems, which contain information about customers and customer requirements, are often integrated with ERP systems and use websites and e-commerce facilities. Within such a system, a customer's order may automatically schedule the required production facilities and order the appropriate components.

3.7 Supply chain management (SCM) systems

Supply chain management (SCM) systems aim to integrate the flow of information between the various companies on a supply chain. If a customer places an order with A, the SCM system will automatically schedule the production and delivery of components from B (A's supplier). Obviously, to operate successfully, participating organisations must have confidence in each other's operations and be willing to swap information.

3.8 Lean manufacturing

However, 'For the past decade, organizations have spent billions of dollars and countless worker-hours installing huge integrated software packages know as enterprise resource planning (ERP) applications. Now many manufacturing companies are realizing that the infrastructure they spent years creating is deficient on their plant floor. The ERP systems of the 1990s have become a liability for many manufacturers because they perpetuate some of the legendary material requirements planning (MRP) problems such as complex bills of materials, inefficient work-flows and unnecessary data collection. A new manufacturing model has emerged that's taking the place of the traditional MRP model. It's called Lean, Flow or Demand-Pull.

Lean manufacturing, a concept with roots in the production processes of Toyota, aims at improving efficiency, eliminating product backlogs and synchronizing production to customer demand rather than a long-term (often incorrect) forecast.'

'Does ERP fit in a LEAN world?', M Bradford, A Mayfield and C Tonney, *Strategic Finance*, May 2001

The point to note is that the **Lean approach** is focused on a **production plan based on actual demand** rather than production being based on a plan which it is hoped demand will follow.

3.9 Optimised production technology (OPT)

One further innovation deserves a brief mention. (Bear in mind though that a new TLA (Three-Letter Acronym) seems to gain favour every few months.) OPT also requires detailed information about inventory levels, product structures, routings, set-up times and operation times for each procedure of each product but it *also* **seeks to optimise the use of bottleneck resources**.

'The OPT philosophy contends that the **primary goal of manufacturing is to make money**. Three important criteria are identified to evaluate progress towards achieving this goal. These are throughput, inventory and operating expenses. The goal is to **maximise throughput** while simultaneously **maintaining or decreasing inventory and operating expenses**.

The OPT approach determines what prevents throughput [of products through the production process] from being higher by **distinguishing between bottleneck and non-bottleneck resources**. A bottleneck might be a machine whose capacity limits the throughput of the whole production process. The aim is to identify bottlenecks and remove them or, of this is not possible, ensure that they are fully utilised at all times. Non-bottleneck resources should be scheduled and operated based on constraints within the system, and should not be used to produce more than the bottlenecks can absorb.

With the OPT approach, it is vitally important to schedule all non-bottleneck resources within the manufacturing system based on the constraints of the system (ie the bottlenecks). For example, if only 70% of the output of a non-bottleneck resource can be absorbed by the following bottleneck resource then 30% of the utilisation of the non-bottleneck is simply concerned with increasing inventory. It can therefore be argued that by operating at the 70% level, the non-bottleneck resource is achieving 100% efficiency.'

(Drury, *Management and Cost Accounting (with BPP's emphasis)*)

Question

Three letter acronyms

Learning outcome: A(vii)

Answer this question without looking back over the preceding sections.

Which of the following has not been discussed in this chapter?

A   MPT
B   MRP
C   OPT
D   ERP

Answer

The correct answer is A.

Question

MRP and ERP

Learning outcome: A(vii)

Explain how MRP and ERP systems can assist the management accountant in preparing budgets, maintaining standard costing systems and presenting variances to management.   (5 marks)

Answer

MRP and ERP systems are production management strategies that are primarily designed to plan enterprise-wide resources. They can assist the management accountant in a variety of ways as follows.

- P systems use a master production schedule to derive details of the parts and materials required at various stages of the production process. The management accountant can use this information as a basis for completing the production cost budget and the underlying budgets (materials cost budget, labour cost budget and so on) for the forthcoming period

- The detailed scheduling of manufacturing and assembly requirements will facilitate preparation of budgets such as the materials purchases budget and this in turn will provide an input to the cash budget

- ERP systems plan enterprise-wide resources. For example even the marketing and personnel functions are integrated so that the management accountant can identify the cash and other resources that will be required by the various business functions and the timing of those requirements

- The detailed schedule of resources required for each product provides the management accountant with the basis for calculating the product standard cost and keeping it up to date if there are any changes to resource specifications

- An ERP system produces information on resource consumption in a real-time environment, thus enabling early comparison with the standard resources according to the detailed schedule and hence rapid feedback of variance information to management

4 Just-in-time (JIT) systems

FAST FORWARD

JIT aims for zero inventory and perfect quality and operates by demand-pull. It consists of **JIT purchasing** and **JIT production** and results in lower investment requirements, space savings, greater customer satisfaction and increased flexibility.

'Traditional' responses to the problems of improving manufacturing capacity and reducing unit costs of production might be described as follows.

- Longer production runs
- Economic batch quantities
- Fewer products in the product range
- More overtime
- Reduced time on preventive maintenance, to keep production flowing

In general terms, longer production runs and large batch sizes should mean less disruption, better capacity utilisation and lower unit costs.

Just-in-time systems challenge such 'traditional' views of manufacture.

Key terms

Just-in-time (JIT) is 'A system whose objective is to produce or to procure products or components as they are required by a customer or for use, rather than for stock. A JIT system is a 'pull' system, which responds to demand, in contrast to a 'push' system, in which stocks act as buffers between the different elements of the system, such as purchasing, production and sales.'

Just-in-time production is 'A system which is driven by demand for finished products whereby each component on a production line is produced only when needed for the next stage'.

Just-in-time purchasing is 'A system in which material purchases are contracted so that the receipt and usage of material, to the maximum extent possible, coincide'.

(CIMA *Official Terminology*)

Although described as a technique in the *Official Terminology*, JIT is more of a **philosophy or approach to management** since it encompasses a **commitment to continuous improvement** and the **search for excellence** in the design and operation of the production management system.

JIT has the following **essential elements**.

Element	Detail
JIT purchasing	Parts and raw materials should be purchased as near as possible to the time they are needed, using small frequent deliveries against bulk contracts.
Close relationship with suppliers	In a JIT environment, the responsibility for the quality of goods lies with the supplier. A long-term commitment between supplier and customer should therefore be established: the supplier is guaranteed a demand for his products since he is the sole supplier and he is able to plan to meet the customer's production schedules. If an organisation has confidence that suppliers will deliver material of 100% quality, on time, so that there will be no rejects, returns and hence no consequent production delays, usage of materials can be matched with delivery of materials and inventories can be kept at near zero levels. Suppliers are also chosen because of their close proximity to an organisation's plant.
Uniform loading	All parts of the productive process should be operated at a speed which matches the rate at which the final product is demanded by the customer. Production runs will therefore be shorter and there will be smaller inventories of finished goods because output is being matched more closely to demand (and so storage costs will be reduced).
Set-up time reduction	Machinery set-ups are non-value-added activities (see below) which should be reduced or even eliminated.
Machine cells	Machines or workers should be grouped by product or component instead of by the type of work performed. The non-value-added activity of materials movement between operations is therefore minimised by eliminating space between work stations. Products can flow from machine to machine without having to wait for the next stage of processing or returning to stores. Lead times and work in progress are thus reduced.
Quality	Production management should seek to eliminate scrap and defective units during production, and to avoid the need for reworking of units since this stops the flow of production and leads to late deliveries to customers. Product quality and production quality are important 'drivers' in a JIT system.
Pull system (*Kanban*)	A *Kanban*, or signal, is used to ensure that products/ components are only produced when needed by the next process. Nothing is produced in anticipation of need, to then remain in inventory, consuming resources.
Preventative maintenance	Production systems must be reliable and prompt, without unforeseen delays and breakdowns. Machinery must be kept fully maintained, and so preventative maintenance is an important aspect of production.
Employee involvement	Workers within each machine cell should be trained to operate each machine within that cell and to be able to perform routine preventative maintenance on the cell machines (ie to be multiskilled and flexible).

Learning outcome: A(vii)

A company is considering changing to a JIT system. Which of the following changes in their working practices are likely to be necessary?

I	More frequent revision of stock control levels and of the economic order quantity
II	Increase in the number of raw material suppliers in order to guarantee supply
III	Selection of suppliers close to the company's manufacturing facility
IV	Increased focus on the accurate forecasting of customer demand
V	Increased quality control activity

A	I and II
B	III, IV and V
C	II, III, IV and V
D	All of them

Answer

The correct answer is B.

Revision of stock controls levels would not be necessary (I) because the control level system would be abandoned completely. Parts and raw materials would be purchased in small frequent deliveries against bulk contracts.

II is not correct because the number of suppliers would be reduced in a JIT environment. There may be a long-term commitment to a single supplier.

III is correct. Suppliers may be chosen because of their close proximity so that they can respond quickly to changes in the company's demands.

IV is correct. Accurate forecasting of demand reduces the need for inventories.

V is correct. Production management will aim to eliminate the occurrence of rejects and defective materials since these situations stop the flow of production.

4.1 Value added

JIT aims to eliminate all **non-value-added costs**. Value is only added while a product is actually being processed. Whilst it is being inspected for quality, moving from one part of the factory to another, waiting for further processing and held in store, value is not being added. Non value-added activities (or **diversionary** activities) should therefore be eliminated.

Key term

'A **value-added** cost is incurred for an activity that cannot be eliminated without the customer's perceiving a deterioration in the performance, function, or other quality of a product. The cost of a picture tube in a television set is value-added.

The costs of those activities that can be eliminated without the customer's perceiving deterioration in the performance, function, or other quality of a product are non-value-added. The costs of handling the materials of a television set through successive stages of an assembly line may be non-value-added. Improvements in plant layout that reduce handling costs may be achieved without affecting the performance, function, or other quality of the television set.' (Horngren)

Question   Value-added activity

Learning outcome: A(viii)

Which of the following is a value-added activity?

A   Setting up a machine so that it drills holes of a certain size
B   Repairing faulty production work
C   Painting a car, if the organisation manufactures cars
D   Storing materials

Answer

The correct answer is C.

The other activities are non-value-adding activities.

Case Study

The following extract from an article in the *Financial Times* illustrates how 'just-in-time' some manufacturing processes can be. The emphasis is BPP's.

'Just-in-time manufacturing is down to a fine art at *Nissan Motor Manufacturing (UK)*. **Stockholding of some components is just ten minutes** - and the holding of all parts bought in Europe is less than a day.

Nissan has moved beyond just-in-time to **synchronous supply** for some components, which means manufacturers deliver these components directly to the production line minutes before they are needed.

These manufacturers do not even receive an order to make a component until the car for which it is intended has started along the final assembly line. Seat manufacturer *Ikeda Hoover*, for example, has about 45 minutes to build seats to specification and deliver them to the assembly line a mile away. It delivers 12 sets of seats every 20 minutes and they are mounted in the right order on an overhead conveyor ready for fitting to the right car.

Nissan has **close relationships with this dozen or so suppliers** and deals exclusively with them in their component areas. It involves them and even their own suppliers in discussions about future needs and other issues. These companies have generally established their own manufacturing units close to the Nissan plant.

Other parts from further afield are collected from manufacturers by *Nissan* several times at fixed times. This is more efficient than having each supplier making individual haulage arrangements.'

4.2 Problems associated with JIT

JIT should not be seen as a panacea for all the endemic problems associated with Western manufacturing. It might not even be appropriate in all circumstances.

   (a)   It is not always easy to predict patterns of demand.

   (b)   JIT makes the organisation far more vulnerable to disruptions in the supply chain.

   (c)   JIT, originated by Toyota, was designed at a time when all of Toyota's manufacturing was done within a 50 km radius of its headquarters. Wide geographical spread, however, makes this difficult.

Case Study

- 'Just-in-time works well during normal business times. Companies that once kept months of safety stock now get by with days, or even hours of materials … . But how about when your industry [high-tech] suddenly undergoes a tremendous boom, and demand far exceeds projections for parts? … Just look at cell phones. The worldwide boom in cellular phone sales wasn't exactly a surprise – sales of these units have been on a fast climb for years. Yet one distributor reports a wait of 18 months to obtain high-frequency transistors for hand held devices.'

  ('Just in time, or just too late?', Doug Bartholomew, *Industry Week,* August 2000)

- The Kobe earthquake in Japan in 1995 severely disrupted industry in areas unaffected by the actual catastrophe. Plants that had not been hit by the earthquake were still forced to shut down production lines less than 24 hours after the earthquake struck because they held no buffer stocks which they could use to cover the shortfall caused by non delivery by the Kobe area suppliers.

- In October 1991 the workforce at the French state-owned car maker *Renault's* gear-box production plant at Cléon went on strike. The day afterwards a British plant had to cease production. Within two weeks *Renault* was losing 60% of its usual daily output. The weaknesses were due to the following.
  - Sourcing components from one plant only
  - Heavy dependence on in-house components
  - Low inventory
  - The fact '...that Japanese-style management techniques depend on stability in labour relations, something in short supply in the French public sector'.

(*Financial Times*, 31 October 1991)

Question   JIT

Learning outcome: A(viii)

Batch sizes within a JIT manufacturing environment may well be smaller than those associated with traditional manufacturing systems.

What costs might be associated with this feature of JIT?

1   Increased set-up costs
2   Opportunity cost of lost production capacity as machinery and the workforce reorganise for a different product
3   Additional materials handling costs
4   Increased administrative costs

A   None of the above
B   1, 2, 3 and 4
C   1 only
D   2 and 3 only

Answer

The correct answer is B.

4.3 Modern versus traditional inventory control systems

There is no reason for the newer approaches to supersede the old entirely. A restaurant, for example, might find it preferable to use the traditional economic order quantity approach for staple non-perishable food items, but adopt JIT for perishable and 'exotic' items. In a hospital a stock-out could, quite literally, be fatal, and JIT would be quite unsuitable.

5 Synchronous manufacturing

Key term

Synchronous manufacturing is a manufacturing philosophy which aims to ensure that all operations within an organisation are performed for the common good of the organisation and that nothing is done unless it improves the bottom line.

It therefore requires managers to **focus on areas of operations which offer the greatest possibilities for global improvements** (such as at a bottleneck resource) rather than improving the process everywhere in the system, which is the JIT philosophy.

Proponents of synchronous manufacturing **regard JIT as unfocused**. They claim that it fails to identify capacity restraints in advance but waits until a problem occurs, which disrupts the entire processing system. Synchronous manufacturing, on the other hand, attempts to **detect problems before they happen** so that the production process and hence throughput are unaffected. According to advocates of synchronous manufacturing, **JIT** fails to focus effectively on bottleneck resources, with the result that **throughput may not be optimal**.

Synchronous manufacturing aims to **develop a production schedule that takes account of the constraints within the processing system**. This involves a detailed analysis of the plant's capabilities and the manufacturing environment with the aim of identifying the system's constraints. Time buffers are then built into the system at strategic points throughout the plant so as to avoid disruption and to ensure that the planned production schedule is met.

FAST FORWARD

Synchronous manufacturing aims to ensure that all operations within an organisation are performed for the common good of the organisation.

6 Total quality management (TQM)

Quality means 'the **degree of excellence of a thing'** - how well made it is, or how well performed if it is a service, how well it serves its purpose, and how it measures up against its rivals. These criteria imply two things.

- That quality is something that **requires care on the part of the provider**.
- That **quality** is largely subjective - it is in the eye of the beholder, the **customer**.

FAST FORWARD

In the context of **Total Quality Management** 'quality' means getting it right first time, and improving continuously.

6.1 The management of quality

The **management** of quality is the process of:

(a) Establishing **standards of quality** for a product or service

(b) Establishing **procedures or production methods** which ought to ensure that these required standards of quality are met in a suitably high proportion of cases

(c) **Monitoring** actual quality

(d) Taking **control action** when actual quality falls below standard

Take the postal service as an example. The postal service might establish a standard that 90% of first class letters will be delivered on the day after they are posted, and 99% will be delivered within two days of posting.

(a) Procedures would have to be established for ensuring that these standards could be met (attending to such matters as frequency of collections, automated letter sorting, frequency of deliveries and number of staff employed).

(b) Actual performance could be monitored, perhaps by taking samples from time to time of letters that are posted and delivered.

(c) If the quality standard is not being achieved, management should take control action (employ more postal workers or advertise the use of postcodes again).

Quality management becomes **total (Total Quality Management (TQM)) when it is applied to everything a business does**.

Key term

Total quality management (TQM) is 'an integrated and comprehensive system of planning and controlling all business functions so that products or services are produced which meet or exceed customer expectations. TQM is a philosophy of business behaviour, embracing principles such as employee involvement, continuous improvement at all levels and customer focus, as well as being a collection of related techniques aimed at improving quality such as full documentation of activities, clear goal setting and performance measurement from the customer perspective.'

(CIMA *Official Terminology*)

Exam focus point

As you learn the mechanics of these new management approaches, try not to view each one in isolation. For example, the pilot paper contained a question requiring students to give reasons why the adoption of TQM is important in a JIT environment.

6.2 Get it right, first time

One of the basic principles of TQM is that the **cost of preventing mistakes is less than the cost of correcting them** once they occur. The aim should therefore be **to get things right first time**. Every mistake, delay and misunderstanding, directly costs an organisation money through **wasted time and effort**, including time taken in pacifying customers. The **lost potential for future sales because of poor customer service must also be taken into account**.

6.3 Continuous improvement

A second basic principle of TQM is dissatisfaction with the *status quo*: the belief that it is **always possible to improve** and so the aim should be to **'get it more right next time'**.

6.4 Quality assurance procedures

Because TQM embraces every activity of a business, quality assurance procedures **cannot be confined to the production process** but must also cover the work of sales, distribution and administration departments, the efforts of external suppliers, and the reaction of external customers.

6.4.1 Quality assurance of goods inwards

The quality of output depends on the quality of input materials, and so quality control should include **procedures for acceptance and inspection of goods inwards and measurement of rejects**. Each supplier can be given a 'rating' for the quality of the goods they tend to supply, and preference with purchase orders can be given to well-rated suppliers. This method is referred to as 'vendor rating'.

Where a **quality assurance scheme** is in place the supplier guarantees the quality of goods supplied and allows the customers' inspectors access while the items are being manufactured. The **onus is on the supplier to carry out the necessary quality checks**, or face cancellation of the contract.

Suppliers' quality assurance schemes are being used increasingly, particularly where extensive sub-contracting work is carried out, for example in the motor industries. One such scheme is **BS EN ISO 9000** certification. A company that gains registration has a certificate testifying that it is operating to a structure of written policies and procedures which are designed to ensure that it can consistently deliver a product or service to meet customer requirements.

6.4.2 Inspection of output

This will take place at various key stages in the production process and will provide a continual check that the production process is under control. The aim of inspection is *not* really to sort out the bad products from the good ones after the work has been done. The **aim is to satisfy management that quality control in production is being maintained.**

The **inspection of samples** rather than 100% testing of all items will keep inspection costs down, and smaller samples will be less costly to inspect than larger samples. The greater the confidence in the reliability of production methods and process control, the smaller the samples will be.

6.4.3 Monitoring customer reaction

Some sub-standard items will inevitably be produced. Checks during production will identify some bad output, but other items will reach the customer who is the ultimate judge of quality. **Complaints ought to be monitored** in the form of letters of complaint, returned goods, penalty discounts, claims under guarantee, or requests for visits by service engineers. Some companies actually survey customers on a regular basis.

6.4.4 Employees and quality

Employees often have a poor attitude towards quality, as a system imposed 'from outside' by non-operational staff and as an implication of lack of trust in workers to maintain quality standards or to apply a control system with objectivity themselves.

Attitudes to quality control and the management of it have, however, been **undergoing changes**.

(a)   As the pace of change in the environment has increased so attention to quality and a commitment to quality standards has become a **vital factor for organisational adaptation and survival**.

(b)   It is being recognised that **workers can be motivated by a positive approach to quality**: producing quality work is a tangible and worthwhile objective. Where responsibility for quality checking has been given to the worker himself (encouraging self-supervision), **job satisfaction may be increased**: it is a kind of job enrichment, and also a sign of trust and respect, because imposed controls have been removed.

(c)   **Non-aversive ways of implementing quality control** have been devised. **Cultural orientation** (the deep 'belief' in quality, filtered down to all operatives) can be enlisted. **Inter-group competition** to meet and beat quality standards, for example, might be encouraged. **Quality circles** may be set up, perhaps with responsibility for implementing improvements which they identify.

Problems can therefore be overcome by **changing people's attitudes** rather than teaching them new tricks. The key issue is to instil **understanding of, and commitment to, working practices that lead to quality**.

Case Study

As part of its TQM programme *BICC Cables* reorganised its factory from its traditional process-based operation into a dedicated product layout. It then launched two separate but related training and development activities, teamwork training and JIT training.

'To implement (JIT) working it was decided to use a firm of consultants in the first manufacturing cell to ensure a comprehensively structured introduction, with our own people working alongside them, and then to implement JIT in the other three cells ourselves.

We decided to create a **game** to convey JIT principles, and all employees in the first cell participated in it. This was followed by a series of **training/information sessions**, during which the importance of bottleneck management and inventory control was emphasised.

Employees rapidly gained an understanding of JIT and learnt the basic lessons that lots of work in progress was not necessary for the factory to be productive and that people did not always have to be busy to be effective. As in the game, we installed **'Kanbans'** on the shopfloor to limit and control the flow of inventory. When the Kanban is full, it acts as a signal to the previous process not to transfer any more work and, if required, to stop the previous process.

This was a difficult idea to take on. In effect we went **against traditional practice** by asking people to stop processes even though there was work to be done and to make themselves available for other work. This focuses attention on where effort needs to be applied to get products dispatched.

This cycle of training and implementation was repeated in the remaining three cells until the complete factory unit was operating along the JIT lines. The use of Kanbans has significantly reduced work in progress, and space has been released which has been used to accommodate new machines.'

6.5 Empowerment

Workers themselves are frequently the best source of information about how (or how not) to improve quality. **Empowerment** therefore has two key aspects.

(a) Allowing workers to have the **freedom to decide how to do** the necessary work, using the skills they possess and acquiring new skills as necessary to be an effective team member.

(b) Making workers **responsible** for achieving production targets and for quality control.

It is important to **question the value of these developments**, however.

'Do employees and management really find 'empowerment' to be liberating? Empirical studies suggest that 'empowerment' often amounts to the delegation of additional duties to employees. Limits have to be placed on what employees can do, so empowerment is often associated with rules, bureaucracy and form-filling. That apart, many employees find most satisfaction from outside work activities and are quite happy to confine themselves to doing what they are told while at work. The proponents of TQM are often very work-centred people themselves and tend to judge others by their own standards.

Do teams contribute to organisational effectiveness? Just calling a group of people who work in the same office 'a team' does not make it a team. A team requires a high level of co-operation and consensus. Many competitive and motivated people find working in a team environment to be uncongenial. It means that every time you want to do anything you have to communicate with and seek approval from fellow team members. In practice, this is likely to involve bureaucracy and form-filling.

... it can be argued that TQM merely moves empowerment from management to employees. It has been argued that the latter cannot be expected to succeed where the former have failed.'

'Quality Streak', Bob Scarlett, *CIMA Insider,* September 2001

6.6 Design for quality

A TQM environment aims to get it right first time, and this means that **quality, not faults, must be designed into the organisation's products and operations from the outset**.

Quality control happens at various stages in the process of designing a product or service.

(a) At the **product design stage**, quality control means trying to design a product or service so that its specifications provide a suitable balance between price and quality (of sales and delivery, as well as manufacture) which will make the product or service competitive.

(b) **Production engineering** is the **process of designing the methods for making a product** (or service) **to the design specification**. It sets out to make production methods as efficient as possible, and to avoid the manufacture of sub-standard items.

(c) **Information systems** should be designed to get the required information to the right person at the right time; **distribution systems** should be designed to get the right item to the right person at the right time; and so on.

6.7 Quality control and inspection

A distinction should be made between **quality control** and **inspection**.

(a) **Quality control** involves setting controls for the process of manufacture or service delivery. It is a aimed at **preventing the manufacture of defective items** or the provision of defective services.

(b) **Inspection** is a technique of **identifying when defective items are being produced at an unacceptable level.** Inspection is usually carried out at three main points.

(i) Receiving inspection - for raw materials and purchased components
(ii) Floor or process inspection for WIP
(iii) Final inspection or testing for finished goods

Question
Quality

Learning outcome: A(viii)

Read the following extract from an article in the *Financial Times* in April 1993, and then list the features and methods of a quality information system that *Lloyds Bank* might have devised to collect information on the impact of the 'service challenge' described here.

'If you telephone a branch of *Lloyds Bank* and it rings five times before there is a reply; if the person who answers does not introduce him or herself by name during the conversation; if you are standing in a queue with more people in it than the number of tills, then something is wrong.'

'If any of these things happen then the branch is breaching standards of customer service set by the bank since last July ... the "service challenge" was launched in the bank's 1,888 branches last summer after being tested in 55 branches in 1990 ...'

'*Lloyds* already has evidence of the impact. Customers were more satisfied with pilot branches in 1991 than with others.'

Answer

A wide variety of answers is possible. The article goes on to explain how the bank is actually going about monitoring the impact of the initiative.

(a) It has devised a 100 point scale showing average satisfaction with branch service.

(b) It conducts a 'first impressions' survey of all new customers.

(c) There is also a general survey carried out every six months which seeks the views of a weighted sample of 350 customers per branch.

(d) A survey company telephones each branch anonymously twice a month to test how staff respond to enquiries about products.

(e) A quarter of each branch's staff answer a monthly questionnaire about the bank's products to test their knowledge.

(f) Groups of employees working in teams in branches are allowed to set their own additional standards. This is to encourage participation.

(g) Branches that underperform are more closely watched by 24 managers who monitor the initiative.

Exam focus point

Your syllabus emphasises the need for you to know about the possible impacts of methods such as TQM on performance measurement.

Examples such as the monitoring of quality at Lloyds Bank might help you to give a practical emphasis to your answer.

7 Costs of quality and cost of quality reports

FAST FORWARD

Quality costs can be analysed into **prevention**, **appraisal**, **internal failure** and **external failure** costs and should be detailed in a **cost of quality report**.

7.1 Costs of quality

When we talk about quality-related costs you should remember that a concern for **good quality saves money**; it is **poor quality that costs money.**

Cost of quality reports highlight the total cost to an organisation of producing products or services that do not conform with quality requirements. Four categories of cost should be reported: prevention costs, appraisal costs, internal failure costs and external failure costs.

Key terms

The **cost of quality** is 'The difference between the actual cost of producing, selling and supporting products or services and the equivalent costs if there were no failures during production or usage'. The cost of quality can be analysed into the following.

Cost of conformance is 'The cost of achieving specified quality standards.

- **Cost of prevention** - the costs incurred prior to or during production in order to prevent substandard or defective products or services from being produced

- **Cost of appraisal** - costs incurred in order to ensure that outputs produced meet required quality standards'

Cost of non-conformance is 'The cost of failure to deliver the required standard of quality.

- **Cost of internal failure** - the costs arising from inadequate quality which are identified before the transfer of ownership from supplier to purchaser

- **Cost of external failure** - the cost arising from inadequate quality discovered after the transfer of ownership from supplier to purchaser'   (CIMA *Official Terminology*)

Quality-related cost	Example
Prevention costs	Quality engineering
	Design/development of quality control/inspection equipment
	Maintenance of quality control/inspection equipment
	Administration of quality control
	Training in quality control
Appraisal costs	Acceptance testing
	Inspection of goods inwards
	Inspection costs of in-house processing
	Performance testing

Quality-related cost	Example
Internal failure costs	Failure analysis Re-inspection costs Losses from failure of purchased items Losses due to lower selling prices for sub-quality goods Costs of reviewing product specifications after failures
External failure costs	Administration of customer complaints section Costs of customer service section Product liability costs Cost of repairing products returned from customers Cost of replacing items due to sub-standard products/marketing errors

The **cost of conformance** is a **discretionary** cost which is incurred with the intention of **eliminating the costs of internal and external failure.** The **cost of non-conformance**, on the other hand, can **only be reduced by increasing the cost of conformance**. The **optimal investment in conformance costs** is when **total costs of quality reach a minimum** (which may be below 100% quality conformance). This is illustrated in the following diagram.

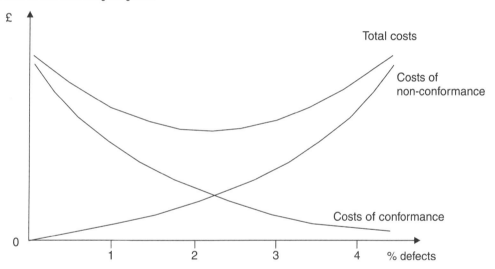

To achieve **0% defects, costs of conformance must be high**. As a **greater proportion of defects are accepted**, however, these costs can be **reduced.** At a level of **0% defects, costs of non-conformance** should be **nil** but these will **increase** as the **accepted level of defects rises.** There should therefore be an **acceptable level of defects** at which the **total costs of quality are at a minimum**.

7.2 Cost of quality reports

Shown below is a typical cost of quality report. **Some figures** in the report, such as the contribution forgone due to sales lost because of poor quality, may have to be **estimated,** but it is better to include an estimate rather than omit the category from the report.

The report has the following **uses**.

(a) By expressing each cost category as a percentage of sales revenue, **comparisons** can be made with previous periods, divisions within the group or other organisations, thereby highlighting problem areas. A comparison of the proportion of external failure costs to sales revenue with the figures for other organisations, for example, can provide some idea of the level of customer satisfaction.

(b) It can be used to make senior management aware of **how much is being spent** on quality-related costs.

(c) It can provide an indication of **how total quality costs could be reduced by a more sensible division of costs between the four categories.** For example, an increase in spending on prevention costs should reduce the costs of internal and external failure and hence reduce total spending.

COST OF QUALITY REPORT
YEAR ENDING 31 DECEMBER 20X0

	£'000	£'000	Cost as % of annual turnover (£10 million)
Prevention costs			
Design of quality control equipment	80		
Quality control training	80		
		160	1.6
Appraisal costs			
Inspection of goods inwards	90		
Inspection of WIP	100		
		190	1.9
Internal failure costs			
Scrap	150		
Rework	200		
		350	3.5
External failure costs			
Returns	500		
Contribution forgone on lost sales	400		
Handling customer complaints	100		
		1,000	10.0
		1,700	17.0

Although cost of quality reports provide a useful summary of the costs, effort and progress of quality, **non-financial quality measures** may be more appropriate for **lower levels of management**. Here are some examples of such measures.

- Number of customer complaints
- Number of warranty claims
- Number of defective units delivered to customers as a percentage of total units delivered

Exam focus point

Remember that the emphasis in your syllabus is not on the detailed mechanics of JIT, TQM etc, but on their impact on performance measurement. Make sure that you could design a cost of quality report for any given scenario.

8 World class manufacturing (WCM)

FAST FORWARD

World class manufacturing (WCM) aims for high quality, fast production, and the flexibility to respond to customer needs.

World class manufacturing (WCM) is a term which was coined in the mid-1980s to **describe the fundamental changes taking place in manufacturing companies** we have been examining. WCM is a very broad term.

Key term

'World Class Manufacturing (WCM) describes the manufacture of high-quality products reaching customers quickly (or the delivery of a prompt and quality service) at a low cost to provide high performance and customer satisfaction.'

Peter J Clarke ('The old and the new in management accounting', *Management Accounting*, June 1995)

The *Official Terminology's* definition of **world class manufacturing** is 'A position of international manufacturing excellence, achieved by developing a culture based on factors such as continuous improvement, problem prevention, zero defect tolerance, customer-driven JIT-based production and total quality management'.

In essence, however, WCM can be taken to have four key elements.

Key element	Description
A new approach to product quality	Instead of a policy of trying to detect defects or poor quality in production as and when they occur, WCM sets out to **identify the root causes of poor quality, eliminate them, and achieve zero defects, that is 100% quality,** thereby incorporating the principles of **TQM.**
Just-in-time manufacturing	See Section 4
Managing people	WCM aims to utilise the skills and abilities of the work force to the full. Employees are given **training** in a variety of skills, so that they can **switch from one task to another**. They are also given more **responsibility** for production scheduling and quality. A **team approach** is encouraged, with strong trust between management and workers.
Flexible approach to customer requirements	The WCM policy is to **develop close relationships** with customers in order to know what their requirements are, supply them on time, with short delivery lead times and change the product mix quickly and develop new products or modify existing products as customer needs change.

A WCM manufacturer will have a clear **manufacturing strategy** aimed at issues such as quality and reliability, short lead times (the time from start to finish of production), flexibility and customer satisfaction. But to compete, the world class manufacturer must appreciate that it is **not just in manufacturing that he must excel**. A **clear understanding** of the relationship between all of the factors which add value to an organisation's products (the **value chain**) is vital.

8.1 The value chain

The value chain is made up of the following.

- Research and development
- Design
- Production
- Marketing

- Distribution
- Customer service
- Customers

It **starts externally** with suppliers, links them to the internal functions of R&D, design, production, marketing, distribution and customer service, and **ends externally** with suppliers.

To improve quality, reduce costs and increase innovation, the manufacturer must ensure that the **functions within the value chain are coordinated** within the overall organisational framework.

Case Study

In January 1993 the *Financial Times* reported the findings of a comparative study of 18 UK and Japanese companies by *Andersen Consulting* and Cambridge University. All of the companies were suppliers of components to the motor industry. The overall finding was that **most of the UK companies lag far behind the 'world class' productivity and quality standards set by the best Japanese companies**. Specific points mentioned included the following.

(a)   UK plants had an average of 2.5 **defects** per 100 components, compared with 2.5 per 10,000 for the best Japanese plants.

(b)   The UK plants typically needed **twice as many employees** to produce the same number of parts.

(c)   The world class plants were making a **more complex and rapidly changing mix of products** than their rivals.

(d)   The world class plants **involved more of their employees** more intensively in problem-solving. In such plants **team leaders** were pivotal, developing the skills of team members as well as taking responsibility for quality and management issues.

(e)   The **organisation of** the production process in world class firms was highly significant. 'It starts with integrating every production step into an uninterrupted flow - so parts travel the minimum distance and hardly wait for the next operation.' Thereafter, 'the discipline governing the flow comes from short set-up times and small lots produced just-in-time, thus eliminating waste and work in progress.' Random interruptions and variability such as machine breakdowns, supplier hiccups or defective parts are eliminated.

(f)   The 'world class' firms had a **tightly integrated supply chain**, marked by minimal stock, frequent deliveries of small volumes of parts, lack of disruption and stable supply volumes. The discipline of the system came from short lead times between order and delivery and building to customer order rather than to accumulate inventory.

Chapter Roundup

- Changes to the **competitive environment**, **product life cycles** and **customer requirements** have had a significant impact on the modern business environment.

- Different approaches for **organising a manufacturing process** include **jobbing industries, batch processing** and **mass production**.

- **Advanced manufacturing technology (AMT)** is a general expression encompassing **computer-aided design (CAD), computer-aided manufacturing (CAM), flexible manufacturing systems (FMS)** and a wide array of innovative computer equipment.

- The **production management strategies** linked to AMT are materials requirement planning (MRPI), manufacturing resource planning (MRPII), enterprise resource planning (ERP), optimised production technology (OPT) and just-in-time (JIT).

- **JIT** aims for zero inventory and perfect quality and operates by demand-pull. It consists of **JIT purchasing** and **JIT production** and results in lower investment requirements, space savings, greater customer satisfaction and increased flexibility.

- **Synchronous manufacturing** aims to ensure that all operations within an organisation are performed for the common good of the organisation.

- In the context of **Total Quality Management** 'quality' means getting it right first time, and improving continuously.

- **Quality costs** can be analysed into **prevention, appraisal, internal failure** and **external failure** costs and should be detailed in a **cost of quality report.**

- **World class manufacturing (WCM)** aims for high quality, fast production, and the flexibility to respond to customer needs.

Quick Quiz

1   *Match the type of production with one of the descriptions (1) to (4).*

Jobbing industries	(1)	Merges the flexibility of the functional layout with the speed and productivity of the product layout
Batch processing	(2)	Uses a product-based layout
Mass/flow production	(3)	Factory is typically laid out on a functional basis
Cellular manufacturing	(4)	Uses functional layout but with a high number of specialised machines

2   *Choose the correct words from those highlighted.*

Materials requirement planning/manufacturing requirement planning/materials resource planning/manufacturing resource planning is concerned with maximising efficiency in the timing of orders for raw materials or parts that are placed with external suppliers and efficient scheduling of the manufacturing and assembly of the end product.

3   *Fill in the blanks in this list of the nine essential elements of JIT.*

(a)   JIT ....
(b)   Close relationships with ....
(c)   Uniform ....

(d)   Set-up time ....

(e)   .... cells

(f)   ....

(g)   .... (Kanban)

(h)   .... maintenance

(i)   .... involvement

4   The cost of inspecting a product for quality is a value-added cost. True or false?

5   *Which of the following is/are correct?*

(a)   Cost of conformance = cost of prevention + cost of internal failure

(b)   Cost of conformance = cost of internal failure + cost of external failure

(c)   Cost of non-conformance = cost of internal failure + cost of external failure

(d)   Cost of conformance = cost of appraisal + cost of prevention

(e)   Cost of non-conformance = cost of prevention + cost of appraisal

(f)   Cost of non-conformance = cost of appraisal + cost of external failure

6   *Match the cost to the correct cost category.*

Costs

(a)   Administration of quality control

(b)   Product liability costs

(c)   Acceptance testing

(d)   Losses due to lower selling prices for sub-quality goods

Cost categories

- Prevention costs
- Appraisal costs
- Internal failure costs
- External failure costs

7   What is an FMS?

A   Fast manufacturing system

B   Flexible manufacturing system

C   Flexible materials system

D   Fixed manufacturing sequence

8   Proponents of synchronous manufacturing are also supporters of JIT. True or false?

9   *Choose the correct words from those highlighted.*

Quality control/inspection is aimed at preventing the manufacture of defective items.

10   What are the four key elements of WCM?

(a)   ....

(b)   ....

(c)   ....

(d)   ....

Answers to Quick Quiz

1   Jobbing industries   - description (3)
    Batch processing   - description (4)
    Mass/flow production   - description (2)
    Cellular manufacturing   - description (1)

2   Materials requirement planning

3   (a)   JIT purchasing
    (b)   Close relationships with suppliers
    (c)   Uniform loading
    (d)   Set-up time reduction
    (e)   Machine cells
    (f)   Quality
    (g)   Pull system (Kanban)
    (h)   Preventative maintenance
    (i)   Employee involvement

4   False

5   (c) and (d) are correct.

6   (a)   Prevention costs
    (b)   External failure costs
    (c)   Appraisal costs
    (d)   Internal failure costs

7   B

8   False. They regard JIT as unfocussed.

9   Quality control

10 A new approach to product quality
    JIT manufacturing
    Managing people
    Flexible approach to customer requirements

Now try the questions below from the Exam Question Bank

Number	Level	Marks	Time
Q7	Examination	5	9 mins
Q8	Examination	5	9 mins

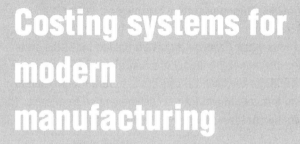

Costing systems for modern manufacturing

Introduction

Having looked at recent developments in manufacturing and business practice, you will now go on to learn about costing systems and performance monitoring systems that have been developed to **suit modern practices.**

The theory of constraints (TOC) provides the basis for the development of throughput accounting (TA) (Sections 1 and 2). As a production system (TOC) and an accounting and performance monitoring system (TA), they are ideally suited to the modern manufacturing environment in which production is an immediate response to customer demand. They aim to maximise the net return on sales. They can also be used in service industries where bottleneck processes can be identified and alleviated.

Backflush accounting (Section 3) is an accounting system that has been specifically designed for use with JIT systems. It cannot be used unless inventory levels are minimal. Its main advantage is the simplification it brings.

Topic list	Learning outcomes	Syllabus references	Ability required
1 The theory of constraints (TOC)	A(iv)	A 8	Comprehension
2 Throughput accounting	A(iv)	A 3	Comp/Application
3 Backflush accounting	A(viii)	A 8	Evaluation

1 The theory of constraints (TOC)

Theory of constraints is a set of concepts developed in the USA which aim to identify the binding constraints in a production system and which strive for evenness of production flow so that the organisation works as effectively as possible. No inventories should be held, except prior to the binding constraint.

The use of a JIT operating system, whether in a manufacturing or service organisation, requires a particular type of costing system. **Throughput accounting** is a technique that has been developed to deal with this. The name was first coined in the late 1980s when *Galloway and Waldron* developed the system in the UK. Throughput accounting is based on the concept of the **theory of constraints** (TOC) which was formulated by Goldratt and Cox in the U.S.A. in 1986. Its key financial concept is to **turn materials into sales as quickly as possible**, thereby maximising throughput and the net cash generated from sales. This is to be achieved by striving for **balance in production processes**, and so **evenness of production flow** is an important aim.

KEY TERMS

Theory of constraints (TOC) is 'An approach to production management which aims to maximise sales revenue less material and variable overhead cost. It focuses on factors such as bottlenecks which act as constraints to this maximisation.'

A bottleneck resource or binding constraint is 'An activity within an organisation which has a lower capacity than preceding or subsequent activities, thereby limiting throughput'.

(CIMA Official Terminology)

1.1 Managing constraints

Goldratt's five steps for dealing with a bottleneck activity are:

Step 1: Identify   Step 4: Elevate
Step 2: Exploit   Step 5: Return to step 1
Step 3: Subordinate

One process will inevitably act as a bottleneck (or limiting factor) and constrain throughput. This is known as a **binding constraint** in TOC terminology.

In order to manage constraints effectively, **Goldratt** has proposed a **five-step process** of ongoing improvement. The process operated as a **continuous loop**.

Step 1   Identify

The first step is to identify the **binding constraint** or bottleneck in the system, ie the activity which is limiting throughput.

Step 2   Exploit

Within the existing constraint managers must **focus on achieving higher throughput from the bottleneck resource**. Until the constraint has been alleviated the immediate focus must be on explaining fully the available capacity. **Output through the binding constraint should never be delayed or held up otherwise sales will be lost**. To avoid this happening **a buffer inventory should be built up immediately prior to the bottleneck** or binding constraint. **This is the only inventory that the business should hold,** with the exception of possibly a

BPP
PROFESSIONAL EDUCATION

very small amount of finished goods inventory and raw materials that are consistent with the JIT approach.

Step 3   Subordinate

All operations should be subordinated to the binding constraint. **Operations prior to the binding constraint should operate at the same speed** as the binding constraint, otherwise work in progress (other than the buffer inventory) will be built up. According to TOC, inventory costs money in terms of storage space and interest costs and so inventory is not desirable. In a traditional production system an organisation will often pay staff a bonus to produce as many units as possible. TOC views this as inefficient since the organisation is paying extra to build up inventory which then costs money to store until it is required. Thus the rate of operation of **non-constraint resources** is subordinated to the rate of operation of the binding constraint.

Step 4   Elevate

Steps should be taken to elevate the system's bottleneck, ie to increase throughput from the binding constraints, for example by purchasing more equipment or improving the efficiency of the operation.

Step 5   Return to Step 1

Once the binding constraint has been eliminated and is no longer binding, return to Step 1 and identify the new binding constraint. **The elimination of one bottleneck will always lead to another**. There will always be a binding constraint, unless capacity is far greater than sales demand or all processes are totally in balance, which is unlikely even if it is a goal to be aimed for.

Key terms

Throughput contribution = sales revenue – direct material cost

Conversion cost (in TOC) = **all operating costs except direct material cost** (ie all costs except totally variable costs)

Investment cost = inventory, equipment, building costs and so on

1.2 Throughput contribution

The aim of TOC is to maximise throughput contribution while keeping conversion and investment costs to a minimum. If a strategy for increasing throughput contribution is being considered it will therefore only be accepted if conversion and investment costs increase by a lower amount than contribution.

Attention!

It is important to realise that **TOC is not an accounting system but a production system.**

2 Throughput accounting

Throughout accounting is the accounting system developed in the UK, based on the theory of constraints and JIT. It measures the throughput contribution per factory hour., It is very similar to marginal costing but can be used to make longer-term decisions about production equipment/capacity.

The concept of throughput accounting has been developed from TOC as an **alternative system of cost and management accounting in a JIT environment**.

Key term

'**Throughput accounting** (TA) is an approach to accounting which is largely in sympathy with the JIT philosophy. In essence, TA assumes that a manager has a given set of resources available. These comprise existing buildings, capital equipment and labour force. Using these resources, purchased materials and parts must be processed to generate sales revenue. Given this scenario the most appropriate financial objective to set for doing this is the maximisation of throughput (Goldratt and Cox, 1984) which is defined as: sales revenue *less* direct material cost.'

(Tanaka, Yoshikawa, Innes and Mitchell, *Contemporary Cost Management*)

The *Official Terminology's* definition of **throughput accounting** is 'A management accounting system which focuses on ways by which the maximum return per unit of bottleneck activity can be achieved'.

TA is different from all other management accounting systems because of what it **emphasises**.

- Firstly **throughput**
- Secondly **inventory minimisation**
- Thirdly **cost control**

TA is based on three concepts.

2.1 Concept 1

In the short run, most costs in the factory (with the exception of materials costs) are fixed. Because TA differentiates between fixed and variable costs it is often compared with marginal costing and **some people argue that there is no difference between marginal costing and throughput accounting.** For this reason TA is sometimes referred to as super variable costing and indeed there are some similarities in the assumptions underlying the two methods. However, on marginal costing direct labour costs are usually assumed to be variable costs. Years ago this assumption was true, but employees are not usually paid piece rate today and they are not laid off for part of the year when there is no work, and so labour cost is not truly variable. If this is accepted the two techniques are identical in some respects, but **marginal costing is generally thought of as being purely a short-term decision-making technique** while **TA, or at least TOC, was conceived with the aim of changing manufacturing strategy to achieve evenness of flow. It is therefore much more than a short-term decision technique.**

Because **TA combines all conversion costs** together and does not attempt to examine them in detail it is particularly **suited to use with activity based costing (ABC)**, which examines the behaviour of these costs and assumes them to be variable in the long run. We will examine ABC in detail in the next chapter.

2.2 Concept 2

In a JIT environment, all inventory is a 'bad thing' and the **ideal inventory level is zero**. Products should not be made unless there is a customer waiting for them. This means **unavoidable idle capacity must be**

accepted in some operations, but not for the operation that is the bottleneck of the moment. There is one exception to the zero inventory policy, being that a buffer inventory should be held prior to the bottleneck process.

2.3 Concept 3

Profitability is determined by the rate at which 'money comes in at the door' (that is, sales are made) and, in a JIT environment, this depends on how quickly goods can be produced to satisfy customer orders. Since the goal of a profit-orientated organisation is to make money, inventory must be sold for that goal to be achieved.

The buffer inventory and any other work in progress or finished goods inventory should be **valued at material cost only** until the output is eventually sold, so that **no value will be added and no profit earned until the sale takes place.** Producing output just to add to work in progress or finished goods inventory creates no profit, and so should not be encouraged.

Question   Throughput accounting versus conventional cost accounting

Learning objective: A(iv)

Throughput accounting versus conventional cost accounting

How are the concepts of throughput accounting a direct contrast to the fundamental principles of conventional cost accounting?   (5 marks)

Answer

Conventional cost accounting	Throughput accounting
Inventory is an asset.	Inventory is *not* an asset. It is a result of unsynchronised manufacturing and is a barrier to making profit.
Costs can be classified either as direct or indirect.	Such classifications are no longer useful.
Product profitability can be determined by deducting a product cost from selling price.	Profitability is determined by the rate at which money is earned.
Profit is a function of costs.	Profit is a function of throughput as well as costs.

2.4 Bottleneck resources

The aim of **modern manufacturing** approaches is to match production resources with the demand for them. This implies that there are **no constraints, termed bottleneck resources** in TA, within an organisation. The throughput philosophy entails the **identification** and **elimination** of these bottleneck resources. Where they **cannot be eliminated production must be limited to the capacity of the bottleneck resource in order to avoid the build-up of work in progress.** If a rearrangement of existing resources or buying-in resources does not alleviate the bottleneck, investment in new equipment may be necessary. The **elimination of one bottleneck is likely to lead to the creation of another** at a previously satisfactory location, however. The **management of bottlenecks** therefore becomes a **primary concern** of the manager seeking to increase throughput.

(a)   There is nothing to be gained by measuring and encouraging the efficiency of machines that do not govern the overall flow of work.

(b)   Likewise, there is little point in measuring the efficiency of production staff working on non-bottleneck processes.

(c)   Bonuses paid to encourage faster working on non-bottleneck processes are wasted and could lead to increased storage costs and more faulty goods.

Other factors that might limit throughput other than a lack of production resources (bottlenecks)

(a)   The existence of an non-competitive selling price.

(b)   The need to deliver on time to particular customers, which may disrupt normal production flow.

(c)   The lack of product quality and reliability, which may cause large amounts of rework or an unnecessary increase in production volume.

(d)   Unreliable material suppliers, which will lead to poor quality products that require rework.

2.5 Identifying the bottleneck resource

It may not always be obvious which is the bottleneck resource and a process of trial and error for a few periods can be an expensive and inefficient way of attempting to identify it.

If the resource constraint is machine capacity, it is possible to identify the constrained machine through the calculation of **machine utilisation rates**.

2.6 Example: machine utilisation rates

A company produces three products using three different machines. The following data is available for the latest period.

	Product L Hours per unit	Product M Hours per unit	Product N Hours per unit
Machine hours required:			
Mixing machine	2	5	3
Cutting machine	3	4	2
Finishing machine	1	2	2
Sales demand	2,700 units	1,200 units	2,500 units

Maximum capacity is as follows.

	Hours available
Mixing machine	22,000
Cutting machine	15,400
Finishing machine	7,300

Required

(a)   Calculate the machine utilisation rate for each machine

(b)   Identify which of the machines is the bottleneck resource

Solution

(a)   Number of machine hours required to fulfil sales demand.

	Product L Hours	Product M Hours	Product N Hours	Total Hours
Mixing machine	5,400	6,000	7,500	18,900
Cutting machine	8,100	4,800	5,000	17,000
Finishing machine	2,700	2,400	5,000	10,100

$$\text{Machine utilisation rate} = \frac{\text{machine hours required to meet sales demand}}{\text{machine hours available}}$$

	Mixing machine	Cutting machine	Finishing machine
Machine utilisation rate	$\frac{18,900}{22,000}$	$\frac{17,900}{15,400}$	$\frac{10,100}{7,300}$
	= 85.9%	116.2%	= 138.3%

(b)   Capacity on the finishing machine is the bottleneck resource. The machine utilisation rate is higher than 100 per cent and it is the largest of the three rates.

2.7 Throughput measures

2.7.1 Return per time period

In a throughput accounting environment, the overall **focus of attention** is the **rate at which the organisation can generate profits**. To monitor this, the return on the throughput through the bottleneck resource is monitored using:

Return per time period $= \dfrac{\text{sales revenue} - \text{material costs}}{\text{time period}}$

This measure shows the **value added** by an organisation during a particular time period. Time plays a crucial role in the measure, so **managers** are strongly **encouraged to remove bottlenecks that might cause production delays**.

2.7.2 Return per time period on bottleneck resource

In throughput accounting, the limiting factor is the bottleneck. The return per time period measure can be adapted and used for **ranking products to optimise production** in the **short term**.

Product return per minute $= \dfrac{\text{sales price} - \text{material costs}}{\text{minutes on key / bottleneck resource}}$

Ranking products on the basis of throughput contribution per minute (or hour) on the bottleneck resource is **similar in concept to maximising contribution per unit of limiting factor**. Such product rankings are for **short-term production scheduling only**. In throughput accounting, bottlenecks should be eliminated and so rankings may change quickly. Customer demand can, of course, cause the bottleneck to change at short notice too.

Rankings by TA product return and by contribution per unit of limiting factor may be different. Which one leads to profit maximisation? The correct approach depends on the variability or otherwise of labour and variable overheads, which in turn depends on the time horizon of the decision. Both are short-term profit maximisation techniques and given that labour is nowadays likely to be fixed in the short term, it could be argued that TA provides the more correct solution. An analysis of variable overheads would be needed to determine their variability.

2.7.3 TA ratio

Products can also be ranked according to the **throughput accounting ratio (TA ratio).**

$$\text{TA ratio } = \frac{\text{throughput contribution or value added per time period}}{\text{conversion cost per time period}}$$

$$= \frac{(\text{sales} - \text{material costs}) \text{ per time period}}{(\text{labour} + \text{overhead}) \text{ per time period}}$$

This measure has the **advantage** of **including the costs involved in running the factory. The higher the ratio, the more profitable the company.**

A profitable product should have a ratio greater than one. If a product's ratio is less than one the organisation is losing money every time that product is produced.

Here's an example. Note the figures are in £ per hour.

	Product A	Product B
	£ per hour	£ per hour
Sales price	100	150
Material cost	(40)	(50)
Throughput	60	100
Conversion cost	(50)	(50)
Profit	10	50
TA ratio	$\frac{60}{50} = 1.2$	$\frac{100}{50} = 2.0$

Profit will be maximised by manufacturing as much of product B as possible.

Question   Product return per factory hour and TA ratio

Learning objective: A(iv)

Each unit of product B requires 4 machine hours. Machine time is the bottleneck resource, there being 650 machine hours available per week.

B is sold for £120 per unit and has a direct material cost of £35 per unit. Total factory costs are £13,000 per week.

Required

Calculate the return per factory hour and the TA ratio for product B.

Answer

Return per factory hour = £(120 − 35)/4 = £21.25
TA ratio = £21.25/£20* = 1.0625
*Cost per factory hour = £13,000/650 = £20

ATTENTION!

If conversion cost cannot be directly allocated to products (because it is not a unit-level manufacturing cost), the TA ratio cannot be calculated and products have to be ranked in terms of throughput contribution per hour or minute of bottleneck resource.

2.7.4 Effectiveness measures and cost control

Traditional efficiency measures such as standard costing variances and labour ratios are **unsuitable** in a TA environment because traditional efficiency should not be encouraged (as the **labour force should not produce just for inventory**).

Effectiveness is a **more important** issue. The **current effectiveness ratio** compares current levels of effectiveness with the standard.

$$\text{Current effectiveness ratio} = \frac{\text{standard minutes of throughput achieved}}{\text{minutes available}}$$

Question   Variances and throughput accounting

Learning objective: A(iv)

Briefly explain whether or not an adverse labour rate variance caused by overtime worked at the bottleneck is a good or bad thing in a throughput accounting environment.   (5 marks)

Answer

In a traditional management accounting environment, adverse variances would be considered bad because they reduce accounting profit below the standard expected for the activity achieved.

In a throughput accounting environment the focus is on maximising throughput contribution while keeping conversion and investment costs to the minimum level possible.

Therefore, in a throughput environment the increased cost of overtime working would be a good thing and would increase reported profits providing the extra labour cost incurred was less than the throughput contribution added.

2.8 Is it good or bad?

TA is seen by some as **too short term**, as all costs other than direct material are regarded as fixed. This is not true. But it does **concentrate on direct material costs** and does nothing for the control of other costs. These characteristics make throughput accounting a **good complement for activity based costing (ABC)**, as ABC focuses on labour and overhead costs. We will cover ABC in detail in the next chapter.

TA attempts to maximise throughput whereas traditional systems attempt to maximise profit. By attempting to maximise throughput an organisation could be producing in excess of the profit-maximising output.

2.9 Where TA helps direct attention

- Bottlenecks
- Key elements in making profits
- Inventory reduction
- Reducing the response time to customer demand
- Evenness of production flow
- Overall effectiveness and efficiency

 Case Study

(a)   An article in *Management Accounting* in April 1992 describes a case study of Garrett Automotive that adopted TA with the particular aim of managing and alleviating bottlenecks in the production process and moving towards 'evenness of flow'. When the project started one particular manufacturing area had three machines with the following outputs:

Machine A 30 units per hour
Machine B 18 units per hour
Machine C 80 units per hour

The production system was certainly not in balance.

As a result of the initial analysis, machine D was moved to assist B and this increased capacity at this point to 21 units per hour. Then machine E was purchased very cheaply and this increased output at B to 26 units per hour. (Machine E paid for itself in just five weeks.) Machine C was due for replacement shortly afterwards and it was replaced with a new and cheaper machine that produced just 26 units per hour. These three changes raised output from 2,025 units to 2,700 units per week and greatly increased profit.

Changing the production process brought considerable financial benefits and changed the reporting emphasis to the critical need to adhere to production schedules and to 'first-time capability' (getting it right first time). The monthly management report was reduced from more than forty pages to five pages and it was made available if requested to all employees. It forced management accounting staff to get back to understanding what is actually happening on the shop floor and to be inventive about performance measures.

(b)   An article in the *Harvard Business Review* September-October 1996 cites the instance of Pratt & Whitney the jet engine manufacturer, which had ten computer controlled grinding machines that were used to shape cast blades. The machines cost $80M and were technical marvels, grinding a blade in just three minutes. They were fed and unloaded by robots but it took eight hours to change the machines so that they could grind a different sort of blade. In addition each blade had to be encased in a special metal alloy to prevent it fracturing during grinding and this was difficult to remove after the process. Twenty two members of staff were required to maintain the complicated computerised control system. As a result of all this, each blade took ten days to pass through the grinding department.

After studies, eight simple grinding machines that did not require the blades to be encased in metal were purchased to replace the computer controlled machines. The time it took to change from grinding one type of blade to the next took just 100 seconds with these machines and it only took the labour of one full-time and one part-time member of staff to feed and control the machines. Processing time increased from three minutes to 75 minutes, however, but this was not a major disadvantage. The factory space required was halved and the time for a blade to pass through the grinding department fell from ten days to 75 minutes.

2.10 Example: throughput accounting

Corrie produces three products, X, Y and Z. The capacity of Corrie's plant is restricted by process alpha. Process alpha is expected to be operational for eight hours per day and can produce 1,200 units of X per hour, 1,500 units of Y per hour, and 600 units of Z per hour.

Selling prices and material costs for each product are as follows.

Product	Selling price $ per unit	Material cost $ per unit	Throughput contribution $ per unit
X	150	70	80
Y	120	40	80
X	300	100	200

Conversion costs are $720,000 per day.

Requirements

(a) Calculate the profit per day if daily output achieved is 6,000 units of X, 4,500 units of Y and 1,200 units of Z.

(b) Determine the efficiency of the bottleneck process given the output in (a).

(c) Calculate the TA ratio for each product.

(d) In the absence of demand restrictions for the three products, advise Corrie's management on the optimal production plan.

Solution

(a) Profit per day = throughput contribution – conversion cost

= [($80 × 6,000) + ($80 × 4,500) + ($200 × 1,200)] – $720,000

= $360,000

(b)

Product	Minutes in alpha per unit	Minutes in alpha per day
X	60/1,200 = 0.05	6,000 × 0.05 = 300
Y	60/1,500 = 0.04	4,500 × 0.04 = 180
Z	60/600 = 0.10	1,200 × 0.10 = 120
		600

Total hours = 600 minutes ÷ 60 = 10 hours

Hours available = 8, hours produced = 10, ∴ Efficiency = 125%

(c) TA ratio = throughput contribution per factory hour/conversion cost per factory hour

Conversion cost per factory hour = $720,000/8 = $90,000

Product	Throughput contribution per factory hour	Cost per factory hour	TA ratio
X	$80 × (60 ÷ 0.05 mins) = $96,000	$90,000	1.07
Y	$80 × (60 ÷ 0.04 mins) = $120,000	$90,000	1.33
Z	$200 × (60 ÷ 0.10 mins) = $120,000	$90,000	1.33

(d) An attempt should be made to remove the restriction on output caused by process alpha's capacity. This will probably result in another bottleneck emerging elsewhere. The extra capacity required to remove the restriction could be obtained by working overtime, making process improvements or product specification changes. Until the volume of throughput can be increased, output should be concentrated upon products Y and Z (greatest TA ratios), unless there are good marketing reasons for continuing the current production mix.

Question

Binding constraints and TA ratio

Learning objective: A(iv)

A company's binding constraint is the capacity of machine M. The throughput accounting (TA) ratio for product P on machine M is 1.4.

Explain how the TA ratio is calculated and state FOUR actions that management could consider to improve the TA ratio for product P. (5 marks)

Answer

The throughput accounting (TA) ratio is calculated as follows.

$$\text{TA ratio} = \frac{\text{throughput per time period}}{\text{conversion cost per time period}} = \frac{(\text{sales} - \text{material costs}) \text{ per time period}}{\text{conversion cost per time period}}$$

Actions that could be considered to improve the TA ratio are as follows.

1. Increase the selling price of product P. This will increase the throughput per time period.

2. Reduce the material cost per unit of product P. This will also increase the throughput per time period.

3. Reduce the total expenditure on conversion costs. This would reduce the conversion cost per time period.

4. Change the working practices on machine M to increase the number of hours of capacity available. This should be achieved without extra conversion cost being incurred, perhaps by altering the method of setting up the machine, to improve productivity. This action would reduce the conversion cost per time period.

Case Study

In 'Accounting for Throughput' (*Management Accounting,* May 1996), Dugdale and Jones discuss the consequences of introducing throughput ideas into the accounting, production and marketing functions of a particular company. The emphasis is BPP's.

(a)   'Measures of efficiency and overhead recovery were no longer considered useful ... The danger of traditional measures causing sub-optimal behaviour was now recognised and the **key measure became 'schedule adherence'** ... The use of schedule adherence was later accompanied by the introduction of a **throughput profit and loss account** ... [which was] extremely simple.

	£
Sales revenue	X
Less: Materials	(X)
Materials price and exchange variances	X
Throughput	X
Less: Expense	(X)
Net profit	X

Gradually other measures were added to cell managers' monthly accounting packages – **days' inventory on-hand, manufacturing cycle time, cost of quality, customer due-date performance**.'

(b)   '... most [cell managers] thought that schedule adherence was a good measure but its credibility depended on the creation of **realistic schedules** ... Without such [financially-based] measures [of departmental performance], many managers considered that they were operating in a measurement vacuum in which they had insufficient information ... It may be that this [creating new local performance measures] is an intractable problem in accounting for throughput.'

(c)   'Whilst there was some disagreement about the use of throughput measures in production there were no such reservations in **marketing**... the move towards marginal cost pricing [throughput accounting being a form of marginal costing, only material costs being treated as variable] and away from absorbed costs and gross margin targets was an unmitigated success.'

2.11 Throughput accounting in service and retail industries

Sales staff have always preferred to use a marginal costing approach so that they can use their discretion on discounts, and **retail organisations** have traditionally thought in terms of sales revenue less the bought in price of goods. The throughput accounting approach is therefore **nothing new** to them.

Throughput accounting can be used very effectively in **support departments and service industries** to **highlight and remove bottlenecks**. For example, if there is a delay in processing a potential customer's application, business can be lost or the potential customer may decide not to proceed. Sometimes credit rating checks are too detailed, slowing the whole procedure unnecessarily and delaying acceptance from say 24 hours to eight days.

A similar problem could occur in hospitals where work that could be done by nurses has to be carried out by doctors. Not only does this increase the cost of the work but it may well cause a bottleneck by tying up a doctor's time unnecessarily.

Question

Product costing versus TA

Learning objective: A(iv)

Here are some statements about traditional product costing. Provide the equivalent statements about throughput accounting.

Statement 1:   Inventory is valued in the financial statements at full production cost.
Statement 2:   Labour, material and variable overheads are treated as variable costs.
Statement 3:   A process is deemed efficient if labour and machine time are fully utilised.
Statement 4:   Value is added when a unit of product is produced.

Answer

1   Inventory is valued at material cost only (ie variable cost).
2   Only direct material is treated as a variable cost.
3   Effectiveness is measured in terms of schedule adherence and meeting delivery dates.
4   Value is added when an item is sold.

3 Backflush accounting

FAST FORWARD

Backflush accounting is a method of accounting that can be used with JIT production systems. It saves a considerable amount of time as it avoids having to make a number of accounting entries that are required by a traditional system.

Backflush accounting is the name given to the method of keeping cost accounts employed if **backflush costing** is used. The two terms are almost interchangeable.

Traditional costing systems use **sequential tracking** (also known as **synchronous tracking**) to track costs sequentially as products pass from raw materials to work in progress, to finished goods and finally to sales. In other words, material costs are charged to WIP when materials are issued to production, direct labour and overhead costs are charged in a similar way as the cost is incurred or very soon after.

If a production system such as **JIT** is used, sequentially tracking means that **all entries are made at almost the same moment** and so a different accounting system can be used. In **backflush costing/accounting, costs are calculated and charged when the product is sold, or when it is transferred to the finished goods store**.

Key term

Backflush costing is 'A method of costing, associated with a JIT production system, which applies cost to the output of a process. Costs do not mirror the flow of products through the production process, but are attached to the output produced (finished goods inventory and cost of sales), on the assumption that such backflushed costs are a realistic measure of the actual costs incurred.'   (CIMA *Official Terminology*)

The CIMA definition above omits the fact that **budgeted or standard costs are used to work backwards to 'flush' out manufacturing costs** for the units produced. (Hence the rather unattractive name for the system!) The application of **standard costs** to finished goods units, or to units sold, is used in order to **calculate cost of goods sold**, thereby **simplifying** the costing system and creating **savings in administrative effort. In a true backflush accounting system, records of materials used and work in progress** are **not required** as material cost can be calculated from either finished goods or goods sold.

Backflush costing runs **counter to the principle enshrined in SSAP 9**, and the staple of cost accounting for decades, that inventory and WIP should be accounted for by calculating cost and net realisable value of 'each item of inventory separately'. The substantial **reduction in inventories that is a feature of JIT** means that **inventory valuation is less relevant,** however, and therefore the **costing system** can be **simplified** to a considerable extent. In the 1980s, Johnson & Kaplan in fact wrote that **management rarely requires a value to be placed on inventory for internal management purposes**, the **value only being required for external reporting**.

Backflush costing is therefore **appropriate** for organisations trying to keep **inventories to the very minimum**. In such circumstances, the **recording** of every little increase in inventory value, as each nut and bolt is added, is simply an expensive and **non-value-added activity** that should be **eliminated**.

3.1 Example: Working backwards from output

To take a **very simplified example**, if backflush costing is used, the management accountant might extract the following information from the monthly accounting transaction records and production records.

	Units		£
Orders completed and despatched in July		196 units	
Orders prepared in advance 1 July		3 units	
Orders prepared in advance 31 July		2 units	
Scrapped items		5 units	
Conversion costs in the month		£250,000	
Material costs in the month		£475,000	

This is enough to place a value on inventories and production as follows.

	Units		£
B/f	(3)	Conversion costs	250,000
Despatched	196	Material costs	475,000
Scrapped	5	Total costs	725,000
C/f	2		
Units produced	200		

Cost per unit is £725,000 divided by 200 units = £3,625

In this case a single process account could be drawn up as follows.

	Dr (£)	Cr (£)
Inventory b/fwd (3 × £3,625)	10,875	
Materials	475,000	
Conversion costs	250,000	
To finished goods (196 × £3,625)		710,500
Losses etc written off to income statement (5 × £3,625)		18,125
Inventory c/fwd (2 × £3,625)		7,250
	735,875	735,875

3.2 Arguments of traditional management accountants

(a)   The figure for **losses** here is **inaccurate**. They would say that in reality the faulty goods would have been scrapped when only partially complete and it is wrong to value them at the same cost as a fully finished good unit.

(b)   Using this approach, the figure for inventories b/fwd and c/fwd will not tie up with the accounts for last month and next month, because the material and conversion costs may be different.

3.3 Reply of modern management accountants

(a)   **Losses** represent only about 2% of total cost and are **not material**. In any case putting a value to them is less **important** than **improving the quality of production procedures** (on the basis of **TQM** practices and non-financial production information) to ensure that they do not occur again.

(b)   **Finished good inventories represent between 1% and 2% of total cost and are immaterial**. Slight discrepancies in valuation methods of b/fwds and c/fwds will amount to a **fraction** of a percentage, and can be written off in the month as a small **variance**.

(c)   Even with computers the **cost of tracing units** every step of the way through production – with 'normal' and 'abnormal' losses, equivalent units and numerous process accounts – **is simply not worth it, in terms of the benefit derived** from the information it provides.

3.4 Variants of backflush costing

(a)   **Trigger points determine when the entries are made in the accounting system**. There will be either one or two trigger points that trigger entries in the accounts.

    (i)   When materials are purchased/received
    (ii)   When goods are completed or when they are sold

In a **true JIT system** where no Inventories are held the **first trigger**, when raw materials are purchased, is **unnecessary**.

(b)   Actual conversion costs are recorded as incurred, just as in conventional recording systems. Conversion costs are applied to products at the second trigger point based on a standard cost. It is assumed that any conversion costs not applied to products are carried forward and disposed of at the period end.

(c)   **Direct labour** is included as an **indirect cost in conversion cost with overheads**. (Production is only required when there is demand for it in a JIT system, and so production labour will be paid regardless of the level of activity.)

(d)   All indirect costs are treated as a fixed period expense.

3.5 Example: accounting entries at different trigger points

The transactions for period 8 20X1 for Clive are as follows.

Purchase of raw materials	£24,990
Conversion costs incurred	£20,220
Finished goods produced (used in methods 2 & 3 only)	4,900 units
Sales	4,850 units

There are no opening inventories of raw materials, WIP or finished goods. The standard cost per unit is made up of £5.10 for materials and £4.20 for conversion costs.

3.6 Solution for 1 trigger point – when goods are sold (method 1)

This is the simplest method of backflush costing. There is only one **trigger point** and that is **when the entry to the cost of goods sold account is required** when the goods are sold. (This method assumes that units are sold as soon as they are produced.)

			£	£
(a)	DEBIT	Conversion costs control	20,220	
	CREDIT	Expense creditors		20,220

Being the actual conversion costs incurred

			£	£
(b)	DEBIT	Cost of goods sold (4,850 × £9.30)	45,105	
	CREDIT	Creditors (4,850 × £5.10)		24,735
	CREDIT	Conversion costs allocated (4,850 × £4.20)		20,370

Being the standard cost of goods sold

			£	£
(c)	DEBIT	Conversion costs allocated	20,370	
	CREDIT	Cost of goods sold		150
	CREDIT	Conversion costs control		20,220

Being the under or over allocation of conversion costs

3.7 Solution for 1 trigger point – when goods are completed (method 2)

This is very similar to the solution above but in this instance the **trigger** is the completion of a unit and its **movement into finished goods store**. The accounting entries are as follows.

			£	£
(a)	DEBIT	Conversion costs control	20,220	
	CREDIT	Expense creditors		20,220

Being the actual conversion costs incurred

			£	£
(b)	DEBIT	Finished goods inventory (4,900 × £9.30)	45,570	
	CREDIT	Creditors (4,900 × £5.10)		24,990
	CREDIT	Conversion costs allocated (4,900 × £4.20)		20,580

Being the standard cost of goods produced

			£	£
(c)	DEBIT	Cost of goods sold (4,850 × £9.30)	45,105	
	CREDIT	Finished goods inventory		45,105

Being the standard cost of goods sold

			£	£
(d)	DEBIT	Conversion costs allocated	20,580	
	CREDIT	Cost of goods sold		360
	CREDIT	Conversion costs control		20,220

Being the under or over allocation of conversion costs

The end of period finished goods inventory balance is £465 (50 × £9.30).

Question

Backflush accounting

Learning objective: A(viii)

RM uses backflush accounting in conjunction with JIT. The system does not include a raw material inventory control account. During control period 7, 300 units were produced and sold and conversation costs of £7,000 incurred. The standard unit cost is £55, which includes material of £25.

What is the debit balance on the cost of goods sold account at the end of control period 7.

A   £16,500
B   £14,500
C   £23,500
D   £18,500

Answer

The correct answer is B.

	£
Conversion cost allocated to cost of goods sold a/c = 300 × (£55 – 25)	9,000
Conversion cost incurred	7,000
Difference set against cost of goods sold a/c	2,000
Standard charge to cost of goods sold a/c (300 × £55)	16,500
Charge to cost of goods sold a/c	14,500

Option A is the standard charge. **Option C** is the sum of conversion cost incurred and the standard charge. **Option D** results from adding the difference instead of deducting it.

3.8 Solution for 2 trigger points – (method 3)

There are two **trigger points**, the **first** when **materials and components are received** and the **other** at the **point of transfer to finished goods**.

			£	£
(a)	DEBIT	Raw materials	24,990	
	CREDIT	Creditors		24,990

Being the purchase of raw materials on credit

			£	£
(b)	DEBIT	Conversion costs control	20,220	
	CREDIT	Expense creditors		20,220

Being the actual conversion costs incurred

			£	£
(c)	DEBIT	Finished goods inventory (4,900 × £9.30)	45,570	
	CREDIT	Raw materials		24,990
	CREDIT	Conversion costs allocated		20,580

Being the standard cost of goods produced

			£	£
(d)	DEBIT	Cost of goods sold (4,850 × £9.30)	45,105	
	CREDIT	Finished goods inventory		45,105

Being the standard cost of goods sold

			£	£
(e)	DEBIT	Conversion costs allocated	20,580	
	CREDIT	Cost of goods sold		360
	CREDIT	Conversion costs control		20,220

Being the under or over allocation of conversion costs

Note that the **WIP account is eliminated** using all methods. In a JIT system the vast majority of manufacturing costs will form part of the cost of sales and will not be deferred in closing inventory values. In such a situation the amount of work involved in tracking costs through WIP, cost of sales and finished goods is unlikely to be justified. This considerably **reduces the volume of transactions recorded** in the internal accounting system.

The successful operation of backflush costing rests upon **predictable levels of efficiency** and **stable material prices and usage**. In other words there should be **insignificant cost variances**.

3.9 Possible problems with backflush costing

(a)   **It is only appropriate for JIT operations** where production and sales volumes are approximately equal.

(b)   Some people claim that it **should not be used for external reporting** purposes. If, however, **inventories are low** or are practically **unchanged** from one accounting period to the next, operating income and inventory valuations derived from backflush accounting will **not be materially different from the results using conventional systems**. Hence, in such circumstances, backflush accounting is acceptable for external financial reporting.

(c)   It is **vital** that adequate production controls exist so that **cost control during the production process is maintained**.

3.10 Advantages of backflush costing

(a)   It is much **simpler**, as there is no separate accounting for WIP.

(b)   Even the **finished goods** account is **unnecessary**, as we demonstrated in the first example above.

(c)   The number of **accounting entries should be greatly reduced**, as are the supporting vouchers, documents and so on.

(d)   The system should **discourage** managers from **producing simply for inventory** since working on material does not add value until the final product is completed or sold.

Question   Backflush accounting and behavioural issues

Learning objective: A(viii)

How might backflush accounting, with goods being sold as the one trigger point, be said to manipulate employees to behave in a certain way?   (5 marks)

Answer

Employees have to concentrate on making sales because cost of sales is the trigger, and so nothing gets recorded until a sale is made.

Unlike in traditional systems, when management can increase profit by producing for finished goods inventory, there is no benefit in producing for inventory.

Exam focus point

Backflush accounting lends itself particularly well to objective testing questions. There was an MCQ on backflush accounting in the pilot paper.

Chapter Roundup

- **Theory of constraints** is a set of concepts developed in the USA which aim to identify the binding constraints in a production system and which strive for evenness of production flow so that the organisation works as effectively as possible. No inventories should be held, except prior to the binding constraint.

- Goldratt's five steps for dealing with a bottleneck activity are:

  Step 1: Identify   Step 4: Elevate
  Step 2: Exploit   Step 5: Return to step 1
  Step 3: Subordinate

- **Throughout accounting** is the accounting system developed in the UK, based on the theory of constraints and JIT. It measures the throughput contribution per factory hour., It is very similar to marginal costing but can be used to make longer-term decisions about production equipment/capacity.

- **Backflush accounting** is a method of accounting that can be used with JIT production systems. It saves a considerable amount of time as it avoids having to make a number of accounting entries that are required by a traditional system.

Quick Quiz

1   Fill in the blanks in the statements below, using the words in the box. Some words may be used twice.

(a)   The theory of constraints is an approach to production management which aims to maximise (1)............. less (2)........ and (3)........... It focuses on factors such as (4)............... which act as (5)....................

(b)   Throughput contribution = (6)............. minus (7) ....

(c)   TA ratio = (8) .... per factory hour ÷ (9) ....per factory hour

> - variable overhead costs
> - bottlenecks
> - material costs
> - sales revenue
> - throughput contribution
> - constraints
> - conversion cost

2   CH Ltd operates a throughput accounting system. Product B sells for £27.99, has a material cost of £7.52 and a conversion cost of £1.91. The product spends 27 minutes on the bottleneck resource. What is the return per factory hour for product B?

A   £45.49
B   £20.47
C   £26.08
D   £57.96

3   Throughput accounting policy is to hold zero inventories throughout all operations

                                                                    True/false (delete as appropriate)

4   Choose the correct words from those highlighted.

(a)   Backflush accounting is a cost accounting system which focuses on the (1) **input/output** of an organisation and then works (2) **forwards/backwards** to allocate costs between cost of goods sold and inventory.

(b)   The point at which a physical activity causes an entry in the accounts which flushes out cost in a backflush system is known as the (3) **trigger point/bottleneck**.

5   A company manufacturing a single product operates a backflush accounting system with two trigger points, one of which is cost of sales. The standard cost of materials is £10 per unit and the standard conversion cost is £15 per unit. At the beginning of the period there are no inventory of any sort, and this is a fairly regular state of affairs. During the period 2,020 units were completed and 2,000 units were sold. What is the balance on the finished goods account at the end of the period?

A   £700   Dr
B   £700   Cr
C   zero
D   £400   Dr

Answers to Quick Quiz

1   1   sales revenue
    2   material costs
    3   variable overhead costs
    4   bottlenecks
    5   constraints
    6   sales revenue
    7   material costs
    8   throughput contribution
    9   conversion cost

2   A   Return per hour = (sales – material cost) per hour on bottleneck resource

    ∴ Return per 27 minutes = £(27.99 – 7.52) = £20.47

    ∴ Return per hour = £20.47 × $\frac{60}{27}$ = £45.49

3   False. A buffer inventory should be held prior to the bottleneck process.

4   (1)   output
    (2)   backwards
    (3)   trigger point

5   C   As cost of sales is a trigger point, the second trigger point must be raw materials purchased. It would be extremely unusual to operate trigger points at finished goods *and* cost of sales in a backflush accounting system and as inventory is not normally held there would be no point

Number	Level	Marks	Time
Q9	Examination	5	9 mins
Q10	Introductory	N/A	N/A
Q11	Introductory	N/A	N/A

Now try the questions below from the Exam Question Bank

Activity based costing

Introduction

In this chapter we look at a third costing system that has been developed to suit modern practices: **activity based costing**.

Basically, activity based costing (ABC) is the **modern alternative to traditional absorption costing**.

Exam questions (both objective test questions and long questions) could ask you to **calculate activity-based costs**, and we show you how to do this in **Section 3**. Or you could get a **discursive question** on the topic, the material for which you will find in the remaining sections of this chapter.

.

Topic list	Learning outcomes	Syllabus references	Ability required
1 The reasons for the development of ABC	A(vi)	A 4	Analysis/evaluation
2 Outline of an ABC system	A(vi)	A 4	Analysis/evaluation
3 Absorption costing versus ABC	A(vi)	A 4	Analysis/evaluation
4 Marginal costing versus ABC	A(vi)	A 4	Analysis/evaluation
5 Introducing an ABC system	A(vi)	A 4	Analysis/evaluation
6 Merits and criticisms of ABC	A(vi)	A 4	Analysis/evaluation

BPP
PROFESSIONAL EDUCATION

1 The reasons for the development of ABC

FAST FORWARD

Traditional costing systems, which assume that all products consume all resources in proportion to their production volumes, tend to **allocate too great a proportion of overheads to high volume products** (which cause relatively little diversity and hence use fewer support services) and **too small a proportion of overheads to low volume products** (which cause greater diversity and therefore use more support services). **Activity based costing (ABC) attempts to overcome this problem**.

The traditional cost accumulation system of **absorption costing** was developed in a time when most organisations produced only a **narrow range of products** and when **overhead costs were only a very small fraction of total costs**, direct labour and direct material costs accounting for the largest proportion of the costs. Errors made in attributing overheads to products were not too significant.

Nowadays, however, with the advent of **advanced manufacturing technology (AMT)**, **overheads** are likely to be far **more important** and in fact direct labour may account for as little as five per cent of a product's cost. It therefore now appears difficult to justify the use of direct labour or direct material as the basis for absorbing overheads or to believe that errors made in attributing overheads will not be significant.

Many resources are used in **non-volume related support activities**, (which have increased due to AMT) such as setting-up, production scheduling, inspection and data processing. These support activities assist the efficient manufacture of a wide range of products (necessary if businesses are to compete effectively) and are **not, in general, affected by changes in production volume**. They tend to **vary in the long term according to the range and complexity** of the products manufactured rather than the volume of output.

The wider the range and the more complex the products, the more support services will be required. Consider, for example, factory X which produces 10,000 units of one product, the Alpha, and factory Y which produces 1,000 units each of ten slightly different versions of the Alpha. Support activity costs in the factory Y are likely to be a lot higher than in factory X but the factories produce an identical number of units. For example, factory X will only need to set-up once whereas Factory Y will have to set-up the production run at least ten times for the ten different products. Factory Y will therefore incur more set-up costs for the same volume of production.

2 Outline of an ABC system

FAST FORWARD

An alternative to the traditional method of accounting for costs - absorption costing - is **activity based costing (ABC)**. ABC involves the identification of the factors (**cost drivers**) which cause the costs of an organisation's major activities. Support overheads are charged to products on the basis of their usage of an activity.

2.1 The definition of ABC

Key term

Activity based costing (ABC) is 'An approach to the costing and monitoring of activities which involves tracing resource consumption and costing final outputs. Resources are assigned to activities and activities to cost objects based on consumption estimates. The latter utilise cost drivers to attach activity costs to outputs '.
(CIMA *Official Terminology*)

The **major ideas** behind activity based costing are as follows.

(a) **Activities cause costs**. Activities include ordering, materials handling, machining, assembly, production scheduling and despatching.

(b) **Producing products creates demand for the activities.**

(c) **Costs** are **assigned** to a product **on the basis of the product's consumption of the activities.**

2.2 The operation of an ABC system

An ABC system operates as follows.

Step 1   Identify an organisation's major activities.

Step 2   Identify the **factors which determine the size of the costs of an activity/cause the costs of an activity**. These are known as **cost drivers.**

> ### Key term
>
> A **cost driver** is 'Any factor which causes a change in the cost of an activity, eg the quality of parts received by an activity is a determining factor in the work required by that activity and therefore affects the resources required. An activity may have multiple cost drivers associated with it.'
>
> (CIMA *Official Terminology*)

Look at the following examples.

Costs	Possible cost driver
Ordering costs	Number of orders
Materials handling costs	Number of production runs
Production scheduling costs	Number of production runs
Despatching costs	Number of despatches

For those **costs that vary with production levels in the short term**, ABC uses **volume-related cost drivers** such as labour or machine hours. The cost of oil used as a lubricant on the machines would therefore be added to products on the basis of the number of machine hours, since oil would have to be used for each hour the machine ran.

Step 3   Collect the costs associated with each cost driver into what are known as cost pools.

> ### Key term
>
> A **cost pool** is 'The point of focus for the costs relating to a particular activity in an activity-based costing system'.
> (CIMA *Official Terminology*)

Step 4   Charge the costs of each cost pool to products on the basis of their usage of the activity (measured by the number of the activity's cost driver a product generates) using a cost driver rate (total costs in cost pool/number of cost drivers).

Question

Learning outcome: A (vi)

Which of the following definitions best describes a cost driver?

A   Any activity which causes an increase in costs
B   A collection of costs associated with a particular activity
C   A cost that varies with production levels
D   Any factor which causes a change in the cost of an activity

Answer

The correct answer is D.

2.3 Transactions analysis

FAST FORWARD

When using ABC, for costs that vary with production levels in the short term, the cost driver will be volume related (labour or machine hours). Overheads that vary with some other activity (and not volume of production) should be traced to products using transaction-based cost drivers such as production runs or number of orders received. One way of classifying these transactions is **logistical, balancing, quality** and **change**.

ABC recognises that factors other than volume can explain the level of overhead. Miller and Vollman ('The Hidden Factory', *Harvard Business Review*, 1985) provided a useful system for analysing the different types of transactions which cause overheads to be incurred.

Types of transaction	Detail
Logistical transactions	Those activities concerned with organising the flow of resources throughout the manufacturing process.
Balancing transactions	Those activities which ensure that demand for and supply of resources are matched.
Quality transactions	Those activities which relate to ensuring that production is at the required level of quality.
Change transactions	Those activities associated with ensuring that customers' requirements (delivery date, changed design and so on) are met.

Note that the primary driver of these transactions is not usually production volume. For example, the level of change transactions might be determined by the number of customers and the number of different product types, rather than by production volume.

Such an analysis provides a better understanding of long-term cost behaviour and allows for the costs associated with particular transactions to be assigned to only those products causing the transactions.

3 Absorption costing versus ABC

FAST FORWARD

Although ABC has obvious merits, a number of criticisms have been raised.

The following example illustrates the point that traditional cost accounting techniques result in a misleading and inequitable division of costs between low-volume and high-volume products, and that ABC can provide a more meaningful allocation of costs.

3.1 Example: activity based costing

Suppose that Cooplan manufactures four products, W, X, Y and Z. Output and cost data for the period just ended are as follows.

	Output units	Number of production runs in the period	Material cost per unit £	Direct labour hours per unit	Machine hours per unit
W	10	2	20	1	1
X	10	2	80	3	3
Y	100	5	20	1	1
Z	100	5	80	3	3
		14			

Direct labour cost per hour   £5

Overhead costs	£
Short run variable costs	3,080
Set-up costs	10,920
Expediting and scheduling costs	9,100
Materials handling costs	7,700
	30,800

Required

Prepare unit costs for each product using conventional costing and ABC.

Solution

Using a **conventional absorption costing approach** and an absorption rate for overheads based on either direct labour hours or machine hours, the product costs would be as follows.

	W £	X £	Y £	Z £	Total £
Direct material	200	800	2,000	8,000	
Direct labour	50	150	500	1,500	
Overheads *	700	2,100	7,000	21,000	
	950	3,050	9,500	30,500	44,000
Units produced	10	10	100	100	
Cost per unit	£95	£305	£95	£305	

* £30,800 ÷ 440 hours = £70 per direct labour or machine hour.

Using **activity based costing** and assuming that the number of production runs is the cost driver for set-up costs, expediting and scheduling costs and materials handling costs and that machine hours are the cost driver for short-run variable costs, unit costs would be as follows.

	W	X	Y	Z	Total
	£	£	£	£	£
Direct material	200	800	2,000	8,000	
Direct labour	50	150	500	1,500	
Short-run variable overheads (W1)	70	210	700	2,100	
Set-up costs (W2)	1,560	1,560	3,900	3,900	
Expediting, scheduling costs (W3)	1,300	1,300	3,250	3,250	
Materials handling costs (W4)	1,100	1,100	2,750	2,750	
	4,280	5,120	13,100	21,500	44,000
Units produced	10	10	100	100	
Cost per unit	£428	£512	£131	£215	

Workings

1	£3,080 ÷ 440 machine hours =	£7 per machine hour
2	£10,920 ÷ 14 production runs =	£780 per run
3	£9,100 ÷ 14 production runs =	£650 per run
4	£7,700 ÷ 14 production runs =	£550 per run

Summary

Product	Conventional costing Unit cost	ABC Unit cost	Difference per unit	Difference in total
	£	£	£	£
W	95	428	+ 333	+3,330
X	305	512	+ 207	+2,070
Y	95	131	+ 36	+3,600
Z	305	215	− 90	−9,000

The figures suggest that the **traditional volume-based absorption costing system is flawed**.

(a) **It underallocates overhead costs to low-volume products** (here, W and X) and **over-allocates overheads to higher-volume products** (here Z in particular).

(b) It **underallocates overhead costs to smaller-sized products** (here W and Y with just one hour of work needed per unit) and **over allocates overheads to larger products** (here X and particularly Z).

3.2 ABC versus traditional costing methods

Both traditional absorption costing and ABC systems adopt the two stage allocation process.

3.2.1 Allocation of overheads

ABC establishes **separate cost pools for support activities** such as despatching. As the costs of these activities are assigned directly to products through cost driver rates, **reapportionment of service department costs is avoided**.

3.2.2 Absorption of overheads

The principal difference between the two systems is the way in which overheads are absorbed into products.

(a) **Absorption costing** most commonly uses two **absorption bases** (labour hours and/or machine hours) to charge overheads to products.

(b)   **ABC** uses **many cost drivers** as absorption bases (number of orders, number of despatches and so on).

Absorption rates under **ABC** should therefore be **more closely linked to the causes of overhead costs.**

3.3 Cost drivers

The **principal idea** of ABC is to **focus attention on what causes costs to increase,** ie the **cost drivers**.

(a)   Those **costs that do vary with production volume,** such as power costs, should be traced to products using production **volume-related cost drivers** as appropriate, such as direct labour hours or direct machine hours. Such costs tend to be **short-term variable overheads** such as power costs.

Overheads which do not **vary** with output but **with some other activity** should be traced to products using **transaction-based cost drivers**, such as number of production runs and number of orders received. Such costs tend to be **long-term variable overheads** (overheads that traditional accounting would classify as fixed).

(b)   Traditional costing systems allow overheads to be related to products in rather more arbitrary ways producing, it is claimed, less accurate product costs.

Question	ABC versus traditional costing

Learning outcome: A(vi)

A company manufactures two products, L and M, using the same equipment and similar processes. An extract of the production data for these products in one period is shown below.

	L	*M*
Quantity produced (units)	5,000	7,000
Direct labour hours per unit	1	2
Machine hours per unit	3	1
Set-ups in the period	10	40
	15	60
Orders handled in the period		

Overhead costs	$
Relating to machine activity	220,000
Relating to production run set-ups	20,000
Relating to handling of orders	45,000
	285,000

Required

Calculate the production overheads to be absorbed by one unit of each of the products using the following costing methods.

(a)   A traditional absorption costing approach using a direct labour hour rate to absorb overheads
(b)   An activity based costing approach, using suitable cost drivers to trace overheads to products

Answer

(a) **Traditional absorption costing approach**

			Direct labour hours
Product L = 5,000 units × 1 hour			5,000
Product M = 7,000 units × 2 hours			14,000
			19,000

$\therefore$ Overhead absorption rate $\qquad$ = $\dfrac{\$285,000}{19,000}$

$\qquad\qquad\qquad\qquad\qquad\qquad\qquad\qquad\qquad$ = $15 per hour

Overhead absorbed would be as follows.

Product L	1 hour × $15	=	$15 per unit
Product M	2 hours × $15	=	$30 per unit

(b) **ABC approach**

		Machine hours
Product L	= 5,000 units × 3 hours	15,000
Product M	= 7,000 units × 1 hour	7,000
		22,000

Using ABC the overhead costs are absorbed according to the **cost drivers**.

	$	
Machine-hour driven costs	220,000 ÷ 22,000 m/c hours	= $10 per m/c hour
Set-up driven costs	20,000 ÷ 50 set-ups	= $400 per set-up
Order driven costs	45,000 ÷ 75 orders	= $600 per order

Overhead costs are therefore as follows.

		Product L £		Product M £
Machine-driven costs	(15,000 hrs × $10)	150,000	(7,000 hrs × $10)	70,000
Set-up costs	(10 × $400)	4,000	(40 × $400)	16,000
Order handling costs	(15 × $600)	9,000	(60 × $600)	36,000
		163,000		122,000
Units produced		5,000		7,000
Overhead cost per unit		$32.60		$17.43

These figures suggest that product M absorbs an unrealistic amount of overhead using a direct labour hour basis. Overhead absorption should be based on the activities which drive the costs, in this case machine hours, the number of production run set-ups and the number of orders handled for each product.

Exam focus point

ABC's appearance in the pilot paper was limited to two relatively straightforward objective testing questions. Both were calculation based, but you should also be prepared for a discursive question on ABC.

4 Marginal costing versus ABC

The main criticism of marginal costing decision making information is that marginal costing analyses cost behaviour patterns according to the volume of production. However, although certain costs may be fixed in relation to the volume of production, they **may in fact be variable in relation to some other cost driver.**

Some commentators argue that only marginal costing provides suitable information for decision making but this is not true. Marginal costing provides a crude method of differentiating between different types of cost behaviour by splitting costs into their variable and fixed elements. However such an analysis can be used only for **short-term decisions** and usually even these have longer-term implications which ought to be considered.

The problem with marginal costing is that it analyses cost behaviour patterns according to the volume of production. However, although certain costs may be fixed in relation to the volume of production, they **may in fact be variable in relation to some other cost driver.** A failure to allocate such costs to individual products could result in incorrect decisions concerning the future management of the products.

The advantage of ABC is that **it spreads costs across products according to a number of different bases.** For example an ABC analysis may show that one particular activity which is carried out primarily for one or two products is expensive. A correct allocation of the costs of this activity may reveal that these particular products are not profitable. If these costs are fixed in relation to the volume of production then they would be treated as **period costs** in a marginal costing system and **written off against the marginal costing contribution for the period.**

The marginal costing system would therefore make no attempt to allocate these 'fixed' costs to individual products and a false impression would be given of the long run average cost of the products.

Thus, marginal costing may provide incorrect decision making information, **particularly in a situation where 'fixed' costs are vary large compared with 'variable' costs.**

5 Introducing an ABC system

ABC should only be introduced if the additional information it provides will result in action that will increase the organisation's overall profitability.

5.1 When should ABC be introduced?

ABC should only be introduced if the **additional information** it provides will **result in action that will increase** the organisation's overall **profitability**. This is most likely to **occur** in situations such as the following, when the **ABC analysis differs significantly from the traditional absorption costing analysis**.

- Production overheads are high in relation to direct costs, especially direct labour.
- Overhead resource consumption is not just driven by production volume.
- There is wide variety in the product range.
- The overhead resource input varies significantly across the product range.

5.2 Analysis of activities

ABC identifies four levels of activities: product level, batch level, product sustaining level and facility sustaining level.

ABC attempts to **relate the incidence of costs to the level of activities undertaken**. A **hierarchy of activities** has been suggested.

Type of activities	Costs are dependent on	Examples
Product level	Volume of production	Machine power
Batch level	Number of batches	Set-up costs
Product sustaining	Existence of a product group/line	Product management
Facility sustaining	Organisation simply being in business	Rent and rates

The difference between a unit product cost determined using traditional absorption costing and one determined using ABC will depend on the proportion of overhead cost which falls into each of the categories above.

    (a)   If most overheads are related to unit level and facility level activities, the costs will be similar.

    (b)   If the overheads tend to be associated with batch or product level activities they will be significantly different.

Consider the following example.

5.3 Example: batch-level activities

XYZ produces a number of products including product D and product E and produces 500 units of each of products D and E every period at a rate of ten of each every hour. The overhead cost is £500,000 and a total of 40,000 direct labour hours are worked on all products. A traditional overhead absorption rate would be £12.50 per direct labour hour and the overhead cost per product would be £1.25.

Production of D requires five production runs per period, while production of E requires 20. An investigation has revealed that the overhead costs relate mainly to 'batch-level' activities associated with setting-up machinery and handling materials for production runs.

There are 1,000 production runs per period and so overheads could be attributed to XYZ's products at a rate of £500 per run.

    •   Overhead cost per D = (£500 × 5 runs)/500 = £5
    •   Overhead cost per E = (£500 × 20 runs)/500 = £20

These overhead costs are activity based and recognise that overhead costs are incurred due to batch level activities. The fact that E has to be made in frequent small batches, perhaps because it is perishable, means that it uses more resources than D. This is recognised by the ABC overhead costs, not the traditional absorption costing overhead costs.

Attention!

As we noted in Chapter 4, in the **modern manufacturing environment**, production often takes place in short, discontinuous production runs and a high proportion of product costs are incurred at the design stage. An increasing proportion of **overhead costs** are therefore **incurred at batch or product level**.

Such an analysis of costs gives management an **indication of the decision level at which costs can be influenced**. For example, a decision to reduce production costs will not simply depend on making a general reduction in output volumes: production may need to be organised to reduce **batch** volumes; a **process** may need to be modified or eliminated; **product lines** may need to be merged or cut out; **facility** capacity may need to be altered.

5.4 ABC in service and retail organisations

ABC has a range of uses and has many advantages over more traditional costing methods. However, the system does have its critics and it is not a panacea for all costing problems.

ABC was **first introduced in manufacturing organisations** but it can equally well be used in **other types of organisation**. For example, the management of the Post Office in the USA recently introduced ABC. They analysed the activities associated with cash processing as follows.

Activities	Examples	Possible cost driver
Unit level	**Accept cash** Processing of cash by bank	Number of transactions **Number of transactions**
Batch level	'Close out' and supervisor review of clerk Deposits Review and transfer of funds	Number of 'close outs' Number of deposits Number of accounts
Product level	Maintenance charges for bank accounts Reconciling bank accounts	Number of accounts Number of accounts

Question

ABC and retail organisations

Learning outcome: A(vi)

List five activities that might be identified n a retail organisation and state one possible cost driver for each of the activities you have identified.

(5 marks)

Answer

Activities	Possible cost driver
Procure goods	Number of orders
Receive goods	Number of orders or pallets
Store goods	Volume of goods
Pick goods	Number of packs
Handle returnables/recyclables	Volume of goods

6 Merits and criticisms of ABC

FAST FORWARD

ABC has a range of users and has many advantages over more traditional costing methods. However, the system does have its critics and it is not used as a panacea for all costing problems.

6.1 Merits of ABC

As you will have discovered when you attempted the question above, there is nothing difficult about ABC. Once the necessary information has been obtained it is similar to traditional absorption costing. This simplicity is part of its appeal. Further merits of ABC are as follows.

(a) The **complexity of manufacturing has increased**, with wider product ranges, shorter product life cycles and more complex production processes. **ABC recognises this complexity with its multiple cost drivers.**

(b) In a more competitive environment, companies must be able to assess product profitability realistically. **ABC facilitates a good understanding of what drives overhead costs.**

(c) In modern manufacturing systems, overhead functions include a lot of non-factory-floor activities such as product design, quality control, production planning and customer services. **ABC is concerned with all overhead costs** and so it takes management accounting beyond its 'traditional' factory floor boundaries.

(d) By controlling the incidence of the cost driver, the level of the **cost** can be **controlled**.

(e) The costs of activities not included in the costs of the products an organisation makes or the services it provides can be considered to be **not contributing to the value of the product/service**. The following questions can then be asked.

- What is the purpose of this activity?
- How does the organisation benefit from this activity?
- Could the number of staff involved in the activity be reduced?

(f) ABC can help with **cost management**. For example, suppose there is a fall in the number of orders placed by a purchasing department. This fall would not impact on the amount of overhead absorbed in a traditional absorption costing system as the cost of ordering would be part of the general overhead absorption rate (assuming no direct link between the overhead absorption basis of, say, direct labour hours, and the number of orders placed). The reduction in the workload of the purchasing department might therefore go unnoticed and the same level of resources would continue to be provided, despite the drop in number of orders. In an ABC system, however, this drop would be immediately apparent because the cost driver rate would be applied to fewer orders.

(g) Many costs are driven by customers (delivery costs, discounts, after-sales service and so on), but traditional absorption costing systems do not account for this. Organisations may be trading with certain customers at a loss but may not realise it because costs are not analysed in a way that reveals the true situation. ABC can be **used in conjunction with customer profitability analysis (CPA)** to determine more accurately the profit earned by servicing particular customers.

> **Key term**
>
> **Customer profitability analysis** (CPA) is 'Analysis of the revenue streams and service costs associated with specific customers or customer groups'. (CIMA *Official Terminology*)

(h) Many **service businesses** have characteristics similar to those required for the successful application of ABC.

- A highly **competitive** market
- **Diversity** of products, processes and customers
- **Significant overhead costs** not easily assigned to individual 'products'
- **Demands placed on overhead resources** by individual 'products' and customers, which are **not proportional to volume**

If ABC were to be used in a hotel, for example, attempts could be made to identify the activities required to support each guest by category and the cost drivers of these activities. The cost of a one-night stay midweek by a businessman could then be distinguished from the cost of a one-night stay by a teenager at the weekend. Such information could prove invaluable for **CPA.**

6.2 Criticisms of ABC

It has been suggested by critics that **activity based costing has some serious flaws.**

(a) Some measure of (arbitrary) cost apportionment may still be required at the cost pooling stage for items like rent, rates and building depreciation.

(b) Can a single cost driver explain the cost behaviour of all items in its associated pool?

(c) On the other hand, the number of cost pools and cost drivers cannot be excessive otherwise an ABC system would be too complex and too expensive.

(d) Unless costs are caused by an activity that is measurable in quantitative terms and which can be related to production output, cost drivers will not be usable. What drives the cost of the annual external audit, for example?

(e) ABC is sometimes introduced because it is fashionable, not because it will be used by management to provide meaningful product costs or extra information. If management is not going to use ABC information, an absorption costing system may be simpler to operate.

6.3 Other uses of ABC

The information provided by analysing activities can support the management functions of planning, control and decision making, provided it is used carefully and with full appreciation of its implications.

6.3.1 Planning

Before an ABC system can be implemented, management must analyse the organisation's activities, determine the extent of their occurrence and establish the relationships between activities, products/services and their cost.

The **information database** produced from such an exercise can then be **used as a basis for forward planning and budgeting**. For example, once an organisation has set its budgeted production level, the database can be used to determine the number of times that activities will need to be carried out, thereby establishing necessary departmental staffing and machine levels. Financial budgets can then be drawn up by multiplying the budgeted activity levels by cost per activity.

This activity-based approach may not produce the final budget figures but it can **provide the basis for different possible planning scenarios**.

6.3.2 Control

The information database also provides an **insight into the way in which costs are structured and incurred in service and support departments**. Traditionally it has been difficult to control the costs of such departments because of the lack of relationship between departmental output levels and departmental cost. With ABC, however, it is possible to **control or manage the costs by managing the activities which underlie them** by monitoring a number of key performance measures.

6.3.3 Decision making

Many of ABC's supporters claim that it can assist with decision making in a number of ways.

- **Provides accurate and reliable cost information**
- Establishes a long-run product cost
- Provides data which can be used to evaluate different ways of delivering business.

It is therefore particularly suited to the following types of decision.

- Pricing
- Promoting or discontinuing products or parts of the business
- Redesigning products and developing new products or new ways to do business

Note, however, that an ABC cost is **not a true cost**, it is **simply a long run average cost** because some costs such as depreciation are still arbitrarily allocated to products. An ABC cost is therefore **not a relevant cost** for all decisions. For example, even if a **product/service ceases** altogether, **some costs** allocated to that product/service using an activity based approach (such as building occupancy costs or depreciation) would **not disappear** just because the product/service had disappeared. Management would need to bear this in mind when making product deletion decisions.

6.4 Activity-based management (ABM)

Although the terms are sometimes used interchangeably, ABM is a broader concept than ABC, being likely to incorporate ABC and activity based budgeting (ABB) which will be covered in a later chapter.

Key term

Activity-based management (ABM) is a 'system of management which uses activity-based cost information for a variety of purposes including cost reduction, cost modelling and customer profitability analysis'.

(CIMA *Official Terminology*)

'It refers to the management philosophy that views the planning, execution and measurement of activities as the key to competitive advantage'.

(Bob Scarlett, CIMA *Insider,* May 2002)

Chapter Roundup

- **Traditional costing systems**, which assume that all products consume all resources in proportion to their production volumes, tend to **allocate too great a proportion of overheads to high volume products** (which cause relatively little diversity and hence use fewer support services) and **too small a proportion of overheads** to low volume products (which cause greater diversity and therefore use more support services). **Activity based costing (ABC) attempts to overcome this problem.**

- An alternative to the traditional method of accounting for costs - absorption costing - is **activity based costing (ABC)**. ABC involves the identification of the factors (**cost drivers**) which cause the costs of an organisation's major activities. Support overheads are charged to products on the basis of their usage of an activity.

- When using ABC, for costs that vary with production levels in the short term, the cost driver will be volume related (labour or machine hours). Overheads that vary with some other activity (and not volume of production) should be traced to products using transaction-based cost drivers such as production runs or number of orders received. One way of classifying these transactions is **logistical, balancing, quality** and **change**.

- Although ABC has obvious merits, a number of criticisms have been raised.

- The main criticism of marginal costing decision making information is that marginal costing analyses cost behaviour patterns according to the volume of production. However, although certain costs may be fixed in relation to the volume of production, they **may in fact be variable in relation to some other cost driver.**

- ABC should only be introduced if the additional information it provides will result in action that will increase the organisation's overall profitability.

- ABC identifies four levels of activities: product level, batch level, product sustaining level and facility sustaining level.

- ABC has a range of uses and has many advantages over more traditional costing methods. However, the system does have its critics and it is not a panacea for all costing problems.

Quick Quiz

1   Choose the correct words from those highlighted.

Traditional costing systems tend to allocate **too great/too small** a proportion of overheads to high volume products and **too great/too small** a proportion of overheads to low volume products.

2   Fill in the blanks.

The major ideas behind ABC are as follows.

(a)   Activities cause ....

(b)   Producing products creates demand for the ....

(c)   Costs are assigned to a product on the basis of the product's consumption of the
....

3   Match the most appropriate cost driver to each cost.

Costs		*Cost driver*
(a)	Set-up costs	Number of machine hours
(b)	Short-run variable costs	Number of production runs
(c)	Materials handling and despatch	Number of orders executed

4   ABC recognises the complexity of modern manufacturing by the use of multiple cost pools. True or false?

5   The use of direct labour hours or direct machine hours to trace costs to products occurs with the use of absorption costing but not with the use of ABC. True or false?

6   The cost driver for quality inspection is likely to be batch size. **True or false?**

7   ABC is not a system that is suitable for use by service organisations. **True or false?**

Answers to Quick Quiz

1   Too great
Too small

2   (a)   Costs
(b)   Activities
(c)   Activities

3   (a)   Number of production runs
(b)   Number of machine hours
(c)   Number of orders executed

4   False. Complexity is recognised by the use of multiple cost drivers.

5   False. The use of volume-related cost drivers should be used for costs that do vary with production volume.

6   False

7   False. It is highly suitable.

Now try the questions below from the Exam Question Bank

Number	Level	Marks	Time
Q12	Examination	20	36 mins
Q13	Examination	5	9 mins
Q14	Examination	5	9 mins

Part B
Standard costing

Standard costing

Introduction

In this chapter we will be looking at **standard costs** and **standard costing.**

Standard costing was covered at Foundation level, where you learned about the principles of standard costing and how to calculate a number of cost and sales variances. We obviously look at the topic in more depth for your studies of this syllabus.

We begin this chapter by reviewing the **main principles of standard costing** in **Section 1**, as well as looking in some detail at the **way in which standard costs are set** in **Section 2**. **Section 3** then looks at the special case of setting standard costs in a service environment.

In **Section 4** we cover the **behavioural implications** of standard costing. The topic is also covered in more detail in Chapters 13 and 14 after you have covered budgetary control (to which standard costing is so closely linked).

Section 5 deals with why costing systems and standard costs must be **reviewed** on a regular basis. **Section 6** provides you with clarification of the **difference between budgets and standards**.

The chapter concludes by addressing some common criticisms of standard costing systems in advanced manufacturing environments.

Topic list	Learning outcomes	Syllabus references	Ability required
1 The uses of standard costing	B(i)	B 1,5	Comprehension
2 Setting standards for manufacturing	B(i)	B 1	Comprehension
3 Setting standards in service industries	B(i)	B 5	Comprehension
4 The behavioural implications of standard costing	B(vi)	B 9	Analysis
5 Updating standards	B(i)	B 1,5	Comprehension
6 Budgets and standards compared	B(i)	B 1,5	Comprehension
7 Criticisms of standard costing	B(i)	B 1,5	Comprehension

1 The uses of standard costing

A **standard** is a **predetermined unit of cost** for inventory valuation, budgeting and control.

1.1 What is a standard cost?

Key term

A **standard cost** is a carefully predetermined estimated unit cost.

Standard costs are usually drawn up for a unit of production or a unit of service rendered but it is also possible to have a standard cost per routine task completed, or a standard cost per £1 of sale. A standard cost per unit of production may include administration, selling and distribution costs, but in many organisations, the assessment of standards is confined to production costs only.

1.2 What is standard costing?

Key term

The CIMA *Official Terminology* definition of **standard costing** is 'A control technique which compares standard costs and revenues with actual results to obtain variances which are used to stimulate improved performance'.

Standard costing is the **preparation of standard costs** to be used in the following circumstances.

(a)   To assist in **setting budgets** and **evaluating managerial performance**.

(b)   To act as a **control device** by establishing standards, highlighting (via **variance analysis**) activities that do not conform to plan and thus alerting management to those areas that may be out of control and in need of corrective action.

(c)   To enable the principle of '**management by exception'** to be practised.

Key term

Management by exception is 'The practice of focusing on activities which require attention and ignoring those which appear to be conforming to expectations'.

(CIMA *Official Terminology*)

A standard cost, when established, is an average expected unit cost. Because it is only an average, actual results will vary to some extent above and below the average. Variances should only be reported where the difference between actual and standard is significant.

(d)   To **provide a prediction of future costs** to be used in decision-making situations.

(e)   To **value inventories and cost production** for cost accounting purposes. It is an alternative method of valuation to methods like FIFO, LIFO or replacement costing.

(f)   To **motivate staff and management** by the provision of challenging targets.

(g)   To **provide guidance on improvement of efficiency** and **minimisation of waste**.

Although the use of standard costs to simplify the keeping of cost accounting records should not be overlooked, we will be **concentrating** on the **control and variance analysis** aspect of standard costing.

1.3 When standard costing is used

Standard costing can be used in a variety of costing situations.

- Batch and mass production
- Process manufacture
- Jobbing manufacture (where there is standardisation of parts)
- Service industries (if a realistic cost unit can be established)

However, the **greatest benefit** from its use can be gained if there is a **degree of repetition** in the production process. It is therefore most suited to **mass production** and **repetitive assembly** work. However, a standard cost can be calculated **per task if there is a similarity of tasks**. In this way standard costing can be used by some **service organisations**.

2 Setting standards for manufacturing

FAST FORWARD

A **standard cost card** shows full details of the standard cost of each product.

2.1 Setting standard costs

A standard cost implies that a standard or target exists for every single element that contributes to the product: the types, usage and prices of materials and parts, the grades, rates of pay and times for the labour involved, the production methods, tools and so on.

The standard cost for each part of the product is recorded on a **standard cost card**.

key term

A **standard cost card** is 'A document or other record detailing, for each individual product, the standard inputs required for production as well as the standard selling price. Inputs are normally divided into material, labour and overhead categories, and both price and quantity information is shown for each.'

(CIMA *Official Terminology*)

An example of a standard cost card is given below.

```
                        STANDARD COST CARD
                      Product: the Splodget, No 12345

                           Cost          Requirement
                                                         Y          Y
Direct materials
     A                 Y2.00 per kg       6 kgs        12.00
     B                 Y3.00 per kg       2 kgs         6.00
     C                 Y4.00 per litre    1 litre       4.00
Others                                                  2.00
                                                                  24.00

Direct labour
  Grade I              Y4.00 per hour     3 hrs        12.00
  Grade II             Y5.40 per hour     5 hrs        27.00
                                                                  39.00
Variable production overheads   Y1.00 per hour   8 hrs             8.00
Fixed production overheads      Y3.00 per hour   8 hrs            24.00
Standard full cost of production                                 95.00
```

Standard costs may be used in **both marginal and absorption costing systems**. The card illustrated has been prepared under an absorption costing system, with selling and administration costs excluded from the standard.

The **responsibility for setting** standard costs should be shared between **managers able to provide the necessary information** about levels of expected efficiency, prices and overhead costs. Standard costs are **usually revised once a year** (to allow for the new overheads budget, inflation in prices, and any changes in expected efficiency of materials usage or of labour). However they may be **revised more frequently if conditions are changing rapidly**.

FAST FORWARD

The standard for each type of cost (labour, material and so on) is made up of a **standard resource price** and a **standard resource usage**.

2.2 Setting standards for materials costs

Direct material prices will be estimated by the purchasing department from their existing knowledge.

- Purchase contracts already agreed
- Pricing discussions with regular suppliers
- Quotations and estimates from potential suppliers
- The forecast movement of prices in the market
- The availability of bulk purchase discounts
- Material quality required

Price inflation can cause difficulties in setting realistic standard prices. Suppose that a material costs £10 per kilogram at the moment, and during the course of the next 12 months, it is expected to go up in price by 20% to £12 per kilogram. **What standard price should be selected?**

- The **current price** of £10 per kilogram
- The **expected price** for the year, say, £11 per kilogram

Either price in would be possible, but neither would be entirely satisfactory.

(a) If the **current price** were used in the standard, the reported price variance would become adverse as soon as prices go up, which might be very early in the year. If prices go up gradually rather than in one big jump, it would be difficult to select an appropriate time for revising the standard.

(b) If an **estimated mid-year price** were used, price variances should be favourable in the first half of the year and adverse in the second half, again assuming that prices go up gradually. Management could only really check that in any month, the price variance did not become excessively adverse (or favourable) and that the price variance switched from being favourable to adverse around month six or seven and not sooner.

Standard costing for materials is therefore more **difficult in times of inflation but it is still worthwhile**.

(a) Usage and efficiency variances will still be meaningful.

(b) Inflation is measurable: there is no reason why its effects cannot be removed from the variances reported.

(c) Standard costs can be revised, so long as this is not done too frequently.

2.3 Setting standards for labour rates

Direct labour rates per hour will be set by discussion with the personnel department and by reference to the payroll and to any agreements on pay rises and/or bonuses with trade union representatives of the employees. A separate average hourly rate or weekly wage will be set for each different labour grade/type of employee (even though individual rates of pay may vary according to age and experience).

2.4 Setting standards for material usage and labour efficiency

To estimate the materials required to make each product (material usage) and also the labour hours required (labour efficiency), **technical specifications** must be prepared for each product by production experts (either in the production department or the work study department).

Material usage and labour efficiency standards are known as **performance standards**.

2.5 Types of performance standard

FAST FORWARD

> **Performance standards** are used to set efficiency targets. There are four types: ideal, attainable, current and basic.

The setting of standards raises the problem of how demanding the standard should be. Should the standard represent a perfect performance or an easily attainable performance? The type of performance standard used can have behavioural implications. There are four types of standard.

Type of standard	Description
Ideal	These are based on **perfect operating conditions**: no wastage, no spoilage, no inefficiencies, no idle time, no breakdowns. Variances from ideal standards are useful for pinpointing areas where a close examination may result in large savings in order to maximise efficiency and minimise waste. However ideal standards are likely to have an unfavourable motivational impact because reported variances will always be adverse. Employees will often feel that the goals are unattainable and not work so hard.

Type of standard	Description
Attainable	These are based on the hope that a standard amount of work will be carried out efficiently, machines properly operated or materials properly used. **Some allowance is made for wastage and inefficiencies**. If well-set they provide a useful psychological incentive by giving employees a realistic, but challenging target of efficiency. The consent and co-operation of employees involved in improving the standard are required.
Current	These are based on **current working conditions** (current wastage, current inefficiencies). The disadvantage of current standards is that they do not attempt to improve on current levels of efficiency.
Basic	These are **kept unaltered over a long period of time**, and may be out of date. They are used to show changes in efficiency or performance over a long period of time. Basic standards are perhaps the least useful and least common type of standard in use.

Ideal standards, attainable standards and current standards each have their supporters and it is by **no means clear which of them is preferable**.

Question
Performance standards

Learning outcome: B(i)

Which of the following statements is not true?

A   Variances from ideal standards are useful for pinpointing areas where a close examination might result in large cost savings.

B   Basic standards may provide an incentive to greater efficiency even though the standard cannot be achieved.

C   Ideal standards cannot be achieved and so there will always be adverse variances. If the standards are used for budgeting, an allowance will have to be included for these 'inefficiencies'.

D   Current standards or attainable standards are a better basis for budgeting, because they represent the level of productivity which management will wish to plan for.

Answer

The correct answer is B.

Statement B is describing ideal standards, not basic standards.

2.6 Setting standards for variable overheads

Standard variable overhead costs are usually charged to products using a standard rate per labour hour, but **in an ABC system any measurable cost driver may be used** to trace overhead costs to products.

Where labour hours are to be used as the basis for charging variable overhead costs, the number of standard labour hours for each product will have already been determined when setting the standard labour costs.

Careful analysis of overhead costs will be necessary in order to determine which costs are variable with the selected measure of activity, and which costs are fixed. Examples of overhead costs that might vary with the number of direct labour hours worked are power costs and the cost of lubricating oils. In order to determine the standard variable overhead cost per hour it will be necessary **to prepare forecasts of the hourly expenditure on each cost separately**. These would then be summed to derive the standard total variable production overhead cost per hour.

2.7 Setting standards for fixed overheads

In a marginal costing system there is no need to determine a standard unit rate for fixed overheads, since these are not attributed to individual units, but are treated as period costs and are charged directly to the income statement.

In an absorption costing system the standard overhead absorption rate is the same as the predetermined overhead absorption rate.

The standard overhead absorption rate will depend on the total value of budgeted overheads for the forthcoming period and on the planned activity or production volume for the period.

Production volume will **depend on two factors**.

    (a)   **Production capacity** (or '**volume capacity**') measured perhaps in standard hours of output.

    (b)   **Efficiency of working**, by labour or machines, allowing for rest time and contingency allowances. This will depend on the type of performance standard to be used (ideal, current, attainable and so on).

Suppose that a department has a workforce of ten employees, each of whom works a 36 hour week to make standard units, and each unit has a standard production time of two hours. The expected efficiency of the workforce is 125%.

    (a)   **Budgeted capacity**, in direct labour hours, would be $10 \times 36 = 360$ production hours per week.

    (b)   **Budgeted efficiency** is 125% so that the workforce should take only 1 hour of actual production time to produce 1.25 standard hours of output.

    (c)   This means in our example that **budgeted output** is 360 production hours × 125% = 450 standard hours of output per week. At two standard hours per unit, this represents production activity or volume of 225 units of output per week.

Output, capacity and efficiency are inter-related items, and you should check your understanding of them by attempting the following problem.

| Question | Linking capacity, efficiency and output |

Learning outcome: B(i)

ABC carries out routine office work in a sales order processing department, and all tasks in the department have been given standard times. There are 40 clerks in the department who work on average 140 hours per month each. The efficiency ratio of the department is 110%.

Required

Calculate the budgeted output in the department.

Answer

Capacity	=	40 × 140 = 5,600 hours per month
Efficiency	=	110%
Budgeted output	=	5,600 × 110% = 6,160 standard hours of work per month

2.7.1 Capacity levels

Capacity levels are needed to establish a standard absorption rate for fixed production overhead, when standard absorption costing is used. Any one of three capacity levels might be used for budgeting.

Key terms

- **Full capacity** is 'output (expressed in standard hours) that could be achieved if sales orders, supplies and workforce were available for all installed workplaces'.

- **Practical capacity** is 'full capacity less an allowance for known unavoidable volume losses'.

- **Budgeted capacity** is 'standard hours planned for the period, taking into account budgeted sales, supplies, workforce availability and efficiency expected'.

(CIMA *Official Terminology*)

(a) **Full capacity** is the **theoretical** capacity, assuming continuous production without any stoppages due to factors such as machine downtime, supply shortages or labour shortages. Full capacity would be associated with **ideal standards**.

(b) **Practical capacity** acknowledges that **some stoppages are unavoidable**, such as maintenance time for machines, and resetting time between jobs, some machine breakdowns and so on. Practical capacity is below full capacity, and would be associated with **attainable standards**.

(c) **Budgeted capacity** is the capacity (labour hours, machine hours) **needed to produce the budgeted output**, and would be associated with **current standards**, which relate to current conditions but may not be representative of normal practical capacity over a longer period of time.

Idle capacity would be defined as the **practical capacity** in a period **less the budgeted capacity** measured in standard hours of output. It represents unused capacity that ought to be available, but which is not needed because the budgeted volume is lower than the practicable volume that could be achieved.

2.8 Setting standards for selling price and margin or contribution

As well as standard costs, standard selling prices and standard margins or contributions can be set. The standard selling price will depend on a number of factors including the following.

- Anticipated market demand
- Competing products and competitors' actions
- Manufacturing costs
- Inflation estimates

The standard sales margin or contribution is the difference between the standard total or variable cost and the standard selling price.

3 Setting standards in service industries

It can be difficult to apply standard costing in a service environment because of the difficulty in establishing a measurable cost unit and the heterogeneous nature of most services.

3.1 Difficulties in applying standard costing in service environments

Standard costing was originally used in manufacturing environments and a criticism levelled at standard costing was its **apparent lack of applicability in service industries**.

The application of standard costing in service industries does have its problems.

- It can be **difficult to establish a measurable cost unit** for some services.

- In some service organisations **every cost unit will be different or heterogeneous**. For example each haircut provided in a salon will be different.

- Since the **human influence is so great** in many services it can be difficult to predict and control the quality of the output and the resources used in its production.

To overcome these problems and enable the application of standard costing for planning and control in service industries it is therefore necessary to do the following.

- **Establish a measurable cost unit**. This is relatively easy in some service organisations. For example in your earlier studies you will have learned about cost units for transport companies, such as a passenger-mile or a tonne-mile, or for hotels, such as a guest-night. (You might recall that these are referred to as **composite cost units**).

- **Attempt to reduce the heterogeneity of services**. If every service provided to the customer is the same as the last then it will be possible to set a standard cost for the service and use this to maximise efficiency and reduce waste.

- **Reduce the element of human influence**. This can be achieved by swapping machines for humans wherever possible.

3.2 McDonaldization

The four dimensions of McDonaldization are calculability, control, efficiency and predictability.

McDonaldization is a term coined by George Ritzer in his 1996 book *'The McDonaldization of Society'*. Ritzer analysed the success of the American hamburger chain and noted that the principles of McDonalds's operations are now being applied to many sectors of society.

The application of McDonaldization in service industries is **assisting the use of standard costing for cost planning and control** because it overcomes the problems referred to above.

Ritzer identified four dimensions of McDonaldization.

- **Calculability**. The content of every McDonalds meal is identical and standardised. Every burger should contain a standard amount of meat, every bun is of the same size and all fries are of the same thickness. **The human element is eliminated as far as possible** in the actual production process in order to make the food in a standard time using standard materials. Human initiative is eliminated in actually putting together the meal at the point of sale through the issuing of standard instructions concerning the content of each type of meal ordered. Thus each meal is a **measurable** standard cost unit for which a **standard cost can be established** and the actual cost can be measured for cost control purposes.

- **Control**. Control over the service is achieved in particular by **reducing the human influence**, which can lead to variation in output and quality. Again, machines and technology substitute for humans: automatic drinks dispensers which measure the exact quantity to be delivered and cash registers which require only one button to be pressed to record the sale of a complete meal are examples of improved control and the reduction of the possibility of human error in the delivery of the service.

- **Efficiency**. Ritzer described efficiency as 'the optimum method of getting from one point to another'. Every McDonalds business is organised to ensure maximum efficiency so that the customer can get exactly what they want as quickly as possible. This **increases customer satisfaction and also increases the company's profitability**.

- **Predictability**. The McDonalds service is the **same in every outlet throughout the world**, whether a meal is purchased in Shanghai or on London. Again this helps with the standardisation of the service and the setting of standard costs throughout the organisation.

Question

Learning outcome: B(ii)

State three service industries where McDonaldization could be applied to standardise the delivery of services.

Answer

Possible service industries where McDonaldization could be applied include the following.

- Exhaust and tyre fitting centres where a detailed manual dictates the activities of operatives for each standard type of fitting

- Call centres, where a machine provides the caller with numbered options from which to select the desired service and the person that answers is using a standard script

- Laboratory testing of blood samples, where the procedures to be followed by laboratory technicians can be standardised.

3.3 Diagnostic related groups

FAST FORWARD

Diagnostic related groups (DRGs) or reference groups are used in the healthcare industry to group together patients with similar lengths of stay and resource requirements. Standard costs can be established for each DRG which can be used for cost planning and control.

The use of standard costing to plan and control costs in the health service has been assisted by the development of **diagnostic related groups (DRGs)** or **reference groups**.

DRGs provide a **system of classifying patients** according to their diagnosis, age and length of stay. This classification helps to determine the resources that should be used to treat and care for the patient.

The concept of DRGs was originally developed in America in order to calculate a **standard cost for each category of patient**. There are more than 500 different possible DRG classifications and the resulting standard cost can be used for billing purposes by the healthcare insurance industry. This means that the insurance company pays the hospital a **standard rate for each DRG** and the hospital would then need to contain its costs below the payment received.

The use of DRGs **enables the principles of standard costing to be applied in the health service in order to maximise efficiency and minimise waste**.

4 The behavioural implications of standard costing

FAST FORWARD

An effective standard costing system should take account of **behavioural implications** in its design.

4.1 Dealing with people

Setting standards and using them as a yardstick for cost control is not simply an exercise in dealing with numbers. It also involves dealing with people, and a standard costing system will only be **effective if it is designed with full understanding of its potential behavioural effects**. We have already seen how the type of performance standard used can have behavioural implications. For example the adverse variances which tend to be reported when ideal standards are used can be demotivating for the individuals who are working to achieve the standard.

4.2 Other behavioural implications to be considered in the design and operation of a standard costing system

(a) **Communication is of the utmost importance**. Because of the technical nature of much of the standard setting process, production employees and their supervisors may need to be involved. This will help to win their support for the resulting standards and they are more likely to be willing to work to achieve them. Moreover, the employees' practical knowledge will contribute towards a more accurate and useful standard for cost planning and control. (There are **disadvantages to participation** in the standard-setting process: staff may make standards too loose; the process takes longer; senior management may not with to devolve responsibility.)

(b) **The variance reporting system should not be used punitively**. There must be no undue pressure or excessive blame attached to the non-achievement of standards. Managers who are treated in this way may resent the use of the standard costing system and thus reduce its effectiveness.

(c) **Care must be taken to distinguish between controllable and non-controllable costs in variance reporting.** It can be demotivating for managers who feel that they are being held responsible for costs and variances over which they cannot exercise control.

(d) **Variance control reports must be produced promptly and accurately**. Inaccuracy will lead to managers losing faith in the value of the information and they may not bother to act upon it. Late information may cause frustration if managers feel that they could have acted earlier if they had known that problems existed.

(e) Standards set should **encourage goal congruence** between individuals and the organisation as a whole.

Key term

Goal congruence is 'In a control system, the state which leads individuals or groups to take actions which are in their self-interest and also in the best interest of the entity'.

(CIMA *Official Terminology*)

A purchasing manager may seek to minimise adverse material price variances and so buy cheap but poor quality material. This will have a detrimental effect on the quantity of material used, the level of rejects and the quality of the final product, none of which are the purchasing manager's immediate problem. They are, however, problems for the organisation as a whole.

Question

Pros and cons of standard costing

Learning outcome: B(i)

(a)   Describe the possible problems which could arise when setting standards.

(b)   List possible advantages of standard costing.   (5 marks)

Answer

(a)   (i)   Deciding how to incorporate inflation into planned unit costs.

      (ii)   Agreeing a short-term labour efficiency standard (current, attainable or ideal).

      (iii) Deciding on the quality of materials to be used (a better quality of material will cost more, but perhaps reduce material wastage).

      (iv)   Deciding on the appropriate mix of component materials, where some change in the mix is possible (for example in the manufacture of foods and drink).

      (v)   Estimating materials prices where seasonal price variations or bulk purchase discounts may be significant.

      (vi)   Finding sufficient time to construct accurate standards. Standard setting can be a time-consuming process.

      (vii) Incurring the cost of setting up and maintaining a system for establishing standards.

      (viii) Dealing with possible behavioural problems. Managers responsible for the achievement of standards might resist the use of a standard costing control system for fear of being blamed for any adverse variances.

      (ix)   Keeping standards realistic and up-to-date.

(b)   (i)   Carefully planned standards are an aid to more accurate budgeting.

      (ii)   Standard costs provide a yardstick against which actual costs can be measured.

      (iii) The setting of standards involves determining the best materials and methods which may lead to economies.

      (iv)   A target of efficiency is set for employees to reach and cost consciousness is stimulated.

      (v)   Variances can be calculated which enable the principle of 'management by exception' to be operated. Only the variances which exceed acceptable tolerance limits need to be investigated by management with a view to control action.

      (vi)   Standard costs and variance analysis can provide a way of motivating managers to achieve better performance. However, care must be taken to distinguish between controllable and non-controllable costs in variance reporting.

5 Updating standards

In general, standards should be **revised** whenever changes of a permanent or reasonably long-term nature occur.

5.1 The need to update standards

When an organisation introduces a system of standard costing, it is quite possible that the standards initially set will not be the most accurate reflection of what occurs 'on average'. **Initial standards** may need **substantial revision** in the early period of a standard costing system's life before they are really useful measures for control purposes.

The evolution of standards does not stop after a couple of accounting periods, however. Standards must be **continuously reviewed** to ensure that they do **mirror** what is **currently happening** and that they are the **most accurate 'average'**.

Out-of-date standards will produce **variances** that are **illogical bases** for planning, control, decision making or performance evaluation. Current operational performance cannot be compared to out-of-date standards.

'Labour and material usage standards normally are set by the industrial engineering department. Material price normally is considered the responsibility of purchasing. Similarly, the labour rates are set by the personnel department. As the production processes change (improve), past standards become less than realistic, and should be revised. It is the responsibility of departments that originally created the standard to inform the accounting department about the need for revising the standards.

But, unfortunately, some managers prefer to keep the old standards because the new improved production process makes their performance look better with old standards.'

(LU Tatikonda, 'Production Managers Need a Course in Cost Accounting', *Management Accounting* (June 1987), published by Institute of Management Accountants, Montvale, N J)

5.2 Improvement of the standard setting process

Standard setting procedures may be refined and extended to enable more accurate standards to be set.

(a)   **Work study** methods may be established within the organisation. These enable accurate estimates of labour time to be made.

(b)   The introduction of **computerised information systems** provides more reliable standards.

With CADCAM (computer-aided design/computer aided manufacture) systems the planning of manufacturing requirements can be **computerised**, with the useful spin-off that standard costs can also be constructed by computer, thus saving administrative time and expense while providing far more accurate standards.

5.3 Revision of standards

In practice standard costs are usually revised **once a year** to allow for the new overheads budget, inflation in prices and wage rates, and any changes in expected efficiency of material usage, labour or machinery.

Some argue that standards should be revised **as soon as there is any change in the basis upon which they were set.** Clearly, for example, if a standard is based on the cost of a material that is no longer available or the use of equipment which has been replaced, it is meaningless to compare actual performance using the new material and equipment with the old standard.

Coates, Rickwood and Stacey in their book *Management Accounting in Practice* put forward the following reasons for revising standards.

    (a)   Manufacturing methods are **significantly** changed due to plant layout, machinery alterations, change in product design, use of different materials, etc.

    (b)   The relationship of normal capacity and actual activity is **significantly** out of balance.

    (c)   The disparity between the standard and expected performance is **so significant** that the standard as a measurement loses its value.

    (d)   An existing standard is discovered to be incorrectly set and a **significant** difference exists.'

(JB Coates, CP Rickwood, RJ Stacey, Management Accounting in Practice, CIMA)

Frequent changes in standards can cause **problems**.

    (a)   They may become **ineffective as motivators and measures of performance,** since it may be perceived that target setters are constantly 'moving the goal posts'.

    (b)   The **administrative effort** may be too time consuming (although the introduction of computer systems renders this objection less forceful).

Coates *et al* concede the following point.

    'Revisions should be **held to a minimum**, despite the fact that standards may not be precise, in order to provide for relative comparisons between operating periods and/or versus budget.'

The most **suitable approach** would therefore appear to be a policy of revising the standards **whenever changes of a permanent and reasonably long-term nature occur**, but not in response to temporary 'blips' in price or efficiency.

6 Budgets and standards compared

FAST FORWARD

Budgets and standards are very similar and interrelated, but there are important differences between them.

You will recall from your earlier studies that a **budget** is a **quantified monetary plan** for a **future period**, which **managers will try to achieve**. Its major function lies in **communicating plans** and **coordinating activities** within an organisation.

On the other hand, a **standard** is a **carefully predetermined quantity target** which can be **achieved in certain conditions**.

Budgets and standards are **similar** in the following ways.

    (a)   They both involve looking to the future and **forecasting** what is likely to happen given a certain set of circumstances.

    (b)   They are both **used for control purposes**. A budget aids control by setting financial targets or limits for a forthcoming period. Actual achievements or expenditures are then compared with the budgets and action is taken to correct any variances where necessary. A standard also achieves control by comparison of actual results against a predetermined target.

As well as being similar, **budgets and standards are interrelated**. For example, a standard unit production cost can act as the basis for a production cost budget. The unit cost is multiplied by the budgeted activity level to arrive at the budgeted expenditure on production costs.

There are, however, **important differences between budgets and standards**.

Budgets	Standards
Gives planned total aggregate costs for a function or cost centre	Shows the unit resource usage for a single task, for example the standard labour hours for a single unit of production
Can be prepared for all functions, even where output cannot be measured	Limited to situations where repetitive actions are performed and output can be measured
Expressed in money terms	Need not be expressed in money terms. For example a standard rate of output does not need a financial value put on it

7 Criticisms of standard costing

FAST FORWARD

Critics argue that standard costing is most appropriate in a standard, stable and repetitive environment and therefore is of limited usefulness in the modern business environment. However, standard costing can be adapted to remain useful for cost planning and control.

7.1 Standard costing in the modern business environment

Critics of standard costing have argued that traditional variance analysis has limited applicability in the modern business environment. The modern business environment is characterised by a need to respond to **customer demands** for **immediate availability of products, shortening product life cycles and higher quality standards**.

Standard costing is most appropriate in a **stable, standardised** and **repetitive** environment and one of the main objectives of standard costing is to ensure that **processes conform to standards**, that they do not vary and that **variances** are **eliminated**. This may seem **restrictive** and **inhibiting** in the business environment of the early twenty first century.

7.2 Standard costing and new technology

Standard costing has **traditionally** been associated with **labour-intensive** operations, but can it be **applied to capital-intensive production too?**

(a) In an AMT environment, the **cost of labour** is a **small proportion** of total costs and so labour rate and efficiency variances will have little control value.

(b) **Fixed costs** represent a **significant** proportion of total costs but there is some **doubt** over the **relevance** of the information provided by **fixed overhead volume variances**.

(c) **Material usage** variances should be virtually non-existent given the accuracy afforded by machines as opposed to human operators.

(d) It is quite possible that, with AMT, **variable overheads** are **incurred** in relation to machine time rather than labour time, and standard costs should reflect this where appropriate.

In an AMT environment, **machine efficiency variances** will be of **value**, however, and standards will still be needed for costing, pricing and budgeting purposes.

7.3 Standard costing and JIT

Some commentators have argued that **traditional variance analysis is unhelpful and potentially misleading** in the modern organisation, and can make managers focus their attention on the wrong issues. Here are just two examples.

(a) **Efficiency variance**. Traditional variance analysis emphasises that adverse efficiency variances should be avoided, which means that managers should try to prevent idle time and keep up production. In a TQM environment, JIT should be used. In these circumstances, manufacturing to eliminate idle time could result in the production of unwanted products that must be held in store and might eventually be scrapped. Efficiency variances could focus management attention on the wrong problems.

(b) **Materials price variance**. In a JIT environment the key issues in materials purchasing are supplier reliability, materials quality, and delivery in small order quantities. Purchasing managers should not be shopping around every month looking for the cheapest price. Many JIT systems depend on long-term contractual links with suppliers, which means that material price variances are not relevant for management control purposes.

7.4 Standard costing and TQM

Standard costing concentrates on **quantity** and ignores other factors contributing to an organisation's effectiveness. In a **total quality** environment, however, quantity is not an issue, **quality** is. Effectiveness in such an environment therefore centres on high quality output (produced as a result of high quality input); the cost of failing to achieve the required level of effectiveness is not measured in variances, but in terms of the **internal and external failure costs** which would not be identified by traditional standard costing analysis.

Standard costing might measure, say, **labour efficiency** in terms of individual tasks and the level of **output**. In a **total quality environment**, labour is most likely to be viewed as a number of **multi-task teams** who are responsible for completion of a part of the production process. The effectiveness of such a team is more appropriately measured in terms of **re-working** required, **returns** from customers, **defects** identified in subsequent stages of production and so on.

In a **TQM** environment there are likely to be **minimal rate variances** if the workforce are paid a guaranteed weekly wage. Fixed price contracts, with suppliers guaranteeing levels of quality, are often a feature, especially if a JIT system is also in place, and so there are likely to be **few, if any, material price and usage variances**.

So **can standard costing and TQM exist together?**

(a) Predetermined standards conflict with the TQM philosophy of continual improvement.

(b) Continual improvements should alter quantities of inputs, prices and so on, whereas standard costing is best used in a stable, standardised, repetitive environment.

(c) Standard costs often incorporate a planned level of scrap in material standards. This is at odds with the TQM aim of 'zero defects' and there is no motivation to 'get it right first time'.

(d) Attainable standards, which make some allowance for wastage and inefficiencies, are commonly set. The use of such standards conflicts with the elimination of waste which is a vital ingredient of a TQM programme.

(e) Standard costing systems make individual managers responsible for the variances relating to their part of the organisation's activities. A TQM programme, on the other hand, aims to make all personnel aware of, and responsible for, the importance of supplying the customer with a quality product.

On the other hand, variance analysis can contribute towards the aim of improved product quality. Can you think how? The following question tests this point.

Question   Variance analysis and product quality

Learning outcome: B(i)

AB has been receiving an increasing number of customer complaints about a general weakness in the quality of its products in recent months. The company believes that its future success is dependent on product quality and it is therefore determined to improve it.

Required

Describe the contribution that variance analysis can make towards the aim of improved product quality.

(5 marks)

Answer

Variance analysis can be used to enhance product quality and to keep track of quality control information. This is because variance analysis measures both the planned use of resources and the actual use of resources in order to compare the two.

As variance analysis is generally expressed in terms of purely quantitative measures, such as quantity of raw materials used and price per unit of quantity, issues of quality would appear to be excluded from the reporting process. Quality would appear to be an excuse for spending more time, say, or buying more expensive raw materials.

Variance analysis, as it currently stands, therefore needs to be **adapted** to take account of quality issues.

(i) Variance analysis reports should routinely include **measures such as defect rates**. Although zero defects will be most desirable, such a standard of performance may not be reached at first. However there should be an expected rate of defects: if this is exceeded then management attention is directed to the excess.

(ii) The **absolute number of defects** should be measured *and* **their type**. If caused by certain materials and components this can shed light on, say, a favourable materials price variance which might have been caused by substandard materials being purchased more cheaply. Alternatively, if the defects are caused by shoddy assembly work this can shed light on a favourable labour efficiency variance if quality is being sacrificed for speed.

(iii) It should also be possible to provide **financial measures for the cost of poor quality**. These can include direct costs such as the wages of inspection and quality control staff, the cost of time in rectifying the defects, and the cost of the materials used in rectification.

(iv) Measures could be built into materials price and variance analysis, so that the **materials price variance** as currently reported includes a **factor reflecting the quality of materials purchased**.

7.5 Other problems with using standard costing in today's environment

(a) Variance analysis concentrates on only a **narrow range of costs**, and does not give sufficient attention to issues such as quality and customer satisfaction.

(b)   Standard costing places **too much emphasis on direct labour costs**. Direct labour is only a small proportion of costs in the modern manufacturing environment and so this emphasis is not appropriate.

(c)   Many of the variances in a standard costing system focus on the control of **short-term variable costs**. In most modern manufacturing environments, the majority of costs, including direct labour costs, tend to be fixed in the short run.

(d)   The use of standard costing relies on the existence of **repetitive operations** and relatively **homogeneous** output. Nowadays many organisations are forced continually to respond to customers' changing requirements, with the result that output and operations are not so repetitive.

(e)   Standard costing systems were **developed** when the **business environment** was more **stable** and **less prone to change**. The current business environment is more dynamic and it is not possible to assume stable conditions.

(f)   Standard costing systems **assume** that **performance to standard is acceptable**. Today's business environment is more focused on continuous improvement.

(g)   Most standard costing systems produce **control statements weekly or monthly**. The modern manager needs much more prompt control information in order to function efficiently in a dynamic business environment.

This long list of criticisms of standard costing may lead you to believe that such systems have little use in today's business environment. Standard costing systems can be adapted to remain useful, however.

Question

The value of standard costing today

Learning outcome: B(i)

Briefly explain ways in which a standard costing system could be adapted so that it is useful in the modern business environment.

(5 marks)

Answer

A standard costing system may be adapted for use in the modern business environment as follows.

(a)   **Non-financial measures** can be included within management control reports. Examples include number of defects, percentage of on-time deliveries, and so on.

(b)   Even when output is not standardised, it may be possible to identify a number of **standard components and activities** whose costs may be controlled effectively by the setting of standard costs and identification of variances.

(c)   The use of computer power enables standards to be **updated rapidly** and more frequently, so that they remain useful for the purposes of control by comparison.

(d)   The use of **ideal standards** and **more demanding performance levels** can combine the benefits of **continuous improvement** and standard costing control.

(e)   Information, particularly of a non-financial nature, can be **produced more rapidly** with the assistance of **computers**. For example the use of on-line data capture can enable the continuous display of real time information on factors such as hours worked, number of components used and number of defects.

7.6 The role in modern business of standards and variances

(a) **Planning**. Even in a TQM environment, budgets will still need to be quantified. For example, the planned level of prevention and appraisal costs needs to be determined. Standards, such as returns of a particular product should not exceed one per cent of deliveries during a budget period, can be set.

(b) **Control**. Cost and mix changes from plan will still be relevant in many processing situations.

(c) **Decision making**. Existing standards can be used as the starting point in the construction of a cost for a new product.

(d) **Improvement and change**. Variance trends can be monitored over time.

Chapter Roundup

- A **standard** is a **predetermined unit of cost** for inventory valuation, budgeting and control.

- A **standard cost card** shows full details of the standard cost of each product.

- The standard for each type of cost (labour, material and so on) is made up of a **standard resource price** and a **standard resource usage**.

- **Performance standards** are used to set efficiency targets. There are four types: ideal, attainable, current and basic.

- It can be difficult to apply standard costing in a service environment because of the difficulty in establishing a measurable cost unit and the heterogeneous nature of most services.

- The four dimensions of McDonaldization are calculability, control, efficiency and predictability.

- Diagnostic related groups (DRGs) or reference groups are used in the healthcare industry to group together patients with similar lengths of stay and resource requirements. Standard costs can be established for each DRG which can be used for cost planning and control.

- An effective standard costing system should take account of **behavioural implications** in its design.

- In general, standards should be **revised** whenever changes of a permanent or reasonably long-term nature occur.

- Budgets and standards are very similar and interrelated, but there are important differences between them.

- Critics argue that standard costing is most appropriate in a standard, stable and repetitive environment and therefore is of limited usefulness in the modern business environment. However, standard costing can be adapted to remain useful for cost planning and control.

Quick Quiz

1 Which one of the following statements is true?

    A   Standard costing is not well suited to mass production.

    B   Standard costing can never be used by service organisations.

    C   Standard costing is most suited to repetitive assembly work.

    D   If there is a degree of repetition in the production process, standard costing should not be used.

2   *Match the types of performance standard to the correct descriptions.*

Performance standards

(a)   Ideal

(b)   Attainable

(c)   Current

(d)   Basic

Descriptions

(1)   If well set, can provide a useful psychological incentive

(2)   Do not attempt to improve on current levels of efficiency

(3)   Least common type of standard in use

(4)   Likely to have an unfavourable motivational effect

3   An attainable standard is based on perfect operating conditions. *True or false?*

4   State Ritzer's four dimensions of McDonaldization.

5   Variance control reports should be produced either promptly or accurately. *True or false?*

6   Standards should be amended every time there is a change in price or efficiency. *True or false?*

7   Fill in the gaps.

(i)   Budgets are prepared for .... costs; standards are for a ....

(ii)   .... can be prepared for all functions; .... are only suitable for repetitive actions where output can be measured.

(iii)   .... are expressed in money terms; .... need not be expressed in money terms.

Answers to Quick Quiz

1   C

2   (a)   4
    (b)   1
    (c)   2
    (d)   3

3   False. An ideal standard is based on perfect operating conditions.

4   Calculability, control, efficiency, predictability

5   False. They should be produced promptly **and** accurately.

6   False. It is probably best to revise standards whenever changes of a permanent or long-term nature occur.

7   (i)   aggregate total
          single task

    (ii)   budgets
           standards

    (iii)   budgets
            standards

Now try the questions below from the Exam Question Bank			
Number	**Level**	**Marks**	**Time**
Q15	Examination	5	9 mins
Q16	Examination	5	9 mins

Variance analysis

Introduction

In your studies for Paper 2 you will have covered the calculation of basic cost and sales variances. Because students often find variance analysis quite difficult (although, really, it isn't) we are going to **go over the basic cost variances** again in detail in **Sections 1 to 5**.

We will be **analysing sales variances in more detail** than you did at Foundation level, and will be looking at the selling price and sales volume variances in **Section 6**. **Section 7** looks at **non-production cost variances**.

This is a **key chapter** in terms of topic **examinability**. Variance calculation and interpretation lends itself well to objective testing or longer calculation-based questions.

In **Chapter 9** we will build on your revision of the basics in this chapter and cover a number of **additional variance analysis topics**. These include splitting the material usage and labour efficiency variances into mix and yield components and preparing statements to reconcile budgeted profit to actual profit using variances.

Topic list	Learning outcomes	Syllabus references	Ability required
1 Variances	B(ii)	B 2, 3, 6	Application/analysis
2 Direct material cost variances	B(ii)	B 2	Application/analysis
3 Direct labour cost variances	B(ii)	B 2	Application/analysis
4 Variable overhead variances	B(ii)	B 2	Application/analysis
5 Fixed overhead variances	B(ii)	B 2	Application/analysis
6 Sales variances	B(ii)	B 6	Application/analysis
7 Non-production cost variances	B(ii)	B 3	Application/analysis

1 Variances

The process by which the total difference between standard and actual results is analysed is known as variance analysis.

Key terms

A **variance** is the 'Difference between planned, budgeted, or standard cost and the actual cost incurred. The same comparisons may be made for revenues'.

(CIMA *Official Terminology*)

Variance analysis is defined in CIMA *Official Terminology* as 'The evaluation of performance by means of variances, whose timely reporting should maximise the opportunity for managerial action'.

When **actual results are better than expected results**, we have a **favourable** variance (F). If, on the other hand, **actual results are worse than expected results**, we have an **adverse** variance (A).

Variances can be divided into three main groups.

- Variable cost variances
    - Direct material
    - Direct labour
    - Variable production overhead
- Fixed production overhead variances
- Sales variances

2 Direct material cost variances

The direct material total variance is the sum of the direct material price variance and the direct material usage variance.

Key terms

The **direct material total variance** is 'A measurement of the difference between the standard material cost of the output produced and the actual cost incurred'.

The **direct material price variance** is 'The difference between the actual price paid for purchased materials and their standard cost'.

The **direct material usage variance** 'Measures efficiency in the use of material, by comparing the standard cost of material used with the standard material cost of what has been produced'.

(CIMA *Official Terminology*)

The **direct material total variance** (the difference between what the output actually cost and what it should have cost, in terms of material) can be **divided into two sub-variances**.

(a)   **The direct material price variance**

This is the difference between what the material purchased did cost and what it should have cost.

(b)   **The direct material usage variance**

This is the **difference between the standard quantity of materials that should have been used for the number of units actually produced, and the actual quantity of materials used, valued at the standard cost per unit of material**. In other words, it is the difference between how much material should have been used and how much material was used, valued at standard cost.

2.1 Example: direct material variances

Product X has a standard direct material cost as follows.

10 kilograms of material Y at £10 per kilogram = £100 per unit of X.

During period 4, 1,000 units of X were manufactured, using 11,700 kilograms of material Y which cost £98,600.

Required

Calculate the following variances.

(a)   The direct material total variance
(b)   The direct material price variance
(c)   The direct material usage variance

Solution

(a)   **The direct material total variance**

This is the difference between what 1,000 units should have cost and what they did cost.

	£
1,000 units should have cost (× £100)	100,000
but did cost	98,600
Direct material total variance	1,400 (F)

The variance is favourable because the units cost less than they should have cost.

Now we can break down the direct material total variance into its two constituent parts: the direct material price variance and the direct material usage variance.

(b)   **The direct material price variance**

This is the difference between what 11,700 kgs should have cost and what 11,700 kgs did cost.

	£
11,700 kgs of Y should have cost (× £10)	117,000
but did cost	98,600
Material Y price variance	18,400 (F)

The variance is favourable because the material cost less than it should have.

(c)   **The direct material usage variance**

This is the difference between how many kilograms of Y should have been used to produce 1,000 units of X and how many kilograms were used, valued at the standard cost per kilogram.

1,000 units should have used (× 10 kgs)	10,000 kgs
but did use	11,700 kgs
Usage variance in kgs	1,700 kgs (A)
× standard cost per kilogram	× £10
Usage variance in £	£17,000 (A)

The variance is adverse because more material than should have been used was used.

(d)   **Summary**

	£
Price variance	18,400 (F)
Usage variance	17,000 (A)
Total variance	1,400 (F)

2.2 Materials variances and opening and closing inventory

Suppose that a company uses raw material P in production, and that this raw material has a standard price of $3 per metre. During one month 6,000 metres are bought for $18,600, and 5,000 metres are used in production. At the end of the month, inventory will have been increased by 1,000 metres. In variance analysis, the problem is to decide the **material price variance**. Should it be calculated on the basis of **materials purchased** (6,000 metres) or on the basis of **materials used** (5,000 metres)?

The answer to this problem depends on **how closing inventories** of the raw materials will be **valued**.

(a)   If they are valued at **standard cost**, (1,000 units at $3 per unit) the price variance is calculated on material **purchases** in the period.

(b)   If they are valued at **actual cost (**FIFO**)** (1,000 units at $3.10 per unit) the price variance is calculated on materials **used in production** in the period.

A **full standard costing system** is usually in operation and therefore the price variance is usually calculated on **purchases** in the period. The variance on the full 6,000 metres will be written off to the costing income statement, even though only 5,000 metres are included in the cost of production.

There are two main **advantages** in extracting the material price variance at the time of **receipt**.

(a)   If variances are extracted at the time of receipt they will be **brought to the attention of managers earlier** than if they are extracted as the material is used. If it is necessary to correct any variances then management action can be more timely.

(b)   Since variances are extracted at the time of receipt, **all inventories will be valued at standard price**. This is administratively easier and it means that all issues from inventories can be made at standard price. If inventories are held at actual cost it is necessary to calculate a separate price variance on each batch as it is issued. Since issues are usually made in a number of small batches this can be a time-consuming task, especially with a manual system.

Question   **Materials price variance**

Learning outcome: B (ii)

What is the price variance based on the information in Paragraph 2.2?

A $3,100 (A)
B $600 (A)
C $3,100 (F)
D $600 (F)

Answer

The correct answer is B.

The price variance would be calculated as follows.

	$
6,000 metres of material P purchased should cost ($\times$ $3)	18,000
but did cost	18,600
Price variance	600 (A)

3 Direct labour cost variances

The direct labour total variance is the sum of the direct labour rate variance and the direct labour efficiency variance.

Key terms

The **direct labour total variance** 'Indicates the difference between the standard direct labour cost of the output which has been produced and the actual direct labour cost incurred'.

The **direct labour rate variance** 'Indicates the actual cost of any change from the standard labour rate of remuneration'.

The **direct labour efficiency variance** 'Indicates the standard labour cost of any change from the standard level of labour efficiency'. (CIMA *Official Terminology*)

The calculation of direct labour variances is very similar to the calculation of direct material variances.

The **direct labour total variance** (the difference between what the output should have cost and what it did cost, in terms of labour) can be **divided into two sub-variances**.

(a) **The direct labour rate variance**

This is similar to the direct material price variance. If is **the difference between the standard cost and the actual cost for the actual number of hours paid for**.

In other words, it is the difference between what the labour did cost and what it should have cost.

(b) **The direct labour efficiency variance**

This is similar to the direct material usage variance. It is the **difference between the hours that should have been worked for the number of units actually produced, and the actual number of hours worked, valued at the standard rate per hour**.

In other words, it is the difference between how many hours should have been worked and how many hours were worked, valued at the standard rate per hour.

3.1 Example: direct labour variances

The standard direct labour cost of product X is as follows.

2 hours of grade Z labour at £5 per hour = £10 per unit of product X.

During period 4, 1,000 units of product X were made, and the direct labour cost of grade Z labour was £8,900 for 2,300 hours of work.

Required

Calculate the following variances.

(a)   The direct labour total variance
(b)   The direct labour rate variance
(c)   The direct labour efficiency (productivity) variance

Solution

(a)   **The direct labour total variance**

This is the difference between what 1,000 units should have cost and what they did cost.

	£
1,000 units should have cost (× £10)	10,000
but did cost	8,900
Direct labour total variance	1,100 (F)

The variance is favourable because the units cost less than they should have done.

Again we can analyse this total variance into its two constituent parts.

(b)   **The direct labour rate variance**

This is the difference between what 2,300 hours should have cost and what 2,300 hours did cost.

	£
2,300 hours of work should have cost (× £5 per hr)	11,500
but did cost	8,900
Direct labour rate variance	2,600 (F)

The variance is favourable because the labour cost less than it should have cost.

(c)   **The direct labour efficiency variance**

1,000 units of X should have taken (× 2 hrs)	2,000 hrs
but did take	2,300 hrs
Efficiency variance in hours	300 hrs (A)
× standard rate per hour	×£5
Efficiency variance in £	£1,500 (A)

The variance is adverse because more hours were worked than should have been worked.

(d)   **Summary**

	£
Rate variance	2,600 (F)
Efficiency variance	1,500 (A)
Total variance	1,100 (F)

3.2 Idle time variance

FAST FORWARD   The **idle time variance** is the number of hours of idle time valued at the standard rate per hour.

A company may operate a costing system in which any idle time is recorded. Idle time may be caused by machine breakdowns or not having work to give to employees, perhaps because of bottlenecks in production or a shortage of orders from customers. When idle time occurs, the labour force is still paid wages for time at work, but no actual work is done. Time paid for without any work being done is unproductive and therefore inefficient. In variance analysis, **idle time is an adverse efficiency variance**.

Key term

The **idle time variance** is 'The standard labour cost of unproductive paid hours, when production was not possible due to factors such as material unavailability, production planning errors or machine breakdown'.

(CIMA *Official Terminology*)

When idle time is recorded separately, it is helpful to provide control information which identifies the cost of idle time separately, and in variance analysis, there will be an idle time variance **as a separate part of the total labour efficiency variance**. The remaining **efficiency variance** will then relate only to the productivity of the labour force during the **hours spent actively working**.

3.3 Example: labour variances with idle time

Refer to the standard cost data in Paragraph 3.1. During period 5, 1,500 units of product X were made and the cost of grade Z labour was £17,500 for 3,080 hours. During the period, however, there as a shortage of customer orders and 100 hours were recorded as idle time.

Required

Calculate the following variances.

(a) The direct labour total variance
(b) The direct labour rate variance
(c) The idle time variance
(d) The direct labour efficiency variance

Solution

(a) **The direct labour total variance**

	£
1,500 units of product X should have cost (× £10)	15,000
but did cost	17,500
Direct labour total variance	2,500 (A)

Actual cost is greater than standard cost. The variance is therefore adverse.

(b) **The direct labour rate variance**

The rate variance is a comparison of what the hours paid should have cost and what they did cost.

	£
3,080 hours of grade Z labour should have cost (× £5)	15,400
but did cost	17,500
Direct labour rate variance	2,100 (A)

Actual cost is greater than standard cost. The variance is therefore adverse.

(c) **The idle time variance**

The idle time variance is the hours of idle time, valued at the standard rate per hour.

Idle time variance = 100 hours (A) × £5 = £500 (A)

Idle time is **always** an **adverse** variance.

(d)   **The direct labour efficiency variance**

The efficiency variance considers the hours actively worked (the difference between hours paid for and idle time hours). In our example, there were (3,080 – 100) = 2,980 hours when the labour force was not idle. The variance is calculated by taking the amount of output produced (1,500 units of product X) and comparing the time it should have taken to make them, with the actual time spent **actively** making them (2,980 hours). Once again, the variance in hours is valued at the standard rate per labour hour.

1,500 units of product X should take (× 2 hrs)	3,000 hrs
but did take (3,080 – 100)	2,980 hrs
Direct labour efficiency variance in hours	20 hrs (F)
× standard rate per hour	× £5
Direct labour efficiency variance in £	£100 (F)

(e)   **Summary**

	£
Direct labour rate variance	2,100 (A)
Idle time variance	500 (A)
Direct labour efficiency variance	100 (F)
Direct labour total variance	2,500 (A)

Attention!

- Remember that, if idle time is recorded, the actual hours used in the **efficiency variance** calculation are the **hours worked and not the hours paid for**.

- If there is a **budgeted level of idle time** and the **actual level** is **less** than the budgeted level, the idle time variance will be **favourable**.

- Some organisations might experience **'expected'** or 'normal' **idle time** at less busy periods, perhaps because demand is seasonal or irregular (but they wish to maintain and pay a constant number of workers). In such circumstances, the **standard** labour rate may **include an allowance for the cost of the expected idle time**. Only the impact of unexpected/abnormal idle time would be included in the idle time variance.

Question
Labour variances

Learning outcome: B(ii)

Growler Ltd is planning to make 100,000 units per period of product AA. Each unit of AA should require 2 hours to produce, with labour being paid £11 per hour. Attainable work hours are less than clock hours, so 250,000 hours have been budgeted in the period.

Actual data for the period was:

Units produced	120,000
Direct labour cost	£3,200,000
Clock hours	280,000

Required

Calculate the following variances.

(a)   Labour rate variance
(b)   Labour efficiency variance
(c)   Idle time variance

Answer

The information means that clock hours have to be multiplied by 200,000/250,000 (80%) in order to arrive at a realistic efficiency variance.

(a)   **Labour rate variance**

	£'000
280,000 hours should have cost (× £11)	3,080
but did cost	3,200
Labour rate variance	120 (A)

(b)   **Labour efficiency variance**

120,000 units should have taken (× 2 hours)	240,000 hrs
but did take (280,000 × 80%)	224,000 hrs
Variance in hours	16,000 hrs (F)
× standard rate per hour	× £11
Labour efficiency variance	£176,000

(c)   **Idle time variance**

280,000 × 20%	56,000 hrs
	× £11
	£616,000 (A)

Question   Idle time and efficiency variances

Learning outcome: B(ii)

There is seasonal demand for CH Ltd's product N. Average idle time during control period 11 is expected to be 10% of hours paid. An allowance for this idle time is included in the standard labour rate, which is €15.30 before the allowance. Standard (productive) time per unit is six labour hours.

During control period 11, 1,800 units of N were manufactured, 13,500 hours were paid for and 12,420 hours actually worked.

What are the idle time and labour efficiency variances?

	Idle time	*Labour efficiency*
A	€ 4,590 (F)	€ 27,540 (A)
B	€ 4,590 (A)	€ 27,540 (F)
C	€ 4,131 (A)	€ 24,786 (A)
D	€ 4,131 (F)	€ 24,786 (F)

Answer

The correct answer is A.

The basic standard rate per hour must be increased to allow for idle time.

Revised standard hourly rate = € 15.30/0.9 = € 17

Variances are now calculated at this revised rate.

Idle time should have been (10% × 13,500 hours paid)	1,350	hrs
but was (13,500 − 12,420)	1,080	hrs
	270	hrs (F)
× standard rate per hour worked	× € 17	
Idle time variance	£4,590	(F)
1,800 units should have taken (× 6 hrs)	10,800	hrs
but did take	12,420	hrs
	1,620	hrs (A)
× standard rate per hour worked	× €17	
Efficiency variance	€ 27,540	(A)

Options C and D have been evaluated at the original standard rate of €15.30.

4 Variable overhead variances

FAST FORWARD

Price (material), **rate** (labour) **and expenditure** (variable overhead) **variances** measure the difference between the actual amount of money paid and the amount of money that should have been paid for the actual quantity of materials or the actual number of hours of labour or variable overheads.

FAST FORWARD

Usage (material) and **efficiency** (labour and variable overhead) **variances** are quantity variances. They measure the difference between the actual physical quantity of materials used or hours taken and the quantities that should have been used or taken for the actual volume of production. These physical differences are then converted into money values by applying the appropriate standard price or rate.

Suppose that the variable production overhead cost of product X is as follows.

2 hours at £1.50 = £3 per unit

During period 6, 400 units of product X were made. The labour force worked 820 hours, of which 60 hours were recorded as idle time. The variable overhead cost was £1,230.

Calculate the following variances.

    (a)   The variable overhead total variance
    (b)   The variable overhead expenditure variance
    (c)   The variable overhead efficiency variance

Since this example **relates to variable production costs**, the total variance is **based on actual units of production**. (If the overhead had been a **variable selling cost**, the variance would be **based on sales volumes**.)

	£
400 units of product X should cost (× £3)	1,200
but did cost	1,230
Variable production overhead total variance	30 (A)

In many variance reporting systems, the variance analysis goes no further, and expenditure and efficiency variances are not calculated. However, the adverse variance of £30 may be explained as the **sum of two factors**.

(a) The hourly rate of spending on variable overheads was higher than it should have been, that is there is an **expenditure variance**.

(b) The labour force worked inefficiently, and took longer to make the output than it should have done. This means that spending on variable overhead was higher than it should have been, in other words there is an **efficiency (productivity) variance**. The variable overhead efficiency variance is exactly the same, in hours, as the direct labour efficiency variance, and occurs for the same reasons.

It is usually assumed that **variable overheads are incurred during active working hours**, but are not incurred during idle time (for example the machines are not running, therefore power is not being consumed, and no indirect materials are being used). This means in our example that although the labour force was paid for 820 hours, they were actively working for only 760 of those hours and so variable overhead spending occurred during 760 hours.

(a) **The variable overhead expenditure variance**

This is the **difference between the amount of variable overhead that should have been incurred in the actual hours actively worked, and the actual amount of variable overhead incurred**.

	£
760 hours of variable overhead should cost (× £1.50)	1,140
but did cost	1,230
Variable overhead expenditure variance	90 (A)

(b) **The variable overhead efficiency variance**

If you already know the direct **labour efficiency variance**, the variable overhead efficiency variance is **exactly the same in hours**, but **priced at the variable overhead rate per hour**. In our example, the efficiency variance would be as follows.

400 units of product X should take (× 2 hrs)	800 hrs
but did take (active hours)	760 hrs
Variable overhead efficiency variance in hours	40 hrs (F)
× standard rate per hour	× £1.50
Variable overhead efficiency variance in £	£60 (F)

(c) **Summary**

	£
Variable overhead expenditure variance	90 (A)
Variable overhead efficiency variance	60 (F)
Variable overhead total variance	30 (A)

5 Fixed overhead variances

Attention!

Fixed overhead variances are the same as material and labour variances in that they **measure the difference between what the output should have cost and what it did cost**. There is a fundamental difference underlying their calculation, however.

Fixed costs do not vary with changes in output (provided output remains within the relevant range). This is a statement of fact since it describes the way in which fixed costs behave. The **budgeted or planned level of fixed costs should therefore be the same whatever the level of output**. So if an organisation budgets fixed costs to be £5,000 for budgeted output of 100 units, the expected fixed costs if actual output is 120 units should still be £5,000.

Contrast this with standard material and labour costs, which vary according to the actual level of output (because they are variable costs).

In this sense there is no equivalent to a usage or efficiency variance when dealing with fixed overheads.

5.1 Fixed overhead variances and marginal costing

FAST FORWARD

The only fixed overhead variance which occurs in a marginal costing system is the fixed overhead expenditure variance.

If the **actual fixed cost differs** from the **planned fixed cost**, the only reason can be that **expenditure** was **higher or lower than planned**.

The **fixed overhead expenditure variance** is therefore the **difference between planned expenditure and actual expenditure**. This is the only fixed overhead variance which occurs if marginal costing is being used.

5.2 Fixed overhead variances and absorption costing

FAST FORWARD

In an absorption costing system, the fixed overhead total variance is the sum of the fixed overhead expenditure variance and the fixed overhead volume variance.

The calculation of fixed overhead variances is slightly more complicated when absorption costing is used.

The fixed overhead total variance in an absorption costing system may be broken down into two parts as usual.

- An **expenditure variance**
- A **volume variance**

In an absorption costing system, **fixed overhead variances** are an attempt to **explain** the **reasons for any under- or over-absorbed overhead.**

Remember that the absorption rate is calculated as budgeted fixed overhead ÷ budgeted level of activity.

Generally the level of activity used in the overhead absorption rate will be units of production or hours of activity. More often than not, if just one product is being produced, the level of activity is in terms of units produced.

You should remember from your earlier studies that if either the budgeted overhead expenditure or the budgeted activity level or both are incorrect then we will have under- or over-absorbed overhead.

5.3 Expenditure variance

The fixed overhead **expenditure variance** measures the under or over absorption caused by the **actual overhead expenditure being different from budget**.

5.4 Volume variance

The fixed overhead **volume variance** measures the under or over absorption caused by the **actual production level being different to the budgeted production level** used in calculating the absorption rate.

Attention!

The **volume variance applies to fixed overhead costs only** and not to variable overheads.

(a)   Variable overheads incurred change with the volume of activity. If the budget is to work for 300 hours and variable overheads are incurred and absorbed at a rate of £6 per hour, the variable overhead budget will be £1,800. If only 200 hours are actually worked, the variable overhead absorbed will be £1,200 and the expected expenditure will also be £1,200, so that there will be no under or over absorption of overhead because of volume changes.

(b)   Fixed overheads are different because the level of expenditure does not change as the number of hours worked varies. If the budget is to work for 300 hours and fixed overheads are budgeted to be £2,400, the fixed overhead absorption rate will be £8 per hour. If actual hours worked are only 200 hours, the fixed overhead absorbed will be £1,600, but expected expenditure will be unchanged at £2,400. There is an under absorption of £800 because of the volume variance of 100 hours shortfall multiplied by the absorption rate of £8 per hour.

5.5 How to calculate the variances

Key terms

- **Fixed overhead total variance** is the difference between fixed overhead incurred and fixed overhead absorbed (the under- or over-absorbed fixed overhead).

- **Fixed overhead expenditure variance** is the difference between the overhead that should have been incurred and that which was incurred. It is calculated as the difference between the budgeted fixed overhead expenditure and actual fixed overhead expenditure.

- **Fixed overhead volume variance** is a measure of the over or under absorption of fixed overhead costs caused by actual production volume differing from that budgeted. It is calculated as the difference between actual and budgeted production/volume multiplied by the standard absorption rate per *unit*.

You should now be ready to work through an example to demonstrate all of the fixed overhead variances.

5.6 Example: fixed overhead variances

Suppose that a company budgets to produce 1,000 units of product E during August. The expected time to produce a unit of E is five hours, and the budgeted fixed overhead is £20,000. The standard fixed overhead cost per unit of product E will therefore be 5 hours at £4 per hour (= £20 per unit). Actual fixed overhead expenditure in August turns out to be £20,450. The labour force manages to produce 1,100 units of product E in 5,400 hours of work.

Required

Calculate the fixed overhead total variance and its sub-variances.

Solution

(a)   **Fixed overhead total variance**

	£
Fixed overhead incurred	20,450
Fixed overhead absorbed (1,100 units × £20 per unit)	22,000
Fixed overhead total variance (= under-/over-absorbed overhead)	1,550 (F)

The variance is favourable because more overheads were absorbed than budgeted.

(b)   **Fixed overhead expenditure variance**

	£
Budgeted fixed overhead expenditure	20,000
Actual fixed overhead expenditure	20,450
Fixed overhead expenditure variance	450 (A)

The variance is adverse because expenditure was greater than budgeted.

(c)   **Fixed overhead volume variance**

The production volume achieved was greater than expected. The fixed overhead volume variance measures the difference at the standard rate.

	£
Actual production at standard rate (1,100 × £20 per unit)	22,000
Budgeted production at standard rate (1,000 × £20 per unit)	20,000
Fixed overhead volume variance	2,000 (F)

The variance is favourable because output was greater than expected.

Question

Fixed overhead variances

Learning outcome: B(ii)

In an absorption costing system the fixed overhead total variance can be analysed into the fixed overhead expenditure variance and the fixed overhead volume variance.
Explain briefly the meaning of each of these three variances in an absorption costing system.

Answer

The fixed overhead total variance in an absorption costing system **evaluates the amount of under- or over-absorbed fixed production overhead for the period**. If the overhead is over-absorbed then the fixed overhead total variance will be favourable. If the overhead is under-absorbed then the variance will be adverse.

The other two variances sum to the fixed overhead total variance and they attempt to evaluate the reason why the fixed production overhead was under or over absorbed.

The expenditure variance is the under or over absorption caused by the expenditure on overheads being different from that budgeted. The variance is calculated as the difference between the budgeted expenditure for the period and the actual expenditure. If the actual expenditure exceeds the budgeted expenditure then this potentially leads to under absorption and the variance is adverse. If the actual expenditure is lower than budgeted then over absorption could result and the variance is favourable.

The volume variance is the under or over absorption caused by the volume of activity being different from that budgeted. The variance is calculated as the difference between budgeted and actual activity, multiplied by the standard overhead absorption rate per unit of activity. If the actual activity is lower than budgeted then this could lead to under absorption and the variance is adverse. If the actual activity is higher than budgeted the potential over absorption means that the variance is favourable.

Question — Variance calculations

Learning outcome: B(ii)

Brian produces and sells one product only, the Blob, the standard cost for one unit being as follows.

	£
Direct material A - 10 kilograms at £20 per kg	200
Direct wages - 5 hours at £6 per hour	30
Fixed overhead	50
Total standard cost	280

The fixed overhead included in the standard cost is based on an expected monthly output of 900 units.

During April the actual results were as follows.

Production	800 units
Material A	7,800 kg used, costing £159,900
Direct wages	4,200 hours worked for £24,150
Fixed overhead	£47,000

Required

(a) Calculate material price and usage variances.
(b) Calculate labour rate and efficiency variances.
(c) Calculate fixed overhead expenditure and volume variances. (20 marks)

Answer

(a) **Material price variance**

	£
7,800 kgs should have cost (× £20)	156,000
but did cost	159,900
Price variance	3,900 (A)

Material usage variance

800 units should have used (× 10 kgs)	8,000 kgs
but did use	7,800 kgs
Usage variance in kgs	200 kgs (F)
× standard cost per kilogram	× £20
Usage variance in £	£4,000 (F)

(b)   **Labour rate variance**

	£
4,200 hours should have cost (× £6)	25,200
but did cost	24,150
Rate variance	1,050 (F)

Labour efficiency variance

800 units should have taken (× 5 hrs)	4,000 hrs
but did take	4,200 hrs
Efficiency variance in hours	200 hrs (A)
× standard rate per hour	× £6
Labour efficiency variance in £	£1,200 (A)

(c)   **Fixed overhead expenditure variance**

	£
Budgeted expenditure (£50 × 900)	45,000
Actual expenditure	47,000
Expenditure variance	2,000 (A)

Fixed overhead volume variance

	£
Budgeted production at standard rate (900 × £50)	45,000
Actual production at standard rate (800 × £50)	40,000
Volume variance	5,000 (A)

Exam focus point

Fixed overhead variances were the topic of MCQ questions in all sittings of the old Paper 8 exam. They are also included in the Pilot Paper for the new syllabus.

6 Sales variances

FAST FORWARD

The **selling** (or **sales**) **price variance** is the difference between what revenue should have been for the quantity sold and the actual revenue.

6.1 Selling price or sales price variance

Key term

The **sales price variance** is 'The change in revenue caused by the actual selling price differing from that budgeted'.   (CIMA *Official Terminology*)

The variance is calculated as the difference between what the sales revenue should have been for the actual quantity sold, and what it was.

Suppose that the standard selling price of product X is £15. Actual sales in year 3 were 2,000 units at £15.30 per unit. The selling price variance is calculated as follows.

	£
Sales revenue from 2,000 units should have been (× £15)	30,000
but was (× £15.30)	30,600
Selling price variance	600 (F)

The variance is favourable because the price was higher than expected.

6.2 Sales volume variance

FAST FORWARD

The sales volume variance in units is the difference between the actual units sold and the budgeted quantity. This variance in units can be valued in one of three ways: in terms of standard revenue, standard gross margin or standard contribution margin.

The sales volume variance in units is calculated as the difference between the actual units sold and the budgeted quantity. This variance in units can be valued in one of three ways.

(a) At the **standard gross profit margin per unit**. This is the **sales volume profit variance** and it measures the change in profit (in an absorption costing system) caused by the sales volume differing from budget.

(b) At the **standard contribution per unit**. This is the **sales volume contribution variance** and it measures the change in profit (in a marginal costing system) caused by the sales volume differing from budget.

(c) At the **standard revenue per unit**. This is the **sales volume revenue variance** and it measures the change in sales revenue caused by sales volume differing from that budgeted.

Suppose that a company budgets to sell 8,000 units of product J for $12 per unit. The standard variable cost per unit is $4 and the standard full cost is $7 per unit. Actual sales were 7,700 units, at $12.50 per unit.

The sales volume variance in units is 300 units adverse (8,000 units budgeted – 7,700 units sold). The variance is adverse because actual sales volume was less than budgeted. The sales volume variance in units can be evaluated in the three ways described above.

(a) Sales volume profit variance = 300 units × standard gross profit margin per unit
= 300 units × $(12 – 7)
= $1,500 (A)

(b) Sales volume contribution variance = 300 units × standard contribution per unit
= 300 units × $(12 – 4)
= $2,400 (A)

(c) Sales volume revenue variance = 300 units × standard revenue per unit
= 300 units × $12
= $3,600 (A)

Note that the sales volume profit variance (in an absorption costing system) and the sales volume contribution variance (in a marginal costing system) can be derived from the sales volume revenue variance, if the profit mark-up percentage and the contribution to sales (C/S) ratio respectively are known.

In our example the profit mark-up percentage is 41.67% ($5/$12) and the C/S ratio is 66.67% ($8/$12).

Therefore the sales volume profit variance and the sales volume contribution variance, derived from the sales volume revenue variance, are as follows.

Sales volume profit variance = $3,600 (A) × 41.67% = $1,500 (A), as above
Sales volume contribution variance = $3,600 (A) × 66.67% = $2,400 (A), as above

Question | Sales **variance**

Learning outcome: B (ii)

Jasper has the following budget and actual figures for year 4.

	Budget	Actual
Sales units	600	620
Selling price per unit	€30	€ 29

Standard full cost of production = €28 per unit. Standard variable cost of production = €19 per unit

Calculate the following sales variances

(a)   Selling price variance
(b)   Sales volume profit variance
(c)   Sales volume contribution variance
(d)   Sales volume revenue variance

Answer

(a)
	£
Sales revenue for 620 units should have been (× £30)	18,600
but was (× £29)	17,980
Selling price variance	620 (A)

(b)
Budgeted sales volume	600 units
Actual sales volume	620 units
Sales volume variance in units	20 units (F)

Sales volume profit variance = 20 units × €(30 – 28) = €40 (F)

(c)   Sales volume contribution variance = 20 units × €(30 – 19) = €220(F)

(d)   Sales volume revenue variance = 20 units × €30 = €600(F)

In this question you were asked to calculate both the sales volume profit variance and the sales volume contribution variance to give you some practice. However the two variances would never be found together in the same system in a real situation. Either a marginal costing system is used, in which case the sale volume contribution variance is calculated, or an absorption costing system is used, in which case a sales volume profit variance is calculated.

6.3 The significance of sales variances

The possible **interdependence** between sales price and sales volume variances should be obvious to you. A reduction in the sales price might stimulate bigger sales demand, so that an adverse sales price variance might be counterbalanced by a favourable sales volume variance. Similarly, a price rise would give a favourable price variance, but possibly at the cost of a fall in demand and an adverse sales volume variance.

It is therefore important in analysing an unfavourable sales variance that the overall consequence should be considered, that is, has there been a counterbalancing favourable variance as a direct result of the unfavourable one?

Question	Sales variances for professional services

Learning outcome: B(ii)

A management consultancy has an IT division which operates a standard absorption costing system. Details from the latest period are as follows.

Standard charge per hour of client services	£180
Standard absorption cost per hour of client service provided	£110
Budgeted hours to be charged to clients per period	780
Actual hours charged to clients during period	730
Actual amount billed to clients during period	£139,800

Calculate the following variances for the period.

(a)   The selling price variance

(b)   The sales volume profit variance

(a)

	£
Sales revenue for 730 hours should have been (x £180)	131,400
but was	139,800
Selling price variance	8,400 (F)

(b)

Budgeted sales volume	780 hours
Actual sales volume	730 hours
Sales volume variance in units	50 hours
× standard profit per unit (£(180 − 110))	× £70
Sales volume profit variance	£3,500 (A)

7 Non-production cost variances

Most **non-production cost variances** can be monitored and controlled using simple expenditure variances.

Non-production costs, such as administration and selling/distribution costs, must **also** be **monitored** and **controlled**.

Some selling/distribution costs may **vary with units sold**, and variances for such costs can be calculated in much the **same way as variable production overhead variances**.

Simple **expenditure variances** may be all that is required for monitoring and controlling **most non-production costs**, however, such as administration.

Chapter Roundup

- The process by which the total difference between standard and actual results is analysed is known as variance analysis.

- The direct material total variance is the sum of the direct material price variance and the direct material usage variance.

- The direct labour total variance is the sum of the direct labour rate variance and the direct labour efficiency variance.

- The **idle time variance** is the number of hours of idle time valued at the standard rate per hour.

- **Price** (material), **rate** (labour) **and expenditure** (variable overhead) **variances** measure the difference between the actual amount of money paid and the amount of money that should have been paid for the actual quantity of materials or the actual number of hours of labour or variable overheads.

- **Usage** (material) and **efficiency** (labour and variable overhead) **variances** are quantity variances. They measure the difference between the actual physical quantity of materials used or hours taken and the quantities that should have been used or taken for the actual volume of production. These physical differences are then converted into money values by applying the appropriate standard price or rate.

- The only fixed overhead variance which occurs in a marginal costing system is the fixed overhead expenditure variance.

- In an absorption costing system, the fixed overhead total variance is the sum of the fixed overhead expenditure variance and the fixed overhead volume variance.

- The **selling** (or **sales**) **price variance** is the difference between what revenue should have been for the quantity sold and the actual revenue.

- The sales volume variance in units is the difference between the actual units sold and the budgeted quantity. This variance in units can be valued in one of three ways: in terms of standard revenue, standard gross margin or standard contribution margin.

- Most **non-production cost variances** can be monitored and controlled using simple expenditure variances.

Quick Quiz

1   An adverse variance occurs when actual results are the same as expected results. *True or false?*

2   *Choose the appropriate words from those highlighted.*

   If material price variances are extracted **at the time of receipt/as the material is used**, they will be brought to the attention of managers earlier than if they are extracted **at the time of receipt/as the material is used**.

   And if variances are extracted **at the time of receipt/as material is used**, all inventories will be valued at **standard price/actual price**, which is administratively easier.

3   Idle time is a favourable efficiency variance. *True or false?*

4   *Match up the variances and the methods of calculation.*

   Variances

   Variable overhead total variance
   Variable overhead expenditure variance
   Variable overhead efficiency variance

Methods of calculation

(a)   The difference between the amount of variable overhead that should have been incurred in the actual hours worked, and the actual amount of variable overhead incurred.

(b)   The labour efficiency variance in hours valued at the standard variable overhead rate per hour.

(c)   The difference between budgeted variable overhead expenditure and actual overhead expenditure.

(d)   The difference between what actual production should have cost in terms of variable overhead, and what it did cost.

(e)   The difference between the labour hours that should have been worked for the actual level of output, and the labour hours actually paid, valued at the standard variable overhead rate per hour.

5   Which of the following statements about the fixed production overhead volume variance is true?

A   It is the same in a standard marginal costing system as in a standard absorption costing system.
B   It does not exist in a standard absorption costing system.
C   It does not exist in a standard marginal costing system.
D   It is the difference between budgeted overhead expenditure and actual overhead expenditure.

6   *Fill in the blank.*

Sales volume profit variance = (actual sales volume – budgeted sales volume) × ....

7   Which of the following is not a suitable basis for valuing the sales volume variance?

A   Selling price
B   Contribution
C   Absorption rate
D   Profit

Answers to Quick Quiz

1   False. It occurs when actual results are worse than expected results.

2   at the time of receipt
as the material is used
at the time of receipt
standard price

3   False. It is an adverse efficiency variance.

4   Total variance (d)
Expenditure variance (a)
Efficiency variance (b)

5   C. This variance does not exist in a standard marginal costing system.

6   Standard profit per unit

7   C   All others are specifically mentioned in the syllabus

Now try the question below from the Exam Question Bank

Number	Level	Marks	Time
Q17	Examination	20	36 mins

Further variance analysis

Introduction

Chapter 8 should have **refreshed your memory** on the basics of standard costing and those variances which you should have covered in your earlier studies. It also introduced you to the calculation of sales price and volume variances.

We begin this chapter by looking at how we can reconcile between **budgeted profit** and **actual profit**, using the range of variances we covered in Chapter 8 to draw up an operating statement.

Section 2 considers the impact on variance analysis of using **marginal costing**, which we covered at various points in the last chapter but will consolidate here.

Section 3 is about what we call the '**backwards approach**' to variance analysis. Basically, this means that you are provided with the variances and have to calculate standard and actual data.

The chapter then moves on to more advanced variance analysis and examines mix and yield variances. When a product requires **two or more materials** in its make-up the materials usage variance can be split into a **materials mix variance** and a **materials yield variance**. Likewise, labour efficiency variances can be split into a **labour mix variance** and a **labour yield variance**. Don't be put off by these new terms. The **basic principle of variance calculation** covered in the previous chapter **still applies**: an actual result is compared with an original standard result.

The chapter concludes with a demonstration of the integration of standard costing with process costing.

Topic list	Learning outcomes	Syllabus references	Ability required
1 Operating statements	A(v), B(iii)	B 2,3,6	Application/analysis
2 Variances in a standard marginal costing system	A(v), B(iii)	B 2,3,6	Application/analysis
3 Working backwards approach to variance analysis	B(ii)	B 2,3,6	Application/analysis
4 Materials mix and yield variances	B(ii)	B 2	Application/analysis
5 Labour mix and yield variances	B(ii)	B 2	Application/analysis
6 Planning and operational variances	B(iv)	B 4	Application/Comprehension
7 Standard process costing	B(iii)	B 6	Application

1 Operating statements

An **operating statement/statement of variances** is a report, usually to senior management, at the end of a control period, reconciling budgeted profit for the period to actual profit.

So far, we have considered how variances are calculated without considering how they combine to **reconcile the difference between budgeted profit and actual profit** during a period. This reconciliation is usually presented as a report to senior management at the end of each control period. The report is called an operating statement or statement of variances.

Key term

The CIMA *Official Terminology* definition of an **operating statement** is 'A regular report for management of actual costs and revenues, as appropriate. Usually compares actual with budget and shows variances'.

An extensive example will now be introduced, both to revise the variance calculations from Chapter 8, and also to show how to combine them into an operating statement.

1.1 Example: variances and operating statements

Sydney manufactures one product, and the entire product is sold as soon as it is produced. There are no opening or closing inventories and work in progress is negligible. The company operates a standard absorption costing system and analysis of variances is made every month. The standard cost card for the product, a boomerang, is as follows.

STANDARD COST CARD - BOOMERANG

		£
Direct materials	0.5 kilos at £4 per kilo	2.00
Direct wages	2 hours at £2.00 per hour	4.00
Variable overheads	2 hours at £0.30 per hour	0.60
Fixed overhead	2 hours at £3.70 per hour	7.40
Standard cost		14.00
Standard profit		6.00
Standing selling price		20.00

Selling and administration expenses are not included in the standard cost, and are deducted from profit as a period charge.

Budgeted output for the month of June year 7 was 5,100 units. Actual results for June year 7 were as follows.

Production of 4,850 units was sold for £95,600.
Materials consumed in production amounted to 2,300 kgs at a total cost of £9,800.
Labour hours paid for amounted to 8,500 hours at a cost of £16,800.
Actual operating hours amounted to 8,000 hours.
Variable overheads amounted to £2,600.
Fixed overheads amounted to £42,300.
Selling and administration expenses amounted to £18,000.

Required

Calculate all variances and prepare an operating statement for the month ended 30 June year 7.

Solution

		£
(a)	2,300 kg of material should cost(× £4)	9,200
	but did cost	9,800
	Material price variance	600 (A)

(b)	4,850 boomerangs should use (× 0.5 kgs)	2,425 kg
	but did use	2,300 kg
	Material usage variance in kgs	125 kg (F)
	× standard cost per kg	× £4
	Material usage variance in £	£ 500 (F)

		£
(c)	8,500 hours of labour should cost (× £2)	17,000
	but did cost	16,800
	Labour rate variance	200 (F)

(d)	4,850 boomerangs should take (× 2 hrs)	9,700 hrs
	but did take (active hours)	8,000 hrs
	Labour efficiency variance in hours	1,700 hrs (F)
	× standard cost per hour	× £2
	Labour efficiency variance in £	£3,400 (F)

(e)	Idle time variance 500 hours (A) × £2	£1,000 (A)

		£
(f)	8,000 hours incurring variable o/hd expenditure should cost (× £0.30)	2,400
	but did cost	2,600
	Variable overhead expenditure variance	200 (A)

(g) Variable overhead efficiency variance in hours is the same as the labour efficiency variance:

1,700 hours (F) × £0.30 per hour	£510 (F)

		£
(h)	Budgeted fixed overhead (5,100 units × 2 hrs × £3.70)	37,740
	Actual fixed overhead	42,300
	Fixed overhead expenditure variance	4,560 (A)

		£
(i)	Actual production at standard rate (4,850 units × £7.40)	35,890
	Budgeted production at standard rate (5,100 units × £7.40)	37,740
	Fixed overhead volume variance	1,850 (A)

(j)	Revenue from 4,850 boomerangs should be (× £20)	97,000
	but was	95,600
	Selling price variance	1,400 (A)

(k) In order to reconcile the budget and actual profit the sales volume variance in units must be valued at the standard profit per unit.

Budgeted sales volume	5,100 units
Actual sales volume	4,850 units
Sales volume variance in units	250 units
× standard profit per unit	× £6 (A)
Sales volume profit variance in £	£1,500 (A)

There are several ways in which an operating statement may be presented. Perhaps the most common format is one which reconciles budgeted profit to actual profit. In this example, **sales and administration costs will be introduced at the end of the statement**, so that we shall **begin with 'budgeted profit before sales and administration costs'**.

Sales variances are reported first, and the **total of the budgeted profit and the two sales variances** results in a figure for **'actual sales minus the standard cost of sales'**. The **cost variances** are then reported, and an **actual profit** (before sales and administration costs) calculated. **Sales and administration costs** are then **deducted** to reach the **actual profit**.

SYDNEY - OPERATING STATEMENT JUNE YEAR 7

	£	£
Budgeted profit before sales and administration costs		30,600
Sales volume profit variance		1,500 (A)
Budgeted profit from actual sales		29,100
Selling price variance		1,400 (A)
Actual sales minus the standard cost of sales		27,700

Cost variances	(F)	(A)	
	£	£	
Material price		600	
Material usage	500		
Labour rate	200		
Labour efficiency	3,400		
Labour idle time		1,000	
Variable overhead expenditure		200	
Variable overhead efficiency	510		
Fixed overhead expenditure		4,560	
Fixed overhead volume		1,850	
	4,610	8,210	3,600 (A)
Actual profit before sales and admin costs			24,100
Sales and administration costs			18,000
Actual profit, June year 7			6,100

Check	£	£
Sales		95,600
Materials	9,800	
Labour	16,800	
Variable overhead	2,600	
Fixed overhead	42,300	
Sales and administration	18,000	
		89,500
Actual profit		6,100

2 Variances in a standard marginal costing system

FAST FORWARD

In a **standard marginal costing system**, there will no fixed overhead volume variance and the sales volume variance will be valued at standard contribution margin, not standard profit margin.

2.1 How marginal costing variances differ from absorption costing variances

At various stages in Chapter 8 we looked at the ways in which variances in a marginal costing system differ from those in an absorption costing system. In this section we will summarise these differences and look at how an operating statement would appear in a marginal costing system.

If an organisation uses **standard marginal costing** instead of standard absorption costing, there will be two differences in the way the variances are calculated.

(a)   In marginal costing, fixed costs are not absorbed into product costs and so there are no fixed cost variances to explain any under or over absorption of overheads. There will, therefore, be **no fixed overhead volume variance**. There will be a fixed overhead expenditure variance which is calculated in exactly the same way as for absorption costing systems.

(b)   The **sales volume variance in units** will be valued at **standard contribution margin** (sales price per unit minus variable costs of sale per unit). It will be called the **sales volume contribution variance.**

Key term

The **sales volume contribution variance** is 'The change in contribution caused by sales volume differing from that budgeted'. (CIMA *Official Terminology*)

Question

Impact of costing system on variances

Learning outcome: B (iii)

What is the monetary difference between absorption costing and marginal costing sales volume variances?

A   Variance in units × selling price per unit
B   Variance in units × contribution per unit
C   Variance in units × fixed overhead absorbed per unit
D   Sales volume × fixed overhead absorbed per unit

Answer

The correct answer is C.

2.2 Preparing a marginal costing operating statement

Returning once again to the example of Sydney, the variances in a system of standard marginal costing would be as follows.

(a)   There is **no fixed overhead volume variance**.

(b)   The standard contribution per unit of boomerang is £(20 – 6.60) = £13.40 and so the **sales volume contribution variance** of 250 units (A) is valued at (× £13.40) = £3,350 (A).

The other variances are unchanged. However, this operating statement differs from an absorption costing operating statement in the following ways.

(a)   It **begins with the budgeted contribution** (£30,600 + budgeted fixed production costs £37,740 = £68,340).

(b)   The subtotal before the analysis of cost variances is **actual sales** (£95,600) **less the standard variable cost of sales** (4,850 × £6.60) = £63,590.

(c)   **Actual contribution** is highlighted in the statement.

(d)   Budgeted fixed production overhead is adjusted by the fixed overhead expenditure variance to show the **actual fixed production overhead expenditure**.

Therefore a **marginal costing** operating statement might look like this.

SYDNEY - OPERATING STATEMENT JUNE YEAR 7

	£	£	£
Budgeted contribution			68,340
Sales volume contribution variance			3,350 (A)
Budgeted contribution from actual sales			64,990
Selling price variance			1,400 (A)
Actual sales minus the standard variable cost of sales			63,590

Variable cost variances	(F)	(A)	
	£	£	
Material price		600	
Material usage	500		
Labour rate	200		
Labour efficiency	3,400		
Labour idle time		1,000	
Variable overhead expenditure		200	
Variable overhead efficiency	510		
	4,610	1,800	
			2,810 (F)
Actual contribution			66,400
Budgeted fixed production overhead			37,740
Expenditure variance			4,560 (A)
Actual fixed production overhead			42,300
Actual profit before sales and administration costs			24,100
Sales and administration costs			18,000
Actual profit			6,100

Notice that the actual profit is the same as the profit calculated by standard absorption costing because there were no changes in inventory levels. Absorption costing and marginal costing do not always produce an identical profit figure.

Question   Operating statement

Learning outcome: B(iii)

MilBri, a manufacturing firm, operates a standard marginal costing system. It makes a single product, LI, using a single raw material AN.

Standard costs relating to LI have been calculated as follows.

Standard cost schedule - LI	Per unit
	£
Direct material, AN, 100 kg at £5 per kg	500
Direct labour, 10 hours at £8 per hour	80
Variable production overhead, 10 hours at £2 per hour	20
	600

The standard selling price of a LI is £900 and MilBri produce 1,020 units a month. Budgeted fixed production overheads are £40,000 per month.

During December, 1,000 units of LI were produced and sold. Relevant details of this production are as follows.

Direct material AN

90,000 kgs costing £720,000 were bought and used.

Direct labour

8,200 hours were worked during the month and total wages were £63,000.

Variable production overhead

The actual cost for the month was £25,000.

Fixed production overhead

The actual expenditure for the month was £41,400

Each LI was sold for £975.

Required

Calculate the following for the month of December and present the results in an operating statement which reconciles the budgeted contribution with the actual gross profit for the month.

(a)   Variable production cost variance
(b)   Direct labour cost variance, analysed into rate and efficiency variances
(c)   Direct material cost variance, analysed into price and usage variances
(d)   Variable production overhead variance, analysed into expenditure and efficiency variances
(e)   Selling price variance
(f)   Sales volume contribution variance
(g)   Fixed production overhead expenditure variance   (20 marks)

Answer

(a)   This is simply a **'total' variance**.

	£
1,000 units should have cost (× £600)	600,000
but did cost (see working)	808,000
Variable production cost variance	208,000 (A)

(b)   **Direct labour cost variances**

	£
8,200 hours should cost (× £8)	65,600
but did cost	63,000
Direct labour rate variance	2,600 (F)

1,000 units should take (× 10 hours)	10,000 hrs
but did take	8,200 hrs
Direct labour efficiency variance in hrs	1,800 hrs (F)
× standard rate per hour	× £8
Direct labour efficiency variance in £	£14,400 (F)

Summary

	£
Rate	2,600 (F)
Efficiency	14,400 (F)
Total	17,000 (F)

(c)   **Direct material cost variances**

	£
90,000 kg should cost (× £5)	450,000
but did cost	720,000
Direct material price variance	270,000 (A)
1,000 units should use (× 100 kg)	100,000 kg
but did use	90,000 kg
Direct material usage variance in kgs	10,000 kg (F)
× standard cost per kg	× £5
Direct material usage variance in £	£50,000 (F)

Summary

	£
Price	270,000 (A)
Usage	50,000 (F)
Total	220,000 (A)

(d)   **Variable production overhead variances**

	£
8,200 hours incurring o/hd should cost (× £2)	16,400
but did cost	25,000
Variable production overhead expenditure variance	8,600 (A)
Efficiency variance in hrs (from (b))	1,800 hrs (F)
× standard rate per hour	× £2
Variable production overhead efficiency variance	£3,600 (F)

Summary

	£
Expenditure	8,600 (A)
Efficiency	3,600 (F)
Total	5,000 (A)

(e)   **Selling price variance**

	£
Revenue from 1,000 units should have been (× £900)	900,000
but was (× £975)	975,000
Selling price variance	75,000 (F)

(f)   **Sales volume contribution variance**

Budgeted sales	1,020 units
Actual sales	1,000 units
Sales volume variance in units	20 units (A)
× standard contribution margin (£(900 − 600))	× £300
Sales volume contribution variance in £	£6,000 (A)

(g)   **Fixed production overhead expenditure variance**

	£
Budgeted expenditure	40,000
Actual expenditure	41,400
Fixed production overhead expenditure variance	1,400 (A)

Workings

	£
Direct material	720,000
Total wages	63,000
Variable production overhead	25,000
	808,000

MilBri – OPERATING STATEMENT FOR DECEMBER

	£	£	£
Budgeted contribution (1,020 × £(900 – 600)			306,000
Sales volume contribution variance			6,000 (A)
Budgeted contribution from actual sales			300,000
Selling price variance			75,000 (F)
Actual sales minus the standard variable cost of sales			375,000

Variable cost variances	(F)	(A)	
Material price		270,000	
Material usage	50,000		
Labour rate	2,600		
Labour efficiency	14,400		
Variable overhead expenditure		8,600	
Variable overhead efficiency	3,600		
	70,600	278,600	208,000 (A)
Actual contribution			167,000
Budgeted fixed production overhead		40,000	
Expenditure variance		1,400 (A)	
Actual fixed production overhead			41,400
Actual gross profit			125,600

Check on actual gross profit:

	£	£
Sales revenue (£975 × 1,000)		975,000
Material cost	720,000	
Labour cost	63,000	
Variable production overhead cost	25,000	
Fixed production overhead cost	41,400	
Actual gross profit		849,400
		125,600

2.3 The inventory adjustment

If **actual sales and production volumes** are **different**, these will be a **closing inventory** value in the actual profit calculation. If these inventories are **valued at actual cost** rather than standard cost, an **inventory adjustment** must be made in **the operating statement**.

Inventory adjustment = difference between inventory at standard cost and inventory at actual cost, where inventory at actual cost = ((units in closing inventory ÷ production volume) × total of actual production costs)

This **difference** is simply **added to the bottom of the operating statement**.

	£	£
Actual profit, with inventory at standard cost		X
Inventory adjustment		
inventory at standard cost	X	
inventory at actual cost	X	
		X
Actual profit, with inventory at actual cost		X

3 Working backwards approach to variance analysis

Exam focus point

Examination questions usually provide you with data about actual results and you have to calculate variances. One way in which your understanding of the topic can be tested, however, is to provide information about variances from which you have to 'work backwards' to determine the actual results. This section should equip you to deal with such questions, which can appear in the objective testing section or as longer questions in the remainder of the paper.

3.1 Example: working backwards

The standard cost card for the trough, one of the products made by Pig, is as follows.

	£
Direct material 16 kgs × £6 per kg	96
Direct labour 6 hours × £12 per hour	72
Fixed production overhead 6 hours × £14 per hour	84
	252

Pig reported the following variances in control period 13 in relation to the trough.

Direct material price: £18,840 favourable
Direct material usage: £480 adverse
Direct labour rate: £10,598 adverse
Direct labour efficiency: £8,478 favourable
Fixed production overhead expenditure: £14,192 adverse
Fixed production overhead volume: £11,592 favourable

Actual fixed production overhead cost £200,000 and direct wages, £171,320. Pig paid £5.50 for each kg of direct material. There was no opening or closing inventories of the material.

Required

Calculate the following.

(a)   Budgeted output
(b)   Actual output
(c)   Actual hours worked
(d)   Average actual wage rate per hour
(e)   Actual number of kilograms purchased and used

Solution

(a) Let budgeted output = q

Fixed production overhead expenditure variance = budgeted overhead − actual overhead

$$= £(84q - 200,000) = £14,192 \text{ (A)}$$

$$\therefore 84q - 200,000 = -14,192$$
$$84q = -14,192 + 200,000$$
$$q = 185,808 \div 84$$
$$\therefore \quad q = 2,212 \text{ units}$$

(b)

	£
Total direct wages cost	171,320
Adjust for variances:	
labour rate	(10,598)
labour efficiency	8,478
Standard direct wages cost	169,200

∴ Actual output = Total standard cost ÷ unit standard cost
= £169,200 ÷ £72
= 2,350 units

(c)

	£
Total direct wages cost	171,320.0
Less rate variance	(10,598.0)
Standard rate for actual hours	160,722.0
÷ standard rate per hour	÷ £12.0
Actual hours worked	13,393.5 hrs

(d) Average actual wage rate per hour = actual wages/actual hours = £171,320/13,393.5 = £12.79 per hour.

(e) Number of kgs purchased and used = x

	£
x kgs should have cost (× £6)	6.0x
but did cost (× £5.50)	5.5x
Direct material price variance	0.5x

∴ £0.5x = £18,840
∴ x = 37,680 kgs

Question   Working backwards

Learning outcome: B (ii)

The standard material content of one unit of product A is 10kgs of material X which should cost £10 per kilogram. In June, 5,750 units of product A were produced and there was an adverse material usage variance of £1,500.

The quantity of material X used in June was

A   56,000 kg
B   57,350 kg
C   57,650 kg
D   59,000 kg

Answer

The correct answer is C.

Let the quantity of material X used = Y

5750 units should have used (× 10kgs)	57,500 kgs
but did use	Y kgs
Usage variance in kgs	(Y – 57,500) kgs
× standard price per kg	× £10
Usage variance in £	£1,500 (A)

$\therefore$ 10(Y – 57,500) = 1,500

Y – 57,500   = 150

$\therefore$ Y   = 57,650 kgs

4 Materials mix and yield variances

FAST FORWARD

When two or more types of material are mixed together to produce a product it is possible to carry out further analysis on the usage variance. The **mix variance** explains how much of the usage variance was caused by a change in the relative proportions of the materials used. The **yield variance** shows how much of the usage variance was caused by using more or less material than the standard allowance.

When a product requires **two or more raw materials** in its make-up, it is often possible to **sub-analyse the materials usage variance** into **materials mix** and **materials yield variances**.

Adding a greater proportion of one material (therefore a smaller proportion of a different material) might make the materials mix cheaper or more expensive. For example the standard mix of materials for a product might consist of the following.

	£
(2/3) 2 kg of material A at £1.00 per kg	2.00
(1/3) 1 kg of material B at £0.50 per kg	0.50
	2.50

It may be possible to change the mix so that one kilogram of material A is used and two kilograms of material B. The new mix would be cheaper.

	£
(1/3) 1 kg of material A	1
(2/3) 2 kg of material B	1
	2

By changing the proportions in the mix, the efficiency of the combined material usage may change. In our example, in making the proportions of A and B cheaper, at 1:2, the product may now require more than three kilograms of input for its manufacture, and the new materials requirement per unit of product might be 3.6 kilograms.

	£
(1/3) 1.2 kg of material A at £1.00 per kg	1.20
(2/3) 2.4 kg of material B at £0.50 per kg	1.20
	2.40

In establishing a materials usage standard, management may therefore have to balance the cost of a particular mix of materials with the efficiency of the yield of the mix.

Once the standard has been established it may be possible to exercise control over the materials used in production by calculating and reviewing mix and yield variances.

'Where substitutions within the mix of materials input to a process are possible, the **[direct material] mix variance** measures the cost of any variation from the standard mix.'

The **direct material yield variance** 'Measures the effect on cost of any difference between the actual material usage and that justified by the output produced'.

(CIMA *Official Terminology*)

4.1 Calculating the variances

FAST FORWARD

The purpose of a mix variance is to provide management with information to help in controlling the proportion of each item actually used. If it is not possible for managers to exercise control over the actual mix of material then there is little to be gained by calculating mix variances.

The mix variance for each material input is based on the following.

(a)   The change in the material's weighting within the overall mix

(b)   Whether the material's unit standard cost is greater or less than the standard weighted average cost of all material inputs.

A **yield variance** is calculated as the **difference between the standard output from what was actually input**, and the **actual output**, valued at the standard cost per unit of output.

4.2 When to calculate mix and yield variances

Mix and yield variances have no meaning, and should never be calculated, unless they are a guide to control action. They are **only appropriate in the following situations**.

(a)   Where **proportions of materials in a mix are changeable and controllable**. If the materials in a mix are in different units, say kilograms and litres, they are obviously completely different and so cannot be substituted for each other.

(b)   Where the **usage variance of individual materials is of limited value because of the variability of the mix**, and a combined yield variance for all the materials together is more helpful for control

It would be **totally inappropriate** to calculate a mix **variance where the materials in the 'mix' are discrete items**. A chair, for example, might consist of wood, covering material, stuffing and glue. These materials are separate components, and it would not be possible to think in terms of controlling the proportions of each material in the final product. The usage of each material must be controlled separately.

4.3 Example: materials usage, mix and yield variances

A company manufactures a chemical, Dynamite, using two compounds Flash and Bang. The standard materials usage and cost of one unit of Dynamite are as follows.

		£
Flash	5 kg at £2 per kg	10
Bang	10 kg at £3 per kg	30
	15 kg	40

In a particular period, 80 units of Dynamite were produced from 500 kg of Flash and 730 kg of Bang.

Required

Calculate the materials usage, mix and yield variances.

Solution

(a)   **Usage variance**

	Flash	Bang
	Flash	*Bang*
80 units of Dynamite should have used	400 kgs	800 kgs
but did use	500 kgs	730 kgs
Usage variance in kgs	100 kgs (A)	70 kgs (F)
× standard cost per kg	× £2	× £3
Usage variance in £	£200 (A)	£210 (F)
Total usage variance		£10 (F)

The total usage variance can be analysed into mix and yield variances.

(b)   **Mix variance**

Actual input = (500 + 730) kgs = 1,230 kgs

Standard mix of actual input

Flash 1/3 × 1,230 kgs =	410 kgs
Bang 2/3 × 1,230 kgs =	820 kgs
	1,230 kgs

	Flash	*Bang*	*Total*
Input should have been	410 kgs	820 kgs	1,230 kgs
but was	500 kgs	730 kgs	1,230 kgs
Variance in kgs	90 kgs (A)	90 kgs (F)	-
× standard price	× £2	× £3	
Variance in £	£180 (A)	£270 (F)	£90 (F)

The **total difference** or mix variance in **kgs** must **always** be **zero** as the mix variance measures the change in the relative proportions of the actual total input. The variance is calculated by comparing the expected mix of the total actual input with the actual mix of the total actual input: the difference between the two totals is zero.

The favourable total variance is due to the greater use in the mix of the cheaper material, Flash. However, this cheaper mix may have an adverse effect on the yield which is obtained from the mix, as we shall now see.

(c)   **Yield variance**

Each unit of output (Dynamite) requires		
	5 kg of Flash, costing	£10
	10 kg of Bang, costing	£30
	15 kg	£40

1,230 kg should have yielded (÷ 15 kg)	82 units of Dynamite
but did yield	80 units of Dynamite
Yield variance in units	2 units (A)
× standard cost per unit of output	× £40
Yield variance in £	£80 (A)

The **adverse** yield variance is due to the **output from the input being less than standard**.

The mix variance and yield variance together add up to the usage variance, which is favourable, because the adverse yield from the mix did not negate the price savings which were made by using proportionately more of the cheaper material.

Attention!

CIMA recommends two approaches to valuing mix variances. **Either or both may be tested**, because both methods are on your syllabus.

The one above (valuing the individual mix variances in units at the **individual standard prices**) is the easier of the two and so, if given a choice, we recommend that it is the approach you use. The second approach is shown below.

Exam focus point

The answer provided to a mix variance question in the pilot paper used the easier approach described above.

4.4 Mix variances: Alternative approach

This approach uses a **weighted average price** to value the individual mix variances in units.

The standard weighted average price of the input materials is £40/15kg = £2.67 per kg.

	Flash	Bang	Total
Input should have been	410 kgs	820 kgs	1,230 kgs
but was	500 kgs	730 kgs	1,230 kgs
Difference in kgs*	90 kgs more	90 kgs less	-
× difference between w.av. price and std price			
£(2.67 – 2)	× £0.67 less		
£(2.67 – 3)		× £0.33 more	
Variance in £**	£60 (F)	£30(F)	£90 (F)

* Here we calculate a **difference in units** (more or less than standard) rather than a variance.

** **To determine whether a mix variance is (A) or (F) using the weighted average method see below.**

	Variance
Input more than standard of a material **costing more** than average	(A)
Input more than standard of a material **costing less** than average	(F)
Input less than standard of a material **costing more** than average	(F)
Input less than standard of a material **costing less** than average	(A)

In this example:

More Flash than standard was input, and Flash **costs** less than the average price, so the variance is **favourable**.

Less Bang than standard was input, and Bang **costs more** than the average price, so the variance is **favourable**.

![pencil icon] **Question**

Learning outcome: B (ii)

The standard materials cost per unit of product D456 is as follows.

		£
Material X	3 kg at £2.00 per kg	6
Material Y	5 kg at £3.60 per kg	18
	8 kg	24

During period 2, 2,000 kg of material X costing £4,100 and 2,400 kg of material Y costing £9,600 were used to produce 500 units of D456.

Required

Calculate price, mix and yield variances.

Answer

Price variances	£
2,000 kg of X should cost (× £2)	4,000
but did cost	4,100
Material X price variance	100 (A)
2,400 kg of Y should cost (× £3.60)	8,640
but did cost	9,600
Material Y price variance	960 (A)

First approach for mix variances

Total quantity used (2,000 + 2,400) kgs = 4,400 kgs
Standard mix for actual use = $^3/_8$ X (1,650 kgs) + $^5/_8$ Y (2,750 kgs) = 4,400 kgs

	X	Y	Total
Input should have been	1,650 kgs	2,750 kgs	4,400 kgs
but was	2,000 kgs	2,400 kgs	4,400 kgs
Variance in kgs	350 kgs (A)	350 kgs (F)	-
× std price per kg	× £2	× £3.60	
Variances in £	£700 (A)	£1,260 (F)	£560 (F)

Alternative approach for mix variances

The alternative method will produce the same total mix variance, but a different split between the mix variance for each material.

The standard weighted average price of the input materials is £24/8 kg = £3 per kg.

	X	Y	Total
Input should have been	1,650 kgs	2,750 kgs	4,400 kgs
but was	2,000 kgs	2,400 kgs	4,400 kgs
Difference in kgs	350 kgs more	350 kgs less	-
× diff between w.av. price and std price			
£(3 – 2)	× £1 less		
£(3 – 3.60)		× £0.60 more	
	£350 (F)	£210 (F)	£560 (F)

Yield variance

Each unit of D456 requires	3 kg	of X, costing	£6
	5 kg	of Y, costing	£18
	8 kg		£24

4,400 kg should have yielded (÷ 8 kg)	550 units
but did yield	500 units
Yield variance in units	50 units (A)
× standard material cost per unit of output	× £24
Yield variance in £	£1,200 (A)

Question
Limitations of mix and yield variances

Learning outcome B (ii)

Explain briefly the limitations of the calculation of materials mix and yield variances.

Answer

Some limitations of the calculation of material mix and yield variances are as follows.

(a)   A **change in the mix** of materials used will almost certainly have an **impact upon the yield**, but this will not be isolated from other causes of the yield variance, such as substandard materials quality.

(b)   If a **favourable mix variance can be established**, without adverse effects upon yield or output quality, the **standard mix is obsolete**.

(c)   Changes in actual unit costs of some ingredients may make a change in mix economically viable. An attempt **to optimise the price variance** may therefore result in an **adverse mix variance**.

(d)   **Changes to the proportions of the input materials** are **assumed** to have **no impact on product quality.**

Summary

- Both methods are based on individual mix **variances in units** calculated as the **difference between actual input and the standard mix of actual input**.

- The **total mix variance in units** is **zero** using **both methods**.

- The **first method values** the individual mix variances in units at the **individual standard prices**.

- The **second method values** the individual mix variances in units at the **difference between the weighted average price and the standard price**.

- The **total mix variance** in £ is the **same** under both methods.

4.5 Deviations from standardised mix

In an exam question under the previous syllabus, candidates were given the percentage deviations for standardised mix and the data used to calculate those deviations. They then had to calculate deviations for a third month and comment on the usefulness of such analysis for operational control.

The question stated that the deviations were shown in weight and were from the standard mix for the quantity input expressed as a percentage of the standardised weight for each ingredient. This sounds complicated but is actually referring to the individual mix variances in units (think about it!). And because source data for the figures shown was provided, candidates could check their understanding of the method of calculation.

Try the question below, to see whether you could have coped with the exam question.

Question   Deviations from standardised mix

Learning outcome: B (ii)

Standard mix for one litre of product J

0.4 litres of ingredient O
0.2 litres of ingredient H
0.5 litres of ingredient N

Actual usage in control period 2

Ingredient O	420 litres
Ingredient H	180 litres
Ingredient N	550 litres
Actual output	1,000 litres

Calculate the percentage deviation from the standardised mix using the method of calculation described above.

Answer

Quantity input = (420 + 180 + 550) = 1,150 litres

Standard mix for the quantity input

The standardised mix for the quantity input is the calculation we carry out to determine the individual mix variances in units. You can check you have done it correctly by ensuring that the sum of the individual components equals total quantity input.

	Standardised mix for quantity input	Litres
O	$1,150 \times (0.4/1.1) =$	418.18
H	$1,150 \times (0.2/1.1) =$	209.09
N	$1,150 \times (0.5/1.1) =$	522.73
		1,150.00

Deviations – absolute

These are simply the differences between the actual input and the standard input calculated above.

	Actual input	Standard mix for actual input(see above)	Deviation (or difference)
	Litres	Litres	Litres
O	420	418.18	1.82 (A)
H	180	209.09	29.09 (F)
N	550	522.73	27.27 (A)
	1,150	1,150.00	–

Deviations as a %

O (1.82/418.18) × 100% = 0.435%
H (29.09/209.09) × 100% = 13.913%
N (27.27/522.73) × 100% = 5.217%

5 Labour mix and yield variances

If more than one type of labour is used in a product, the labour efficiency variance can be analysed further into a **labour mix (team composition) variance** and a **labour yield (team productivity or output) variance.**

Key terms

'Where substitutions between the grades of labour used to operate a process are possible, the **[direct labour] mix variance** measures the cost of any variation from the standard mix'.

The **direct labour yield variance** 'Measures the effect on cost of any difference between the actual labour hours worked and the hours justified by output produced'.

(CIMA *Official Terminology*)

The labour mix variance is also known as the **team composition variance**, the labour yield variance as the **labour output variance** or **team productivity variance**.

The calculations are the same as those required for materials mix and yield variances.

5.1 Example: labour mix variances

Two grades of labour work together in teams to produce product X. The standard composition of each team is five grade A employees paid at £6 per hour and three grade B employees paid at £4 per hour. Output is measured in standard hours and expected output is 95 standard hours for 100 hours worked in total. During the last period, 2,280 standard hours of output were produced using 1,500 hours of grade A labour (costing £9,750) and 852 hours of grade B labour (costing £2,982).

Required

Calculate all possible labour variances.

Solution

Initial working

Calculation of **standard rate per hour of output**

Labour grade

			£
A	5.00	hours × £6 =	30
B	3.00	hours × £4 =	12
	8.00	hours	42
Less 5%	0.40	hours	
	7.60	hours	

∴ Standard rate per hour of output = £42/7.6 = £5.5263 per standard hour

Direct labour total variance

	£
2,280 standard hours of output should have cost (× £5.5263)	12,600
but did cost	12,732
Direct labour total variance	132 (A)

Direct labour rate variance

		A £		*B* £
Hours worked should have cost	(1,500 × £6)	9,000	(852 × £4)	3,408
but did cost		9,750		2,982
Direct labour rate variance		750 (A)		426 (F)
Total direct labour rate variance			£324 (A)	

Direct labour efficiency variance

		A		*B*
2,280 standard hours of output should take an input of	(2,280 ÷ 0.95 × ⁵/₈)	1,500 hrs	(2,280 ÷ 0.95 × ³/₈)	900 hrs
but did take		1,500 hrs		852 hrs
Efficiency variance in hours		-		48 hrs (F)
× standard rate per hour		× £6		× £4
		-		£192 (F)

The **labour efficiency variance** can be analysed further into the **team composition** variance (the **labour mix** variance) and the **team productivity** variance (the **labour yield** variance).

Team composition (labour mix) variance

Again there are two approaches to valuing the variance.

Approach 1

Total actual hours = 1,500 + 852 = 2,352 hours

Standard mix of actual input

		Hrs
A	5/8 × 2,352 =	1,470
B	3/8 × 2,352 =	882
		2,352

	A	B	Total
Mix should have been	1,470 hrs	882 hrs	2,352 hrs
but was	1,500 hrs	852 hrs	2,352 hrs
Mix variance in hrs	30 hrs (A)	30 hrs (F)	-
× std rate per hour	× £6	× £4	
Mix variance in £	£180 (A)	£120 (F)	£60 (A)

Approach 2

The standard weighted rate per hour of labour is £42/8 = £5.25 per hour.

	A	B	Total
Mix should have been	1,470 hrs	882 hrs	2,352 hrs
but was	1,500 hrs	852 hrs	2,352 hrs
Difference	30 hrs more	30 hrs less	-

× difference between weighted average price and standard price

£(5.25 − 6)	× £0.75 more		
£(5.25 − 4)		× £1.25 less	
Mix variance in £	£22.50 (A)	£37.50 (A)	£60 (A)

Team productivity (labour yield) variance

2,352 hours of work should have produced (× 0.95)	2,234.4 std hrs
but did produce	2,280.0 std hrs
Team productivity variance in hrs	45.6 std hrs (F)
× std rate per std hr	× £5.5263
Team productivity variance in £	£252 (F)

Question Labour mix variances

Learning outcome: B (ii)

A firm has established the following standard composition of a team of its staff performing the year end audit of a medium-sized company.

	Standard hours to perform audit	Rate per hour $	Standard labour cost of audit $
Audit manager	30	450	13,500
Junior auditors	120	170	20,400
Audit clerks	50	50	2,500
	200		36,400

A year end audit has just been completed for company X and the hours recorded in respect of each grade of staff are as follows.

	Actual hours to perform audit
Audit manager	27
Junior auditors	125
Audit clerks	58
	210

Required

Calculate the following labour variances for the company X audit.

(a)   The labour efficiency variance
(b)   The labour yield variance
(c)   the labour mix variance, using the average valuation basis

Answer

(a)   **Labour efficiency variance**

	Audit manager	Junior auditors	Audit clerks	Total $
Audit should take	30 hrs	120 hrs	50 hrs	
but did take	27 hrs	125 hrs	58 hrs	
Efficiency variance in hours	3 hrs (F)	5 hrs (A)	8 hrs (A)	
× standard rate per hour	× $450	× $170	× $50	
	$1,350 (F)	$850 (A)	$400 (A)	$100 (A)

(b)   **Labour yield variance**

Standard weighted average labour rate per hour $= \dfrac{\$36,400}{200}$

$= \$182$

Audit should have taken	200 hrs
but did take	210 hrs
Labour yield variance in hours	10 hours (A)
× standard rate per hour	× $182
Labour yield variance	$1,820 (A)

(c)   **Labour mix variance**

	Audit manager	Junior auditor	Audit clerks	Total
Mix should have been	31.5 hrs	126.0 hrs	52.5 hrs	210.0 hrs
but was	27.0 hrs	125.0 hrs	58.0 hrs	210.0 hrs
Difference	4.5 hrs less	1.0 hr less	5.5 hrs more	–

× difference between weighted average rate and standard rate

$(450 – 182)	× $268 more			
$(170 – 182)		× $12 less		
$(50 – 182)			× $132 less	
Mix variance in $	$1,206 (F)	$12 (A)	$726 (F)	$1,920 (F)

6 Planning and operational variances

To date in your studies, we have been looking at variances which are calculated using what we will call the **conventional approach** to variance analysis, whereby an **actual cost** is **compared** with an **original standard cost**. In this section of the chapter we will be examining **planning** and **operational variances**. They are not really alternatives to the conventional approach, they merely provide a much **more detailed analysis**.

A planning and operational variance attempts to **divide a total variance** (which has been calculated conventionally) into a group of **variances** which have arisen because of **inaccurate planning or faulty standards (planning variances)** and a group of **variances** which have been caused by **adverse or favourable operational performance (operational variances)**.

Key terms

A **planning variance** (or **revision variance**) compares an original standard with a revised standard that should or would have been used if planners had known in advance what was going to happen.

An **operational variance** (or **operating variance**) compares an actual result with the revised standard.

Ex ante means original budget/standard.

Ex post means revised budget/standard.

Planning and operational variances are based on the principle that variances ought to be reported by taking as the **main starting point**, not the original standard, but a **standard** which can be seen, in hindsight, to be the **optimum** that should have been **achievable**.

Exponents of this approach argue that the monetary value of variances ought to be a realistic reflection of what the causes of the variances have cost the organisation. In other words they should show the cash (and profit) gained or lost as a consequence of operating results being different to what should have been achieved. Variances can be valued in this way by **comparing actual results with a realistic standard or budget**. Such variances are called **operational variances**.

Planning variances arise because the **original standard and revised more realistic standards are different** and have nothing to do with operational performance. In most cases, it is unlikely that anything could be done about planning variances: they are **not controllable by operational managers but by senior management**.

In other words the **cause of a total variance** might be one or both of the following.

- Adverse or favourable operational performance (**operational variance**)
- Inaccurate planning, or faulty standards (**planning variance**)

Key terms

The CIMA *Official Terminology* defines an **operational variance** as 'A classification of variances in which non-standard performance is defined as being that which differs from an *ex post* standard. Operational variances can relate to any element of the standard product specification.'

The CIMA *Official Terminology* defines **planning variances** as 'A classification of variances caused by *ex ante* budget allowances being changed to an *ex post* basis. They are also known as revision variances.'

6.1 Calculating total planning and operational variances

We will begin by looking at how to split a total cost variance into its planning and operational components.

6.2 Example: total cost planning and operational variances

At the beginning of 20X0, WB set a standard marginal cost for its major product of £25 per unit. The standard cost is recalculated once each year. Actual production costs during August 20X0 were £304,000, when 8,000 units were made.

With the benefit of hindsight, the management of WB realises that a more realistic standard cost for current conditions would be £40 per unit. The planned standard cost of £25 is unrealistically low.

Required

Calculate the planning and operational variances.

Solution

With the benefit of hindsight, the **realistic standard should have been £40**. The variance caused by favourable or adverse **operating** performance should be calculated by comparing actual results against this realistic standard.

	£
Revised standard cost of actual production (8,000 × £40)	320,000
Actual cost	304,000
Total **operational** variance	16,000 (F)

The variance is favourable because the actual cost was lower than would have been expected using the revised basis.

The **planning** variance reveals the extent to which the original standard was at fault.

		£
Revised standard cost	8,000 units × £40 per unit	320,000
Original standard cost	8,000 units × £25 per unit	200,000
Planning variance		120,000 (A)

It is an adverse variance because the original standard was too optimistic, overestimating the expected profits by understating the standard cost. More simply, it is adverse because the revised cost is much higher than the original cost.

	£
Planning variance	120,000 (A)
Operational variance	16,000 (F)
Total	104,000 (A)

If **traditional variance analysis** had been used, the total cost variance would have been the same, but **all the 'blame' would appear to lie on actual results** and operating inefficiencies (rather than some being due to faulty planning).

	£
Standard cost of 8,000 units (× £25)	200,000
Actual cost of 8,000 units	304,000
Total cost variance	104,000 (A)

Question   Total planning and operational variances

Learning outcome: B (iv)

Suppose a budget is prepared which includes a raw materials cost per unit of product of £2 (2 kg of copper at £1 per kg). Due to a rise in world prices for copper during the year, the average market price of copper rises to £1.50 per kg. During the year, 1,000 units were produced at a cost of £3,250 for 2,200 kg of copper.

The planning and operational variances are

	Operational variance	Planning variance
A	£250 (A)	£1,000 (A)
B	£250 (A)	£1,100 (A)
C	£250 (F)	£1,000 (F)
D	£250 (A)	£1,000 (F)

Answer

The correct answer is A.

Operational variance

	£
Actual cost (for 1,000 units)	3,250
Revised standard cost (for 1,000 units) (2,000 kg × £1.50)	3,000
Total operational variance	250 (A)

Planning variance

	£
Revised standard cost (1,000 × 2 kg × £1.50)	3,000
Original standard cost (1,000 × 2 kg × £1)	2,000
Total planning variance	1,000 (A)

6.3 Operational price and usage variances

So far we have only considered planning and operational variances in total, without carrying out the usual two-way split. In **Question: total planning and operational variances** above, for instance, we identified a total operational variance for materials of £250 without considering whether this operational variance could be split between a usage variance and a price variance.

This is not a problem so long as you retain your grasp of knowledge you already possess. You know that a **price** variance measures the difference between the actual amount of money paid and the amount of money that should have been paid for that quantity of materials (or whatever). Thus, in our example:

	£
Actual price of actual materials (2,200 kg)	3,250
Revised standard price of actual materials (£1.50 × 2,200 kg)	3,300
Operational price variance	50 (F)

The variance is favourable because the materials were purchased more cheaply than would have been expected.

Similarly, a **usage** variance measures the difference between the actual physical quantity of materials used or hours taken and the quantities that should have been used or taken for the actual volume of production. Those physical differences are then converted into money values by applying the appropriate standard cost.

In our example we are calculating **operational variances**, so we are not interested in planning errors. This means that the **appropriate standard cost is the revised standard cost** of £1.50.

Actual quantity should have been	2,000 kgs
but was	2,200 kgs
Operational usage variance in kgs	200 kgs (A)
× revised standard cost per kg	× £1.50
Operational usage variance in £	£300 (A)

The two variances of course reconcile to the total variance as previously calculated.

	£
Operational price variance	50 (F)
Operational usage variance	(300) (A)
Total operational variance	250 (A)

6.4 Operational variances for labour and overheads

Precisely the same argument applies to the calculation of operational variances for labour and overheads, and the examples already given should be sufficient to enable you to do the question below.

Question   Planning and operational variances

Learning outcome B(iv)

A new product requires three hours of labour per unit at a standard rate of £6 per hour. In a particular month the budget is to produce 500 units. Actual results were as follows.

Hours worked	1,700
Production	540 units
Wages cost	£10,500

Within minutes of production starting it was realised that the job was extremely messy and the labour force could therefore claim an extra 25p per hour in 'dirty money'.

Required

What are the planning and operational variances?

	Planning	Operational rate	Operational efficiency
A	£405 (F)	£125 (F)	£500 (A)
B	£405 (A)	£125 (F)	£500 (A)
C	£405 (F)	£300 (A)	£500 (F)
D	£405 (A)	£300 (F)	£480 (A)

Answer

The correct answer is B.

Keep calm and calculate the *total* variance in the normal way to begin with. Then you will understand what it is that you have to analyse. Next follow through the workings shown above, substituting the figures in the exercise for those in the example.

	£
Total labour variance	
540 units should have cost (× 3 hrs × £6)	9,720
but did cost	10,500
	780 (A)

	£
Planning variance	
Revised standard cost (540 × 3 hrs × £6.25)	10,125
Original standard cost (540 × 3 hrs × £6.00)	9,720
	405 (A)

	£
Operational rate variance	
Actual cost of actual hrs	10,500
Revised standard cost of actual hrs (1,700 × £6.25)	10,625
	125 (F)
Operational efficiency variance	
540 units should have taken (× 3 hrs)	1,620 hrs
but did take	1,700 hrs
Operational efficiency variance in hours	80 hrs
× revised standard rate per hour	× £6.25
Operational efficiency variance in £	£500 (A)

6.5 Planning variances and sub-variances

In the examples described so far, there has only been one 'planning error' in the standard cost. When two planning errors occur, there may be some difficulty in deciding how much of the total planning variance is due to each separate error.

6.6 Example: two planning errors

A company estimates that the standard direct labour cost for a product should be £20 (4 hours × £5 per hour). Actual production of 1,000 units took 6,200 hours at a cost of £23,800. In retrospect, it is realised that the standard cost should have been 6 hours × £4 per hour = £24 per unit.

Required

Calculate the planning and operational variances.

Solution

(a) **Operational variances**

(i)		
	1,000 units should take (× 6 hours)	6,000 hrs
	but did take	6,200 hrs
	Efficiency variance in hours	200 hrs (A)
	× revised standard cost per hour	× £4 (A)
	Efficiency variance in £	£800 (A)

(ii)		£
	6,200 hours should cost (× £4)	24,800
	but did cost	23,800
	Rate variance	1,000 (F)

(iii)	Check:	£
	Actual costs	23,800
	Revised standard cost (1,000 units × £24)	24,000
	Total operational variance (800 (A) + 1,000 (F))	200 (F)

(b) **Planning variance**

	£
Revised standard cost 1,000 units × 6 hours × £4	24,000
Original standard cost 1,000 units × 4 hours × £5	20,000
Planning variance	4,000 (A)

Commentary

Within the total planning variance, there are two separate variances.

- A **planning efficiency variance** of 1,000 units × (6 – 4) hours or 2,000 hours (A).
- A **planning rate variance** of £1 per hour (F).

The problem, however, is to put a **value** to these sub-variances. This can be done in either of **two ways**.

(a)

		£
		10,000 (A)
Planning efficiency variance	2,000 hours (A) × original price of £5	
Planning rate variance	£1 per hour (F) × revised standard efficiency of 6,000 hours	6,000 (F)
Total		4,000 (A)

(b)

		£
		8,000 (A)
Planning efficiency variance	2,000 hours (A) × revised rate of £4	
Planning rate variance	£1 per hour (F) × original efficiency of 4,000 hours	4,000 (F)
Total		4,000 (A)

Since the analysis can be done either way, it is **doubtful whether there is much value in splitting the total planning variance**. However, this point may be examinable and is worth learning. The following question provides an example of when there may be some point in carrying out the analysis.

Question   Planning variances and sub-variances

Learning outcome: B(iv)

The standard materials cost of a product is 3 kg × £1.50 per kg = £4.50. Actual production of 10,000 units used 28,000 kg at a cost of £50,000. In retrospect it was realised that the standard materials cost should have been 2.5 kg per unit at a cost of £1.80 per kg (so that the *total* cost per unit was correct).

Required

Calculate the planning and operational variances in as much detail as possible, giving alternative analyses of planning variances.

Answer

As always, calculate the *total* materials variance first, to give you a point of reference. Then follow through the workings above.

Total materials variance	£
10,000 units should have cost (× £4.50)	45,000
but did cost	50,000
	5,000 (A)

Operational price variance	£
28,000 kg should cost (× £1.80)	50,400
but did cost	50,000
	400 (F)

Operational usage variance

10,000 units should use (× 2.5 kgs)	25,000 kgs
but did use	28,000 kgs
Variance in Kgs	3,000 kgs (A)
× standard rate per kg	× £1.80
	£5,400 (A)

Planning variance

Either

	£
Planning price variance (5,000 kgs (F) × £1.50)	7,500 (F)
Planning usage variance (£0.30(A) × 25,000 kgs)	7,500 (A)
	–

or

	£
Planning price variance (5,000 kgs (F) × £1.80)	9,000 (F)
Planning usage variance (£0.30 (A) × 30,000 kgs)	9,000 (A)
	–

6.7 Planning and operational sales variances

Our final calculations in this chapter deal with planning and operational sales variances.

6.8 Example: planning and operational sales variances

Dimsek budgeted to make and sell 400 units of its product, the role, in the four-week period no 8, as follows.

	£
Budgeted sales (100 units per week)	40,000
Variable costs (400 units × £60)	24,000
Contribution	16,000
Fixed costs	10,000
Profit	6,000

At the beginning of the second week, production came to a halt because inventories of raw materials ran out, and a new supply was not received until the beginning of week 3. As a consequence, the company lost one week's production and sales. Actual results in period 8 were as follows.

	£
Sales (320 units)	32,000
Variable costs (320 units × £60)	19,200
Contribution	12,800
Fixed costs	10,000
Actual profit	2,800

In retrospect, it is decided that the optimum budget, given the loss of production facilities in the third week, would have been to sell only 300 units in the period.

Required

Calculate appropriate planning and operational variances.

Solution

The **planning** variance **compares the revised budget** with the **original budget**.

Revised sales volume, given materials shortage	300 units
Original budgeted sales volume	400 units
Planning variance in units of sales	100 units(A)
× standard contribution per unit	× £40
Planning variance in £	£4,000 (A)

Arguably, **running out of raw materials is an operational error** and so the loss of sales volume and contribution from the materials shortage is an opportunity cost that could have been avoided with better purchasing arrangements. The operational variances are variances calculated in the usual way, except that actual results are compared with the revised standard or budget. There is a sales volume contribution variance which is an **operational variance**, as follows.

Actual sales volume	320 units
Revised sales volume	300 units
Operational sales volume variance in units	20 units (F)
(possibly due to production efficiency or marketing efficiency)	
× standard contribution per unit	× £40
	£800 (F)

These variances can be used as **control information** to reconcile budgeted and actual profit.

	£	£
Operating statement, period 8		
Budgeted profit		6,000
Planning variance	4,000 (A)	
Operational variance – sales volume contribution	800 (F)	
		3,200 (A)
Actual profit in period 8		2,800

You will have noticed that in this example sales volume variances were **valued at contribution forgone**, and there were no fixed cost volume variances. This is because contribution forgone, in terms of lost revenue or extra expenditure incurred, is the nearest equivalent to **opportunity cost** which is readily available to management accountants (who assume linearity of costs and revenues within a relevant range of activity).

Question	Sales planning and operational variances

Learning outcome: B(iv)

KSO budgeted to sell 10,000 units of a new product during 20X0. The budgeted sales price was £10 per unit, and the variable cost £3 per unit.

Although actual sales in 20X0 were 10,000 units and variable costs of sales were £30,000, sales revenue was only £5 per unit. With the benefit of hindsight, it is realised that the budgeted sales price of £10 was hopelessly optimistic, and a price of £4.50 per unit would have been much more realistic.

Required

Calculate planning and operational variances.

Answer

The only variances are selling price variances.

Planning (selling price) variance

	Total
	£
Revised budget (10,000 × £4.50)	45,000
Original budget (10,000 × £10.00)	100,000
Planning variance	55,000 (A)

The original variance was too optimistic and so the planning variance is an adverse variance.

Operational (selling price) variance

	£
Actual sales (10,000 × £5)	50,000
Revised sales (10,000 × £4.50)	45,000
Operational (selling price) variance	5,000 (F)

The total difference between budgeted and actual profit of £50,000 (A) is therefore analysed as follows.

	£
Operational variance (selling price)	5,000 (F)
Planning variance	55,000 (A)
	50,000 (A)

6.9 The value of planning and operational variances

Advantages of a system of planning and operational variances

(a) The analysis highlights those variances which are **controllable** and those which are **non-controllable**.

(b) **Managers' acceptance** of the use of variances for performance measurement, and their **motivation**, is likely to increase if they know they will not be held responsible for poor planning and faulty standard setting.

(c) The **planning and standard-setting processes** should improve; standards should be more accurate, relevant and appropriate.

(d) Operational variances will provide a **'fairer' reflection of actual performance**.

The limitations of planning and operational variances, which must be overcome if they are to be applied in practice.

(a) It is difficult to **decide in hindsight** what the **realistic standard** should have been.

(b) It may become **too easy to justify all the variances as being due to bad planning**, so no operational variances will be highlighted.

(c) Establishing realistic revised standards and analysing the total variance into planning and operational variances can be a **time consuming** task, even if a spreadsheet package is devised.

(d) Even though the intention is to provide more meaningful information, **managers may be resistant** to the very idea of variances and refuse to see the virtues of the approach. Careful presentation and explanation will be required until managers are used to the concepts.

6.10 Management reports involving planning and operational variances

The format of a management report that includes planning and operational variances should be tailored to the information requirements of the managers who receive it.

From the **point of view of senior management** reviewing performance as a whole, a layout that identifies **all of the planning variances together**, and then **all of the operational variances** may be most illuminating. The difference due to planning is the responsibility of the planners, and the remainder of the difference is due to functional managers.

One possible layout is shown below.

OPERATING STATEMENT PERIOD 1

	£	£
Original budget contribution		X
Planning variances		
Material usage	X	
Material price	X	
Labour efficiency	X	
Labour idle time	X	
Labour rate	X	
Selling price	X̲	
		X̲
Revised budget contribution		X
Sales volume contribution variance		X
Revised standard contribution from sales achieved		X̲
Operational variances	X	
Selling price	X	
Material usage	X	
Material price	X	
Labour efficiency	X	
Labour rate	X	
Variable overhead expenditure	X	
Variable overhead efficiency	X̲	
		X̲
Actual contribution		X
Less: fixed costs budget	X	
expenditure variance	X̲	
		X̲
Actual margin		X̲

7 Standard process costing

7.1 Standard cost method of inventory valuation

As well a the FIFO and average cost methods of valuation of process work in progress (WIP) that you learned about in Chapter 3, your syllabus also requires you to be able to **integrate standard cost methods** with process costing.

Standard process costing might seem much easier to you than process costing with FIFO or weighted average costing. The basic rules are as follows.

(a)   All finished output is valued at standard cost.

(b)   All closing WIP is valued at standard cost, but since closing WIP is only part-complete, we value the **equivalent units** in closing WIP at standard cost.

(c)   There is no normal loss, no abnormal loss and no abnormal gain in standard process costing. Instead, there are variances.

Efficiency and usage variances are calculated by taking the equivalent units of production in the period as the actual output in the period. The equivalent units are **calculated in the same way as for the FIFO method.**

The labour efficiency and material usage variances will be recorded in the process account. Other cost variances, ie material price, labour rate and all the overhead variances, might appear in the process account but are more likely to appear in the materials account, labour control account or overhead control account.

7.2 Example: standard process costing

Micksamess manufactures a chemical, X24 in a single process. The standard cost per kilo of X24 is as follows.

		£
Direct materials	1.2 kilos × £5 per kilo	6
Direct labour	0.25 hrs × £8 per hr	2
Fixed overheads	0.25 hrs × £12 per hr	3
Standard cost per kilo of X24		11

Budgeted output per period is 1,000 kilos of X24 and budgeted fixed costs are therefore £3,000.

Actual costs and production details in period 11 are as follows.

Opening WIP   200 kilos, 100% complete for direct materials, and 60% complete for labour and overhead.

Total finished output of X24 in period 11: 1,100 kilos

(a)   **Materials price variance**

	£
1,500 kilos of material should cost (× £5)	7,500
but did cost	7,350
Price variance	150 (F)

(b)   **Materials usage variance**

1,300 equivalent units of X24 should use (× 1.2)	1,560 kilos
but did use	1,500 kilos
Usage variance, in kilos	60 kilos (F)
× standard price per kilo	× £5
Usage variance, In £	£300 (F)

(c)   **Direct labour rate variance**

	£
570 hours of labour should cost (× £4)	2,280
but did cost	2,400
Rate variance	120 (A)

(d)   Direct labour efficiency variance

1,060 equivalent units of X24 should take (× 0.25)	265 hrs
but did take	285 hrs
Efficiency variance, in hours	20 hrs (A)
× standard rate per hour	× £8
Efficiency variance, in £	£160

(e)   Fixed overhead expenditure variance

	£
Budgeted fixed overhead	3,000
Actual fixed overhead	2,900
Expenditure variance	100 (F)

(f)   Fixed overhead volume variance

	£
Actual production at standard are (1,060 × £3)	3,180
Budgeted production at standard rate (1,000 × £3)	3,000
Fixed overhead volume variance	180 (F)

The process account can now be prepared.

PROCESS ACCOUNT

	£		£
Opening WIP	1,800	Finished goods	
Materials (1,500 kg × £5)	7,500	(1,10 units × £11)	12,100
Labour (285 hours × £8)	2,280	Labour efficiency variance	160
Overhead (265 std hours × £12)	3,180	Closing WIP	2,800
Materials usage variance	300		
	15,060		15,060

Notice that the overhead absorption is based on standard hours. The same result would have been achieved by absorbing the overheads on a unit basis (1,060 equivalent units × £3 = £3,180).

Closing WIP   400 kilos, 100% complete for direct materials, and 20% complete for labour and overhead.

	£
Direct materials purchased and used: 1,500 kilos, cost	7,350
Direct labour: 285 hours, cost	2,400
Fixed overhead	2,900
Total actual costs	12,650

Required

(a)   Calculate the following for period 11.

    (i)   The total cost of finished output

    (ii)   The value of closing WIP

    (iii)   The variances for the period

(b)   Prepare the account for the process for the period.

Solution

Workings

	Total units	Equivalent units of work in period 11			
		Materials		*Labour and overhead*	
Opening WIP	200	0	(40%)		80
Fully worked units	900	900			900
Total finished output	1,100	900			980
Closing WIP	400	400	(20%)		80
	1,500	1,300			1,060

Total cost of finished output. Output is valued at standard cost

1,100 kilos × £11 per kilo (standard) = £12,100

Valuation of WIP. Closing WIP is valued at the standard cost of its equivalent units. The material element of WIP could be costed at the cost per kilo of material **input** (ie £5 per kilo) are at the cost per kilo of output (ie £6 per kilo). It is easier to cost the materials in WIP at the cost per kilo of **output** material, because this avoids the need to calculate a standard loss on the materials in opening WIP brought forward at the start of period and completed during the period.

	Materials		*Labour and overhead*		*Total*
		£		£	£
Closing WIP	400 × £6	2,400	80 × £5	400	3,800
Opening WIP	200 × £6	1,200	120 × £5	600	1,800

Variances. The usage and efficiency variances are calculated by taking actual production period 11 as 1,300 equivalent units of materials and 1,060 equivalent units of direct labour and fixed overhead.

The variances for material price and labour rate are recorded in the stores control account and wages control account respectively. The overhead volume and expenditure variances are recorded in the overhead control account.

Variance summary

	£	£
Standard cost of output in period 11		
1300 equivalent units of material (× £6)	7,800	
1060 equivalent units of labour and overhead (× £5)	5,300	
		13,100
Variances		
Direct material price	150 (F)	
Direct material usage	300 (F)	
Direct labour rate	120 (a)	
Direct labour efficiency	160 (A)	
Fixed overhead expenditure	100 (F)	
Fixed overhead volume	180 (F)	
Total cost variances		450 (F)
Actual costs		12,650

Question   Standard process costing

Learning outcome: B(iii)

Raw Emotion, a perfume manufacturer, uses standard process costing. The standard cost pert litre of raw emotion is as follows.

		£
Direct materials	1.4 litres at £9 per litre	12.60
Direct labour	1 hour at £6	6.00
Fixed overheads	1 hour at $5.40	5.40
		24.00

Budgeted output is 2,500 litres of raw emotion.

Actual production details and cots for May were as follows.

Opening WIP: 500 litres; 100% complete in respect of direct materials and 50% complete for both labour and overheads

Closing WIP: 700 litres, complete for materials, but only 35% complete for labour and overhead

Total finished output was 2,750 litres.

	£
Direct materials purchased and used (3,450 litres)	29,325
Direct labour (2,800 hours)	17,360
Fixed overhead	14,000
	60,685

Required

Prepare the process account for May using standard process costing.

Answer

PROCESS ACCOUNT

	£		£
Opening WIP (W3)	9,150	Finished output (W2)	66,000
Materials (W4)	31,050	Labour efficiency variance (W5)	330
Labour (W5)	16,800	Closing WIP	11,613
Overhead (W6)	14,823		
Materials usage variance (W4)	6,120		
	77,943		77,943

Workings

1 **Statement of equivalent units**

				Equivalent units		Labour and
	Total units		Materials			overhead
Opening WIP	500	0%	0	50%		250
Fully worked units	2,250		2,250			2,250
Total output	2,750		2,250			2,500
Closing WIP	700	100%	700	35%		245
	3,450		2,950			2,745

2 **Cost of finished output**

2,750 ÷ £24 = £66,000.

3 **WIP**

Opening WIP	£
Direct materials (500 × £12.60)	6,300
Direct labour (250 × £6.00)	1,500
Fixed overhead (250 × £5.40)	1,350
	9,150

Closing WIP	£
Direct materials (700 × £12.60)	8,820
Direct labour (245 × £6)	1,470
Fixed overhead (245 × £5.40)	1,323
	11,613

4 Materials

Materials price variance	£
3,450 litres should cost (× £9)	31,050
but did cost	29,325
Price variance	1,725 (F)

Materials usage variance	
2,950 equivalent units should use (× 1.4)	4,130 litres
but did use	3,450 litres
Usage variance in litres	680 litres (F)
× standard price per kg	× £9
Usage variance in £	£6,120 (F)

5 Labour

	£
2,800 hours should cost (× £6)	16,800
but did cost	17,360
Labour rate variance	560 (A)

2,745 equivalent units should take	2,745 hrs
but did take	2,800 hrs
Labour efficiency variance in hours	55 hrs (A)
× standard rate	× £6
Labour efficiency variance in £	£330 (A)

6 Fixed overheads

	£
Budgeted fixed overhead (2,500 × 1 × £5.40)	13,500
Actual fixed overhead	14,000
Expenditure variance	550 (A)

	£
Actual production at standard rate (2,745 × £5.40)	14,823
Budgeted production at standard rate (2,500 × £5.40)	13,500
Fixed overhead volume variance	1,323 (F)

7.3 The advantages of standard process costing

Standard process costing has certain advantages over the FIFO and weighted average methods of process costing.

(a)   Variance information can be used for management control purposes.

(b)   It is relatively easy to calculate the cost of finished output and closing WIP.

(c)   It avoids the comparative difficulties of calculating (and understanding) abnormal loss and abnormal loss/gain.

Chapter Roundup

- An **operating statement/statement of variances** is a report, usually to senior management, at the end of a control period, reconciling budgeted profit for the period to actual profit.

- In a **standard marginal costing system**, there will no fixed overhead volume variance and the sales volume variance will be valued at standard contribution margin, not standard profit margin.

- When two or more types of material are mixed together to produce a product it is possible to carry out further analysis on the usage variance. The **mix variance** explains how much of the usage variance was caused by a change in the relative proportions of the materials used. The **yield variance** shows how much of the usage variance was caused by using more or less material than the standard allowance.

- The purpose of a mix variance is to provide management with information to help in controlling the proportion of each item actually used. If it is not possible for managers to exercise control over the actual mix of material then there is little to be gained by calculating mix variances.

- If more than one type of labour is used in a product, the labour efficiency variance can be analysed further into a **labour mix (team composition) variance** and a **labour yield (team productivity or output) variance.**

- A planning and operational variance attempts to **divide a total variance** (which has been calculated conventionally) into a group of **variances** which have arisen because of **inaccurate planning or faulty standards (planning variances)** and a group of **variances** which have been caused by **adverse or favourable operational performance** (operational variances).

Quick Quiz

1   *Put the following items in the correct order so as to provide a reconciliation between budgeted contribution and actual profit.*

   Actual sales and admin costs
   Actual fixed production overhead
   Variable cost variances
   Sales variances
   Fixed production overhead expenditure variance
   Actual contribution
   Actual profit
   Budgeted fixed production overhead
   Actual sales minus the standard variable cost of sales
   Budgeted contribution
   Actual profit before sales and admin costs

2   Which of the following statements about the materials mix variance is true?

   A   It should only be calculated if the proportions in the mix are controllable.
   B   In quantity, it is always the same as the usage variance.
   C   In quantity, it is always zero whatever method of calculation is used
   D   It can only be calculated for a maximum of three materials in the mix.

3   *Fill in the blanks.*

   Materials .... variance = materials mix variance + materials .... variance.

4   The labour mix variance is sometimes known as the team mix variance and the labour yield variance is sometimes known as the team yield variance. True or false?

5   The material cost for an actual production level of 510 units was £32,130. There was a material price variance of £1,020 (A) and the standard price per kg was £6.10. How many kgs of material were used?

    A   5,100 kgs
    B   5,434 kgs
    C   5,267 kgs
    D   Impossible to tell from the information provided

6   In an operational and planning approach to variance analysis, which standards are used to calculate the operational variances?

    Ex ante standards ☐

    Ex post standards ☐

7   *Choose the correct words from those highlighted*

A planning variance compares the **revised budget/original budget** with the **original budget/actual result.**

Answers to Quick Quiz

1		£	£
Budgeted contribution			X
Sales variances			X
Actual sales minus standard variable cost of sales			X
Variable cost variances			X
Actual contribution			X
Budgeted fixed production overhead		X	
Fixed production overhead expenditure variance		X	
Actual fixed production overhead			X
Actual profit before sales and admin costs			X
Actual sales and admin costs			X
Actual profit			X

2   A

3   Materials usage variance = materials mix variance + materials yield variance.

4   False. They are sometimes known as the team composition variance and the team productivity variance.

5	A	Total actual material cost	£32,130
		Price variance	£(1,020)
		Standard price for actual usage	£31,110
		÷ standard cost per kg	÷ £6.10
		Actual kgs used	5,100

6   Ex post standards

7   Revised budget
Original budget

Now try the questions below from the Exam Question Bank

Number	Level	Marks	Time
Q18	Introductory	n/a	10 mins
Q19	Introductory	n/a	36 mins
Q20	Examination	20	36 mins
Q21	Examination	20	36 mins

Interpretation of management control information

Introduction

The **calculation of variances** in itself **does little to help management**. Managers need to know whether or not a variance should be investigated, why the variance might have occurred, what it means and whether its occurrence is linked to any other reported variance. They therefore **need to know how to investigate and interpret variances, and how to assess any interdependence between them**. Sections 1 to 4 will explain how this is done.

In **Section 1** we will look at the issues that need to be considered before management decide **whether they need to look into the occurrence of a variance** more closely.

The **models** which can be used to determine whether or not a variance is worthy of **investigation** are covered in **Section 2**. You may need to think back to your *Business Maths* studies at Foundation level here!

Joint variances, which arise when both price and quantity of inputs differ from standards, are covered briefly in **Section 3**. Such variances are of particular relevance when allocating responsibility for the occurrence of variances.

Section 4 provides you with lots of information about **why variances might occur** and looks in particular at the meaning of fixed overhead variances.

Benchmarking, the topic of **Section 6**, is another comparison exercise, involving comparison against best available performance, whether that be inside or outside the organisation.

This chapter's contents are more likely to appear in **Sections B and C** than Section A.

This ends our study of standard costing. In **Part B** we move on to **budgeting**. Watch out for **variances** making an important **reappearance** when you study budgetary control!

Topic list	Learning outcomes	Syllabus references	Ability required
1 To investigate or not to investigate?	B(ii)(v)	B 7	Application/analysis
2 Variance investigation models	B(ii)(v)	B 7	Application/analysis
3 Joint variances: the controllability principle	B(ii)(v)	B 7	Application/analysis
4 Interpreting variances	B(ii)(v)	B 7	Application/analysis
5 Capacity ratios	B(v)	B 7	Application/analysis
6 Benchmarking	B(v)	B 8	Application/analysis

1 To investigate or not to investigate?

FAST FORWARD

Before investigating variances management should bear in mind **materiality, controllability, variance trend, cost, interrelationships** and **performance standards**.

Before management decide whether or not to investigate a particular variance, there are a number of factors which should be considered.

Materiality

Small variations in a single period are bound to occur and **are unlikely to be significant**. Obtaining an 'explanation' is likely to be time-consuming and irritating for the manager concerned. The explanation will often be 'chance', which is not, in any case, particularly helpful. For such variations further investigation is not worthwhile.

Controllability

Controllability must also influence the decision whether to investigate further. If there is a general worldwide price increase in the price of an important raw material there is **nothing that can be done internally** to control the effect of this. If a central decision is made to award all employees a 10% increase in salary, staff costs in division A will increase by this amount and the variance is not controllable by division A's manager. Uncontrollable variances call for a **change in the plan**, not an investigation into the past.

Variance trend

If, say, an efficiency **variance** is £1,000 adverse in month 1, the obvious conclusion is that the process is **out of control** and that corrective action must be taken. This may be correct, but what if the same variance is £1,000 adverse every month? The **trend** indicates that the process is **in control** and the standard has been wrongly set. Suppose, though, that the same variance is consistently £1,000 adverse for each of the first six months of the year but that production has steadily fallen from 100 units in month 1 to 65 units by month 6. The variance trend in absolute terms is constant, but relative to the number of units produced, efficiency has got steadily worse.

Cost

The likely cost of an investigation needs to be weighed against the cost to the organisation of allowing the variance to continue in future periods.

Interrelationship of variances

Quite possibly, individual variances should not be looked at in isolation. One variance might be inter-related with another, and much of it might have occurred only because the other, inter-related, variance occurred too. When two variances are **interdependent (interrelated) one** will usually be **adverse** and the other **one favourable**. Here are some examples.

Interrelated variances	Explanation
Materials price and usage	If cheaper materials are purchased in order to obtain a favourable price variance, materials wastage might be higher and an adverse usage variance will occur. If the cheaper material is more difficult to handle, there might be an adverse labour efficiency variance too.
	If more expensive material is purchased, however, the price variance will be adverse but the usage variance might be favourable.

Interrelated variances	Explanation
Labour rate and efficiency	If employees in a workforce are paid higher rates for experience and skill, using a highly skilled team might lead to an adverse rate variance and possibly a favourable efficiency variance. In contrast, a favourable rate variance might indicate a larger-than-expected proportion of inexperienced workers which could result in an adverse labour efficiency variance, and perhaps poor materials handling and high rates of rejects and hence an adverse materials usage variance.
Selling price and sales volume	We looked at this in Chapter 8.
Materials mix and yield variance	If the mix is cheaper than standard, there may be a resulting lower yield, so that a favourable mix variance might be offset by an adverse yield variance. Alternatively, a mix which is cheaper than standard might have no effect on yield, but the end product might be of sub-standard quality. Sales volumes might then be affected, or sales prices might have to be reduced to sell off the output that customers are not willing to buy at the normal price.

Because management accountants analyse total variances into component elements, ie materials price and usage, labour rate, idle time, efficiency, and so on, they should not lose sight of the overall 'integrated' picture of events, and any interdependence between variances should be reported whenever it is suspected to have occurred.

Question
Interdependence between variances

Learning outcome: B (ii)

There is likely to be interdependence between an adverse labour rate variance and

A   a favourable materials usage variance
B   an adverse fixed overhead expenditure variance
C   an adverse selling price variance
D   none of the above

Answer

The correct answer is A.

A higher paid and hence more skilled workforce could use materials most efficiently.

Exam focus point

'Interpretation of variances: interrelationship, significance' is a specific syllabus topic. You could be required to perform calculations *and* to analyse and explain your results.

FAST FORWARD

The **efficiency variance** reported in any control period, whether for materials or labour and overhead, will **depend on the efficiency level in the standard cost**.

The performance standard used

(a)   If an **ideal standard** is used, **variances** will always be **adverse**.

(b)   If an **attainable standard** is used, or a **current** standard, we should expect **small variances around the standard** from one period to the next, which may not necessarily be significant.

(c)   Management might set a **target** standard **above the current** standard but **below the ideal** standard of efficiency. In such a situation, there will probably be adverse efficiency variances, though not as high as if ideal standards were used. However, if there is **support from the workforce** in trying to improve efficiency levels to the new standard, management would hope to see the **adverse efficiency variances gradually diminish** period by period, until the workforce eventually achieves 100% efficiency at the target standard level.

It is therefore necessary to make a judgement about what an adverse or favourable efficiency variance signifies, in relation to the 'toughness' of the standard set. **Trends** in efficiency variances, that is gradual improvements or deteriorations in efficiency, should be monitored, because these might be more informative than the variance in a single control period.

1.1 Management signals from variance trend information

FAST FORWARD

Individual variances should not be looked at in isolation since one variance might be **interrelated** with another, and much of the variance might have occurred only because the other, interrelated variance occurred too.

Variance analysis is a means of assessing performance, but it is only a method of signalling to management areas of possible weakness where control action might be necessary. It does not provide a ready-made diagnosis of faults, nor does it provide management with a ready-made indication of what action needs to be taken. It merely **highlights items for possible investigation**.

Individual variances should not be looked at in isolation. As an obvious example, a favourable sales price variance is likely to be accompanied by an adverse sales volume variance: the increase in price has caused a fall in demand. We now know in addition that sets of variances should be scrutinised for a number of successive periods if their full significance is to be appreciated.

Signals that may be extracted from variance trend information

(a)   Materials price variances may be favourable for a few months, then shift to adverse variances for the next few months and so on. This could indicate that prices are **seasonal** and perhaps stock could be built up in cheap seasons.

(b)   Regular, perhaps fairly slight, increases in adverse price variances usually indicate the workings of general **inflation**. If desired, allowance could be made for general inflation when flexing the budget.

(c)   Rapid large increases in adverse price variances may suggest a sudden **scarcity** of a resource. It may soon be necessary to seek out cheaper substitutes.

 Question   Trends in variances

Learning outcome: B(ii)

A production department has experienced an improving trend in reported labour efficiency variances but a worsening trend in machine running expenses. Suggest possible reasons for these trends and comment on the management action that may be necessary.   (5 marks)

Gradually improving labour efficiency variances may signal that the employees were inexperienced at first and that the standard time was set based upon measures taken in the early stages of production. However the employees are now **increasing in speed as they learn the task** and the efficiency variances are improving as a result.

Alternatively the improving trend could indicate the success of a recently introduced **productivity bonus scheme** which has not been incorporated into the standard cost.

In either case opportunities should be sought to encourage the trend and the standard cost should be revised if it is to remain useful for control purposes.

Another reason, which may be connected with the increased machine running expense, is that employees are operating the machine at a higher speed than expected in the standard, thus **improving the rate of output** and the labour efficiency variance, but increasing the machine running expenses. Management will need to investigate the overall effect of these changes on total costs and on the product quality.

The worsening trend in machine running expenses may be the result of operating the machines at a faster speed than standard, thus **increasing the power costs**. Another possible cause is that the **equipment may be deteriorating** and will soon need repair or even replacement. Management will need to investigate whether repair or replacement of the machine is necessary.

These are just a few examples. Note that in each case it is suggested that the **variance trend be used as feedforward control information** (covered in Chapter 13), anticipating future problems before they occur.

1.1.1 Percentage variance charts

A trend in variances is often easier to appreciate when the variances are presented as percentages. These percentages become even easier to interpret and understand when presented graphically.

1.2 Example: percentage variance charts

The standard cost of a material is £15 per kg and the standard usage for one unit of product B is 10 kgs. In the first six months of the year actual usage and costs and associated variances have been as follows.

	Output Units	Usage Kgs	Cost £	Price variances £	Usage variances £
January	30	300	4,800	300 (A)	-
February	40	425	6,800	425 (A)	375 (A)
March	35	385	6,160	385 (A)	525 (A)
April	42	465	6,975	-	675 (A)
May	38	420	6,300	-	600 (A)
June	40	435	6,525	-	525 (A)

Required

(a) Calculate the price and usage variances in percentage terms (based on standard cost or usage).
(b) Comment on the trend as revealed by the absolute and percentage variances.
(c) Present a percentage variance chart of the data.

Solution

(a)

	Price variances %	Usage variances %
January	6 $^2/_3$ (A)	0
February	6 $^2/_3$ (A)	6.25 (A)
March	6 $^2/_3$ (A)	10.00 (A)
April	-	10.70 (A)
May	-	10.50 (A)
June	-	8.75 (A)

(b) The absolute price variances indicate that suppliers were charging more than had been anticipated but the price charged appears to be fluctuating. The percentage measures show that there was a temporary blip of a constant amount in the first quarter of the year. Perhaps a bulk discount was not being claimed, and corrective action was taken in April.

There is less to choose between the two approaches for the usage variance. The process seems to have gone out of control in February but corrective action appears to be bringing it back under control. Both absolute and percentage measures show this, but the percentage measures more clearly indicate that the control action is working (compare June and March).

(c)

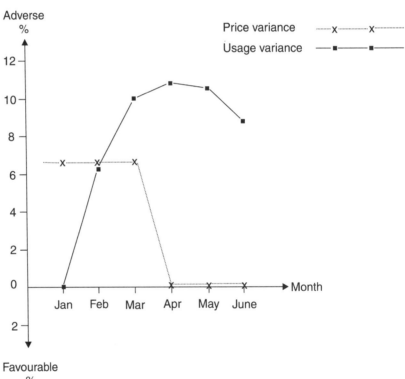

Question   Percentage variance chart

Learning outcome: B (ii)

What conclusion could you reach from the following percentage variance chart?

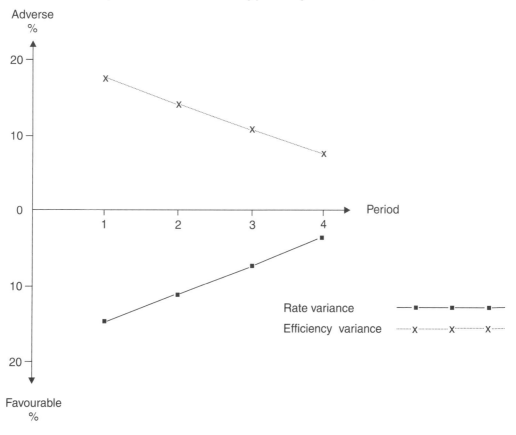

Answer

These variances could be interrelated. As the labour rate has increased (reducing favourable percentage rate variance), the efficiency has tended more closer to standard levels (reducing percentage adverse efficiency variance).

Since both variances are tending towards a zero percentage it may not be necessary to undertake detailed investigation at this stage.

(Such conclusions may not have been immediately apparent from absolute figures.)

Attention!

A variance may represent a small percentage of the standard value but involve significant amounts of money. Both percentages and absolute values should therefore be considered when analysing variances.

1.3 Why might actual and standard performance differ?

Actual and standard performance might differ because of measurement errors, out of date standards, efficient or inefficient operations and/or random or chance fluctuations.

Here are some common reasons.

(a)   **Measurement errors**

In examination questions there is generally no question of the information that you are given being wrong. In practice, however, it may be extremely difficult to establish that 1,000 units of product A used 32,000 kg of raw material X. Scales may be **misread**, the **pilfering** or **wastage** of materials may go unrecorded, items may be wrongly classified (as material X3, say, when material X8 was used in reality), or employees may make **'cosmetic' adjustments** to their records to make their own performance look better than it really was.

Unless an investigation leads to an improvement in the accuracy of the recording system, it is **unlikely that there will be any benefit from the investigation** if the cause of the difference is found to be a measurement error.

(b)   **Out of date standards**

(i)   Price standards are likely to become out of data quickly when frequent changes to the costs of inputs occur or in periods of high **inflation**. In such circumstances an investigation of variances is likely to highlight a general change in market prices rather than efficiencies or inefficiencies in acquiring resources.

(ii)   Standards may also be out of date where operations are subject to **technological development**. **Investigation** of this type of variance **will provide feedback** on the inaccuracy of the standard and highlight the need to frequently review and update standards so that subsequent performance does not deviate from that expected.

(c)   **Efficient or inefficient operations**

Such problems as spoilage or idle time, better quality material or more highly skilled labour are all likely to affect the efficiency of operations and hence cause variances. **Investigation** of variances in this category should highlight the causes of the inefficiency or efficiency and **lead to corrective action** to eliminate the inefficiency being repeated or action to compound the benefits of the efficiency.

(d)   **Random or chance fluctuations**

(i)   A **standard is an average figure**: really it represents the midpoint of a range of possible values and therefore **individual measurements** taken at specific times are **likely to deviate unpredictably within the predictable range**.

(ii)   As long as the variance falls within this range, it will be classified as a random or chance fluctuation and will **not require investigating**.

2 Variance investigation models

2.1 Rule-of-thumb model

> Variance investigation models involve the **rule-of-thumb** model, the **statistical significance model** and **statistical control charts**.

This involves **deciding a limit** and if the size of a **variance is within the limit**, it should be considered **immaterial**. Only if it exceeds the limit is it considered materially significant, and worthy of investigation.

In practice many managers believe that this approach to deciding which variances to investigate is perfectly adequate. However, it has a number of **drawbacks**.

(a)   Should variances be investigated if they exceed 10% of standard? Or 5%? Or 15%?

(b)   Should a **different fixed percentage be applied to favourable and unfavourable variances**?

(c)   Suppose that the fixed percentage is, say, 10% and an important category of expenditure has in the past been very closely controlled so that adverse variances have never exceeded, say, 2% of standard. Now if adverse variances suddenly shoot up to, say, **8% or 9%** of standard, there might well be **serious excess expenditures incurred that ought to be controlled**, but with the fixed percentage limit at 10%, the variances would not be 'flagged' for investigation.

(d)   **Unimportant categories** of low-cost expenditures might be loosely controlled, with variances commonly exceeding 10% in both a favourable and adverse direction. These would be regularly - and **unnecessarily - flagged for investigation**.

(e)   Where actual expenditures have **normal and expected wide fluctuations** from period to period, but the 'standard' is a fixed expenditure amount, variances will be **flagged for investigation unnecessarily often**.

(f)   There is **no attempt to consider the costs and potential benefits of investigating variances** (except insofar as the pre-set percentage is of 'material significance').

(g)   The **past history of variances in previous periods is ignored**. For example, if the pre-set percentage limit is set at 10% and an item of expenditure has regularly exceeded the standard by, say, 6% per month for a number of months in a row, in all probability there is a situation that ought to warrant control action. Using the pre-set percentage rule, however, the variance would never be flagged for investigation in spite of the cumulative adverse variances.

Some of the difficulties can be overcome by **varying the pre-set percentage from account to account** (for example 5% for direct labour efficiency, 2% for rent and rates, 10% for sales representatives' expenditure, 15% for postage costs, 5% for direct materials price, 3% for direct materials usage and so on). On the other hand, some difficulties, if they are significant, can only be overcome with a different cost-variance investigation model.

2.2 Statistical significance model

Historical data are used to **calculate** both a standard as **an expected average** and the **expected standard deviation** around this average when the process is under control. An **in-control process** (process being material usage, fixed overhead expenditure and so on) is one in which any resulting **variance is simply due to random fluctuations** around the expected outcome. An **out-of-control process**, on the other hand, is one in which **corrective action can be taken to remedy any variance**.

By assuming that variances that occur are normally distributed around this average, a **variance will be investigated if it is** *more* **than a distance from the expected average that the estimated normal distribution suggests is likely if the process is in control**. (Note that such a variance would be deemed significant.)

(a)   A 95% or 0.05 significance level rule would state that variances should be investigated if they exceed 1.96 standard deviations from the standard.

(b)   A 99% or 0.01 significance level rule would state that variances should be investigated if they exceed 2.58 standard deviations from the standard. This is less stringent than a 0.05 significance level rule.

(c)   For simplicity, 1.96 and 2.58 standard deviations can be rounded up to 2 and 3 standard deviations respectively.

For example data could be collected and analysed to reveal the following pattern.

Standard hours per unit	6 hours
Standard deviation per unit	0.5 hours

Assume that a 0**.05 significance level** rule is in use.

Suppose that 100 units are made and take 640 hours. The efficiency variance would be 40 hours (A). The standard deviation is 0.5 hours for one unit and $0.5 \times \sqrt{100} = 5$ hours for 100 units. Since 40 hours (A) is **8 standard deviations** from the standard of 600 hours, the efficiency variance should be **investigated**.

Question

Investigating variances

Learning outcome: B (ii), (v)

Data has been collected and analysed and reveals that transport costs per month are Y25,000, with a standard deviation of Y2,000. A 0.01 significance rule is in use. Actual travel expenses are Y28,750. Should the resulting variance be investigated?

Answer

Variance = Y3,750 (A) = 1.875 standard deviations

The variance would not be investigated.

The statistical significance rule has two principal **advantages** over the rule of thumb approach.

(a)   **Important costs** that normally vary by only a small amount from standard will be **signalled for investigation if variances increase significantly**.

(b)   Costs that **usually fluctuate by large amounts will not be signalled** for investigation unless variances are extremely large.

The main **disadvantage** of the statistical significance rule is the problem of assessing standard deviations in expenditure.

2.3 Statistical control charts

By marking variances and control limits on a control chart, **investigation** is signalled not only when a particular **variance exceeds the control limit** (since it would be non-random and worth investigating) but also when the **trend of variances shows a progressively worsening movement** in actual results (even though the variance in any single control period has not yet overstepped the control limit).

The x̄ **control chart** is based on the principle of the statistical significance model. For each cost item, a chart is kept of monthly variances and **tolerance limits are set at 1, 2 or 3 standard deviations**.

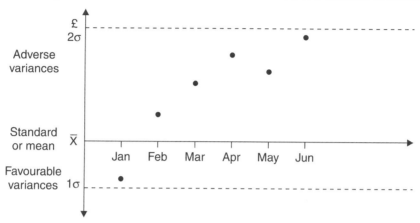

In this example, variances do not exceed the tolerance limits in any month, but the chart shows a worsening of variances over time, and so management might decide that an investigation is warranted, perhaps when it exceeds an inner warning limit.

Using a **cusum chart, the cumulative sum of variances** over a long period of time **is plotted**. If the variances are not significant, these 'sums' will simply fluctuate in a random way above and below the average to give a total or cumulative sum of zero. But if significant variances occur, the cumulative sum will start to develop a positive or negative drift, and when it exceeds a set tolerance limit, the situation must be investigated.

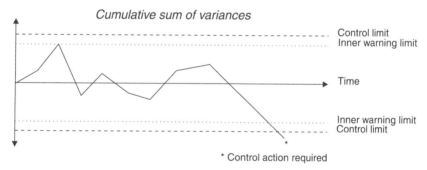

The **advantage** of the multiple period approach over the single period approach is that **trends are detectable earlier**, and control action would be introduced sooner than might have been the case if only current-period variances were investigated.

3 Joint variances: the controllability principle

A **joint** or **composite variance** should be reported to each of the managers jointly responsible for it.

Suppose that a company makes a standard product, which uses six kilograms of material at £2 per kilogram. If actual output during a period is 100 units, which uses 640 kilograms at a cost of £2.30 per kilogram, the variances would be calculated as follows.

	£
640 kilograms should cost (× £2)	1,280
but did cost (× £2.30)	1,472
Price variance	192 (A)

100 units should use (× 6 kgs)	600 kg
but did use	640 kg
Usage variance in kgs	40 kg (A)
× standard cost per kg	× £2
Usage variance in £	£80 (A)

The **usage variance** would probably be **reported to the production manager**, and the **price variance** to the **purchasing manager**. Each would be held responsible for 'controlling' their respective variance item.

This traditional method of reporting fails to show that some of the price variance could have been avoided by the production manager. If the usage of materials had not been adverse, there would have been no need to buy the extra 40 kilograms of material, and the savings would have been 40 kg × £2.30 = £92. The purchasing manager could also have avoided the variance, of course, by buying all the materials at £2 per kilogram. This means that the **excess purchase price of the excess usage of materials could have been avoided by either the purchasing manager or the production manager**.

The name sometimes given to this **adverse price of adverse usage* is a joint or composite variance**, and it may be shown in a diagram as follows.

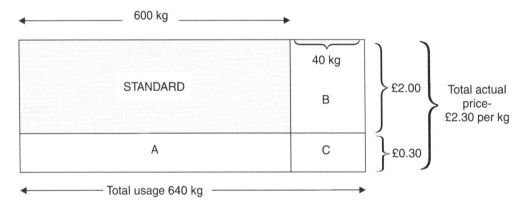

(* A **composite variance could also apply to labour rate and labour efficiency variances**.)

(a)   The traditional price variance is A + C (£192 (A)).

(b)   The traditional usage variance is B (£80(A)).

(c)   However, the composite variance, C, is £0.30 per kg × 40 kg (A) = £12 (A), and so we might argue as follows.

   (i)   The purchasing manager should be responsible for A + 2C (£204 (A)).
   (ii)   The production manager should be responsible for B + C (£92 (A)).

In other words, the composite variance should be reported to each of the managers jointly responsible for it.

This is an application of the **controllability principle** in variance reporting. The principle is that managers should only be held responsible for costs over which they can exercise control. We will return to study this principle in more depth in Chapter 13 and in section 4 below.

A **joint variance** is 'A variance which is caused by both the prices and quantities of inputs differing from the specifications in the original standard'.

(CIMA *Official Terminology*)

4 Interpreting variances

4.1 Material price variances

An adverse material price variance may be partly due to inflation and therefore not wholly within the buying management's control.

An **adverse** price variance would suggest that the **managers responsible for buying decisions have paid too much for the materials**, and should be more careful in future. There are **reasons** why a large adverse or favourable price variance might occur, however, which are **outside the buying management's control**.

Reason	Comment
Inflation	This was discussed in Chapter 7.
Seasonal variations in prices	If material prices fluctuate seasonally, the standard price might be an average price for the year as a whole, on the assumption that it is impractical to buy a whole year's supply in the cheap season and store it until needed. In such a situation, price variances should be favourable for purchases in the cheap season and adverse for purchases in the more expensive season.
Rush orders	If buying managers are asked to make an order for immediate delivery, they might have to forgo a bulk purchase discount, or pay more for the quick supply lead time. The responsibility for the resulting adverse price variance should therefore belong to whoever made the rush order necessary in the first place.

Price variances should be **reported in the period when the purchases are made**, not when the materials are issued from stores and used. This is mainly because control information about price variances ought to be made available as soon as possible after the buying decision which gave rise to the variance, that is when the materials are bought.

4.1 Materials usage variances

A materials usage variance indicates that the quantity of materials consumed was larger or smaller than standard. It could indicate that materials **wastage** was higher or lower than it should have been or that the quantity of **rejects** was above or below standard. Wastage costs money, and should be kept to a minimum. The size of a materials usage variance, however, just like the size of a labour efficiency variance, **depends on the standard rate of usage** (or efficiency) and **whether the standard was attainable or ideal.**

In certain circumstances it could be worthwhile calculating mix and yield variances in order to carry out further analysis.

4.2 Labour rate variances

It might be tempting to think that the rate variance is something that operational managers can do little about, since rates of pay will be agreed at a senior level. A rate variance might, however, be due to **unexpected overtime working** (with overtime paid at a premium rate) or **productivity bonuses** added on to basic rates. To some extent, these should be **controllable by operational managers.**

4.3 Labour efficiency variances

The labour efficiency variance indicates that the actual production time needed to do the work was longer or less than expected. Inefficiency costs money: after all, if it takes three hours to make a unit of product instead of two hours, the unit cost of production will be higher and the profit from selling the unit will be less.

A standard time for labour to produce an item of work will normally take into account contingency allowances for down time and rest periods. Whether or not there is an allowance for these factors will depend on the type of performance standard used (ideal, attainable and so on). In a production industry based on batch production or jobbing work, the standard time will include an allowance for setting up times and clearing up times for each batch or job finished.

An **adverse** labour efficiency variance might indicate **poor labour productivity** in a period, for which a badly-motivated workforce or weak supervision might be to blame, but other causes of a variance might be as follows.

- Excessively **high down times**, due to a serious machine break down, or a bottleneck in production which left many of the workforce idle and waiting for work

- **Shorter batch runs** than expected, which increase the amount of setting up time and cleaning up time between batches, when no physical output is being produced

4.4 Overhead variances

Variances are supposed to provide management with control information. For example, an adverse material price variance of £100 tells management that the material used cost £100 more than it should have cost. But what about information provided by overhead variances? What control information can managers get from the fact that there is an adverse fixed overhead volume variance of £450? The information is not nearly so clear or understandable as that provided by labour and material variances, is it? But why is this?

4.4.1 Fixed overhead volume variance

Unlike expenditure variances or variable cost efficiency variances, the fixed overhead volume variance is **not a true reflection of the extra or lower cash spending** by an organisation as a result of the variance occurring. This is because the variance is valued in terms of overhead absorption rates; the estimates used in the calculation of these rates are often quite arbitrary but it is these absorption rates which determine the value assigned to the overhead volume variance.

Together with the expenditure variance, the fixed overhead volume variance shows the under- or over-absorbed fixed overhead. Under/over absorption is simply a book balancing exercise, however, which occurs as a result of the cost ascertainment process of absorption costing, and the level of under-/over-absorbed overhead depends on the accuracy of the original estimates used in calculating the absorption rates. The level of under/over absorption is not control information, it is simply a figure used to balance the books.

Perhaps the overhead volume variance would be more useful, however, if the losses or gains in output were valued in terms of contribution rather than in terms of absorption rates (which have arbitrary elements and were designed for quite a different purpose). The existence of a fixed overhead volume variance can therefore be important; it is only the monetary value given to the variance that can be misleading to managers.

4.4.2 Variable overhead efficiency variance

This arises because labour is either more or less efficient than standard. Variable production overheads tend to be incurred in direct proportion to production hours worked, and so if the workforce spends too much time on a job, it will incur not only more labour cost than it should, but also more variable overhead cost too.

4.4.3 Expenditure variances

The **fixed overhead expenditure variance** probably provides the **most useful** management information as the size of the variance can be said to be controllable.

(a)   It does have its limitations, however. It is made up of a price component and a usage component. It can therefore vary if there are changes in charges (for example salary increases) or if quantities change (for example if more staff are taken on).

(b)   For such variances to have any practical value as a control measure, the variances for each cost centre need to be calculated, and reported to the managers responsible. Within each overhead cost centre, the manager should be able to analyse the total variance into indirect materials cost variances, indirect labour cost variances and excess or favourable spending on other items, such as depreciation, postage and so on.

4.5 Selling price variance

This is perhaps the variance with the **most obvious meaning**. A selling price variance indicates by how much actual selling prices of products or services have exceeded or been less than standard.

Selling price variances will be **common**. Many companies sell their products to customers at a discount, with the size of the discount depending on the size of the order or who the customer is. (For example, regular customers might be given a minimum discount on their purchases, regardless of order quantity). The standard selling price might ignore discounts altogether, or it might have an allowance for the average expected discount. In either event, the actual sales prices and standard sales prices will usually differ.

4.6 Sales volume variance

A sales volume variance will result in **higher-than-expected sales revenue if it is favourable, but there will be an off-setting increase in the cost of sales**. Similarly, an adverse sales volume variance will result in lower-than-expected sales revenue, but there will be an offsetting reduction in the cost of sales.

The **net effect** of a sales volume variance is an **increase or reduction in profitability**, which is valued in terms of profit margin when a standard absorption costing system is in use and in terms of contribution margin, when a standard marginal costing system is in use.

4.7 Summary

Variance	Favourable	Adverse
Material price	Unforeseen discounts received Greater care in purchasing Change in material standard	Price increase Careless purchasing Change in material standard
Material usage	Material used of higher quality than standard More efficient use of material Errors in allocating material to jobs	Defective material Excessive waste or theft Stricter quality control Errors in allocating material to jobs
Labour rate	Use of workers at a rate of pay lower than standard	Wage rate increase
Idle time	**The idle time variance is always adverse**	Machine breakdown Illness or injury to worker
Labour efficiency	Output produced more quickly than expected because of worker motivation, better quality materials etc Errors in allocating time to jobs	Lost time in excess of standard Output lower than standard set because of lack of training, sub-standard materials etc Errors in allocating time to jobs
Fixed overhead expenditure	Savings in costs incurred More economical use of services	Increase in cost of services used Excessive use of services Change in type of service used

Overhead expenditure variances ought to be traced to the individual cost centres where the variances occurred.

Variance	Favourable	Adverse
Fixed overhead volume	Production or level of activity greater than budgeted	Production or level of activity less than budgeted

Question

Reasons for variances

Learning outcomes: B (ii), (v)

M absorbs fixed production overhead at a predetermined rate based on budgeted output. Extracts from the variance analysis for April are as follows.

Fixed production overhead expenditure variance   £6,000 (F)
Fixed production overhead volume variance   £1,000 (A)

Consider the following statements concerning production in April.

Statement

1   The fixed production overhead was over-absorbed by £5,000
2   Production output was higher than budget
3   Production overhead expenditure was £6,000 lower than budgeted

Which of these statements are consistent with the reported variances?

PROFESSIONAL EDUCATION

A   Statements 1 and 3 only
B   Statements 2 and 3 only
C   Statements 1 and 3 only
D   Statements 1, 2 and 3 only

Answer

The correct answer is D.

Statement 1 is correct because over-absorbed fixed overhead is represented by a favourable total overhead variance.

If the production output was higher than budget, the volume variance would be favourable. Statement 2 is incorrect.

The expenditure variance is favourable therefore actual overhead expenditure was lower than budgeted.

Statement 3 is correct.

Question   Standard costing and inflation

Learning outcome: B(ii)

Jot down ideas for answering the following questions.

(a)   Explain the problems concerning control of operations that a manufacturing company can be
       expected to experience in using a standard costing system during periods of rapid inflation.

                                                                                      (5 marks)

(b)   Suggest three methods by which the company could try to overcome the problems to which you
       have referred in answer to (a) above, indicating the shortcomings of each method.   (5 marks)

Answer

(a)   (i)   Inflation should be budgeted for in standard prices. But **how** can the rate of inflation and the
               timing of inflationary increases be accurately **estimated**? Who decides **how much
               inflationary 'allowance'** should be added to each manager's expenditure budget?

       (ii)   How can actual expenditure be judged against a **realistic 'standard' price level**. Ideally,
               there would be an external price index (for example, one published by the Office for National
               Statistics) but even external price indices are not reliable guides to the prices an
               organisation ought to be paying.

       (iii)   The existence of inflation tends to **eliminate the practical value of price variances** as a
               pointer to controlling spending.

       (iv)   Inflation affects operations more directly. Usually costs go up before an organisation can
               put up the prices of its own products to customers. Inflation therefore tends to **put pressure
               on a company's cash flows**.

       (v)   To provide useful and accurately-valued variances (accurate efficiency variances as well as
               reliable price variances) the **standard costs ought to be revised frequently**. This would be
               an administrative burden on the organisation.

(vi)   If the organisation uses standard costs for pricing or inventory valuation, frequent revisions of the standard would be necessary to keep prices ahead of costs or inventories sensibly valued.

(b)   To overcome the problems, we could suggest the following.

(i)   **Frequent revision** of the standard costs. **Problem** - the administrative burden.

(ii)   **Incorporating estimates** of the rate of inflation and the timing of inflation into budget expenditure allowances and standard costs. **Problem** - accurate forecasting.

(iii)   Constructing **internal indices** of material prices to measure what actual price levels should have been. **Problem** - the administrative burden of constructing and maintaining the index.

(iv)   A **determined effort** by management to **keep costs down**, and resist unnecessary spending. Cost control can minimise the damaging effects of price inflation. **Problem** - obtaining the cooperation of all management and employees in cost control efforts.

5 Capacity ratios

FAST FORWARD

Capacity ratios provide similar information to fixed overhead variances.

As well as reporting to managers concerning the monetary value of standard costing variances, capacity ratios may also be calculated.

5.1 Example: capacity ratios

Given the following information, calculate an idle capacity ratio, a production volume ratio and an efficiency ratio and explain their meanings.

Full capacity	10,000 standard hours	Standard hours produced	6,500
Practical capacity	8,000 standard hours	Actual hours worked	7,000
Budgeted capacity	7,500 standard hours		

Solution

Idle capacity ratio $= \dfrac{\text{Practical capacity} - \text{budgeted capacity}}{\text{Practical capacity}} \times 100\%$

$= \dfrac{8,000 - 7,500}{8,000} \times 100\% = 6.25\%.$

This means that 6.25% of practical capacity will be unused because budgeted volume is lower than the volume that could be achieved.

Production volume ratio $= \dfrac{\text{Standard hours produced}}{\text{Budgeted capacity}} \times 100\%$

$= \dfrac{6,500}{7,500} \times 100\% = 86^2/_3\%$

This means actual output was only $86^2/_3\%$ of budgeted output.

$$\text{Efficiency ratio} = \frac{\text{Standard hours produced}}{\text{Actual hours worked}} \times 100\% = \frac{6,500}{7,000} \times 100\% = 92.86\%$$

This means that the labour force were working at 92.86% efficiency.

6 Benchmarking

FAST FORWARD

Benchmarking is an attempt to identify best practices and by comparison of operations to achieve improved performance.

We have seen how standard costing achieves control by the comparison of actual results with a pre-determined standard.

Benchmarking is another type of comparison exercise through which an organisation attempts to improve performance. The idea is to seek the best available performance against which the organisation can monitor its own performance.

Key term

CIMA's *Official Terminology* defines **benchmarking** as 'The establishment, through data gathering, of targets and comparators, through whose use relative levels of performance (and particularly areas of underperformance) can be identified. By the adoption of identified best practices it is hoped that performance will improve.'

CIMA lists four types of benchmarking.

Type	Description
Internal benchmarking	A method of comparing one operating unit or function with another within the same industry
Functional benchmarking	Internal functions are compared with those of the best external practitioners of those functions, regardless of the industry they are in (also known as operational or generic benchmarking)
Competitive benchmarking	Information is gathered about direct competitors, through techniques such as reverse engineering*
Strategic benchmarking	A type of competitive benchmarking aimed at strategic action and organisational change

* **Reverse engineering**: buying a competitor's product and dismantling it, in order to understand its content and configuration

From this list you can see that a benchmarking exercise **does not necessarily have to involve the comparison of operations with those of a competitor**. Indeed, it might be difficult to persuade a direct competitor to part with any information which is useful for comparison purposes. Functional benchmarking, for example, does not always involve direct competitors. For instance a railway company may be identified as the 'best' in terms of on-board catering, and an airline company that operates on different routes could seek opportunities to improve by sharing information and comparing their own catering operations with those of the railway company.

A 1994 survey of the *The Times* Top 1,000 companies (half of which were in manufacturing) revealed that the business functions most subjected to benchmarking in the companies using the technique were **customer services, manufacturing, human resources and information services.**

6.1 Obtaining information

Financial information about competitors is **easier** to acquire than non-financial information. Information about **products** can be obtained from **reverse engineering**, **product literature**, **media comment** and **trade associations**. Information about **processes** (how an organisation deals with customers or suppliers) is more **difficult** to find.

Such information can be obtained from **group companies** or possibly **non-competing organisations in the same industry** (such as the train and airline companies mentioned above).

6.2 Why use benchmarking?

6.2.1 For setting standards

Benchmarking allows **attainable standards** to be established following the examination of both **external and internal information**. If these standards are **regularly reviewed** in the light of information gained through benchmarking exercises, they can become part of a programme of **continuous improvement** by becoming increasingly demanding.

6.2.2 Other reasons

(a) Its flexibility means that it can be used in both the public and private sector and by people at different levels of responsibility.

(b) Cross comparisons (as opposed to comparisons with similar organisations) are more likely to expose radically different ways of doing things.

(c) It is an effective method of implementing change, people being involved in identifying and seeking out different ways of doing things in their own areas.

(d) It identifies the processes to improve.

(e) It helps with cost reduction.

(f) It improves the effectiveness of operations.

(g) It delivers services to a defined standard.

(h) It provides a focus on planning.

(i) It can provide early warning of competitive disadvantage.

(j) It should lead to a greater incidence of team working and cross-functional learning.

Benchmarking works, it is claimed, for the following reasons.

(a) The comparisons are carried out by the managers who have to live with any changes implemented as a result of the exercise.

(b) Benchmarking focuses on improvement in key areas and sets targets which are challenging but 'achievable'. What is *really* achievable can be discovered by examining what others have achieved: managers are thus able to accept that they are not being asked to perform miracles.

Learning outcome: B (v)

We've looked at the advantages of benchmarking. Can you think of any disadvantages?

Answer

- Difficulties in deciding which activities to benchmark
- Identifying the 'best in class' for each activity
- Persuading other organisations to share information
- Successful practices in one organisation may not transfer successfully to another
- The danger of drawing incorrect conclusions from inappropriate comparisons

Chapter Roundup

- Before investigating variances management should bear in mind **materiality**, **controllability**, **variance trend**, **cost**, **interrelationships** and **performance standards**.

- The **efficiency variance** reported in any control period, whether for materials or labour and overhead, will **depend on the efficiency level in the standard cost**.

- Individual variances should not be looked at in isolation since one variance might be **interrelated** with another, and much of the variance might have occurred only because the other, interrelated variance occurred too.

- **Actual and standard performance might differ** because of measurement errors, out of date standards, efficient or inefficient operations and/or random or chance fluctuations.

- **Variance investigation models** involve the **rule-of-thumb** model, the **statistical significance model** and **statistical control charts**.

- A **joint** or **composite variance** should be reported to each of the managers jointly responsible for it.

- An adverse material price variance may be partly due to inflation and therefore not wholly within the buying management's control.

- Capacity ratios provide similar information to fixed overhead variances.

- **Benchmarking** is an attempt to identify best practices and by comparison of operations to achieve improved performance.

Quick Quiz

1   Favourable variances are never worthy of investigation because they result in profit increases. *True or false?*

2   Which of the following is not a reason why actual and standard performance might differ?

   A   Measurement errors
   B   Realistic standards
   C   Efficient or inefficient operations
   D   Random or chance fluctuations

3   *Choose the correct words from those highlighted.*

   A **cusum/cumus** chart plots **individual/the cumulative sum of** variances **over a period of time/on a one-off basis**.

4   The following variances were reported for period 1.

   Direct labour rate   £2,800 adverse
   Direct labour efficiency   £1,350 favourable

   Which of the following statements are consistent with these variances?

   A   Direct labour achieved levels of efficiency which were higher than standard, an   Consistent
       paid bonuses at higher rates than standard   Not consistent

   B   The original standard labour rate was unrealistically low because it failed to tal   Consistent
       wage inflation   Not consistent

   C   The production manager elected to use more skilled labour at a higher hourly i   Consistent
       budgeted   Not consistent

5   If ideal standards are used, reported efficiency variances will tend to be favourable. *True or false?*

6   *Match the type of benchmarking to the descriptions.*

   Type of benchmarking

   Internal; functional; competitive; strategic

   Descriptions

   (a)   Information is gathered about direct competitors

   (b)   Internal functions are compared with those of the best external practitioners of those functions, regardless of the industry they are in

   (c)   One operating unit or function is compared with another within the same industry

   (d)   A type of competitive benchmarking aimed at strategic action and organisational change

7   The joint variance based on the excess labour rate over the standard rate of the excess number of hours worked over standard is the responsibility of the production manager. *True or false?*

Answers to Quick Quiz

1   False

2   B. Out of date standards would cause a difference.

3   A cusum chart plots the cumulative sum of variances over a period of time.

4   All of the statements are consistent with the reported variances.

5   False. They will tend to be adverse.

6   Internal benchmarking   (c)
     Functional benchmarking   (b)
     Competitive benchmarking   (a)
     Strategic benchmarking   (d)

7   True – although it is also the responsibility of the manager responsible for labour rates.

Now try the question below from the Exam Question Bank

Number	Level	Marks	Time
Q22	Examination	20	36 mins

Part C
Budgeting

Budgets

Introduction

This chapter begins a new topic, **budgeting**. You will meet the topic at all stages of your future examination studies and so it is vital that you get a firm grasp of it now.

You may recognise much of this chapter from your *Management Accounting Fundamentals* studies at Foundation level. You have already covered most of the topics in this chapter at a basic level and so we have included a couple of deemed knowledge boxes on the most straightforward areas.

The chapter begins by explaining the **reasons for operating a budgetary planning and control system** (**Section 1**), explains some of the **key terms** associated with budgeting and reminds you of the steps in the preparation of a master budget (**Section 2**).

You should have already covered **budget preparation** (including the preparation of cash budgets) but we will look at some more complex examples in **Sections 4 and 5**.

Section 6 looks at how the master budget is evaluated by calculating **key metrics**.

Section 7 explains how the budgeting process does not stop once the master budget has been prepared but is a **constant task** of the management accountant.

A number of **alternative approaches to budgeting** are reviewed in **Section 8**, while **Section 9** looks at how to budget in an uncertain environment.

Our study of budgeting continues in Chapter 12 with a look at forecasting.

Topic list	Learning outcomes	Syllabus references	Ability required
1 Budgetary planning and control systems	C(i)(v)	C 4	Comprehension
2 The preparation of budgets	C(i)(vi)	C 5	Application/evaluation
3 The sales budget	C(i)(vi)	C 5	Application/evaluation
4 Production and related budgets	C(i)(vi)	C 5	Application/evaluation
5 Cash budgets	C(i)(vi)	C 5	Application/evaluation
6 The master budget: calculating key metrics	C(iv)	C 6	Application/evaluation
7 Monitoring procedures	C(ix)	C 4	Comprehension
8 Alternative approaches to budgeting	C(vi)	C 5, 6	Application/evaluation
9 Budgeting in an uncertain environment	C(vii)	C 3	Application/evaluation

1 Budgetary planning and control systems

A **budget** is a quantified plan of action for a forthcoming accounting period. A **budget** is a plan of what the organisation is aiming to achieve and what is has set as a target whereas a **forecast** is an estimate of what is likely to occur in the future

Key term

The **budget** is 'a quantitative statement for a defined period of time, which may include planned revenues, expenses, assets, liabilities and cash flows. A budget provides a focus for the organisation, aids the co-ordination of activities and facilitates planning'.   (CIMA *Official Terminology*)

There is, however, little point in an organisation simply preparing a budget for the sake of preparing a budget. A beautifully laid out budgeted income statement filed in the cost accountant's file and never looked at again is worthless. The organisation should gain from both the actual preparation process and from the budget once it has been prepared.

The **objectives** of a budgetary planning and control system are as follows.

–   To ensure the achievement of the organisation's objectives
–   To compel planning
–   To communicate ideas and plans
–   To coordinate activities
–   To provide a framework for responsibility accounting
–   To establish a system of control
–   To motivate employees to improve their performance

Budgets are therefore not prepared in isolation and then filed away but are the fundamental components of what is known as the **budgetary planning and control system**. A budgetary planning and control system is essentially a system for ensuring **communication**, **coordination** and **control** within an organisation. Communication, coordination and control are general objectives: more information is provided by an inspection of the specific objectives of a budgetary planning and control system.

Objective	Comment
Ensure the achievement of the organisation's objectives	Objectives are set for the organisation as a whole, and for individual departments and operations within the organisation. Quantified expressions of these objectives are then drawn up as targets to be achieved within the timescale of the budget plan.
Compel planning	This is probably the most important feature of a budgetary planning and control system. Planning forces management to look ahead, to set out detailed plans for achieving the targets for each department, operation and (ideally) each manager and to anticipate problems. It thus prevents management from relying on ad hoc or uncoordinated planning which may be detrimental to the performance of the organisation. It also helps managers to **foresee potential threats or opportunities**, so that they may **take action now** to avoid or minimise the effect of the threats and to take full advantage of the opportunities.

Objective	Comment
Communicate ideas and plans	A formal system is necessary to ensure that each person affected by the plans is aware of what he or she is supposed to be doing. Communication might be one-way, with managers giving orders to subordinates, or there might be a two-way dialogue and exchange of ideas.
Coordinate activities	The activities of different departments or sub-units of the organisation need to be coordinated to ensure maximum integration of effort towards common goals. This concept of coordination implies, for example, that the purchasing department should base its budget on production requirements and that the production budget should in turn be based on sales expectations. Although straightforward in concept, coordination is remarkably difficult to achieve, and there is often **'sub-optimality'** and conflict between departmental plans in the budget so that the efforts of each department are not fully integrated into a combined plan to achieve the company's best targets.
Provide a framework for responsibility accounting	Budgetary planning and control systems require that managers of **budget centres** are made responsible for the achievement of budget targets for the operations under their personal control.
Establish a system of control	A budget is a **yardstick** against which actual performance is monitored and assessed. Control over actual performance is provided by the comparisons of actual results against the budget plan. Departures from budget can then be investigated and the reasons for the departures can be divided into **controllable** and **uncontrollable** factors.
Motivate employees to improve their performance	The interest and commitment of employees can be retained via a system of feedback of actual results, which lets them know how well or badly they are performing. The identification of controllable reasons for departures from budget with managers responsible provides an incentive for improving future performance.
Provide a framework for authorisation	Once the budget has been agreed by the directors and senior managers it acts as an authorisation for each budget holder to incur the costs included in the budget centre's budget. **As long as the expenditure is included in the formalised budget** the budget holder can carry out day to day operations without needing to seek separate authorisation for each item of expenditure.
Provide a basis for performance evaluation	As well as providing a yardstick for control by comparison, the monitoring of actual results compared with the budget can provide a basis for **evaluating the performance of the budget holder.** As a result of this evaluation the manager might be rewarded, perhaps with a financial bonus or promotion. Alternatively the evaluation process might highlight the need for more investment in staff development and training.

Exam focus point

A huge range of exam questions could be asked on the contents of this chapter. You could get a long budget preparation question or (perhaps more likely) a discursive question on the relevance of one or more of the alternative approaches to budgeting. Cash budgeting could easily be examined in the MCQ section.

2 The preparation of budgets

Having seen why organisations prepare budgets, we will now turn our attention to the mechanics of budget preparation. We will begin by defining and explaining a number of terms.

2.1 Planning

Key term

Planning is described in the *Official Terminology* as 'The establishment of objectives, and the formulation, evaluation and selection of the policies, strategies, tactics and action required to achieve them. Planning comprises long-term/strategic planning, and short-term operation planning. The latter is usually for a period of up to one year'.

The overall planning process therefore covers both the long and short term.

Type of planning	Detail
Strategic/corporate/ long-range planning	Covers periods longer than one year and involves 'The formulation, evaluation and selection of strategies for the purpose of preparing a long-term plan of action to attain objectives'. (CIMA *Official Terminology*).
Budgetary/short-term tactical planning	Involves preparing detailed plans, which generally cover one year, for an organisation's functions, activities and departments. Works within the framework set by the strategic plans and converts those strategic plans into action.
Operation planning	Planning on a very short-term or day-to-day basis and is concerned with planning how an organisation's resources will be used. Works within the framework set by the budgetary plans and converts the budgetary plans into action.

2.1.1 The value of long-term planning

A **budgetary planning and control system** operating in **isolation** without any form of long-term planning as a framework is **unlikely to produce maximum potential benefits** for an organisation.

(a) **Without stated long-term objectives**, managers **do not know what they should be trying to achieve** and so there are **no criteria against which to assess possible courses of action**.

(b) Without long-term planning, budgets may simply be based on a sales forecast. Performance can therefore only be judged in terms of previous years' results, **no analysis of the organisation's potential** having been carried out.

(c) Many business **decisions need to be taken on a long-term basis**. For instance, **new products** cannot simply be introduced when sales of existing products begin to decline. Likewise, **capital equipment** cannot necessarily be purchased and installed in the short term if production volumes start to increase.

(d) With long-term planning, **limiting factors** (other than sales) which might arise can possibly be anticipated, and avoided or overcome.

2.2 The budget period

The **budget period** is 'The period for which a budget is prepared and used, which may then be sub-divided into control periods'. (CIMA *Official Terminology*)

Except for capital expenditure budgets, the budget period is commonly the accounting year (sub-divided into 12 or 13 control periods).

2.3 The budget manual

The **budget manual** is a collection of instructions governing the responsibilities of persons and the procedures, forms and records relating to the preparation and use of budgetary data.

Likely contents of a budget manual	Examples
An explanation of the objectives of the budgetary process	• The purpose of budgetary planning and control • The objectives of the various stages of the budgetary process • The importance of budgets in the long-term planning and administration of the enterprise
Organisational structures	• An organisation chart • A list of individuals holding budget responsibilities
Principal budgets	• An outline of each • The relationship between them
Administrative details of budget preparation	• Membership and terms of reference of the budget committee • The sequence in which budgets are to be prepared • A timetable
Procedural matters	• Specimen forms and instructions for their completion • Specimen reports • Account codes (or a chart of accounts) • The name of the budget officer to whom enquiries must be sent

2.4 The responsibility for preparing budgets

The initial responsibility for preparing the budget will normally be with the managers (and their subordinates) who will be carrying out the budget, selling goods or services and authorising expenditure. However, the budget is normally set as part of a longer process, involving the authorisation of set targets by senior management and the negotiation process with the budget holders. This is further examined in chapter 13. Depending on the size of the organisation there may be a large number of **budget centres** and a separate **budget holder** would be responsible for setting and achieving the budget for the centre. In Chapter 13 we will return to consider how the hierarchy of budget centres ensure the coordination of all the functional budgets into the overall **master budget**.

Examples of the functional budgets that would e prepared and **the managers responsible for their preparation** are as follows.

(a)   The **sales manager** should draft the **sales budget** and **selling overhead** cost centre budgets.

(b)   The **purchasing manager** should draft the **material purchases** budget.

(c)   The **production manager** should draft the **direct production** cost budgets.

(d)   Various **cost centre managers** should prepare the individual production, administration and distribution cost centre budgets for their own cost centre.

(e)   The **cost accountant** will **analyse** the budgeted overheads to determine the overhead absorption rates for the next budget period.

2.5 Budget committee

The **budget committee** is the coordinating body in the preparation and administration of budgets.

The **coordination** and **administration** of budgets is usually the responsibility of a **budget committee** (with the managing director as chairman).

(a)   The budget committee is assisted by a **budget officer** who is usually an accountant. Every part of the organisation should be represented on the committee, so there should be a representative from sales, production, marketing and so on.

(b)   **Functions of the budget committee**

- **Coordination** of the preparation of budgets, which includes the issue of the budget manual

- **Issuing of timetables** for the preparation of functional budgets

- **Allocation of responsibilities** for the preparation of functional budgets

- **Provision of information** to assist in the preparation of budgets

- **Communication of final budgets** to the appropriate managers

- **Comparison** of actual results with budget and the investigation of variances

- **Continuous assessment** of the budgeting and planning process, in order to improve the planning and control function

2.6 Budget preparation

Let us now look at the steps involved in the preparation of a budget. The procedures will differ from organisation to organisation, but the step-by-step approach described in this chapter is indicative of the steps followed by many organisations. The preparation of a budget may take weeks or months, and the budget committee may meet several times before the functional budgets are co-ordinated and the master budget is finally agreed.

The CIMA *Official Terminology* defines a **departmental/functional budget** as 'A budget of income and/or expenditure applicable to a particular function.

A function may refer to a department or a process. Functional budgets frequently include:

- Production cost budget (based on a forecast of production and plant utilisation)
- Marketing cost budget, sales budget
- Personnel budget
- Purchasing budget
- Research and development budget'

2.7 The principal budget factor

The **principal budget factor** should be identified at the beginning of the budgetary process, and the budget for this is prepared before all the others.

The first task in the budgetary process is to identify the **principal budget factor**. This is also known as the **key** budget factor or **limiting** budget factor.

The **principal budget factor** is the factor which limits the activities of an organisation.

Likely principal budget factors

(a) The **principal budget factor** is usually **sales demand**: a company is usually restricted from making and selling more of its products because there would be no sales demand for the increased output at a price which would be acceptable/profitable to the company.

(b) Other possible factors

- Machine capacity
- Distribution and selling resources
- The availability of key raw materials
- The availability of cash.

Once this factor is defined then the remainder of the budgets can be prepared. For example, if sales are the principal budget factor then the production manager can only prepare his budget after the sales budget is complete.

Management may not know what the limiting budget factor is until a draft budget has been attempted. The first draft budget will therefore usually begin with the preparation of a draft sales budget.

Steps in the preparation of a budget

Step 1.   Identification of **principal/key/limiting budget factor**

Step 2.   Preparation of a **sales budget,** assuming that sales is the principal budget factor (in units and in sales value for each product, based on a sales forecast)

Step 3.   Preparation of a **finished goods inventory budget** (to determine the planned change in finished goods inventory levels)

Step 4.   Preparation of a **production budget** (calculated as sales + closing inventory – opening inventory)

Step 5.   Preparation of **budgets for production resources**

* Materials usage
* Machine usage
* Labour

Step 6.   Preparation of a **raw materials inventory budget** (to determine the planned change in raw materials inventory levels)

Step 7.   Preparation of a **raw materials purchases budget** (calculated as usage + inventory – opening inventory)

Step 8.   Preparation of **overhead cost budgets** (such as production, administration, selling and distribution and R&D)

Step 9.   Calculation of **overhead absorption rates** (if absorption costing is used)

Step 10.   Preparation of a **cash budget** (and others as required, **capital expenditure** and **working capital** budgets)

Step 11.   Preparation of a **master budget** (budgeted income statement and budgeted balance sheet)

Remember that it is **unlikely** that the execution of the **above steps** will be **problem-free** as data from one budget becomes an input in the preparation of another budget. For example, the materials purchases budget will probably be used in preparing the payables budget. The payables budget will then become an input to the cash budget, and so on. The budgets must therefore be **reviewed in relation to one another**. Such a review may indicate that some budgets are out of balance with others and need modifying so that they will be compatible with other conditions, constraints and plans. The budget officer must identify such inconsistencies and bring them to the attention of the manager concerned.

Alternatively, there may have been a **change in one of the organisational policies**, such as a change in selling prices, which will need to be **incorporated into the budget**. The revision of one budget may lead to the revision of all budgets. This process must continue until all budgets are acceptable and co-ordinated with each other.

If such changes are made manually, the process can be very time consuming and costly. Computer **spreadsheets** can help immensely.

Question

Learning outcome: C (vi)

A company that manufactures and sells a range of products, with sales potential limited by market share, is considering introducing a system of budgeting.

Required

(a)   List (in order of preparation) the functional budgets that need to be prepared.

(b)   State which budgets will comprise the master budget.

(c)   Consider how the work outlined in (a) and (b) can be coordinated in order for the budgeting process to be successful.

Answer

(a)   The **sequence of budget preparation** will be roughly as follows.

    •   Sales budget. (The market share limits demand and so sales is the principal budget factor. All other activities will depend upon this forecast.)

    •   Finished goods inventory budget (in units)

    •   Production budget (in units)

    •   Production resources budgets (materials, machine hours, labour)

    •   Overhead budgets for production, administration, selling and distribution, research and development and so on

Other budgets required will be the capital expenditure budget, the working capital budget (receivables and payables) and, very importantly, the cash budget.

(b)   The **master budget** is the summary of all the functional budgets. It often includes a summary income statement and balance sheet.

(c)   Procedures for preparing budgets can be contained in a **budget manual** which shows which budgets must be prepared when and by whom, what each functional budget should contain and detailed directions on how to prepare budgets including, for example, expected price increases, rates of interest, rates of depreciation and so on.

The formulation of budgets can be coordinated by a **budget committee** comprising the senior executives of the departments responsible for carrying out the budgets: sales, production, purchasing, personnel and so on.

The budgeting process may also be assisted by the use of a **spreadsheet/computer budgeting package**.

3 The sales budget

We have already established that, for many organisations, the principal budget factor is sales volume. The sales budget is therefore **often the primary budget** from which the majority of the other budgets are derived.

Before the sales budget can be prepared a sales forecast has to be made. A **forecast** is an estimate of what is likely to occur in the future. A budget, in contrast, is a plan of what the organisation is aiming to achieve and what it has set as a target. We will be looking at forecasting techniques in detail in the next chapter.

On the basis of the sales forecast and the production capacity of the organisation, a sales budget will be prepared. This may be subdivided, possible subdivisions being by product, by sales area, by management responsibility and so on.

Once the sales budget has been agreed, related budgets can be prepared.

4 Production and related budgets

If the principal budget factor was production capacity then the production budget would be the first to be prepared. To assess whether production is the principal budget factor, the **production capacity available** must be determined, taking account of a number of factors.

- **Available labour**, including idle time, overtime and standard output rates per hour

- **Availability of raw materials** including allowances for losses during production

- **Maximum machine hours available**, including expected idle time and expected output rates per machine hour

It is, however, normally sales volume that is the constraint and therefore the production budget is usually prepared after the sales budget and the finished goods inventory budget.

The production budget will show the quantities and costs for each product and product group and will tie in with the sales and inventory budgets. This co-ordinating process is likely to show any shortfalls or excesses in capacity at various times over the budget period.

If there is likely to be a **shortfall** then consideration should be given to how this can be avoided. Possible **options** include the following.

- Overtime working
- Subcontracting
- Machine hire
- New sources of raw materials

A significant shortfall means that production capacity is, in fact, the limiting factor.

If **capacity exceeds sales volume** for a length of time then consideration should be given to **product diversification**, a **reduction in selling price** (if demand is price elastic) and so on.

Once the production budget has been finalised, the labour, materials and machine budgets can be drawn up. These budgets will be based on budgeted activity levels, planned inventory positions and projected labour and material costs.

4.1 Example: the production budget and direct labour budget

Landy manufactures two products, A and B, and is preparing its budget for 20X3. Both products are made by the same grade of labour, grade Q. The company currently holds 800 units of A and 1,200 units of B in inventory, but 250 of these units of B have just been discovered to have deteriorated in quality, and must therefore be scrapped. Budgeted sales of A are 3,000 units and of B 4,000 units, provided that the company maintains finished goods inventories at a level equal to three months' sales.

Grade Q labour was originally expected to produce one unit of A in two hours and one unit of B in three hours, at an hourly rate of £2.50 per hour. In discussions with trade union negotiators, however, it has been agreed that the hourly wage rate should be raised by 50p per hour, provided that the times to produce A and B are reduced by 20%.

Required

Prepare the production budget and direct labour budget for 20X3.

Solution

The expected time to produce a unit of A will now be 80% of 2 hours = 1.6 hours, and the time for a unit of B will be 2.4 hours. The hourly wage rate will be £3, so that the direct labour cost will be £4.80 for A and £7.20 for B (thus achieving a saving for the company of 20p per unit of A produced and 30p per unit of B).

(a) **Production budget**

		Product A			Product B	
		Units	Units		Units	Units
Budgeted sales			3,000			4,000
Closing inventories	($^3/_{12}$ of 3,000)	750		($^3/_{12}$ of 4,000)	1,000	
Opening inventories (minus inventories scrapped)		800			950	
(Decrease)/increase in inventories						50
			(50)			
Production			2,950			4,050

(b) **Direct labour budget**

	Grade Q	Cost
	Hours	£
2,950 units of product A	4,720	14,160
4,050 units of product B	9,720	29,160
Total	14,440	43,320

It is assumed that there will be no idle time among grade Q labour which, if it existed, would have to be paid for at the rate of £3 per hour.

> **Exam focus point**
>
> You are unlikely to get straightforward budget preparation questions at Managerial level given that the topic is initially covered at an earlier level but the syllabus does require you to understand the creation of budgets.

4.2 The standard hour

> **Key term**
>
> A **standard hour** or standard minute is 'The amount of work achievable at standard efficiency levels in an hour or minute'.   (CIMA *Official Terminology*)

This is a useful concept in budgeting for labour requirements. For example, budgeted **output of different products or jobs** in a period could be converted into standard hours of production, and a labour budget constructed accordingly.

Standard hours are particularly useful when management wants to monitor the production levels of a variety of dissimilar units. For example product A may take five hours to produce and product B, seven hours. If four units of each product are produced, instead of saying that total output is eight units, we could state the production level as (4 × 5) + (4 × 7) standard hours = 48 standard hours.

4.3 Example: direct labour budget based on standard hours

Truro manufactures a single product, Q, with a single grade of labour. Its sales budget and finished goods inventory budget for period 3 are as follows.

Sales	700 units
Opening inventories, finished goods	50 units
Closing inventories, finished goods	70 units

The goods are inspected only when production work is completed, and it is budgeted that 10% of finished work will be scrapped.

The standard direct labour hour content of product Q is three hours. The budgeted productivity ratio for direct labour is only 80% (which means that labour is only working at 80% efficiency).

The company employs 18 direct operatives, who are expected to average 144 working hours each in period 3.

Required

(a)   Prepare a production budget.

(b)   Prepare a direct labour budget.

(c)   Comment on the problem that your direct labour budget reveals, and suggest how this problem might be overcome.

Solution

(a)   **Production budget**

	Units
Sales	700
Add closing inventory	70
	770
Less opening inventory	50
Production required of 'good' output	720
Wastage rate	10%

Total production required $720 \times \dfrac{100\,^*}{90} = 800$ units

(* Note that the required adjustment is 100/90, not 110/100, since the waste is assumed to be 10% of total production, not 10% of good production.)

(b)   Now we can prepare the **direct labour budget**.

Standard hours per unit	3
Total standard hours required = 800 units × 3 hours	2,400 hours
Productivity ratio	80%

Actual hours required $2,400 \times \dfrac{100}{80} = 3,000$ hours

(c)   If we look at the **direct labour budget** against the information provided, we can identify the problem.

	Hours
Budgeted hours available (18 operatives × 144 hours)	2,592
Actual hours required	3,000
Shortfall in labour hours	408

The (draft) budget indicates that there will not be enough direct labour hours to meet the production requirements.

(d)   **Overcoming insufficient labour hours**

(i)   **Reduce the closing inventory** requirement below 70 units. This would reduce the number of production units required.

(ii)   Persuade the workforce to do some **overtime** working.

(iii)   Perhaps **recruit** more direct labour if long-term prospects are for higher production volumes.

(iv)   **Improve** the **productivity** ratio, and so reduce the number of hours required to produce the output.

(v)   If possible, **reduce** the **wastage** rate below 10%.

4.4 Example: the material purchases budget

Tremor manufactures two products, S and T, which use the same raw materials, D and E. One unit of S uses 3 litres of D and 4 kilograms of E. One unit of T uses 5 litres of D and 2 kilograms of E. A litre of D is expected to cost Y3 and a kilogram of E Y7.

Budgeted sales for 20X2 are 8,000 units of S and 6,000 units of T; finished goods in inventory at 1 January 20X2 are 1,500 units of S and 300 units of T, and the company plans to hold inventories of 600 units of each product at 31 December 20X2.

Inventories of raw material are 6,000 litres of D and 2,800 kilograms of E at 1 January, and the company plans to hold 5,000 litres and 3,500 kilograms respectively at 31 December 20X2.

The warehouse and stores managers have suggested that a provision should be made for damages and deterioration of items held in store, as follows.

Product S :   loss of 50 units
Product T :   loss of 100 units
Material D :   loss of 500 litres
Material E :   loss of 200 kilograms

Required

Prepare a material purchases budget for the year 20X2.

Solution

To calculate material purchase requirements, it is first of all necessary to calculate the budgeted production volumes and material usage requirements.

	Product S		Product T	
	Units	Units	Units	Units
Sales		8,000		6,000
Provision for losses		50		100
Closing inventory	600		600	
Opening inventory	1,500		300	
(Decrease)/increase in inventory		(900)		300
Production budget		7,150		6,400

	Material D Litres	Material D Litres	Material E Kg	Material E Kg
Usage requirements				
To produce 7,150 units of S		21,450		28,600
To produce 6,400 units of T		32,000		12,800
Usage budget		53,450		41,400
Provision for losses		500		200
		53,950		41,600
Closing inventory	5,000		3,500	
Opening inventory	6,000		2,800	
(Decrease)/increase in inventory		(1,000)		700
Material purchases budget		52,950		42,300

	Material D		Material E	
Cost per unit	Y3 per litre		Y7 per kg	
Cost of material purchases	Y158,850		Y296,100	
Total purchases cost		Y454,950		

Question

Learning outcome: C (vi)

J purchases a basic commodity and then refines it for resale. Budgeted sales of the refined product are as follows.

	April	May	June
Sales in kg	9,000	8,000	7,000

- The basic raw material costs £3 per kg.

- Material losses are 10% of finished output.

- The target month-end raw material inventory level is 5,000 kg plus 25% of the raw material required for next month's budgeted production.

- The target month-end inventory level for finished goods is 6,000 kg plus 25% of next month's budgeted sales.

What are the budgeted raw material purchases for April?

A 8,500 kg
B 9,350 kg
C 9,444.25 kg
D 9,831.25 kg

Answer

The correct answer is B.

	March kg	April kg	May kg
Required finished inventory:			
Base inventory	6,000	6,000	6,000
+ 25% of next month's sales	2,250	2,000	1,750
= Required inventory	8,250	8,000	7,750
Sales for month		9,000	8,000
		17,000	15,750
Less: opening inventory		8,250	8,000
Required finished production		8,750	7,750
+ 10% losses = raw material required		9,625	8,525

Required material inventory:		
Base inventory	5,000.00	5,000.00
+ 25% of material for next month's production	2,406.25	2,131.25
= Required closing material inventory	7,406.25	7,131.25
Production requirements		9,625.00
		16,756.25
Less: opening inventory		7,406.25
Required material purchases		9,350.00

4.5 Non-production overheads

In the modern business environment, an increasing proportion of overheads are not directly related to the volume of production, such as administration overheads and research and development costs.

4.6 Key decisions in the budgeting process for non-production overheads

Deciding which fixed costs are committed (will be incurred no matter what) and which fixed costs will depend on management decisions.

Deciding what factors will influence the level of variable costs. Administration costs for example may be partly governed by the number of orders received.

5 Cash budgets

FAST FORWARD

Cash budgets show the expected receipts and payments during a budget period and are a vital management planning and control tool.

Key term

A **cash budget** is 'A detailed budget of estimated cash inflows and outflows incorporating both revenue and capital items'. (CIMA *Official Terminology*)

5.1 The usefulness of cash budgets

The cash budget is one of the most important planning tools that an organisation can use. It shows the **cash effect of all plans made within the budgetary process** and hence its preparation can lead to a **modification of budgets** if it shows that there are insufficient cash resources to finance the planned operations.

It can also give management an indication of **potential problems** that could arise and allows them the opportunity to take action to avoid such problems. A cash budget can show **four positions**. Management will need to take appropriate action depending on the potential position.

Cash position	Appropriate management action
Short-term surplus	• Pay suppliers early to obtain discount • Attempt to increase sales by increasing receivables and inventories • Make short-term investments
Short-term deficit	• Increase payables

Cash position	Appropriate management action
	• Reduce receivables • Arrange an overdraft
Long-term surplus	• Make long-term investments • Expand • Diversify • Replace/update non-current assets
Long-term deficit	• Raise long-term finance (such as via issue of share capital) • Consider shutdown/disinvestment opportunities

Exam focus point

A cash budgeting question in an examination could ask you to recommend appropriate action for management to take once you have prepared the cash budget. Ensure your advice takes account both of whether there is a surplus or deficit and whether the position is long or short term.

5.2 What to include in a cash budget

A cash budget is prepared to show the expected receipts of cash and payments of cash during a budget period.

Sources of cash receipts

- Cash sales
- Payments by customers for credit sales
- The sale of property, plant and equipment
- The issue of new shares or loan inventory and less formalised loans
- The receipt of interest and dividends from investments outside the business

Remember that bad debts will **never be received in cash** and doubtful debts may not be received so you have to adjust if necessary for such items.

Although all the **receipts** above would affect a cash budget they would **not all appear in the income statement**.

(a)   The issue of new shares or loan inventory is a balance sheet item.

(b)   The cash received from an asset affects the balance sheet, and the profit or loss on the sale of an asset, which appears in the income statement, is not the cash received but the difference between cash received and the written down value of the asset at the time of sale.

Reasons for paying cash

- Purchase of inventories
- Payroll costs or other expenses
- Purchase of capital items
- Payment of interest, dividends or taxation

Not all payments are **income statement items**. The purchase of property, plant and equipment and the payment of VAT affect the balance sheet. Some costs in the income statement such as profit or loss on sale of non-current assets or depreciation are not cash items but are costs derived from accounting conventions.

In addition, the **timing** of cash receipts and payments **may not coincide** with the recording of income statement transactions. For example, a dividend might be declared in the results for year 6 and shown in the income statement for that year, but paid in cash in year 7.

Cash budgets are most effective if they are treated as **rolling budgets**. We will be looking at rolling budgets in more detail later in this chapter.

Steps in the preparation of a cash budget

- Set up a proforma cash budget.

	Month 1	Month 2	Month 3
	£	£	£
Cash receipts: Receipts from customers	X	X	X
Loan etc	X	X	X
	X	X	X
Cash payments: Payments to suppliers	X	X	X
Wages etc	X	X	X
	X	X	X
Opening balance	X	X	X
Net cash flow (receipts - payments)	X	X	X
Closing balance	X	X	X

- Enter the figures that can be entered straightaway (receipts or payments that you are told occur in a specific month)

- Sort out cash receipts from customers.

  - Establish budgeted sales month by month.

  - Establish the length of credit period taken by customers, using the following formula to calculate it if necessary.

    Receivables collection period (no of days credit)

    $$= \frac{\text{average (or year - end) receivables during period}}{\text{total credit sales in period}} \times \text{no of days in period}$$

  - Hence determine when budgeted sales revenue will be received as cash (by considering cash receipts from customers, ignoring any provision for doubtful debts).

  - Establish when opening receivables will pay.

- Establish when any other cash income will be received.

- Sort out cash payments to suppliers.

  - Establish production quantities and materials usage quantities each month.

  - Establish materials inventory changes and hence the quantity and cost of materials purchases each month.

  - Establish the length of credit period taken from suppliers, using the following formula to calculate it if necessary.

    Payables payment period (no of days credit)

    $$= \frac{\text{average (or year - end) payables during period}}{\text{total purchases on credit in period}} \times \text{no of days in period}$$

  - Hence calculate when cash payments to suppliers will be made and when the amount due to opening payables will be paid.

- Establish when any other cash payments (excluding non-cash items such as depreciation) will be made.

5.3 Example: income statement and cash budget

Penny operates a retail business. Purchases are sold at cost plus 33$\frac{1}{3}$%.

(a)

	Budgeted sales in month £	Labour cost in month £	Expenses incurred in month £
January	40,000	3,000	4,000
February	60,000	3,000	6,000
March	160,000	5,000	7,000
April	120,000	4,000	7,000

(b)   It is management policy to have sufficient inventory in hand at the end of each month to meet half of next month's sales demand.

(c)   Suppliers for materials and expenses are paid in the month after the purchases are made/expenses incurred. Labour is paid in full by the end of each month. Labour costs and expenses are treated as period costs in the income statement.

(d)   Expenses include a monthly depreciation charge of £2,000.

(e)   (i)   75% of sales are for cash.
       (ii)   25% of sales are on one month's credit.

(f)   The company will buy equipment costing £18,000 for cash in February and will pay a dividend of £20,000 in March. The opening cash balance at 1 February is £1,000.

Required

(a)   Prepare a cash budget for February and March.
(b)   Prepare an income statement for February and March.

Solution

(a)   CASH BUDGET

	February £	March £
Receipts		
Receipts from sales	55,000 (W1)	135,000 (W2)
Payments		
Trade payables	37,500 (W3)	82,500 (W3)
Expense payables	2,000 (W4)	4,000 (W4)
Labour	3,000	5,000
Equipment purchase	18,000	-
Dividend	–	20,000
Total payments	60,500	111,500
Receipts less payments	(5,500)	23,500
Opening cash balance b/f	1,000	(4,500)*
Closing cash balance c/f	(4,500)*	19,000

Workings

1

		£
Receipts in February	75% of Feb sales (75% × £60,000)	45,000
	25% of Jan sales (25% × £40,000)	10,000
		55,000

2

		£
Receipts in March	75% of Mar sales (75% × £160,000)	120,000
	25% of Feb sales (25% × £60,000)	15,000
		135,000

3   Purchases

		January £	February £
For Jan sales	(50% of £30,000)	15,000	
For Feb sales	(50% of £45,000)	22,500	(50% of £45,000) 22,500
For Mar sales		–	(50% of £120,000) 60,000
		37,500	82,500

These purchases are paid for in February and March.

4   Expenses

Cash expenses in January (£4,000 – £2,000) and February (£6,000 – £2,000) are paid in February and March respectively. Depreciation is not a cash item.

(b)   INCOME STATEMENT

	February £	February £	March £	March £
Sales		60,000		160,000
Cost of purchases (75%)		45,000		120,000
Gross profit		15,000		40,000
Less: Labour	3,000		5,000	
Expenses	6,000		7,000	
		9,000		12,000
Net profit		6,000		28,000

Attention!

(a) The asterisks show that the **cash balance at the end of February** is **carried forward** as the **opening cash balance for March**.

(b) The fact that profits are made in February and March **disguises** the fact that there is a **cash shortfall** at the end of February.

(c) Steps should be taken either to ensure that an **overdraft facility** is available for the cash shortage at the end of February, or to **defer certain payments** so that the overdraft is avoided.

(d) Some payments must be made on due dates (payroll, taxation and so on) but it is possible that other payments can be delayed, depending on the requirements of the business and/or the goodwill of suppliers.

5.4 A comparison of profit and cash flows

Look at the example above. Had you noticed that the total profit of £34,000 differs from the total receipts less total payments (£18,000). Profit and cash flows during a period need not be the same amount and, in fact, are actually more likely to be different.

(a) **Sales** and **cost of sales** are recognised in an **income statement** as soon as they are **made/incurred**. The **cash budget** does not show figures for sales and cost of sales but is concerned with **cash actually received** from customers and **paid** to suppliers.

(b)   An **income statement** may include **accrued** amounts for rates, insurance and other expenses. In the **cash budget** such amounts will appear in full in the **period in which they are paid**. There is no attempt to apportion payments to the period to which they relate.

(c)   Similarly an **income statement** may show a charge for **depreciation**. This is not a cash expense and will never appear in a cash budget. The **cash budget** will show **purchase of a non-current asset** as a payment in the **period when the asset is paid for**, and may also show the proceeds on disposal of a non-current asset as a receipt of cash. No attempt is made to allocate the purchase cost over the life of the asset.

Question   Cash budgets (receipts)

Learning outcome: C (vi)

X will begin trading on 1 January 20X3. The following sales revenue is budgeted for January to March 20X3.

January	February	March
€13,000	€17,000	€10,000

Five per cent of sales will be for cash. The remainder will be credit sales. A discount of 5% will be offered on all cash sales. The payment pattern for credit sales is expected to be as follows.

Invoices paid in the month after sale	75%
Invoices paid in the second month after sale	23%
Bad debts	2%

Invoices are issued on the last day of each month.

The amount budgeted to be received from customers in March 20X3 is

A   €15,428
B   €15,577.50
C   €15,928
D   €16,065.50

Answer

The correct answer is A.

	Received in March €
Cash sales (5% × €10,000) × 95%	475.00
February sales (€17,000 × 95%) × 75%	12,112.50
January sales (€13,000 × 95%) × 23%	2,840.50
	15,428.00

Question   Analysis of cash budget

Learning outcome: C (vi)

You are presented with the following cash budget for your organisation for the period January to June 20X2.

CASH BUDGET

	January $	February $	March $	April $	May $	June $
Cash receipts						
Cash sales	44,000	52,000	56,000	60,000	64,000	72,000
Credit sales	48,000	60,000	66,000	78,000	84,000	90,000
	92,000	112,000	122,000	138,000	148,000	162,000
Cash payments						
Purchases	60,000	80,000	90,000	110,000	130,000	140,000
Wages						
75%	12,000	15,000	18,000	21,000	24,000	27,000
25%	3,000	4,000	5,000	6,000	7,000	8,000
Overheads	10,000	15,000	15,000	15,000	20,000	20,000
Dividends			20,000			
Capital expenditure			30,000			40,000
	85,000	114,000	178,000	152,000	181,000	235,000
b/f	15,000	22,000	20,000	(36,000)	(50,000)	(83,000)
Net cash flow	7,000	(2,000)	(56,000)	(14,000)	(33,000)	(73,000)
c/f	22,000	20,000	(36,000)	(50,000)	(83,000)	(156,000)

Prior to the preparation of the cash budget, the managing director had been pleased with the functional budgets because they showed sales increasing by more than 100% in the period under review. In order to achieve this he had arranged a bank overdraft with a ceiling of $50,000 to accommodate the increased inventory levels and wage bill for overtime worked.

Required

Comment upon the cash budget in the light of your managing director's comments and offer advice.

Answer

The overdraft arrangements are quite inadequate to service the cash needs of the business over the six-month period. If the figures are realistic then action should be taken now to avoid difficulties in the near future. The following are **possible courses of action**.

(a) Activities could be curtailed.

(b) Other sources of cash could be explored, for example a long-term loan to finance the capital expenditure and a factoring arrangement to provide cash due from receivables more quickly.

(c) Efforts to increase the speed of debt collection could be made.

(d) Payments to suppliers could be delayed.

(e) The dividend payments could be postponed (the figures indicate that this is a small company, possibly owner-managed).

(f) Staff might be persuaded to work at a lower rate in return for, say, an annual bonus or a profit-sharing agreement.

(g) Extra staff might be taken on to reduce the amount of overtime paid.

(h) The inventory holding policy should be reviewed; it may be possible to meet demand from current production and minimise cash tied up in inventories.

This question has demonstrated the use of a cash budget for feedforward control, which you will learn more about in Chapter 13.

6 The master budget: calculating key metrics

6.1 The role of the master budget

The **master budget** is a summary of the functional (subsidiary) budgets and cash budget and includes a budgeted profit and loss account and a budgeted balance sheet.

Key term

The **master budget** is 'The budget into which all subsidiary budgets are consolidated, normally comprising budgeted profit and loss account, budgeted balance sheet and budgeted cash flow statement. These documents, and the supporting subsidiary budgets, are used to plan and control activities for the following year'. (CIMA *Official Terminology*)

It is this master budget which is **submitted** to senior managers or directors for their approval. If the master budget is **approved** as an acceptable plan for the forthcoming budget period then it acts as an **instruction and authorisation** to budget managers, to allow them to take action to achieve their budgets.

If the master budget is not approved as an acceptable plan then it will be returned to the budget committee for amendment. The **amended** master budget will then be reviewed again by senior management. Thus, budgeting is an **iterative process** and it may be necessary to perform many iterations before an acceptable, workable budget is adopted and approved.

6.2 Using key metrics to evaluate performance

A **key metric** is a term used to describe **an important measure in assessing performance,** whether budgeted or actual. Key metrics will vary from one organisation to another and an indicator which is a key metric for one organisation might not be a key metric for another organisation. Similarly, within the same organisation the key metrics may change over time, depending upon the changing circumstances of the organisation and the environment in which it operates.

Another term which is often used instead of key metrics is **key performance indicators (KPIs).**

In assessing the draft master budget to decide whether to accept and authorise it as an acceptable plan for the forthcoming period the senior managers will review a number of key metrics calculated from the draft master budget.

Targets will be set for each of the key metrics and if the draft budget does not meet each of the targets then it will be returned to the budget committee for revision.

Key metrics might be calculated for a number of areas including the following.

(a)   Profitability
(b)   Asset utilisation
(c)   Liquidity

6.3 Calculating key metrics for profitability

Key metrics for profitability might include the following.

(a)   **Return on capital employed** = (profit from operations/net assets) x 100%
      This ratio might also be referred to as **return on net assets.**

(b)   **Profit margin** = (profit from operations/revenue) x 100%

(c)   **Contribution to sales ratio**

6.4 Example: calculating key metrics for profitability

GD has established the following key metrics in order to assess profitability in the budgetary plans for the forthcoming budget period.

Return on capital employed = 22%
Profit margin = 12%
Contribution to sales ratio = 36%

Extracts from GD's master budget are as follows.

	$'000
Budgeted balance sheet extracts	
Non-current assets	3,500
Current assets (including inventory 1,440)	3,780
Current liabilities	2,320
Budgeted income statement extracts	
Revenue	6,980
Contribution	2,560
Profit from operations	990

Required

Assess whether senior management would approve the budget in terms of the key metrics for profitability.

Solution: calculating key metrics for profitability

Capital employed (in $'000)	= non-current assets + current assets − current liabilities
	= 3,500 + 3,780 − 2,320
	= 4,960
ROCE	= (990/4,960) × 100% = 20.0%
Profit margin	= (990/6,980) × 100% = 14.2%
Contribution to sales ratio	= (2,560/6,980) × 100% = 36.7%

Senior management would not approve the budget because, although it achieves the key metrics in terms of the profitability of sales, it does not achieve a sufficient return on capital employed.

6.5 The link between profitability and asset turnover/utilisation

In this example the return on capital employed metric was not achieved because the asset turnover ratio was too low.

Asset turnover monitors how efficient the company is in generating sales from its assets or capital employed. The asset turnover ratio is calculated as follows.

Asset turnover   = revenue/net assets
For GD, asset turnover = 6,980/4,960 = 1.4 times

Although GD has not specifically established a key metric for asset turnover it is implied from those given because of the connection between the return on net assets/capital employed and the asset turnover.

ROCE = profit margin × asset turnover

$$\frac{\text{Profit from operations}}{\text{Net assets}} = \frac{\text{profit from operations}}{\text{revenue}} \times \text{revenue}$$

In other words, a certain return on capital employed could be achieved either by earning a high profit margin but generating a relatively low turnover from the assets used, or by generating a high turnover from the assets but doing so at a low profit margin, or by any combination of higher or lower ratios.

For GD's budget, ROCE (20%) = profit margin (14.2%) × asset turnover (1.4 times)

Looking at the key metrics, the implied key metric for asset turnover is 1.8 times, using the formula as shown.

GD's key metrics: ROCE (22%) =profit margin (12%) × asset turnover (1.8 times)

GD's managers now know that, in order to achieve the key metric for return on capital employed, they need to **focus on improving asset turnover** but without affecting the budgeted profit margin.

6.6 Asset utilisation ratios

More detail might be sought on the utilisation of the various assets in order to be able to pinpoint where there is room for improvement in order to achieve the key metric for asset turnover. **Turnover can be measured for any individual category of assets** including non-current assets and inventory.

$$\text{Non-current asset turnover} = \frac{\text{revenue}}{\text{non} - \text{current assets}}$$

$$\text{Inventory turnover} = \frac{\text{cost of goods sold}}{\text{inventory}}$$

Notice that the inventory turnover ratio uses cost of goods sold as the numerator, rather than revenue for the period. This is because the inventory is valued at cost therefore the ratio is comparing like with like. However, if the information is not available concerning the cost of goods sold then **the revenue figure may be used instead.**

Question

Evaluating key metrics

Learning outcome: C(iv)

Using the data for GD in the example above, determine whether the key metric of 2.3 times for non-current asset turnover is achieved for the budget period. Advise management on any action they might take.

(5 marks)

Non-current asset turnover = 6,980/3,500 = 2.0 times

This is lower than the key metric of 2.3 times therefore the budget **would not be acceptable as a formalised plan for the forthcoming period.**

The relevant budget managers would need to look for **ways of improving this key metric**. The areas they might investigate include the following.

(a)   **Increase the budgeted revenue**. As long as this can be achieved without needing to invest in more non-current assets then the ratio will improve. However it will be necessary to ensure that the increase in revenue is achieved without a significant increase in costs, otherwise the profit margin will be adversely affected.

(b)   **Reduce the budgeted level of non-current assets.** If this can be achieved without a detrimental effect on revenue then the non-current asset turnover will improve. Perhaps budgeted purchases of non-current assets can be postponed or managers may be able to identity under-utilised assets which can be exploited further or else sold.

6.7 Liquidity ratios

Liquidity is a measure of the organisation's ability to meet its short-term obligations in cash. The monitoring of liquidity therefore focuses on the current assets and current liabilities.

The two key ratios used to monitor liquidity are as follows.

(a)   Current ratio = current assets/current liabilities
(b)   Acid test or quick ratio = current assets excluding inventory/current liabilities

The current ratio is concerned with whether an organisation can cover its current liabilities with its current assets. A ratio of less than 1.0 means that the organisation cannot do so but this does not necessarily mean that there are liquidity problems. Plenty of retail organisations thrive on a ratio of less than 1.0. They can do this because they sell their products largely for cash and their inventory turnover rates are relatively high.

The acid test ratio is concerned with whether an organisation can cover its current liabilities without needing to resort to selling the inventory. For some organisations the inventory is not a particularly liquid asset, ie it cannot be sold quickly in order to meet short term liabilities. Therefore this ratio really is an acid test of an organisation's ability to meet its current liabilities.

6.8 Example: calculating key metrics for liquidity

GD has established the following key metrics in order to assess liquidity in the budgetary plans for the forthcoming budget period.

Current ratio   = 1.5
Acid test/quick ratio   = 1.0

Assess whether senior management would approve the budget in terms of the key metrics for liquidity.

Solution: calculating key metrics for liquidity

Current ratio   = 3,780/2,320 = 1.6
Acid test ratio   = (3,780 – 1,440)/2,320 = 1.0

The senior managers would approve the budget from the point of view of the liquidity key metrics.

7 Monitoring procedures

FAST FORWARD

The budgeting process does not end for the forthcoming year once the budget period has begun: budgeting should be seen as a **continuous and dynamic process.**

The budgeting process does not stop once the budgets have been agreed. **Actual results should be compared on a regular basis with the budgeted results.** The frequency with which such comparisons are made depends very much on the organisation's circumstances and the sophistication of its control systems but it should occur at least **monthly**. Management should receive a report detailing the differences and should investigate the reasons for the differences. If the **differences** are **within the control** of management, **corrective action** should be taken to bring the reasons for the difference under control and to ensure that such inefficiencies do not occur in the future. We will look at this procedure in more detail in Chapter 13.

The differences may have occurred, however, because the budget was **unrealistic** to begin with or because the actual conditions did not reflect those anticipated (or could have possibly been anticipated). This would therefore **invalidate** the remainder of the budget.

Because the original budget was unrealistic or because of changes in anticipated conditions, the budget committee may need to reappraise the organisation's future plans and may need to adjust the budget to take account of such changes. The **revised budget** then represents a revised statement of formal operating plans for the remaining portion of the budget period.

Attention!

The important point to note is that the budgetary process does not end for the current year once the budget period has begun: budgeting should be seen as a **continuous and dynamic process**.

8 Alternative approaches to budgeting

8.1 Incremental budgeting

The **traditional approach** to budgeting is to **base next year's budget on the current year's results plus an extra amount for estimated growth or inflation next year.** This approach is known as **incremental budgeting** since it is concerned mainly with the increments in costs and revenues which will occur in the coming period.

Learning outcome: C(vi)

CP produces two products, X and Y. In the year ended 30 April 20X1 it produced 4,520 X and 11,750 Y and incurred costs of £1,217,200.

The costs incurred are such that 60% are variable. 70% of these variable costs vary with the number of X produced, with the remainder varying with the output of Y.

The budget for the three months to 31 October 20X1 is being prepared using an incremental approach based on the following.

- All costs will be 5% higher than the average paid in the year ended 30 April 20X1
- Efficiency levels will be unchanged
- Expected output

    X   1,210 units
    Y   3,950 units

What is the budgeted cost for the output of X (to the nearest £100) for the three months ending 31 October 20X1?

A   £100
B   £127,800
C   £536,800
D   £134,200

Answer

The correct answer is D.

Proportion of actual annual costs related to X = £1,217,200 × 0.6 × 0.7 = £511,224

Proportion applicable to three-month period = £511,224/4 = £127,806

Inflated cost = £127,806 × 1.05 = £134,196

Option A is the budgeted cost per X. If you selected **option B** you forgot to inflate the cost. If you selected **option C**, you forgot to reduce the annual cost to a quarterly cost.

Incremental budgeting is a reasonable procedure if current operations are as effective, efficient and economical as they can be. It is also appropriate for budgeting for costs such as staff salaries, which may be estimated on the basis of current salaries plus an increment for inflation and are hence administratively fairly easy to prepare.

Learning outcome: C(vi)

Explain what is meant by incremental budgeting and discuss its suitability for budgeting for rent costs and for advertising expenditure.   (5 marks)

Answer

Incremental budgeting is a method of setting budgets whereby **the latest period's budget is used as a base for preparing the budget for the forthcoming period.** Adjustments are made for any expected changes, for example changes in staffing levels or in the level of activity.

Incremental budgeting may be appropriate for budgeting for rent because the rent cost for the forthcoming period may be **estimated on the basis of the current rent plus an increment for the annual rent increase.**

Incremental budgeting might not be appropriate for budgeting for advertising expenditure because such expenditure is not so easily quantifiable and is more discretionary in nature. Using incremental budgeting for advertising expenditure could allow **slack (unnecessary expenditure)** and wasteful spending to creep into the budget. Simply adding an increment to the current year's budget **does not force managers to question whether the current level of expenditure is necessary.** Furthermore there will be a tendency for the relevant manager to **ensure that the current budget is spent**, in case the allowance is removed for the forthcoming year, if it is not spent this year.

In general, however, it is an **inefficient form of budgeting** as it **encourages slack** and **wasteful spending** to creep into budgets. Past inefficiencies are perpetuated because cost levels are rarely subjected to close scrutiny.

To ensure that inefficiencies are not concealed, however, alternative approaches to budgeting have been developed. One such approach is **zero base budgeting (ZBB)**.

8.2 Zero base budgeting

FAST FORWARD
- The principle behind **zero base budgeting** is that the budget for each cost centre should be prepared from 'scratch' or zero. Every item of expenditure must be justified to be included in the budget for the forthcoming period.
- There is a three-step approach to ZBB.
    - Define **decision packages**
    - Evaluate and rank packages
    - Allocate resources
- ZBB is particularly useful for budgeting for discretionary costs.

8.2.1 The principles of ZBB

ZBB rejects the assumption inherent in incremental budgeting that this year's activities will continue at the same level or volume next year, and that next year's budget can be based on this year's costs plus an extra amount, perhaps for expansion and inflation.

Key term

Zero base budgeting is 'A method of budgeting which requires each cost element to be specifically justified, as though the activities to which the budget relates were being undertaken for the first time. Without approval the budget allowance is zero.'

(CIMA *Official Terminology*)

In reality, however, managers do not have to budget from zero, but can **start from their current level of expenditure and work downwards**, asking what would happen if any particular aspect of current expenditure and current operations were removed from the budget. In this way, every aspect of the budget is examined in terms of its cost and the benefits it provides and the selection of better alternatives is encouraged.

8.2.2 Implementing ZBB

The implementation of ZBB involves a number of steps but of greater importance is the **development of a questioning attitude** by all those involved in the budgetary process. Existing practices and expenditures must be challenged and searching questions asked.

- Does the activity need to be carried out?
- What would be the consequences if the activity were not carried out?
- Is the current level of provision adequate?
- Are there alternative ways of providing the function?
- How much should the activity cost?
- Is the expenditure worth the benefits achieved?

The three steps of ZBB

Step 1 Define decision packages, comprehensive descriptions of specific organisational activities (decision units) which management can use to evaluate the activities and rank them in order of priority against other activities. There are two types.

(a) Mutually exclusive packages contain alternative methods of getting the same job done. The best option among the packages must be selected by comparing costs and benefits and the other packages are then discarded.

(b) Incremental packages divide one aspect of an activity into different levels of effort. The 'base' package will describe the minimum amount of work that must be done to carry out the activity and the other packages describe what additional work could be done, at what cost and for what benefits.

EXAMPLE

Suppose that a cost centre manager is preparing a budget for maintenance costs. He might first consider two mutually exclusive packages. Package A might be to keep a maintenance team of two men per shift for two shifts each day at a cost of £60,000 per annum, whereas package B might be to obtain a maintenance service from an outside contractor at a cost of £50,000. A cost-benefit analysis will be conducted because the quicker repairs obtainable from an in-house maintenance service might justify its extra cost. If we now suppose that package A is preferred, the budget analysis must be completed by describing the incremental variations in this chosen alternative.

- The **'base' package** would describe the minimum requirement for the maintenance work. This might be to pay for one man per shift for two shifts each day at a cost of £30,000.

- **Incremental package 1** might be to pay for two men on the early shift and one man on the late shift, at a cost of £45,000. The extra cost of £15,000 would need to be justified, for example by savings in lost production time, or by more efficient machinery.

- **Incremental package 2** might be the original preference, for two men on each shift at a cost of £60,000. The cost-benefit analysis would compare its advantages, if any, over incremental package 1; and so on.

Question ZBB

Learning outcome: C (vi)

What might the base package and incremental packages for a personnel department cover?

	Base	Incremental
A	Recruitment	Training
B	Dismissal	Recruitment
C	Training	Pension administration
D	Pension administration	Recruitment

Answer

The correct answer is A.

The base package might cover the recruitment and dismissal of staff. Incremental packages might cover training, pension administration, trade union liaison, staff welfare and so on.

Step 2 **Evaluate and rank each activity (decision package)** on the basis of its benefit to the organisation. This can be a lengthy process. Minimum work requirements (those that are essential to get a job done) will be given high priority and so too will work which meets legal obligations. In the accounting department these would be minimum requirements to operate the payroll, purchase ledger and sales ledger systems, and to maintain and publish a satisfactory set of accounts.

Step 3 **Allocate resources** in the budget according to the funds available and the evaluation and ranking of the competing packages.

8.2.3 The advantages and limitations of ZBB

Advantages of ZBB

- It is possible to identify and **remove inefficient or obsolete operations.**
- It forces employees to **avoid wasteful expenditure**.
- It can **increase motivation**.
- It **responds to changes in the business environment.**
- ZBB **documentation provides** an in-depth **appraisal of an organisation's operations.**
- It **challenges the status quo**.
- In summary, ZBB should result in a **more efficient allocation of resources**.

The major **disadvantage** of ZBB is the **volume of extra paperwork** created. The assumptions about costs and benefits in each package must be continually updated and new packages developed as soon as new activities emerge. The following problems might also occur.

(a) **Short-term benefits** might be **emphasised** to the detriment of long-term benefits.

(b) It may give the impression **that all decisions have to be made in the budget**. Management must be able to meet unforeseen opportunities and threats at all times, however, and must not feel restricted from carrying out new ideas simply because they were not approved by a decision package, cost benefit analysis and the ranking process.

(c)   It may be a **call for management skills** both in constructing decision packages and in the ranking process **which the organisation does not possess**. Managers may therefore have to be trained in ZBB techniques.

(d)   The organisation's **information systems may not be capable of providing suitable information**.

(e)   **The ranking process can be difficult**. Managers face three common problems.

   (i)   A large number of packages may have to be ranked.

   (ii)   It can be difficult to rank packages which appear to be equally vital, for legal or operational reasons.

   (iii)   It is difficult to rank activities which have qualitative rather than quantitative benefits - such as spending on staff welfare and working conditions.

In summary, perhaps the **most serious drawback to ZBB is that it requires a lot of management time and paperwork**. One way of obtaining the benefits of ZBB but of overcoming the drawbacks is to apply it selectively on a rolling basis throughout the organisation. This year finance, next year marketing, the year after personnel and so on. In this way all activities will be thoroughly scrutinised over a period of time.

Question   Base and incremental packages

Learning outcome: C (vi)

What might the base and incremental packages cover in your department if your organisation used ZBB?

8.2.4 Using ZBB

ZBB is not particularly suitable for direct manufacturing costs, which are usually budgeted using standard costing, work study and other management planning and control techniques. ZBB is best applied to **support expenses**, that is expenditure incurred in departments which exist to support the essential production function. These support areas include marketing, finance, quality control, personnel, data processing, sales and distribution. In many organisations, these expenses make up a large proportion of the total expenditure. These activities are less easily quantifiable by conventional methods and are more **discretionary** in nature. We return to the problem of budgeting for discretionary costs later in this section.

ZBB can also be successfully applied to **service industries** and **not-for-profit organisations** such as local and central government, educational establishments, hospitals and so on, and in any organisation where alternative levels of provision for each activity are possible and costs and benefits are separately identifiable.

Question   Using ZBB

Learning outcome: C(vi)

You work for a large multinational company which manufactures weedkillers. It has been decided to introduce zero base budgeting (ZBB) in place of the more traditional incremental budgeting. The manager of the research and development department has never heard of ZBB.

Required

Write a report to the manager of the research and development department which explains the following.

(a)	How zero base budgeting techniques differ from traditional budgeting	(5 marks)
(b)	How ZBB may assist in planning and controlling discretionary costs	(5 marks)
(c)	How ZBB will help to control budgetary slack	(5 marks)

Answer

REPORT

To: R&D manager
From: Management accountant   Date: 01.01.X3
Subject: Zero base budgeting

(a)   The **traditional approach** to budgeting works from the premise that last year's activities will continue at the same level or volume, and that next year's budget can be based on last year's costs plus an extra amount to allow for expansion and inflation. The term 'incremental' budgeting is often used to describe this approach.

   Zero base budgeting (ZBB) quite literally works from a zero base. The approach recognises that every activity has a cost and insists that there must be quantifiable benefits to justify the spending. ZBB expects managers to choose the best method of achieving each task on a cost-benefit basis. Activities must be ranked in order of priority.

(b)   **Discretionary cost** is 'expenditure whose value is a matter of policy', that is, it is not vital to the continued existence of an organisation in the way that, say, raw materials are to a manufacturing business. ZBB was developed originally to help management with the difficult task of allocating resources in precisely such areas. Research and development is a frequently cited example; others are advertising and training.

   Within a research and development department ZBB will establish priorities by ranking the projects that are planned and in progress. Project managers will be forced to consider the benefit obtainable from their work in relation to the costs involved. The result may be an overall increase in R&D expenditure, but only if it is justified.

   It is worth mentioning that when R&D costs are subsequently being monitored care is needed in interpreting variances. A favourable expenditure variance may not be a good thing: it may mean that not enough is being spent on R&D activity.

(c)   **Budgetary slack** may be defined as the **difference between the minimum necessary costs and the costs built into the budget or actually incurred**. One of the reasons why, under traditional budgeting, an extra amount is added to last year's budget may be because managers are overestimating costs to avoid being blamed in the future for overspending and to make targets easier to achieve. Slack is a protective device and it is self-fulfilling because managers will subsequently ensure that their actual spending rises to meet the (overestimated) budget, in case they are blamed for careless budgeting.

   In an R&D department a further incentive to include slack is the nature of the work. Managers may well have 'pet' projects in which their personal interest is so strong that they tend to ignore the benefit or lack of benefit to the organisation which is funding them.

   The ZBB approach, as described in (a) above, clearly will not accept this approach: all expenditure has (in theory) to be justified in cost-benefit terms in its entirety in order to be included in next year's budget. In practice it is more likely that managers will start from their current level of expenditure as usual, but ZBB requires them to work downwards, asking what would happen if any particular element of current expenditure and current operations were removed from the budget.

8.3 Programme planning and budgeting systems

PPBS is particularly useful for public sector and non-profit-seeking organisations.

A programme planning and budgeting system (PPBS) sets a budget in terms of **programmes** (groups of activities with common objectives). By focusing on objectives, the budget is therefore **orientated towards the ultimate output of the organisation**. This contrasts with the traditional approach to budgeting, which focuses on inputs (such as material and labour).

Such an approach is therefore particularly useful for **public sector** and **not-for-profit** organisations, such as government departments, schools, hospitals and charities, to ensure that expenditure is **focused** on programmes and activities that generate the most **beneficial results**. This is of particular value at a time when there is increasing public demand for **accountability** by such organisations: donors to charities have recently expressed concern over the high proportion of donations used to pay administrative expenses. PPBS allows people (taxpayers and donors) to see where their money is going and how it has been spent.

Disadvantages of using traditional budgeting for public sector and not-for-profit organisations

(a) Activities often span several years but the emphasis is on annual figures.

(b) It is difficult to incorporate into a budget report planned or actual achievements (number of sufferers helped, level of education and so on) as these achievements tend to be non-financial in nature.

(c) Costs relating to a particular objective are spread across a number of cost categories. For example, the costs relating to an objective of a police force to protect people and property from traffic hazards might be allocated to a variety of traditional cost categories – personnel, transport, administration, training and so on. It would be impossible to tell how much was spent, or authorised, to achieve that objective.

(d) There is no evidence as to how effectively or efficiently resources are being used.

PPBS would overcome these problems as the emphasis would be on objectives and the best use of resources to achieve effectiveness over the medium to long term.

PPBS approach

Step 1 Review long-term objectives (such as, for a police force, protect persons and property and deal with offenders).

Step 2 Set out the programmes of activities needed to achieve the objectives (such as police patrol on foot, police patrol in vehicles and so on).

Step 3 Evaluate the alternative programmes in terms of costs and benefits and select the most appropriate programmes.

Step 4 Analyse the programmes selected, finding out (for example) what would happen to the level of achievement of objectives if resources allocated to a particular programme were reduced by, say, 10%.

8.4 Discretionary costs

A **discretionary** (or **managed** or **policy**) **cost** is 'A cost whose amount within a time period is determined by, and is easily altered by, a decision taken by the appropriate budget holder'.

(CIMA *Official Terminology*)

8.4.1 Budgeting for discretionary costs

It is much easier to set budgets for **engineered costs** (costs for which there is a **demonstrable relationship between the input** to a process and the **output** of that process) than for **discretionary costs** (costs for which there is **no clear relationship between the input and output of a process**, often because the **output is difficult to measure**, in terms of quantity and/or quality). It is obviously easier to budget for direct material costs (engineered cost) than for the cost of the accounts department (discretionary cost).

Budgeting for discretionary costs can be made **easier** by **converting them into engineered costs**.

- Develop suitable output measures
- Understand how input impacts on output

For example, by analysing the work undertaken to process an invoice for payment, an **average time** for dealing with an invoice can be established and the relationship between the number of invoices processed and the resources required to do this ascertained.

The analysis required for **activity based costing** will also add to an understanding of the relationship between the inputs and outputs of a process.

If a discretionary cost cannot be converted into an engineered cost, ZBB or PPBS will be needed.

8.4.2 Control of discretionary costs

Discretionary costs **cannot be controlled on the basis of outputs** because of the difficulty in specifying outputs in financial terms. In order to set minimum standards of performance, some measure of output is needed, however. An accounts department may be required to pay invoices within two weeks of receipt, for example.

Inputs can be **controlled**, however, if the **budget** acts as a device to ensure financial resources allocated to the activity are not exceeded.

8.5 Rolling budgets

FAST FORWARD

- **Rolling budgets** (continuous budgets) are budgets which are continuously updated by adding a further period (say a month or a quarter) and deducting the earliest period.
- **Cash budgets** are usually prepared on a rolling basis.

CIMA's *Official Terminology* defines a **rolling budget** as 'A budget continuously updated by adding a further accounting period (month or quarter) when the earliest accounting period has expired.'

Rolling budgets are also called **continuous budgets**. They are particularly **useful** when an organisation is facing a **period of uncertainty** so that it is difficult to prepare accurate forecasts. For example it may be difficult to estimate the level of inflation for the forthcoming period.

Rolling budgets are an attempt to prepare **targets and plans** which are **more realistic** and **certain**, particularly with a regard to price levels, by shortening the period between preparing budgets.

Instead of preparing a **periodic budget annually** for the full budget period, budgets would be prepared, say, every one, two or three months (four, six, or even twelve budgets each year). Each of these budgets would plan for the next twelve months so that the current budget is extended by an extra period as the current period ends: hence the name rolling budgets. **Cash budgets** are usually prepared on a rolling basis.

Suppose, for example, that a rolling budget is prepared every three months. The first three months of the budget period would be planned in great detail, and the remaining nine months in lesser detail, because of the greater uncertainty about the longer-term future.

(a)   The first continuous budget would show January to March Year 1 in detail, and April to December Year 1 in less detail.

(b)   At the end of March, the first three months of the budget would be removed and a further three months would be added at the end for January to March Year 2.

(c)   The remaining nine months for April to December Year 1 would be updated in the light of current conditions, adding more detail to the earliest three months, April to June Year 1.

The detail in the first three months would be principally important for the following.

- **Planning** working capital and short-term resources (cash, materials, labour and so on)

- **Control**: the budget for each control period should provide a more reliable yardstick for comparison with actual results.

Question   Rolling budgets

Learning outcome: C (vi)

What advantages and disadvantages of rolling budgets can you think of?

Answer

The **advantages** are as follows.

(a)   They reduce the element of uncertainty in budgeting. If a high rate of inflation or major changes in market conditions or any other change is likely which cannot be quantified with accuracy, rolling budgets concentrate detailed planning and control on short-term prospects where the degree of uncertainty is much smaller.

(b)   They force managers to reassess the budget regularly, and to produce budgets which are up to date in the light of current events and expectations.

(c)   Planning and control will be based on a recent plan instead of an annual budget that might have been made many months ago and which is no longer realistic.

(d)   There is always a budget which extends for several months ahead. For example, if rolling budgets are prepared quarterly there will always be a budget extending for the next 9 to 12 months. If rolling budgets are prepared monthly there will always be a budget for the next 11 to 12 months. This is not the case when annual budgets are used.

The **disadvantages** of rolling budgets can be a deterrent to using them.

(a) A system of rolling budgets calls for the routine preparation of a new budget at regular intervals during the course of the one financial year. This involves more time, effort and money in budget preparation.

(b) Frequent budgeting might have an off-putting effect on managers who doubt the value of preparing one budget after another at regular intervals, even when there are major differences between the figures in one budget and the next.

Key term

Activity based budgeting is 'A method of budgeting based on an activity framework and utilising cost driver data in the budget-setting and variance feedback processes.' (CIMA *Official Terminology*)

At its **simplest**, activity based budgeting (ABB) is merely the **use of costs determined using** ABC **as a basis for preparing budgets**.

A budget for an activity is therefore based on the budgeted number of the activity's cost driver × the appropriate cost driver rate. For example, if an organisation expects to place 500 orders and the rate per order is £100, the budgeted cost of the ordering activity will be 500 × £100 = £50,000.

Implementing ABC leads to the realisation that the **business as a whole** needs to be **managed** with far more reference to the behaviour of activities and cost drivers identified.

(a) **Traditional budgeting may make managers 'responsible' for activities which are driven by factors beyond their control**: the cost of setting-up new personnel records and of induction training would traditionally be the responsibility of the personnel manager even though such costs are driven by the number of new employees required by managers other than the personnel manager.

(b) The **budgets for costs not directly related to production** are often traditionally set using an **incremental approach** because of the difficulty of linking the activity driving the cost to production level. But this assumes that all of the cost is unaffected by any form of activity level, which is often not the case in reality. Some of the costs of the purchasing department, for example, will be fixed (such as premises costs) but some will relate to the number of orders placed or the volume of production, say. Surely the budget for the purchasing department should take some account of the expected number of orders?

More **formally**, therefore, ABB involves **defining the activities** that underlie the financial figures in each function and using the level of activity to decide **how much resource should be allocated,** how well it is being **managed** and to explain **variances** from budget.

Claimed results of using ABB

(a) Different activity levels will provide a foundation for the base package and incremental packages of ZBB.

(b) The organisation's overall strategy and any actual or likely changes in that strategy will be taken into account because ABB attempts to manage the business as the sum of its interrelated parts.

(c) Critical success factors (an activity in which a business must perform well if it is to succeed) will be identified and key metrics devised to monitor progress towards them.

(d)   The focus is on the whole of an activity, not just its separate parts, and so there is more likelihood of getting it right first time. For example, what is the use of being able to produce goods in time for their despatch date if the budget provides insufficient resources for the distribution manager who has to deliver them.

(e)   Traditional accounting tends to focus on the nature of the costs being incurred (the input side) and traditional budgeting tends to mirror this. ABB emphasises the activities that are being achieved (the outputs).

9 Budgeting in an uncertain environment

9.1 Budgets for worst possible, best possible and most likely outcomes

In an uncertain environment, the **three tier approach** to budgeting or **sensitivity analysis** can be used.

When some future events are uncertain and the performance of the organisation depends on how these future events turn out, one way of budgeting is to prepare three budgets.

(a)   The **most likely outcome budget**, which will start off as the **master budget**.

(b)   A budget for the **worst possible or pessimistic outcome**. The 'worst possible' should be for a **realistic** worst outcome, based on the assumption that key events or outcomes which are uncertain at the time of budgeting will turn out for the worst.

(c)   A budget for the **best possible outcome**.

9.2 Example: most likely, pessimistic and optimistic budgets

Suppose that Netcord is a company which makes and sells tennis rackets. Its sales for the past few years, and its profits, have been constant as follows.

	£
Sales	1,500,000
Variable costs	500,000
Contribution	1,000,000
Fixed costs	800,000
Profit	200,000

In preparing a budget for the next year, there is uncertainty about several key points.

(a)   Netcord has tendered for two contracts, each to supply an overseas customer. The sales value of contract A is £500,000, that of contract B £300,000. For each of these orders, variable costs (including selling and shipping costs) would be 40% of sales value. Total fixed costs would be unaffected by the order. The company hopes to win both orders, but thinks it more likely that it will win contract A but not contract B.

(b)   A new product, a model of squash racket, is due to be launched next year. Expected sales are £30,000 per month, with variable costs of 50% of sales, and fixed costs of £5,000 per month. The most likely launch date for the new product is in mid-year (ie six months into the year) but it could be launched as early as the end of month 4 or as late as the end of month 9.

(c)   Although it is expected that sales price and costs will not go up, there is a reasonable possibility that variable costs on the current product range will go up by 10%.

Required

Prepare a most likely, a pessimistic and an optimistic budget.

Solution

The most likely, optimistic and pessimistic assumptions are shown.

Most likely	Optimistic	Pessimistic
Win contract A	Win contract A	Don't win contract A
Don't win contract B	Win contract B	Don't win contract B
New product after 6 months	New product after 4 months	New product after 9 months
No change in costs	No change in costs	Variable costs up 10%

	Most likely		Optimistic		Pessimistic	
	£'000	£'000	£'000	£'000	£'000	£'000
Normal sales, current product	1,500		1,500		1,500	
Variable costs	500		500		550	
Contribution		1,000		1,000		950
Overseas contracts						
Sales	500		800		0	
Variable costs (40%)	200		320		0	
Contribution		300		480		0
Squash rackets						
Sales	180		240		90	
Variable costs (50%)	90		120		45	
Contribution		90		120		45
Total contribution		1,390		1,600		995
Fixed costs						
Squash rackets	30		40		15	
Other	800		800		800	
		830		840		815
Profit		560		760		180

The 'most likely' budget will probably be adopted as the master budget, but the management of Netcord could **use the three budgets** as follows.

(a)   To assess the likely effect of actual outcomes (for example winning contract A).

(b)   To identify by how much each uncertain outcome might affect profits, and do whatever they can to try to avoid the worst outcome if profits would be particularly badly affected.

In this example, it is fairly clear that winning contract A is the most important 'uncertain outcome' and management might wish to think about ways in which they can improve their chances of winning it.

9.3 The suitability of the three tier approach

The most likely/worst possible/best possible (or **three tier**) **approach** to budgeting is best suited to situations where there are only a **few uncertain outcomes**. When there are a **large number of outcomes** which cannot be predicted with any reasonable confidence, having just three budgets will probably be too simplistic and not really helpful to management. In such circumstances, **spreadsheet** packages can be used. We look at this topic at the end of the next chapter.

9.4 Sensitivity analysis

Suppose W Ltd expects to sell 500 units of product N in control period 2 at £75 per unit. There is some uncertainty over the unit variable cost, however, which could be anywhere between £30 and £50, with £40 as the 'expected' outcome. Fixed costs are £20,000.

One way of carrying out a sensitivity analysis on this information would be graphically (using **worst case/best case/expected results**).

Worst case

	£
Sales (500 × £75)	37,500
Variable costs (500 × £50)	(25,000)
Fixed costs	(20,000)
Loss	(7,500)

Best case

	£
Sales	37,500
Variable costs (500 × £30)	(15,000)
Fixed costs	(20,000)
Profit	2,500

Expected

	£
Sales	37,500
Variable costs (500 × £40)	(20,000)
Fixed costs	(20,000)
Loss	(2,500)

The graph indicates that the operation remains **profitable over just 25% of possible outcomes**. The graphical presentation therefore gives an impression of the possible impact of the uncertainty.

9.5 Expected values

If probabilities can be assigned to the three possible outcomes in the three tier approach then it is possible to calculate the **expected value** of the outcome. You studied expected values in Paper 3c but we will review the basics here.

Key term

An **expected value or** (EV) is a weighted average value, based on probabilities.

If the probability of an outcome of an event is p, then the expected number of times that this outcome will occur in n events (the expected value) is equal to n × p.

For example, suppose that the probability that a transistor is defective is 0.02. How many defectives would we expect to find in a batch of 4,000 transistors?

EV   = 4,000 × 0.02
      = 80 defectives

9.6 Example: expected values

The annual sales of product J ay be as follows.

	Units	Probability
Worst case	4,000	0.1
Best case	9,200	0.2
Most likely case	6,400	0.7
		1.0

Required

Calculate the expected annual sales volume.

Key focus point

Notice that the total probability of all possible outcomes is 1.0. The examiner expected candidates to know this in an MCQ on the pilot paper.

Solution

The EV of annual sales is calculated by multiplying each possible outcome (volume of annual sales) by the probability that this outcome will occur.

Units	Probability	Expected value Units
4,000	0.1	400
9,200	0.2	1,840
6,400	0.7	4,480
Expected value of annual sales		6,720

 Question   Expected sales

Learning outcome: C (vii)

The demand for product S next period will depend on bank interest rates. If interest rates increase the sales volume will be 5,100 units. If interest rates decrease the sales volume will be 7,600 units. If interest rates remain unaltered the sales volume will be 6,200 units.

The latest estimates are that there is a 60% probability that interest rates will rise and no possibility that they will remain unaltered.

Required

Calculate the expected sales volume of product S next period.

Answer

Interest rates	Sales volume	Probability	Expected value
	Units		Units
Increase	5,100	0.60	3,060
Remain the same	6,200	0.00	0
Decrease	7,600	0.40	3,040
		1.00	6,100

The expected sales volume is 6,100 units.

Chapter Roundup

- A **budget** is a quantified plan of action for a forthcoming accounting period. A **budget** is a plan of what the organisation is aiming to achieve and what is has set as a target, whereas a **forecast** is an estimate of what is likely to occur in the future

- The **objectives** of a budgetary planning and control system are as follows.

    - To ensure the achievement of the organisation's objectives
    - To compel planning
    - To communicate ideas and plans
    - To coordinate activities
    - To provide a framework for responsibility accounting
    - To establish a system of control
    - To motivate employees to improve their performance

- The **budget committee** is the coordinating body in the preparation and administration of budgets.

- The **principal budget factor** should be identified at the beginning of the budgetary process, and the budget for this is prepared before all the others.

- **Cash budgets** show the expected receipts and payments during a budget period and are a vital management planning and control tool.

- The **master budget** is a summary of the functional (subsidiary) budgets and cash budget and includes a budgeted profit and loss account and a budgeted balance sheet.

- The budgeting process does not end for the forthcoming year once the budget period has begun: budgeting should be seen as a **continuous and dynamic process.**

- The principle behind **zero base budgeting** is that the budget for each cost centre should be prepared from 'scratch' or zero. Every item of expenditure must be justified to be included in the budget for the forthcoming period.

- There is a three-step approach to ZBB.

    - Define **decision packages**
    - Evaluate and rank packages
    - Allocate resources

- ZBB is particularly useful for budgeting for discretionary costs.

- **PPBS** is particularly useful for public sector and non-profit-seeking organisations.

- **Rolling budgets** (continuous budgets) are budgets which are continuously updated by adding a further period (say a month or a quarter) and deducting the earliest period.

- **Cash budgets** are usually prepared on a rolling basis.

- In an uncertain environment, the **three tier approach** to budgeting or **sensitivity analysis** can be used.

Quick Quiz

1   Which of the following is not an objective of a system of budgetary planning and control?

   A   To establish a system of control
   B   To coordinate activities
   C   To compel planning
   D   To motivate employees to maintain current performance levels

2   Sales is always the principal budget factor and so it is always the first budget to be prepared. *True or false?*

3   *Choose the appropriate words from those highlighted.*

   A **forecast/budget** is an **estimate/guarantee** of what is **likely to occur in the future/has happened in the past.**

   A **forecast/budget** is a **quantified plan/unquantified plan/guess** of what the organisation is aiming to **achieve/spend**.

4   *Fill in the blanks.*

   When preparing a production budget, the quantity to be produced is equal to sales ……………….. opening inventory ……………….. closing inventory.

5   Which of the following should be included in a cash budget?

	Include	Do not include
Funds from the issue of share capital		
Revaluation of a fixed asset		
Receipt of dividends from outside the business		
Depreciation of production machinery		
Bad debts written off		
Repayment of a bank loan		

6   What are the three components of the master budget?

   1   …………………………………..

   2   …………………………………..

   3   …………………………………..

7   Match the description to the type of budget.

   Types of budget

   Incremental budget; rolling budget; zero base budget

   Description

   (a)   Next year's budget is based on the current year's results plus an extra amount for estimated growth or inflation next year.

   (b)   Each item in the budget is specifically justified, as though each activity were being undertaken for the first time.

   (c)   The budget is continuously updated by adding a further accounting period when the earliest accounting period has expired.

8   Once a budget period has started, assuming a system of rolling budgets is **not** in operation, the original budget should never be adjusted. *True or false?*

9   What are the three tiers of the three tier approach to budgeting?

1   …………………………………..

2   …………………………………..

3   …………………………………..

Answers to Quick Quiz

1   D. The objective is to motivate employees to *improve* their performance.

2   False. The budget for the principal budget factor must be prepared first, but sales is not always the principal budget factor.

3   A forecast is an estimate of what is likely to occur in the future.

     A budget is a quantified plan of what the organisation is aiming to achieve.

4   When preparing a production budget, the quantity to be produced is equal to sales minus opening inventory plus closing inventory.

5

	Include	Do not include
Funds from the issue of share capital	✓	
Revaluation of a fixed asset		✓
Receipt of dividends from outside the business	✓	
Depreciation of production machinery		✓
Bad debts written off		✓
Repayment of a bank loan	✓	

6   Budgeted cash flow, budgeted profit and loss account and budgeted balance sheet.

7   Incremental budget (a); rolling budget (c); zero base budget (b).

8   False. If the budget is found to be unrealistic or if actual conditions do not reflect those that could possibly have been anticipated, the remainder of the budget may be invalid and the budget committee may need to adjust it.

9   Most likely outcome
     Worst possible outcome
     Best possible outcome

Now try the questions below from the Exam Question Bank

Number	Level	Marks	Time
Q23	Examination	20	36 mins
Q24	Examination	5	9 mins

Preparing forecasts for budgetary plans

Introduction

In Chapter 11 we saw how to prepare budgets but we have not yet looked at where the figures which go into the budgets come from. As we will see in this chapter, to produce a budget calls for the **preparation of forecasts of costs and revenues**. Various quantitative techniques can assist with these **'number-crunching' aspects of budgeting.** This chapter aims to provide an understanding of those techniques. Note that the techniques will be described within their budgetary context.

We will be covering **two principal forecasting techniques** in this chapter, **regression analysis** and **time series analysis**. Regression analysis can be applied to costs and revenues while time series analysis is generally applied to revenue.

MCQs on forecasting techniques are **likely**. **Longer questions** could **involve both regression analysis and time series analysis**. For example, you might have to apply seasonal variations to a trend determined using regression analysis.

'What if?' analysis, covered in Section 10, is specifically mentioned in the syllabus and so work through the section with care.

Much of this chapter will be **revision** from your 3c *Business Mathematics* paper, but work through all of the material slowly and carefully to ensure that you have a thorough knowledge of quantitative forecasting techniques.

Our study of budgeting continues in the next chapter, the third and final one on the topic.

Topic list	Learning outcomes	Syllabus references	Ability required
1 Forecasting using historical data	C(ii)(iii)	C 1,2	Application
2 Linear regression analysis	C(ii)	C 1	Application
3 Scatter diagrams and correlation	C(ii)	C 2,3	Application
4 Sales forecasting	C(ii)	C 1	Application
5 Regression and forecasting	C(ii)	C 1	Application
6 The components of time series	C(ii)	C 1	Application
7 Finding the trend	C(ii)	C 1	Application
8 Finding the seasonal variations	C(ii)	C 1	Application
9 Time series analysis and forecasting	C(ii)	C 1	Application
10 Using spreadsheet packages to build business models	C(vii)	C 3	Application/evaluation
11 Forecasting problems	C(ii)	C 1,2	Application

1 Forecasting using historical data

- A number of quantitative methods may be used by the management accountant to obtain information for inclusion in budgets.

- Before using any technique based on past data, the past data must be assessed for appropriateness for the intended purpose. There is no point in using a 'sophisticated' technique with unreliable data.

Numerous techniques have been developed for using past costs incurred as the basis for forecasting future values. These techniques range from simple arithmetic and visual methods to advanced computer-based statistical systems. With all techniques, however, there is the **presumption that the past will provide guidance to the future**. Before using any extrapolation techniques, the **past data** must therefore be critically examined to **assess their appropriateness for the intended purpose**. The following checks should be made.

(a)   The **time period** should be long enough to include any periodically paid costs but short enough to ensure that averaging of variations in the level of activity has not occurred.

(b)   The **data** should be examined to ensure that any non-activity level factors affecting costs were roughly the same in the past as those forecast for the future. Such factors might include changes in technology, changes in efficiency, changes in production methods, changes in resource costs, strikes, weather conditions and so on. Changes to the past data are frequently necessary.

(c)   The **methods of data collection** and the accounting policies used should not introduce bias. Examples might include depreciation policies and the treatment of by-products.

(d)   Appropriate choices of **dependent** and **independent variables** must be made.

The two forecasting methods which we are going to look at (the scatter diagram method and linear regression analysis) are based on the assumption that a **linear relationship** links levels of cost and levels of activity.

Knowledge brought forward from earlier studies

Linear relationships

- A **linear relationship** can be expressed in the form of an equation which has the general form Y = a + bX

    where   Y is the **dependent** variable, depending for its value on the value of X

    X is the **independent** variable, whose value helps to determine the corresponding value of y

    a is a **constant**, a fixed amount

    b is a constant, being the **coefficient of X** (that is, the number by which the value of X should be multiplied to derive the value of Y)

- If there is a linear relationship between total costs and level of activity, Y = total costs, X = level of activity, a = fixed cost (the cost when there is no activity level) and b = variable cost per unit.

- The graph of a linear equation is a **straight line** and is determined by two things, the **gradient** (or slope) of the straight line and the point at which the straight line crosses the Y axis (the **intercept**).

> - Gradient = b in the equation $Y = a + bX = (Y_2 - Y_1)/(X_2 - X_1)$ where (X_1, Y_1), (X_2, Y_2) are two points on the straight line
>
> - Intercept = a in the equation $Y = a + bX$

1.1 The high-low method

An important technique that you have already learned to analyse linear cost behaviour patterns is the **high-low method**. Have a go at the following question to ensure that you remember how to use it. Some of the cost and revenue behaviour patterns are quite complicated so you will need to prepare careful workings.

Question   Analysing cost behaviour and projecting revenues and costs

Learning outcome: C(iii)

The manager of a nail salon is using the results of two recent periods to forecast the revenues and costs for a forthcoming period. The results for the two periods to be used as a basis for forecasting are as follows.

	Period 1		Period 2	
Activity				
Number of manicures		240		305
Number of pedicures		180		246
	£	£	£	£
Revenue		9,780		11,574.00
Materials	756		991.80	
Staff salaries	5,100		6,862.00	
Utilities	712		856.10	
Laundry	466		570.80	
Rent	430		430.00	
Other	375		375.00	
		7,839		10,085.70
Profit		1,941		1,488.30

The manager has ascertained the following information.

1 Activity in period 2 increased substantially above the normal activity because all customers received a ten per cent discount. this discount will not be offered in period 4 and the prices of all manicures will be increased by £1 from their period 1 level.

2 The variable element of all costs varies in direct proportion to the total number of manicures and pedicures.

3 All staff are paid a fixed salary, plus a bonus for each customer. the fixed element of staff salary costs increases by £1,500 per period once total activity reaches 450 manicures and pedicures because of the need to employ temporary staff.

4 The variable element of laundry costs is expected to increase by 50% in period 4.

5 Forecast activity for period 4 is as follows.

- 265 manicures
- 165 pedicures

Required

Prepare a forecast profit statement for period 4.

Answer

Forecast profit statement for period 4

	£	£
Revenue (W1)		10,220
Materials (W2)	774	
Staff salaries (W3)	5,120	
Utilities (W4)	723	
Laundry (W5)	646	
Rent	430	
Other	375	
		8,068
Profit		2,152

Workings

1   Analyse revenue patterns

Let the normal price of a manicure be £m

Let the normal price of a pedicure be £p

$$240m + 180p = 9,780 \qquad (1)$$
$$(305 \times 09m) + (246 \times 0.9p) = 11,574$$
$$275.5m + 221.4p = 11,574 \qquad (2)$$
$$(1) \div 240 \quad m + 0.75\,p = 40,75$$

Substitute form in (2)
$$274.5(40.75 - 0.75p) + 221.4p = 11,574$$
$$11,185.875 - 205.875p + 221.4p = 11,574$$
$$11,185.875 + 15.525p = 11,574$$
$$p = 25$$

Substitute in (1)
$$240m + (180 \times 25) = 9,780$$
$$240m = 9,780 - 4,500$$
$$m = 22$$

∴ Revenue forecast for period 4:

		£
Manicures: (£22 + 1) × 265	=	6,095
Pedicures: £25 × 165	=	4,125
		10,220

2   Material costs

Period 1	£756/420	= £1.80 per unit
Period 2	£991.80/551	= £1.80 per unit

This is a wholly variable cost

Forecast for period 4 = £1.80 × (265 + 165) = £774

3   Staff salaries

To use the high-low method it will be necessary to eliminate the effect of the step in fixed costs that occurs at the 450 total activity level.

	Units		£
High activity	551	(£6,862 − £1,500)	5,362
Low activity	420		5,100
	131		262

Variable cost per unit = £262/131 = £2 (the staff bonus)

Substitute in low activity:

Fixed cost   = £5,100 − (420 × £2)
              = £4,260

Forecast for 430 total units in period 4 = £4,260 + (430 × £2)
                                      = £5,120

4   Utilities

	Units	£
High activity	551	856.10
Low activity	420	712.00
	131	144.10

Variable cost per unit   = £144.10/131 = £1.10

Substitute in low activity:

Fixed cost   = £712 − (420 × £1.10)
                   = £250

Forecast for period 4   = £250 + (430 × £1.10)
                        = £723

5   Laundry

	Units	£
High activity	551	570.80
Low activity	420	466.00
	131	104.80

Variable cost per unit   = £104.80/131 = £0.80

Substitute on low activity:

Fixed cost   = £466 − (420 × £0.80)
                   = £130

Forecast for period 4   = £130 + (430 × £0.80 × 1.5)
                        = £646

2 Linear regression analysis

FAST FORWARD

Linear regression analysis (least squares technique) involves determining a **line of best fit.**

You will have learned simple linear regression analysis in your Paper 3c studies. However, 'regression' is specifically mentioned in the Paper P1 syllabus therefore we will start from basics in this Text.

Linear regression analysis, also known as the **'least squares technique'**, is a **statistical method** of estimating costs using historical data from a number of previous accounting periods. The analysis is used to derive a **line of best fit which has the general form**

Y = a + bX where

Y, the dependent variable = total cost

X, the independent variable = the level of activity

a, the intercept of the line on the Y axis = the fixed cost

b, the gradient of the line = the variable cost per unit of activity.

Historical data is collected from previous periods and adjusted to a common price level to remove inflationary differences. This provides a number of readings for activity levels (X) and their associated costs (Y). Then, by substituting these readings into the formulae below for a and b, estimates of the fixed cost and variable cost per unit are provided.

Formula provided in the exam

If $Y = a + bX$, $b = \dfrac{n\Sigma YX - \Sigma X\Sigma Y}{n\Sigma X^2 - (\Sigma X)^2}$ and $a = \overline{Y} - b\overline{X}$

where $\overline{X}, \overline{Y}$ are the average values of X and Y and n is the number of pairs of data for X and Y.

These formulae are provided in the exam. An example will help to illustrate this technique.

2.1 Example: least squares method

The transport department of Norwest Council operates a large fleet of vehicles. These vehicles are used by the various departments of the Council. Each month a statement is prepared for the transport department comparing actual results with budget. One of the items in the transport department's monthly statement is the cost of vehicle maintenance. This maintenance is carried out by the employees of the department. To facilitate control, the transport manager has asked that future statements should show vehicle maintenance costs analysed into fixed and variable costs.

Data from the six months from January to June year 2 inclusive are given below.

Year 2	Vehicle maintenance cost £	Vehicle running hours
January	13,600	2,100
February	15,800	2,800
March	14,500	2,200
April	16,200	3,000
May	14,900	2,600
June	15,000	2,500

Required

Analyse the vehicle maintenance costs into fixed and variable costs, based on the data given, utilising the least squares method.

Solution

If $Y = a + bX$, where Y represent costs and X represents running hours (since costs depend on running hours) then $b = (n\Sigma XY - \Sigma X\Sigma Y)/(n\Sigma X^2 - (\Sigma X)^2)$, when n is the number of pairs of data, which is 6 in this problem.

X	Y	XY	X²
'000 hrs	£'000		
2.1	13.6	28.56	4.41
2.8	15.8	44.24	7.84
2.2	14.5	31.90	4.84
3.0	16.2	48.60	9.00
2.6	14.9	38.74	6.76
2.5	15.0	37.50	6.25
15.2	90.0	229.54	39.10

Variable cost per hour, b $= (6(229.54) - (15.2)(90.00))/(6(39.1) - (15.2)^2)$

$= (1,377.24 - 1,368)/(234.6 - 231.04) = 9.24/3.56 = £2.60$

Fixed costs (in £'000), a $= \overline{Y} - b\overline{X} = (\Sigma Y/n) - (b\Sigma X/n) = (90/6) - (2.6(15.2)/6) = 8.41$ approx, say £8,400

Question

Regression analysis

Learning outcome: C(ii)

You are given the following data for output at a factory and costs of production over the past five months.

Month	Output '000 units	Costs £'000
	X	y
1	20	82
2	16	70
3	24	90
4	22	85
5	18	73

Required

(a) Calculate an equation to determine the expected cost level for any given output volume.
(b) Prepare a budget for total costs if output is 22,000 units.

Answer

(a) *Workings*

X	Y	XY	X²
20	82	1,640	400
16	70	1,120	256
24	90	2,160	576
22	85	1,870	484
18	73	1,314	324
ΣX = 100	ΣY = 400	ΣXY = 8,104	ΣX² = 2,040

n = 5 (There are five pairs of data for x and y values)

b = $(n\Sigma XY - \Sigma X\Sigma Y)/(n\Sigma X^2 - (\Sigma X)^2) = ((5 \times 8,104) - (100 \times 400))/((5 \times 2,040) - 100^2)$

= $(40,520 - 40,000)/(10,200 - 10,000) = 520/200 = 2.6$

a = $\overline{Y} - b\overline{X} = (400/5) - (2.6 \times (100/5)) = 28$

$$Y = 28 + 2.6X$$

where Y = total cost, in thousands of pounds and X = output, in thousands of units.

(b)   If the output is 22,000 units, we would expect costs to be 28+ 2.6 × 22 = 85.2 = £85,200.

2.2 The conditions suited to the use of linear regression analysis

Conditions which should apply if linear regression analysis is to be used to estimate costs

(a)   A **linear cost function should be assumed**. This assumption can be tested by measures of reliability, such as the correlation coefficient and the coefficient of determination (which ought to be reasonably close to 1). We will be looking at these concepts later in the chapter.

(b)   When calculating a line of best fit, there will be a range of values for X. In the question above, the line Y = 28 + 2.6X was predicted from data with output values ranging from X = 16 to X = 24. Depending on the degree of correlation between X and Y, we might safely use the estimated line of best fit to forecast values for Y, provided that the value of X remains within the range 16 to 24. We would be on less safe ground if we used the equation to predict a value for Y when X = 10, or 30, or any other value outside the range 16 to 24, because we would **have to assume that costs behave in the same way outside the range of x values used to establish the line in the first place.**

Key terms

- **Interpolation** means using a line of best fit to predict a value within the two extreme points of the observed range.

- **Extrapolation** means using a line of best fit to predict a value outside the two extreme points.

(c)   The **historical data** for cost and output should be **adjusted to a common price level** (to overcome cost differences caused by inflation) and the historical data should also be **representative of current technology, current efficiency levels and current operations** (products made).

(d)   As far as possible, **historical data should be accurately recorded** so that variable costs are properly matched against the items produced or sold, and fixed costs are properly matched against the time period to which they relate. For example, if a factory rental is £120,000 per annum, and if data is gathered monthly, these costs should be charged £10,000 to each month instead of £120,000 in full to a single month.

(e)   Management should either be **confident that conditions** which have existed in the past **will continue into the future or amend the estimates** of cost produced by the linear regression analysis to **allow for expected changes** in the future.

(f)   As with any forecasting process, the **amount of data available is very important**. Even if correlation is high, if we have fewer than about ten pairs of data, we must regard any forecast as being somewhat unreliable.

(g)   It must be assumed that the **value of one variable, Y, can be predicted or estimated from the value of one other variable, X.**

Learning outcome: C(ii)

The relationship between total operating cost and quantity produced (in a manufacturing company) is given by the linear regression model TC = 5,000 + 500Q, where TC = total operating cost (in £) per annum and Q = quantity produced per annum (kg).

Explain five reservations that you might have about relying on the above model for budgetary planning purposes.

(5 marks)

Answer

(a)   The reliability of the model is unknown if we do not know the correlation coefficient. A low correlation would suggest that the model may be unreliable.

(b)   The model is probably valid only over a certain range of quantity produced. Outside this range, the relationship between the two variables may be very different.

(c)   The model is based on past data, and assumes that what has happened in the past will happen in the future.

(d)   The model assumes that a linear relationship exists between the quantity produced per annum and the total operating costs per annum. It is possible that a non-linear relationship may exist.

(e)   The fixed costs of £5,000 per annum may be misleading if they include an element of allocated costs.

Exam focus point

In an exam you could be given a regression equation which you need to use to determine the expected or standard cost for an actual level of activity. By comparing this standard cost with an actual cost provided you can then establish a total cost variance.

3 Scatter diagrams and correlation

3.1 The scatter diagram method of forecasting

FAST FORWARD

Scatter diagrams can be used to estimate the fixed and variable components of costs.

By this method of cost estimation, cost and activity data are plotted on a graph. A **'line of best fit'** is then drawn. This line should be drawn through the middle of the plotted points as closely as possible so that the distance of points above the line are equal to distances below the line. Where necessary costs should be adjusted to the same indexed price level to allow for inflation.

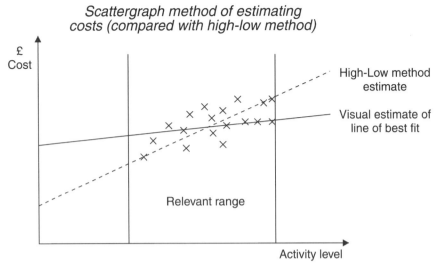

Scattergraph method of estimating costs (compared with high-low method)

The fixed cost is the intercept of the line of best fit on the vertical axis. Suppose the fixed cost is £500 and that one of the plotted points (which is very close to the line or actually on it) represents output of 100 units and total cost of £550. The variable cost of 100 units is therefore calculated as £(550 – 500) = £50 and so the variable cost per unit is £0.50. The equation of the line of best fit is therefore *approximately* Y = 500 + 0.5X.

If the company to which this data relate wanted to forecast total costs when output is 90 units, a forecast based on the equation would be 500 + (0.5 × 90) = £545. Alternatively the **forecast could be read directly from the graph using the line of best fit.**

The disadvantage of the scatter diagram method is that the cost line is drawn by visual judgement and so is a **subjective approximation**. The subjectivity is very clear from the diagram, which demonstrates how **different** our estimates of fixed and variable costs would be if we used the **high-low method** of cost analysis.

3.2 Correlation

FAST FORWARD

Correlation describes the extent to which the values of two variables are related. Two variables might be **perfectly** correlated, **partly** correlated or **uncorrelated**. The correlation may be **positive** or **negative**. The degree of correlation between two variables can be measured using the **Pearsonian coefficient of correlation, r**. The **coefficient of determination** indicates the variations in the dependent variable that can be explained by variations in the independent variable.

Attention!

Although your Paper P1 syllabus does not specifically mention correlation, it does include regression analysis. The successful application of linear regression models depends on X and Y being closely linearly related. Therefore an understanding of correlation is essential to the ability to discuss the quality or reliability of a forecast prepared using regression techniques.

(a)

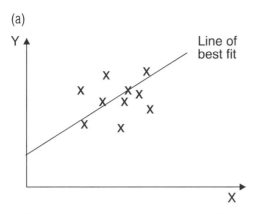

(b)

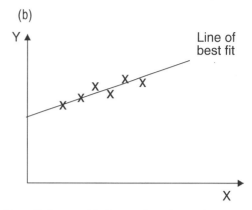

In the scatter diagrams above, you should agree that a line of best fit is more likely to reflect the 'real' relationship between X and Y in (b) than in (a). In (b), the pairs of data are all close to the line of best fit, whereas in (a), there is much more scatter around the line.

In the situation represented in scatter diagram (b), forecasting the value of Y from a given value for X would be more likely to be accurate than in the situation represented in (a). This is because there would be greater correlation between X and Y in (b) than in (a).

Key term

Correlation is the degree to which change in one variable is related to change in another - in other words, the interdependence between variables.

3.3 Degrees of correlation

Two variables might be **perfectly correlated**, **partly correlated**, **uncorrelated** or subject to **non-linear correlation**.

Perfect correlation

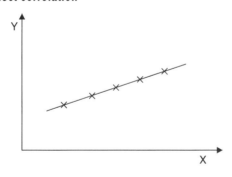

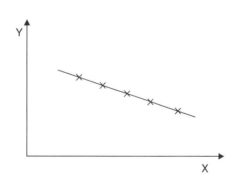

All the pairs of values lie on a straight line. An **exact linear relationship** exists between the two variables.

Partial correlation

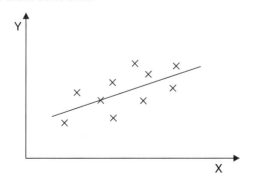

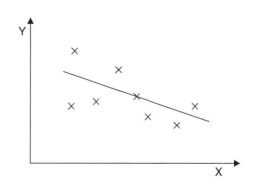

In the left hand diagram, although there is no exact relationship, **low values of X tend to be associated with low values of Y, and high values of X with high values of Y**.

In the right hand diagram, there is no exact relationship, but **low values of X tend to be associated with high values of Y and vice versa.**

No correlation

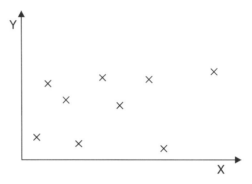

The values of these two variables are not correlated with each other.

Non-linear or curvilinear correlation

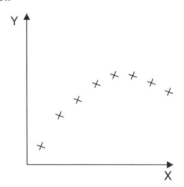

There is a relationship between X and Y since the points are on an obvious curve but it is not a linear relationship.

3.3.1 Positive and negative correlation

Correlation, whether perfect or partial, can be **positive** or **negative**.

> **Key terms**
>
> - **Positive correlation** is the type of correlation where low values of one variable are associated with low values of the other, and high values of one variable are associated with high values of the other.
>
> - **Negative correlation** is the type of correlation where low values of one variable are associated with high values of the other, and high values of one variable with low values of the other.

3.4 Measures of correlation

3.4.1 The coefficient of correlation, r

The **degree of correlation between two variables** can be measured using the **Pearsonian coefficient of correlation** (also called the **product moment correlation coefficient**).

r has a value between –1 (perfect negative correlation) and +1 (perfect positive correlation). If r = 0 then the variables are uncorrelated.

Formula provided in the exam

The **coefficient of correlation**, r, is calculated as follows.

$$r = \frac{n\Sigma XY - \Sigma X\Sigma Y}{\sqrt{[n\Sigma X^2 - (\Sigma X)^2][n\Sigma Y^2 - (\Sigma Y)^2]}}$$

The examiner has confirmed that the formula for the correlation coefficient would be **provided** in the exam if it were required.

Look back at the example in Paragraph 2.1. Suppose that we wanted to know the correlation between vehicle maintenance costs and vehicle running hours. We can use a lot of the calculation in Paragraph 2.1 to determine r.

$$r = \frac{6(229.54) - (15.2)(90.0)}{\sqrt{[6(39.1) - (15.2)^2][6\Sigma y^2 - (90.0)^2]}}$$

$$= \frac{1,377.24 - 1,368}{\sqrt{[(234.6 - 231.04)(6\Sigma y^2 - 8,100)]}}$$

All we need to calculate is ΣY^2.

							Total
Y (£'000)	13.60	15.80	14.50	16.20	14.90	15.00	90.00
Y^2	184.96	249.64	210.25	262.44	222.01	225.00	1,354.30

$$r = \frac{9.24}{\sqrt{(3.56)(6 \times (1,354.30) - 8,100)}} = 0.96$$

A **fairly high degree of positive correlation** between X (vehicle running hours) and Y (vehicle maintenance cost) is indicated here **because r is quite close to +1**.

3.4.2 The coefficient of determination, r^2

Key term

The **coefficient of determination** is a measure of the proportion of the change in the value of one variable that can be explained by variations in the value of the other variable.

In our example, $r^2 = (0.96)^2 = 0.9216$, and so 92% of variation in the value of Y (cost) can be explained by a linear relationship with X (running hours). This leaves only 8% of variations in y to be predicted from other factors. It is therefore **likely that vehicle** running hours could be used with a high degree of confidence to predict costs during a period.

3.5 Correlation and causation

If two variables are well correlated this may be due to pure chance or there may be a reason for it. The **larger the number of pairs of data**, the **less likely it is that the correlation is due to chance**, though that possibility should never be ignored.

If there is a reason, it may not be causal. Monthly net income is well correlated with monthly credit to a person's bank account, for the logical (rather than causal) reason that for most people the one equals the other. **Even if there is a causal explanation** for a correlation, it **does not follow that variations in the value of one variable cause variations in the value of the other**. Sales of ice cream and of sunglasses are well correlated, not because of a direct causal link but because the weather influences both variables.

Having said this, it is of course possible that where two variables are correlated, there is a direct causal link to be found.

3.6 The interactions of r^2 and r with linear regression

The successful application of linear regression models depends on X and Y being closely linearly related. r measures the strength of the linear relationship between two variables but **what numerical value of r is suggestive of sufficient linearity in data to allow one to proceed with linear regression?** The lower the value of r, the less chance of forecasts made using linear regression being adequate.

If there is a perfect linear relationship between the two variables ($r = \pm1$), we can predict y from any given value of X with great confidence. If correlation is high (for example r = 0.9), the actual values will all be quite close to the regression line and so predictions should not be far out. If correlation is below about 0.7, predictions will only give a very rough guide to the likely value of Y.

If r = 0.75, say, you may feel that the linear relationship between the two variables is fairly strong. But $r^2 = 56.25\%$ indicates that only just over half of the variations in the dependent variable can be explained by a linear relationship with the independent variable. The low figure could be because a non-linear relationship is a better model for the data or because extraneous factors need to be considered. It is a **common rule of thumb that $r^2 \geq 80\%$ indicates that linear regression may be applied for the purpose of forecasting.**

4 Sales forecasting

Sales forecasting techniques include asking sales personnel, market research, and using mathematical models and techniques.

The sales budget is frequently the first budget prepared since **sales is usually the principal budget factor**, but before the sales budget can be prepared a sales forecast has to be made. Sales forecasting is complex *and* difficult and involves the consideration of a number of factors including the following.

- Past sales patterns
- The economic environment
- Results of market research
- Anticipated advertising during the budget period
- Competition
- Changing consumer taste
- New legislation
- Distribution and quality of sales outlets and personnel
- Pricing policies and discounts offered
- Legislation
- Environmental factors

As well as bearing in mind those factors, management can use a number of forecasting methods, often combining them to reduce the level of uncertainty.

Method	Detail
Sales personnel	They can be asked to provide estimates.
Market research	Especially relevant for new products or services.
Mathematical models	Set up so that repetitive computer simulations can be run which permit managers to review the results that would be obtained in various circumstances.
Mathematical techniques	See later in this chapter.

5 Regression and forecasting

When **regression analysis** is used for **forecasting sales**, the years (or days or months) become the x variables in the regression formulae by numbering them from 1 upwards.

The same regression techniques as those considered earlier in the chapter can be used to **calculate a regression line (a trend line) for a time series**. A time series is simply a series of figures or values recorded over time (such as total annual costs for the last ten years). The determination of a trend line is particularly useful in forecasting. (We will be looking at time series and trend lines in more detail in the next section.)

The **years (or days or months) become the X variables in the regression formulae** by **numbering them from 1 upwards**.

5.1 Example: regression and forecasting

Sales of product B over the seven year period from year 1 to year 7 were as follows.

Year	Year 1	Year 2	Year 3	Year 4	Year 5	Year 6	Year 7
Sales of B ('000 units)	22	25	24	26	29	28	30

There is high correlation between time and the volume of sales.

Required

Calculate the trend line of sales, and forecast sales in year 8 and year 9.

Solution

Workings

Year	X	Y	XY	X[2+]
1	1	22	22	1
2	2	25	50	4
3	3	24	72	9
4	4	26	104	16
5	5	29	145	25
6	6	28	168	36
7	7	30	210	49
	$\Sigma X = 28$	$\Sigma Y = 184$	$\Sigma XY = 771$	$\Sigma X^2 = 140$

n = 7

Where Y = a + bX

b = $((7 \times 771) - (28 \times 184))/((7 \times 140) - (28 \times 28)) = 245/196 = 1.25$

a = $(184/7) - ((1.25 \times 28)/7) = 21.2857$, say 21.3

Y = $21.3 + 1.25X$ where X = 1 in year 1, X = 2 in year 2 and so on.

Using this trend line, predicted sales in year 8 (X = 8) would be $21.3 + 1.25 \times 8 = 31.3 = 31,300$ units.

Similarly, for year 9 (X = 9) predicted sales would be $21.3 + 1.25 \times 9 = 32.55 = 32,550$ units.

6 The components of time series

A **time series** records a series of figures or values over time. A time series has four components: a **trend**, **seasonal variations**, **cyclical variations** and **random variations**.

Key term

A **time series** is a series of figures or values recorded over time.

Examples of time series

- Output at a factory each day for the last month
- Monthly sales over the last two years
- The Retail Prices Index each month for the last ten years

Key term

A graph of a time series is called a **historigram**.

(Note the 'ri'; this is not the same as a histogram.) For example, consider the following time series.

Year	Year 0	Year 1	Year 2	Year 3	Year 4	Year 5	Year 6
Sales (£'000)	20	21	24	23	27	30	28

The historigram is as follows.

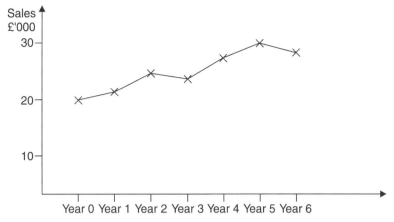

The horizontal axis is always chosen to represent time, and the vertical axis represents the values of the data recorded.

Components of a time series

- A **trend**

- **Seasonal variations** or fluctuations

- Cycles, or **cyclical variations**

- Non-recurring, **random variations**, caused by unforeseen circumstances such as a change in government, a war, technological change or a fire

6.1 The trend

FAST FORWARD

Trend values can be distinguished from seasonal variations by a process of **moving averages**.

Key term

The **trend** is the underlying long-term movement over time in values of data recorded.

In the following examples of time series, there are three types of trend.

Year	Output per labour hour Units	Cost per unit £	Number of employees
4	30	1.00	100
5	24	1.08	103
6	26	1.20	96
7	22	1.15	102
8	21	1.18	103
9	17	1.25	98
	(A)	(B)	(C)

(a) In time series **(A)** there is a **downward trend** in the output per labour hour. Output per labour hour did not fall every year, because it went up between year 5 and year 6, but the long-term movement is clearly a downward one.

(b) In time series **(B)** there is an **upward trend** in the cost per unit. Although unit costs went down in year 7 from a higher level in year 6, the basic movement over time is one of rising costs.

(c) In time series **(C)** there is **no clear movement** up or down, and the number of employees remained fairly constant. The trend is therefore a static, or level one.

6.2 Seasonal variations

Seasonal variations are short-term fluctuations in recorded values, due to different circumstances which affect results at different times of the year, on different days of the week, at different times of day, or whatever.

Here are two examples of seasonal variations.

(a) Sales of ice cream will be higher in summer than in winter.

(b) The telephone network may be heavily used at certain times of the day (such as mid-morning and mid-afternoon) and much less used at other times (such as in the middle of the night).

Seasonal is a term which may appear to refer to the seasons of the year, but its meaning in time series analysis is somewhat broader, as the examples given above show.

6.3 Example: a trend and seasonal variations

The number of customers served by a company of travel agents over the past four years is shown in the following historigram.

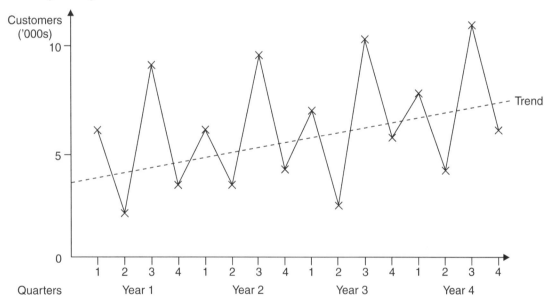

In this example, there would appear to be large seasonal fluctuations in demand, but there is also a basic upward trend.

6.4 Cyclical variations

Cyclical variations are **medium-term changes in results caused by circumstances which repeat in cycles**. In business, cyclical variations are commonly associated with economic cycles, successive booms and slumps in the economy. Economic cycles may last a few years. Cyclical variations are longer term than seasonal variations.

6.5 Summarising the components

In practice a time series could incorporate all of the four features we have been looking at and, to make reasonably accurate forecasts, the four features often have to be isolated. We can begin the process of isolating each feature by summarising the components of a time series as follows.

The **actual time series, Y= T + S + C + R**

where **Y = the actual time series**   **C = the cyclical component**
        T = the trend series   **R = the random component**
        S = the seasonal component

Though you should be aware of the cyclical component, it is unlikely that you will be expected to carry out any calculation connected with isolating it. The mathematical model which we will use, the **additive model**, therefore excludes any reference to C and is **Y = T + S + R**.

We will begin by looking at how to find the trend in a time series.

7 Finding the trend

Look at these monthly sales figures.

Year 6	*August*	*September*	*October*	*November*	*December*
Sales (£'000)	0.02	0.04	0.04	3.20	14.60

It looks as though the business is expanding rapidly - and so it is, in a way. But when you know that the business is a Christmas card manufacturer, then you see immediately that the January sales will no doubt slump right back down again.

It is obvious that the business will do better in the Christmas season than at any other time - that is the seasonal variation. Using the monthly figures, how can he tell whether or not the business is doing well overall - whether there is a rising sales trend over time other than the short-term rise over Christmas?

One possibility is to compare figures with the equivalent figures of a year ago. However, many things can happen over a year to make such a comparison misleading - new products might now be manufactured and prices will probably have changed.

In fact, there are a number of ways of overcoming this problem of distinguishing trend from seasonal variations. One such method is called **moving averages**. This method attempts to **remove seasonal (or cyclical) variations from a time series by a process of averaging so as to leave a set of figures representing the trend**.

A **moving average** is an average of the results of a fixed number of periods. Since it is an average of several time periods, it is **related to the mid-point of the overall period**.

7.1 Example: moving averages

Year	Sales
	Units
0	390
1	380
2	460
3	450
4	470
5	440
6	500

Required

Take a moving average of the annual sales over a period of three years.

Solution

(a)   Average sales in the three year period year 0 – year 2 were (390 + 380 + 460)/3 = 1,230/3 = 410. This average relates to the middle year of the period, year 1.

(b)   Similarly, average sales in the three year period year 1 – year 3 were (380 + 460 + 450)/3 = 1,290/3 = 430. This average relates to the middle year of the period, year 2.

(c)   The average sales can also be found for the periods year 2 - year 4, year 3 - year 5 and year 4 - year 6, to give the following.

Year	Sales	Moving total of 3 years sales	Moving average of 3 years sales (÷ 3)
0	390		
1	380	1,230	410
2	460	1,290	430
3	450	1,380	460
4	470	1,360	453
5	440	1,410	470
6	500		

Note the following points.

(i)   The **moving average series has five figures** relating to years 1 to 5. The **original series had seven figures** for years 0 to 6.

(ii)   There is an upward trend in sales, which is more noticeable from the series of moving averages than from the original series of actual sales each year.

The above example averaged over a three-year period. Over what period should a moving average be taken? The answer to this question is that the **moving average which is most appropriate will depend on the circumstances and the nature of the time series**.

(a)   A moving average which takes an **average of the results in many time periods will represent results over a longer term** than a moving average of two or three periods.

(b)   On the other hand, with a moving average of results in many time periods, the **last figure in the series will be out of date by several periods**. In our example, the most recent average related to year 5. With a moving average of five years' results, the final figure in the series would relate to year 4.

(c)   When there is a **known cycle** over which seasonal variations occur, such as all the days in the week or all the seasons in the year, the **most suitable moving average would be one which covers one full cycle**.

7.2 Moving averages of an even number of results

In the previous example, **moving averages were taken of the results in an *odd* number of time periods,** and the **average then related to the mid-point of the overall period**.

If a **moving average** were taken of results in an **even number of time periods**, the basic technique would be the same, but the mid-point of the overall period would not relate to a single period. For example, suppose an average were taken of the following four results.

Spring	120	
Summer	90	average 115
Autumn	180	
Winter	70	

The average would relate to the mid-point of the period, between summer and autumn.

The trend line average figures need to relate to a particular time period; otherwise, seasonal variations cannot be calculated. To overcome this difficulty, we take a **moving average of the moving average**. An example will illustrate this technique.

7.3 Example: moving averages over an even number of periods

Calculate a moving average trend line of the following results of Linden.

Year	Quarter	Volume of sales '000 units
5	1	600
	2	840
	3	420
	4	720
6	1	640
	2	860
	3	420
	4	740

Solution

A moving average of four will be used, since the volume of sales would appear to depend on the season of the year, and each year has four quarterly results. The moving average of four does not relate to any specific period of time; therefore a second moving average of two will be calculated on the first moving averages.

Year	Quarter	Actual volume of sales '000 units (A)	Moving total of 4 quarters' sales '000 units (B)	Moving average of 4 quarters' sales '000 units (B ÷ 4)	Mid-point of 2 moving averages Trend line '000 units (C)
5	1	600			
	2	840			
	3	420	2,580	645.0	650.00
	4	720	2,620	655.0	657.50
6	1	640	2,640	660.0	660.00
	2	860	2,640	660.0	662.50
	3	420	2,660	665.0	
	4	740			

By taking a mid point (a moving average of two) of the original moving averages, we can relate the results to specific quarters (from the third quarter of year 5 to the second quarter of year 6).

Question

Learning outcome: C (ii)

Actual sales volumes during years 3 and 4 were as follows.

Year	Quarter	Actual sales volume '000 units
3	1	47
	2	59
	3	92
	4	140
4	1	35
	2	49
	3	89
	4	120

What trend figures can be calculated from the information above?

Year	Quarter	A	B	C	D
3	2	338	-	-	84.50
	3	326	83.000	84.50	81.50
	4	316	80.250	81.50	79.00
4	1	313	78.625	79.00	78.25
	2	293	75.750	78.25	73.25
	3	-	-	73.25	-

Answer

The correct answer is B.

Year	Quarter	Actual sales '000 units	Moving total of 4 quarters' sales '000 units	Moving average '000 units	Mid-point Trend '000 units
3	1	47			
	2	59			
			338	84.5	
	3	92			83.000
			326	81.5	
	4	140			80.250
			316	79.0	
4	1	35			78.625
			313	78.25	
	2	49			75.750
			293	73.25	
	3	89			
	4	120			

8 Finding the seasonal variations

Seasonal variations can be estimated using the **additive** model or the **proportional (multiplicative) model**.

Once a trend has been established we can find the seasonal variations. As we saw earlier, the additive model for time series analysis is Y = T + S + R. We can therefore write Y – T = S + R. In other words, if we deduct the trend series from the actual series, we will be left with the seasonal and residual components of the time series. If we assume that the random component is relatively small, and hence negligible, the **seasonal component can be found as S = Y – T,** the **de-trended series.**

The actual and trend sales for Linden (as calculated in Example 7.3) are set out below. The **difference between the actual results for any one quarter (Y) and the trend figure for that quarter (T)** will be the seasonal variation for that quarter.

Year	Quarter	Actual	Trend	Seasonal variation
5	1	600		
	2	840		
	3	420	650.00	–230.00
	4	720	657.50	62.50
6	1	640	660.00	–20.00
	2	860	662.50	197.50
	3	420		
	4	740		

Suppose that seasonal variations for the third and fourth quarters of year 6 and the first and second quarters of year 7 are –248.75, 62.50, –13.75 and 212.50 respectively. The variation between the actual result for a particular quarter and the trend line average is not the same from year to year, but an **average of these variations can be taken**.

Year	Q_1	Q_2	Q_3	Q_4
5			–230.00	62.50
6	–20.00	197.50	–248.75	62.50
7	–13.75	212.50		
Total	–33.75	410.00	–478.75	125.00
Average (÷ 2)	–16.875	205.00	–239.375	62.50

Variations around the basic trend line should cancel each other out, and add up to zero. At the moment, they do not. We therefore **spread the total of the variations** (11.25) **across the four quarters** (11.25 ÷ 4) **so that the final total of the variations sum to zero.**

	Q_1	Q_2	Q_3	Q_4	Total
Estimated quarterly variations	– 16.8750	205.0000	–239.3750	62.5000	11.250
Adjustment to reduce variations to 0	–2.8125	–2.8125	–2.8125	–2.8125	–11.250
Final estimates of quarterly variations	–19.6875	202.1875	–242.1875	59.6875	0
These might be rounded as follows	QI: –20,	QI: 202,	QI:-242,	QI: 60,	Total: 0

8.1 Seasonal variations using the proportional model

The method of estimating the seasonal variations in the above example was to use the differences between the trend and actual data. This model **assumes that the components of the series are independent** of each other, so that an increasing trend does not affect the seasonal variations and make them increase as well, for example.

The alternative is to use the **proportional model** whereby each actual figure is expressed as a proportion of the trend. Sometimes this method is called the **multiplicative model**.

The **trend component** will be the **same whichever model is used** but the values of the **seasonal and random components** will **vary according to the model being applied**.

Example 7.3 can be reworked on this alternative basis. The trend is calculated in exactly the same way as before but we need a different approach for the seasonal variations. The proportional model is $Y = T \times S \times R$ and, just as we calculated $S = Y - T$ for the additive model (Example 7.3) we can calculate $S = Y/T$ for the proportional model.

Year	Quarter	Actual (Y)	Trend (T)	Seasonal percentage (Y/T)
5	1	600		
	2	840		
	3	420	650.00	0.646
	4	720	657.50	1.095
6	1	640	660.00	0.970
	2	860	662.50	1.298
	3	420		
	4	740		

Suppose that seasonal variations for the next four quarters are 0.628, 1.092, 0.980 and 1.309 respectively. The summary of the seasonal variations expressed in proportional terms is therefore as follows.

Year	Q_1 %	Q_2 %	Q_3 %	Q_4 %
5			0.646	1.095
6	0.970	1.298	0.628	1.092
7	0.980	1.309		
Total	1.950	2.607	1.274	2.187
Average	0.975	1.3035	0.637	1.0935

Instead of summing to zero, as **with the additive approach**, the **averages should sum (in this case) to 4.0, 1.0 for each of the four quarters.** They actually sum to 4.009 so 0.00225 has to be deducted from each one.

	Q_1	Q_2	Q_3	Q_4
Average	0.97500	1.30350	0.63700	1.09350
Adjustment	−0.00225	−0.00225	−0.00225	−0.00225
Final estimate	0.97275	1.30125	0.63475	1.09125
Rounded	0.97	1.30	0.64	1.09

Note that the **proportional model is better than the additive model when the trend is increasing or decreasing over time**. In such circumstances, seasonal variations are likely to be increasing or decreasing too. The additive model simply adds absolute and unchanging seasonal variations to the trend figures whereas the proportional model, by multiplying increasing or decreasing trend values by a constant seasonal variation factor, takes account of changing seasonal variations.

9 Time series analysis and forecasting

Forecasts can be made by calculating a **trend line** (using moving averages or linear regression), using the trend line to forecast future trend line values, and adjusting these values by the **average seasonal variation** applicable to the future period.

By extrapolating a trend and then adjusting for seasonal variations, forecasts of future values can be made.

Making forecasts of future values

Step 1   Find a trend line using moving averages or using linear regression analysis (see Section 5).

Step 2   Use the trend line to forecast future trend line values.

Step 3   **Adjust these values by the average seasonal variation applicable to the future period, to determine the forecast for that period**. With the additive model, add (or subtract for negative variations) the variation. With the multiplicative model, multiply the trend value by the variation proportion.

Extending a trend line outside the range of known data, in this case forecasting the future from a trend line based on historical data, is known as **extrapolation**.

9.1 Example: forecasting

The sales (in £'000) of swimwear by a large department store for each period of three months and trend values found using moving averages are as follows.

Quarter	Year 4		Year 5		Year 6		Year 7	
	Actual	Trend	Actual	Trend	Actual	Trend	Actual	Trend
	£'000	£'000	£'000	£'000	£'000	£'000	£'000	£'000
First			8		20	40	40	57
Second			30	30	50	45	62	
Third			60	31	80	50	92	
Fourth	24		20	35	40	54		

Using the additive model, seasonal variations have been determined as follows.

Quarter 1	Quarter 2	Quarter 3	Quarter 4
−£18,250	+£2,750	+£29,750	−£14,250

Required

Predict sales for the last quarter of year 7 and the first quarter of year 8, stating any assumptions.

Solution

We might guess that the trend line is rising steadily, by (57 − 40)/4 = 4.25 per quarter in the period 1st quarter year 6 to 1st quarter year 7 (57 being the prediction in 1st quarter year 7 and 40 the prediction in 1st quarter year 6). Since the trend may be levelling off a little, a quarterly increase of +4 in the trend will be assumed.

		Trend	Seasonal variation	Forecast
1st quarter	Year 7	57		
4th quarter	Year 7 (+ (3 × 4))	69	−14.25	54.75
1st quarter	Year 8 (+ (4 × 4))	73	−18.25	54.75

Rounding to the nearest thousand pounds, the forecast sales are £55,000 for each of the two quarters.

Note that you could actually plot the trend line figures on a graph, extrapolate the trend line into the future and read off forecasts from the graph using the extrapolated trend line.

If we had been using the proportional model, with an average variation for (for example) quarter 4 of 0.8, our prediction for the fourth quarter of year 7 would have been $69 \times 0.8 = 55.2$, say £55,000.

Question

Regression analysis and seasonal variations

Learning outcomes: C (vii)

The trend in a company's sales figures can be described by the linear regression equation $Y = 780 + 4X$, where X is the month number (with January year 3 as month 0) and Y is sales in thousands of pounds. The average seasonal variation for March is 106%.

The forecast sales for March year 5 (to the nearest £'000) are

A   £890,000
B   £933,000
C   £937,000
D   £941,000

Answer

The correct answer is C.

X = 26

Forecast $= 1.06 \times [780 + (4 \times 26)] = 937.04 = £937,040$ or about £937,000.

10 Using spreadsheet packages to build business models

FAST FORWARD

Spreadsheet packages can be used to build business models to assist the forecasting and planning process.

Key term

A **spreadsheet** is 'The term commonly used to describe many of the modelling packages available for microcomputers, being loosely derived from the likeness to a "spreadsheet of paper" divided into rows and columns'.   (CIMA *Computing Terminology*)

It is a type of general purpose software package with **many business applications**, not just accounting ones. It **can be used to build a model**, in which data is presented in **cells** at the intersection of these **rows and columns**. It is up to the model builder to determine what data or information should be presented in the spreadsheet, how it should be presented and how the data should be manipulated by the spreadsheet program. The most widely used spreadsheet packages are Lotus 1-2-3 and Excel.

The idea behind a spreadsheet is that the model builder should **construct a model as follows**.

(a) Identify what data goes into each row and column and by **inserting text** (for example, column headings and row identifications).

(b) **Specify how the numerical data in the model should be derived**. Numerical data might be derived using one of the following methods.

(i) **Insertion into the model via keyboard input.**

(ii) **Calculation from other data in the model** by means of a formula specified within the model itself. The model builder must insert these formulae into the spreadsheet model when it is first constructed.

(iii) **Retrieval from data on a disk file** from another computer application program or module.

10.1 The advantages of spreadsheets

The uses of spreadsheets are really only limited by your imagination, and by the number of rows and columns in the spreadsheet, but some of the more **common accounting applications** are listed below.

- Balance sheets
- Cash flow analysis/forecasting
- General ledger
- Inventory records
- Job cost estimates
- Market share analysis and planning

- Profit projections
- Profit statements
- Project budgeting and control
- Sales projections and records
- Tax estimation

The great value of spreadsheets derives from their **simple format** of rows, columns and worksheets of data, and the ability of the data **users to have direct access themselves** to their spreadsheet model via their own PC. For example, an accountant can construct a cash flow model with a spreadsheet package on the PC on his desk: he can **create** the model, **input** the data, **manipulate** the data and **read or print the output** direct. He will also have fairly **instant access** to the model whenever it is needed, in just the time it takes to load the model into his PC. Spreadsheets therefore bring computer modelling within the everyday reach of data users.

10.2 The disadvantages of spreadsheets

Spreadsheets have disadvantages if they are not properly used.

(a) A **minor error in the design** of a model at any point can **affect the validity of data** throughout the spreadsheet. Such errors can be very difficult to trace.

(b) Even if it is properly designed in the first place, it is very **easy to corrupt** a model by accidentally changing a cell or inputting data in the wrong place.

(c) It is possible to **become over-dependent on them**, so that simple one-off tasks that can be done in seconds with a pen and paper are done on a spreadsheet instead.

(d) The possibility for experimentation with data is so great that it is possible to **lose sight of the original intention** of the spreadsheet.

(e) Spreadsheets **cannot take account of qualitative factors** since they are invariably difficult to quantify. Decisions should not be made on the basis of quantitative information alone.

In summary, spreadsheets should be seen as a **tool in planning and decision making**. The user must make the decision.

In 'Spreadsheets and databases as budgeting tools' (CIMA *Student*, July 1999), Bob Scarlett expanded on the limitations of spreadsheets for budgeting. (The emphasis is BPP's.)

'The process of creating a budget in a large organisation is a **complex** operation. Each area in the organisation needs to prepare a plan and these plans need to be **collated and consolidated**. The system must then accommodate **adjustments** on a **top-down** and **bottom-up** basis. A budgeting operation based on spreadsheets has the following **problems**:

- It is **inflexible** and **error prone**. A large number of spreadsheets can be linked and consolidated but this process presents many difficulties. Calculations are complex and mistakes are easily made. Random 'what if' analyses across centres may become very difficult to carry out.

- It is a **single-user tool in a multi-user environment**. A large number of spreadsheet users are involved using similar templates over periods of weeks. This involves massive duplication of effort and gives rise to risks relating to loss of data integrity and consistency of structure.

- It **lacks 'functionality'**. There are many users in the budget management process ranging from cost centre managers to the chief financial officer. All require ready access to the system in order to input data to it and draw information from it. The budget controller must be able to track revisions. Spreadsheet based systems are notorious for complexity – and they can be anything but easy to use.

Spreadsheet-based budgeting systems may be perfectly adequate for the small and simple operation. However, the limitations of such systems may become increasingly apparent as larger and more complex operations are considered.'

10.3 'What if?' analysis

'What if?' analysis involves changing the values of the forecast variables to see the effect on the forecast outcome. The information provided helps managers to understand the sensitivity of the forecast to the value of the variables.

Once a model has been constructed the consequences of changes or amendments to budget/plan assumptions may be tested by asking **'what if?' questions, a form of sensitivity analysis**. For example, a spreadsheet may be used to develop a cash flow model, such as that shown below.

	A	B	C	D
		Month 1	*Month 2*	*Month 3*
1				
2	Sales	1,000	1,200	1,440
3	Cost of sales	(650)	(780)	(936)
4	Gross profit	350	420	504
5				
6	Receipts:			
7	Current month	600	720	864
8	Previous month	-	400	480
9		-	-	-
10		600	1,120	1,344
11	Payments	(650)	(780)	(936)
12		(50)	340	408
13	Balance b/f	-	(50)	290
14	Balance c/f	(50)	290	698

Typical 'what if?' questions for sensitivity analysis

(a)   What if the cost of sales is 68% of sales revenue, not 65%?

(b)   What if payment from debtors is received 40% in the month of sale, 50% one month in arrears and 10% two months in arrears, instead of 60% in the month of sale and 40% one month in arrears?

(c)   What if sales growth is only 15% per month, instead of 20% per month?

Using the spreadsheet model, the answers to such questions can be obtained simply and quickly, using the editing facility in the program. The information obtained should **provide management with a better understanding of what the cash flow position in the future might be**, and **what factors are critical to ensuring that the cash position remains reasonable**. For example, it might be found that the cost of sales must remain less than 67% of sales value to achieve a satisfactory cash position.

Attention!

'What if?' analysis is specifically mentioned on your Paper P1 syllabus. Although we have discussed the analysis in the context of spreadsheets, it can obviously be performed manually - but much more slowly and probably inaccurately! Your syllabus requires you to **calculate** the consequences of 'what if' scenarios, so make sure you try part (b) in the next question.

Question
Spreadsheets

Learning outcome: C (vii)

(a)   Write out the formulae that would appear in column C of the spreadsheet shown above.

(b)   Comment on the effect on the cash balances if *all* of the 'what if?' conditions listed in Paragraph 10.3 applied. Perform the calculations manually, then if you have access to a spreadsheet package, you could use it to check your answer.

(c)   Which cells in column C would have to be changed, and how, if the 'what if?' conditions applied?

(d)   How could the design of the spreadsheet model be improved to facilitate sensitivity analysis?

Answer

(a)   C2:   B2*1.2   C10:   @ SUM(C7..C9) or = SUM (C7...C9)
        C3:   C2*0.65   C11:   C3
        C4:   C2 + C3   C12:   C10 + C11
        C7:   C2*0.6C13:   B14
        C8:   B2*0.4C14:   C12 + C13

Note that the figures are entered into each cell as either positive or negative and so C4, for example, is calculated by *adding* 1,200 and -780.

(b)

A	B		C		D
	Month 1		*Month 2*		*Month 3*
Sales	1,000	(+15%)	1,150	(+15%)	1,323
Cost of sales (68%)	680		782		900
Gross profit	320		368		423
Receipts					
Current month (40%)	400		460		529
Previous month (50%)	–		500		575
Two months in arrears (10%)	–		–		100
	400		960		1,204
Payments	(680)		(782)		(900)
	(280)		178		304
Balance b/f	–		(280)		(102)
Balance c/f	(280)		(102)		202

The cash position would be substantially worse if all of the 'what if?' conditions occurred simultaneously. Although the cash balance would become positive during month 3, the closing balance would be much lower. If these conditions were to apply then management would need to make arrangements to finance a large short-term deficit during months 1 and 2.

(c)   C2:   B2*1.15
      C3:   C2*0.68
      C7:   C2*0.4
      C8:   B2*0.5
      C9:   Blank (but D9 would have B2*0.1)

(d)   It would be much easier to conduct sensitivity analysis if the items that are variable were allocated specific cells outside the body of the cash flow table. For example rows 15 - 19 could contain the following.

	A	B
15	Cost of sales/Sales	0.68
16	Receipts - current month	0.40
17	- 1 month in arrears	0.50
18	- 2 months in arrears	0.10
19	Sales growth	1.15

The formulae in row C would then read as follows.

C2   B2*B19
C3   C2*B15
C7   C2*B16
C8   B2*B17
C9   A2*B18

(Note that B17, for example, is an absolute cell address whereas C2 is a relative cell address.)

Further sensitivity analysis could be conducted simply by changing the values in cells B15 - B19, rather than having to rewrite each column each time a variable is changed.

10.4 Analysing relationships

One of the major **assumptions** in **linear regression analysis** is that there is a **linear relationship** between the dependent and independent variables.

The relationship might be **curvilinear**, however. A curvilinear relationship can be expressed in the form **Y = aX^b** (where Y is the dependent variable, X is the independent variable and a and b are constants).

Before the advent of computers and spreadsheet packages, if we knew that a linear relationship did not exist between, say, cumulative sales (Y) and time (X), we would have needed to use logarithms to find the value of b. ('a' would be sales in the first time period.)

Nowadays, fortunately, a **spreadsheet** package can be used to carry out a series of **repetitive calculations** (substituting the given value of a and the given values of X into Y = aX^b and changing the value of b until the results with a particular value of b are close to the given values of Y).

The resulting equation can then be used for **forecasting** purposes.

10.5 Management reporting

10.5.1 The impact of computer packages

We have looked at the use of spreadsheet packages in budgeting. But what has been the **impact of computer packages in general** on accountants and managers?

(a) **Data** can be provided **more quickly** and in **more detail**.
(b) **Consolidation** of monthly management accounts is **quicker** and **more complete**.
(c) As we have seen, **'what if' analysis** is far easier to carry out.

10.5.2 Monthly reporting

Monthly reports are now **produced more quickly**. The vast majority of organisations prepare management accounts at least once a month, and preparation rarely takes more than ten working days (preparation sometimes taking only five days or less from the period end).

Reports are **more detailed**, often including both **financial and non-financial data**. The majority of **requests** for additional information can be **met**.

Presentation is more **professional**.

Reporting systems are often **broadly standard** across organisations as a result of internal reviews. Such reviews have led to a general **rise in the standards of reporting**, although they have been criticised as offering **standard solutions to unique problems**.

In large organisations reports now contain **lots more figures**. As well as profit for the period just ended, they cover forecast profit, cash flow, working capital and the balance sheet and include reams of non-financial data.

10.5.3 Implications of these developments

Information overload occurs because of the ease with which information can be provided. Reporting by exception is frequently not applied.

There is continuing focus on **information about internal activities** of the organisation, so that monthly reporting remains a system for internal review and control rather than an aid to short-term decision making.

The **level of detail should not be greater than the accuracy of the data**. It is questionable whether period-end cut off procedures and accounting for accruals have improved in line with faster reporting. Systems for recording indirect costs (which in the past did not need to be overly accurate given the small proportion of total costs they represented) may need improvement.

11 Forecasting problems

All forecasts are subject to error, but the likely errors vary from case to case.

- The **further into the future** the forecast is for, the **more unreliable** it is likely to be.
- The **less data** available on which to base the forecast, the **less reliable** the forecast.
- The **pattern** of trend and seasonal variations **may not continue** in the future.
- **Random variations** may upset the pattern of trend and seasonal variation.

There are a number of changes that also may make it difficult to forecast future events.

Type of change	Examples
Political and economic changes	Changes in interest rates, exchange rates or inflation can mean that future sales and costs are difficult to forecast.
Environmental changes	The opening of high-speed rail links might have a considerable impact on some companies' markets.
Technological changes	These may mean that the past is not a reliable indication of likely future events. For example new faster machinery may make it difficult to use current output levels as the basis for forecasting future production output.
Technological advances	Advanced manufacturing technology is changing the cost structure of many firms. Direct labour costs are reducing in significance and fixed manufacturing costs are increasing. This causes forecasting difficulties because of the resulting changes in cost behaviour patterns, breakeven points and so on.
Social changes	Alterations in taste, fashion and the social acceptability of products can cause forecasting difficulties.

Chapter Roundup

- A number of quantitative methods may be used by the management accountant to obtain information for inclusion in budgets.

- Before using any technique based on past data, the past data must be assessed for appropriateness for the intended purpose. There is no point in using a 'sophisticated' technique with unreliable data.

- **Linear regression analysis** (least squares technique) involves determining a **line of best fit.**

- **Scatter diagrams** can be used to estimate the fixed and variable components of costs.

- **Correlation** describes the extent to which the values of two variables are related. Two variables might be **perfectly** correlated, **partly** correlated or **uncorrelated**. The correlation may be **positive** or **negative**. The degree of correlation between two variables can be measured using the **Pearsonian coefficient of correlation**, **r**. The **coefficient of determination** indicates the variations in the dependent variable that can be explained by variations in the independent variable.

- **Sales forecasting** techniques include asking sales personnel, market research, and using mathematical models and techniques.

- When **regression analysis** is used for **forecasting sales**, the years (or days or months) become the x variables in the regression formulae by numbering them from 1 upwards.

- A **time series** records a series of figures or values over time. A time series has four components: a **trend**, **seasonal variations**, **cyclical variations** and **random variations**.

- **Trend** values can be distinguished from seasonal variations by a process of **moving averages**.

- **Seasonal variations** can be estimated using the **additive** model or the **proportional** (**multiplicative**) model.

- **Forecasts** can be made by calculating a **trend line** (using moving averages or linear regression), using the trend line to forecast future trend line values, and adjusting these values by the **average seasonal variation** applicable to the future period.

- **Spreadsheet packages** can be used to build business models to assist the forecasting and planning process.

- **'What if?' analysis** involves changing the values of the forecast variables to see the effect on the forecast outcome. The information provided helps managers to understand the sensitivity of the forecast to the value of the variables.

Quick Quiz

1 In the equation $Y = a + bX$, which is the dependent variable?

A Y
B a
C b
D X

2 *Fill in the missing words.*

Extrapolation involves using a .... of best .... to predict a value .... the two extreme points of the observed range.

3 Between sales of suntan cream and sales of cold drinks, one would expect (assuming spending money to be unlimited)

A positive, but spurious, correlation
B negative, but spurious, correlation
C positive correlation indicating direct causation
D negative correlation indicating direct causation

4 Which of the following statements is/are true of the coefficient of determination?

	True	False
(a) It is the square of the Pearsonian coefficient of correlation		
(b) It can never quite equal 1		
(c) If it is high, this proves that variations in one variable cause variations in the other		

5 *Choose the appropriate words from those highlighted.*

When using **regression analysis/analytical regression** for forecasting, the X variables are the **years (or days or months)/the level of sales (or costs)**.

6 What are the four components of a time series?

A Trend, seasonal variations, cyclical variations, relative variations
B Trend, systematic variations, cyclical variations, relative variations
C Trend, systematic variations, seasonal variations, random variations
D Trend, seasonal variations, cyclical variations, random variations

7 The multiplicative model expresses a time series as Y = T + S + R. *True or false?*

8 A time series for weeks 1 to 12 has been analysed into a trend and seasonal variations, using the additive model. The trend value is 84 + 0.7w, where w is the week number. The actual value for week 9 is 88.7. What is the seasonal variation for week 9?

A 90.3
B −1.6
C 1.6
D 6.3

9 *List six factors to consider when forecasting sales.*

1 ....

2 ....

3 ....

4 ....

5 ....

6 ....

10 *Complete the following table.*

Year	Quarter	Actual volume of sales Units	Moving total of 4 quarters' sales Units	Moving average of 4 quarters' sales Units	Trend
3	1	1,350			
	2	1,210			
	3	1,080			
	4	1,250			
4	1	1,400			
	2	1,260			
	3	1,110			
	4	1,320			

11 How would you write the spreadsheet formula that produced 40% of the sum of cells D17 and D18?

A 0.4*D17+D18
B 40*D17+D18
C 40*(D17+D18)
D 0.4*(D17+D18)

12 The further into the future the forecast is for, the more reliable it is likely to be. *True or false?*

Answers to Quick Quiz

1 A

2 Line; fit; outside.

3 A. When cold drinks sell well, so will suntan cream. Neither sales level causes the other; both are caused by the weather.

4 Statement (a) is true. The coefficient of determination is r^2
   Statement (b) is false. r can reach 1 or –1, so r^2 can reach 1
   Statement (c) is false. Correlation does not prove a causal link

5 regression analysis
   years (or days or months)

6 D

7 False. The multiplicative model expresses a time series as $Y = T \times S \times R$

8 B. For week 9, the trend value is $84 + (0.7 \times 9) = 90.3$

   The seasonal variation is actual – trend = 88.7 – 90.3, = –1.6, indicating that the value for week 9 is below what one might expect from the trend.

9 Here are some examples.

   - Past sales patterns
   - The economic environment
   - Results of market research
   - Anticipated advertising during the budget period
   - Competition
   - Changing consumer taste
   - New legislation
   - Distribution and quality of sales outlets and personnel
   - Pricing policies and discounts offered

- Legislation
- Environmental factors

10

Year	Quarter	Actual volume of sales Units	Moving total of 4 quarters' sales Units	Moving average of 4 quarters' sales Units	Trend
3	1	1,350			
	2	1,210			
	3	1,080	4,890	1,222.5	1,228.75
	4	1,250	4,940	1,235.0	1,241.25
4	1	1,400	4,990	1,247.5	1,251.25
	2	1,260	5,020	1,255.0	1,263/75
	3	1,110	5,090	1,272.5	
	4	1,320			

11 D

12 False. It is likely to be more unreliable.

Now try the questions below from the Exam Question Bank			
Number	**Level**	**Marks**	**Time**
Q25	Examination	n/a	n/a
Q26	Examination	5	9 mins
Q27	Examination	5	9 mins

Budgetary control and performance measurement

Introduction

This chapter continues the budgeting theme and looks at budgetary control.

Budgetary control is the comparison of actual results with budgeted results. **Variances** are calculated to identify the differences between actual and budgeted results and these differences are reported to management so that appropriate **action** can be taken.

Such an approach relies upon a system of **flexible** (as opposed to **fixed**) **budgets**. We look at the **difference** between the two types in **Section 1**. **Flexible budgets** are vital for both planning and control and **Section 2** shows how they are constructed and **Section 3** looks at their use in the overall **budgetary control process**.

Section 4 examines the argument that a manager should not be responsible for a variance he cannot **control**. **Section 5** looks at two **types of control** which can be used once budgetary control statements have been prepared.

The chapter then considers the **behavioural implications** of operating a budgetary control system. As in all studies of human behaviour, it is difficult to draw concrete conclusions. There is, however, one point which is agreed: **budgeting is more than a mathematical technique**.

The chapter concludes with a review of the criticisms of budgeting and the recommendations of the advocates of the **balances scorecard** and **'beyond budgeting'**.

Topic list	Learning outcomes	Syllabus references	Ability required
1 Fixed and flexible budgets	C(xi)	C 7	Evaluation
2 Preparing flexible budgets	C(xi)	C 7	Evaluation
3 Flexible budgets and budgetary control	C(xi)	C 7	Evaluation
4 Controllable and uncontrollable costs	C(viii)(ix)	C 7	Comprehension
5 Feedback and feedforward control mechanisms	C(x)	C 7	Comprehension
6 Behavioural implications of budgeting	C(xiii)	C 8	Evaluation
7 Participation and performance evaluation	C(xiii)	C 8	Evaluation
8 The use of budgets as targets	C(xiii)	C 9	Evaluation
9 The management accountant and motivation	C(xiii)	C 8	Evaluation
10 The balanced scorecard	C(xii)	C 9	Analysis
11 Beyond budgeting	C(xiv)	C 9	Evaluation

1 Fixed and flexible budgets

Fixed budgets remain unchanged regardless of the level of activity; **flexible budgets** are designed to flex with the level of activity.
Flexible budgets are prepared using marginal costing and so mixed costs must be split into their fixed and variable components (possibly using the **high/low method**).

1.1 Fixed budgets

The master budget prepared before the beginning of the budget period is known as the **fixed** budget. By the term 'fixed', we do not mean that the budget is kept unchanged. Revisions to a fixed master budget will be made if the situation so demands. The term 'fixed' means the following.

(a)   The budget is prepared on the basis of an estimated volume of production and an estimated volume of sales, but no plans are made for the event that actual volumes of production and sales may differ from budgeted volumes.

(b)   When actual volumes of production and sales during a control period (month or four weeks or quarter) are achieved, a fixed budget is not adjusted (in retrospect) to represent a new target for the new levels of activity.

The major purpose of a fixed budget lies in its use at the planning stage, when it seeks to define the broad objectives of the organisation.

Key term

CIMA's *Official Terminology* definition is 'A budget which is normally set prior to the start of an accounting period, and which is not changed in response to subsequent changes in activity or costs/revenues. Fixed budgets are generally used for planning purposes.'   (CIMA *Official Terminology*)

Fixed budgets (in terms of a **pre-set expenditure limit**) are also useful for **controlling any fixed cost**, and **particularly non-production fixed costs** such as advertising, because such costs should be unaffected by changes in activity level (within a certain range).

1.2 Flexed budgets

 Comparison of a fixed budget with the actual results for a different level of activity is of little use for **budgetary control purposes**. Flexible budgets should be used to show what cost and revenues should have been for the actual level of activity. Differences between the flexible budget figures and actual results are **variances**.

Key term

A **flexible budget** is 'A budget which, by recognising different cost behaviour patterns, is designed to change as volume of activity changes'.   (CIMA *Official Terminology*)

Two uses of flexible budgets

(a)   **At the planning stage**. For example, suppose that a company expects to sell 10,000 units of output during the next year. A master budget (the fixed budget) would be prepared on the basis of these expected volumes. However, if the company thinks that output and sales might be as low as 8,000 units or as high as 12,000 units, it may prepare **contingency**

flexible budgets, at volumes of, say 8,000, 9,000, 11,000 and 12,000 units, and then assess the possible outcomes. This is an example of the use of **'what if?' analysis** that you studied in Chapter 12.

(b) **Retrospectively.** At the end of each control period, flexible budgets can be used to compare actual results achieved with what results should have been under the circumstances. Flexible budgets are an essential factor in budgetary control.

   (i) Management needs to know about how good or bad actual performance has been. To provide a measure of performance, there must be a yardstick (budget/ standard) against which actual performance can be measured.

   (ii) Every business is dynamic, and actual volumes of output cannot be expected to conform exactly to the fixed budget. Comparing actual costs directly with the fixed budget costs is meaningless.

   (iii) For useful control information, it is necessary to compare actual results at the actual level of activity achieved against the results that should have been expected at this level of activity, which are shown by the flexible budget.

2 Preparing flexible budgets

Knowledge brought forward from earlier studies

The preparation of flexible budgets

- The first step in the preparation of a flexible budget is the determination of **cost behaviour patterns**, which means deciding whether costs are fixed, variable or semi-variable.

- Fixed costs will remain constant as activity levels change.

- For non-fixed costs, divide each cost figure by the related activity level. If the cost is a **linear variable cost**, the cost per unit will remain constant. If the cost is a **semi-variable cost**, the unit rate will reduce as activity levels increase.

- Split semi-variable costs into their fixed and variable components using the **high/low method** or the **scattergraph method**.

- Calculate the **budget cost allowance** for each cost item as budget cost allowance = budgeted fixed cost* + (number of units produced/sold × variable cost per unit)**.

   * nil for totally variable cost ** nil for fixed cost

Key term

The **budget cost allowance/flexed budget** is 'The budgeted cost ascribed to the level of activity achieved in a budget centre in a control period. It comprises variable costs in direct proportion to volume achieved and fixed costs as a proportion of the annual budget.'

(CIMA *Official Terminology*)

2.1 Example: fixed and flexible budgets

Suppose that Gemma expects production and sales during the next year to be 90% of the company's output capacity, that is, 9,000 units of a single product. Cost estimates will be made using the high-low method and the following historical records of cost.

Units of output/sales	Cost of sales
	Yen
9,800	44,400
7,700	38,100

The company's management is not certain that the estimate of sales is correct, and has asked for flexible budgets to be prepared at output and sales levels of 8,000 and 10,000 units. The sales price per unit has been fixed at Y5 .

Required

Prepare appropriate budgets.

Solution

If we assume that within the range 8,000 to 10,000 units of sales, all costs are fixed, variable or mixed (in other words there are no stepped costs, material discounts, overtime premiums, bonus payments and so on) the fixed and flexible budgets would be based on the estimate of fixed and variable cost.

		Yen
Total cost of 9,800 units	=	44,400
Total cost of 7,700 units	=	38,100
Variable cost of 2,100 units	=	6,300

The variable cost per unit is Yen 3.

		Yen
Total cost of 9,800 units	=	44,400
Variable cost of 9,800 units (9,800 × Yen 3)	=	29,400
Fixed costs (all levels of output and sales)	=	15,000

The fixed budgets and flexible budgets can now be prepared as follows.

	Flexible budget 8,000 units Yen	Fixed budget 9,000 units Yen	Flexible budget 10,000 units Yen
Sales (× Yen 5)	40,000	45,000	50,000
Variable costs (× Yen 3)	24,000	27,000	30,000
Contribution	16,000	18,000	20,000
Fixed costs	15,000	15,000	15,000
Profit	1,000	3,000	5,000

Have a go at the following question. It is more complicated than the last example because it includes inflation. You will need to recall your studies of index numbers from Paper 3(c) *Business Mathematics.*

High-low method

Learning outcome: C(xi)

Rice and Faull Ltd has recorded the following total costs during the last five years.

Year	Output volume Units	Total cost £	Average price level index
0	65,000	145,000	100
1	80,000	179,000	112
2	90,000	209,100	123
3	60,000	201,600	144
4	75,000	248,000	160

The expected costs in year 5 when output is 85,000 units and the average price level index is 180 will be

A   £165,000
B   £185,625
C   £207,850
D   £297,000

Answer

The correct answer is D

Price levels should be adjusted to a common basis, say index level 100.

(a)

	Output	Total cost £	Cost at price level index = 100 £
High level	90,000 units	209,100 × (100/123)	= 170,000
Low level	60,000 units	201,600 × (100/144)	= 140,000
Variable cost	30,000 units		= 30,000

The variable cost is therefore £1 per unit.

(b)   Use the variable cost to determine the fixed cost.

	£
Total cost of 90,000 units (Index 100)	170,000
Variable cost of 90,000 units (× £1)	90,000
Fixed costs (Index 100)	80,000

(c)   Costs in year 5 for 85,000 units will be as follows.

	£
Variable costs (Index 100)	85,000
Fixed costs (Index 100)	80,000
Total costs (Index 100)	165,000

At year 5 price levels (Index 180) = £165,000 ×(180/100) = £297,000

Exam focus point

The pilot paper included a short objective test question which required the use of the high/low method to analyse a semi-variable cost. The budget cost allowance had to be determined for a given output and used to determine the overhead expenditure variance, but inflation was not involved on this occasion.

2.2 The need for flexible budgets

We have seen that flexible budgets may be prepared in order to plan for variations in the level of activity above or below the level set in the fixed budget. It has been suggested, however, that since many cost items in modern industry are fixed costs, the value of flexible budgets in planning is dwindling.

(a)   In many manufacturing industries, plant costs (depreciation, rent and so on) are a very large proportion of total costs, and these tend to be fixed costs.

(b)   Wage costs also tend to be fixed, because employees are generally guaranteed a basic wage for a working week of an agreed number of hours.

(c)   With the growth of service industries, labour (wages or fixed salaries) and overheads will account for most of the costs of a business, and direct materials will be a relatively small proportion of total costs.

Flexible budgets are nevertheless necessary, and even if they are not used at the planning stage, they must be used for budgetary control variance analysis.

3 Flexible budgets and budgetary control

FAST FORWARD

Budgetary control is based around a system of **budget centres**. Each centre has its own budget which is the responsibility of the **budget holder**.

Key term

The CIMA *Official Terminology* defines **budgetary control** as 'The establishment of budgets relating the responsibilities of executives to the requirements of a policy, and the continuous comparison of actual with budgeted results, either to secure by individual action the objectives of that policy or to provide a basis for its revision'.

In other words, individual managers are held responsible for investigating differences between budgeted and actual results, and are then expected to take corrective action or amend the plan in the light of actual events.

It is therefore vital to ensure that valid comparisons are being made. Consider the following example.

3.1 Example:

Penny manufactures a single product, the Darcy. Budgeted results and actual results for May are as follows.

	Budget	Actual	Variance
Production and sales of the Darcy (units)	7,500	8,200	
	£	£	£
Sales revenue	75,000	81,000	6,000 (F)
Direct materials	22,500	23,500	1,000 (A)
Direct labour	15,000	15,500	500 (A)
Production overhead	22,500	22,800	300 (A)
Administration overhead	10,000	11,000	1,000 (A)
	70,000	72,800	2,800 (A)
Profit	5,000	8,200	3,200 (F)

Note. (F) denotes a favourable variance and (A) an unfavourable or adverse variance.

In this example, the variances are meaningless for the purposes of control. All costs were higher than budgeted but the volume of output was also higher; it is to be expected that actual variable costs would be greater those included in the fixed budget. However, it is not possible to tell how much of the increase is due to **poor cost control** and how much is due to the **increase in activity**.

Similarly it is not possible to tell how much of the increase in sales revenue is due to the increase in activity. Some of the difference may be due to a difference between budgeted and actual selling price but we are unable to tell from the analysis above.

For control purposes we need to know the answers to questions such as the following.

- Were actual costs higher than they should have been to produce and sell 8,200 Darcys?
- Was actual revenue satisfactory from the sale of 8,200 Darcys?

Instead of comparing actual results with a fixed budget which is based on a different level of activity to that actually achieved, the correct approach to budgetary control is to compare actual results with a budget which has been **flexed** to the actual activity level achieved.

Suppose that we have the following estimates of the behaviour of Penny's costs.

(a) Direct materials and direct labour are variable costs.

(b) Production overhead is a semi-variable cost, the budgeted cost for an activity level of 10,000 units being £25,000.

(c) Administration overhead is a fixed cost.

(d) Selling prices are constant at all levels of sales.

Solution

The **budgetary control analysis** should therefore be as follows.

	Fixed budget	Flexible budget	Actual results	Variance
Production and sales (units)	7,500	8,200	8,200	
	£	£	£	£
Sales revenue	75,000	82,000 (W1)	81,000	1,000(A)
Direct materials	22,500	24,600 (W2)	23,500	1,100 (F)
Direct labour	15,000	16,400 (W3)	15,500	900 (F)
Production overhead	22,500	23,200 (W4)	22,800	400 (F)
Administration overhead	10,000	10,000 (W5)	11,000	1,000 (A)
	70,000	74,200	72,800	1,400 (F)
Profit	5,000	7,800	8,200	400 (F)

Workings

1. Selling price per unit = £75,000 ÷ 7,500 = £10 per unit
   Flexible budget sales revenue = £10 × 8,200 = £82,000

2. Direct materials cost per unit = £22,500 ÷ 7,500 = £3
   Budget cost allowance = £3 × 8,200 = £24,600

3. Direct labour cost per unit = £15,000 ÷ 7,500 = £2
   Budget cost allowance = £2 × 8,200 = £16,400

4. Variable production overhead cost per unit
   = £(25,000 – 22,500)/(10,000 – 7,500)
   = £2,500/2,500 = £1 per unit
   ∴ Fixed production overhead cost = £22,500 – (7,500 × £1) = £15,000
   ∴ Budget cost allowance = £15,000 + (8,200 × £1) = £23,200

5   Administration overhead is a fixed cost and hence budget cost allowance = £10,000

Comment

(a)   In selling 8,200 units, the expected profit should have been, not the fixed budget profit of £5,000, but the flexible budget profit of £7,800. Instead actual profit was £8,200 ie £400 more than we should have expected.

One of the reasons for this improvement is that, given output and sales of 8,200 units, the cost of resources (material, labour etc) was £1,400 lower than expected. (A comparison of the fixed budget and the actual costs in Example 3.1 appeared to indicate that costs were not being controlled since all of the variances were adverse).

In Chapter 8 you saw how these total cost variances can be analysed to reveal how much of the variance is due to lower resource prices and how much is due to efficient resource usage.

(b)   The sales revenue was, however, £1,000 less than expected because a lower price was charged than budgeted.

We know this because flexing the budget has eliminated the effect of changes in the volume sold, which is the only other factor that can affect sales revenue. You have probably already realised that this variance of £1,000 (A) is a **selling price variance**.

The lower selling price could have been caused by the increase in the volume sold (to sell the additional 700 units the selling price had to fall below £10 per unit). We do not know if this is the case but without flexing the budget we could not know that a different selling price to that budgeted had been charged. Our initial analysis in Paragraph 3.3 had appeared to indicate that sales revenue was ahead of budget.

The difference of £400 between the flexible budget profit of £7,800 at a production level of 8,200 units and the actual profit of £8,200 is due to the net effect of cost savings of £1,400 and lower than expected sales revenue (by £1,000).

The difference between the original budgeted profit of £5,000 and the actual profit of £8,200 is the total of the following.

(a)   The savings in resource costs/lower than expected sales revenue (a net total of £400 as indicated by the difference between the flexible budget and the actual results).

(b)   The effect of producing and selling 8,200 units instead of 7,500 units (a gain of £2,800 as indicated by the difference between the fixed budget and the flexible budget). This is the **sales volume contribution variance**.

A **full variance analysis statement** would be as follows.

	£	£
Fixed budget profit		5,000
Variances		
Sales volume	2,800 (F)	
Selling price	1,000 (A)	
Direct materials cost	1,100 (F)	
Direct labour cost	900 (F)	
Production overhead cost	400 (F)	
Administration overhead cost	1,000 (A)	
		3,200 (F)
Actual profit		8,200

If management believes that any of the variances are large enough to justify it, they will investigate the reasons for their occurrence to see whether any corrective action is necessary. You learned about identifying the significance of variances in Chapter 10.

Question | Flexible budget

Learning outcome: C(xi)

Flower budgeted to sell 200 units and produced the following budget.

	£	£
Sales		71,400
Variable costs		
Labour	31,600	
Material	12,600	
		44,200
Contribution		27,200
Fixed costs		18,900
Profit		8,300

Actual sales turned out to be 230 units, which were sold for £69,000. Actual expenditure on labour was £27,000 and on material £24,000. Fixed costs totalled £10,000.

Required

Prepare a flexible budget that will be useful for management control purposes.

Answer

	Budget 200 units £	Budget per unit £	Flexed budget 230 units £	Actual 230 units £	Variance £
Sales	71,400	357	82,110	69,000	13,110 (A)
Variable costs					
Labour	31,600	158	36,340	27,000	9,340 (F)
Material	12,600	63	14,490	24,000	9,510 (A)
	44,200	221	50,830	51,000	
Contribution	27,200	136	31,280	18,000	13,280 (A)
Fixed costs	18,900		18,900	10,000	8,900 (F)
Profit	8,300		12,380	8,000	4,380 (A)

3.2 Flexible budgets, control and computers

The production of flexible budget control reports is an area in which computers can provide invaluable assistance to the cost accountant, calculating flexed budget figures using fixed budget and actual results data and hence providing detailed variance analysis. For control information to be of any value it must be produced quickly: speed is one of the many advantages of computers.

3.3 Flexed budgets using ABC data

Instead of flexing budgets according to the number of units produced or sold, in an ABC environment it is possible to use **more meaningful bases for flexing the budget**. The budget cost allowance for each activity can be determined according to the number of **cost drivers**.

Suppose the budget for a production department for a given period is as follows.

	£
Wages	220,000
Materials	590,000
Equipment	20,000
Power, heat and light	11,000
	841,000

This budget gives little indication of the link between the level of activity in the department and the costs incurred, however.

Suppose the activities in the department have been identified as sawing, hammering, finishing, reworking and production reporting. The budget might therefore be restated as follows.

Activities	Cost driver	Budgeted cost per unit of cost driver £	Budgeted no of cost drivers	Budget £
Sawing	Number of units sawed	50.00	5,000	250,000
Hammering	Number of units hammered together	10.00	35,000	350,000
Finishing	Number of sq metres finished	0.50	400,000	200,000
Reworking	Number of items reworked	12.40	2,500	31,000
Production reporting	Number of reports	400.00	25	10,000
				841,000

Advantages of this approach

(a)   Costs classified as fixed in the first budget can now be seen to be variable and hence can be more readily controlled.

(b)   The implications of increases/decreases in levels of activity are immediately apparent. For example, if acceptable quality levels were raised so that an additional 200 units per annum were reworked, budgeted costs would increase by $200 \times £12.40 = £2,480$.

A **flexible budget** would be prepared as follows.

	Actual no of cost drivers	Budgeted cost per unit of cost driver £	Flexed budget £	Actual cost £	Variance £
Sawing	6,000	50.00	300,000	297,000	3,000 (F)
Hammering	40,000	10.00	400,000	404,000	4,000 (A)
Finishing	264,400	0.50	132,200	113,200	19,000 (F)
Reworking	4,500	12.40	55,800	56,100	300 (A)
Production reporting	30	400.00	12,000	13,700	1,700 (A)
			900,000	884,000	16,000 (F)

3.4 The link between standard costing and budget flexing

The calculation of standard cost variances and the use of a flexed budget to control costs and revenues are **very similar in concept**.

For example, a direct material total variance in a standard costing system is calculated by **comparing the material cost that should have been incurred for the output achieved, with the actual cost that was incurred**.

Exactly the same process is undertaken when a budget is flexed to provide a basis for comparison with the actual cost: **the flexible budget cost allowance for material cost is the same as the cost that should**

have been incurred for the activity level achieved. In the same way as for standard costing, this is then compared with the actual cost incurred in order to practice control by comparison.

However, there are differences between the two techniques.

(a) **Standard costing variance analysis is more detailed**. The total material cost variance is analysed further to determine how much of the total variance is caused by a difference in the price paid for materials (the material price variance) and how much is caused by the usage of material being different from the standard (the material usage variance). In flexible budget comparisons only total cost variances are derived.

(b) **For a standard costing system to operate it is necessary to determine a standard unit cost for all items of output**. All that is required to operate a flexible budgeting system is an understanding of the cost behaviour patterns and a measure of activity to use to flex the budget cost allowance for each cost element.

4 Controllable and uncontrollable costs

Controllable costs are those which can be influenced by the budget holder. **Uncontrollable costs** cannot be so influenced.

In order to prepare a budget for an organisation as a whole, individual budgets have to be prepared for sub-sections of the organisation, such as individual departments, products or activities.

Key term

A **budget centre** is defined in CIMA *Official Terminology* as 'A section of an entity for which control may be exercised and budgets prepared'.

Budgetary control is based around a system of budget centres. Each budget centre will have its own budget and a manager will be responsible for managing the budget centre and ensuring that the budget is met.

The **selection of budget centres** in an organisation is therefore a **key first step in setting up a control system**. What should the budget centres be? What income, expenditure and/or capital employment plans should each budget centre prepare? And how will measures of performance for each budget centre be made?

A well-organised system of control should have the following features.

Feature	Explanation
A hierarchy of budget centres	If the organisation is quite large a hierarchy is needed. Subsidiary companies, departments and work sections might be budget centres. Budgets of each section would then be consolidated into a departmental budget, departmental budgets in turn would be consolidated into the subsidiary's budget, and the budgets of each subsidiary would be **combined into a master budget** for the group as a whole.
Clearly identified responsibilities for achieving budget targets	Individual managers should be made responsible for achieving the budget targets of a particular budget centre.

Feature	Explanation
Responsibilities for revenues, costs and capital employed	Budget centres should be organised so that all the revenues earned by an organisation, all the costs it incurs, and all the capital it employs are made the responsibility of someone within the organisation, at an appropriate level of authority in the management hierarchy.

Budgetary control and budget centres are therefore part of the overall system of **responsibility accounting** within an organisation.

Key term

Responsibility accounting is a system of accounting that segregates revenue and costs into areas of personal responsibility in order to monitor and assess the performance of each part of an organisation.

4.1 The controllability principle

We saw in Chapter 7 that care must be taken to distinguish between controllable costs and uncontrollable costs in variance reporting. The controllability principle is that managers of responsibility centres should only be held accountable for costs over which they have some influence. From a motivation point of view this is important because it can be very demoralising for managers who feel that their performance is being judged on the basis of something over which they have no influence. It is also important from a control point of view in that control reports should ensure that information on costs is reported to the manager who is able to take action to control them.

Key term

A **controllable cost** is 'A cost which can be influenced by its budget holder'.

(CIMA *Official Terminology*)

Responsibility accounting attempts to associate costs, revenues, assets and liabilities with the managers most capable of controlling them. As a system of accounting, it therefore distinguishes between controllable and uncontrollable costs.

Most **variable costs** within a department are thought to be **controllable in the short term** because managers can influence the efficiency with which resources are used, even if they cannot do anything to raise or lower price levels.

A cost which is not controllable by a junior manager might be controllable by a senior manager. For example, there may be high direct labour costs in a department caused by excessive overtime working. The junior manager may feel obliged to continue with the overtime to meet production schedules, but his senior may be able to reduce costs by hiring extra full-time staff, thereby reducing the requirements for overtime.

A cost which is not controllable by a manager in one department may be controllable by a manager in another department. For example, an increase in material costs may be caused by buying at higher prices than expected (controllable by the purchasing department) or by excessive wastage (controllable by the production department) or by a faulty machine producing rejects (controllable by the maintenance department).

Some costs are **non-controllable**, such as increases in expenditure items due to inflation. Other costs are **controllable, but in the long term rather than the short term**. For example, production costs might be reduced by the introduction of new machinery and technology, but in the short term, management must attempt to do the best they can with the resources and machinery at their disposal.

4.1.1 The controllability of fixed costs

It is often assumed that all fixed costs are non-controllable in the short run. This is not so.

(a)   **Committed fixed costs** are those costs arising from the possession of plant, equipment, buildings and an administration department to **support the long-term needs of the business**. These costs (depreciation, rent, administration salaries) are largely **non-controllable in the short term** because they have been committed by longer-term decisions affecting longer-term needs. When a company decides to cut production drastically, the long-term committed fixed costs will be reduced, but only after redundancy terms have been settled and assets sold.

(b)   **Discretionary fixed costs**, such as advertising and research and development costs, are incurred as a result of a top management decision, but could be **raised or lowered at fairly short notice** (irrespective of the actual volume of production and sales).

Question		Discretionary costs

Learning outcomes: C(viii), (ix)

Which of the following is an example of a discretionary cost?

A   Material costs
B   Advertising expenditure
C   Cost of heating and lighting
D   Salaries

Answer

The correct answer is B.

A discretionary cost is a cost whose amount, within a particular time period, is determined by, and can be altered by, the budget holder.

4.1.2 Controllability and apportioned costs

Managers should only be held accountable for costs over which they have some influence. This may seem quite straightforward in theory, but it is not always so easy in practice to distinguish controllable from uncontrollable costs. **Apportioned overhead costs provide a good example**.

Suppose that a manager of a production department in a manufacturing company is made responsible for the costs of his department. These costs include **directly attributable overhead items** such as the costs of indirect labour employed in the department and indirect materials consumed in the department. The department's overhead costs also include an apportionment of costs from other cost centres, such as rent and rates for the building it shares with other departments and a share of the costs of the maintenance department.

Should the production manager be held accountable for any of these apportioned costs?

(a)   Managers should not be held accountable for costs over which they have no control. In this example, apportioned rent and rates costs would not be controllable by the production department manager.

(b)   Managers should be held accountable for costs over which they have some influence. In this example, it is the responsibility of the maintenance department manager to keep maintenance costs within budget. But their costs will be partly variable and partly fixed, and the variable cost element will depend on the volume of demand for their services. If the production department's staff treat their equipment badly we might expect higher repair costs, and the production department manager should therefore be made accountable for the repair costs that his department makes the maintenance department incur on its behalf.

(c)   Another argument for charging the production department with some of the costs of the maintenance department is that it prevents the production department from viewing the maintenance services as 'free services'. Over-use would be discouraged and the production manager is more likely to question the activities of the maintenance department and the result might be a reduction overall in maintenance costs or the provision of more efficient maintenance services.

Question   Committed and discretionary costs

Learning outcomes: C(viii), (ix)

Try to discover some of your organisation's committed fixed costs and discretionary fixed costs. You will then be able to use them as examples in the exam.

4.1.3 Controllability and dual responsibility

Quite often a particular cost might be the **responsibility of two or more managers**. For example, raw materials costs might be the responsibility of the purchasing manager (prices) and the production manager (usage). A **reporting system must allocate responsibility appropriately**. The purchasing manager must be responsible for any increase in raw materials prices whereas the production manager should be responsible for any increase in raw materials usage.

Attention!

You can see from these descriptions that there are **no clear cut rules** as to which costs are controllable and which are uncontrollable. Each situation and cost must be reviewed separately and a decision taken according to the effect on the control value of the information and its behavioural impact.

4.2 Budgetary control reports

If the **budget holders** (managers of budget centres) are to attempt to meet budgets they must receive regular budgetary control reports so that they can monitor the budget centre's operations and take any necessary control action.

The **amount of detail** included in reports will **vary** according to the needs of management. In general terms, there should be **sufficient detail** within the reports to **motivate the individual manager to take the most appropriate action** in all circumstances. A form of **exception reporting** can be used for **top management,** reports just detailing significant variances.

5 Feedback and feedforward control mechanisms

5.1 Feedback

The term **'feedback'** is used to describe both the process of reporting back control information to management and the control information itself. In a business organisation, it is information produced from within the organisation **(management control reports)** with the purpose of helping management and other employees with control decisions.

(a) **Single loop feedback**, normally expressed as feedback, is the feedback of relatively small variations between actual and plan in order that corrective action can bring performance in line with planned results. This implies that the existing plans will not change. This type of feedback is associated with budgetary control and standard costing.

(b) **Double loop feedback**, also known as **higher level feedback**, ensures that plans, budgets, organisational structures and the control systems themselves are revised to meet changes in conditions.

(c) Feedback will most often be **negative:** targets were missed and this was **not** what was required. It may, however, be **positive:** targets were missed, but other targets were hit which were better than those we were aiming at. Negative feedback would result in control action to get back onto target. Positive feedback means that the target should be moved.

5.2 The feedback loop in the control cycle

Exam focus point

The suggested answer supplied with the pilot paper included a diagram of the control loop as a part of an answer describing the main features of a feedback loop. The use of a diagram can save a lot of writing if you can sketch one quickly.

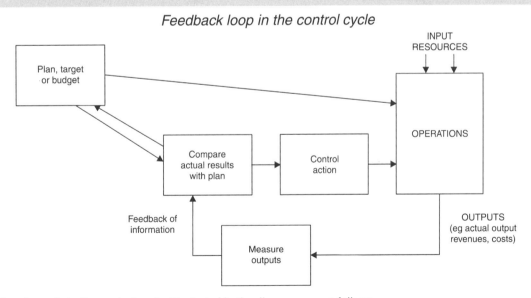

Feedback loop in the control cycle

The elements in the control cycle, illustrated in the diagram, are as follows.

Step 1   **Plans and targets are set for the future**. These could be long-, medium- or short-term plans. Examples include budgets, profit targets and standard costs.

Step 2   **Plans are put into operation**. As a consequence, materials and labour are used, and other expenses are incurred.

Step 3   **Actual results are recorded and analysed.**

Step 4   **Information about actual results is fed back** to the management concerned, often in the form of accounting reports. This reported information is **feedback**.

Step 5   **The feedback is used by management to compare** actual results with the plan or targets (what should be or should have been achieved).

Step 6   By comparing actual and planned results, management can then do one of three things, depending on how they see the situation.

    (a)   **They can take control action**. By identifying what has gone wrong, and then finding out why, corrective measures can be taken.

    (b)   **They can decide to do nothing**. This could be the decision when actual results are going better than planned, or when poor results were caused by something which is unlikely to happen again in the future.

    (c)   **They can alter the plan or target** if actual results are different from the plan or target, and there is nothing that management can do (or nothing, perhaps, that they want to do) to correct the situation.

It may be helpful at this stage to relate the control system to a **practical example, such as monthly sales.**

Step 1   A **sales budget** or plan is prepared for the year.

Step 2   Management **organises the business's resources** to achieve the budget targets.

Step 3   At the end of each month, **actual results** are **reported back to management**.

Step 4   Managers **compare actual results against the plan.**

Step 5   Where necessary, they **take corrective action to adjust the workings of the system**, probably by amending the inputs to the system.

- Salespeople might be asked to work longer hours.
- More money might be spent on advertising.
- Some new price discounts might be decided.
- Delivery periods to customers might be reduced by increasing output.

Where appropriate the sales plan may be revised, up or down.

5.3 Feedforward control

Feedforward control is based on comparing original targets or actual results with a **forecast** of future results.

Feedforward control is 'The forecasting of differences between actual and planned outcomes, and the implementation of action, before the event, to avoid such differences'. (CIMA *Official Terminology*)

Most control systems make use of a comparison between results of the current period (historical costs) and the planned results. Past events are therefore used as a means of controlling or adjusting future activity. A major criticism of this approach to control activity is that it is backward looking.

Consider, however, a **cash budget**. This is used to identify likely peaks and troughs in cash balances, and if it seems probable that, say, a higher overdraft facility will be needed later in the year, control action will be taken in advance of the actual need, to make sure that the facility will be available. This is an example of **feedforward control**, that is, control based on comparing original targets or actual results with a **forecast** of future results. You saw an example of a cash budget being used for feedforword control in Chapter 11.

The 'information revolution', which has arisen from computer technology, management information systems theory and the growing use of quantitative techniques has widened the scope for the use of this control technique. Forecasting models can be constructed which enable regular revised forecasts to be prepared about what is now likely to happen in view of changes in key variables (such as sales demand, wage rates and so on). You studied forecasting in Chapter 12.

If regular forecasts are prepared, managers will have both the current forecast and the original plan to guide their action. The original plan may or may not be achievable in view of the changing circumstances. The current forecast indicates what is expected to happen in view of these circumstances.

Examples of control comparisons

Step 1   **Current forecast versus plan.** What action must be taken to get back to the plan, given the differences between the current forecast and the plan? Is any control action worthwhile?

Step 2   If **control action** is **planned**, the current forecast will need to be amended to take account of the effects of the control action and a **revised forecast** prepared.

Step 3   The next comparison should then be **revised forecast versus plan** to determine whether the plan is now expected to be achieved.

Step 4   A comparison between the **original current forecast** and the **revised forecast** will show what the expected effect of the control action will be.

Step 5   At the **end of a control period**, actual results will be analysed and two comparisons may be made.

- **Actual results versus the revised forecast.** Why did differences between the two occur?

- **Actual results so far in the year versus the plan.** How close are actual results to the plan?

Step 6   At the same time, a **new current forecast** should be prepared, and the cycle of comparisons and control action may begin again.

It is in this way that costs are constantly controlled and monitored.

6 Behavioural implications of budgeting

Used correctly a budgetary control system can **motivate** but it can also produce undesirable **negative reactions**.

There are basically two ways in which a budget can be set: from the **top down** (**imposed** budget) or from the **bottom up** (**participatory** budget). Many writers refer to a third style (**negotiated**).

Attention!

Much of Sections 6 to 9 applies equally to the operation of systems of standard costing.

The purpose of a budgetary control system is to assist management in planning and controlling the resources of their organisation by providing appropriate control information. The information will only be valuable, however, if it is interpreted correctly and used purposefully by managers *and* employees.

The correct use of control information therefore depends not only on the content of the information itself, but also on the behaviour of its recipients. This is because control in business is exercised by people. Their attitude to control information will colour their views on what they should do with it and a number of behavioural problems can arise.

(a)   The **managers who set the budget** or standards are **often not the managers** who are then made **responsible for achieving budget targets**.

(b)   The **goals of the organisation as a whole**, as expressed in a budget, **may not coincide with the personal aspirations of individual managers**.

(c)   **Control is applied at different stages by different people**. A supervisor might get weekly control reports, and act on them; his superior might get monthly control reports, and decide to take different control action. Different managers can get in each others' way, and resent the interference from others.

6.1 Motivation

Motivation is what makes people behave in the way that they do. It comes from individual attitudes, or group attitudes. Individuals will be motivated by personal desires and interests. These may be in line with the objectives of the organisation, and some people 'live for their jobs'. Other individuals see their job as a chore, and their motivations will be unrelated to the objectives of the organisation they work for.

It is therefore vital that the goals of management and the employees harmonise with the goals of the organisation as a whole. This is known as **goal congruence**. Although obtaining goal congruence is essentially a behavioural problem, **it is possible to design and run a budgetary control system which will go some way towards ensuring that goal congruence is achieved**. Managers and employees must therefore be favourably disposed towards the budgetary control system so that it can operate efficiently.

The management accountant should therefore try to ensure that employees have positive attitudes towards **setting budgets, implementing budgets** (that is, putting the organisation's plans into practice) and feedback of results (**control information**).

6.1.1 Poor attitudes when setting budgets

If managers are involved in preparing a budget, poor attitudes or hostile behaviour towards the budgetary control system can begin at the **planning stage.**

(a)   Managers may **complain that they are too busy** to spend much time on budgeting.

(b)   They may **build 'slack' into their expenditure estimates**.

(c)   They may argue that **formalising a budget plan on paper is too restricting** and that managers should be allowed flexibility in the decisions they take.

(d)   They may set budgets for their budget centre and **not coordinate** their own plans with those of other budget centres.

(e)   They may **base future plans on past results**, instead of using the opportunity for formalised planning to look at alternative options and new ideas.

On the other hand, **managers may not be involved in the budgeting process**. Organisational goals may not be communicated to them and they might have their budget decided for them by senior management or administrative decision. It is **hard for people to be motivated to achieve targets set by someone else.**

6.1.2 Poor attitudes when putting plans into action

Poor attitudes also arise **when a budget is implemented**.

(a)   Managers might **put in only just enough effort** to achieve budget targets, without trying to beat targets.

(b)   A formal budget might **encourage rigidity and discourage flexibility**.

(c)   **Short-term planning** in a budget **can draw attention away from the longer-term consequences** of decisions.

(d)   There might be **minimal cooperation and communication** between managers.

(e)   Managers will often try to make sure that they **spend up to their full budget allowance, and do not overspend**, so that they will not be accused of having asked for too much spending allowance in the first place.

(f)   Particularly in **service departments and public sector organisations,** where performance is assessed by comparing actual and budget spending, managers may consider the **budget** as a **sum of money that has to be spent**. A manager of a local authority department might be given an annual budget of £360,000. The manager knows that he will be punished for spending more than £360,000 but that if he spends less than £300,000 his budget will probably be reduced next year, leading to a loss of status and making his job more difficult next year. To ensure he does not overspend he may spend £26,000 a month for 11 months of the year (by reducing the provision of the department's service), building up a contingency fund of (11 × £4,000) £44,000 to be used in case of emergencies. In the final month of the year he would then need to spend (£(44,000 + 30,000)) £74,000 to ensure his whole budget was used (perhaps by using extra labour and/or high quality materials). The manager's **behaviour** has therefore been **distorted by the control system**.

6.1.3 Poor attitudes and the use of control information

The **attitude of managers towards the accounting control information** they receive **might reduce the information's effectiveness**.

(a)   Management accounting control reports could well be seen as having a relatively **low priority** in the list of management tasks. Managers might take the view that they have more pressing jobs on hand than looking at routine control reports.

(b)   Managers might **resent control information**; they may see it as **part of a system of trying to find fault with their work**. This resentment is likely to be particularly strong when budgets or standards are imposed on managers without allowing them to participate in the budget-setting process.

(c)   If budgets are seen as **pressure devices** to push managers into doing better, control reports will be resented.

(d)   Managers **may not understand the information** in the control reports, because they are unfamiliar with accounting terminology or principles.

(e)   Managers might have a **false sense of what their objectives should be**. A production manager might consider it more important to maintain quality standards regardless of cost. He would then dismiss adverse expenditure variances as inevitable and unavoidable.

(f)   **If there are flaws in the system of recording actual costs**, managers will dismiss control information as unreliable.

(g)   **Control information** might be **received weeks after the end of the period to which it relates**, in which case managers might regard it as out-of-date and no longer useful.

(h)   Managers might be **held responsible for variances outside their control**.

It is therefore obvious that accountants and senior management should try to implement systems that are acceptable to budget holders and which produce positive effects.

6.1.4 Pay as a motivator

Many researchers agree that **pay can be an important motivator**, when there is a formal link between higher pay (or other rewards, such as promotion) and achieving budget targets. Individuals are likely to work harder to achieve budget if they know that they will be rewarded for their successful efforts. There are, however, problems with using pay as an incentive.

(a)   A serious problem that can arise is that **formal reward and performance evaluation systems can encourage dysfunctional behaviour**. Many investigations have noted the tendency of managers to pad their budgets either in anticipation of cuts by superiors or to make the subsequent variances more favourable. And there are numerous examples of managers making decisions in response to performance indices, even though the decisions are contrary to the wider purposes of the organisation.

(b)   The targets must be challenging, but fair, otherwise individuals will become dissatisfied. **Pay can be a demotivator as well as a motivator**!

7 Participation and performance evaluation

> FAST FORWARD
>
> There are three ways of using budgetary information to evaluate managerial performance (**budget constrained style, profit conscious style, non-accounting style**).
>
> In certain situations it is useful to prepare an **expectations budget** and an **aspirations budget**.
>
> Management and the management accountant require strategies and methods for dealing with the **tensions** and **conflict** resulting from the **conflicting purposes** of a budget.

7.1 Participation

It has been argued that **participation** in the budgeting process **will improve motivation** and so will improve the quality of budget decisions and the efforts of individuals to achieve their budget targets (although obviously this will depend on the personality of the individual, the nature of the task (narrowly defined or flexible) and the organisational culture).

There are basically two ways in which a budget can be set: from the **top down** (imposed budget) or from the **bottom up** (participatory budget).

7.2 Imposed style of budgeting

Key term

An **imposed/top-down budget** is 'A budget allowance which is set without permitting the ultimate budget holder to have the opportunity to participate in the budgeting process'.   (CIMA *Official Terminology*)

In this approach to budgeting, **top management prepare a budget with little or no input from operating personnel** which is then imposed upon the employees who have to work to the budgeted figures.

The times when imposed budgets are effective

- In newly-formed organisations
- In very small businesses
- During periods of economic hardship
- When operational managers lack budgeting skills
- When the organisation's different units require precise coordination

There are, of course, advantages and disadvantages to this style of setting budgets.

(a)   **Advantages**

- Strategic plans are likely to be incorporated into planned activities.
- They enhance the coordination between the plans and objectives of divisions.
- They use senior management's awareness of total resource availability.
- They decrease the input from inexperienced or uninformed lower-level employees.
- They decrease the period of time taken to draw up the budgets.

(b)   **Disadvantages**

(i)   Dissatisfaction, defensiveness and low morale amongst employees. It is hard for people to be motivated to achieve targets set by somebody else.

(ii)   The feeling of team spirit may disappear.

(iii)   The acceptance of organisational goals and objectives could be limited.

(iv)   The feeling of the budget as a punitive device could arise.

(v)   Managers who are performing operations on a day to day basis are likely to have a better understanding of what is achievable.

(vi)   Unachievable budgets could result if consideration is not given to local operating and political environments. This applies particularly to overseas divisions.

(vii)   Lower-level management initiative may be stifled.

7.3 Participative style of budgeting

Key term

Participative/bottom-up budgeting is 'A budgeting system in which all budget holders are given the opportunity to participate in setting their own budgets'.   (CIMA *Official Terminology*)

In this approach to budgeting, **budgets are developed by lower-level managers who then submit the budgets to their superiors**. The budgets are based on the lower-level managers' perceptions of what is achievable and the associated necessary resources.

Question

Participative budgets

Learning outcome: C(xiii)

In what circumstances might participative budgets *not* be effective?

A   In centralised organisations
B   In well-established organisations
C   In very large businesses
D   During periods of economic affluence

Answer

The correct answer is A.

An imposed budget is likely to be most effective in a centralised organisation.

As well as in the circumstances in B, C and D, participative budgets are also effective when operational management have strong budgeting skills and when the organisation's different units act autonomously.

Advantages of participative budgets

- They are based on information from employees most familiar with the department.
- Knowledge spread among several levels of management is pulled together.
- Morale and motivation is improved.
- They increase operational managers' commitment to organisational objectives.
- In general they are more realistic.
- Co-ordination between units is improved.
- Specific resource requirements are included.
- Senior managers' overview is mixed with operational level details.
- Individual managers' aspiration levels are more likely to be taken into account.

Disadvantages of participative budgets

- They consume more time.
- Changes implemented by senior management may cause dissatisfaction.
- Budgets may be unachievable if managers are not qualified to participate.
- They may cause managers to introduce budgetary slack and budget bias.
- They can support 'empire building' by subordinates.
- An earlier start to the budgeting process could be required.
- Managers may set 'easy' budgets to ensure that they are achievable.

7.4 Negotiated style of budgeting

At the two extremes, budgets can be dictated from above or simply emerge from below but, in practice, different levels of management often agree budgets by a process of negotiation. In the imposed budget approach, operational managers will try to negotiate with senior managers the budget targets which they consider to be unreasonable or unrealistic. Likewise senior management usually review and revise budgets presented to them under a participative approach through a process of negotiation with lower level managers. **Final budgets are therefore most likely to lie between what top management would really like and what junior managers believe is feasible.** The budgeting process is hence a **bargaining process** and it is this bargaining which is of vital importance, **determining whether the budget is an effective management tool or simply a clerical device**.

7.5 Performance evaluation

A very important **source of motivation to perform well** (to achieve budget targets, perhaps, or to eliminate variances) is, not surprisingly, being **kept informed about how actual results are progressing, and how actual results compare with target**. Individuals should not be kept in the dark about their performance.

The information fed back about actual results should have the qualities of good information.

Question

Good information

Learning outcome: C(xiii)

Cast your mind back to your earlier studies. Which of the following is not a quality of good information?

A   Relevant
B   Complete
C   Timely
D   Cheap

Answer

The correct answer is D.

Good information is not necessarily cheap. The cost of providing it should be less than the value of the benefits it provides, however.

Here are the qualities of good information.

- Relevance
- Accuracy
- Inspires confidence
- Timely
- Cost of provision less than the value of benefits provided

- Completeness
- Clarity
- Appropriately communicated (channel and recipient)
- Manageable volume

Features of feedback

(a) Reports should be **clear** and **comprehensive**.

(b) The **'exception principle'** should be applied so that **significant variances** are highlighted for investigation.

(c) Reports should identify the **controllable** costs and revenues, which are the items that can be directly influenced by the manager who receives the report. It can be demotivating if managers feel that they are being held responsible for items which are outside their control and which they are unable to influence.

(d) Reports should be **timely**, which means they must be produced in good time to allow the individual to take control action before any adverse results get much worse.

(e) Information should be **accurate** (although only accurate enough for its purpose as there is no need to go into unnecessary detail for pointless accuracy).

(f) Reports should be communicated to the manager who has **responsibility** and **authority** to act on the matter.

Surprisingly research evidence suggests that **all too often accounting performance measures lead to a lack of goal congruence**. Managers seek to improve their performance on the basis of the indicator used, even if this is not in the best interests of the organisation as a whole. For example, a production manager may be encouraged to achieve and maintain high production levels and to reduce costs, particularly if his or her bonus is linked to these factors. Such a manager is likely to be highly motivated. But the need to maintain high production levels could lead to high levels of slow-moving inventory, resulting in an adverse effect on the company's cash flow. (This is another example of **behaviour being distorted by the control system**.)

The **impact of an accounting system on managerial performance** depends ultimately on how the information is used. Research by Hopwood has shown that there are three distinct ways of using budgetary information to evaluate managerial performance.

Style of evaluation	Comment
Budget constrained	'The manager's performance is primarily evaluated upon the basis of his ability to continually meet the budget on a short-term basis. This criterion of performance is stressed at the expense of other valued and important criteria and the manager will receive unfavourable feedback from his superior if, for instance, his actual costs exceed the budgeted costs, regardless of other considerations.'
Profit conscious	'The manager's performance is evaluated on the basis of his ability to increase the general effectiveness of his unit's operations in relation to the long-term purposes of the organisation. For instance, at the cost centre level one important aspect of this ability concerns the attention which he devotes to reducing long-run costs. For this purpose, however, the budgetary information has to be used with great care in a rather flexible manner.'
Non-accounting	'The budgetary information plays a relatively unimportant part in the superior's evaluation of the manager's performance.'

A summary of the effects of the three styles of evaluation is as follows.

	Style of evaluation		
	Budget constrained	Profit conscious	Non-accounting
Involvement with costs	HIGH	HIGH	LOW
Job-related tension	HIGH	MEDIUM	MEDIUM
Manipulation of the accounting reports (**bias**)	EXTENSIVE	LITTLE	LITTLE
Relations with the supervisor	POOR	GOOD	GOOD
Relations with colleagues	POOR	GOOD	GOOD

Research has shown no clear preference for one style over another.

7.6 Budget slack

Key term

Budget slack is 'The intentional overestimation of expenses and/or underestimation of revenues in the budgeting process'.   (CIMA *Official Terminology*)

In the process of preparing budgets, managers might **deliberately overestimate costs and underestimate sales**, so that they will not be blamed in the future for overspending and poor results.

In controlling actual operations, managers must then **ensure that their spending rises to meet their budget**, otherwise they will be 'blamed' for careless budgeting.

A typical situation is for a manager to **pad the budget** and waste money on non-essential expenses so that he uses all his budget allowances. The reason behind his action is the fear that unless the allowance is fully spent it will be reduced in future periods thus making his job more difficult as the future reduced budgets will not be so easy to attain. Because inefficiency and slack are allowed for in budgets, achieving a budget target means only that costs have remained within the accepted levels of inefficient spending.

Budget bias can **work in the other direction** too. It has been noted that, after a run of mediocre results, some managers **deliberately overstate revenues and understate cost estimates**, no doubt feeling the need to make an immediate favourable impact by promising better performance in the future. They may merely delay problems, however, as the managers may well be censured when they fail to hit these optimistic targets.

Yet again this is an example of **control systems distorting the processes they are meant to serve**.

8 The use of budgets as targets

Once decided, budgets become targets. As targets, they can motivate managers to achieve a high level of performance. But **how difficult should targets be**? And how might people react to targets of differing degrees of difficulty in achievement?

(a) There is likely to be a **demotivating** effect where an **ideal standard** of performance is set, because adverse efficiency variances will always be reported.

(b) A **low standard of efficiency** is also **demotivating**, because there is no sense of achievement in attaining the required standards, and there will be no impetus for employees to try harder to do better than this.

(c) A **budgeted level of attainment** could be 'normal': that is, the **same as the level that has been achieved in the past**. Arguably, this level will be **too low**. It might **encourage budgetary slack**.

It has been argued that **each individual has a personal 'aspiration level'**. This is a level of performance in a task with which the individual is familiar, which the individual undertakes for himself to reach. This aspiration level might be quite challenging and if individuals in a work group all have similar aspiration levels it should be possible to incorporate these levels within the official operating standards.

Some care should be taken, however, in applying this.

(a) If a manager's **tendency to achieve success is stronger than the tendency to avoid failure**, budgets with **targets of intermediate levels of difficulty** are the most motivating, and stimulate a manager to better performance levels. Budgets which are either too easy to achieve or too difficult are de-motivating, and managers given such targets achieve relatively low levels of performance.

(b) A manager's **tendency to avoid failure might be stronger than the tendency to achieve success**. (This is likely in an organisation in which the budget is used as a pressure device on subordinates by senior managers). Managers might then be discouraged from trying to achieve budgets of intermediate difficulty and tend to avoid taking on such tasks, resulting in poor levels of performance, worse than if budget targets were either easy or very difficult to achieve.

It has therefore been suggested that in a situation where budget targets of an intermediate difficulty *are* motivating, such targets ought to be set if the purpose of budgets is to motivate; however, although budgets which are set for **motivational purposes** need to be stated in terms of **aspirations rather than expectations**, budgets for planning and decision purposes need to be stated in terms of the best available estimate of expected actual performance. The **solution** might therefore be to have **two budgets**.

(a) A **budget for planning and decision making based on reasonable expectations**.

(b) A second **budget for motivational purposes**, with **more difficult targets of performance** (that is, targets of an intermediate level of difficulty).

These two budgets might be called an **'expectations budget'** and an **'aspirations budget'** respectively.

9 The management accountant and motivation

We have seen that budgets serve many purposes, but in some instances their purposes can conflict and have an effect on management behaviour. Management and the management accountant therefore require strategies and methods for dealing with the resulting tensions and conflict. For example, should targets be adjusted for uncontrollable and unforeseeable environmental influence? But what is then the effect on motivation if employees view performance standards as changeable?

Can performance measures and the related budgetary control system ever **motivate managers** towards achieving the organisation's goals?

(a) Accounting measures of performance **can't provide a comprehensive assessment** of what a person has achieved for the organisation.

(b) It is unfair as it is usually **impossible to segregate controllable and uncontrollable components of performance**.

(c) Accounting **reports tend to concentrate on short-term achievements**, to the exclusion of the long-term effects.

(d) Many accounting **reports try to serve several different purposes**, and in trying to satisfy several needs actually satisfy none properly.

The management accountant does not have the authority to do much on his or her own to improve hostile or apathetic attitudes to control information. There has to be support, either from senior management or from budget centre managers. However, the management accountant can do quite a lot to improve and then maintain the standard of a budgetary control reporting system.

(a) **How senior management can offer support**

    (i) Making sure that a **system of responsibility accounting is adopted** as discussed in Section 4 of this chapter.

    (ii) Allowing **managers to have a say in formulating their budgets**.

    (iii) Offering **incentives** to managers who meet budget targets.

    (iv) **Not regarding budgetary control information as a way of apportioning blame**.

(b) **Budget centre managers should accept their responsibilities**. In-house training courses could be held to encourage a collective, cooperative and positive attitude among managers.

(c) **How the management accountant can improve (or maintain) the quality of the budgetary control system**

    (i) **Develop a working relationship with operational managers**, going out to meet them and discussing the control reports.

    (ii) **Explain the meaning of budgets and control reports**.

    (iii) **Keep accounting jargon in these reports to a minimum.**

    (iv) Make **reports clear and to the point**, for example using the principle of reporting by exception.

    (v) Provide control information with a **minimum of delay.**

    (vi) **Make control information as useful as possible**, by distinguishing between directly attributable and controllable costs over which a manager should have influence and apportioned or fixed costs which are unavoidable or uncontrollable.

    (vii) Make sure that **actual costs are recorded accurately**.

    (viii) Ensure that **budgets are up-to-date**, either by having a system of rolling budgets, or else by updating budgets or standards as necessary, and ensuring that standards are 'fair' so that control information is realistic.

Attention!

There are no ideal solutions to the conflicts caused by the operation of a budgetary control system. Management and the management accountant have to develop their own ways of dealing with them, taking into account their organisation, their business and the personalities involved.

Question

Behavioural aspects of budget participation

Learning outcome: C(xiii)

Discuss the behavioural aspects of participation in the budgeting process and any difficulties you might envisage. (5 marks)

Answer

The level of participation in the budgeting process can vary from zero participation to a process of group decision making. There are a number of behavioural aspects of participation to consider.

(a)   **Communication**. Managers cannot be expected to achieve targets if they do not know what those targets are. Communication of targets is made easier if managers have participated in the budgetary process from the beginning.

(b)   **Motivation**. Managers are likely to be better motivated to achieve a budget if they have been involved in compiling it, rather than having a dictatorial budget imposed on them.

(c)   **Realistic targets**. A target must be achievable and accepted as realistic if it is to be a motivating factor. A manager who has been involved in setting targets is more likely to accept them as realistic. In addition, managers who are close to the operation of their departments may be more aware of the costs and potential savings in running it.

(d)   **Goal congruence**. One of the best ways of achieving goal congruence is to involve managers in the preparation of their own budgets, so that their personal goals can be taken into account in setting targets.

Although participative budgeting has many advantages, difficulties might also arise.

(a)   **Pseudo-participation**. Participation may not be genuine, but merely a pretence at involving managers in the preparation of their budgets. Managers may feel that their contribution is being ignored, or that the participation consists of merely obtaining their agreement to a budget which has already been decided. If this is the case then managers are likely to be more demotivated than if there is no participation at all.

(b)   **Coordination**. If participative budgeting is well managed it can improve the coordination of the preparation of the various budgets. There is, however, a danger that too many managers will become involved so that communication becomes difficult and the process become complex.

(c)   **Training**. Some managers may not possess the necessary skill to make an effective contribution to the preparation of their budgets. Additional training may be necessary, with the consequent investment of money and time. It may also be necessary to train managers to understand the purposes and advantages of participation.

(d)   **Slack**. If budgets are used in a punitive fashion for control purposes then managers will be tempted to build in extra expenditure to provide a 'cushion' against overspending. It is easier for them to build in slack in a participative system.

10 The balanced scorecard

The **balanced scorecard approach** to the provision of information focuses on four different perspectives: customer, financial, internal, and innovation and learning.

So far in our discussion we have focussed on performance measurement and control from a financial point of view. Another approach, originally developed by Kaplan and Norton, is the use of what is called a 'balanced scorecard' consisting of a **variety of indicators both financial and non-financial**.

Key term

The **balanced scorecard approach** is 'An approach to the provision of information to management to assist strategic policy formulation and achievement. It emphasises the need to provide the user with a set of information which addresses all relevant areas of performance in an objective and unbiased fashion. The information provided may include both financial and non-financial elements, and cover areas such as profitability, customer satisfaction, internal efficiency and innovation.' (CIMA *Official Terminology*)

The balanced scorecard focuses on **four different perspectives**, as follows.

Perspective	Question	Explanation
Customer	What do existing and new customers value from us?	Gives rise to targets that matter to customers: cost, quality, delivery, inspection, handling and so on.
Internal	What processes must we excel at to achieve our financial and customer objectives?	Aims to improve internal processes and decision making.
Innovation and learning	Can we continue to improve and create future value?	Considers the business's capacity to maintain its competitive position through the acquisition of new skills and the development of new products.
Financial	How do we create value for our shareholders?	Covers traditional measures such as growth, profitability and shareholder value but set through talking to the shareholder or shareholders direct.

Performance targets are set once the key areas for improvement have been identified, and the balanced scorecard is the **main monthly report**.

The scorecard is **'balanced'** in the sense that managers are required to **think in terms of all four perspectives**, to **prevent improvements being made in one area at the expense of** another.

The types of measure which may be monitored under each of the four perspectives include the following. The list is not exhaustive but it will give you an idea of the possible scope of a balanced scorecard approach. The measures selected, particularly within the internal perspective, will vary considerably with the type of organisation and its objectives.

Perspective	Measures	
Customer	• New customers acquired • Customer complaints	• On-time deliveries • Returns
Internal	• Quality control rejects • Average set-up time	• Speed of producing management information
Innovation and learning	• Labour turnover rate • Percentage of revenue generated by new products and services • Average time taken to develop new products and services	
Financial	• Return on capital employed • Cash flow	• Revenue growth • Earnings per share

Broadbent and Cullen (in Berry, Broadbent and Otley, ed, *Management Control*, 1995) identify the following **important features** of this approach.

- It looks at both **internal and external matters** concerning the organisation.
- It is **related to the key elements of a company's strategy**.
- **Financial and non-financial measures** are linked together.

The balanced scorecard approach may be particularly useful for performance measurement in organisations which are unable to use simple profit as a performance measure. For example the **public sector** has long been forced to use a **wide range of performance indicators**, which can be formalised with a balanced scorecard approach.

Question

Learning outcome: C (xii)

To which perspective of the balanced scorecard could the measure 'training days per employee' be most appropriately applied?

A   Customer
B   Internal
C   Innovation and learning
D   Financial

Answer

The correct answer is C.

10.1 Problems

As with all techniques, problems can arise when it is applied.

Problem	Explanation
Conflicting measures	Some measures in the scorecard such as research funding and cost reduction may naturally conflict. It is often difficult to determine the balance which will achieve the best results.
Selecting measures	Not only do appropriate measures have to be devised but the number of measures used must be agreed. Care must be taken that the impact of the results is not lost in a sea of information.
Expertise	Measurement is only useful if it initiates appropriate action. Non-financial managers may have difficulty with the usual profit measures. With more measures to consider this problem will be compounded.
Interpretation	Even a financially-trained manager may have difficulty in putting the figures into an overall perspective.
Too many measures	The ultimate objective for commercial organisations is to maximise profits or shareholder wealth. Other targets should offer a guide to achieving this objective and not become an end in themselves.

11 Beyond budgeting

FAST FORWARD

The **Beyond Budgeting Round Table** have proposed that traditional budgeting should be abandoned. They have publicised ten main criticisms of the traditional process.

11.1 Criticisms of budgeting

In our discussion of the budgetary planning process we have come across many difficulties with budgets and criticisms of how they are used in organisations. The large amount of material on behavioural issues in this chapter should help you to appreciate the real danger that budgets can cause unintended dysfunctional behaviour that needs to be guarded against in organisations.

The Beyond Budgeting Round Table (BBRT) is an independent research collaborative that has put forward the proposition that budgeting, as most organisations practice it, should be abandoned. Their website at www.bbrt.org lists the following ten criticisms of budgeting.

(a) **Budgets are time consuming and expensive**. Even with the support of computer models it is estimated that the budgeting process uses up to 20 to 30 per cent of senior executives' and financial managers' time.

(b) **Budgets provide poor value to users**. Although surveys have shown that some managers feel that budgets give them control, a large majority of financial directors wish to reform the budgetary process because they feel that finance staff spend too much time on 'lower value added activities'

(c) **Budgets fail to focus on shareholder value**. Most budgets are set on an incremental basis as an acceptable target agreed between the manager and the manager's superior. Managers may be rewarded for achieving their short term budgets and will not look to the longer term or take risks, for fear of affecting their own short term results.

(d) **Budgets are too rigid and prevent fast response**. Although most organisations do update and revise their budgets at regular intervals as the budget period proceeds the process is often too slow compared with the pace at which the external environment is changing.

(e) **Budgets protect rather than reduce costs**. Once a manager has an authorised budget he can spend that amount of resource without further authorisation. A 'use it or lose it' mentality often develops so that managers will incur cost unnecessarily. This happens especially towards the end of the budget period in the expectation that managers will not be permitted to carry forward any unused resource into the budget for next period.

(f) **Budgets stifle product and strategy innovation**. The focus on achieving the budget discourages managers from taking risks in case this has adverse effects on their short term performance. Managers do not have the freedom to respond to changing customer needs in a fast changing market because the activity they would need to undertake is not authorised in their budget.

(g) **Budgets focus on sales targets rather than customer satisfaction**. The achievement of short term sales forecasts becomes the focus of most organisations. However this does not necessarily result in customer satisfaction. The customer may be sold something **inappropriate to their needs**, as in recent years in the UK financial services industry. Alternatively if a manager has already met the sales target for a particular period they might try to **delay sales to the next period**, in order to give themselves a 'head start' towards achieving the target for the next period. Furthermore there is an incentive towards the end of a period, if a manager feels that the sales target is not going to be achieved for the period, to **delay sales until the next period**, and thus again have a head start towards achieving the target for the next period. All of these actions, focusing on sales targets rather than customer satisfaction, will have a detrimental effect on the organisation in the longer term.

(h) **Budgets are divorced from strategy**. Most organisations monitor the monthly results against the short term budget for the month. What is needed instead is a system of monitoring the longer term progress against the organisation's strategy.

(i)   **Budgets reinforce a dependency culture**. The process of planning and budgeting within a framework devolved from senior management perpetuates a culture of dependency. Traditional budgeting systems, operated on a centralised basis, do not encourage a culture of **personal responsibility**.

(j)   **Budgets lead to unethical behaviour**. For example we have seen in this chapter a number of opportunities for dysfunctional behaviour such as **building slack into the budget** in order to create an easier target for achievement.

11.2 Beyond Budgeting concepts

The two fundamental concepts of the **Beyond Budgeting** approach are the use of **adaptive management processes** rather than fixed annual budgets and a move to a more decentralised way of managing the business with a culture of personal responsibility.

Two fundamental concepts underlie the Beyond Budgeting approach advocated by BBRT.

(a)   **Use adaptive management processes rather than the more rigid annual budget**. Traditional annual plans tie managers to predetermined actions which are not responsive to current situations. Managers should instead be planning on a **more adaptive**, rolling basis but with the focus on cash forecasting rather than purely on cost control. Performance is monitored against world-class benchmarks, competitors and previous periods.

(b)   **Move towards devolved networks rather than centralised hierarchies**. The emphasis is on encouraging a culture of personal responsibility by delegating decision making and performance accountability to line managers.

11.3 Adaptive management processes

An adaptive management process **does not tie a manager to the achievement of a fixed target** but instead expects managers to deliver **continuous performance improvement in response to changing conditions**. Planning is undertaken on a continuous, participative basis.

Evaluation of a manager's performance is based on **relative improvement** and this evaluation is carried out using a **range of relative performance indicators with hindsight**, ie taking account of the conditions under which the manager was operating.

Managers are **given the resources** they need as they are required and horizontal **cross-company activities are coordinated** to respond to customer demand.

11.4 Devolved organisations

In a devolved organisation managers are enabled and encouraged to make their own local decisions in order to achieve results, **within a governance framework based on clear principles and boundaries**. Managers are not restricted to a specific agreed plan but **can use their own initiative and local knowledge** to achieve the organisation's goals. They are expected to make decisions that create value and are fully **accountable for customer satisfaction** and for **achieving a high level of relative success**.

The emphasis in information systems is on openness and 'one truth' throughout the organisation, thus **encouraging ethical behaviour** that is beneficial to the organisation.

The ability of managers to act immediately, without the restriction of a fixed plan, but **within clear principles, values and strategic boundaries** enables the organisation to respond quickly to identified opportunities and threats.

Learning outcome: C(xiv)

Identify THREE criticisms that are levelled at the traditional budgeting process by advocates of techniques that are 'beyond budgeting' and explain how the traditional budgeting process can be adapted to address these criticisms.

(5 marks)

Answer

Three criticisms that could be addressed by adapting the traditional budgeting process are as follows.

(a)   Budgets are time consuming and expensive.

(b)   Budgets protect rather than reduce costs.

(c)   Budgets focus on sales targets rather than customer satisfaction.

The traditional budgeting process can be operated in a fashion that addresses these criticisms as follows.

(a)   **Budgets are time consuming and expensive**

A traditional budgeting system need not be more expensive and time consuming than the adaptive management process advocated as a Beyond Budgeting concept. Managers need to appreciate that the cost of obtaining information should not exceed the benefit to be derived from it. A culture of '**sufficiently accurate**' should be encouraged in budget managers and they should understand that their task is to quantify the costs to be incurred in their area **in order to achieve the organisation's strategy**. This does not necessitate a separate forecast for every paperclip and staple, down to the nearest penny, but budgets can instead be prepared to the nearest thousand or to the nearest million, depending on the size of the organisation.

(b)   **Budgets protect rather than reduce costs**

The attitude of senior managers needs to change in order to prevent unnecessary expenditure and slack being built into the budget. If a budget manager has not used all of their allocated budget resource during a period they should not expect to lose that resource in the next period. **Each manager should be able to request the resource needed to achieve the organisation's strategy**, regardless of the expenditure incurred in the latest period or the amount that was included in the original budget. Thus a 'use it or lose it' culture can be avoided.

Slack can also be avoided by **using budgetary control reports in a less punitive and rigid manner**. If managers believe they are going to be admonished for exceeding the budget expenditure or they are not going to be allowed more resource than stated in their original budget then they will build in slack at the planning stage in order to provide some leeway.

(c)   **Budgets focus on sales targets rather than customer satisfaction**

The punitive use of budgetary control reports will again aggravate this situation. Managers must be given the opportunity to justify any sales shortfalls and should not be penalised for any shortfalls that are beyond their control. The use of **non-financial performance measures** combined with the financial budgetary control reports will assist in moving managers' focus away from the sales targets. For example managers' performance could be assessed on a combination of sales targets and the level of customer satisfaction achieved.

Chapter Roundup

- **Fixed budgets** remain unchanged regardless of the level of activity; **flexible budgets** are designed to flex with the level of activity.

- **Flexible budgets** are prepared using marginal costing and so mixed costs must be split into their fixed and variable components (possibly using the **high/low method**).

- Comparison of a fixed budget with the actual results for a different level of activity is of little use for **budgetary control purposes**. Flexible budgets should be used to show what cost and revenues should have been for the actual level of activity. Differences between the flexible budget figures and actual results are **variances**.

- Budgetary control is based around a system of **budget centres**. Each centre has its own budget which is the responsibility of the **budget holder**.

- **Controllable costs** are those which can be influenced by the budget holder. **Uncontrollable costs** cannot be so influenced.

- The term **'feedback'** is used to describe both the process of reporting back control information to management and the control information itself. In a business organisation, it is information produced from within the organisation **(management control reports)** with the purpose of helping management and other employees with control decisions.

- **Feedforward control** is based on comparing original targets or actual results with a **forecast** of future results.

- Used correctly a budgetary control system can **motivate** but it can also produce undesirable **negative reactions**.

- There are basically two ways in which a budget can be set: from the **top down (imposed** budget) or from the **bottom up (participatory** budget). Many writers refer to a third style (**negotiated**).

- There are three ways of using budgetary information to evaluate managerial performance (**budget constrained style**, **profit conscious style**, **non-accounting style**).

- In certain situations it is useful to prepare an **expectations budget** and an **aspirations budget**.

- Management and the management accountant require strategies and methods for dealing with the **tensions** and **conflict** resulting from the **conflicting purposes** of a budget.

- The **balanced scorecard approach** to the provision of information focuses on four different perspectives: customer, financial, internal, and innovation and learning.

- The **Beyond Budgeting Round** Table have proposed that traditional budgeting should be abandoned. They have publicised ten main criticisms of the traditional process.

- The two fundamental concepts of the **Beyond Budgeting** approach are the use of **adaptive management processes** rather than fixed annual budgets and a move to a more decentralised way of managing the business with a culture of personal responsibility.

Quick Quiz

1   *Fill in the blanks.*

    A flexible budget is a budget which, by recognising ...., is designed to
.... as the level of activity changes.

2   An extract of the costs incurred at two different activity levels is shown. Classify the costs according to
their behaviour patterns and show the budget cost allowance for an activity of 1,500 units.

		1,000 units	2,000 units	Type of cost	Budget cost allowance for 1,500 units
		£	£		£
(a)	Fuel	3,000	6,000	....	....
(b)	Photocopying	9,500	11,000	....	....
(c)	Heating	2,400	2,400	....	....
(d)	Direct wages	6,000	8,000	....	....

3   What is the controllability principle?

4   Feedforward control is based on comparing original targets or actual results with a forecast of future
results. *True or false?*

5   *Match the descriptions to the budgeting style.*

    Description

    (a)   Budget allowances are set without the involvement of the budget holder

    (b)   All budget holders are involved in setting their own budgets

    (c)   Budget allowances are set on the basis of discussions between budget holders and those to whom
they report

    Budgeting style

    Negotiated budgeting
Participative budgeting
Imposed budgeting

6   *Choose the appropriate words from those highlighted.*

    An **expectations/aspirations** budget would be most useful for the purposes of planning and decision
making based on reasonable expectations, whereas an **aspirations/expectations** budget is more
appropriate for improving motivation by setting targets of an intermediate level of difficulty.

7   In the context of a balanced scorecard approach to performance measurement, to which of the four
perspectives does each measure relate?

    Performance measure   *Perspective*

    (a)   Time taken to develop new products   ....
    (b)   Percentage of on-time deliveries   ....
    (c)   Average set-up time   ....
    (d)   Return on capital employed   ....

8   *Choose the appropriate words from those highlighted.*

    The correct approach to budgetary control is to compare **actual/budgeted** results with a budget that has
been flexed to the **actual/budgeted** level of activity.

9   Not all fixed costs are non-controllable in the short term. *True or false?*

10   What is goal congruence (in terms of organisational control systems)?

   A   When the goals of management and employees harmonise with the goals of the organisation as a whole

   B   When the goals of management harmonise with the goals of employees

   C   When the work-related goals of management harmonise with their personal goals

   D   When an organisation's goals harmonise with those of its customers

11   For each organisation there is an ideal solution to the conflicts caused by the operation of a budgetary control system and it is the responsibility of the management accountant to find that solution. True or false?

12   Which of the following is **not** consistent with the concepts of the Beyond Budgeting approach?

   A   Continuous forecasting
   B   Participative planning
   C   Centralised decision making
   D   Relative performance measures

Answers to Quick Quiz

1   cost behaviour patterns
    flex or change

2   (a)   Variable £4,500
    (b)   Semi-variable £10,250
    (c)   Fixed £2,400
    (d)   Semi-variable £7,000

3   The principle that managers should only be held responsible for costs that they have direct control over.

4   True

5   (a)   Imposed budgeting
    (b)   Participative budgeting
    (c)   Negotiated budgeting

6   expectations
    aspirations

7   (a)   Learning
    (b)   Customer
    (c)   Internal
    (d)   Financial

8   actual
    actual

9   True. Discretionary fixed costs can be raised or lowered at fairly short notice.

10   A

11   False. There are no ideal solutions. Management and the management accountant have to develop their own ways of dealing with the conflicts, taking into account the organisation, the business and the personalities involved.

12   C

Now try the questions below from the Exam Question Bank

Number	Level	Marks	Time
Q28	Examination	5	9 mins
Q29	Examination	5	9 mins
Q30	Examination	20	36 mins

Control and performance measurement of responsibility centres

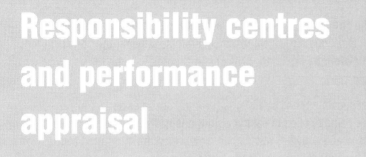

Responsibility centres and performance appraisal

Introduction

In this chapter we look again at a system of **responsibility accounting**. We look at the way that **organisation structure** can be devised to **assist management control** and at the ways in which the **performance** of various part of the organisation could be assessed.

Section 1 deals with discussion of the various types of responsibility centre that can be used in a system of responsibility accounting. **Sections 2 to 5** deal with the calculation and evaluation of return on investment, residual income and economic value added and with discussion of their behavioural implications.

Topic list	Learning outcomes	Syllabus references	Ability required
1 Responsibility centres	D(i)(ii)(iii)	D1	Application/analysis
2 Return on investment (ROI)	D(iv)	D3	Application
3 ROI and decision making	D(v)	D3	Analysis
4 Residual income (RI)	D(iv)(v)	D3	Application/analysis
5 Economic value added ® (EVA)	D(iv)(v)	D3	Application/analysis

1 Responsibility centres

1.1 Divisionalisation

There are a number of advantages and disadvantages to **divisionalisation**. The principal disadvantage is that it can lead to dysfunctional decision making and a lack of goal congruence.

In general a large organisation can be **structured in one of two ways: functionally** (all activities of a similar type within a company, such as production, sales, research, are placed under the control of the appropriate departmental head) or **divisionally** (split into divisions in accordance with the products which are made or services which are provided).

Divisional managers are therefore responsible for all operations (production, sales and so on) relating to their product, the functional structure being applied to each division. It is quite possible, of course, that only part of a company is divisionalised and activities such as administration are structured centrally on a functional basis with the responsibility of providing services to *all* divisions.

1.2 Decentralisation

In general, a **divisional structure will lead to decentralisation** of the decision-making process and divisional managers may have the freedom to set selling prices, choose suppliers, make product mix and output decisions and so on. Decentralisation is, however, a matter of degree, depending on how much freedom divisional managers are given.

1.3 Advantages of divisionalisation

(a)   Divisionalisation can **improve** the **quality of decisions** made because divisional managers (those taking the decisions) have good knowledge of local conditions and should therefore be able to make more informed judgements. Moreover, with the personal incentive to improve the division's performance, they ought to take decisions in the division's best interests.

(b)   **Decisions should be taken more quickly** because information does not have to pass along the chain of command to and from top management. Decisions can be made on the spot by those who are familiar with the product lines and production processes and who are able to react to changes in local conditions quickly and efficiently.

(c)   The authority to act to improve performance should **motivate divisional managers**.

(d)   Divisional organisation **frees top management** from detailed involvement in day-to-day operations and allows them to devote more time to strategic planning.

(e)   Divisions provide **valuable training grounds for future members of top management** by giving them experience of managerial skills in a less complex environment than that faced by top management.

(f)   In a large business organisation, the **central head office will not have the management resources or skills to direct operations closely enough itself**. Some authority must be delegated to local operational managers.

1.4 Disadvantages of divisionalisation

(a)   A danger with divisional accounting is that the business organisation will divide into a number of self-interested segments, each acting at times against the wishes and interests of other segments. Decisions might be taken by a divisional manager in the best interests of his own part of the business, but against the best interest of other divisions and possibly against the interests of the organisation as a whole.

A task of **head office** is therefore to try to **prevent dysfunctional decision making** by individual divisional managers. To do this, head office must reserve some power and authority for itself so that divisional managers cannot be allowed to make entirely independent decisions. A **balance** ought to be kept **between decentralisation** of authority to provide incentives and motivation, **and retaining centralised authority** to ensure that the organisation's divisions are all working towards the same target, the benefit of the organisation as a whole (in other words, **retaining goal congruence** among the organisation's separate divisions).

Key term

Goal congruence is '... the state which leads individuals or groups to take actions which are in their self-interest and also in the best interest of the entity'.

(CIMA *Official Terminology*)

(b)   It is claimed that the **costs of activities that are common** to all divisions such as running the accounting department **may be greater** for a divisionalised structure than for a centralised structure.

(c)   **Top management**, by delegating decision making to divisional managers, may **lose control** since they are not aware of what is going on in the organisation as a whole. (With a good system of performance evaluation and appropriate control information, however, top management should be able to control operations just as effectively.)

1.5 Responsibility accounting

FAST FORWARD

Responsibility accounting is the term used to describe decentralisation of authority, with the performance of the decentralised units measured in terms of accounting results.

With a system of responsibility accounting there are three types of **responsibility centre: cost centre; profit centre; investment centre**.

The creation of divisions allows for the operation of a system of responsibility accounting as we saw in Chapter 13.

There are a number of types of responsibility accounting unit, or responsibility centre that can be used within a system of responsibility accounting.

In the weakest form of **decentralisation** a system of cost centres might be used. As decentralisation becomes stronger the responsibility accounting framework will be based around profit centres. In its **strongest form investment centres are used**.

Type of responsibility centre	Manager has control over ...	Principal performance measures
Cost centre	Controllable costs	Variance analysis Efficiency measures
Revenue centre	Revenues only	Revenues

Type of responsibility centre	Manager has control over ...	Principal performance measures
Profit centre	Controllable costs Sales prices (including transfer prices)	Profit
Contribution centre	As for profit centre except that expenditure is reported on a marginal cost basis	Contribution
Investment centre	Controllable costs Sales prices (including transfer prices) Output volumes Investment in non-current assets and working capital	Return on investment Residual income Other financial ratios

Exam focus point

The four types of responsibility centre that are specifically mentioned in the syllabus are cost, revenue, profit and investment centres.

1.6 Cost centres

A cost centre manager is responsible for, and has control over, the costs incurred in the cost centre. The manager has **no responsibility for earning revenues** or for **controlling the assets and liabilities of the centre**.

Cost centre organisations can be relatively easy to establish, because as you will recall from your earlier studies a cost centre is any part of the organisation to which costs can be separately attributed. A cost centre **forms the basis for building up cost records** for cost measurement, budgeting and control.

Functional departments such as product on, personnel and marketing might be treated as cost centres and made responsible for their costs.

A performance report for a cost centre might look like this.

```
COST CENTRE X
PERFORMANCE REPORT FOR THE PERIOD

Budgeted activity                                   (units)
Actual activity                                     (units)
```

	Budgeted costs (original) $	Budgeted costs (flexed) $	Actual costs $	Variance $
Material costs				
Labour costs				
Variable overhead costs				
Depreciation costs				
etc				

Two important points to note about this report are as follows.

(a)   The report should include **only controllable costs**, which we discussed in Chapter 13, although as we saw there is a case for also providing information on certain **uncontrollable**

costs. However, there should be a **clear distinction** in the report between controllable costs and uncontrollable costs.

(b)   The actual costs are compared with a budget that has been **flexed to the actual activity level achieved**. We saw in Chapter 13 that this approach provides better information, for the purposes of both control and motivation.

The use of flexible budget information is appropriate for control comparisons in production cost centres but the costs attributed to **discretionary cost centres** are more difficult to control. Examples of discretionary cost centres include advertising, research and development and training cost centres. Management has a **significant amount of discretion** as the amount to be budgeted for the particular activity in question.

Moreover, there is no optimum relationship between the inputs (as measured by the costs incurred) and the outputs achieved. **Fixed budgets** must be used for the control of discretionary costs.

Question   Responsibility accounting

Learning outcome: D(ii)

Explain the meaning and importance of controllable costs, uncontrollable costs and budget cost allowance in the context of a system of responsibility accounting.   (5 marks)

Answer

In a system of responsibility accounting costs and revenues are **segregated into areas of personal responsibility** in order to monitor and assess the performance of each part of an organisation.

Controllable costs are those costs which are within the control of the manager of a responsibility centre whereas uncontrollable costs are **outside the control** of the centre manager.

A budget cost allowance is the **cost that should be incurred** in a responsibility centre **for the actual activity level that was achieved**. It is the flexible budget cost that is obtained by flexing the variable cost allowance in line with changes in the level of activity.

All three items are important from a point of view of **control** and **motivation**.

Better cost control is achieved if those areas that a manager can control (controllable costs) are **highlighted separately** from those costs that the manger cannot control (uncontrollable costs). Better cost control is also achieved through **more meaningful variances** that are obtained by comparing a realistic flexible budget cost allowance with the actual results that were achieved.

Motivation of managers is improved if uncontrollable items are analysed separately, since otherwise they will feel they are **being held accountable for something over which they have no control**. Similarly the realistic flexible budget of comparison is more likely to have a positive motivational impact because a **more meaningful** comparative measure of actual performance is obtained.

1.7 Revenue centres

The manager of a revenue centre is responsible only for raising revenue but has no responsibility for forecasting or controlling costs. An example of a revenue centre might be a sales centre.

Revenue centres are often used for control purposes in not-for-profit organisations such as charities. For example a revenue centre manager may have responsibility for revenue targets **within a overall fund-**

raising exercise, but that manager does not control the costs incurred. Such responsibility would pass to a more senior manager to whom the revenue centre manager reports.

1.8 Profit centres

For a profit centre organisation structure to be established it is necessary to identify units of the organisation to which both revenues and costs can be separately attributed. Revenues might come from sales of goods and services to **external customers**, or from goods and services **provided to other responsibility centres within the organisation**. These internal 'sales' are charged at a notional selling price or **transfer price**. We will return to look at transfer prices in detail in Chapter 15.

A profit centre's performance report, in the same way as that for a cost centre, would identify separately the controllable and non-controllable costs. A profit centre performance report might look like this.

PROFIT CENTRE Y
INCOME STATEMENT FOR THE PERIOD

	Budget £'000	Actual £'000	Variance £'000
Sales revenue	X	X	
Variable cost of sales	(X)	(X)	
Contribution	X	X	
Directly attributable/controllable fixed costs			
Salaries	X	X	
Stationery costs	X	X	
	etc	etc	
	(X)	(X)	
Gross profit (directly attributable/controllable)	X	X	
Share of uncontrollable costs (eg head office costs)	(X)	(X)	
Net profit	X	X	

Again, the budget for the sales revenue and variable cost of sales will be **flexed according to the activity level achieved**.

The variances could be analysed in further detail for the profit centre manager.

Notice that three different 'profit levels' are highlighted in the report.

(a) Contribution, which is within the control of the profit centre manager

(b) Directly attributable gross profit, which is also within the manager's control

(c) Net profit, which is after charging certain uncontrollable costs and which is therefore not controllable by the profit centre manager.

1.9 Attributable costs and controllable costs

In the example of profit centre Y we have assumed that all attributable costs are controllable costs. Although this is usually the case some care is needed before this assumption is made.

In responsibility accounting, an attributable cost is **a cost that can be specifically identified with a particular responsibility centre**. No arbitrary apportionment is necessary to share the cost over a number of different responsibility centres.

You can see therefore that **most attributable costs will be controllable costs**. An example of an attributable fixed cost is the salary of the supervisor working in a particular responsibility centre.

However, think about the depreciation of the equipment in profit centre Y. This is certainly **attributable to the profit centre**, but is it a controllable cost? The answer is probably 'no'. It is unlikely that the manager has control over the level of investment in equipment in profit centre Y, otherwise the centre would be classified as an investment centre.

Therefore it might be necessary to include a third measure of 'profit' in our performance report, which would be the controllable profit before the deduction of those costs which are attributable to the profit centre, but which are not controllable by the profit centre manager.

Exam focus point

If an exam question requires you to prepare a performance report for a responsibility centre, read the information carefully to distinguish controllable attributable and non-controllable costs, and then state clearly any assumptions you need to make in order to distinguish between them.

1.10 Investment centres

FAST FORWARD

An **investment centre** manager has responsibility for capital investment in the centre.

Where a manager of a division or strategic business unit is **allowed some discretion about the amount of investment undertaken** by the division, assessment of results by profit alone (as for a profit centre) is clearly inadequate. The profit earned must be related to the amount of capital invested. Such divisions are sometimes called investment centres for this reason. Performance is measured by **return on capital employed (ROCE)**, often referred to as **return on investment (ROI)** and other subsidiary ratios, or by **residual income (RI)**.

Key term

An **investment centre** is 'A profit centre with additional responsibilities for capital investment and possibly for financing, and whose performance is measured by its return on investment'.

(CIMA *Official Terminology*)

Managers of **subsidiary companies will often be treated as investment centre** managers, accountable for profits and capital employed. Within each subsidiary, the major divisions might be treated as profit centres, with each divisional manager having the authority to decide the prices and output volumes for the products or services of the division. Within each division, there will be departmental managers, section managers and so on, who can all be treated as cost centre managers. All managers should receive regular, periodic performance reports for their own areas of responsibility.

The amount of **capital employed** in an investment centre should consist only of **directly attributable non-current assets and working capital (net current assets)**.

(a) Subsidiary companies are often required to remit spare cash to the central treasury department at group head office, and so directly attributable working capital would normally consist of inventories and receivables less payables, but minimal amounts of cash.

(b)   If an investment centre is apportioned a share of head office non-current assets, the amount of capital employed in these assets should be recorded separately because it is not directly attributable to the investment centre or controllable by the manager of the investment centre.

2 Return on investment (ROI)

The performance of an investment centre is usually monitored using either or both of return on investment (ROI) (also known as return on capital employed (ROCE) and residual income (RI).

ROI is generally regarded as the **key performance measure.** The main reason for its **widespread use** is that it **ties in directly with the accounting process**, and is identifiable from the income statement and balance sheet. However it does have limitations, as we will see later in this chapter.

Key term

Return on investment (ROI) (or **return on capital employed (ROCE)**) shows how much profit has been made in relation to the amount of capital invested and is calculated as (profit/capital employed) × 100%.

For example, suppose that a company has two investment centres A and B, which show results for the year as follows.

	A	B
	£	£
Profit	60,000	30,000
Capital employed	400,000	120,000
ROI	15%	25%

Investment centre A has made double the profits of investment centre B, and in terms of profits alone has therefore been more 'successful'. However, B has achieved its profits with a much lower capital investment, and so has earned a much higher ROI. This suggests that B has been a more successful investment than A.

2.1 Measuring ROI

There is no generally agreed method of calculating ROI and it can have **behavioural implications** and lead to dysfunctional decision making when used as a guide to investment decisions. It focuses attention on short-run performance whereas investment decisions should be evaluated over their full life.

ROI can be measured in different ways.

2.1.1 Profit after depreciation as a % of net assets employed

This is probably the **most common method**, but it does present a problem. If an investment centre maintains the same annual profit, and keeps the same assets without a policy of regular replacement of non-current assets, its ROI will increase year by year as the assets get older. This **can give a false impression of improving performance over time**.

For example, the results of investment centre X, with a policy of straight-line depreciation of assets over a 5-year period, might be as follows.

Year	Non-current assets at cost £'000	Depreciation in the year £'000	NBV (mid year) £'000	Working capital £'000	Capital employed £'000	Profit £'000	ROI
0	100			10	110		
1	100	20	90	10	100	10	10.0%
2	100	20	70	10	80	10	12.5%
3	100	20	50	10	60	10	16.7%
4	100	20	30	10	40	10	25.0%
5	100	20	10	10	20	10	50.0%

This table of figures is intended to show that an investment centre can **improve its ROI** year by year, simply **by allowing its fixed assets to depreciate**, and there could be a **disincentive to** investment centre managers to **reinvest in new or replacement assets**, because the centre's ROI would probably fall.

Question

ROI calculation (1)

Learning outcome: D(iv)

A new company has non-current assets of £460,000 which will be depreciated to nil on a straight line basis over 10 years. Net current assets will consistently be £75,000, and annual profit will consistently be £30,000. ROI is measured as return on net assets.

Required

Calculate the company's ROI in years 2 and 6.

Answer

Year 2 – 6.4%
Year 6 – 10.6%

A further disadvantage of measuring ROI as profit divided by net assets is that, for similar reasons, it is not **easy to compare** fairly the **performance of investment centres**.

For example, suppose that we have two investment centres.

	Investment centre P £	Investment centre P £	Investment centre Q £	Investment centre Q £
Working capital		20,000		20,000
Non-current assets at cost	230,000		230,000	
Accumulated depreciation	170,000		10,000	
Net book value		60,000		220,000
Capital employed		80,000		240,000
Profit		£24,000		£24,000
ROI		30%		10%

Investment centres P and Q have the same amount of working capital, the same value of non-current assets at cost, and the same profit. But P's non-current assets have been depreciated by a much bigger amount (presumably P's non-current assets are much older than Q's) and so P's ROI is three times the size of Q's ROI. The conclusion might therefore be that P has performed much better than Q. This comparison, however, would not be 'fair', because the **difference in performance might be entirely attributable to the age of their non-current assets**.

The arguments for using net book values for calculating ROI

(a)   It is the **'normally accepted'** method of calculating ROI.

(b)   Organisations are continually buying new non-current assets to replace old ones that wear out, and so on the whole, the **total net book value** of all non-current assets together **will remain fairly constant** (assuming nil inflation and nil growth).

2.1.2 Profit after depreciation as a % of gross assets employed

Instead of measuring ROI as return on net assets, we could measure it as return on gross assets. This would **remove the problem of ROI increasing over time as non-current assets get older**.

If a company acquired a non-current asset costing £40,000, which it intends to depreciate by £10,000 pa for 4 years, and if the asset earns a profit of £8,000 pa after depreciation, ROI might be calculated on net book values or gross values, as follows.

Year	Profit	NBV(mid-year value)	ROI based on NBV	Gross value	ROI based on gross value
	£	£		£	
1	8,000	35,000	22.9%	40,000	20%
2	8,000	25,000	32.0%	40,000	20%
3	8,000	15,000	53.3%	40,000	20%
4	8,000	5,000	160.0%	40,000	20%

The ROI based on **net book value** shows an **increasing trend over time**, simply because the asset's value is falling as it is depreciated. The ROI based on gross book value suggests that the asset has **performed consistently** in each of the four years, which is probably a more valid conclusion.

Question	ROI calculation (2)

Learning outcome: D(iv)

Repeat **Question: ROI calculation (1)**, measuring ROI as return on gross assets.

Answer

Year 2 – 5.6%
Year 6 – 5.6%

However, using gross book values to measure ROI has its **disadvantages**. Most important of these is that measuring ROI as return on gross assets ignores the age factor, and **does not distinguish between old and new assets**.

(a)   **Older non-current assets** usually **cost more to repair and maintain**, to keep them running. An investment centre with old assets may therefore have its profitability reduced by repair costs, and its ROI might fall over time as its assets get older and repair costs get bigger.

(b)   **Inflation** and **technological change alter the cost of non-current assets**. If one investment centre has non-current assets bought ten years ago with a gross cost of £1 million, and another investment centre, in the same area of business operations, has non-current assets bought very recently for £1 million, the quantity and technological character of the non-current assets of the two investment centres are likely to be very different.

2.1.3 Constituent elements of the investment base

Although we have looked at how the investment base should be valued, we need to consider its appropriate constituent elements.

(a) If a **manager's performance is being evaluated**, only those **assets** which can be **traced directly to the division** and are **controllable by the manager should be included**. Head office assets or investment centre assets controlled by head office should not be included. So, for example, only those cash balances actually maintained within an investment centre itself should be included.

(b) If it is **the performance of the investment centre that is being appraised, a proportion of the investment in head office assets would need to be included** because an investment centre could not operate without the support of head office assets and administrative backup.

2.1.4 Profits

We have looked at how to define the asset base used in the calculations but what about profit? If the **performance of the investment centre manager is being assessed** it should seem reasonable to **base profit on the revenues and costs controllable by the manager** and exclude service and head office costs except those costs specifically attributable to the investment centre. If it is the **performance of the investment centre that is being assessed, however, the inclusion of general service and head office costs would seem reasonable**.

2.1.5 Tangible and intangible assets

The management accountant is free to capitalise or expense intangible assets. When significant expenditure on an **intangible asset** (such as an advertising campaign) which is expected to provide future benefits is expensed, profits will be reduced and ROI/RI artificially depressed. In the future, the investment should produce significant cash inflows and the ROI/RI will be artificially inflated. **Such expenditure** should therefore be **capitalised so as to smooth out performance measures and to eradicate the risk of drawing false conclusions from them**. The calculation of EVA, which we will learn about later in this chapter, does just this.

A **comparison of the performance of manufacturing divisions and service divisions** should be **treated with caution**. The majority of a **manufacturing division's assets** will be **tangible** and therefore are **automatically capitalised** whereas the treatment of a **service division's** mostly **intangible assets** is **open to interpretation**.

2.1.6 Massaging the ROI

If a manager's large bonus depends on ROI being met, the manager may feel pressure to massage the measure. The **asset base** of the ratio can be **altered** by **increasing/decreasing payables and receivables** (by **speeding up or delaying payments and receipts**).

3 ROI and decision making

3.1 New investments

If investment centre performance is judged by ROI, we should expect that the managers of investment centres will probably decide to undertake new capital investments **only if these new investments are likely to increase the ROI of their centre**.

Suppose that an investment centre, A, currently makes a return of 40% on capital employed. The manager of centre A would probably only want to undertake new investments that promise to yield a return of 40% or more, otherwise the investment centre's overall ROI would fall.

For example, if investment centre A currently has assets of £1,000,000 and expects to earn a profit of £400,000, how would the centre's manager view a new capital investment which would cost £250,000 and yield a profit of £75,000 pa?

	Without the new investment	*With the new investment*
Profit	£400,000	£475,000
Capital employed	£1,000,000	£1,250,000
ROI	40%	38%

The **new investment** would **reduce the investment centre's ROI** from 40% to 38%, and so the investment centre manager would probably decide **not to undertake** the new investment.

If the group of companies of which investment centre A is a part has a target ROI of, say, 25%, the new investment would presumably be seen as **beneficial for the group as a whole**. But even though it promises to yield a return of 75,000/250,000 = 30%, which is above the group's target ROI, it would still make investment centre A's results look worse. The manager of investment centre A would, in these circumstances, be motivated to do not what is best for the organisation as a whole, but what is **best for his division.**

ROI should not be used to guide investment decisions but there is a difficult motivational problem. If management performance is measured in terms of ROI, any decisions which benefit the company in the long term but which reduce the ROI in the immediate short term would reflect badly on the manager's reported performance. In other words, **good investment decisions would make a manager's performance seem worse than if the wrong investment decision were taken instead**.

3.2 Extended example: ROI and decision-making

At the end of 20X3, Division S (part of a group) had a book value of non-current assets of £300,000 and net current assets of £40,000. Net profit before tax was £64,000.

The non-current assets of Division S consist of five separate items each costing £60,000 which are depreciated to zero over 5 years on a straight-line basis. For each of the past years on 31 December it has bought a replacement for the asset that has just been withdrawn and it proposes to continue this policy. Because of technological advances the asset manufacturer has been able to keep his prices constant over time. The group's cost of capital is 15%.

Required

Assuming that, except where otherwise stated, there are no changes in the above data, deal with the following separate situations.

(a)   Division S has the opportunity of an investment costing £60,000, and yielding an annual profit of £10,000.

      (i)   Calculate its new ROI if the investment were undertaken.

      (ii)   State whether the manager of division S would recommend that the investment be undertaken.

(b)   Division S has the opportunity of selling, at a price equal to its written-down book value of £24,000, an asset that currently earns £3,900 p.a.

      (i)   Calculate its new ROI if the asset were sold.

      (ii)   State whether the manager of division S would recommend the sale of the asset.

Solution in general

The question does not state whether capital employed should include a valuation of non-current assets at gross historical cost or at net book value. It is assumed that net book value is required. It is also assumed that the non-current asset which has just been bought as a replacement on 31 December 20X3 has not been depreciated at all.

Exam focus point

It is worth stating assumptions such as these at the start of a solution to questions of this sort. If the problem has not been properly defined, clarify your own assumptions and definitions for the benefit of the marker of your exam script!

The gross book value of the 5 fixed asset items is 5 × £60,000 = £300,000.

	£
Net book value of asset just bought on 31.12.X3	60,000
NBV of asset bought 1 year earlier	48,000
NBV of asset bought 2 years earlier	36,000
NBV of asset bought 3 years earlier	24,000
NBV of asset bought 4 years earlier	12,000
NBV of all 5 non-current assets at 31.12.X3	180,000
Net current assets	40,000
Total capital employed, Division S	220,000

Solution to part (a)

Part (i)

Begin with a comparison of the existing ROI (which is presumably the typical ROI achieved each year under the current policy of asset replacement) and the ROI with the new investment.

    Existing ROI = (64/220) × 100% = 29.1%

For the ROI with the new investment it is assumed that the full asset cost of £60,000 should be included in the capital employed, although the asset will obviously be depreciated over time. It is also assumed that the additional profit of £10,000 is net of depreciation charges.

    ROI with new investment = ((64 + 10)/(220 + 60)) × 100% = 26.4%

If the investment centre manager based his investment decisions on whether an investment would increase or reduce his ROI, he would not want to make the additional investment. This investment has a **marginal ROI** of (10/60) × 100% = 16.7%, which is **above the group's cost of capital but below Division S's current ROI** of 29.1%. Making the investment would therefore lower the Division's average ROI.

Part (ii)

This example **illustrates the weakness of ROI as a guide to investment decisions**. An investment centre manager might want an investment to show a good ROI from year 1, when the new investment has a high net book value. In the case of Division S, the average net book value of the asset over its full life will be 50% of £60,000 = £30,000, and so the average ROI on the investment over time will be (£10,000/£30,000) × 100% = 33.3% which is greater than the cost of capital.

Presumably, however, the Division S manager would not want to wait so long to earn a good ROI, and wants to protect his division's performance in the short run as well as the long run. therefore he would not recommend that the investment be undertaken.

Solution to part (b)

Part (b) of the question deals with a disinvestment proposal, compared to an acquisition in part (a). The same basic principles apply.

The **ROI if the asset is sold** is ((64 − 3.9)/(220 − 24)) × 100% = 30.7%

This compares favourably with the Division's current average ROI of 29.1%, and so if the manager of Division S made his divestment decisions on the basis of ROI, he would **presumably decide to get rid of the asset**.

However, the decision would be misguided, because **decisions should not be based on the short-term effects on ROI**.

The asset which would be sold earns a ROI of (3.9/24) × 100% = 16.3%, which is higher than the group's cost of capital, but lower than the Division S average.

On the assumption that the asset would earn £3,900 after depreciation for the two remaining years of its life, its ROI next year would be (3.9/12) × 100% = 32.5% which again is higher than the cost of capital.

4 Residual income (RI)

RI can sometimes give results that avoid the **behavioural** problem of **dysfunctionality**. Its weakness is that it does not facilitate comparisons between investment centres nor does it relate the size of a centre's income to the size of the investment.

An alternative way of measuring the performance of an investment centre, instead of using ROI, is residual income (RI). **Residual income** is a **measure of the centre's profits after deducting a notional or imputed interest cost**.

(a)   The centre's profit is **after deducting depreciation** on capital equipment.

(b)   The imputed cost of capital might be the organisation's cost of borrowing or its weighted average cost of capital.

Key term

Residual income (RI) is 'Pre-tax profits less an imputed interest charge for invested capital. Used to assess divisional performance'.
                                                        (CIMA *Official Terminology*)

Question

Learning outcome: D(iv)

A division with capital employed of £400,000 currently earns an ROI of 22%. It can make an additional investment of £50,000 for a 5 year life with nil residual value. The average net profit from this investment would be £12,000 after depreciation. The division's cost of capital is 14%.

What are the residual incomes before and after the investment?

	Before investment	After investment
A	£144,000	£163,000
B	22%	14%
C	£32,000	£37,000
D	14%	22%

Answer

The correct answer is C.

	Before investment £	After investment £
Divisional profit (£400,000 x 22%)	88,000	100,000
Imputed interest		
(400,000 × 0.14)	56,000	
(450,000 × 0.14)		63,000
Residual income	32,000	37,000

Option A: The imputed interest has been added to divisional profit, rather than deducted.

Options B and D: Residual income is a monetary amount.

4.1 The advantages and weaknesses of RI compared with ROI

The advantages of using RI

(a) Residual income will **increase** when investments earning above the cost of capital are undertaken and investments earning below the cost of capital are eliminated.

(b) Residual income is **more flexible** since a different cost of capital can be applied to investments with **different risk** characteristics.

The **weakness** of RI is that it **does not facilitate comparisons** between investment centres nor **does it relate the size of a centre's income to the size of the investment**.

4.2 RI versus ROI: marginally profitable investments

Residual income will increase if a new investment is undertaken which earns a profit in excess of the imputed interest charge on the value of the asset acquired. Residual income will go up even if the investment only just exceeds the imputed interest charge, and this means that 'marginally profitable' investments are likely to be undertaken by the investment centre manager.

In contrast, when a manager is judged by ROI, a marginally profitable investment would be less likely to be undertaken because it would reduce the average ROI earned by the centre as a whole.

4.3 Example: residual income and decision making

In the previous example in Paragraph 3.15, **whereas ROI would have worsened with the new investment opportunity (part (a)) and improved with the disinvestment (part (b)), residual income would have done the opposite** – improved with the new investment and worsened with the disinvestment.

The figures would be:

(a)   *Part (a)*

	Without new investment £	Investment £	With new investment £
Profit before notional interest	64,000	10,000	74,000
Notional interest (15% of £340,000)	51,000	9,000*	60,000
	13,000	1,000	14,000

* 15% of £60,000

If the manager of Division S were **guided by residual income** into making decisions, he would **approve the new investment**.

(b)   *Part (b)*

	Without disinvestment £	Disinvestment £	With disinvestment £
Profit before notional interest	64,000	3,900	60,100
Notional interest	51,000	3,600 *	47,400
Residual income	13,000	300	12,700

*15% of £24,000

If the investment centre manager is guided by residual income, he would decide to **keep the asset** instead of selling it off.

Residual income **does not always point to the right investment decision**. However, residual income is **more likely than ROI to improve when managers make correct investment/divestment decisions**, and so is probably a 'safer' basis than ROI on which to measure performance.

4.4 Example: ROI versus residual income

Suppose that Department H has the following profit, assets employed and an imputed interest charge of 12% on operating assets.

	£	£
Operating profit	30,000	
Operating assets		100,000
Imputed interest (12%)	12,000	
Return on investment		30%
Residual income	18,000	

Suppose now that an additional investment of £10,000 is proposed, which will increase operating income in Department H by £1,400. The effect of the investment would be:

	£	£
Total operating income	31,400	
Total operating assets		110,000
Imputed interest (12%)	13,200	
Return on investment		28.5%
Residual income	18,200	

If the Department H manager is made responsible for the department's performance, he would **resist the new investment if he were to be judged on ROI**, but would **welcome the investment if he were judged according to RI**, since there would be a marginal increase of £200 in residual income from the investment, but a fall of 1.5% in ROI.

The marginal investment offers a return of 14% (£1,400 on an investment of £10,000) which is above the 'cut-off rate' of 12%. Since the original return on investment was 30%, the marginal investment will reduce the overall divisional performance. Indeed, any marginal investment offering an accounting rate of return of less than 30% in the year would reduce the overall performance.

Exam focus point

Examination questions on residual income may focus on the sort of behavioural aspects of investment centre measurement that we have discussed above, for example why it is considered necessary to use residual income to measure performance rather than ROI, and why residual income might influence an investment centre manager's investment decisions differently.

Question

Responsibility centres

Learning outcome: D(i)

Explain the difference between cost, revenue, profit and investment centres in a system of responsibility accounting? (5 marks)

Answer

The main differences between the four types of responsibility centre lie in the following.

(a)   The items over which the responsibility centre manager has control.

(b)   The performance measures which are appropriate to assess the responsibility manager's performance

Cost centre

The cost centre manager has control over the **controllable costs** of the centre only. There is no opportunity to earn revenue, therefore suitable control measures are **variance analysis** (based on a **flexible budget** where appropriate) and **efficiency measures** (such as productivity and efficiency ratios).

Revenue centre

The revenue centre manager has control over the **revenue earned** by the centre. There is no opportunity to exercise control over costs, therefore a suitable control measure is the **budgetary comparison** (flexed if appropriate) **of the actual and budgeted revenue.**

Profit centre

The profit centre manager has control over the **controllable costs** in the same way as a cost centre manager, but he also has the opportunity to **earn revenue** (whether internal or external) and therefore has control over the **profit earned by the centre**.

Suitable performance measures include the **controllable profit** and the **controllable profit margin percentage.**

Investment centre

The investment centre manager has control over **all the same items as a profit centre manager** but in addition he can control the level of investment in the centre, in terms of working capital (net current assets) and non-current assets.

Appropriate performance measures therefore **relate the controllable profit earned to the level of controllable investment in the centre**, for example the return on investment or the residual income earned.

5 Economic value added ® (EVA)

EVA ® is an alternative absolute performance measure. It is similar to RI and is calculated as follows.

EVA = net operating profit after tax (NOPAT) less capital charge

where the capital charge = weighted average cost of capital × net assets

Economic value added (EVA) is a registered trade mark owned by Stern Stewart & co. It is a specific type of residual income (RI) calculated as follows.

> EVA = net operating profit after tax (NOPAT) less capital charge
> where the capital charge = weighted average cost of capital x net assets

You can see from the formula that the calculation of EVA is very similar to the calculation of RI.

EVA and RI are similar because both result in an absolute figure which is calculated by subtracting an imputed interest charge from the profit earned by the investment centre. However there are differences as follows.

(a) The profit figures are calculated differently. EVA is based on an '**economic profit**' which is derived by making a series of adjustments to the accounting profit.

(b) The notional capital charges use **different bases for net assets**. The replacement cost of net assets is usually used in the calculation of EVA.

The calculation of EVA is different to RI because the net assets used as the basis of the imputed interest charge are usually valued at their **replacement cost** and are **increased by any costs that have been capitalised** (see below).

There are also differences in the way that NOPAT is calculated compared with the profit figure that is used for RI, as follows.

(a) Costs which would normally be treated as expenses, but which are considered within an EVA calculation as **investments building for the future**, are added back to NOPAT to derive a figure for 'economic profit'. These costs are included instead as assets in the figure for net assets employed, ie as investments for the future. Costs treated in this way include items such as **goodwill, research and development expenditure and advertising costs**.

(b) Adjustments are sometimes made to the depreciation charge, whereby accounting depreciation is added back to the profit figures, and **economic depreciation** is subtracted instead to arrive at NOPAT. Economic depreciation is a charge for the fall in asset value due to wear and tear or obsolescence.

(c) Any lease charges are excluded from NOPAT and added in as a part of capital employed.

Another point to note about the calculation of NOPAT, which is the same as the calculation of the profit figure for RI, is that **interest** is excluded from NOPAT because interest costs are taken into account in the capital charge.

5.1 Example: calculating EVA

An investment centre has reported operating profits of $21 million. This was after charging $4 million for the development and launch costs of a new product that is expected to generate profits for four years. Taxation is paid at the rate of 25% of the operating profit.

The company has a risk adjusted weighted average cost of capital of 12% per annum and is paying interest at 9% per annum on a substantial long term loan.

The investment centre's non-current asset value is $50 million and the net current assets have a value of $22 million. The replacement cost of the non-current assets is estimated to be $64 million.

Required

Calculate the investment centre's EVA for the period.

Solution

Calculation of NOPAT

	$ million
Operating profit	21
Add back development costs	4
Less one year's amortisation of development costs ($4 million/4)	(1)
	24
Taxation at 25%	(6)
NOPAT	18

Calculation of economic value of net assets

	$ million
Replacement cost of net assets ($22 million + $64 million)	86
Add back investment in new product to benefit future	3
Economic value of net assets	89

Calculation of EVA

The capital charge is based on the **weighted average cost of capital**, which takes account of the cost of share capital as well as the cost of loan capital. Therefore the correct interest rate is 12%.

	$ million
NOPAT	18.00
Capital charge (12% × $89 million)	(10.68)
EVA	7.32

5.2 Advantages of EVA

The advantages of EVA include the following.

(a) Maximisation of EVA will create real wealth for the shareholders.

(b) The adjustments within the calculation of EVA mean that the measure is based on figures that are closer to cash flows than accounting profits. Hence EVA may be **less distorted by the accounting policies selected**.

(c) The EVA measure is an absolute value which is easily understood by non-financial managers.

(d)   If management are assessed using performance measures based on traditional accounting policies they may be unwilling to invest in areas such as advertising and development for the future because **such costs will immediately reduce the current year's accounting profit**. EVA recognises such costs as investments for the future and thus they do not immediately reduce the EVA in the year of expenditure.

5.3 Disadvantages of EVA

EVA does have some drawbacks.

(a)   It is still a **relatively short term measure** which can encourage managers to focus on short term performance.

(b)   EVA is based on historical accounts which may be of **limited use as a guide to the future**. In practice also the influences of accounting policies on the starting profit figure may not be completely negated by the adjustments made to it in the EVA model.

(c)   Making the necessary adjustments can be problematic as sometimes a **large number of adjustments** are required.

(d)   Investment centres which are larger in size may have larger EVA figures for this reason. **Allowance for relative size** must be made when comparing the relative performance of investment centres.

Question

Calculating EVA

Learning outcome: D(iv)

Division D operates as an investment centre. The book value of the non-current assets is €83,000 but their replacement value is estimated to be €98,000. Working capital in the division has a value of €19,000.

Latest operating profits for the division were €18,500, after charging historical cost depreciation of €8,100 and the costs of a major advertising campaign which amounted to €6,000. The advertising campaign is expected to boost revenues for two years.

An economic depreciation charge for the period would have been €12,300.

The risk adjusted weighted cost of capital for the company is 11% per annum.

Required

Calculate the EVA for Division D. Ignore taxation.

Answer

	€
Operating profit	18,500
Add back historical cost depreciation	8,100
Less economic depreciation	(12,300)
Add back advertising costs	6,000
Less amortisation of advertising costs (€6,000/2)	(3,000)
NOPAT (ignoring taxation)	17,300
Replacement value of non-current assets	98,000
Working capital	19,000
Add investment in advertising to benefit next year	3,000
Economic value of net assets	120,000
NOPAT	17,300
Capital charge (11% × €120,000)	13,200
EVA	4,100

Chapter Roundup

- There are a number of advantages and disadvantages to **divisionalisation**. The principal disadvantage is that it can lead to dysfunctional decision making and a lack of goal congruence.

- **Responsibility accounting** is the term used to describe decentralisation of authority, with the performance of the decentralised units measured in terms of accounting results.

- With a system of responsibility accounting there are three types of **responsibility centre: cost centre; profit centre; investment centre**.

- An **investment centre** manager has responsibility for capital investment in the centre.

- The performance of an investment centre is usually monitored using either or both of **return on investment (ROI)** (also known as return on capital employed (ROCE) and **residual income (RI).**

- There is no generally agreed method of calculating ROI and it can have **behavioural implications** and lead to dysfunctional decision making when used as a guide to investment decisions. It focuses attention on short-run performance whereas investment decisions should be evaluated over their full life.

- RI can sometimes give results that avoid the **behavioural** problem of **dysfunctionality**. Its weakness is that it does not facilitate comparisons between investment centres nor does it relate the size of a centre's income to the size of the investment.

- EVA ® is an alternative absolute performance measure. It is similar to RI and is calculated as follows.

  EVA = net operating profit after tax (NOPAT) less capital charge

  where the capital charge = weighted average cost of capital × net assets

- EVA and RI are similar because both result in an absolute figure which is calculated by subtracting an imputed interest charge from the profit earned by the investment centre. However there are differences as follows.

  (a) The profit figures are calculated differently. EVA is based on an **'economic profit'** which is derived by making a series of adjustments to the accounting profit.

  (b) The notional capital charges use **different bases for net assets**. The replacement cost of net assets is usually used in the calculation of EVA.

Quick Quiz

1   *Fill in the table below.*

Type of responsibility centre	Manager has control over ...	Principal performance measures

2   Over which of the following can an investment centre manager exercise control?

   I   Controllable costs in the division
   II   Selling prices of the division's output
   III   The division's output volumes
   IV   Investment in the division's non-current assets and working capital

   A   All of them
   B   II and III
   C   I only
   D   IV only

3   *Choose the correct words from those highlighted.*

   ROI based on profits as a % of net assets employed will (1) **increase/decrease** as an asset gets older and its book value (2) **increases/reduces**. This could therefore create an (3) **incentive/disincentive** to investment centre managers to reinvest in new or replacement assets.

4   An investment centre with capital employed of £570,000 is budgeted to earn a profit of £119,700 next year. A proposed non-current asset investment of £50,000, not included in the budget at present, will earn a profit next year of £8,500 after depreciation. The company's cost of capital is 15%. What is the budgeted ROI and residual income for next year, both with and without the investment?

	ROI	*Residual income*
Without investment	....	....
With investment	....	....

5   'The use of residual income in performance measurement will avoid dysfunctional decision making because it will always lead to the correct decision concerning capital investments.' *True or false?*

6   *Choose the correct words from those highlighted.*

   If accounting ROI is used as a guideline for investment decisions, it **should be/should not be** looked at over the full life of the investment. In the short term, the accounting ROI is likely to be **high/low** because the net book value of the asset will be **high/low**.

7   EVA is calculated as operating profit less a capital charge. *True/false.*

Answers to Quick Quiz

1

Type of responsibility centre	Manager has control over ...	Principal performance measures
Cost centre	Controllable costs	Variance analysis Efficiency measures
Revenue centre	Revenues only	Revenues
Profit centre	Controllable costs Sales prices (including transfer prices)	Profit
Contribution centre	As for profit centre except that expenditure is reported on a marginal cost basis	Contribution
Investment centre	Controllable costs Sales prices (including transfer prices) Output volumes Investment in non-current and current assets	Return on investment Residual income Other financial ratios

2   A

3   (a)   increase
     (b)   reduces
     (c)   disincentive

4   *ROI*   *Residual income*
     Without investment   21.0%   £34,200
     With investment   20.7%   £35,200

5   False

6   should be
     low
     high

7   False. EVA = NOPAT less a capital charge

Now try the questions below from the Exam Question Bank			
Number	**Level**	**Marks**	**Time**
Q31	Introductory	n/a	n/a
Q32	Examination	20	36 mins
Q33	Examination	20	36 mins

Transfer pricing

Introduction

In this chapter we will continue our study of responsibility centres by looking at the operation of a transfer pricing system.

Sections 1 and 2 provide you with a **framework** for your study of the remainder of the chapter. **Sections 3 to 7** cover the **various approaches** to transfer pricing required in particular circumstances, while **Section 9** provides a useful summary of these sections.

Sections 9 and 10 are based on **specific transfer pricing topics** mentioned in the syllabus.

This is quite a long chapter but we have included **'summary' boxes** throughout the chapter – make sure you are happy with the contents of them before you move on.

Topic list	Learning outcomes	Syllabus references	Ability required
1 The basic principles of transfer pricing	D(vi)	D 5	Comprehension
2 General rules	D(vi)	D 5	Comprehension
3 The use of market price as a basis for transfer prices	D(vii)	D 6	Comprehension
4 Transfer pricing with an imperfect external market	D(vii)	D 6	Comprehension
5 Standard cost versus actual cost	D(vii)	D 6	Comprehension
6 Transfer pricing when there is no external market for the transferred item	D(vii)	D 6	Comprehension
7 Transfer pricing and changing costs/prices	D(vii)	D 6	Comprehension
8 Identifying the optimal transfer price	D(vii)	D 6	Comprehension
9 Negotiated transfer prices	D(vii)	D 6	Comprehension
10 International transfer pricing	D(vii)	D 7	Comprehension

1 The basic principles of transfer pricing

FAST FORWARD

Transfer prices are a way of promoting **divisional autonomy**, ideally without prejudicing the **measurement of divisional performance** or discouraging **overall corporate profit maximisation**.

Transfer prices should be set at a level which ensures that profits for the organisation as a whole are maximised.

In Chapter 14 we saw that the revenue earned in a profit centre need not necessarily be a result of sales external to the organisation. **Transfer pricing** is used when divisions of an organisation need to charge other divisions of the same organisation for goods and services they provide to them. For example, subsidiary A might make a component that is used as part of a product made by subsidiary B of the same company, but that can also be sold to the external market, including makers of rival products to subsidiary B's product. There will therefore be two sources of revenue for A.

    (a)   External sales revenue from sales made to other organisations

    (b)   Internal sales revenue from sales made to other responsibility centres within the same organisation, valued at the transfer price

Key term

A **transfer price** is 'The price at which goods or services are transferred between different units of the same company'.
        (CIMA *Official Terminology*)

1.1 Three problems with transfer pricing

1.1.1 Maintaining the right level of divisional autonomy

Transfer prices are particularly appropriate for **profit centres** because if one profit centre does work for another the size of the transfer price will affect the costs of one profit centre and the revenues of another.

However, a danger with profit centre accounting is that the business organisation will **divide into a number of self-interested segments**, each acting at times against the wishes and interests of other segments. Decisions might be taken by a profit centre manager in the best interests of his own part of the business, but against the best interests of other profit centres and possibly the organisation as a whole.

A task of **head office** is therefore to try to **prevent dysfunctional decision making** by individual profit centres. To do this, head office must reserve some power and authority for itself and so **profit centres cannot be allowed to make entirely autonomous decisions**.

Just how much authority head office decides to keep for itself will vary according to individual circumstances. **A balance** ought to be kept **between divisional autonomy** to provide incentives and motivation, and **retaining centralised authority** to ensure that the organisation's profit centres are all working towards the same target, the benefit of the organisation as a whole (in other words, **retaining goal congruence** among the organisation's separate divisions).

1.1.2 Ensuring divisional performance is measured fairly

Profit centre managers tend to put their own profit performance above everything else. Since profit centre performance is measured according to the profit they earn, no profit centre will want to do work for another and incur costs without being paid for it. Consequently, profit centre managers are likely to dispute the size of transfer prices with each other, or disagree about whether one profit centre should do work for another or not. Transfer prices **affect behaviour and decisions** by profit centre managers.

1.1.3 Ensuring corporate profits are maximised

When there are disagreements about how much work should be transferred between divisions, and how many sales the division should make to the external market, there is presumably a **profit-maximising level of output and sales for the organisation as a whole**. However, unless each profit centre also maximises its own profit at this same level of output, there will be inter-divisional disagreements about output levels and the profit-maximising output will not be achieved.

1.1.4 The ideal solution

Ideally a transfer price should be set at a level that overcomes these problems.

   (a)   The transfer price should provide an 'artificial' selling price that enables the **transferring division to earn a return for its efforts**, and the **receiving division to incur a cost for benefits received**.

   (b)   The transfer price should be set at a level that enables **profit centre performance** to be **measured 'commercially'**. This means that the transfer price should be a fair commercial price.

   (c)   The transfer price, if possible, should encourage profit centre managers to agree on the amount of goods and services to be transferred, which will also be at a level that is consistent with the aims of the organisation as a whole such as **maximising company profits**.

In practice it is difficult to achieve all three aims.

Question   Divisional autonomy

Learning outcome: D(vi)

   (a)   What do you understand by the term 'divisional autonomy'?

   (b)   What are the likely behavioural consequences of a head office continually imposing its own
           decisions on divisions?   (5 marks)

Answer

   (a)   The term refers to the right of a division to govern itself, that is, the **freedom to make decisions without consulting a higher authority first and without interference from a higher body**.

   (b)   Decentralisation recognises that those closest to a job are the best equipped to say how it should be done and that people tend to perform to a higher standard if they are given responsibility. Centrally-imposed decisions are likely to **make managers feel that they do not really have any authority** and therefore that they **cannot be held responsible for performance**. They will therefore **make less effort** to perform well.

Question   Benefits of transfer pricing

Learning outcome D(vi)

The transfer pricing system operated by a divisional company has the potential to make a significant contribution towards the achievement of corporate financial objectives.

Required
Explain the potential benefits of operating a transfer pricing system within a divisionalised company.

Answer

Potential benefits of operating a transfer pricing system within a divisionalised company include the following.

(a)   It can lead to **goal congruence** by motivating divisional managers to make decisions, which improve divisional profit and improve profit of the organisation as a whole.

(b)   It can prevent **dysfunctional decision making** so that decisions taken by a divisional manager are in the best interests of his own part of the business, other divisions and the organisation as a whole.

(c)   Transfer prices can be set at a level that enables divisional performance to be measured 'commercially'. A transfer pricing system should therefore report a level of divisional profit that is a **reasonable measure of the managerial performance** of the division.

(d)   It should ensure that **divisional autonomy** is not undermined. A well-run transfer pricing system helps to ensure that a balance is kept between divisional autonomy to provide incentives and motivation, and centralised authority to ensure that the divisions are all working towards the same target, the benefit of the organisation as a whole.

2 General rules

FAST FORWARD

The **limits within which transfer prices should fall** are as follows.

- **The minimum**. The sum of the supplying division's marginal cost and opportunity cost of the item transferred.

- **The maximum**. The lowest market price at which the receiving division could purchase the goods or services externally, less any internal cost savings in packaging and delivery.

The **minimum** results from the fact that the **supplying division will not agree to transfer if the transfer price is less than the marginal cost + opportunity cost of the item transferred** (because if it were the division would incur a loss).

The **maximum** results from the fact that the **receiving division will buy the item at the cheapest price possible**.

2.1 Example: general rules

Division X produces product L at a marginal cost per unit of £100. If a unit is transferred internally to division Y, £25 contribution is foregone on an external sale. The item can be purchased externally for £150.

- **The minimum**. Division X will not agree to a transfer price of less than £(100 + 25) = £125 per unit.

- **The maximum**. Division Y will not agree to a transfer price in excess of £150.

The difference between the two results (£25) represents the savings from producing internally as opposed to buying externally.

2.1.1 Opportunity cost

The **opportunity cost** included in determining the lower limit will be one of the following.

(a)　The maximum contribution forgone by the supplying division **in transferring internally rather than selling goods externally**

(b)　The contribution forgone by **not using the same facilities** in the producing division **for their next best alternative use**

If there is **no external market** for the item being transferred, and **no alternative uses for** the division's facilities, the **transfer price = standard variable cost of production**.

If there is an **external market** for the item being transferred and **no alternative, more profitable use** for the facilities in that division, the **transfer price = the market price**.

3 The use of market price as a basis for transfer prices

FAST FORWARD

If **variable costs and market prices are constant**, regardless of the volume of output, a **market-based transfer price** is the ideal transfer price.

If an **external market price exists** for transferred goods, profit centre managers will be aware of the price they could obtain or the price they would have to pay for their goods on the external market, and they would inevitably **compare** this price **with the transfer price**.

3.1 Example: transferring goods at market value

A company has two profit centres, A and B. A sells half of its output on the open market and transfers the other half to B. Costs and external revenues in an accounting period are as follows.

	A £	B £	Total £
External sales	8,000	24,000	32,000
Costs of production	12,000	10,000	22,000
Company profit			10,000

Required

What are the consequences of setting a transfer price at market value?

Solution

If the transfer price is at market price, A would be happy to sell the output to B for £8,000, which is what A would get by selling it externally instead of transferring it.

	A £	A £	B £	B £	Total £
Market sales		8,000		24,000	32,000
Transfer sales		8,000		–	
		16,000		24,000	
Transfer costs		–	8,000		
Own costs	12,000		10,000		22,000
		12,000		18,000	
Profit		4,000		6,000	10,000

The **transfer sales of A are self cancelling with the transfer cost of B**, so that the total profits are unaffected by the transfer items. The transfer price simply spreads the total profit between A and B.

Consequences

(a)   A earns the same profit on transfers as on external sales. B must pay a commercial price for transferred goods, and both divisions will have their profit measured in a fair way.

(b)   A will be indifferent about selling externally or transferring goods to B because the profit is the same on both types of transaction. B can therefore ask for and obtain as many units as it wants from A.

A **market-based** transfer price therefore seems to be the **ideal** transfer price.

3.2 Adjusted market price

Internal transfers are often **cheaper** than external sales, with **savings** in selling and administration costs, bad debt risks and possibly transport/delivery costs. It would therefore seem reasonable for the **buying division to expect a discount** on the external market price. The transfer price might be slightly less than market price, so that **A and B could share the cost savings** from internal transfers compared with external sales. It should be possible to reach agreement on this price and on output levels with a minimum of intervention from head office.

3.3 The merits of market value transfer prices

3.3.1 Divisional autonomy

In a decentralised company, divisional managers should have the **autonomy** to make output, selling and buying **decisions which appear to be in the best interests of the division's performance.** (If every division optimises its performance, the company as a whole must inevitably achieve optimal results.) Thus a **transferor division should be given the freedom to sell output on the open market,** rather than to transfer it within the company.

'Arm's length' transfer prices, which give profit centre managers the freedom to negotiate prices with other profit centres as though they were independent companies, will tend to result in a market-based transfer price.

3.3.2 Corporate profit maximisation

In most cases where the transfer price is at market price, **internal transfers** should be **expected**, because the **buying division** is likely to **benefit** from a better quality of service, greater flexibility, and dependability of supply. **Both divisions** may **benefit** from cheaper costs of administration, selling and transport. A market price as the transfer price would therefore **result in decisions which would be in the best interests of the company or group as a whole**.

3.3.3 Divisional performance measurement

Where a **market price exists**, but the **transfer price is a different amount** (say, at standard cost plus), divisional managers will **argue** about the volume of internal transfers.

For example, if division X is expected to sell output to division Y at a transfer price of £8 per unit when the open market price is £10, its manager will decide to sell all output on the open market. The manager of division Y would resent the loss of his cheap supply from X, and would be reluctant to buy on the open market. A wasteful situation would arise where X sells on the open market at £10, where Y buys at £10, so that administration, selling and distribution costs would have been saved if X had sold directly to Y at £10, the market price.

3.4 The disadvantages of market value transfer prices

Market value as a transfer price does have certain **disadvantages**.

(a) The **market price may be a temporary one**, induced by adverse economic conditions, or dumping, or the market price might depend on the volume of output supplied to the external market by the profit centre.

(b) A transfer price at market value might, under some circumstances, **act as a disincentive to use up any spare capacity** in the divisions. A price based on incremental cost, in contrast, might provide an incentive to use up the spare resources in order to provide a marginal contribution to profit.

(c) Many products **do not have an equivalent market price** so that the price of a similar, but not identical, product might have to be chosen. In such circumstances, the option to sell or buy on the open market does not really exist.

(d) There might be an **imperfect external market** for the transferred item, so that if the transferring division tried to sell more externally, it would have to reduce its selling price.

Summary

If a **perfect external market** exists, **market price** is the **ideal** transfer price.

4 Transfer pricing with an imperfect external market

FAST FORWARD

If transfer prices are set at variable cost with an imperfect external market, the supplying division does not cover its fixed costs. **Dual pricing** or a **two-part tariff system** can be used in an attempt to overcome this problem.

If **transfers** are made at actual cost instead of **standard cost**, there is no incentive for the supplying division to control costs as they can all be passed on to the receiving division.

Cost-based approaches to transfer pricing are often used in practice, because in practice the following conditions are common.

(a) There is **no external market** for the product that is being transferred (see Section 5).

(b) Alternatively, although there is an external market, it is an **imperfect** one because the market price is affected by such factors as the amount that the company setting the transfer price supplies to it, or because there is only a limited external demand. We cover this situation in this section.

In either case there will **not be a suitable market price** upon which to base the transfer price. Another basis must therefore be used.

4.1 Transfer prices based on full cost

Under this approach, unsurprisingly, the **full cost** (including fixed production overheads absorbed) that has been incurred by the supplying division in making the intermediate product is charged to the receiving division. If a **full cost plus approach** is used a **profit margin is also included** in this transfer price.

Suppose a company has two profit centres, A and B. A can only sell half of its maximum output of 800 units externally because of limited demand. It transfers the other half of its output to B which also faces limited demand. Costs and revenues in an accounting period are as follows.

	A £	B £	Total £
External sales	8,000	24,000	32,000
Costs of production in the division	13,000	10,000	23,000
Profit			9,000

Division A's costs included fixed production overheads of £4,800 and fixed selling and administration costs of £1,000.

There are no opening or closing inventories. It does not matter, for this illustration, whether marginal costing or absorption costing is used. For the moment, we shall ignore the question of whether the current output levels are profit-maximising and congruent with the goals of the company as a whole.

If the transfer price is at full cost, A in our example would have 'sales' to B of £6,000 ((£13,000 – 1,000) × 50%). Selling and administration costs are not included as these are not incurred on the internal transfers. This would be a cost to B, as follows.

	A £	A £	B £	B £	Company as a whole £
Open market sales		8,000		24,000	32,000
Transfer sales		6,000		–	
Total sales, inc transfers		14,000		24,000	
Transfer costs			6,000		
Own costs	13,000		10,000		23,000
Total costs, inc transfers		13,000		16,000	
Profit		1,000		8,000	9,000

The **transfer sales of A are self-cancelling with the transfer costs of B** so that total profits are **unaffected by the transfer items**. The transfer price simply spreads the total profit of £9,000 between A and B.

The obvious **drawback** to the transfer price at cost is that **A makes no profit** on its work, and the manager of division A would much prefer to sell output on the open market to earn a profit, rather than transfer to B, regardless of whether or not transfers to B would be in the best interests of the company as a whole. Division A needs a profit on its transfers in order to be motivated to supply B; therefore transfer pricing at cost is inconsistent with the use of a profit centre accounting system.

4.1.1 Sub-optimal decisions

Note, also, that as the level of transfer price increases, its effect on division B could lead to suboptimalisation problems for the organisation as a whole.

For example, suppose division B could buy the product from an outside supplier for £10 instead of paying £15 (£6,000/(800/2)) to division A. This transfer price would therefore force division B to buy the product externally at £10 per unit, although it could be manufactured internally for a variable cost of £(13,000 – 4,800 – 1,000)/800 = £9 per unit.

Although division B (the buying division) would save £(15 – 10) = £5 per unit by buying externally, the organisation as a whole would lose £400 as follows.

	Per unit £
Marginal cost of production	9
External purchase cost	10
Loss if buy in	1

The overall loss on transfer/purchase of 400 units is therefore 400 × £1 = £400.

This loss of £1 per unit assumes that any other use for the released capacity would produce a benefit of less than £400. If the 400 units could also be sold externally for £20 per unit, the optimal decision for the organisation as a whole would be to buy in the units for division B at £10 per unit.

	Per unit £
Market price	20
Marginal cost	9
Contribution	11
Loss if buy-in	(1)
Incremental profit	10

The overall incremental profit would therefore be 400 × £10 = £4,000.

4.2 Transfer prices based on full cost plus

If the transfers are at cost plus a margin of, say, 10%, A's sales to B would be £6,600 (£13,000 −1,000) × 50% × 1.10).

	A £	A £	B £	B £	Total £
Open market sales		8,000		24,000	32,000
Transfer sales		6,600		–	
		14,600		24,000	
Transfer costs			6,600		
Own costs	13,000		10,000		23,000
		13,000		16,600	
Profit		1,600		7,400	9,000

Compared to a transfer price at cost, **A gains some profit** at the expense of B. However, A makes a bigger profit on external sales in this case because the profit mark-up of 10% is less than the profit mark-up on open market sales. The choice of 10% as a profit mark-up was arbitrary and unrelated to external market conditions.

The transfer price **fails on all three criteria** (divisional autonomy, performance measurement and corporate profit measurement) for judgement.

(a) Arguably, the transfer price does not give A fair revenue or charge B a reasonable cost, and so their profit **performance is distorted**. It would certainly be unfair, for example, to compare A's profit with B's profit.

(b) Given this unfairness it is likely that the **autonomy** of each of the divisional managers is **under threat.** If they cannot agree on what is a fair split of the external profit a decision will have to be imposed from above.

(c) It would seem to give A an incentive to sell more goods externally and transfer less to B. This may or **may not be in the best interests of the company as a whole**.

In fact we can demonstrate that the method is **flawed from the point of view of corporate profit maximisation**. Division A's total production costs of £12,000 include an element of fixed costs. Half of division A's total production costs are transferred to division B. However from the point of view of division B the cost is entirely variable.

The cost per unit to A is £15 (£12,000 ÷ 800) and this includes a fixed element of £6 (£4,800 ÷ 800), while division B's own costs are £25 (£10,000 ÷ 400) per unit, including a fixed element of £10 (say). The **total variable cost is really** £9 + £15 = **£24**, but from division **B's point of view** the **variable cost** is £15 + £(25 − 10) = **£30**. This means that division B will be unwilling to sell the final product for less than £30, whereas any price above £24 would make a contribution to overall costs. Thus, if external prices for the final product fall, B might be tempted to cease production.

4.3 Transfer prices based on variable or marginal cost

A variable or marginal cost approach entails charging the variable cost (which we assume to be the same as the marginal cost) that has been incurred by the supplying division to the receiving division. As above, we shall suppose that A's cost per unit is £15, of which £6 is fixed and £9 variable.

	A £	A £	B £	B £	Company as a whole £	Company as a whole £
Market sales		8,000		24,000		32,000
Transfer sales		3,600		–		
		11,600		24,000		
Transfer costs	–		3,600			
Own variable costs	7,200		6,000		13,200	
Own fixed costs	5,800		4,000		9,800	
Total costs and transfers		13,000		13,600		23,000
(Loss)/Profit		(1,400)		10,400		9,000

4.3.1 Divisional autonomy, divisional performance measurement and corporate profit maximisation

(a)   This result is **deeply unsatisfactory for the manager of division** A who could make an additional £4,400 (£(8,000 – 3,600)) profit if no goods were transferred to division B, but all were sold externally.

(b)   Given that the manager of division A would prefer to transfer externally, **head office** are likely to have to **insist** that internal transfers are made.

(c)   For the company overall, external transfers only would cause a large fall in profit, because division B could make no sales at all.

Point to note. Suppose no more than the current £8,000 could be earned from external sales and the production capacity used for production for internal transfer would remain idle if not used. Division A would be indifferent to the transfers at marginal cost as they do not represent any benefit to the division.

If more than the £8,000 of revenue could be earned externally (ie division A could sell more externally than at present), division A would have a strong disincentive to supply B at marginal cost.

4.3.2 Covering fixed costs

The problem is that with a transfer price at variable cost the **supplying division does not cover its fixed costs.**

Ways in which this problem can be overcome

(a)   Use a transfer price based on variable cost and, at the end of the period, the supplying division is credited with a share of the overall profit arising from the final sale of the transferred goods. This **dual pricing** system seems fairer but it will be necessary to determine the share of profits centrally, thus **undermining divisional autonomy.**

(b)   A further variation on **dual pricing**, where an external market exists, is to credit the selling division with the market price for transfers made, but debit the buying division with the variable or marginal cost. This can be effective in avoiding dysfunctional behaviour and sub-optimal decisions, but it can be administratively cumbersome.

(c)   A **two-part tariff system** can be used. Transfer prices are set at variable cost and once a year there is a **transfer of a fixed fee as a lump sum payment to the supplying division**, representing an allowance for its fixed costs. This method risks sending the message to the supplying division that it need not control its fixed costs, however, because the company will subsidise any inefficiencies. On the other hand, if fixed costs are incurred because spare capacity is kept available for the needs of other divisions, it is reasonable to expect those other divisions to pay a fee if they 'booked' that capacity in advance but later failed to utilise it. But the main problem with this approach is that it is likely to **conflict with divisional autonomy**.

5 Standard cost versus actual cost

When a transfer price is based on cost, **standard cost** should be used, not actual cost. A transfer of actual cost would give no incentive to **control costs**, because they could all be passed on. Actual cost-*plus* transfer prices might even encourage the manager of A to overspend, because this would increase the divisional profit, even though the company as a whole (and division B) suffers.

Suppose, for example, that A's costs in our example should have been £13,000, but actually were £16,000. Transfers (50% of output) would cost £8,000 actual, and the cost plus transfer price is at a margin of 10% (£8,000 × 110% = £8,800).

	A			B	Total
	£	£	£	£	£
Market sales		8,000		24,000	32,000
Transfer sales		8,800		–	
		16,800		24,000	
Transfer costs		–	8,800		
Own costs	16,000		10,000		26,000
		16,000		18,800	
Profit		800		5,200	6,000

A's overspending by £3,000 has reduced the total profits from £9,000 to £6,000.

In this example, B must bear much of the cost of A's overspending, which is clearly unsatisfactory for responsibility accounting. If, however, the transfer price were at standard cost plus instead of actual cost plus, the transfer sales would have been £6,600 (£(13,000 – 1,000) × 50% × 110%), regardless of A's overspending.

	A			B	Total
	£	£	£	£	£
Market sales		8,000		24,000	32,000
Transfer sales		6,600		–	
		14,600		24,000	
Transfer costs		–	6,600		
Own costs	16,000		10,000		
		16,000		16,600	26,000
Profit/(loss)		(1,400)		7,400	6,000

The entire cost of the overspending by A of £3,000 is now borne by division A itself as a comparison with the figures in Section 4.2 above will show.

6 Transfer pricing when there is no external market for the transferred item

When there is **no external market** for the item being transferred, the transfer price should be greater than or equal to the variable cost in the supplying division but less than or equal to the selling price minus variable costs (net marginal revenue) in the receiving division.

If there is **no similar item sold on an external market**, and if the **transferred item** is a **major product of the transferring division**, there is a strong argument that **profit centre accounting is a waste of time**. Profit centres cannot be judged on their commercial performance because there is no way of estimating what a fair revenue for their work should be. It would be more appropriate, perhaps, to treat the transferring division as a cost centre, and to judge performance on the basis of cost variances.

If **profit centres are established**, in the **absence of a market price**, the **optimum transfer price is likely to be one based on standard cost plus**, but only provided that the **variable cost per unit and selling price per unit are unchanged at all levels of output**. A standard cost plus price would motivate divisional managers to increase output and to reduce expenditure levels.

6.1 Example: standard cost plus as a transfer price in the absence of an external market

Motivate has two profit centres, P and Q. P transfers all its output to Q. The variable cost of output from P is £5 a unit, and fixed costs are £1,200 a month. Additional processing costs in Q are £4 a unit for variable costs, plus fixed costs of £800 a month. Budgeted production is 400 units a month, and the output of Q sells for £15 a unit.

Required

Determine the range of prices from which the transfer price (based on standard full cost plus) should be selected, in order to motivate the managers of both profit centres to both increase output and reduce costs.

Solution

Any transfer price based on standard cost plus will motivate managers to cut costs, because favourable variances between standard costs and actual costs will be credited to the division's profits. Managers of each division will also be willing to increase output (above the budget) provided that it is profitable to do so.

(a)   The **manager of P** will **increase output if the transfer price exceeds the variable cost** of £5 a unit.

(b)   The **manager of Q** will **increase output if the transfer price is less than the difference between the fixed selling price (£15)** and the **variable costs** in **Q** itself. This amount of £11 (£15 – £4) is sometimes called **net marginal revenue**.

The range of prices is therefore between £5.01 and £10.99.

Check

Suppose the transfer price is £9. With absorption based on the budgeted output of 400 units what would divisional profits be if output and sales are 400 units and 500 units?

Overheads per unit are £1,200/400. The full cost of sales is £(5 + 3) = £8 in division P. In division Q, full cost is £(4 + 2) = £6, plus transfer costs of £9.

(a)   At 400 units:

	P £	Q £	Total £
Sales	–	6,000	6,000
Transfer sales	3,600	–	
Transfer costs	–	(3,600)	
Own full cost of sales	(3,200)	(2,400)	(5,600)
	400	0	400
Under-/over-absorbed overhead	0	0	0
Profit/(loss)	400	0	400

(b)   At 500 units:

	P £	Q £	Total £
Sales	–	7,500	7,500
Transfer sales	4,500	–	–
Transfer costs	–	(4,500)	–
Own full cost of sales	(4,000)	(3,000)	(7,000)
	500	0	500
Over-absorbed overhead	300	200	500
Profit/(loss)	800	200	1,000

Increasing output improves the profit performance of both divisions and the company as a whole, and so decisions on output by the two divisions are likely to be **goal congruent**.

Summary

When there is **no external market** for the item being transferred, the **transfer price** should be **greater than or equal to** the **variable cost** in the **supplying** division but **less than or equal to** the selling price minus variable costs (**net marginal revenue**) in the **receiving** division.

7 Transfer pricing and changing costs/prices

FAST FORWARD

When **unit costs and prices are not constant at all levels of output**, there will be a profit-maximising level above which total revenue will start to decline. The ideal transfer price is one which motivates profit centre managers to produce at the optimum level of output for the organisation. This level may be below full capacity. The transfer price set should enable individual divisions to maximise their profits at this level of output. The transfer price which achieves this is unlikely to be market based or cost based.

7.1 No external market for the transferred item

If **cost behaviour patterns change** and the **selling price** to the **external market (for the receiving division's product)** is **reduced at higher levels of output**, there will be a **profit-maximising level of output**: to produce more than an 'optimum' amount would cause reductions in profitability.

Under such circumstances, the ideal transfer price is one which would motivate profit centre managers to produce at the optimum level of output, and neither below nor above this level.

7.2 Example: the profit-maximising transfer price

MCMR has two divisions, S and T. There is no external intermediate market and so S transfers all its output to T, which finishes the work. Costs and revenues at various levels of capacity are as follows.

Output	S costs	T revenues	T costs	T net revenues	Profit
Units	£	£	£	£	£
600	600	3,190	240	2,950	2,350
700	700	3,530	280	3,250	2,550
800	840	3,866	336	3,530	2,690
900	1,000	4,180	400	3,780	2,780
1,000	1,200	4,480	480	4,000	2,800 *
1,100	1,450	4,780	580	4,200	2,750
1,200	1,800	5,070	720	4,350	2,550

Company profits are maximised at £2,800 with output of 1,000 units. But if we wish to select a transfer price in order to establish S and T as profit centres, what transfer price would motivate the managers of S and T together to produce 1,000 units, no more and no less?

Discussion and solution

The transfer price will act as revenue to S and as a cost to T.

(a)   **S will continue to produce more output until** the costs of additional production exceed the transfer price revenue, that is where the **marginal cost exceeds the transfer price**.

(b)   **T will continue to want to receive more output from S until** its net revenue from further processing is not sufficient to cover the additional transfer price costs, that is where its **net marginal revenue is less than the transfer price**.

	Division S	Division T
Output	Marginal costs	Net marginal revenues
Units	£	£
600	–	–
700	100	300
800	140	280
900	160	250
1,000	200	220
1,100	250	200
1,200	350	150

Since S will continue to produce more output if the transfer price exceeds the marginal cost of production, a **price of at least £200 per 100 units (£2 per unit) is required to 'persuade' the manager of S to produce as many as 1,000 units**. A price in excess of £250 per 100 units would motivate the manager of S to produce 1,100 units or more.

By a similar argument, T will continue to want more output from S if the net marginal revenues exceed the transfer costs from S. **If T wants 1,000 units, the transfer price must be less than £220 per 100 units**. However, if the transfer price is lower than £200 per 100 units, T will ask for 1,100 units from S in order to improve its divisional profit further.

Summary

(a)   The total company profit is maximised at 1,000 units of output.

(b)   Division S will want to produce 1,000 units, no more and no less, if the transfer price is between £200 to £250 per 100 units, or £2 and £2.50 per unit.

(c)   Division T will want to receive and process 1,000 units, no more and no less, if the transfer price per unit is between £2 and £2.20.

(d)   A transfer price must therefore be selected in the **range £2.00 to £2.20 per unit** (exclusive).

Summary

When there is **no external market for the transferred item** and **changing costs/prices** for the final output, the **transfer** price should be **greater than or equal** to the **marginal cost in the supplying division** but **less than or equal** to the **net marginal revenue in the receiving division**.

Question — Transfer pricing and changing costs/prices (no external market)

Learning outcome: D(vii)

Explain how the following figures are calculated, or arrived at.

(a)   Example 7.2 – T net revenues
(b)   Example 7.2 Discussion and solution (b) – Division S marginal costs
(c)   Example 7.2 Discussion and solution (b) – Division T net marginal revenue
(d)   Example 7.2 – a transfer price of £2.10 per unit

Answer

(a)   T revenues minus T costs
(b)   S costs for 700 units minus S costs for 600 units (and so on)
(c)   T net revenues for 700 units minus T net revenues for 600 units (and so on)
(d)   See Example 7.2 Discussion and solution

This exercise is to make sure that you were following the argument.

7.3 With an external market for the transferred item

7.3.1 Imperfect external market

The approach is essentially the same as the one shown above, except that the supplying division may also have income, and so its marginal revenue needs to be taken into account.

7.4 Example: profit maximisation with an imperfect external market

IMP makes hand-built sports cars. The company has two divisions, M and N. The output of division M can either be sold externally or transferred to division N which turns it into a version for the USA. Due to competition from Japanese car makers the US market is giving poor returns at present. Cost and marginal revenues at various levels of output are as follows.

	M	*M*	*M*	*N*
Cars produced	Total cost	Marginal cost	Marginal revenue	Net marginal revenue
	£'000	£'000	£'000	£'000
1	18	18	20 (1)	18 (2)
2	26	8	16 (3)	12 (4)
3	35	9	12 (5)	6
4	45	10	8 (6) will not be built	0
5	56	11	4	(6)
6	68	12	0	(12)
7	81	13	(4)	(18)
8	95	14	(8)	0

Required

Determine the optimal output level.

Solution

(a)   In this situation, for any individual car, **marginal revenue will be received by division M** *or* **net marginal revenue will be received by division N. The same car cannot be sold twice!**

(b)   Marginal revenue is the extra amount received for each additional car sold into M's market (or net marginal revenue is the extra amount for additional cars in N's market). Thus the marginal revenue for three cars in M's market is £12,000 only if all three cars have been sold in M's market. If three are produced but one is sold in N's market, the marginal revenue for M for the other two is £16,000.

(c)   For each car produced a decision must therefore be made as to which market to sell it in, and this will be done according to which market offers the higher marginal revenue.

(d)   As shown by the numbers in brackets, the first car is sold in M's market, the second in N's, the third in M's, and the fourth and fifth in either. By the time six cars have been produced and shared out between the two markets the marginal cost has risen to £12,000. This is greater than the marginal revenue obtainable from either market (£8,000 in M, £6,000 in N).

(e)   The sixth car will therefore not be built. Division M will produce five units and sell three cars itself and transfer two to division N. The transfer price must be more than £11,000 to meet M's marginal cost, but less than £12,000 otherwise division N will not buy it.

Summary

When there is an **imperfect external market for the transferred item** and changing costs/prices for the final output, the transfer **price** should again **fall between marginal cost in the supplying division** and **net marginal revenue in the receiving division.**

We now need to consider whether the profit-maximising transfer price should be set using the same approach if **supplies of the transferred item are limited.**

7.5 Example: Maximising profits when the transferred item is in short supply

Suppose that one month division M suffered a two-week strike and was only able to produce two cars. If it follows normal policy and transfers the second to division N, its own results for the month will be as follows.

		£'000
Sales	– own	20
	– transfers	11
		31
Total cost		26
		5

However, if division M keeps the second car and sells both in its own market it will earn £36,000 in total (£20,000 + £16,000) increasing its own divisional profit by £5,000.

From the point of view of the company this is a bad decision. If the second car is transferred to division N it can be sold for £18,000. Overall revenue and profit will increase by £2,000 ((£18,000 – 16,000)).

Attention!

Where there is a **capacity constraint** resulting in short supplies of the product, **a transfer price based on matching marginal cost and marginal revenue will not encourage corporate profit maximisation.**

The only way to be sure that a profit maximising transfer policy will be implemented is to **dictate the policy from the centre**.

7.5.1 Perfect external market

The approach is the same as that used for an imperfect external market except that marginal revenue for the supplying division is constant at the market price for all volumes of output.

7.6 Example: profit maximisation with a perfect external market

We will use the example of IMP again but this time the market price achieved by M is £10,000. The costs and marginal revenues at various levels of output are as follows.

Cars produced	M Total cost £'000	M Marginal cost £'000	M Marginal revenue £'000	N Net marginal revenue £'000
1	18	18	10 (3)	18 (1)
2	26	8	10 (4)	12 (2)
3	35	9	10	6
4	45	10	10	0
5	56	11	10	(6)
6	68	12	10	(12)
7	81	13	10	(18)
8	95	14	10	0

Marginal cost is greater than marginal revenue in either market by the fifth car, so four cars will be built, two sold by M and two transferred to be sold by N. As seen earlier, the market price will be the transfer price.

Summary

When there is a **perfect external market for the transferred item** and **changing costs/prices** for the final output, profits are maximised when **market price** is used on the transfer price.

Question   Profit-maximising transfer price

Learning outcome: D(vii)

Divisions J and A are in M Group. Division J manufactures part N. Three units of part N are used in product Z manufactured by Division A. Division J has no external customers for part N. Division J transfers part N to Division A at variable cost (£35 per part) plus 50%. The variable cost to Division A of manufacturing product Z is £50 per unit. This £50 does not include the cost of part N transferred from Division J.

Division A can sell the following number of units of product Z, earning the associated levels of marginal revenue.

Units sold	1	2	3	4
Marginal revenue	£270	£240	£210	£180

How many units of product Z should management of Division A sell if they wish to maximise divisional profit?

A   1
B   2
C   3
D   4

Answer

The correct answer is C.

Variable cost of parts for Division A's product Z = £35 × 3 = £105.

Transfer price = £105 × 150% = £157.50

Division A's variable cost per unit of Z = £50

Total variable/marginal cost to division A = £207.50

Division A will sell until marginal cost = marginal revenue.

It will therefore sell 3 units.

8 Identifying the optimal transfer price

Throughout the chapter we have been leading up to the following guiding rules for identifying the optimal transfer price.

(a)   The **ideal transfer price** should **reflect the opportunity cost** of sale to the supply division and the opportunity cost to the buying division. Unfortunately, full information about opportunity costs may not be easily obtainable in practice.

(b)   Where a **perfect external market price exists and unit variable costs and unit selling prices are constant**, the **opportunity cost** of transfer will be **external market price** or **external market price less savings in selling costs**.

(c)   In the **absence of a perfect external market price for the transferred item**, but when **unit variable costs are constant**, and the **sales price per unit of the end-product is constant**, the **ideal transfer price** should reflect the opportunity cost of the resources consumed by the supply division to make and supply the item and so should be at **standard variable cost + opportunity cost of making the transfer**.

(d) When **unit variable costs and/or unit selling prices are not constant,** there will be a **profit-maximising level of output** and the **ideal transfer price** will only be found by sensible **negotiation** and careful **analysis**.

    (i) Establish the output and sales quantities that will optimise the profits of the company or group as a whole.

    (ii) Establish the transfer price at which both profit centres would maximise their profits at this company-optimising output level.

There may be a range of prices within which both profit centres can agree on the output level that would maximise their individual profits and the profits of the company as a whole. Any price within the range would then be 'ideal'.

Question   Optimal transfer prices

Learning outcome: D(vii)

You should try to learn the above rules, and refer back to the appropriate part of the chapter if you are not sure about any point. Read through the rules again and then answer these questions.

(a) In what situation should the transfer price be the external market price?

(b) How should the transfer price be established when there are diseconomies of scale and prices have to be lowered to increase sales volume?

(c) What is the ideal transfer price?

(d) In what circumstances should the transfer price be standard variable cost + the opportunity cost of making the transfer?

9 Negotiated transfer prices

FAST FORWARD

If divisional managers are allowed to **negotiate transfer prices** with each other, the agreed price may be finalised from a mixture of accounting arithmetic, negotiation and compromise.

A transfer price based on opportunity cost is often difficult to identify, for lack of suitable information about costs and revenues in individual divisions.

In this case it is likely that transfer prices will be set by means of negotiation. The agreed price may be finalised from a mixture of accounting arithmetic, politics and compromise.

(a) A negotiated price might be based on market value, but with some reductions to allow for the internal nature of the transaction, which saves external selling and distribution costs.

(b) Where one division receives near-finished goods from another, a negotiated price might be based on the market value of the end product, minus an amount for the finishing work in the receiving division.

9.1 Behavioural implications

Even so, inter-departmental **disputes** about transfer prices are likely to arise and these may need the **intervention or mediation of head office** to settle the problem. Head office management may then **impose a price** which maximises the profit of the company as a whole. On the other hand, head office management might restrict their intervention to the **task of keeping negotiations in progress** until a transfer price is eventually settled. The **more head office has to impose** its own decisions on profit centres, the less **decentralisation of authority** there will be and the **less effective the profit centre system** of accounting will be for **motivating** divisional managers.

10 International transfer pricing

Problems associated with currency exchange rates, taxation, import tariffs, exchange control, anti-dumping legislation and competitive pressures arise **with transfer pricing in multinational companies**.

As we have seen, the level at which a transfer price should be set is not a straightforward decision for organisations. The situation is even less clear cut for organisations operating in a number of countries, when even more factors need to be taken into consideration. Moreover, the manipulation of profits through the use of transfer pricing is a common area of confrontation between multinational organisations and host country governments.

Factor	Explanation
Exchange rate fluctuation	The value of a transfer of goods between profit centres in different countries could depend on fluctuations in the currency exchange rate.
Taxation in different countries	If taxation on profits is 20% of profits in Country A and 50% of profits in Country B, a company will presumably try to 'manipulate' profits (by means of raising or lowering transfer prices or by invoicing the subsidiary in the high-tax country for 'services' provided by the subsidiary in the low-tax country) so that profits are maximised for a subsidiary in Country A, by reducing profits for a subsidiary in Country B. Artificial attempts at reducing tax liabilities could, however, upset a country's tax officials if they discover it and may lead to some form of penalty. Many tax authorities have the power to modify transfer prices in computing tariffs or taxes on profit, although a genuine arms-length market price should be accepted.
Import tariffs/customs duties	Suppose that Country A imposes an import tariff of 20% on the value of goods imported. A multi-national company has a subsidiary in Country A which imports goods from a subsidiary in Country B. In such a situation, the company would minimise costs by keeping the transfer price to a minimum value.
Exchange controls	If a country imposes restrictions on the transfer of profits from domestic subsidiaries to foreign multinationals, the restrictions on the transfer can be overcome if head office provides some goods or services to the subsidiary and charges exorbitantly high prices, disguising the 'profits' as sales revenue, and transferring them from one country to the other. The ethics of such an approach should, of course, be questioned.
Anti-dumping legislation	Governments may take action to protect home industries by preventing companies from transferring goods cheaply into their countries. They may do this, for example, by insisting on the use of a fair market value for the transfer price.
Competitive pressures	Transfer pricing can be used to enable profit centres to match or undercut local competitors.

Factor	Explanation
Repatriation of funds	By inflating transfer prices for goods sold to subsidiaries in countries where inflation is high, the subsidiaries' profits are reduced and funds repatriated, thereby saving their value.
Minority shareholders	Transfer prices can be used to reduce the amount of profit paid to minority shareholders by artificially depressing a subsidiary's profit.

10.1 The pros and cons of different transfer pricing bases

(a) A transfer price at **market value** is usually encouraged by the tax and customs authorities of both host and home countries as they will receive a fair share of the profits made but there are problems with its use.

    (i) Prices for the same product may vary considerably from one country to another.

    (ii) Changes in exchange rates, local taxes and so on can result in large variations in selling price.

    (iii) A division will want to set its prices in relation to the supply and demand conditions present in the country in question to ensure that it can compete in that country.

(b) A transfer price at **cost** is usually acceptable to tax and customs authorities since it provides some indication that the transfer price approximates to the real cost of supplying the item and because it indicates that they will therefore receive a fair share of tax and tariff revenues. Cost-based approaches do not totally remove the suspicion that the figure may have been massaged because the choice of the type of cost (full actual, full standard, actual variable, marginal) can alter the size of the transfer price.

(c) In a multinational organisation, **negotiated** transfer prices may result in overall sub-optimisation because no account is taken of factors such as differences in tax and tariff rates between countries.

Question   International transfer pricing

Learning outcome: D (vii)

RBN is a UK parent company with an overseas subsidiary. The directors of RBN wish to transfer profits from the UK to the overseas company. They are considering changing the level of the transfer prices charged on goods shipped from the overseas subsidiary to UK subsidiaries and the size of the royalty payments paid by UK subsidiaries to the overseas subsidiary.

In order to transfer profit from the UK to the overseas subsidiary, the directors of RBN should

A   increase both the transfer prices and royalty payments
B   increase the transfer prices but decrease the royalty payments
C   decrease the transfer prices but increase the royalty payments
D   decrease both the transfer prices and royalty payments

Answer

The correct answer is A.

To increase the overseas subsidiary's profit, the transfer price needs to be higher (since it is the overseas subsidiary doing the selling) and the royalty payments by the UK subsidiaries to the overseas subsidiary company should also be higher. Both would add to the overseas subsidiary's revenue without affecting its costs.

Question

More international transfer pricing

Learning outcome: D (vii)

LL Multinational transferred 4,000 units of product S from its manufacturing division in the USA to the selling division in the UK in the year to 31 December.

Each unit of S cost $350 to manufacture, the variable cost proportion being 75%, and was sold for £600. The UK division incurred marketing and distribution costs of £8 per unit. The UK tax rate was 30% and the exchange rate £ = $1.5.

If the transfers were at variable cost, what was the UK division's profit after tax?

A   £1,668,000
B   £1,167,600
C   £922,600
D   £1,751,400

Answer

The correct answer is B.

	£
External sales (£600 × 4,000)	2,400,000
Variable cost (transfer price of ($350 × 75%/$1.5) × 4,000)	700,000
Marketing and distribution costs (£8 × 4,000)	32,000
Profit before tax	1,668,000
Tax at 30%	500,400
Profit after tax	1,167,600

Option A is the profit before tax. If you selected **option C** you forgot to transfer the variable cost into £. **Option D** is the correct answer but in $.

A study by Ernst and Young of 210 multinationals found that 49% were being investigated over transfer pricing, while 83% had been involved in a transfer pricing dispute at some time.

> 'Transfer pricing is big business ... The figures involved are sometimes huge. During the 1992 presidential campaign, Bill Clinton claimed that $45bn in tax revenue could be raised from foreign-based enterprises operating in the US which were unfairly allocating their profits by transfer pricing distortions.'
>
> (J Kelly, *Financial Times,* 23 November 1995)

 Case Study

The following descriptions are taken from Christopher Pass's article 'Transfer Pricing in **Multinational** Companies' which appeared in the September 1994 edition of *Management Accounting*.

'In 1993 Nissan agreed to pay 'penalty taxes' of Y17bn (£106m) to the US Internal Revenue Services (IRS) following an IRS investigation which concluded that Nissan had avoided US taxes by transferring part of its US profits to Japan in the early 1990s. The IRS's main contention was that Nissan had set transfer prices on its passenger cars and trucks imported from Japan at 'unrealistically' high levels and as a result declared lower profits in the US than it should have done. What constitutes a 'fair' or 'realistic' transfer price is, as we have indicated above, open to question. In the USA, the common Japanese practice of charging relatively low prices to build market share over the longer term is viewed with some scepticism and hence has raised suspicions regarding 'unfair' transfer pricing practices.

The NTA alleged that many US and European concerns had deliberately under-recorded profits earned in Japan both by charging 'excessive' transfer prices to their local subsidiaries for materials imported from their parent companies, and by levying 'excessive' royalty payments on their Japanese subsidiaries.

The NTA imposed a penalty tax of Y15bn (£96m) on Cola-Cola for 'unfair' transfer pricing practices and for applying excessive brand and marketing royalty payments transferred to its US parent company over the period 1990-92; while Ciba-Geigy was charged a penalty tax of Y5.7bn (£38m) and Roche Y10bn (£64m) for engaging in manipulative transfer pricing over a similar three year period. Hoechst has been 'fined' an undisclosed amount which it is appealing against before a Japan-Germany inter-governmental tax authority.'

10.2 Example: international transfer pricing

Division W, which is part of the XYZ group, is based in country A and has the capacity to manufacture 100,000 units of product B each year. The variable cost of producing a unit of B is £15 and the division can sell 85,000 units externally per annum at £25 per unit.

Division D is part of the same group and in based in country L. Division D purchases 40,000 units of product B each year from O (which is not part of XYZ group), which is also based in country L. D pays a sterling equivalent of £20 per unit.

If division D were to purchase product B from division W, division W would set a transfer price of £22. Given that there are no selling costs involved in transferring units to division D, this would give division W the same contribution on internal and external sales.

Division W would give priority to division D and so the orders from some external customers would not be met.

Required

Determine from whom division D should purchase product B in each of the following circumstances if the aim is to maximise group profit.

(a) The tax rate in country A is 30% and the tax rate in country L is 40%.
(b) The tax rate in country A is 60% and the tax rate in country L is 15%.

You may assume that changes in contribution can be used as a basis of calculating changes in tax charges and that division D is able to absorb any tax benefits from the profit it generates on other activities.

Solution

We need to consider the relevant costs, which are the changes in contribution and tax paid.

 BPP PROFESSIONAL EDUCATION   431

	£'000	(a)	(b)
Current position			
D buys 40,000 units from O @ £20 per unit	(800)		
These purchases reduce D's tax liability by			
£800,000 × 40%		320	
£800,000 × 15%			120
W sells 85,000 units @ £(25 – 15) = £10			
contribution per unit	850		
W's tax on this contribution			
£850,000 × 30%		(255)	
£850,000 × 60%			(510)
If D buys from W			
D buys 40,000 units @ £22 per unit	(880)		
These purchases reduce D's tax liability by			
£880,000 × 40%		352	
£880,000 × 15%			132
W sells 100,000 units @ £10 contribution per unit	1,000,000		
W's tax on this contribution			
£1,000,000 × 30%		(300)	
£1,000,000 × 60%			(600)

Summary

	(a)	(b)
If D switches to W		
Decrease in D's contribution		
£((880) – (800))	(80)	(80)
Decrease in D's tax liability		
£(352 – 320)	32	
£(132 – 120)		12
Increase in W's contribution		
£(1,000,000 – 850,000)	150	150
Increase in W's tax liability		
£((300) – (255))	(45)	
£((600) – (510))		(90)
Net gain to XYZ group	57	(8)

∴ Division D should purchase from Division W to maximise group profit in scenario (a) but from O in scenario (b).

> **Attention!**
>
> The figures in the summary above are calculated by deducting the cashflow arising in the current position from the cashflows if D buys from W.

10.3 Currency management

When subsidiaries in different countries trade with each other it will be necessary to **decide which currency will be used for the transfer price**.

If the transfer price is set in one of the subsidiaries' home currencies and there is a movement in the exchange rate then one of the subsidiaries will make a **loss on exchange of foreign currencies**.

10.4 Example: transfer prices and exchange rate losses

A subsidiary in the UK sells product P to a US subsidiary. Details are as follows.

	Per unit
Transfer price	$21
Cost incurred in UK subsidiary	£9

At the date that the transfer price was agreed the exchange rate was £1 = $1.50.

The US subsidiary incurs additional costs of $3 per unit to convert product P for sale in the US, at a selling price of $29 per unit.

Due to a weakening of the dollar against the pound, the exchange rate is now £1 = $1.80.

Required

Calculate the effect of the change I exchange rate on the profit per unit earned by each subsidiary, if the agreed transfer price was fixed in terms of:

(a)   Dollars
(b)   Pounds sterling

Solution

When exchange rate is £1 = $1.50

	UK subsidiary £ per unit	US subsidiary $ per unit
Selling price of product ($21 ÷ 1.50)	14	29
Costs incurred in subsidiary - internal	(9)	(3)
- transfer		(21)
Profit per unit	5	5

When exchange rate is £1 = $1.80. Transfer price fixed in dollars ($21)

	UK subsidiary £ per unit	US subsidiary $ per unit
Selling price of product ($21 ÷ 1.80)	11.67	29
Costs incurred in subsidiary - internal	(9.00)	(3)
- transfer		(21)
Profit per unit	2.67	5

When exchange rate is £1 = $1,80. Transfer price fixed in pounds sterling

	UK subsidiary £ per unit		US subsidiary $ per unit
Selling price of product	14		29.00
Costs incurred in subsidiary - internal	(9)		(3.00)
- transfer		(£14 × 1.80)	(25.20)
Profit per unit	5		0.80

Thus the weakening dollar had a detrimental effect on the UK subsidiary when the transfer price was fixed in dollars, but a detrimental effect to the UK subsidiary when the transfer price was fixed in pounds sterling.

As well as having a behavioural impact this could also affect the taxation of the whole group. If a particular currency weakens, as in this example, then the selection of the correct currency for the transfer price can ensure that currency translation losses occur in the subsidiary which pays the higher rate of taxation.

Chapter Roundup

- Transfer prices are a way of promoting **divisional autonomy**, ideally without prejudicing the **measurement of divisional performance** or discouraging **overall corporate profit maximisation**.

- Transfer prices should be set at a level which ensures that profits for the organisation as a whole are maximised.

- The **limits** within which transfer prices should fall are as follows.

  - **The minimum**. The sum of the supplying division's marginal cost and opportunity cost of the item transferred.

  - **The maximum**. The lowest market price at which the receiving division could purchase the goods or services externally, less any internal cost savings in packaging and delivery.

- If **variable costs and market prices are constant**, regardless of the volume of output, a **market-based transfer price** is the ideal transfer price.

- If transfer prices are set at variable cost with an imperfect external market, the supplying division does not cover its fixed costs. **Dual pricing** or a **two-part tariff system** can be used in an attempt to overcome this problem.

- If **transfers** are made at actual cost instead of **standard cost**, there is no incentive for the supplying division to control costs as they can all be passed on to the receiving division.

- When there is **no external market** for the item being transferred, the transfer price should be greater than or equal to the variable cost in the supplying division but less than or equal to the selling price minus variable costs (net marginal revenue) in the receiving division.

- When **unit costs and prices are not constant at all levels of output**, there will be a profit-maximising level above which total revenue will start to decline. The ideal transfer price is one which motivates profit centre managers to produce at the optimum level of output for the organisation. This level may be below full capacity. The transfer price set should enable individual divisions to maximise their profits at this level of output. The transfer price which achieves this is unlikely to be market based or cost based.

- If divisional managers are allowed to **negotiate transfer prices** with each other, the agreed price may be finalised from a mixture of accounting arithmetic, negotiation and compromise.

- Problems associated with currency exchange rates, taxation, import tariffs, exchange control, anti-dumping legislation and competitive pressures arise **with transfer pricing in multinational companies**.

Quick Quiz

1   *Put ticks in the appropriate column to highlight whether or not a transfer price should fulfil each of the following criteria.*

	Criteria should be fulfilled	Criteria should not be fulfilled
Should encourage dysfunctional decision making		
Should encourage output at an organisation-wide profit-maximising level		
Should encourage divisions to act in their own self interest		
Should encourage divisions to make entirely autonomous decisions		
Should enable the measurement of profit centre performance		
Should reward the transferring division		
Should be a reasonable cost for receiving division		
Should discourage goal congruence		

PROFESSIONAL EDUCATION

2   *Fill in the gaps.*

Market value as a transfer price has certain disadvantages.

(a)   The market price might be ...., induced by adverse economic conditions, say.

(b)   There might be an .... external market, so that if the transferring division tried to sell more externally, it would have to reduce its selling price.

(c)   Many products do not have ....

3   Division P transfers its output to division Q at variable cost. Once a year P charges a fixed fee to Q, representing an allowance for P's fixed costs. This type of transfer pricing system is commonly known as

A   Dual pricing
B   Negotiated transfer pricing
C   Opportunity cost based transfer pricing
D   Two-part tariff transfer pricing

4   Profits are maximised when marginal cost is equal to marginal revenue. True or false?

5   *Choose the correct words from those highlighted.*

When transfer prices are based on opportunity costs, opportunity costs are either the (1) **contribution/profit** forgone by the (2) **receiving/supplying** division in transferring (3) **internally/externally** rather than (4) **selling externally/transferring internally**, or the (5) **profit/contribution** forgone by not using the relevant facilities for their (6) **next best/cheapest/most profitable** alternative use.

6   *Choose the correct words from those highlighted.*

Taxation on profits in country C is charged at a higher rate than in country D. When goods are transferred from a subsidiary in country C to a subsidiary in country D it would be beneficial, from the point of view of the whole organisation, to charge a (1) **higher/lower** transfer price so that the total taxation cost for the organisation is (2) **higher/lower**.

7   Transfer prices based on standard cost provide an incentive for the receiving division to control costs. *True or false?*

8   In which of the following circumstances is there a strong argument that profit centre accounting is a waste of time?

A   When the transferred item is also sold on an external market

B   When the supplying division is based in a different country to head office

C   If the transferred item is a major product of the supplying division

D   If there is no similar product sold on an external market and the transferred item is a major product of the supplying division

9   *Choose the correct words from those highlighted.*

The more head office has to impose its own decisions on profit centres, the **more/less** decentralisation of authority there will be and the **more/less** effective the profit centre system of accounting will be for motivating divisional managers.

Answers to Quick Quiz

1

	Criteria should be fulfilled	Criteria should not be fulfilled
Should encourage dysfunctional decision making		✓
Should encourage output at an organisation-wide profit-maximising level	✓	
Should encourage divisions to act in their own self interest		✓
Should encourage divisions to make entirely autonomous decisions		✓
Should enable the measurement of profit centre performance	✓	
Should reward the transferring division	✓	
Should be a reasonable cost for receiving division	✓	
Should discourage goal congruence		✓

2   (a)   temporary
    (b)   imperfect
    (c)   an equivalent market price

3   D

4   True

5   (1)   contribution
    (2)   supplying
    (3)   internally
    (4)   selling externally
    (5)   contribution
    (6)   next best

6   (1)   lower
    (2)   lower

7   False. They provide an incentive to the supplying division.

8   D

9   less
    less

Now try the question below from the Exam Question Bank

Number	Level	Marks	Time
Q34	Examination	20	36 mins

Mathematical
tables

Tables

Area under the normal curve

This table gives the area under the normal curve between the mean and the point Z standard deviations above the mean. The corresponding area for deviations below the mean can be found by symmetry.

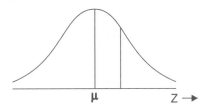

$Z = \dfrac{(x-\mu)}{\sigma}$	0.00	0.01	0.02	0.03	0.04	0.05	0.06	0.07	0.08	0.09
0.0	.0000	.0040	.0080	.0120	.0160	.0199	.0239	.0279	.0319	.0359
0.1	.0398	.0438	.0478	.0517	.0557	.0596	.0636	.0675	.0714	.0753
0.2	.0793	.0832	.0871	.0910	.0948	.0987	.1026	.1064	.1103	.1141
0.3	.1179	.1217	.1255	.1293	.1331	.1368	.1406	.1443	.1480	.1517
0.4	.1554	.1591	.1628	.1664	.1700	.1736	.1772	.1808	.1844	.1879
0.5	.1915	.1950	.1985	.2019	.2054	.2088	.2123	.2157	.2190	.2224
0.6	.2257	.2291	.2324	.2357	.2389	.2422	.2454	.2486	.2517	.2549
0.7	.2580	.2611	.2642	.2673	.2704	.2734	.2764	.2794	.2823	.2852
0.8	.2881	.2910	.2939	.2967	.2995	.3023	.3051	.3078	.3106	.3133
0.9	.3159	.3186	.3212	.3238	.3264	.3289	.3315	.3340	.3365	.3389
1.0	.3413	.3438	.3461	.3485	.3508	.3531	.3554	.3577	.3599	.3621
1.1	.3643	.3665	.3686	.3708	.3729	.3749	.3770	.3790	.3810	.3830
1.2	.3849	.3869	.3888	.3907	.3925	.3944	.3962	.3980	.3997	.4015
1.3	.4032	.4049	.4066	.4082	.4099	.4115	.4131	.4147	.4162	.4177
1.4	.4192	.4207	.4222	.4236	.4251	.4265	.4279	.4292	.4306	.4319
1.5	.4332	.4345	.4357	.4370	.4382	.4394	.4406	.4418	.4429	.4441
1.6	.4452	.4463	.4474	.4484	.4495	.4505	.4515	.4525	.4535	.4545
1.7	.4554	.4564	.4573	.4582	.4591	.4599	.4608	.4616	.4625	.4633
1.8	.4641	.4649	.4656	.4664	.4671	.4678	.4686	.4693	.4699	.4706
1.9	.4713	.4719	.4726	.4732	.4738	.4744	.4750	.4756	.4761	.4767
2.0	.4772	.4778	.4783	.4788	.4793	.4798	.4803	.4808	.4812	.4817
2.1	.4821	.4826	.4830	.4834	.4838	.4842	.4846	.4850	.4854	.4857
2.2	.4861	.4864	.4868	.4871	.4875	.4878	.4881	.4884	.4887	.4890
2.3	.4893	.4896	.4898	.4901	.4904	.4906	.4909	.4911	.4913	.4916
2.4	.4918	.4920	.4922	.4925	.4927	.4929	.4931	.4932	.4934	.4936
2.5	.4938	.4940	.4941	.4943	.4945	.4946	.4948	.4949	.4951	.4952
2.6	.4953	.4955	.4956	.4957	.4959	.4960	.4961	.4962	.4963	.4964
2.7	.4965	.4966	.4967	.4968	.4969	.4970	.4971	.4972	.4973	.4974
2.8	.4974	.4975	.4976	.4977	.4977	.4978	.4979	.4979	.4980	.4981
2.9	.4981	.4982	.4982	.4983	.4984	.4984	.4985	.4985	.4986	.4986
3.0	.49865	.4987	.4987	.4988	.4988	.4989	.4989	.4989	.4990	.4990
3.1	.49903	.4991	.4991	.4991	.4992	.4992	.4992	.4992	.4993	.4993
3.2	.49931	.4993	.4994	.4994	.4994	.4994	.4994	.4995	.4995	.4995
3.3	.49952	.4995	.4995	.4996	.4996	.4996	.4996	.4996	.4996	.4997
3.4	.49966	.4997	.4997	.4997	.4997	.4997	.4997	.4997	.4997	.4998
3.5	.49977									

Present value table

Present value of £1 ie (1+r)-n where r = interest rate, n = number of periods until payment or receipt.

Periods					Interest rates (r)					
(n)	1%	2%	3%	4%	5%	6%	7%	8%	9%	10%
1	0.990	0.980	0.971	0.962	0.952	0.943	0.935	0.926	0.917	0.909
2	0.980	0.961	0.943	0.925	0.907	0.890	0.873	0.857	0.842	0.826
3	0.971	0.942	0.915	0.889	0.864	0.840	0.816	0.794	0.772	0.751
4	0.961	0.924	0.888	0.855	0.823	0.792	0.763	0.735	0.708	0.683
5	0.951	0.906	0.863	0.822	0.784	0.747	0.713	0.681	0.650	0.621
6	0.942	0.888	0.837	0.790	0.746	0.705	0.666	0.630	0.596	0.564
7	0.933	0.871	0.813	0.760	0.711	0.665	0.623	0.583	0.547	0.513
8	0.923	0.853	0.789	0.731	0.677	0.627	0.582	0.540	0.502	0.467
9	0.914	0.837	0.766	0.703	0.645	0.592	0.544	0.500	0.460	0.424
10	0.905	0.820	0.744	0.676	0.614	0.558	0.508	0.463	0.422	0.386
11	0.896	0.804	0.722	0.650	0.585	0.527	0.475	0.429	0.388	0.350
12	0.887	0.788	0.701	0.625	0.557	0.497	0.444	0.397	0.356	0.319
13	0.879	0.773	0.681	0.601	0.530	0.469	0.415	0.368	0.326	0.290
14	0.870	0.758	0.661	0.577	0.505	0.442	0.388	0.340	0.299	0.263
15	0.861	0.743	0.642	0.555	0.481	0.417	0.362	0.315	0.275	0.239
16	0.853	0.728	0.623	0.534	0.458	0.394	0.339	0.292	0.252	0.218
17	0.844	0.714	0.605	0.513	0.436	0.371	0.317	0.270	0.231	0.198
18	0.836	0.700	0.587	0.494	0.416	0.350	0.296	0.250	0.212	0.180
19	0.828	0.686	0.570	0.475	0.396	0.331	0.277	0.232	0.194	0.164
20	0.820	0.673	0.554	0.456	0.377	0.312	0.258	0.215	0.178	0.149

Periods					Interest rates (r)					
(n)	11%	12%	13%	14%	15%	16%	17%	18%	19%	20%
1	0.901	0.893	0.885	0.877	0.870	0.862	0.855	0.847	0.840	0.833
2	0.812	0.797	0.783	0.769	0.756	0.743	0.731	0.718	0.706	0.694
3	0.731	0.712	0.693	0.675	0.658	0.641	0.624	0.609	0.593	0.579
4	0.659	0.636	0.613	0.592	0.572	0.552	0.534	0.516	0.499	0.482
5	0.593	0.567	0.543	0.519	0.497	0.476	0.456	0.437	0.419	0.402
6	0.535	0.507	0.480	0.456	0.432	0.410	0.390	0.370	0.352	0.335
7	0.482	0.452	0.425	0.400	0.376	0.354	0.333	0.314	0.296	0.279
8	0.434	0.404	0.376	0.351	0.327	0.305	0.285	0.266	0.249	0.233
9	0.391	0.361	0.333	0.308	0.284	0.263	0.243	0.225	0.209	0.194
10	0.352	0.322	0.295	0.270	0.247	0.227	0.208	0.191	0.176	0.162
11	0.317	0.287	0.261	0.237	0.215	0.195	0.178	0.162	0.148	0.135
12	0.286	0.257	0.231	0.208	0.187	0.168	0.152	0.137	0.124	0.112
13	0.258	0.229	0.204	0.182	0.163	0.145	0.130	0.116	0.104	0.093
14	0.232	0.205	0.181	0.160	0.141	0.125	0.111	0.099	0.088	0.078
15	0.209	0.183	0.160	0.140	0.123	0.108	0.095	0.084	0.074	0.065
16	0.188	0.163	0.141	0.123	0.107	0.093	0.081	0.071	0.062	0.054
17	0.170	0.146	0.125	0.108	0.093	0.080	0.069	0.060	0.052	0.045
18	0.153	0.130	0.111	0.095	0.081	0.069	0.059	0.051	0.044	0.038
19	0.138	0.116	0.098	0.083	0.070	0.060	0.051	0.043	0.037	0.031
20	0.124	0.104	0.087	0.073	0.061	0.051	0.043	0.037	0.031	0.026

Cumulative present value table

This table shows the present value of £1 per annum, receivable or payable at the end of each year for n years $\dfrac{1-(1+r)^{-n}}{r}$.

Periods					Interest rates (r)					
(n)	1%	2%	3%	4%	5%	6%	7%	8%	9%	10%
1	0.990	0.980	0.971	0.962	0.952	0.943	0.935	0.926	0.917	0.909
2	1.970	1.942	1.913	1.886	1.859	1.833	1.808	1.783	1.759	1.736
3	2.941	2.884	2.829	2.775	2.723	2.673	2.624	2.577	2.531	2.487
4	3.902	3.808	3.717	3.630	3.546	3.465	3.387	3.312	3.240	3.170
5	4.853	4.713	4.580	4.452	4.329	4.212	4.100	3.993	3.890	3.791
6	5.795	5.601	5.417	5.242	5.076	4.917	4.767	4.623	4.486	4.355
7	6.728	6.472	6.230	6.002	5.786	5.582	5.389	5.206	5.033	4.868
8	7.652	7.325	7.020	6.733	6.463	6.210	5.971	5.747	5.535	5.335
9	8.566	8.162	7.786	7.435	7.108	6.802	6.515	6.247	5.995	5.759
10	9.471	8.983	8.530	8.111	7.722	7.360	7.024	6.710	6.418	6.145
11	10.368	9.787	9.253	8.760	8.306	7.887	7.499	7.139	6.805	6.495
12	11.255	10.575	9.954	9.385	8.863	8.384	7.943	7.536	7.161	6.814
13	12.134	11.348	10.635	9.986	9.394	8.853	8.358	7.904	7.487	7.103
14	13.004	12.106	11.296	10.563	9.899	9.295	8.745	8.244	7.786	7.367
15	13.865	12.849	11.938	11.118	10.380	9.712	9.108	8.559	8.061	7.606
16	14.718	13.578	12.561	11.652	10.838	10.106	9.447	8.851	8.313	7.824
17	15.562	14.292	13.166	12.166	11.274	10.477	9.763	9.122	8.544	8.022
18	16.398	14.992	13.754	12.659	11.690	10.828	10.059	9.372	8.756	8.201
19	17.226	15.679	14.324	13.134	12.085	11.158	10.336	9.604	8.950	8.365
20	18.046	16.351	14.878	13.590	12.462	11.470	10.594	9.818	9.129	8.514

Periods					Interest rates (r)					
(n)	11%	12%	13%	14%	15%	16%	17%	18%	19%	20%
1	0.901	0.893	0.885	0.877	0.870	0.862	0.855	0.847	0.840	0.833
2	1.713	1.690	1.668	1.647	1.626	1.605	1.585	1.566	1.547	1.528
3	2.444	2.402	2.361	2.322	2.283	2.246	2.210	2.174	2.140	2.106
4	3.102	3.037	2.974	2.914	2.855	2.798	2.743	2.690	2.639	2.589
5	3.696	3.605	3.517	3.433	3.352	3.274	3.199	3.127	3.058	2.991
6	4.231	4.111	3.998	3.889	3.784	3.685	3.589	3.498	3.410	3.326
7	4.712	4.564	4.423	4.288	4.160	4.039	3.922	3.812	3.706	3.605
8	5.146	4.968	4.799	4.639	4.487	4.344	4.207	4.078	3.954	3.837
9	5.537	5.328	5.132	4.946	4.772	4.607	4.451	4.303	4.163	4.031
10	5.889	5.650	5.426	5.216	5.019	4.833	4.659	4.494	4.339	4.192
11	6.207	5.938	5.687	5.453	5.234	5.029	4.836	4.656	4.486	4.327
12	6.492	6.194	5.918	5.660	5.421	5.197	4.988	4.793	4.611	4.439
13	6.750	6.424	6.122	5.842	5.583	5.342	5.118	4.910	4.715	4.533
14	6.982	6.628	6.302	6.002	5.724	5.468	5.229	5.008	4.802	4.611
15	7.191	6.811	6.462	6.142	5.847	5.575	5.324	5.092	4.876	4.675
16	7.379	6.974	6.604	6.265	5.954	5.668	5.405	5.162	4.938	4.730
17	7.549	7.120	6.729	6.373	6.047	5.749	5.475	5.222	4.990	4.775
18	7.702	7.250	6.840	6.467	6.128	5.818	5.534	5.273	5.033	4.812
19	7.839	7.366	6.938	6.550	6.198	5.877	5.584	5.316	5.070	4.843
20	7.963	7.469	7.025	6.623	6.259	5.929	5.628	5.353	5.101	4.870

Probability

$A \cup B$ = A **or** B. $A \cap B$ = A **and** B (overlap). P(B/A) = probability of B, **given** A.

Rules of addition

If A and B are *mutually exclusive*: $P(A \cup B) = P(A) + P(B)$
If A and B are **not** mutually exclusive: $P(A \cup B) = P(A) + P(B) - P(A \cap B)$

Rules of multiplication

If A and B are *independent*: $P(A \cap B) = P(A) * P(B)$
If A and B are **not** independent: $P(A \cap B) = P(A) * P(B/A)$

E(X) = expected value = probability * payoff

Quadratic equations

If $aX^2 + bX + c = 0$ is the general quadratic equation, then the two solutions (roots) are given by

$$X = \frac{-b \pm \sqrt{b^2 - 4ac}}{2a}$$

Descriptive statistics

Arithmetic mean

$$\bar{x} = \frac{\sum x}{n} \text{ or } \bar{x} = \frac{\sum fx}{\sum f}$$

Standard deviation

$$\sqrt{\frac{\sum (x - \bar{x})^2}{n}}$$

$$SD = \sqrt{\frac{\sum fx^2}{\sum f} - \bar{x}^2} \text{ (frequencydistribution)}$$

Index numbers

Price relative = 100 * P_1 / P_0

Quantity relative = 100 * Q_1 / Q_0

Price: $\dfrac{\sum W \times P_1 / P_0}{\sum W} \times 100$ where W denotes weights

Quantity: $\dfrac{\sum W \times Q_1 / Q_0}{\sum W} \times 100$ where W denotes weights

Time series

Additive model: Series = Trend + Seasonal + Random

Multiplicative model: Series = Trend * Seasonal * Random

Linear regression and correlation

The linear regression equation of Y on X is given by:

$Y = a + bX$ *or*

$Y - \overline{Y} = b(X - \overline{X})$, where

$$b = \frac{\text{Covariance}(XY)}{\text{Variance}(X)} = \frac{n\sum XY - (\sum X)(\sum Y)}{n\sum X^2 - (\sum X)^2}$$

and $a = \overline{Y} - b\overline{X}$,

or solve $\quad \sum Y = na + b\sum X$

$\qquad\qquad \sum XY = a\sum X + b\sum X^2$

Coefficient of correlation (r)

$$r = \frac{\text{Covariance}(XY)}{\sqrt{\text{VAR}(X).\text{VAR}(Y)}}$$

$$= \frac{n\sum XY - (\sum X)(\sum Y)}{\sqrt{[n\sum X^2 - (\sum X)^2][n\sum Y^2 - (\sum Y)^2]}}$$

$$R(\text{rank}) = 1 - \left[\frac{6\sum d^2}{n(n^2 - 1)}\right]$$

Financial mathematics

Compound Interest (Values and Sums)

Future Value of S_1 of a sum X, invested for n periods, compounded at r% interest:

$$S = X[1 + r]^n$$

Annuity

Present value of an annuity of £1 per annum receivable or payable, for n years, commencing in one year, discounted at r% per annum:

$$PV_s = \frac{1}{r}\left[1 - \frac{1}{[1+r]^n}\right]$$

Perpetuity

Present value of £1 per annum, payable or receivable in perpetuity, commencing in one year discounted at r% per annum

$$PV = \frac{1}{r}$$

Objective test questions and answers

1   Which of the following statements about standards is/are true?

    I   Can be prepared for all functions, even where output cannot be measured
    II   Must be expressed in money terms
    III   Aids control by setting financial targets or limits for a forthcoming period
    IV   Should be revised every time prices or levels of efficiency change

    A None of the above   B All of the above   C III and IV   D I, II and IV

(2 marks)

2   JPM has recorded the following data in budget working papers.

Activity	Overhead cost
Labour hours	£
22,000	108,740
24,000	115,080
28,000	127,760
36,000	153,120

In control period 11, 30,600 labour hours were actually worked and the actual overhead cost was £154,952.

What is the total overhead expenditure variance?

    A £18,950 (A)   B £57,950 (A)   C £24,800 (A)   D £136,002 (A)

(2 marks)

The following information relates to questions 3 and 4.

The standard cost and selling price structure for the single product that is made by CD is as follows.

	£ per unit
Selling price	82
Variable cost	(47)
Fixed production overhead	(29)
	6

The budgeted level of production and sales is 3,200 units per month.

Extract from the actual results for March

Fixed production overhead volume variance	£8,700 favourable
Fixed production overhead expenditure variance	£2,200 adverse
Inventory levels reduced by 200 units during the period.	

3   What was the actual expenditure on fixed production overhead during March?

    A £86,300   B £90,600   C £92,800   D £95,000

(2 marks)

4   What was the actual sales volume during March?

    A 2,900 units   B 3,300 units   C 3,500 units   D 3,700 units

(2 marks)

5   What is budgetary slack?

     A   The difference between the costs built into the budget and the costs actually incurred.
     B   The difference between the minimum necessary costs and the costs actually incurred.
     C   The sum of the minimum necessary costs and the costs built into the budget.
     D   The difference between the flexible budget and the costs actually incurred.

     (2 marks)

6   Sales of product D during 20X0 (control periods 1 to 13) were noted and the following totals calculated.

     $\Sigma X = 91$ $\Sigma Y = 1{,}120$ $\Sigma XY = 9{,}247$ $\Sigma X^2 = 819$

     There is a high correlation between time and volume of sales. Using a suitable regression line, what is the predicted sales level of product D in control period 4 of 20X1, when a seasonal variation of −13 is relevant?

     A   552   B   158   C   150   D   176

7   At the beginning of May 20X3, LB held an inventory of 1,680 units of product C. On 30 April 20X4 the inventory level was 1,120 units. The standard cost of product C is as follows.

	£
Material (15 kgs × £6)	90
Labour (4 hrs × £11)	44
Variable overhead (4 hrs × £20)	80
Fixed overhead (4 hrs × £32)	128
	342

     The profit reported in the management accounts for the twelve months ended 30 April 20X4 was £1,219,712. If LB used marginal costing, what profit would have been reported for the period?

     A   £1,148,032
     B   £1,219,712
     C   £1,291,392
     D   It cannot be determined from the information provided   (2 marks)

8   Which of the following statements about throughput accounting and the theory of constraints (TOC) is/are true?

     1   In TOC, a binding constraint is an activity which has a higher capacity than preceding or subsequent activities, thereby limiting throughput.

     2   A buffer stock is permissible within TOC.

     3   In TOC, throughput contribution = sales revenue − labour cost

     4   In throughput accounting, profitability is determined by the rate at which money is earned.

     A   All of the above
     B   2 and 3
     C   3 only
     D   2 and 4   (2 marks)

9   Y operates a system of backflush costing and has recorded the following transactions for control period 3.

Purchase of raw materials	£54,340
Conversion costs incurred	£67,210
Finished goods produced	286 units
Sales	270 units

There were no opening inventories of raw materials, WIP or finished goods. No variances arose during control period 3.

Assuming that the trigger point for recording costs is when goods are completed, which of the following is the correct double entry to record the standard cost of goods sold

A	DEBIT	Finished goods inventory	£114,750	
	CREDIT	Cost of sales		£114,750
B	DEBIT	Cost of sales	£121,550	
	CREDIT	Finished goods inventory		£121,550
C	DEBIT	Finished goods inventory	£67,210	
	CREDIT	Conversion costs		£67,210
D	DEBIT	Cost of sales	£114,750	
	CREDIT	Finished goods inventory		£114,750

(2 marks)

10 Division J of NZ produced the following results in the last financial year.

	£'000
Net profit	720
Capital employed: non-current assets	3,000
Capital employed: net current assets	200

For performance appraisal purposes, all divisional assets are valued at original cost. The division is considering a project which will increase annual net profit by £50,000 but will require average inventory levels to increase by £60,000 and non-current assets to increase by £200,000. NZ imposes a 16% capital charge on its divisions.

Given these circumstances, will the appraisal criteria return on investment (ROI) and residual income (RI) motivate division J management to accept the project?

	ROI	RI
A	Yes	Yes
B	Yes	No
C	No	No
D	No	Yes

(2 marks)

11 A company manufactures a single product and has produced the following flexed budget for the year.

	Level of activity		
	70%	80%	90%
	$	$	$
Direct materials	17,780	20,320	22,860
Direct labour	44,800	51,200	57,600
Production overhead	30,500	32,000	33,500
Administration overhead	17,000	17,000	17,000
Total cost	110,080	120,520	130,960

Calculate the total budget cost allowance at 45% activity.

(3 marks)

12   The following data relates to the Columba group, a company with several divisions. Division D produces a single product which it sells to Division R and also to organisations outside the Columba group.

	Division D sales to Division R $	Division D external sales $
Sales revenue at £70 per unit		700,000
Sales revenue at £60 per unit	300,000	
Variable costs at £36 per unit	180,000	360,000
Contribution	120,000	340,000
Fixed costs	100,000	240,000
Profit	20,000	100,000

The Columba group profit is $550,000

A supplier offers to supply 3,000 units at $50 each to Division R.

Divisional managers of Columba are given freedom of choice for selling and buying decisions, and their performance is judged solely according to divisional profitability.

Calculate the profit for Division D and for Columba if Division D does not match the lower price offered by the external supplier and cannot increase its external sales, and Division R chooses to purchase from the external supplier.   (4 marks)

The following information relates to questions 13 and 14

Northfields makes a product in a single process. The following data is available for the latest period.

Opening WIP: 1,200 units Valued as follows:	£	Closing WIP: 600 units Degree of completion:	%
Material	14,400	Material	100
Labour	7,200	Labour	50
Overhead	2,400	Overhead	30

Units added and costs incurred during the period:

Material: 3,000 units	£36,000
Labour:	£20,100
Overhead:	£8,940
Losses:	nil

Northfields uses the weighted average method of stock valuation.

13   Calculate the value of the units transferred to finished goods.   (2 marks)

14   Calculate the value of the closing work in progress.   (4 marks)

The following information relates to questions 15 and 16

A firm of financial consultants offers short revision courses on taxation and auditing for professional exams. The firm has budgeted annual overheads totalling £152,625. Until recently the firm had applied overheads on a volume basis, based on the number of course days offered. The firm has no variable costs and the only direct costs are the consultants' own time which they divide equally between the two courses. The firm is considering the possibility of adopting an ABC system and has identified the overhead costs as shown below.

	£
Centre hire	62,500
Enquiries administration	27,125
Brochures	63,000

The following information relates to the past year and is expected to remain the same for the coming year.

Course	No of courses sold	Duration of course	No of enquiries per course	No of brochures printed per course
Auditing	50	2 days	175	300
Taxation	30	3 days	70	200

All courses run with a maximum number of students (30), as it is deemed that beyond this number the learning experience is severely diminished, and the same centre is used for all courses at a standard daily rate. The firm has the human resources to run only one course at any one time.

15   Calculate the overhead cost per course for both auditing and taxation using traditional volume based absorption costing.   (2 marks)

16   Calculate the overhead cost per course for both auditing and taxation using Activity Based Costing.   (3 marks)

The following information relates to questions 17 and 18

Product B requires 4.5 kg of material per unit. The standard price of the material is €6 per kg. The budgeted production for last month was 750 units. Actual results were as follows.

Material used	2,250 kg
Production	780 units
Material cost	€14,175

Due to worldwide increases in the price of the material used it was realised, after the month had ended, that a more realistic material standard price would have been €6.50 per kg.

17   (a)   Explain what is meant by a planning variance.   (2 marks)

        (b)   Calculate planning and operational variances for material costs for the month.   (3 marks)

18   State three possible causes of the operational usage variance you have calculated   (3 marks)

The following information relates to questions 19 and 20

The master budget of PQ reveals the following information,

Balance sheet extracts

	£'000
Current assets (including inventory 1,950)	3,470
Current liabilities	1,790

Budgeted invoice statement extracts

	£'000
Revenue	7,550
Profit from operations	1,240
Return on capital employed	24%

19   Calculate the total asset turnover ratio.   (2 marks)

20   Calculate the quick or acid test ratio to assess PQ's liquidity.   (2 marks)

1   **The correct answer is A.**

I   The use of standards is limited to situations where repetitive actions are performed and output can be measured.

II   Standards need not be expressed in monetary terms.

III   Standards achieve control by comparison of actual results against a predetermined target.

IV   The most suitable approach is probably to revise standards whenever changes of a permanent and reasonably long-term nature occur.

2   **The correct answer is A.**

Determine fixed cost using high-low method

	Hrs	£
Highest activity level	36,000	153,120
Lowest activity level	22,000	108,740
Difference	14,000	44,380

∴ Variable cost per hour   = £44,380/14,000
    = £3.17

∴ Fixed cost (substituting in lowest activity level)

        = £(108,740 − (22,000 × £3.17)
        = £39,000

	£	£
Expenditure should have been:		
Fixed	39,000	
Variable (30,600 × £3.17)	97,002	
		136,002
but was		154,952
Variance		18,950 (A)

If you selected option B, you forgot to include the budgeted fixed overhead.

If you selected option C, you performed a pro-rata calculation on the budgeted cost for 36,000 hours to determine the budgeted cost at actual activity level.

Option D is what expenditure should have been.

3   **The correct answer is D.**

	£
Budgeted fixed overhead expenditure (3,200 units × £29)	92,800
Fixed production overhead expenditure variance	2,200 (A)
Actual fixed production overhead expenditure	95,000

If you selected option A, you adjusted the budgeted overhead unnecessarily for the fixed overhead volume variance.

If you selected option B, you had the right idea about adjusting the budgeted overhead for the expenditure variance, but you should have added the variance rather than subtracting it.

If you selected option C, you chose the budgeted fixed overhead expenditure for the month.

4   **The correct answer is D.**

	Units
Budgeted production	3,200
Volume variance in units (£8,700 ÷ £29)	300 (F)
Actual production for March	3,500
Reduction in inventory volume	200
Actual sales for March	3,700

If you selected option A, you subtracted the volume variance in units from the budgeted production. However the volume variance is favourable and so the actual production must be higher than budgeted.

If you selected option B, you subtracted the inventory reduction from the actual production volume. However if inventories reduce, sales volume must be higher than production volume.

Option C is the actual production for March. Since the inventory volume altered, sales must be different from the production volume.

5   **The correct answer is B.**

6   **The correct answer is C.**

During 20X0, there are 13 control periods and so n = 13. The regression line is Y = a + bX.

$$b = \frac{n\Sigma XY - \Sigma X\Sigma Y}{n\Sigma X^2 - (\Sigma X)^2}$$

$$= \frac{(13 \times 9,247) - (91 \times 1,120)}{(13 \times 819) - (91)^2}$$

$$= 7.731$$

$$a = \frac{\Sigma Y}{n} - \frac{b\Sigma X}{n}$$

$$= \frac{1,120}{13} - \frac{(7.731 \times 91)}{13}$$

$$= 32.037$$

Regression line is Y = 32.037 + 7.731X

Control period 4 of 20X1, X = 17

∴ Y = 32.037 + (7.731 × 17) = 163 units

Adjusting by the seasonal variation of –13, predicted sales = 163 – 13 = 150 units

If you chose option A, you mixed up your 'a' and 'b' values and forgot the seasonal adjustment.

If you chose option B, you used X = 18.

If you chose option D, you added the seasonal variation instead of deducting it.

7   **The correct answer is C.**

Inventory levels have fallen so marginal costing reports the higher profit.

	£
Absorption costing profit	1,219,712
+ fixed overhead included in inventory level change	
((1,680 – 1,120) × £128)	71,680
Marginal costing profit	1,291,392

If you chose option A, you deducted the fixed overhead included in the inventory level change. If inventory levels decrease, absorption costing will report the lower profit because as well as the fixed overhead absorbed during the period, fixed overhead which had been carried forward in opening inventory is released and included in cost of sales.

Option B is the absorption costing profit. The marginal costing profit must be different, however, because there has been a change in inventory levels.

8   **The correct answer is D.**

Statement 1 is incorrect because a binding constraint is an activity which has a lower capacity than preceding or subsequent activities

Statement 3 is incorrect because throughput contribution = sales revenue – material cost

9   **The correct answer is D.**

Standard cost per unit = £(54,340 + 67,210)/286 units = £425

If you chose option A you got the double entry the wrong way round. If you chose option B you simply totalled the costs incurred. Option C ignores the material costs.

10   **The correct answer is D.**

Current ROI = (720/3,200) × 100% = 22.5%
New ROI = ((720 + 50)/(3,200 + 260)) × 100% = 22.25%
New ROI is lower and so will not motivate management to accept the project.

Current RI in £'000 = 720 – (0.16 × 3,200) = 208
New RI in £'000 = (720 + 50) – (0.16 × (3,200 + 260)) = 216.4
New RI is higher and so will motivate management to accept the project.

11   **The correct answer is $83,980**

Variable costs

	$ per 1%	$
Direct materials	254	11,430
Direct labour	640	28,800
Production overhead	150 (W)	6,750
		46,980

Fixed costs

	$	
Production overhead	20,000 (W)	
Administration overhead	17,000	
		37,000
		83,980

Working

Production overhead is a semi-variable cost.

Range of activity = 90% – 70% = 20%

Range of cost = $(33,500 – 30,500) = $3,000

Variable cost per 1% change in activity = $3,000/20 = $150

Fixed cost = $33,500 – (90 × $150) = $20,000

12 **The correct answer is profit for Division D = $48,000; profit for Columbia Group = $508,000**

Division R will buy the 3,000 units externally at a price of $50 per unit, leaving it with only 2,000 units to buy from Division D at $60 per unit.

Profits of Division D

	$'000
Contribution from external sales	340
Contribution from sales to Division R	48
	388
Fixed costs	340
Profit	48

The group as a whole will be paying $(50 − 36) = $14 per unit extra for each unit that Division R purchases externally, thus reducing Columba's profits by 3,000 × $14 = $42,000.

Columba's profit will therefore reduce to $550,000 − $42,000 = $508,000.

13 **The correct answer is £79,200**

Equivalent units

	Total units	Materials		Labour		Overhead	
Finished output*	3,600	3,600		3,600		3,600	
Closing WIP	600	(100%)	600	(50%)	300	(30%)	180
	4,200		4,200		3,900		3,780

* 3,000 units input + opening WIP 1,200 units − closing WIP 600 units

Costs per equivalent unit

	Materials £	Labour £	Overhead £	Total
Opening stock	14,400	7,200	2,400	
Added during period	36,000	20,100	8,940	
Total cost	50,400	27,300	11,340	
Equivalent units	4,200	3,900	3,780	
Cost per equivalent unit	£12	£7	£3	£22

Value of units transferred to finished goods = 3,600 × £22
= £79,200

14 **The correct answer is £9,840**

Value of closing work in progress:

		£
Materials	600 equivalent units × £12	7,200
Labour	300 equivalent units × £7	2,100
Overhead	180 equivalent units × £3	540
		9,840

15 **The correct answer is auditing £1,606.58 per course; taxation £2,409.87 per course.**

	Auditing	Taxation	Total
Number of courses sold	50	30	
Duration of course (days)	2	3	
Number of course days	100	90	190

Overhead cost per course day $= \dfrac{£152,625}{190} = £803.29$

Overhead cost per course

Auditing   £803.29 × 2 days = £1,606.58
Taxation   £803.29 × 3 days = £2,409.87

16   **The correct answer is auditing £1,995.40 per course; taxation £1,761.85 per course.**

Centre hire cost per course day = $\dfrac{£62,500}{190\,*}$ = £328.95

* See working in question 15.

Enquiries administration cost per enquiry = $\dfrac{£27,125}{(50 \times 175) + (30 \times 70)}$ = £2.50

Brochure cost per brochure printed = $\dfrac{£63,000}{(50 \times 300) + (30 \times 200)}$ = £3

Overhead costs per course using ABC

		Auditing £ per course		Taxation £ per course
Centre hire at £328.95 per day	(× 2)	657.90	(× 3)	986.85
Enquiries admin at £2.50 per enquiry	(× 175)	437.50	(× 70)	175.00
Brochures at £3 per brochure printed	(× 300)	900.00	(× 200)	600.00
		1,995.40		1,761.85

17   (a)   A planning variance calculates the difference in standard cost arising due to changes from the original standard that are not controllable by operational managers because they are caused by planning errors. In the scenario described a planning variance has arisen because of the worldwide increase in material prices. This is outside the control of operational managers and should therefore be analysed separately from variance related to operational performance.

(b)   **Planning variance**

	€
Revised standard cost (780 × 4.5kg × €6.50)	22,815
Original standard cost (780 × 4.5kg × €6.00)	21,060
	1,755 (A)

Operational price variance

	€
Actual cost of actual kg used	14,175
Revised standard cost of actual kg (2,250 × €6.50)	14,625
	450 (F)

Operational usage variance

780 units should have used (× 4.5 kg)	3,510 kg
but did use	2,250 kg
Operational usage variance in kg	1,260 kg (F)
× revised standard price per kg	× €6.50
Operational usage variance in €	€8,190 (F)

18   Three possible courses of a favourable operational usage variance are as follows.

(a)   The material was of a higher quality than in the standard therefore wastage was lower than standard.

(b)   The original standard usage per unit was set too low.

(c)   The direct labour were more highly skilled than standard and therefore they used the material more efficiently than standard.

19   **The correct answer is 1.5 times**

Profit margin   = (1,240/7,550) × 100% = 16.4%

ROCE   = profit margin × asset turnover

∴ Asset turnover   = ROCE/profit margin
                       = 24.0/16.4
                       = 1.5 times

20   **The correct answer is 0.8**

Acid test ratio   = (3,470 − 1,950)/1,790
                   = 1,520/1,790
                   = 0.8

BPP
PROFESSIONAL EDUCATION

Exam question bank

1 Marginal and absorption costing compared

36 mins

Learning outcome A(i)

TLF manufactures a single product, the Claud. The following figures relate to the Claud for a one-year period.

	50%	100%
Activity level		
Sales and production (units)	400	800
	€	€
Sales	8,000	16,000
Production costs: variable	3,200	6,400
fixed	1,600	1,600
Sales and distribution costs:		
variable	1,600	3,200
fixed	2,400	2,400

The normal level of activity for the year is 800 units. Fixed costs are incurred evenly throughout the year, and actual fixed costs are the same as budgeted.

There were no inventories of Claud at the beginning of the year.

In the first quarter, 220 units were produced and 160 units sold.

REQUIREMENTS

(a) Calculate the fixed production costs absorbed by Clauds in the first quarter if absorption costing is used. **3 Marks**

(b) Calculate the under/over recovery of overheads during the quarter. **3 Marks**

(c) Calculate the profit using absorption costing. **6 Marks**

(d) Calculate the profit using marginal costing. **5 Marks**

(e) Explain why there is a difference between the answers to (c) and (d). **3 Marks**

(Total = 20 Marks)

2 Production overhead control account

Learning outcome A(iii)

Briefly outline the differences between the operation of a production overhead control account in a marginal costing accounting system compared with an absorption costing system. **(5 Marks)**

3 Work in progress control account

Learning outcome A(iii)

Briefly describe the accounting entries that would be made in a work in progress control account to record the costs of production in an absorption costing system within a jobbing environment. **(5 Marks)**

4 Fertiliser

36 mins

Learning outcome A(iii)

XYZ is a chemical processing company which uses two processes to convert three raw materials W, X and Y into a final product Z which is used as a fertiliser in the farming industry. In the second process a by-product is produced, which can be sold without additional processing for £2 per kg.

At 30 September 20X3 there was work in progress of 8,400 kg in the second process, the cost of which was made up as follows.

	£
Process 1	8,720
Materials	2,000
Labour	3,600
Overhead	7,200
	21,520

The following data relates to October 20X3.

(a) Direct wages incurred

Process 1	£17,160
Process 2	£8,600

(b) Direct materials issued to production

Process 1	10,500 kg of W costing	£4,960
	7,200 kg of X costing	£14,700
Process 2	4,050 kg of Y costing	£16,562

(c) Completed output from the two processes

Process 1	13,100 kg
Process 2: Product Z	20,545 kg
By-product B	481 kg

(d) Closing work in progress (100% complete as to materials but only 50% complete as to conversion cost)

Process 1	2,000 kg
Process 2	1,500 kg

(e) Expected normal losses (caused by evaporation and occurring at the end of processing)

Process 1	15% of throughput
Process 2	8% of throughput

Note. Throughput equals opening work in progress plus materials introduced less closing work in progress. The losses have no resale value.

(f) Production overhead is absorbed using the following absorption rates

Process 1	150% of direct labour cost
Process 2	200% of direct labour cost

REQUIREMENT

Prepare the accounts for each of the two processes for the month of October 20X3.   **(Total Marks = 20)**

5 Losses in process costing

Learning outcome A(iii)

In a process environment it is common for the output from a process to be less than the process input. In accounting for such process losses it is usual to distinguish between normal process losses and abnormal process losses or gains.

Explain briefly why such a distinction is made and how process losses are valued and accounted for in a process costing system.   **(5 Marks)**

6 The concept of equivalent units
Learning outcome A(iii)

Explain what is meant by the concept of equivalent units. Use simple figures to demonstrate the application of the concept in a process environment. **(5 Marks)**

7 Just in time systems
Learning outcome A(iii)

State FIVE financial benefits of a Just in Time (JIT) system. **(5 Marks)**

8 Costs of quality
Learning outcome A(iii)

A consequence of the introduction of just-in-time manufacturing methods is usually increased quality costs. Briefly describe the four categories of quality costs. **(5 Marks)**

9 Throughput accounting
Learning outcome A(iii)

Throughput accounting has been described as 'super variable costing'.

Explain why throughput accounting is sometimes described in this way and identify briefly the differences between throughput accounting and marginal or variable cost accounting. **(5 Marks)**

10 WAQ
Learning outcome A(iv)

WAQ produces a single product, X, which passes through three different processes, A, B and C. The throughput per hour of the three processes is 12, 10 and 15 units of X respectively. The company works an 8-hour day, 6 days a week, 48 weeks a year. The selling price of X is £150 per unit and its material cost is £30 per unit. Conversion costs are planned to be £24,000 per week.

REQUIREMENTS

(a) Determine the throughput accounting (TA) ratio per day.

(b) Calculate how much the company could spend on equipment to improve the throughput of process B if it wished to recover its costs in the following time periods.

2 years
12 weeks

(c) Calculate the revised TA ratio if this money is spent.

11 TXL
Learning outcome A(iii)

TXL manufactures a single product. Standard costs for materials and conversion costs are £40 and £30 per unit respectively. The company uses a backflush accounting system with two trigger points: raw materials purchased and goods transferred to finished goods store. At the beginning of March there was no opening inventory of raw materials or WIP and at the end of the month there was no WIP.

Other data for the month

Number of completed production units	15,000
Number of products sold	14,000
Raw materials purchased	£630,000
Conversion costs incurred	£470,000

REQUIREMENTS

Prepare summary journal entries for March assuming that there were no material cost variances and without writing off under or over absorbed conversion costs.

Explain how you would modify the accounting system if the company switched to a total JIT system. Prepare specimen journal entries using the data above and the new trigger point(s). Write off the under- or over-absorbed conversion costs.

12 KH

36 mins

Learning outcome A(vi)

KH is a fairly new company at the leading edge of paint-spraying technology. Presently it has three customers - G, F and R - whose bare metal products are finished by KH.

G's products require 7 coats of paint, F's 6 coats and R's 5 coats. Because the products are different shapes and sizes different quantities of paint are needed.

Customer	Litres
G	7.6
F	8.6
R	6.3

Paint is delivered in batches of various sizes, depending upon the finish required.

Production details for each product are budgeted as follows for the coming month.

	G	F	R
Units sprayed	5,400	4,360	3,600
Batches of paint required	27	20	40
Machine attendant time	30 mins	45 mins	75 mins
Cost of paint per unit	£15.20	£11.18	£18.90

Machine attendants are paid £5.30 per hour.

Overhead costs are absorbed on a labour hour basis. The following overheads are anticipated in the coming month.

	£
Paint stirring and quality control	24,081
Electricity	104,700
Filling of spraying machines	64,914

REQUIREMENTS

(a) Calculate the unit cost to KH of each sprayed product for the coming month showing each cost element separately.

(b) Given the following additional information calculate the unit cost to KH on an activity based costing approach.

Activity	Cost driver
Paint stirring and quality control	Batches of paint
Electricity	Coats of paint
Filling of spraying machines	Litres of paint

(c)   Using the costs calculated for parts (a) and (b) as illustration describe the role in activity based costing of cost drivers.   **(Total Marks = 20)**

13 ABC v traditional absorption costing   Learning outcome A(vi)

Explain briefly FOUR situations where a product unit cost calculated using an ABC system is likely to differ significantly from the unit cost for the same product calculated using a traditional absorption costing system based on direct labour hours.   **(5 Marks)**

14 ABC in the modern environment   Learning outcome A(vi)

Explain briefly the reasons why ABC is particularly suitable in a modern business environment and any situations where it is not appropriate.   **(5 Marks)**

15 Setting standard costs   Learning outcome B(i)

Critics of standard costing argue that it is of limited usefulness for cost control in an inflationary environment.

Comment on this statement and explain whether or not you agree with it.   **(5 Marks)**

16 The behavioural implications of setting standard costs
Learning outcome: B(ii)

Explain how the type of performance standard used when setting standard costs can have a behavioural impact on the managers who are responsible for achieving the standards.   **(5 Marks)**

17 DS   36 mins
Learning outcome B(ii)

DS manufactures a brand of tennis racket, the W, and a brand of squash racket, the B. The budget for October was as follows.

		W	B
Production (units)		4,000	1,500
Direct materials:	wood (£0.30 per metre)	7 metres	5 metres
	gut (£1.50 per metre)	6 metres	4 metres
Other materials		£0.20	£0.15
Direct labour (£3 per hour)		30 mins	20 mins
Overheads			
Variable:			£
power			1,500
maintenance			7,500
			9,000
Fixed:			
supervision			8,000
heating and lighting			1,200
rent			4,800
depreciation			7,000
			21,000

Variable overheads are assumed to vary with standard hours produced.

Actual results for October were as follows.

| Production: | W | 3,700 units |
| | B | 1,890 units |

Direct materials, bought and used:		£
wood	37,100 metres	11,000
gut	29,200 metres	44,100
other materials		1,000
Direct labour	2,200 hours	6,850
Power		1,800
Maintenance		6,900
Supervision		7,940
Heating and lighting		1,320
Rent		4,800
Depreciation		7,000
		92,710

REQUIREMENT

Calculate the cost variances for October. Assume that a standard absorption costing system is in operation. **(Total Marks = 20)**

18 Reconciliation

Learning outcome B(iii)

Incorporate the cost variances calculated in question 17 above into an operating statement, reconciling the standard and actual cost of production for the month. **5 Marks**

19 HP

36 mins

Learning outcome B(ii)

HP manufactures a special floor tile which measures ½m × ¼m × 0.01m. The tiles are manufactured in a process which requires the following standard mix.

Material	Quantity	Price	Amount
	kg	£	£
A	40	1.50	60
B	30	1.20	36
C	10	1.40	14
D	20	0.50	10
			120

Each mix should produce 100 square metres of floor tiles of 0.01m thickness. During April, the actual output was 46,400 tiles from the following input.

Material	Quantity	Price	Amount
	kg	£	£
A	2,200	1.60	3,520
B	2,000	1.10	2,200
C	500	1.50	750
D	1,400	0.50	700
			7,170

REQUIREMENT

Calculate the following variances for the month of April.

(a)   Cost variance for each material
(b)   Price variance for each material
(c)   Mix variance using the individual valuation basis
(d)   Yield variance in total   **(Total Marks = 20)**

20 Wimbrush   **36 mins**

Learning outcome B(iv)

The management of Wimbrush feel that standard costing and variance analysis have little to offer in the reporting of some of the activities of their firm.

'Although we produce a range of fairly standardised products' states the accountant of Wimbrush, 'prices of many of our raw materials are apt to change suddenly and comparison of actual prices with predetermined, and often unrealistic, standard prices is of little use.

For example, consider the experience over the last accounting period of two of our products, Widgets and Splodgets. To produce a Widget we use 5 kg of X and our plans were based on a cost of X of £3 per kg. Due to market movements the actual price changed and if we had purchased efficiently the cost would have been £4.50 per kg.

Production of Widgets was 2,000 units and usage of X amounted to 10,800 kg at a total cost of £51,840.

A Splodget uses raw material Z but again the price of this can change rapidly. It was thought that Z would cost £30 per tonne but in fact we only paid £25 per tonne and if we had purchased correctly the cost would have been less as it was freely available at only £23 per tonne. It usually takes 1.5 tonnes of Z to produce 1 Splodget but our production of 500 Splodgets used only 700 tonnes of Z.

So you can see that with our particular circumstances the traditional approach to variance analysis is of little use and we don't use it for materials although we do use it for reporting on labour and variable overhead costs.'

REQUIREMENTS:

(a)   Analyse the material variances for both Widgets and Splodgets, utilising the following.

    (i)   Traditional variance analysis
    (ii)   An approach which distinguishes between planning and operational variances   **12 Marks**

(b)   Write brief notes which do the following.

    (i)   Explain the approach to variance analysis which distinguishes between planning and operational variances.

    (ii)   Indicate the extent to which this approach is useful for firms in general and for Wimbrush Ltd in particular.   **8 Marks**

                                      (Total Marks = 20)

21 M

M operates a standard absorption costing system in respect of its only product. The standard cost card of this product for the budget year ending 31 December 20X0 is as follows.

	£	£
Selling price		120.00
Direct material A (5 kgs)	12.50	
Direct material B (10 kgs)	40.00	
Direct wages (3 hours)	18.00	
Variable overhead (3 hours)	9.00	
Fixed overhead* (3 hours)	15.00	
		94.50
Profit/unit		25.50

*Fixed overhead is absorbed on the basis of direct labour hours. Budgeted fixed overhead costs are £180,000 for the year. Cost and activity levels are budgeted to be constant each month.

During January 20X0, when budgeted sales and production were 1,000 units, the following actual results were achieved.

	£
Sales (900 units)	118,800
Production costs (1,050 units)	
Direct material A (5,670 kg)	14,742
Direct material B (10,460 kg)	38,179
Direct wages (3,215 hours)	19,933
Variable overhead	10,288
Fixed overhead	15,432

With the benefit of hindsight you now know that direct labour received a pay increase of 3 per cent which was not allowed for in the standard cost. The original standard is to be used for inventory valuation.

You have also confirmed with the production manager that the nature of the production method is such that direct materials A and B are mixed together to produce the final product.

All materials were purchased and used during January.

REQUIREMENTS:

(a) Prepare for the production manager a statement that reconciles the budgeted and actual profits for January 20X0 using the following variances.

    (i)   Sales volume profit
    (ii)   Sales price
    (iii)   Direct material price
    (iv)   Direct material mix using the average valuation basis
    (v)   Direct material yield
    (vi)   Direct labour rate, analysed between planning and operating effects
    (vii)   Direct labour efficiency
    (viii) Variable production overhead expenditure
    (ix)   Variable production overhead efficiency
    (x)   Fixed production overhead expenditure
    (xi)   Fixed production overhead volume

    Variances should be calculated so as to provide useful information to the production manager

(Total Marks = 20)

22 Benchmarking

36 mins

Relevant information with regard to the operation of the sales order department of MM is as follows.

- A team of staff deals with existing customers in respect of problems with orders or with prospective customers enquiring about potential orders.

- The processing of orders requires communication with the production and despatch functions of the company.

- The nature of the business is such that there is some despatching of part orders to customers which helps reduce inventory holding costs and helps customers in their work flow management.

- Sales literature is sent out to existing and prospective customers by means of a monthly mailshot.

The activity matrix below shows the budget for the sales order department.

Activity cost matrix - sales order department

Cost element	Total cost £'000	Customer negotiations £'000	Processing of orders Home £'000	Processing of orders Export £'000	Implementing despatches £'000	Sales literature £'000	General admin £'000
Salaries	500	80	160	100	90	20	50
Stores/supplies	90		16	6	8	60	
IT	70	10	30	20	10		
Sundry costs	80	8	10	6	20	10	26
Total	740	98	216	132	128	90	76
Volume of activity	2,000 customers	3,000 negotiations	5,000 orders	1,200 orders	11,500 despatches		

MM has decided to acquire additional computer software with internet links in order to improve the effectiveness of the sales order department. The cost to the company of this initiative is estimated at £230,000 pa.

If the proposed changes are implemented, there will be cost and volume changes to activities in the sales order department and it is estimated that the following activity cost matrix will result.

Activity cost matrix - sales order department after the proposed changes

Cost element	Total cost £'000	Customer negotiations £'000	Processing of orders Home £'000	Processing of orders Export £'000	Implementing despatches £'000	Sales literature £'000	General admin £'000
Salaries	450	72	144	90	81	18	45
Stores/supplies	54	-	16	6	8	24	-
IT	300	40	120	80	40	20	-
Sundry costs	106	16	11	10	33	10	26
Total	910	128	291	186	162	72	71
Volume of activity	2,600 customers	6,000 negotiations	5,500 orders	2,000 orders	18,750 despatches		

Recent industry average statistics for sales order department activities in businesses of similar size, customer mix and product mix are as follows.

Cost per customer per year	£300
Cost per home order processed	£50
Cost per export order processed	£60
Cost per despatch	£8
Sales literature cost per customer	£35
Average number of orders per customer per year	4.1
Average number of despatches per order	3.3

REQUIREMENT:

Prepare an analysis (both discursive and quantitative/monetary as appropriate) which examines the implications of the IT initiative. The analysis should include a benchmarking exercise on the effectiveness of the sales order department against both its current position and the industry standards provided. You should incorporate comment on additional information likely to improve the relevance of the exercise.

(Total Marks = 20)

Approaching the answer

Look for key words and ask questions of the information given to you. This is illustrated here.

Relevant information with regard to the operation of the sales order department of MM is as follows.

> Is this back-ground or will it have an impact?

- A team of staff deals with existing customers in respect of problems with orders or with prospective customers enquiring about potential orders.

- The processing of orders requires communication with the production and despatch functions of the company.

- The nature of the business is such that there is some despatching of part orders to customers which helps reduce inventory holding costs and helps customers in their work flow management.

- Sales literature is sent out to existing and prospective customers by means of a monthly mailshot.

> Ah! ABC

The activity matrix below shows the budget for the sales order department.

Activity cost matrix - sales order department

> These are the activities

Cost element	Total cost £'000	Customer negotiations £'000	Processing of orders Home £'000	Processing of orders Export £'000	Implementing despatches £'000	Sales literature £'000	General admin £'000
Salaries	500	80	160	100	90	20	50
Stores/supplies	90		16	6	8	60	
IT	70	10	30	20	10		
Sundry costs	80	8	10	6	20	10	26
Total	740	98	216	132	128	90	76
Volume of activity	2,000 customers	3,000 negotiations	5,000 orders	1,200 orders	11,500 despatches		

> These are the cost drivers

MM has decided to acquire additional computer software with internet links in order to improve the effectiveness of the sales order department. The cost to the company of this initiative is estimated at £230,000 pa.

If the proposed changes are implemented, there will be cost and volume changes to activities in the sales order department and it is estimated that the following activity cost matrix will result.

Activity cost matrix - sales order department after the proposed changes

This shows the effect of the software initiative

These two costs are the only ones to fall

Cost element	Total cost £'000	Customer negotiations £'000	Processing of orders Home £'000	Processing of orders Export £'000	Implementing despatches £'000	Sales literature £'000	General admin £'000
Salaries	450	72	144	90	81	18	45
Stores/supplies	54	-	16	6	8	24	-
IT	300	40	120	80	40	20	-
Sundry costs	106	16	11	10	33	10	26
Total	910	128	291	186	162	72	71
Volume of activity	2,600 customers	6,000 negotiations	5,500 orders	2,000 orders	18,750 despatches		

The volume of all cost drivers has increased post IT initiative

Recent industry average statistics for sales order department activities in businesses of similar size, customer mix and product mix are as follows.

Why have we got these statistics?

Cost per customer per year	£300
Cost per home order processed	£50
Cost per export order processed	£60
Cost per despatch	£8
Sales literature cost per customer	£35
Average number of orders per customer per year	4.1
Average number of despatches per order	3.3

REQUIREMENT

This is what the report must look at

Prepare an analysis (both discursive and quantitative/monetary as appropriate) which examines the implications of the IT initiative. The analysis should include a benchmarking exercise on the effectiveness of the sales order department against both its current position and the industry standards provided. You should incorporate comment on additional information likely to improve the relevance of the exercise.

So we compare the position post IT initiative with the current position and industry standards

Don't forget this

(Total Marks = 20)

Strange word to use? Does it mean the point of the exercise?

ANSWER PLAN

Not all the points you notice will necessarily be relevant, and you may also find that you do not have time to mention all the points in your answer. Now you should prioritise your points in a more formal answer plan and then write your answer.

- Calculate indicators for MM – current and post-IT
- Tabulate activity measures for MM – current and post-IT
- Compare indicators/activity measures
- Additional information required and comment on relevance
- Conclusion?

23 Calculating key metrics

36 mins

Learning outcome C(iv)

The following summary information is taken from the draft master budget of WQ for the forthcoming period.

Income statement for the year ended 31 December 20X6

	€'000
Revenue	4,350
Cost of sales	2,880
Gross profit	1,470
Distribution expenses	440
Administration expenses	560
Profit from operations	470

Balance sheet as at 31 December 20X6

	€'000	€'000
ASSETS		
Non-current assets		1,560
Current assets		
Inventory	440	
Receivables	120	
Bank	295	
		855
		2,415
EQUITY AND LIABILITIES		
Capital and reserves		1,725
Non-current liabilities		450
Current liabilities		240
		2,415

Cash budget (extracts)

	Jan – Mar €'000	Apr – Jun €'000	July – Sept €'000	Oct – Dec €'000
Cash receipts	1,120	1,050	1,330	1,090
Cash payments				
Operating expenses	980	1,020	940	900
Purchase of non-current assets		450		
Dividends	120			
Income tax		105		
Total payments	1,100	1,575	940	900
B/f	220	240	(285)	105
Net cash flow	20	(525)	390	190
C/f	240	(285)	105	295

The master budget is to be assessed according to the following key metrics.

(a)	Return on capital employed	23.0%
(b)	Profit margin	10.0%
(c)	Net asset turnover	2.3 times
(d)	Non-current asset turnover	2.5 times
(e)	Inventory turnover	9.0 times
(f)	Current ratio	3.0
(g)	Acid test ratio	0.9
(h)	Maximum overdraft	€180,000

REQUIREMENT

Assess the master budget in terms of these key metrics and prepare notes for the senior management concerning the acceptability of the master budget as a plan for the forthcoming period. Recommend actions that may be considered to rectify any areas where the key metrics are not achieved.

(Total marks = 20)

24 The purposes of budgeting
Learning outcomes C (i)(v)

Two purposes of budgeting could be to establish a system of control and to provide a framework for authorisation.

Explain how there may be a conflict between these two purposes in an effective budgetary planning and control system. **(5 Marks)**

25 PF
Learning outcomes C (ii)

The manager of PF with responsibility for monitoring sales of product XN30 is convinced that the levels of sales is on a rising trend, but that it is seasonal, with more sales at some times of the year than at others. The manager has gathered the following data about sales in recent years. Trend values are shown in brackets.

Sales (thousands of units of product XN30)

Year	Spring	Summer	Autumn	Winter
20X3			250	340
20X4	186 (281)	343 (285)	263 (289)	357 (293)
20X5	203 (297)	358 (302)	278 (305)	380 (307)
20X6	207 (311)	371 (313)	290 (317)	391 (320)
20X7	222	383		

REQUIREMENTS

(a) Show the actual sales level and the trend line on a historigram.
(b) Establish seasonal deviations from the trend.
(c) Estimate what the level of sales might be in the autumn and winter of 20X7.

26 'What if' analysis
Learning outcomes C(i)(vii)

Explain briefly what is meant by 'what if' analysis in the context of budgetary planning and outline any weaknesses in the approach. **(5 Marks)**

27 Calculating projected costs and revenues
Learning outcomes C(ii)(iii)

Describe briefly how historical data may be assessed for its suitability as the basis for forecasting future costs and revenues. **(5 Marks)**

28 Balanced scorecard

Learning outcome C(xii)

For each perspective of the balanced scorecard, suggest ONE key performance indicator that could be monitored by a company that provides training courses to the general public, and explain why each might be a useful indicator.

(5 Marks)

29 Responsibility accounting

Learning outcome C(viii)

Explain the importance of an established system of responsibility accounting in the construction of functional budgets that support the overall master budget.

(5 Marks)

30 Presentation

36 mins
Learning outcomes B(ii)(iii) C(xi)

The following statement has been produced for presentation to the general manager of Department X.

	Month ended 31 October 20X0		
	Original budget	Actual result	Variance
	£	£	£
Sales	600,000	550,000	(50,000)
Direct materials	150,000	130,000	20,000
Direct labour	200,000	189,000	11,000
Production overhead			
Variable with direct labour	50,000	46,000	4,000
Fixed	25,000	29,000	(4,000)
Variable selling overhead	75,000	72,000	3,000
Fixed selling overhead	50,000	46,000	4,000
Total costs	550,000	512,000	38,000
Profit	50,000	38,000	(12,000)
Direct labour hours	50,000	47,500	
Sales and production units	5,000	4,500	

Note. There are no opening and closing inventories.

The general manager says that this type of statement does not provide much relevant information for him. He also thought that the profit for the month would be well up to budget and was surprised to see a large adverse profit variance.

REQUIREMENTS

(a)   Re-draft the above statement in a form which would be more relevant for the general manager.

(7 Marks)

(b)   Calculate all sales, material, labour and overhead variances and reconcile to the statement produced in (a).

(13 Marks)

(Total Marks = 20)

31 Divisional performance

(a)   Compare and contrast the use of residual income and return on investment in divisional performance measurement, stating the advantages and disadvantages of each.

(b)   Division Y of Chardonnay currently has capital employed of £100,000 and earns an annual profit after depreciation of £18,000. The divisional manager is considering an investment of £10,000 in an asset which will have a ten-year life with no residual value and will earn a constant annual profit after depreciation of £1,600. The cost of capital is 15%.

Calculate the following and comment on the results.

(i)   The return on divisional investment, before and after the new investment
(ii)   The divisional residual income before and after the new investment
(iii)   The net present value of the new investment

32 B and C

36 mins

Learning outcomes C(iv)(v)

The following figures for the years ending 31 December 20X4 and 20X3 relate to the B and C divisions of Cordeline.

The return on capital employed (ROCE) figure is the basis for awarding a 20% bonus to the manager of B division (actual ROCE/target ROCE). The below target ROCE for C division has resulted in a zero bonus award to its manager.

	Division			
	B		C	
	20X4	20X3	20X4	20X3
	£'000	£'000	£'000	£'000
Sales	9,850	7,243	4,543	2,065
Profit before interest and taxes (PBIT)	1,336	1,674	924	363
Included in profit calculation:				
Depreciation for year	960	919	1,300	251
Net book value (NBV) of non-current assets*	5,540	6,000	7,700	2,600
Original cost of non-current assets	12,600	12,100	9,500	3,100
Replacement cost of non-current assets	25,000	24,500	9,750	3,350
New investment in non-current assets	500	750	6,400	2,400
Cost of capital	8%	8%	8%	8%
Return on capital employed**	24%	28%	12%	14%
Target return on capital	20%	20%	20%	20%

* Net book value is original cost less accumulated depreciation to date.

** Cordeline consider ROCE for bonus purposes to be PBIT as a % of NBV.

REQUIREMENT

Cordeline's board are meeting to review the company's management performance appraisal and reward system. Prepare a short paper for the board, drawing on the above information, which contains the following.

(a)   An explanation of possible counter-productive behaviour resulting from using the current ROCE calculation for performance appraisal   **(14 Marks)**

(b)   A revised ROCE measure together with justification for your suggestion   **(6 Marks)**

(Total Marks = 20)

33 MPL

36 mins

Learning outcomes C(ix)(xi) D(iii)

MPL is a company specialising in providing consultancy services to the catering industry. The operating statement for period 5 for the IT division is as follows. The division operates as a profit centre.

	Budget	Actual	Variance
Chargeable consultancy hours	2,400	2,500	100
	€	€	€
Central administration costs – fixed	15,000	15,750	750 (A)
Consultants' salaries – fixed	80,000	84,000	4,000 (A)
Casual wages – variable	960	600	360 (F)
Motor and travel costs – fixed	4,400	4,400	-
Telephone – fixed	600	800	200 (A)
Telephone – variable	2,000	2,150	150 (A)
Printing, postage & stationery – variable	2,640	2,590	50 (F)
Depreciation of equipment – fixed	3,200	3,580	380 (A)
Total costs	108,800	113,870	5,070 (A)
Fees charged	180,000	200,000	20,000 (F)
Profit	71,200	86,130	14,930 (F)

While the manager of the IT division is pleased that the actual profit exceeded the budget expectation she is interested to know how this has been achieved. After the budget had been issued to her she had queried the meaning of variable costs and had been told that they were variable in direct proportion to chargeable consultancy hours.

REQUIREMENTS

As the newly appointed management accountant, prepare a report addressed to the board of directors of MPL which:

(a) Explains the present approach to budgeting adopted in MPL and discusses the advantages and disadvantages of involving consultants in the preparation of future budgets; **(8 Marks)**

(b) Critically discusses the format of the operating statement for period 5; **(5 Marks)**

(c) Prepare an alternative statement for the profit centre which distinguishes clearly between controllable profit and attributable profit and which provides a realistic measure of the variances for the period. State any assumptions you make. **(7 Marks)**

(Total Marks = 20)

34 Transfer pricing

36 mins

Learning outcome D(vii)

(a) A company operates two divisions, Able and Baker. Able manufactures two products, X and Y. Product X is sold to external customers for £42 per unit. The only outlet for product Y is Baker.

Baker supplies an external market and can obtain its semi-finished supplies (product Y) from either Able or an external source. Baker currently has the opportunity to purchase product Y from an external supplier for £38 per unit. The capacity of division Able is measured in units of output, irrespective of whether product X, Y or combination of both are being manufactured. The associated product costs are as follows.

	X	Y
Variable costs per unit	32	35
Fixed overheads per unit	5	5
Total unit costs	37	40

REQUIREMENT

Using the above information, provide advice on the determination of an appropriate transfer price for the sale of product Y from division Able to division Baker under the following conditions.

(i)   When division Able has spare capacity and limited external demand for product X

(3 Marks)

(ii)   When division Able is operating at full capacity with unsatisfied external demand for product X

(4 Marks)

(b)   A group has two companies, K, which is operating at just above 50% capacity and L, which is operating at full capacity (7,000 production hours).

L produces two products, X and Y, using the same labour force for each product. For the next year its budgeted capacity involves a commitment to the sale of 3,000 kg of Y, the remainder of its capacity being used on X. Direct costs of these two products are as follows.

	X		Y	
	£ per kg		£ per kg	
Direct materials	18		14	
Direct wages	15	(1 production hour)	10	($^2/_3$ production hour)

The company's overhead is £126,000 per annum relating to X and Y in proportion to their direct wages. At full capacity £70,000 of this overhead is variable. L prices its products with a 60% mark-up on its total costs.

For the coming year, K wishes to buy from L 2,000 kg of product X which it proposes to adapt and sell, as product Z, for £100 per kg. The direct costs of adaptation are £15 per kg. K's total fixed costs will not change, but variable overhead of £2 per kg will be incurred.

REQUIREMENTS

As group management accountant, make the following recommendations.

(i)   The range of transfer prices, if any, at which 2,000 kg of product X should be sold to K

(ii)   The other points that should be borne in mind when making any recommendations about transfer prices in the above circumstances   **(13 Marks)**

(Total Marks = 20)

Exam answer bank

BPP
PROFESSIONAL EDUCATION

1 Marginal and absorption costing compared

(a) $$\frac{\text{Budgeted fixed production costs}}{\text{Budgeted output (normal level of activity)}} = \frac{\text{€1,600}}{800 \text{ units}}$$

Absorption rate = €2 per unit produced.

During the quarter, the fixed production overhead absorbed was 220 units × €2 = £440.

(b)

	€
Actual fixed production overhead	400 (¼ of £1,600)
Absorbed fixed production overhead	440
Over absorption of overhead	40

(c)   **Profit for the quarter, absorption costing**

	€	€
Sales (160 × €20)		3,200
Production costs		
Variable (220 × €8)	1,760	
Fixed (absorbed overhead (220 × €2))	440	
Total (220 × €10)	2,200	
Less closing inventories (60 × €10)	600	
Production cost of sales	1,600	
Adjustment for over-absorbed overhead	40	
Total production costs		1,560
Gross profit		1,640
Less: sales and distribution costs		
variable (160 × €4)	640	
fixed (¹⁄₄ of €2,400)	600	
		1,240
Net profit		400

(d)   **Profit for the quarter, marginal costing**

	€	€
Sales		3,200
Variable production costs	1,760	
Less closing inventories (60 × €8)	480	
Variable production cost of sales	1,280	
Variable sales and distribution costs	640	
Total variable costs of sales		1,920
Total contribution		1,280
Less:		
Fixed production costs incurred	400	
Fixed sales and distribution costs	600	
		1,000
Net profit		280

(e)   The difference in profit is due to the different valuations of closing inventory. In absorption costing, the 60 units of closing inventory include absorbed fixed overheads of €120 (60 × €2) , which are therefore costs carried over to the next quarter and not charged against the profit of the current quarter. In marginal costing, all fixed costs incurred in the period are charged against profit.

	€
Absorption costing profit	400
Fixed production costs carried forward in inventory values	120
Marginal costing profit	280

2 Production overhead control account

Pass marks. Whenever you are asked to discuss the difference between marginal costing and absorption costing, remember that the difference between the two systems lies solely in their **treatment of fixed production overhead**. Absorption costing includes fixed production overhead in the production cost of units whereas marginal costing treats fixed production overhead as a **period cost** and charges the cost in total to the income statement each period.

The production overhead control account is used as a 'collecting place' for production overhead before further analysis is undertaken. Production overheads incurred are debited to the account in both systems.

The differences between the two systems occur in the analysis of the production overhead once it has been collected in the debit side of the account.

Absorption costing system

In an absorption costing system the overhead to be absorbed by the output in the period is calculated using a pre-determined overhead absorption rate. The absorbed overhead is credited out of the overhead control account and debited to the work in progress account.

The remaining balance on the production overhead control account represents the under-/over-absorbed overhead for the period. A credit balance represents an over absorption which is credited to the income statement. A debit balance is an under absorption which is debited to the income statement.

Marginal costing system

In a marginal costing system a distinction is made between fixed and variable overhead in the production overhead control account. The fixed production overhead is credited out of the overhead control account and debited directly to the income statement. The fixed overhead is not absorbed into production costs. The variable production overhead is credited out of the overhead control account and debited to the work in progress account, to be included in the unit cost of production for the period. There will be no remaining balance on the overhead control account because under or over absorption of overheads does not occur in a marginal costing system.

3 Work in progress control account

Pass marks. It is important to relate your answer specifically to a jobbing environment. Don't just produce a general essay on the workings of a work in progress account.

Since production is undertaken to customer requirements there is unlikely to be any finished goods inventory. Also remember that the work in progress control account is a summary account of all the different work in progress accounts for the jobs currently being worked on.

The work in progress (WIP) control account in a job environment represents a summary of all of the costs incurred on jobs in progress during the period.

- The cost of direct materials issued to the various jobs are totalled and debited to the WIP control account

- The direct labour cost incurred on all jobs is totalled and debited to the WIP control account

- The production overhead absorbed by all jobs, using a predetermined overhead absorption rate, is debited to the WIP control account

- The total production cost of jobs completed during the period is credited to the WIP control account and transferred directly to the cost of sales account. There would usually be no account for finished goods inventory in a job environment, since no inventories of finished goods are held

- The balance on the WIP control account at the end of the period represents the total of the work in progress value of all jobs in progress at the end of the period

4 Fertiliser

Pass marks. We'll analyse this question using the **four-step approach** to process costing questions set out in the Study Text. The first thing we need to establish, however, is the WIP valuation method adopted by the company. The definition of throughput indicates that ABC Ltd uses the **weighted average method** as no distinction is made between opening WIP and units introduced.

Step 1 for process 1 **Determine output and losses and prepare a statement of equivalent units**

You need to ensure that output + closing WIP + normal loss = material introduced. If it doesn't, there must be an abnormal loss or gain. Here the balancing figure is an abnormal loss. Units of normal loss are valued at zero equivalent units but units of abnormal loss are taken to be one full equivalent unit each.

Step 2 for process 1 **Calculate cost per unit of output, losses and WIP and prepare a statement of cost per equivalent unit**

Simply divide the costs by the appropriate number of equivalent units. Don't forget to include the production overhead at 150% of direct wages cost.

Step 3 for process 1 **Calculate total cost of output, losses and WIP and prepare a statement of evaluation**

Value the equivalent units derived in Step 1 at the cost per equivalent unit derived in Step 2. Remember that units of normal loss have no value.

Step 4 for process 1 **Complete account**

In this question you were only required to prepare process accounts but in other questions you may need to draw up accounts for scrap, abnormal loss and so on. The process account simply shows how the quantity and cost of the various inputs (on the debit side of the account) are spread across the various outputs (on the credit side). The figures for inputs are provided in the question, the figures for outputs are derived in step 3. Don't forget to include normal loss in terms of quantity.

Step 1 for process 2

For this process you have to include the opening WIP when calculating the normal loss. (There was no opening WIP in process 1.) You also have an extra output of by-product B. In calculating the equivalent units remember that the by-product is treated in the same way as the normal loss. It does not carry any of the process costs.

Step 2 for process 2

You need to include the various costs included in opening WIP and the cost of the material introduced from process 1. Again the by-product is treated the same as the normal loss. Its value is deducted from the materials cost column.

Step 3 for process 2

The approach here is exactly as for process 1. The by-product is valued at its resale value.

Step 4 for process 2

The inputs need to include the opening WIP and the material introduced from process 1.

PROCESS 1

Step 1   STATEMENT OF EQUIVALENT UNITS

	Total Kgs	Material Kgs	Conversion costs Kgs
Output to process 2	13,100	13,100	13,100
Closing WIP	2,000	2,000	1,000
Normal loss (15% × (10,500 + 7,200 – 2,000))	2,355	-	-
Abnormal loss (balancing figure)	245	245	245
Material introduced	17,700	15,345	14,345

Step 2   STATEMENT OF COST PER EQUIVALENT UNIT

	Material		Conversion costs
Costs incurred during period (£(4,960 + 14,700))	£19,660	(£(17,160 + 25,740))	£42,900
Equivalent units of production	15,345		14,345
Cost per equivalent unit	£1.2812		£2.9906

Step 3   STATEMENT OF EVALUATION

	Material Equiv units	£	Conversion costs Equiv units	£	Total £
Fully worked units	13,100	16,784	13,100	39,177	55,961
Closing WIP	2,000	2,562	1,000	2,990	5,552
Abnormal loss	245	314	245	733	1,047
	15,345	19,660	14,345	42,900	62,560

Step 4   PROCESS 1

	Kgs	£		Kgs	£
Raw material			Process 2 account	13,100	55,961
W	10,500	4,960	Normal loss	2,355	-
X	7,200	14,700	Abnormal loss	245	1,047
		19,660	Closing work in		
Wages		17,160	progress	2,000	5,552
Production overhead					
(150% × £17,160)		25,740			
	17,700	62,560		17,700	62,560

PROCESS 2

Step 1   STATEMENT OF EQUIVALENT UNITS

	Total Kgs	Process 1 material Kgs	Conversion costs Kgs
Finished goods: Product Z	20,545	20,545	20,545
Product B	481	-	-
Closing WIP	1,500	1,500	750
Normal loss (8% × (8,400 + 13,100 + 4,050 – 1,500))	1,924	-	-
Abnormal loss (balancing figure)	1,100	1,100	1,100
	25,550	23,145	22,395

Step 2   STATEMENT OF COST PER EQUIVALENT UNIT

	Process 1/material		Conversion costs	
Opening WIP	£(8,720 + 2,000)	£10,720	£(3,600 + 7,200)	£10,800
Costs incurred during period	£(55,961 + 16,562)	£72,523	£(8,600 + 17,200)	£25,800
Less by-product value (£2 × 481 kg)		£(962)		
		£82,281		£36,600
Equivalent units		23,145		22,395
Cost per equivalent unit		£3.5550		£1.6343

Step 3   STATEMENT OF EVALUATION

	Process 1/Materials		Conversion costs		Total
	Equiv units	£	Equiv units	£	£
Fully worked units	20,545	73,037	20,545	33,577	106,614
Closing WIP	1,500	5,333	750	1,226	6,559
Abnormal loss	1,100	3,911	1,100	1,797	5,708
	23,145	82,281	22,395	36,600	118,881

Step 4   PROCESS 2

	Kgs	£		Kgs	£
Opening WIP	8,400	21,520	Finished goods control		
Process 1 account	13,100	55,961	account:	20,545	106,614
Raw material	4,050	16,562	product Z		962
			by-product B	481	
Wages		8,600	Normal loss	1,924	-
Production overhead			Abnormal loss	1,100	5,708
(200% × £8,600)		17,200	Closing WIP	1,500	6,559
	25,550	119,843		25,550	118,881

5 Losses in process costing

> **Pass marks**. As well as being able to apply the process costing method you must also be able to explain clearly **why** you undertake the various steps in valuing the different parts of the output. If you are getting in a muddle with your explanation it can sometimes help to make up **simple** figures to demonstrate the concepts. However don't take so long with your figures that you run out of time. For five marks the time allocation is only about nine minutes so you need to gather your thoughts quickly and produce a concise answer.

When a certain level of loss is expected in a process, an allowance is made for **normal loss**, ie an expected level of loss for a given volume of activity.

If losses are greater than the expected or normal level the excess loss is an **abnormal loss**. If losses are less than the expected or normal level the difference is an **abnormal gain**.

A distinction is made between normal losses and abnormal losses and gains so that the abnormal events can be **costed separately**. The occurrence of an abnormal loss or gain therefore does not affect the unit cost of good production and the cost of abnormal events is highlighted separately for management attention.

The normal loss units **do not absorb any of the production costs**. They have either zero value, or if they can be sold as scrap they are valued at their scrap value and this amount is subtracted from the total process costs for the period, ie credited to the process account.

Abnormal losses and gains are **valued separately at the same rate as good units** and their scrap value is not included in the calculation of the process costs for the period. The full cost of abnormal losses and gains is transferred from the process account to a separate account. Their scrap value is then offset against this cost and the net balance on the account is transferred to the income statement.

6 The concept of equivalent units

Pass marks. In this question you are asked to use simple figures to illustrate your explanation. Don't make life difficult for yourself and ensure that you do keep the figures simple. Notice how our cost per equivalent unit is a nice round number. Don't decide on a figure for 'costs incurred during period' until you know the equivalent units produced. You can then choose a 'nice' cost per equivalent unit, with costs incurred as the balancing figure.

In a process costing environment the unit cost of output is determined by averaging out the costs incurred over the number of units produced in the period.

The averaging procedure results in a cost per unit produced in the period. However this unit rate would be distorted if no account was taken of units which are only part complete, ie work in progress.

This problem is overcome by using the concept of **equivalent units**, whereby work in progress is valued according to its degree of completion. A simple example will demonstrate the application of this concept.

Period 1

Opening work in progress	nil
Closing work in progress	1,000 units; 25% complete
Units transferred to next process	24,000
Cost incurred during period	£84,875

Equivalent units produced   =   24,000 + (1,000 × 25%)
                                =   24,250

Cost per equivalent unit   =   £84,875/24,250
                                =   £3.50

This unit cost would be applied to the completed units and to the incomplete units in progress, resulting in the following valuations.

Units transferred to next process = 24,000 × £3.50   = £84,000
Closing work in process = 250 equivalent units × £3.50   = £875

The 1,000 units in progress are therefore treated as the equivalent of 250 complete units, ie 1,000 × 25% = 250 equivalent units.

7 Just in time systems

Pass marks. We have stated more than the five financial benefits required by the question, so that you can use them for revision practice, if required. In the exam you will be wasting valuable time if you provide more than the required number of benefits.

JIT systems have a number of financial **benefits**.

- Increase in labour productivity due to labour being multiskilled and carrying out preventative maintenance

- Reduction of investment in plant space

- Reduction in costs of storing inventory

- Reduction in risk of inventory obsolescence

- Lower investment in inventory

- Reduction in costs of handling inventory

- Reduction in costs associated with scrap, defective units and reworking

- Higher revenue as a result of reduction in lost sales following failure to meet delivery dates (because of improved quality)

- Reduction in the costs of setting up production runs

- Higher revenues as a result of faster response to customer demands

8 Costs of quality

Pass marks. The question asks for a brief description of the four categories of cost. It would not be sufficient to simply list them. It's a good idea to provide an example of each in case your description is a little muddled! Remember the time allowance is about nine minutes so this should give you a rough idea of how much you need to write.

The four categories of cost are prevention costs, appraisal costs, internal failure costs and external failure costs.

Prevention costs

The costs incurred prior to production commencing or during the production process in order to prevent the occurrence of sub-standard output. For example the cost of training quality control personnel.

Appraisal costs

The costs incurred to ascertain whether outputs meet the required quality standards. For example the cost of inspecting goods inwards.

Internal failure costs

The costs incurred as a result of the failure to achieve quality standards before the output is transferred to the customer. For example the cost of re-working output identified as sub-standard.

External failure costs

The costs incurred as a result of sub-standard quality output discovered after the output is transferred to the customer. For example the cost of repairing products returned from customers.

9 Throughput accounting

> **Pass marks**. You are asked for a brief identification of the differences between the two systems. A good form of presentation for your answer would be bullet points, which are much quicker to use in an exam than an essay format. However it is important that your bullet points are not so brief that they do not provide the necessary explanation.

Throughput accounting (TA) **differentiates between fixed and variable costs** in the same way that a system of marginal costing does. However it **goes further** in its analysis of costs to argue that **only a very limited number of costs are actually variable in the short run**. This is the reason for the coining of the term 'super variable costing' to describe TA.

There are a number of differences between TA and marginal or variable cost accounting.

- Both systems distinguish between fixed and variable costs in reporting profit and valuing inventories, but **TA treats only material cost as variable**.

- In a marginal costing system, labour cost would normally be treated as a variable cost to be included in the unit cost in the valuation of inventory. In a TA system **labour cost is treated as a fixed cost** and is combined with all other operating expenses to be written off as a **period cost**.

- Inventory in a marginal costing system is valued at total variable production cost. In a TA system all inventory is valued at material cost only.

- The focus of a marginal costing system is the **provision of information for short term decision making**. TA, or the Theory of Constraints on which it was based, was conceived with the aim of **changing manufacturing strategy to achieve evenness of flow**.

10 WAQ

> **Pass marks**. A full question on **throughput accounting** is unlikely, with throughput accounting calculations being more likely to appear in Section A as **MCQs**. These part questions are just the sort of calculations you could be required to do for an MCQ.
>
> In (a) the **throughput accounting ratio** is based on the **process** with the **lowest throughput** per day.
>
> In (b) you need to work out how many **extra units** would be produced over two years, and the extra **contribution** on these units, if the bottleneck were eliminated. This gain should **correspond** to the **possible investment**.

(a)

	Process A	Process B	Process C
Throughput per hour (units)	12	10	15
Throughput per day (units)	96	80	120
Throughput contribution per unit		£120	

$$\text{Throughput accounting ratio} = \frac{£120 \times 80 \text{ units}}{£24,000/6}$$

$$= 2.4$$

(b) (i)   Gain if bottleneck at process B is eliminated = 96 – 80 units = 16 units per day.
Gain over two years = 16 units × 6 days × 48 weeks × 2 × £120 = £1,105,920
Therefore £1.1 million could be spent if the cost were to be recovered over two years.

(ii)   Gain over 12 weeks = 16 units × 6 days × 12 weeks × £120 = £138,240

       Therefore £0.14 million could be spent if the cost were to be recovered over 12 weeks.

(c)   **TA ratio** = $\dfrac{96 \text{ units} \times £120}{4,000} = \dfrac{11,250}{4,000} = 2.88$

11 TXL

> **Pass marks.** A question solely on backflush costing is unlikely in the exam and this question serves to highlight whether or not you understand the basic workings of a system of backflush accounting.
>
> Note in (a) that the **finished goods and cost of goods sold accounts** are **debited** with the **standard cost** of goods produced and sold.
>
> In (b) there would be **no raw material stock** because **JIT** was being used and hence **no raw materials control account**.

(a)

	Debit £	Credit £
Raw materials	630,000	
Creditors control		630,000
Being the purchase of direct materials		
Conversion cost control	470,000	
Creditors, etc		470,000
Being the conversion costs incurred		
Finished goods	1,050,000	
Raw materials		600,000
Conversion costs absorbed		450,000
Being the standard cost of completed goods		
Cost of goods sold	980,000	
Finished goods		980,000
Being the standard cost of goods sold		

(b)   There would be no raw material stock and so there would be only one trigger point which would be either transfer to finished goods or sale of goods. The following entries are based on the sale of goods as the trigger price.

	Debit £	Credit £
Conversion cost control	470,000	
Creditors, etc a/c		470,000
Being the conversion costs incurred		
Cost of goods sold	980,000	
Raw materials		560,000
Conversion cost absorbed		420,000
Being the standard cost of goods sold		
Conversion cost control		470,000
Conversion cost absorbed	420,000	
Cost of goods sold	50,000	
Being the under absorption of conversion costs		

12 KH

> **Pass marks**. The level of calculations required in this question means that it is probably a bit too easy to be classified as exam standard, but nevertheless it provides you with an excellent opportunity to practice calculating product costs using ABC.
>
> The only real difficulty in the ABC calculations is making sure that you use the **correct bases for sharing out the overheads**. Paint stirring and quality control is shared out on the basis of batches, the figures for which are given in the question. An easy mistake to make with **electricity** would be to divide the overhead in the ratio of number of coats of paint but that would not be correct: G's products have substantially more costs overall because more G units are sprayed overall. The cost should therefore be apportioned on the basis of **total coats**. For sharing out the cost of filling of spraying machines you need to work out the total litres of paint used.
>
> Don't forget to make use of your **answers to (a) and (b)** to **illustrate** your answer to (c). Your arguments will carry a lot more weight if you can back them up with examples.

(a)   **Unit cost using absorption costing**

	G	F	R
	£	£	£
Paint	15.20	11.18	18.90
Labour (W1)	2.65	3.98	6.63
Stirring and quality control (W2)	1.15	1.73	2.88
Electricity (W2)	5.00	7.50	12.50
Filling of machines (W2)	3.10	4.65	7.75
	27.10	29.04	48.66

(b)   **Unit cost using activity based costing**

	G	F	R
	£	£	£
Paint	15.20	11.18	18.90
Labour	2.65	3.98	6.63
Stirring and quality control (W3)	1.38	1.27	3.08
Electricity (W3)	8.94	7.66	6.39
Filling of machines (W3)	4.87	5.52	4.04
	33.04	29.61	39.04

(c)   **Cost drivers** are activities or transactions that are significant determinants of cost, in other words the activities that cause costs to occur. Activity based costing acknowledges that some costs vary not with volume of output but with some other cost driver.

The logic of this approach is clearly illustrated by the facts given in the question. If paint delivered is stirred and inspected in batches, then it is the number of batches rather than units or labour hours that determine how much stirring and inspection is to be done.

The use of electricity best illustrates the **difference between the two methods** in this example. Under absorption costing R's products absorb the largest part of the electricity overhead because R's involve more labour time than the other products. Under activity based costing R's have the smallest share of the electricity overhead, recognising that use of labour time and consumption of electricity are not necessarily related. (Note that R's use more different batches of paint than the other products: the labour time is probably spent adjusting the machinery while it is idle rather than operating it and using electricity.)

The **consequences of adopting activity based costing** are a significant change in the unit cost of R's mainly at the expense of G's. This will have implications for valuing work in progress and also for pricing the service and assessing its overall validity.

Workings

1   *Labour cost per unit*

	G	F	R
Labour hours per unit	0.50	0.75	1.25
Rate per hour	£5.30	£5.30	£5.30
Cost per unit	£2.65	£3.98	£6.63

2   *Overheads - absorption costing*

	G	F	R	Total
Units	5,400	4,360	3,600	13,360
Labour hours/unit	0.5	0.75	1.25	
Total labour hours	2,700	3,270	4,500	10,470

	Total overhead £	Total hours Hrs	Rates per hour £
Paint stirring and quality control	24,081	10,470	2.30
Electricity	104,700	10,470	10.00
Filling of spraying machines	64,914	10,470	6.20

	G £	F £	R £
Stirring @ £2.30 per hour ($\times$ 0.5/0.75/1.25)	1.15	1.73	2.88
Electricity @ £10 per hour	5.00	7.50	12.50
Filling @ £6.20 per hour	3.10	4.65	7.75

3   Overheads - activity based costing

(a)   Paint stirring and quality control

	G	F	R	Total
Units	5,400	4,360	3,600	
Batches	27	20	40	87
Share of overhead (27:20:40)	£7,473	£5,536	£11,072	£24,081
Per unit	£1.38	£1.27	£3.08	

(b)   Electricity

	G	F	R	Total
Coats per unit	7	6	5	
Total coats	37,800	26,160	18,000	81,960
Share of overhead	£48,288	£33,418	£22,994	£104,700
Per unit	£8.94	£7.66	£6.39	

(c)   Filling

	G	F	R	Total
Litres per unit	7.6	8.6	6.3	
Total litres	41,040	37,496	22,680	101,216
Share of overhead	£26,321	£24,048	£14,545	£64,914
Per unit	£4.87	£5.52	£4.04	

13 ABC v traditional absorption costing

> **Pass marks**. You may have thought of other, equally valid situations in which the product cost would be different. The important thing is to think about the differences between the ways in which the two systems absorb overheads and this will give you the basis for identifying where unit cost differences are likely to occur.

Four situations where the product unit cost is likely to differ significantly are as follows.

1   **Where production overhead costs are high in relation to direct costs, in particular direct labour cost**. If production overheads do not represent a significant proportion of total costs then different methods of allocating overheads to products would not have a significant impact on the resulting total unit cost.

2   **Where the product range is wide and diverse**. If products are all very similar then a different analysis of overheads in unlikely to produce a significant difference in the relative overhead cost allocation.

3   **Where the amount of overhead resources used by products varies across the product range**. Some products may place a much greater burden on certain activities than other products. The traditional labour hour-based overhead absorption is not likely to reflect this different pattern of overhead resource input and the resulting unit cost would be significantly different from the unit cost resulting from an ABC system. The ABC system would reflect the different pattern of resource consumption.

4   **Where direct labour hours are not the primary driver of overhead resource consumption**. Certain overhead costs may be driven by something other than labour hours, such as the number of batches or the number of quality control inspections. If these costs are significant then an ABC analysis will produce a different unit cost from that resulting from a traditional overhead absorption system based on direct labour hours.

14 ABC in the modern environment

> **Pass marks**. If the question does not specifically state how many reasons or situations you should explain then, for five marks, you can usually assume that you should make an absolute minimum of five separate points. Try to draw on aspects of the modern environment that you have learned about, for example JIT and throughput. Remember to explain your points reasonably fully, within the time constraint. You cannot expect the examiner to guess what you mean from a few brief words.

Reasons for suitability

(a)   Most modern organisations tend to have a high level of overhead costs, especially relating to support services such as maintenance and data processing. ABC, by the use of carefully chosen cost drivers, traces these overheads to product lines in a more logical and less arbitrary manner than traditional absorption costing.

(b)   The determination and use of cost drivers helps to measure and improve the efficiency and effectiveness of support departments.

(c)   Many costs included in general overheads can actually be traced to specific JIT lines and/or product lines using ABC. This improves product costing and cost management because the costs are made the responsibility of the line manager.

(d) ABC forces the organisation to ask such searching questions as 'What causes the demand for the activity?', 'What does the department achieve?', 'Does it add value?' and so on.

(e) ABC systems may encourage reductions in throughput time and inventory and improvements in quality.

Unsuitable situations

(a) A number of businesses have recently been split into several small autonomous sections. In this situation there may be no need for a sophisticated costing system such as ABC because staff should be aware of cost behaviour.

(b) ABC can work against modern manufacturing methods such as JIT. JIT seeks to reduce set-up time so that very small batches can be made economically.

(c) The aim of set-up time reduction is to allow more set-ups, not just to reduce set-up costs. The use of a cost driver based on the number of set-ups will therefore work against JIT principles as it will tend to encourage larger batches.

15 Setting standard costs

> **Pass marks**. Be prepared to see both sides of the argument in a question such as this. A good approach is to present a brief discussion which both agrees and disagrees with the statement. However if the question asks you to state whether or not you agree with the statement then you must ensure that you actually do so.

Price inflation can indeed cause difficulties in setting realistic standard prices.

If **current prices** are used in the standard cost then **reported price variances would become adverse as soon as prices increase**. It would be difficult to tell at any point whether an adverse variance was because of inefficient purchasing or because of unavoidable price rises.

On the other hand, if annual standard costs are set then an **estimated mid-year price** might be used in the standard cost. This would result in **favourable price variances in the first half of the year and adverse variances in the second half**, assuming that prices increase gradually. Again, **control action would be impaired** because it would be difficult to highlight those variances which were controllable and those which were caused by unavoidable price inflation.

I would agree that standard costing can be difficult to apply in inflationary conditions but **this does not mean that its application is not worthwhile**, for the following reasons.

- **Usage and efficiency variances would still be meaningful**

- **It is possible to measure inflation**; there is no reason why its effects cannot be removed from the variances reported to management

- **Standard costs can be revised more frequently** than annually, in order to keep them up to date as a yardstick for current performance.

16 The behavioural implications of setting standard costs

Pass marks. Try not to be too general in your answer. You will earn marks for mentioning specific types of performance standard, such as attainable and current standards.

There are four main types of performance standard that can be used when setting standards for factors such as material usage and labour efficiency. They are as follows.

- Ideal standard
- Attainable standard
- Current standard
- Basic standard

The potential behavioural impact of the standards lies in the **level of allowance that is made for inefficiencies**.

The ideal standard is based on **perfect operating conditions**. No allowance is made for wastage, breakdowns, idle time and so on. While this might be the ultimate aim of operations and it does help to highlight the cost of inefficiencies, it is **not achievable in most situations**. Therefore an ideal standard will usually result in adverse variances. This can be **demotivating** for managers since no matter how hard they try their performance results will always be adverse. The behavioural impact could be that managers will **work less hard than they might have done** if some allowance had been made for unavoidable losses, etc.

The current standard is based on **current working conditions**. This might not have a desirable motivational impact because it does not provide managers with any sort of target to work towards. There will be **no sense of achievement** in meeting the standard cost targets.

It is generally accepted that the best behavioural impact results from the use of an attainable performance standard. This is based on an **efficient level of operation** that is achievable in efficient operating conditions. A reasonable allowance is made for losses, machine breakdowns and so on. The standard can be set **high enough that there is a sense of achievement in meeting the standard, but not so high that it has a demotivating impact**.

Thus, careful selection of an appropriate performance standard can have a desirable impact on human behaviour.

17 DS

Pass marks. Although this is a long question which requires a lot of calculations (there are two products, three types of material and two variable overheads) and covers all of the variances we have been looking at in Chapter 8, it is **not really exam standard**. For a start, the requirement is **straightforward** (prepare an operating statement). Secondly, **only basic variances are examined**, a real exam question being likely to incorporate mix and yield or planning and operational variances.

Nevertheless, this is an extremely **good practice question** as it does cover all the basic variances.

The price and usage variance calculations were straightforward, although you may have got stuck trying to calculate a **usage variance for other materials**. This was **impossible** as you were not given standard usage information. You could therefore only calculate an overall cost variance for other materials.

Because you were not provided with a breakdown of the actual hours worked on the individual products, you had to work out the standard time for actual production for each product, add them together and then compare the total with the actual figure provided.

BPP)))
PROFESSIONAL EDUCATION

The question did not specify that **variable overheads were incurred in line with labour hours** but, in the absence of further information, you had to make that **assumption**. You could then calculate a total variable overhead cost per standard hour (the sum of (budgeted expenditure/total budgeted labour hours) for each overhead), which could be used in the variable overhead expenditure and efficiency variance calculations. Again, the question did not provide you with **a fixed overhead absorption rate** so you needed to **calculate** one (using the budgeted hours from the variable overhead calculation). Once you had done this the fixed overhead variances were not difficult to calculate (if you could remember how to calculate them!). Don't worry if you have difficulty in calculating the fixed overhead variances, as their meaning is not as easy to grasp as that of the variable cost variances. Remember you are trying to determine **why the overhead absorbed is not the same as the overhead incurred**.

This might be because there is a **difference between budgeted expenditure and actual expenditure** (expenditure variance) or because there is a **difference between budgeted volume and actual volume** (volume variance).

Materials price variance

	£	£
37,100 metres of wood should cost (× £0.30)	11,130	
but did cost	11,000	
Wood price variance		130 (F)
29,200 metres of gut should cost (× £1.50)	43,800	
but did cost	44,100	
Gut price variance		300 (A)
Wood and gut price variance		170 (A)

Material usage variance

		Wood		Gut
3,700 units of W should use	(× 7m)	25,900 m	(× 6 m)	22,200 m
1,890 units of B should use	(× 5m)	9,450 m	(× 4 m)	7,560 m
		35,350 m		29,760 m
Together they did use		37,100 m		29,200 m
Material usage variance in metres		1,750 m(A)		560 m (F)
× standard cost per metre		× £0.30		× £1.50
Material usage variance				
Wood		£525 (A)		
Gut				£840 (F)

Other materials cost variance

	£
3,700 units of W should cost (× £0.20)	740.00
1,890 units of B should cost (× £0.15)	283.50
	1,023.50
Together they did cost	1,000.00
Other materials cost variance	23.50 (F)

Direct labour rate

	£
2,200 hours of labour should cost (× £3)	6,600
but did cost	6,850
Direct labour rate variance	250 (A)

Direct labour efficiency

3,700 units of W should take (× 30 minutes)	1,850 hrs
1,890 units of B should take (× 20 minutes)	630 hrs
	2,480 hrs
Together they did take	2,200 hrs
Efficiency variance in hrs	280 hrs (F)
× standard rate per hour	× × £3
Direct labour efficiency variance	£840 (F)

Variable overhead costs

	Hours	Units
Budgeted hours: W	2,000	4,000
B	500	1,500
	2,500	

	£
Power cost per standard hour (£1,500 ÷ 2,500 hrs)	0.60
Maintenance cost per standard hour (£7,500 ÷ 2,500 hrs)	3.00
	3.60

Variable overhead efficiency variance

= (as labour) 280 hours (F) × £3.60 = £1,008 (F)

	£	£
Variable overhead cost of 2,200 hours should be (× £3.60)		7,920
but was: power	1,800	
maintenance	6,900	
		8,700
Variable overhead expenditure variance		780 (A)

Fixed overhead

Budgeted fixed costs	£21,000
Budgeted hours (see calculation for variable overheads)	2,500 hrs
Absorption rate per hour	£8.40

Fixed overhead expenditure variance

	Budgeted expenditure £	Actual expenditure £	Expenditure variance £
Supervision	8,000	7,940	60 (F)
Heating and lighting	1,200	1,320	120 (A)
Rent	4,800	4,800	-
Depreciation	7,000	7,000	-
Total	21,000	21,060	60 (A)

Fixed overhead volume variance

	£	£
Actual production at standard rates		
W (3,700 × £8.40 × 1/2 hr)	15,540	
B (1,890 × £8.40 × $\frac{1}{3}$ hr)	5,292	
Budgeted production at standard rates		20,832
W (4,000 × £8.40 × 1/2 hr)	16,800	
B (1,500 × £8.40 × $\frac{1}{3}$ hr)	4,200	21,000
		168 (A)

Calculation of unit standard costs

	W	B
	£ per unit	£ per unit
Direct materials: wood	2.10	1.50
gut	9.00	6.00
Other materials	0.20	0.15
Direct labour	1.50	1.00
Variable overhead at £3.60 per hour	1.80	1.20
Fixed overhead at £8.40 per hour	4.20	2.80
Total standard cost per unit	18.80	12.65

18 Reconciliation

Pass marks. Your **operating statement** needed to **reconcile** the **standard cost of output** (standard cost per unit × actual output) with **actual cost of output** (given in the question). You therefore needed to work out the standard unit cost of each product, the information for which you had derived in the course of your variance calculations in question 17 or had been given in the question.

The reconciliation allowed you to **check** that your variance calculations were correct. Don't waste time in the exam going back over all of your calculations if it does not reconcile, however, unless you have a few free minutes at the end.

Operating statement for October

		(F) £	(A) £	£
Standard cost of actual output:	W 3,700 × £18.80			69,560.00
	B 1,890 × £12.65			23,908.50
				93,468.50
Cost variances				
Wood price		130		
Gut price			300	
Wood usage			525	
Gut usage		840		
Other materials cost		23.50		
Direct labour rate			250	
Direct labour efficiency		840		
Variable overhead efficiency		1,008		
Variable overhead expenditure			780	
Fixed overhead expenditure			60	
Fixed overhead volume			168	
		2,841.50	2,083	758.50 (F)
Actual cost of output				92,710.00

19 HP

Workings

The area of one floor tile is ½ × ¼ = 0.125 sq m. In a standard batch of 100 sq m there will be 800 tiles. The standard cost per tile is therefore as follows.

Material	Quantity	Price	Std cost
	kg	£	£
A	0.0500	1.50	0.0750
B	0.0375	1.20	0.0450
C	0.0125	1.40	0.0175
D	0.0250	0.50	0.0125
	0.1250	1.20	0.1500

(a) **Cost variance**

	A	B	C	D	Total
	£	£	£	£	£
46,400 tiles should cost	3,480	2,088	812	580	6,960
but did cost	3,520	2,200	750	700	7,170
Cost variance	40(A)	112(A)	62(F)	120(A)	210(A)

(b) **Price variance**

		Should	Did	Price variance	
Material	Quantity	cost	cost	Per kg	Total
	kg	£	£	£	£
A	2,200	1.50	1.60	0.10 (A)	220 (A)
B	2,000	1.20	1.10	0.10 (F)	200 (F)
C	500	1.40	1.50	0.10 (A)	50 (A)
D	1,400	0.50	0.50	-	-
Total price variance					70 (A)

(c) **Mix variance**

Actual input = (2,200 + 2,000 + 500 + 1,400) kgs = 6,100 kg

Standard mix of actual input

A	40/100 × 6,100 kgs =	2,440 kgs
B	30/100 × 6,100 kgs =	1,830 kgs
C	10/100 × 6,100 kgs =	610 kgs
D	20/100 × 6,100 kgs =	1,220 kgs
		6,100 kgs

Material	Mix should have been kg	But was kg	Variance kg	× std price £	Mix variance £
A	2,440	2,200	240 (F)	1.50	360 (F)
B	1,830	2,000	170 (A)	1.20	204 (A)
C	610	500	110 (F)	1.40	154 (F)
D	1,220	1,400	180 (A)	0.50	90 (A)
	6,100	6,100	-		220 (F)

If you used the alternative valuation method (ie using a weighted average price of £120/100 kg = £1.20 per kg), you would have the following variances: A £72 (F); B £0; C £22 (F); D £126 (F).

(d) **Yield variance**

Each unit of output (800 tiles) requires

40	kg of A, costing	£60
30	kg of B, costing	£36
10	kg of C, costing	£14
20	kg of D, costing	£10
100 kg		£120

6,100 kgs should have yielded (× 800 tiles/100 kgs)	48,800 tiles
but did yield	46,400 tiles
	2,400 tiles (A)
× standard cost per tile	× £0.15
	£360 (A)

20 Wimbrush

Pass marks. Part (a)(i) should have caused you no problems, but you may have found part (a)(ii) more difficult.

Operational variances are calculated by **comparing a revised standard with an actual result**, so you cannot work out these variances until you have **established the revised standard**.

Planning variances are calculated by **comparing an original standard with a revised standard** and are based on actual production volumes. If a **revised** standard is **greater** than an **original** standard, the planning variance is **adverse** because the original standard was too optimistic, overstating the profits but understanding the realistic cost.

If you have time in an exam, you could work out 'traditional' variances based on original standards and actual results. As our summary shows, the **sum** of the **operational** variances and the **planning** variance should total the **'traditional'** variance.

If you can answer **part (b)** successfully then you understand the whole concept of planning and operational variances. Use your answer, if you are happy with it, as a **summary for revision purposes**. If you aren't happy with it maybe you should attempt part (b) again.

(a) (i) **Traditional variance analysis**

2,000 Widgets should use (× 5 kg)	10,000 kg
but did use	10,800 kg
Material X usage variance in kgs	800 kg (A)
× standard cost per kg	× £3
Material X usage variance in £	£2,400 (A)

	£
10,800 kg of X should cost (× £3)	32,400
but did cost	51,840
Material X price variance	19,440 (A)

500 Splodgets should use (×1.5 tonnes)	750 tonnes
but did use	700 tonnes
Material Z usage variance in tonnes	50 tonnes (F)
× standard cost per tonne	× £30
Material Z usage variance in £	£1,500 (F)

	£
700 tonnes of Z should cost (× £30)	21,000
but did cost (× £25)	17,500
Material Z price variance	3,500 (F)

Summary	Material X variances £	Material Z variances £	Total £
Price variance	19,440 (A)	3,500 (F)	15,940 (A)
Usage variance	2,400 (A)	1,500 (F)	900 (A)
	21,840 (A)	5,000 (F)	16,840 (A)

(ii) **Planning and operational variances**

Widgets: the revised standard was 5 kg at £4.50 per kg

	£
10,800 kg of X should have cost (× £4.50)	48,600
but did cost	51,840
Material X price variance (operational variance)	3,240 (A)

Usage variance for X = 800 kg (A) × £4.50 = **(operational variance)**   3,600 (A)

The **planning variance** is calculated as follows.

	£
Original standard (using X) 2,000 units × 5 kg × £3 =	30,000
Revised standard (using X) 2,000 units × 5 kg × £4.50 =	45,000
Planning variance £1.50 (A) per kg, or	15,000 (A)

Splodgets: the revised realistic standard is 1.5 tonnes of Z at £23 =   £34.50

	£
700 tonnes of Z should cost (× £23)	16,100
did cost (× £25)	17,500
Material Z price variance (operational variance)	1,400 (A)

Material Z usage variance = 50 tonnes (F) × £23 = **(operational variance)**   £1,150 (F)

Planning variance

	£
Original standard 500 units × 1.5 tonnes × £30 per tonne =	22,500
Revised standard 500 units × 1.5 tonnes × £23 per tonne =	17,250
Total planning variance (£7 per tonne (F)) or	5,250 (F)

Summary	Material X £	Material Z £	Total £
Price variance	3,240 (A)	1,400 (A)	4,640 (A)
Usage variance	3,600 (A)	1,150 (F)	2,450 (A)
Operational variances	6,840 (A)	250 (A)	7,090 (A)
Planning variances	15,000 (A)	5,250 (F)	9,750 (A)
Total variances	21,840 (A)	5,000 (F)	16,840 (A)

(b)   (i)   The distinction between planning and operational variances is a development of the opportunity cost approach to variance analysis. *Demski* argued that **more helpful and meaningful information will be provided for management control decisions** if variances are reported using an ex-post (revised) standard, that is a **standard which in hindsight should have been used**, when the actual standard used (or the budget) is unrealistic for the conditions which actually prevailed. Thus, when it is realised in retrospect that the planned standard is inaccurate, a more realistic (ex-post) standard should be used to calculate operational variances. The **final reconciliation between budgeted and actual profit** would then be made as a **planning variance**, which measures the **extent to which the budget targets are at fault** because the original standard used was incorrect. (A planning variance is similar to a budget revision variance.)

(ii)   The **opportunity cost approach** may be useful to companies by **indicating more clearly the actual loss sustained by faults which gave rise to the particular variances**. There is an attempt to equate variance with the amount of profit or loss sustained, which traditional variances often fail to do. Examples are as follows.

(1)   Traditional absorption costing variances for sales volume and production volume do not show the true effect of the variations from budget on company profitability.

(2)   When a standard is incorrect, traditional variances will mislead managers about the true costs incurred. In the case of Wimbrush the error in the original standard price of material X means that traditional variances would have reported a misleading variance to the purchasing department for price, and a mis-valuation of the usage variance would report the cost of the adverse usage of material X and the favourable usage of Z incorrectly.

Planning and operational variances attempt to **indicate** the following constructively.

(1)   What the real cost of variances should be.

(2)   Which of these variances might have been controllable by better management performance and which were unavoidable.

(3)   The effect on financial targets of a failure to construct realistic standards.

The approach is only different from traditional variance analysis, however, when the revised and original standards are different.

21 M

> **Pass marks.** You may have put a different interpretation on the question.
>
> - You may have valued the sales volume variance at the revised profit per unit of £24.96 (although the question did say that the original standard should be used for inventory valuation), giving variance of £2,496 (A)
>
> - You may have based the labour rate planning variance on 1,000 units × 3 hours × £0.18, giving a variance of £540 (A)
>
> - Yu would then have had to make an adjustment for the planning variance left in inventory of (1,050 – 900) units × £0.54 = £81

(a)   *Workings*

(i)

Budgeted sales volume	1,000 units
Actual sales volume	900 units
Variance in units	100 units (A)
× Standard profit per unit	£25.50
Sales volume variance	£2,550 (A)

(ii)

	£
900 units should have sold for (× £120)	108,000
but did sell for	118,800
Sales price variance	10,800 (F)

(iii)   *Material A*

	£
5,670 kgs should have cost (× £2.50)	14,175
but did cost	14,742
Material A price variance	567 (A)

Material B

	£
10,460 kgs should have cost (× £4)	41,840
but did cost	38,179
Material B price variance	3,661 (F)

(iv)   Standard weighted average cost   = standard cost/standard quantity
                                           = £(40 + 12.50)/(5 + 10) kgs
                                           = £3.50 per kg

Actual input = (5,670 + 10,460) kgs = 16,130 kgs

Standard mix of actual input

A = 16,130 × 5/15 =	5,376.67 kgs
B = 16,130 × 10/15 =	10,753.33 kgs
	16,130.00

		Actual input	Standard Mix of actual input	Difference	× difference between w. av. price and std price		Variance
		Kgs	Kgs	Kgs		£	£
A		5,670	5,376.67	293.33	(£3.50 – £2.50)	1.00	293.33 (F)
B		10,460	10,753.33	(293.33)	(£3.50 – £4.00)	(0.50)	146.67 (F)
		16,130	16,130.00	-			440.00 (F)

(v) 16,130 kg should have yielded (÷ 15)   1,075.33 units
          but did yield   1,050.00 units
     Yield variance in units   25.33
     × standard cost per unit of output   × £52.50
     Yield variance in £   £1,330 (A)

(vi) Revised labour rate £6 × 103% = £6.18

                                                                                         £
      Revised standard cost (1,050 units × 3hrs × £6.18)   19,467
      Original standard cost (1,050 units × 3hrs × £6)   18,900
                                                                                       567 (A)

                                                                                         £
      With revised standard, 3,215 hours should have cost (× £6 × 103%)   19,869
           but did cost   19,933
      Labour rate operating variance   64 (A)

(vii)
                                                                                         £
      1,050 units should have taken (× 3hrs)   3,150 hrs
      but did take   3,215 hrs
      Variance in hrs   65 hrs (A)
      × revised standard rate per hr (× £6 × 103%)   × £6.18
      Labour efficiency variance   £402 (A)

(viii)
                                                                                         £
      3,215 hours of variable overhead should have cost (× £3)   9,645
      but did cost   10,288
      Variable production overhead expenditure variance   643 (A)

(ix)
      1,050 units should have taken (× 3hrs)   3,150 hrs
      but did take   3,215 hrs
      Variance in hrs   65 hrs (A)
      × standard rate per hr   × £3
      Variable production overhead efficiency variance   £195 (A)

(x)
                                                                                         £
      Budgeted expenditure (£180,000/12)   15,000
      Actual expenditure   15,432
      Fixed production overhead expenditure variance   432 (A)

(xi)
                                                                                         £
      Actual production at standard rate (1,050 × £15 per unit)   15,750
      budgeted production at standard rate (1,000 × £15 per unit)   15,000
      Fixed overhead volume variance   750 (F)

PROFIT RECONCILIATION STATEMENT (BUDGET TO ACTUAL) JANUARY 20X0

			£
Budgeted profit (1,000 units × £25.50)			25,500
Planning variances: labour rate			567 (A)
Revised budgeted profit			24,933
Sales volume variance			2,550 (A)
Revised standard profit from sales achieved			22,383

Operating variances	£	£	
	(F)	(A)	
Sales price	10,800		
Material price - A		567	
- B	3,661		
Material mix - A	420		
- B	20		
Material yield		1,330	
Labour rate		64	
Labour efficiency		402	
Variance production overhead expenditure		643	
Variable production overhead efficiency		195	
Fixed production overhead expenditure		432	
Fixed production overhead volume	750		
	15,651	3,633	12,018 (F)
Actual profit			34,401

We can do a check on the actual profit figure in the reconciliation statement by calculating actual profit based on the figures given in the exam. Closing inventory is to be valued at standard cost.

Pass mark. Only do this if you have time in the exam – perhaps at the very end if you have five minutes to spare.

Check	£	£
Sales		118,800
Costs incurred	98,574	
Closing inventory (150 × £94.50)	(14,175)	
		84,399
Actual profit		34,401

22 Benchmarking

By comparing various indicators drawn from the budget before the implementation of the IT initiative with both those drawn from the budget after its implementation and recent industry average statistics, the **effectiveness of the sales order department** can be assessed.

	Industry average		MM Current	Post - IT
Cost per customer per year	£300	(W1)	£370.00	£350.00
Cost per home order processed	£50	(W2)	£43.20	£52.91
Cost per export order processed	£60	(W3)	£110.00	£93.00
Cost per despatch	£8	(W4)	£11.13	£8.64
Sales literature cost per customer	£35	(W5)	£45.00	£27.69
Average no. of orders per customer pa	4.1	(W6)	3.10	2.88
Average no. of despatches per order	3.3	(W7)	1.85	2.50

	Industry average	MM Current	Post - IT
Activity measures			
Number of customers		2,000	2,600
Number of negotiations		3,000	6,000
Number of home orders		5,000	5,500
Number of export orders		1,200	2,000
Number of despatches		11,500	18,750

Workings

1	Total cost ÷ number of customers
2	Cost of processing home orders ÷ number of orders
3	Cost of processing export orders ÷ number of orders
4	Cost of implementing despatches ÷ number of despatches
5	Sales literature cost ÷ number of customers
6	Number of orders (home + export) ÷ number of customers
7	Number of despatches ÷ number of orders (home and export)

The implementation of the IT initiative will cause **customer numbers** to increase by 30% to 2,600, **home orders** to increase by 10% to 5,500 and **export orders** to increase by 67% to 2,000. Industry average statistics are not available for these measures and so it is impossible to tell whether MM's level of business is below, in line with or above what one would expect.

The implementation of the IT initiative should cause the **cost per customer per year** to fall by 5.4% (£20) but this cost is still 16.7% (£50) above the industry average.

The IT initiative is likely to cause the **cost per home order processed** to increase by 22.5% (£9.71), causing it to move from below the industry average of £50 to above it. The **cost per export order processed** should fall as a result of the IT initiative (by 15.5% from £110 to £93), but it is still way above the industry average of £60.

After the implementation of the IT initiative the **export orders will be 27% of total orders**, compared with 19% before the implementation. An industry average statistic would enable us to ascertain whether this represents a common trend or an increasing market share for MM.

The **average number of orders per customer per annum** was below the industry average of 4.1 before the implementation of the IT initiative but has dropped even further from 3.1 to 2.88.

Despite the increase in customer numbers (which might have led to inefficiencies, additional fixed costs and so on), the IT initiative has led to a significant drop (38.47%) in the **sales literature cost per customer** from £45 to £27.69, bringing it under the industry average cost of £35.

Although the IT initiative has led to a 22.4 % fall in the **cost per despatch**, from £11.13 to £8.64, the industry average is still lower at £8. If the majority of the despatch costs are fixed in nature, the fall in the cost per despatch could well be due to the increase in despatches to 18,750.

The question indicated that the **despatching of part orders** to customers is to the benefit of both customers and the company as it helps to reduce MM's inventory holding costs and helps customers in their work flow management. The implementation of the IT initiative has caused the **average number of despatches per order** to move to the advantage of customers and the company, increasing from 1.85 to 2.5, but it still falls short of the industry average of 3.3.

It would also be useful to have information which would allow us to ascertain **whether additional contribution will be earned** as a result of the IT initiative to cover its cost for the year.

23 Calculating key metrics

> **Pass marks.** The formula to be used in calculating the key metrics may be supplied in the exam, in which case you should insert the correct figures carefully and then study the formula to see the significance of the result you have calculated. If the formula is not supplied it is important that you **state the formula you are using** for your calculations. The examiner may have been expecting a slightly different calculation but as long as yours is sensible and logical and it does measure the relevant metric as requested then you should earn all the marks available.

(a) Return on capital employed
$$= \text{(profit from operations/net assets)} \times 100\%$$
$$= (470/(2{,}415 - 240)) \times 100\%$$
$$= 21.6\%$$

(b) Profit margin
$$= \text{(profit from operations/revenue)} \times 100\%$$
$$= (470/4{,}350) \times 100\%$$
$$= 10.8\%$$

(c) Net asset turnover
$$= \text{revenue/net assets}$$
$$= 4{,}350/(2{,}415 - 240)$$
$$= 2.0 \text{ times}$$

(d) Non-current asset turnover
$$= \text{revenue/non-current assets}$$
$$= 4{,}350/1{,}560$$
$$= 2.8 \text{ times}$$

(e) Inventory turnover
$$= \text{cost of goods sold/inventory}$$
$$= 2{,}880.440$$
$$= 6.5 \text{ times}$$

(f) Current ratio
$$= \text{current assets/current liabilities}$$
$$= 855/240$$
$$= 3.6$$

(g) Acid test ratio
$$= \text{current assets excluding inventory/current liabilities}$$
$$= (855 - 440)/240$$
$$= 1.7$$

Notes for senior management

Summary of key metrics

		Budgeted	Target
(a)	Return on capital employed	21.6%	23.0%
(b)	Profit margin	10.8%	10.0%
(c)	Net asset turnover	2.0 times	2.3 times
(d)	Non-current asset turnover	2.8 times	2.5 times
(e)	Inventory turnover	6.5 times	9.0 times
(f)	Current ratio	3.6	3.0
(g)	Acid test ratio	1.7	0.9

Overdraft: the maximum overdraft budgeted at the end of June is €285,000 which exceeds the target of maximum €180,000. The situation could be much worse than shown, since we only have quarter end data and the overdraft could in fact be larger during the intervening period.

(a) The return on capital employed is below the target due to a **budgeted net asset turnover which is lower than the target for the year**.

(b)   The budgeted profit margin is slightly above the target metric and this **helps to partly negate the shortfall on net asset turnover**.

(c)   The budgeted net asset turnover is below target. Opportunities need to be sought to either **increase revenue or to reduce the level of net assets**. However, inventories should be aimed for (see later) but there may also be room for improvement in the level of receivables.

(d)   Non-current asset turnover is budgeted to be higher than the target metric. Therefore the **improvement in net asset turnover must come from more efficient management of the elements of working capital**.

(e)   Inventory turnover is much lower than target. Improvement is needed here. The **level of investment in inventories must be reduced**, but without an adverse effect o revenues. Perhaps the number of lines could be reduced or forecasting procedures could be improved in order to reduce the need to hold high buffer inventories.

(f)   The current ratio is budgeted to be higher than target. Although this means that the liquidity is sound there may be a **wasteful level of resource invested in current assets**. This is reflected in the low rate of inventory turnover.

(g)   The acid test ratio is also above target, which suggests that **either receivables or cash could be reduced**, while still remaining within the target for liquidity. This reduction would assist achievement of the target net asset turnover, but must be achieved without an adverse effect on revenue.

(h)   The cash budget reveals a **short term cash flow problem** in the quarter April to June. The problem may continue into July and August but it is not possible to tell from the information available. By the end of September the **budgeted cash balances are back to acceptable levels**. Action needs to be taken to avoid the large overdraft. It may be possible to **delay the purchase of the non-current assets**, or perhaps **improved credit terms can be negotiated**. Delaying this large payment of €450,000 will avid the large overdraft completely.

24 The purposes of budgeting

Pass marks. It is best to set your answer in context by first explaining briefly how budgets fulfil each of the purposes, before going on to describe how the two purposes might conflict.

Budgeting provides a system of control by providing a **yardstick** against which actual performance can be monitored and assessed.

A budgeting system provides a framework for authorisation by **delegating authority** to each budget holder to incur the costs included in the budget centre's budget.

There may be a conflict between these two purposes because the delegated authority may **encourage managers to incur the expenditure in their budget** even when it is not necessary. They may do this perhaps because the budget is set on an **incremental basis** and they are concerned that if they do not spend the budget then they will not be given the same allowance in the next budget. Alternatively they may feel that their **expertise in forecasting** would be subject to scrutiny if they do not spend all the budget expenditure that they had originally forecast was necessary.

This unnecessary expenditure **negates the control aspect**. If the actual expenditure is not above the budget then expenditure may be deemed to be under control, when the actual is compared with the budget. However if some of the actual expenditure is unnecessary, as described above, then **expenditure is not controlled in reality.**

25 PF

> **Pass marks**. This question provides you with valuable practice in determining seasonal variations and forecasting.
>
> We have used the **additive** model and have adjusted the total of the seasonal variations to zero. If you have used the **multiplicative** model you would need to **adjust the totals so that they sum to four**. Given that time series analysis is **not** an **exact** science, you can round the adjusted variations to integer values, but remember to keep the total of the variations to zero.
>
> For part (c) you need to determine the quarterly change in the trend line. Over 11 quarters it increases by 39, which means that the increase per quarter is roughly 3,500. During **20X6** the increase has been **3,000** per quarter, however, so we will use 3,000 as our quarterly increase. Again you do not need to be too accurate.
>
> Make sure that you are aware of the **assumptions** and **limitations** of time series analysis, as this is just the type of issue that you could be called upon to discuss in the exam.

(a)   **Graph of sales**

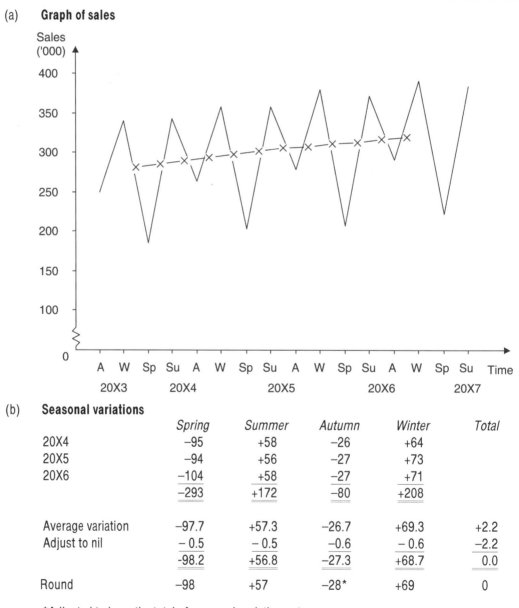

(b)   **Seasonal variations**

	Spring	Summer	Autumn	Winter	Total
20X4	−95	+58	−26	+64	
20X5	−94	+56	−27	+73	
20X6	−104	+58	−27	+71	
	−293	+172	−80	+208	
Average variation	−97.7	+57.3	−26.7	+69.3	+2.2
Adjust to nil	− 0.5	− 0.5	−0.6	− 0.6	−2.2
	−98.2	+56.8	−27.3	+68.7	0.0
Round	−98	+57	−28*	+69	0

*Adjusted to keep the total of seasonal variations at zero.

PROFESSIONAL EDUCATION

(c)   The **trend line shows increases in sales of about three thousand per quarter**, and so a forecast of sales will be based on this assumption.

			Trend line	Variation	Forecast
20X6	Winter	Trend line value	320		
20X7	Autumn	Estimate 320 + (3 × 3)	329	−28	301
	Winter	Estimate 320 + (4 × 3)	332	+69	401

The **forecasts** of sales, based on the calculations and assumptions here, are **301,000 units of product XN30 in autumn 20X7** and **401,000 units of products XN30 in winter 20X7**.

26 'What if' analysis

> **Pass marks**. Your syllabus requires you to develop a **critical approach** to the use of management accounting techniques so you must always be prepared to think about any **limitations** in the techniques you have learned. Make sure that your answer **addresses clearly each separate part of this question**.

Budgetary planning relies on managers' forecasts of a number of variables, ranging from the selling price and volume of sales to the level of advertising expenditure and the costs of cleaning the factory. Any of these forecasts could be incorrect and **managers may wish to know the effect of any changes in the forecast variables**.

'What if' analysis is designed to show the effect of changes in forecast variables. The variables are altered by a predetermined amount to see the effect that the alteration will have on the budgeted outcome. For example the questions could be asked 'what if the selling price is increased by five per cent' or 'what if inventory levels are reduced by ten per cent'. The budget forecasts would be recalculated, usually using a computer spreadsheet model, so that managers can see the impact of these possible changes in the forecast variables.

Weaknesses in the approach include the following.

(a)   The analysis **does not examine the probability that any particular variation in costs or revenues might occur**.

(b)   The analysis may reveal as critical, **factors over which managers have no control**. Thus the analysis is not a helpful guide for management action.

(c)   The analysis **does not in itself provide a decision rule**. Managers still need to use their judgement to lay down parameters for acceptability.

27 Calculating projected costs and revenues

> **Pass marks**. Criticising the use of historical data for forecasting has always been popular with management accounting examiners! You would be well advised to commit to memory a list of factors to adapt in answer this sort of question.

The following checks should be made on historical data before it can be used as a basis for forecasting future costs and revenues.

(a)   **Conditions that existed in the past should be the same as those expected in the future**. If this is not the case then the data should be **adjusted for any factors that affect the figures other than the level of activity**. For example the effect of any changes in technology, fashion, resource costs, weather conditions and so on should be eliminated from the historical data before it can be used.

(b)   The **time period** of the historical data should be long enough to include any costs that are paid periodically but short enough to ensure that averaging of variations in the level of activity has not occurred.

(c)   The **methods of data collection** used to assemble the historical data should not have introduced bias.

(d)   The **accounting methods** used in the historical data should be the same as those to be used in the future. For example the same inventory valuation policy and the same depreciation policy should be used.

(e)   Appropriate choices should be made of **dependent** and **independent variables**. For example the independent variable must be capable of measurement and it must be possible to forecast it with reasonable accuracy.

28 Balanced scorecard

> **Pass marks**. We have provided more than one measure for each perspective but you must **not** do this in the exam otherwise you will waste time. You may have thought of other measures that are just as useful but the two key points to remember is that your measures must be **measurable** and **useful**. There is no point in thinking up with the most wonderful item to be monitored if it would not be feasible to collect the relevant data. Also, once the performance indicator is reported to management it **must initiate appropriate action**. There is nothing to be gained by reporting information to managers that they will not be able to act upon.
>
> You might find it difficult at times to decide in which perspective a certain measure belongs. Don't worry about this. There will often be overlap between the perspectives. If you think of a measure just try to put it into the most sensible category and try to ensure that your measures are not all too similar.
>
> Don't forget to explain **why** each measure might be a useful indicator.

Performance indicators that might usefully be monitored by a training company include the following.

Customer perspective

- number of customer complaints; monitors customer satisfaction
- average time to complete a booking; monitors customer service

Innovation and learning perspective

- training expenditure per employee; monitors ability to update staff and lecturer skills
- percentage of revenue generated by new courses; monitors ability to maintain competitiveness by continual development

Internal perspective

- number of courses cancelled due to lack of demand; monitors ability to publicise available courses adequately and forecast the demand in the training market
- response time in producing management accounting information; monitors ability to maintain competitiveness by keeping management informed

Financial perspective

- return on capital employed; monitors ability to create value for the shareholders
- revenue growth; monitors ability to maintain market share

29 Responsibility accounting

Pass marks. A good exam technique with this type of question is to quickly clarify all of the main technical terms at the beginning of your answer. But don't take too long on this; you have only nine minutes at the very most to write out your complete answer.

Responsibility accounting is a system of accounting that identifies **specific areas of responsibility** or budget centres for all costs incurred by or revenues earned by an organisation. Functional budgets are budgets prepared for each department or process within an organisation. These functional budgets are then summarised to produce the overall summary or master budget for the whole organisation.

The main function of the system of responsibility accounting is **to identify clear responsibilities** for preparing and achieving budget targets. An individual manager is made responsible for each budget centre and for ensuring that their budget coordinates with all others that are affected by or affect their own activities. **The budgeting process cannot begin without such a system of defined responsibilities**. If individual responsibilities are not clarified at the outset then there may be duplication of effort, some areas may be overlooked completely and managers would not know who to consult when they require information about specific areas of the business.

A clearly defined hierarchy of budget centres is necessary in order to **consolidate and coordinate the master budget for the whole organisation**. The hierarchy can consist of a responsibility centre for each section, department or subsidiary company. For example in a large group the budget for each section would be summarised into a budget for each function. The functional budgets in turn would be summarised or consolidated into the subsidiary company's budget and the individual subsidiaries' budgets would then be summarised into an overall master budget for the group.

The hierarchy of individual budget centres should be organised to ensure that all the revenues earned by an organisation, all the costs it incurs, and all the capital it employs are made the responsibility of someone within the organisation, at an appropriate level in the hierarchy.

30 Presentation

Pass marks. The **comparison of the actual results for 4,500 units with the budget data for 5,000** units is not particularly useful for the general manager. It is **not possible to tell whether cost and revenue differences are caused by changes in activity or by changes in expenditure**. A **flexible budget presentation** would be more relevant, presented in **marginal costing format** to **highlight the more easily controlled variable costs**.

In (b), the **variances** are **calculated** using **marginal costing principles**. This means that there will be **no variance for fixed production overhead volume**. The other main difference compared with absorption costing variances is that the **sales volume variance** is **valued** at the **standard *contribution* per unit**.

Note how we have shown the **variance between actual results** and firstly **contribution in the flexed budget**, then **profit in the flexed budget** and finally the **original budget**. There is no sales volume variance against the flexed budget because the very **process of flexing** removes any difference between budgeted volume and actual volume.

(a)

	Original budget for 5,000 units £'000	Flexed budget for 4,500 units £'000	Actual result £'000	Variance against flexed budget £'000
Sales	600	540.0	550	10
less variable costs				
Direct materials	150	135.0	130	5.0
Direct labour	200	180.0	189	(9.0)
Production overh'd	50	45.0	46	(1.0)
Selling overhead	75	67.5	72	(4.5)
Total variable cost	475	427.5	437	(9.5)
Contribution	125	112.5	113	0.5
less fixed overhead:				
Production	25	25.0	29	(4.0)
Selling	50	50.0	46	4.0
Profit	50	37.5	38	0.5

(Flexed budget variable costs: $\times \frac{4,500}{5,000}$)

Note. Variances in brackets are adverse.

(b)   *Workings*

1   Standard contribution per unit:

	for 5,000 units	£ per unit
Sales price	£600,000	120
Direct materials	£150,000	30
Direct labour	£200,000	40
Variable production overhead	£50,000	10
Variable selling overhead	£75,000	15
Standard contrib'n per unit		25

2   Standard labour rate per hour = £200,000/50,000 = £4 per hour

3   Standard variable production overhead per hour = £50,000/50,000 = £1 per hour

Variances (*Note.* Variances in brackets are adverse)

			Variance against flexed budget
		£	£
(i)	**Selling price variance**		
	Margin on 4,500 units should have been	112,500	
	but was (£(550,000 – 427,500))	122,500	
			10,000
(ii)	**Direct material cost variance**		
	No further analysis than that in (a) possible		5,000
(iii)	**Direct labour rate variance**		
		£	
	47,500 hrs should cost (× £4)	190,000	
	but did cost	189,000	
			1,000
	Direct labour efficiency variance		
	4,500 units should have taken (× 10 hrs)	45,000 hrs	
	but did take	47,500 hrs	
	Variance in hours	2,500 hrs	
	× standard rate per hour	× £4	
			(10,000)
(iv)	**Variable production overhead efficiency variance**		
	2,500 hrs × standard rate per hour (× £1)		(2,500)
	Variable production overhead expenditure variance		
		£	
	47,500 hrs should cost (× £1)	47,500	
	but did cost	46,000	
			1,500
(v)	**Variable selling overhead expenditure variance**		
		£	
	4,500 units should cost (× £15)	67,500	
	but did cost	72,000	
			(4,500)
Total contribution variance			500
(vi)	**Fixed production overhead expenditure variance**		
	= budget expenditure – actual expenditure		
	= £(25,000 – 29,000)		(4,000)
(vii)	**Fixed selling overhead expenditure variance**		
	= budget expenditure – actual expenditure		
	= £(50,000 – 46,000)		4,000
Variance against flexed budget			
			500
(viii)	**Sales volume variance**	= [actual units – budget units] × std contribution/unit	
		= (4,500 – 5,000) × £25	(12,500)
Variance against original budget			(12,000)

31 Divisional performance

> **Pass marks.** What a nice question we've given you to go with this chapter. For parts (a) and (b) you simply need to regurgitate knowledge you should have picked up directly from the text, no application skills are required at all.
>
> That being said, it is vital that you do not learn the advantages and disadvantages of ROI and RI in a parrot fashion as they underlie the very core of the chapter. You **must understand how and why ROI affects managerial behaviour,** for example. You are just as likely to get a written question on this area as a calculation-based one.
>
> The calculations required in (b) should not have caused you any problems.

(a)   The **residual income (RI)** for a division is calculated by deducting from the divisional profit an imputed interest charge, based on the investment in the division.

The **return on investment (ROI)** is the divisional profit expressed as a percentage of the investment in the division.

Both methods use the **same basic figure for profit and investment**, but **residual income** produces an **absolute** measure whereas the **return on investment** is expressed as a **percentage**.

Both methods suffer from **disadvantages** in measuring the profit and the investment in a division which include the following.

(i)   Assets must be valued consistently at historical cost or at replacement cost. Neither valuation basis is ideal.

(ii)   Divisions might use different bases to value inventory and to calculate depreciation.

(iii)   Any charges made for the use of head office services or allocations of head office assets to divisions are likely to be arbitrary.

In addition, **return on investment** suffers from the following **disadvantages**.

(i)   Rigid adherence to the need to maintain ROI in the short term can discourage managers from investing in new assets, since average divisional ROI tends to fall in the early stages of a new investment. Residual income can overcome this problem by highlighting projects which return more than the cost of capital.

(ii)   It can be difficult to compare the percentage ROI results of divisions if their activities are very different: residual income can overcome this problem through the use of different interest rates for different divisions.

(b)   (i)   **Return on divisional investment (ROI)**

	Before investment	After investment
Divisional profit	£18,000	£19,600
Divisional investment	£100,000	£110,000
Divisional ROI	18.0%	17.8%

The ROI will fall in the short term if the new investment is undertaken. This is a problem which often arises with ROI, as noted in part (a) of this solution.

(ii) **Divisional residual income**

	Before investment £	After investment £
Divisional profit	18,000	19,600
Less imputed interest: £100,000 × 15%	15,000	
£110,000 × 15%		16,500
Residual income	3,000	3,100

The residual income will increase if the new investment is undertaken. The use of residual income has highlighted the fact that the new project returns more than the cost of capital (16% compared with 15%).

32 B and C

Pass marks. Part (a) requires both regurgitation of book knowledge and **application of the data provided** in the question to illustrate your answer. The examiner needs evidence that you can apply the techniques and principles you have learnt to particular scenarios.

We suggested use of **ROCE based on gross book value of assets** in part (b) as this overcomes the counterproductive behaviour caused by the current approach.

Paper for board meeting to review the company's performance appraisal and reward system

(a) *Possible counter-productive behaviour resulting from using the current ROCE calculation for performance appraisal*

Under the current method of performance appraisal, managers are judged on the basis of the ROCE that their divisions earn, the ROCE being calculated using the net book value of non-current assets. The use of ROCE as a method of appraising performance has disadvantages, whilst there are additional disadvantages of using ROCE based on the net book value of non-current assets.

(i) As managers are judged on the basis of the ROCE that their divisions earn each year, they are likely to be motivated into taking decisions which increase the division's short-term ROCE and rejecting projects which reduce the short-term ROCE even if the project is in excess of the company's target ROCE and hence is desirable from the company's point of view.

Suppose that the manager of B division was faced with a proposed project which had a projected return of 21%. He would be likely to reject the project because it would reduce his division's overall ROCE to below 24%. The investment would be desirable from Cordeline's point of view, however, because its ROCE would be in excess of the company's target ROCE of 20%. This is an example of sub-optimality and a lack of goal congruence in decision making.

(ii) A similar misguided decision would occur if the manager of C division, say, was worried about the low ROCE of his division and decided to reduce his investment by scrapping some assets not currently being used. The reduction in both depreciation charge and assets would immediately improve the ROCE. When the assets were eventually required, however, the manager would then be obliged to buy new equipment.

(iii) The current method bases the calculation of ROCE on the net book value of assets. If a division maintains the same annual profits and keeps the same asset without a policy of regular replacement of non-current assets, its ROCE will increase year by year as the assets get older. Simply by allowing its assets to depreciate a divisional manager is able to give a false impression of improving performance over time.

The level of new investment in non-current assets by C division was over three times that of B division in 20X3 and nearly 13 times that of B division in 20X4. B division is using old assets that have been depreciated to a much greater extent than those of C division and hence the basis of the ROCE calculation is much lower. Consequently it is able to report a much higher ROCE.

(iv)   The method used to calculate ROCE therefore also provides a disincentive to divisional mangers to reinvest in new or replacement assets because the division's ROCE would probably fall. From the figures provided it is obvious that C division has replaced assets on a regular basis, the difference between original and replacement costs of its assets being small. The manager of B division, on the other hand, has not replaced assets, there being a marked difference between original and replacement cost of the division's assets.

(v)   A further disadvantage of measuring ROCE as profit divided by the net book value of assets is that it is not easy to compare fairly the performance of one division with another. Two divisions might have the same amount of working capital, the same value of non-current assets at cost and the same profit. But if one division's assets have been depreciated by a much bigger amount, perhaps because they are older, that division's ROCE will be bigger.

In some respects this is the case with B and C divisions. Both the profit and the original asset cost of C division are about the same proportion of B division's profit and original asset cost but the ROCE of B division is twice that of C division.

The use of ROCE per se and ROCE calculated using the net book value of assets therefore produces a number of examples of counter-productive behaviour.

(b)   *A revised ROCE measure*

Instead of using the net book value of non-current assets to calculate ROCE, it could be calculated using the gross book value of non-current assets. This would remove the problem of ROCE increasing over time as assets get older and will enable comparisons to be made more fairly.

Using the alternative method, the ROCE for the two divisions in the two years would be as follows.

B	20X3	13.8%
	20X4	10.6%
C	20X3	11.7%
	20X4	9.7%

Although B division still has a greater ROCE, the difference between the ROCE of the two divisions is much less.

33 MPL

Pass marks. The key point to note in the scenario detail is that budgets are issued to the responsibility centre managers, implying that an **imposed system** of budgeting is in place. Make sure that you do discuss the advantages **and disadvantages** of participation as requested in the question, as all too often students focus on just the advantages, seeing a participative approach as the panacea for all organisational ills.

In part (c) you will need to distinguish between controllable and uncontrollable costs. Attributable profit is the profit after all attributable costs have been deducted. Controllable profit is profit before deduction of uncontrollable costs.

(a)

REPORT

To: Board of Directors of MPL
From: Management accountant
Date: 23 April 20X0
Subject: Budgeting

This report considers our present approach to budgeting, including the appropriateness of the format of the opening statement currently prepared.

(a)   **Present approach to budgeting**

Given that the budgets are **'issued to' budget holders**, they clearly have very **little or no input to the budget process**. Budgets are **set centrally by senior management** and are **imposed** on managers without the managers participating in their preparation.

Although there are advantages to such an approach (for example, strategic plans are likely to be incorporated into planned activities, there is little input from inexperienced or uninformed employees and the period of time taken to draw up the budgets is shorter), **dissatisfaction, defensiveness and low morale** amongst employees who must work with the budgets is often apparent. The budget may be seen as a **punitive device** and **initiative may be stifled.** More importantly, however, it is **difficult for people to be motivated to achieve targets that have been set by somebody else.**

- **Targets** that are **too difficult** will have a **demotivating** effect because **adverse efficiency variances** will always be reported.

- **Easy targets** are also **demotivating** because there is **no sense of achievement** in attaining them.

- **Targets set at the same levels as have been achieved in the past** will be too low and might **encourage budgetary slack**.

Academics have argued that each individual has a **personal 'aspiration level'** which the individual undertakes for himself to reach, and so it may be more appropriate to adopt a **participative approach** to budgeting. Budgets would be developed by the budget holders and would be based on their perceptions of what is achievable and the associated necessary resources.

Managers are more likely to be **motivated** to achieve targets that they have set themselves and overall the budgets are likely to be more **realistic** (as senior management's overview of the business is mixed with operational level details and the expectations of both senior management and the budget holders are considered).

Allowing participation in the budget-setting process is **time consuming**, however, and can produce **budget bias.** It is generally assumed that the bias will operate in one direction only, consultants building **slack** into their budgets so targets are easy to achieve. But **bias can work in two directions.** Optimistic forecasts may be made with the intention of pleasing senior management, despite the risk of displeasing them when optimistic targets are not met.

(b)   **Format of the operating statement**

The current format of the operating statement classifies costs as either fixed or variable in relation to the number of chargeable consultancy hours and compares expected costs for the budgeted number of chargeable consultancy hours with actual costs incurred.

For **control purposes**, however, there is little point in comparing costs and revenues for the budgeted numbers of chargeable hours with actual costs and revenues if budgeted and actual hours differ. Rather, the **costs that should have been incurred given the actual number of chargeable consultancy hours should be compared with the actual costs incurred.** Although fixed costs should be the same regardless of the hours charged, such a comparison requires **variable costs to be flexed** to the actual activity level. More appropriate **variances** could then be calculated and denoted as either **adverse or favourable.**

The report should also **distinguish** between those **costs** which are **controllable** by the profit centre manager and those which are **uncontrollable.** The manager's attention will then be focused on those variances for which they are responsible and which, if significant, require action.

(c) **Assumptions**

    (i) Central administration costs are not directly attributable to the profit centre and they are outside the control of the profit centre manager.

    (ii) Depreciation of equipment is an attributable cost, since it ca be specifically identified with the profit centre. However, it is not a controllable cost since the profit centre manager has no control over investment decisions.

Revised operating statement for period 5

	Original budget	Flexed budget	Actual	Variance
Chargeable consultancy hours	2,400	2,500	2,500	100
	€	€	€	€
Fees charged	180,000	187,500	200,000	12,500 (F)
Variable costs				
Casual wages	960	1,000	600	400 (F)
Telephone	2,000	2,083	2,150	67 (A)
Printing, postage and stationery	2,640	2,750	2,590	160 (F)
	5,600	5,833	5,340	493 (F)
Contribution	174,400	181.667	194,660	12,993 (F)
Controllable fixed costs				
Consultant's salaries	80,000	80,000	84,000	4,000 (A)
Motor and travel costs	4,400	4,400	4,400	-
Telephone	600	600	800	200 (A)
	85,000	65,000	89,200	4,200 (A)
Controllable profit	89,400	96,667	105,460	8,793 (F)
Attributable uncontrollable fixed cost	3,200	3,200	3,580	380 (A)
Attributable profit	86,200	93,467	101,880	8,413 (F)
Uncontrollable fixed cost	15,000	15,000	15,750	750 (A)
Division net profit	71,200	78,467	86,130	(7,663) (F)

34 TRANSFER PRICING

Pass marks. If you can answer **part (a)** successfully then there is every chance that you really understand transfer pricing. The reasoning required is not at all difficult but goes to the very **heart of the topic**. If you couldn't answer part (a) yourself, work through our answer really carefully until you understand what's going on.

The **first thing** to do in part (b)(i) is to **calculate** the **unit costs** and **selling price** of product X. We are told that overheads are apportioned to X and Y in proportion to direct wages. Since hourly rates for labour are the same for both products, the same results will be obtained by **apportioning** the **overheads** according to **labour hours**.

The **next step** is to work out **whether** or not the 2,000 kgs of product **X** should be **sold** to **K**. This depends on whether product Z earns a **positive contribution** based on an appropriate **relevant** cost.

Finally, the range of transfer prices can be established. You will need to use your **common sense** in this part of the question in terms of suggesting an appropriate level of **variable costs** that may be **saved** with **internal** transfers.

As usual we have included a **discursive** requirement. We know that it is tempting just to read our answer and tell yourself that you would be able to reproduce something similar in the exam, but it doesn't work like that. You must **practice** these requirements as conscientiously as the numerical ones.

(a)   (i)   **Division Able has spare capacity and limited external demand for product X**

In this situation, the incremental cost to the company of producing product Y is £35. It costs division Baker £38 to buy product Y from the external market and so it is cheaper by £3 per unit to buy from division Able.

The transfer price needs to be fixed at a price above £35 both to provide some incentive to division Able to supply division Baker and to provide some contribution towards fixed overheads. The transfer price must be below £38 per unit, however, to encourage division Baker to buy from division Able rather than from the external supplier.

The transfer price should therefore be set in the range above £35 and below £38 and at a level so that both divisions, acting independently and in their own interests, would choose to buy from and sell to each other.

(ii)   **Division Able is operating at full capacity with unsatisfied external demand for product X**

If division Able chooses to supply division Baker rather than the external market, the **opportunity cost** of such a decision must be incorporated into the transfer price.

For every unit of product Y produced and sold to division Baker, division Able will lose £10 (£(42-32)) in contribution due to not supplying the external market with product X. The relevant cost of supplying product Y in these circumstances is therefore £45 (£(35 + 10)). It is therefore in the interests of the company as a whole if division Baker sources product Y externally at the cheaper price of £38 per unit. Division Able can therefore continue to supply external demand at £42 per unit.

The company can ensure this happens if the transfer price of product Y is set above £38, thereby encouraging division Baker to buy externally rather than from division Able.

(b) (i) **Product X**

	£ per kg
Direct materials	18.00
Direct wages	15.00
Variable overhead ((£70,000/7,000 hours) × 1 hr)	10.00
	43.00
Fixed overhead ((£56,000/7,000 hours) × 1 hr)	8.00
	51.00
Profit mark up 60%	30.60
Selling price	81.60

If product X is used by K in manufacturing product Z, the **opportunity cost** to the company is the sales revenue forgone, £81.60 per kg.

Relevant cost per kg of Z = £81.60 + £15 adaptation + £2 variable overhead = £98.60
Contribution per kg of Z = £100 – £98.60 = £1.40 per kg

Product Z earns a positive contribution and therefore 2,000 kg of product X should be sold to K.

We can now consider the **transfer price**.

£81.60 would be the arm's length price at which a transfer could be made, and this price would make K aware of the full opportunity cost of using X to make product Z.

However, K may argue that certain variable costs may be saved with internal transfers, for instance packaging, credit control and transport costs. If these are, say, £3 per kg, then the transfer price could be reduced by £3 + 60% = £4.80, to say £(81.60 – 4.80) = £76.80.

K is also likely to be unhappy that L is taking a much larger profit mark up, 60% compared with £1.40/£17 × 100% = 8.2% mark up on K's costs.

However, it is unlikely that K can justify a substantial reduction in the transfer price, because of the opportunity costs involved.

The **suggested range of transfer prices** is therefore £76.80 to £81.60 per kg.

(ii) **Other points which should be borne in mind when making any recommendations about transfer prices in these circumstances**

(1) What are the personal goals and aspirations of the individual managers, and the consequent motivational impact of any transfer price?

(2) Are there any other uses for L's and K's facilities?

(3) What will be the short-term and long-term effect on L's sales, if 2,000 kg of product X are withdrawn from the external market?

(4) What is the likely effect of the new product on the morale of K's staff, who must be aware of the current under-utilisation of capacity?

(5) What are the long-term prospects for product Z?

(6) Can the constraint on production hours in L be removed without any significant effect on unit costs?

(7) The forecast profit margin on Product Z is fairly small. It may therefore be risky to rely on this forecast for a new product.

Pilot Paper

MANAGERIAL LEVEL

MANAGEMENT ACCOUNTING PILLAR

PAPER P1 – MANAGEMENT ACCOUNTING – PERFORMANCE MANAGEMENT

Pilot paper

This is a Pilot Paper and is intended to be an indicative guide for tutors and students of the style and type of questions that are likely to appear in future examinations. It does not seek to cover the full range of the syllabus learning outcomes for this subject.

Management Accounting Performance Evaluation will be a three hour paper with two compulsory sections (50 marks and 30 marks respectively) and one section with a choice of questions for 20 marks.

INSTRUCTIONS TO CANDIDATES

You are allowed three hours to answer this question paper.
Answer the NINETEEN objective test questions in section A   *Answer ALL PARTS of the question from section B*   *Answer ONE question only from two in Section C*

SECTION A – 50 MARKS

ANSWER ALL SUB-QUESTIONS

Questions 1.1 to 1.10 are worth 2 marks each (20 marks in total)

Questions 1.11 to 1.19 are worth 30 marks in total

Required:

On the indicative ANSWER SHEET, enter either your answer in the space provided where the sub-question requires a written response, or place a circle "O" around the letter that gives the correct answer to the sub-question where a list of distractors has been provided.

If you wish to change your mind about an answer to such a sub-question, block out your first answer completely and then circle another letter. You will not receive marks if more than one letter is circled.

Space has been provided on the four-page answer sheet for workings. If you require further space, please use the last page of your answer book and clearly indicate which question(s) these workings refer to.

You must detach the answer sheet from the question paper and attach it to the front cover of your answer book before you hand it to the invigilators at the end of the examination.

Question One

The following data are given for questions **1.1** and **1.2** below

Trafalgar Limited budgets to produce 10,000 units of product D12, each requiring 45 minutes of labour. Labour is charged at £20 per hour, and variable overheads at £15 per labour hour. During September 2003, 11,000 units were produced. 8,000 hours of labour were paid at a total cost of £168,000. Variable overheads in September amounted to £132,000.

1.1 What is the correct labour efficiency variance for September 2003?

    A   £5,000   Adverse

    B   £5,000   Favourable

    C   £5,250   Favourable

    D   £10,000   Adverse

1.2 What is the correct variable overhead expenditure variance for September 2003?

    A   £3,750   Favourable

    B   £4,125   Favourable

    C   £12,000   Adverse

    D   £12,000   Favourable

1.3 Which of the following definitions best describes "Zero-Based Budgeting"?

A A method of budgeting where an attempt is made to make the expenditure under each cost heading as close to zero as possible.

B A method of budgeting whereby all activities are re-evaluated each time a budget is formulated.

C A method of budgeting that recognises the difference between the behaviour of fixed and variable costs with respect to changes in output and the budget is designed to change appropriately with such fluctuations.

D A method of budgeting where the sum of revenues and expenditures in each budget centre must equal zero.

1.4 Copenhagen plc is an insurance company. Recently there has been concern that too many quotations have been sent to clients either late or containing errors.

The department concerned has responded that it is understaffed, and a high proportion of current staff has recently joined the firm. The performance of this department is to be carefully monitored.

Which ONE of the following non-financial performance indicators would NOT be an appropriate measure to monitor and improve the department's performance?

A Percentage of quotations found to contain errors when checked.

B Percentage of quotations not issued within company policy of three working days.

C Percentage of department's quota of staff actually employed.

D Percentage of budgeted number of quotations actually issued.

1.5 Nile Limited is preparing its sales budget for 2004. The sales manager estimates that sales will be 120,000 units if the Summer is rainy, and 80,000 units if the Summer is dry. The probability of a dry Summer is 0·4.

What is the expected value for sales volume for 2004?

A 96,000 units

B 100,000 units

C 104,000 units

D 120,000 units

1.6 MN plc uses a Just-in-Time (JIT) system and backflush accounting. It does not use a raw material stock control account. During April, 1,000 units were produced and sold. The standard cost per unit is £100: this includes materials of £45.

During April, conversion costs of £60,000 were incurred.

What was the debit balance on the cost of goods sold account for April?

A £90,000

B £95,000

C £105,000

D £110,000

1.7 Division A transfers 100,000 units of a component to Division B each year.

The market price of the component is £25 per unit.

Division A's variable cost is £15 per unit.

Division A's fixed costs are £500,000 each year.

What price per unit would be credited to Division A for each component that it transfers to Division B under marginal cost pricing and under two-part tariff pricing (where the Divisions have agreed that the fixed fee will be £200,000)?

	Marginal cost pricing	Two-part tariff pricing
A	£15	£15
B	£25	£15
C	£15	£17
D	£25	£17

1.8 Which of the following statements are true?

(i) A flexible budget can be used to control operational efficiency.

(ii) Incremental budgeting can be defined as a system of budgetary planning and control that measures the additional costs that are incurred when there are unplanned extra units of activity.

(iii) Rolling budgets review and, if necessary, revise the budget for the next quarter to ensure that budgets remain relevant for the remainder of the accounting period.

A (i) and (ii) only

B (ii) and (iii) only

C (iii) only

D (i) only

1.9 Green division is one of many divisions in Colour plc. At its year-end, the fixed assets invested in Green were £30 million, and the net current assets were £5 million. Included in this total was a new item of plant that was delivered three days before the year end. This item cost £4 million and had been paid for by Colour, which had increased the amount of long term debt owed by Green by this amount.

The profit earned in the year by Green was £6 million before the deduction of £1·4 million of interest payable to Colour.

What is the most appropriate measure of ROI for the Green division?

A 13·1%

B 14·8%

C 17·1%

D 19·4%

1.10 Division G has reported annual operating profits of £20·2 million. This was after charging £3 million for the full cost of launching a new product that is expected to last three years. Division G has a risk adjusted cost of capital of 11% and is paying interest on a substantial bank loan at 8%. The historical cost of the assets in Division G, as shown on its balance sheet, is £60 million, and the replacement cost has been estimated at £84 million.

Ignore the effects of taxation.

What would be the EVA for Division G?

A   £15·40 million

B   £15·48 million

C   £16·60 million

D   £12·96 million

(Total for sub-questions 1.1 –1.10 = 20 marks)

Required:

Each of the sub-questions numbered **1.11** to **1.19** below require a brief written response.

This response should be in note form and should not exceed 50 words.

Write your answers to these sub-questions in your answer book.

1.11 The overhead costs of RP Limited have been found to be accurately represented by the formula

$$y = £10,000 + £0·25x$$

where y is the monthly cost and x represents the activity level measured as the number of orders.

Monthly activity levels of orders may be estimated using a combined regression analysis and time series model:

$$a = 100,000 + 30b$$

where a represents the de-seasonalised monthly activity level and b represents the month number.

In month 240, the seasonal index value is 108.

Required:

Calculate the overhead cost for RP Limited for month 240 to the nearest £1,000.   **(3 marks)**

1.12 The following data have been extracted from the budget working papers of WR Limited:

Activity (machine hours)	Overhead cost £
10,000	13,468
12,000	14,162
16,000	15,549
18,000	16,242

In November 2003, the actual activity was 13,780 machine hours and the actual overhead cost incurred was £14,521.

Required:

Calculate the total overhead expenditure variance for November 2003.   **(4 marks)**

The following data are given for questions 1.13 and 1.14 below

DRP Limited has recently introduced an Activity Based Costing system. It manufactures three products, details of which are set out below:

	Product D	Product R	Product P
Budgeted annual production (units)	100,000	100,000	50,000
Batch size (units)	100	50	25
Machine set-ups per batch	3	4	6
Purchase orders per batch	2	1	1
Processing time per unit (minutes)	2	3	3

Three cost pools have been identified. Their budgeted costs for the year ending 31 December 2004 are as follows:

Machine set-up costs	£150,000
Purchasing of materials	£70,000
Processing	£80,000

1.13 Calculate the annual budgeted number of:

  (a) batches

  (b) machine set-ups

  (c) purchase orders

  (d) processing minutes

(2 marks)

1.14 Calculate the budgeted overhead unit cost for Product R for inclusion in the budget for 2004.

(4 marks)

The following data are given for questions 1.15 and 1.16 below

SW plc manufactures a product known as the TRD100 by mixing two materials. The standard material cost per unit of the TRD100 is as follows:

			£
Material X	12 litres @	£2·50	30
Material Y	18 litres @	£3·00	54

In October 2003, the actual mix used was 984 litres of X and 1,230 litres of Y. The actual output was 72 units of TRD100.

1.15 Calculate the total material mix variance for October 2003. **(3 marks)**

1.16 Calculate the total material yield variance for October 2003. **(2 marks)**

The following data are given for questions 1.17 and 1.18

A company produces three products using three different machines. No other products are made on these particular machines. The following data is available for December 2003.

Product	A	B	C
Contribution per unit	£36	£28	£18
Machine hours required per unit			
Machine 1	5	2	1.5
Machine 2	5	5.5	1.5
Machine 3	2.5	1	0.5
Estimated sales demand (units)	50	50	60

Maximum machine capacity in December will be 400 hours per machine.

Total factory cost in December 2003 is £3,200.

1.17 (a) Calculate the machine utilisation rates for each machine for December 2003. **(2 marks)**

(b) Identify which of the machines is the bottleneck machine. **(2 marks)**

1.18 (a) State the recommended procedure given by Goldratt in his "Theory of Constraints" for dealing with a bottleneck activity. **(2 marks)**

(b) Calculate the optimum allocation of the bottleneck machine hours to the three products.

(3 marks)

1.19 Explain three circumstances where the First in, First out (FIFO) valuation method of process costing will give very similar results to the Weighted Average valuation method. **(3 marks)**

(Total for sub-questions 1.11 – 1.19 = 30 marks)

(Total for Section A = 50 marks)

SECTION B – 30 MARKS

ANSWER ALL PARTS OF THIS QUESTION – ALL PARTS CARRY EQUAL MARKS

Question Two

(a)   Briefly outline the main features of "feedback control", and the "feedback loop" and explain how, in practice, the procedures of feedback control can be transformed into "feed-forward control".

(b)   Give FOUR reasons why the adoption of Total Quality Management (TQM) is particularly important within a Just-in-Time (JIT) production environment.

(c)   Briefly outline the advantages and disadvantages of allowing profit center managers to participate actively in the setting of the budget for their units.

(d)   Explain and discuss the similarities and differences between Residual Income and Economic Value Added as methods for assessing the performance of divisions.

(e)   Define the "controllability principle" and give arguments for and against its implementation in determining performance measures.

(f)   Discuss the problems that arise specifically when determining transfer prices where divisions are located in different countries.

(Total = 30 marks)

SECTION C – ANSWER ONE QUESTION ONLY

BOTH QUESTIONS CARRY 20 MARKS

Question Three

Marshall Limited operates a business that sells advanced photocopying machines and offers on-site servicing. There is a separate department that provides servicing. The standard cost for one service is shown below along with the operating statements for the Service Department for the six months to 30 September 2003. Each service is very similar and involves the replacement of two sets of materials and parts.

Marshall Limited's budgets for 5,000 services per month.
Standard cost for one service

	£
Materials – 2 sets @ £20 per set	40
Labour – 3 hours @ £11 per hour	33
Variable overheads – 3 hours @ £5 per hour	15
Fixed overheads – 3 hours @ £8 per hour	24
Total standard cost	112

Operating Statements for six months ending 30 September 2003

Months	1	2	3	4	5	6	Total
Numbers of services per month	5,000	5,200	5,400	4,800	4,700	4,500	29,600
	£	£	£	£	£	£	£
Flexible budget costs	560,000	582,400	604,800	537,600	526,400	504,000	3,315,500
Less: Variances							
Materials							
Price	5, 150F	3,090F	1,100F -	2,040A	-5,700A	-2,700A	-1,100A
Usage	-6,000A	2,000F	-4,000A	-12,000A	-2,000A	0	-22,000A
Labour							
Rate	26,100F	25,725F	27,331F	18,600F	17,400F	15,515F	130,671F
Efficiency	5,500F	9,900F	12,100F	-12,100A	-4,400A	-1,000A	0
Variable overheads:							
Spending	-3,500A	-3,500A	-2,500A	-4,500A	500F	2,500F	-11,000A
Efficiency	2,500F	4,500F	5,500F	-5,500A	-2,000A	-5,000A	0
Fixed overheads:							
Expenditure	-3,000A	-5,000A	-5,000A	-15,000A	5,000F	5,000F	-18,000A
Volume	0	4,800F	9,600F	- 4,800A	7,200A	-12,000A	-9,600A
Actual costs	533,250	540,885	560,669	574,940	524,800	511,685	3,246,229

Note: "A" = adverse variance; "F" = favourable variance

Required:

(a) Prepare a summary financial statement showing the overall performance of the Service Department for the six months to 30 September 2003. **(4 marks)**

(b) Write a report to the Operations Director of Marshall Limited commenting on the performance of the Service Department for the six months to 30 September 2003.

531

Suggest possible causes for the features you have included in your report and state the further information that would be helpful in assessing the performance of the department.   **(16 marks)**
(Total = 20 marks)

Question Four

PQR plc is a chemical processing company. The company produces a range of solvents by passing materials through a series of processes. The company uses the First In First Out (FIFO) valuation method.

In Process 2, the output from Process 1 (XP1) is blended with two other materials (P2A and P2B) to form XP2. It is expected that 10% of any new input to Process 2 (that is, transfers from Process 1 plus Process 2 materials added) will be immediately lost and that this loss will have no resale value. It is also expected that in addition to the loss, 5% of any new input will form a by-product, Z, which can be sold without additional processing for £2·00 per litre.

Data from Process 2 for November 2003 was as follows:

Opening work in process

Process 2 had 1,200 litres of opening work in process. The value and degree of completion of this was as follows:

	£	%degree of completion
XP1	1,560	100
P2A	1,540	100
P2B	750	100
Conversion costs	3,790	40
	7,640	

Input

During November, the inputs to Process 2 were:

	£
XP1 5,000 litres	15,679
P2A 1,200 litres	6,000
P2B 3,000 litres	4,500
Conversion costs	22,800

Closing work in process

At the end of November, the work in process was 1,450 litres. This was fully complete in respect of all materials, but only 30% complete for conversion costs.

Output

The output from Process 2 during November was:

Z	460 litres
XP2	7,850 litres

Required:

Prepare the Process 2 account for November 2003.   **(17 marks)**

Note: **3 marks** will be awarded for presentation.

(Total = 20 marks)

Answer sheet

Indicative answer sheet for section a – Sub question 1.1 to 1.10

On the indicative ANSWER SHEET, enter either your answer in the space provided where the sub-question requires a written response, or place a circle "O" around the letter that gives the correct answer to the sub-question where a list of distractors has been provided.

If you wish to change your mind about an answer to such a sub-question, block out your first answer completely and then circle another letter. You will not receive marks if more than one letter is circled.

Space has been provided on the four-page answer sheet for workings. If you require further space, please use the last page of your answer book and clearly indicate which question(s) these workings refer to.

You must detach the answer sheet from the question paper and attach it to the front cover of your answer book before you hand it to the invigilators at the end of the examination.

1.1	A	B	C	D
1.2	A	B	C	D
1.3	A	B	C	D
1.4	A	B	C	D
1.5	A	B	C	D
1.6	A	B	C	D
1.7	A	B	C	D
1.8	A	B	C	D
1.9	A	B	C	D
1.10	A	B	C	D

Pilot paper
Answers

Section A

1.1 B The correct labour efficiency variance is calculated as follows, comparing budgeted hours with actual hours spent for the production achieved.

((11,000units × 0.75hrs) − 8000hrs) × £20 per hr = £5000 Favourable

1.2 C The correct variable overhead variance is calculated by comparing the budgeted variable overheads per labour hour worked with the actual variable overheads incurred during the month.

(8000 hours × £15 per labour hour − £132,000) = £12,000 Adverse

1.3 B

1.4 D The percentage of budgeted number of quotations actually issued is not a relevant non-financial performance indicator in this case as the concerns relate to the **accuracy** and **timing** of the quotations sent, **not the numbers issued.**

1.5 C If the probability of a dry summer is 0.4 the probability of a wet summer is 0.6. Therefore the expected value for sales is calculated as follows:

80,000 × 0.4 + 120,000 × 0.6 = 104,000 units

1.6 C The conversion cost allocated per unit is £55. (This is the standard cost of £100 per unit minus the material cost of £45) .

For 1000 units the conversion cost allocated should be £55,000. The actual conversion cost incurred is £60,000. The total debit on the cost of goods sold account is £105,000 being the total of material costs of £ 45,000 plus £ 60,000 in conversion costs.

1.7 A Under marginal cost transfer pricing, the variable cost of £15 per unit is used.

The two part tariff transfer price system will also use the marginal cost of £15 per unit.

1.8 D

1.9 D The ROI will exclude the £4m plant not available as an earning asset during the year. By excluding it from fixed assets we would also be excluding the increase in long term debt owed to Green by a corresponding amount.

Fixed assets + net current assets = Capital + reserves + long term loans

The components of the numerator in an ROI calculation should be consistent with the components of the denominator. In this case the profit used would be gross of interest incurred as the denominator includes both capital and reserves and long term loans.

Thus ROI will be £6 million / (£35 million − £ 4 million) = 19.4%

1.10 D EVA = net operating profit after tax less capital charge. The launch costs should be spread over three years. Therefore the £3 million relating to these has to be added back to profit and £1 million relating to the current year should be deducted. The capital charge should be based on the replacement cost of the net assets multiplied by the risk adjusted cost of capital.

EVA = (£20.2 + £30 − £1.0) − (£84 million × 11%) = £12.96 million

1.11 Orders are estimated as follows, using the given formula which combines regression analysis and a time series model.

Number of orders = (100,000 + 240 × 30) × Index value
               = (100,000 + 240 × 30) × 1.08
               = £115,776

The overhead cost was represented by

y   =   £10,000 + £0.25   where **X** = number of orders = £115,775

    =   £10,000 + £0.25 × 115,775 = £39,000

1.12   The overhead cost given, includes both fixed and variable costs. Fixed and variable budgeted overhead costs can be separated using the High/Low method.

	Hours	£
High	18,000	16,242
Low	10,000	13,462
	8,000	2,774

The variable cost per machine hour can be estimated as $\dfrac{£2,774}{8,000}$ = £0.34675

The fixed cost is £10,000 being the difference between variable overheads of 10,000 × 0.34675 and fixed overheads of £13,468.

The total overhead variance for November is : Fixed overhead + Variable overhead for quality achieved – total actual overhead cost incurred.

	£
£13,468 – (10,000 × 0.34675) =	14,778
Total actual overhead cost incurred	14,521
	257F

1.13   (a)   To find the annual number of batches, the budgeted annual production in units for each product is divided up by the batch size in units.

    Budgeted number of batches

Product D (100,000/100)	=	1,000
Product R (100,000/50)	=	2,000
Product P (50,000/25)	=	2,000
		5,000

   (b)   To find the annual budgeted number of machine setups, we multiply the annual number of batches for each product in (a) above by the machine set-ups per batch.

    Budgeted machine set-ups:

Product D (1,000 × 3)	=	3,000
Product R (2,000 × 4)	=	8,000
Product P (2,000 × 6)	=	12,000
		23,000

   (c)   To find the annual budgeted number of purchase orders we multiply the number of batches from (a) above with the purchase order per batch.

    Budgeted number of purchase orders:

Product D (1,000 × 2)	=	2,000
Product R (2,000 × 1)	=	2,000
Product P(2,000 × 1)	=	2,000
		6,000

   (d)   The annual budgeted number of processing minutes is calculated by multiplying the budgeted annual production in units per product with the processing time per units in minutes.

Budgeted processing minutes:

Product D (100,000 × 2)	=	200,000	
Product R (100,000 × 3)	=	300,000	
Product P (50,000 × 3)	=	150,000	
		650,000	minutes

1.14 Budgeted cost/set-up for product R:

$$= \frac{£150,000}{23,000} = £6.52 \qquad \text{Budgeted unit cost of R: } = \frac{£6.25 \times 4}{50} = £0.52$$

$$= \frac{£70,000}{6,000} = £11.67 \qquad \text{Budgeted unit cost of R: } = \frac{£11.67 \times 4}{50} = £0.30$$

Budgeted processing cost per minute:

$$= \frac{£80,000}{650,000} = £0.12$$

Total budgeted cost of R per unit is:

		£
		£
Set-up costs	=	0·52
Purchasing costs	=	0·23
Processing costs	=	0·36
Total cost	=	0.87 per unit

1.15 Product TRD100

	Actual mix Litres	Standard mix Litres	Difference Litres	Price £	Variance £
X	984	885·6	98·4 (A)	2·50	246·0 (A)
Y	1,230	1,328·4	98·4 (F)	3·00	295·2 (F)
Total	2,214	2,214·0	nil		49·2 (F)

1.16 Expected output of product TRD100 $\dfrac{2,214}{30}$ = 7.38 units

Actual output = 72.0 units

Shortfall = 1.8 units

1.8 unit × £84/unit = £151.2(A)

An alternative would be only 73 complete units of output were expected, thus the shortfall would be 1 unit. The variance would be 1·0 x £84 per unit = £84 adverse.

1.17 (a) Machine utilisation rates

		Product		
Required machine hours	A	B	C	Total
Machine 1	1,200	400	200	1,800
Machine 2	1,800	600	300	2,700
Machine 3	600	200	100	900

Utilisation rates:

Machine 1 (440/400)	=	112%
Machine 2 (615/400)	=	169%
Machine 3 (205/400)	=	56%

(b) Machine 2 is the bottleneck machine as it has the highest utilisation of all three machines at 169%.

1.18 (a) One process will inevitably act as a bottleneck (or limiting factor) and constrain throughput. This is known as a binding constraint in TOC terminology.

In order to manage constraints effectively, Goldratt has proposed a five-step process of ongoing improvement. The process operated as a continuous loop.

- Identify

    The first step is to identify the binding constraint or bottleneck in the system, ie the activity which is limiting throughput.

- Exploit

    Within the existing constraint managers must focus on achieving higher throughput from the bottleneck resource. Until the constraint has been alleviated the immediate focus must be on explaining fully the available capacity. Output through the binding constraint should never be delayed or held up otherwise sales will be lost. To avoid this happening a buffer inventory should be built up immediately prior to the bottleneck or binding constraint. This is the only inventory that the business should hold, with the exception of possibly a very small amount of finished goods inventory and raw materials that are consistent with the JIT approach.

- Subordinate

    All operations should be subordinated to the binding constraint. Operations prior to the binding constraint should operate at the same speed as the binding constraint, otherwise work in progress (other than the buffer inventory) will be built up. According to TOC, inventory costs money in terms of storage space and interest costs and so inventory is not desirable. In a traditional production system an organisation will often pay staff a bonus to produce as many units as possible. TOC views this as inefficient since the organisation is paying extra to build up inventory which then costs money to store until it is required. Thus the rate of operation of non-constraint resources is subordinated to the rate of operation of the binding constraint.

- Elevate

    Steps should be taken to elevate the system's bottleneck, ie to increase throughput from the binding constraints, for example by purchasing more equipment or improving the efficiency of the operation.

- Return to Step 1

    Once the binding constraint has been eliminated and is no longer binding, return to Step 1 and identify the new binding constraint. The elimination of one bottleneck will always lead to another. There will always be a binding constraint, unless capacity is far greater than sales demand or all processes are totally in balance, which is unlikely even if it is a goal to be aimed for.

(b)   Optimal allocation would be on the basis of contribution from the bottle neck resource.

Product	A	B	C
Contribution per unit	£12	£10	£6
Machine 2 hours	9	3	1.5
Contribution per machine hour	£1.33	£3.33	£4.00
Ranking	3	2	1

Thus allocation on this ranking

Product C	200 units	using	300 hours
Product B	200 units	using	600 hours
			900 hours used
Product A	77* units	using	693 hours
			1,593 hours

* 700/9 77.8 units, thus 77 units

1.19 • When the conversion costs inclosing WIP at the end of the period is relatively low compared with the total conversion costs incurred during the period. In this circumstance, even if costs fluctuate dramatically from one period to the next, the costing treatment of the relatively small amount of conversion cost brought forward in opening and closing WIP would not have a significant effect on the final unit cost

• When the conversion percentage for work in progress is relatively constant between periods. In this circumstance the amount of work done on the opening and closing WIP is relatively constant each period.

• When opening and closing WIP are very small when compared to sales in the period.

Section B

Question 2

(a)

Feedback loop in the control cycle

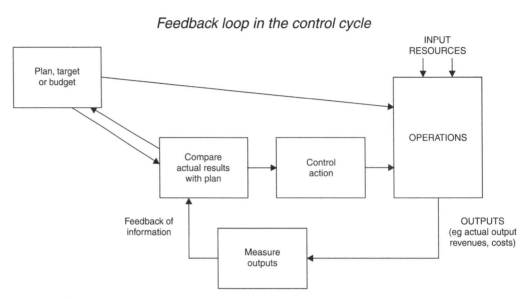

The term "feedback control " refers to the monitoring of outputs achieved against desired or target outputs, making a comparison and taking appropriate action as a result where necessary. In a budgeting context, *feedback control* is exercised by comparing an ex ante target (budget) against an ex post output (actual performance).

Through this process of comparison, any significant variations are investigated and one of two courses of action taken. Either corrective action is taken to ensure that the target is met by actual performance in future periods or the target is changed if it is is concluded that it was not realistically achievable.

The "feedback loop" refers to the feedback represented by the loop above whereby corrective action brings actual performance in line with planned results. A criticism of this approach is that it is reactive and backward looking comparing historical costs with planned results. Past events are used as a means of controlling future activity.

The "feed-forward" control has been developed to counter this argument. In feed-forward control instead of actual outputs being compared against planned results and taking whatever corrective action is necessary, planned results are compared against predictions or forecasts at any future time. The result is that control is being proactive and forward looking.

(b)   Total Quality Management (TQM) is a term used to describe a customer oriented process that places great emphasis on quality and the provision of products and services on a timely basis and of consistently high quality. TQM is particularly important in a JIT environment for the following reasons.

As JIT requires very little or no stock to be held the suppliers must be able to be totally relied upon both in terms of quality and timing to deliver the required goods. This is because under JIT there will normally be no alternative inventory to be relied on.

JIT requires very precise planning because it aims to produce the right quantity at the right time only when needed . A close working relationship with suppliers is therefore vital. TQM is important because of its emphasis on customer service and timely delivery.

The consequences of sub-standard goods and delays in delivery are amplified in a JIT environment because JIT aims to maintain the flow of materials and production with minimum stoppages and minimum storage of goods.

Where JIT is operated with a Pull (Kanban) system for stock replacement whereby products and components are only produced when needed by the next process with nothing produced in anticipation of need, deliveries to exact specification and at very short notice are essential.

(c) Advantages and disadvantages of allowing profit centre managers to participate actively in the setting of the budgets for their units.

Main advantages of participation are as follows :

- When unit costs are relatively constant from one period to the next with unit cost fluctuation minimal. In this circumstance the separate analysis of each period's costs using FIFO would produce a similar result to the weighting average method.

- Acceptance and commitment

- If profit centre managers participate in setting the targets they are more likely to accept these and show more commitment towards achieving them.

- Narrowing the knowledge and information gap

- The detailed knowledge of day to day operations that profit managers have will enable more effective and relevant targets to be set. This process of information sharing will lead to the setting of optimal targets, taking into account both organisational and operational constraints and opportunities and making variance analysis more meaningful.

- Motivation and improved performance

- Research findings confirm that participation increases job satisfaction, improves work related attitudes and leads to better performance.

Potential disadvantages of participation

- The process of participation may be more time consuming in some circumstances participation may lead to less difficult targets or the introduction of budget slack.

- Research has shown certain people to react better to an imposed budget

(d) Residual income (RI) is an alternative way of measuring the performance of an investment centre. **RI is a measure of the centre's profits after deducting a notional or imputed interest cost**.

(i) The centre's profit is after deducting depreciation on capital equipment.

(ii) The imputed cost of capital might be the organisation's cost of borrowing or its weighted average cost of capital.

Unlike return on investment (ROI) which is a percentage or relative measure, RI is an absolute measure.

EVA ® is an alternative absolute performance measure. It is similar to RI and is calculated as follows.

EVA = net operating profit after tax (NOPAT) less capital charge

where the capital charge = weighted average cost of capital × net assets

Economic value added (EVA) is a registered trade mark owned by Stern Stewart & co. It is a specific type of residual income (RI) calculated as follows.

EVA = net operating profit after tax (NOPAT) less capital charge
where the capital charge = weighted average cost of capital x net assets

You can see from the formula that the calculation of EVA is very similar to the calculation of RI.

EVA and RI are similar because both result in an absolute figure which is calculated by subtracting an imputed interest charge from the profit earned by the investment centre. However there are differences as follows.

(i)   The profit figures are calculated differently. EVA is based on an 'economic profit' which is derived by making a series of adjustments to the accounting profit.

(ii)   The notional capital charges use different bases for net assets. The replacement cost of net assets is usually used in the calculation of EVA.

The calculation of EVA is different to RI because the net assets used as the basis of the imputed interest charge are usually valued at their replacement cost and are increased by any costs that have been capitalised (see below).

There are also differences in the way that NOPAT is calculated compared with the profit figure that is used for RI, as follows.

(i)   Costs which would normally be treated as expenses, but which are considered within an EVA calculation as investments building for the future, are added back to NOPAT to derive a figure for 'economic profit'. These costs are included instead as assets in the figure for net assets employed, ie as investments for the future. Costs treated in this way include items such as goodwill, research and development expenditure and advertising costs.

(ii)   Adjustments are sometimes made to the depreciation charge, whereby accounting depreciation is added back to the profit figures, and economic depreciation is subtracted instead to arrive at NOPAT. Economic depreciation is a charge for the fall in asset value due to wear and tear or obsolescence.

(iii)   Any lease charges are excluded from NOPAT and added in as a part of capital employed.

Another point to note about the calculation of NOPAT, which is the same as the calculation of the profit figure for RI, is that interest is excluded from NOPAT because interest costs are taken into account in the capital charge.

(e)   The controllability principle refers to the degree of influence that a specific manager has over costs, revenue and related items.

The basis for the controllability principle is that managers of responsibility centres should only be held accountable for costs over which they have some influence. Under this principle, a divisional manager would not be held responsible for the allocation of central costs to his department if he has no control over the magnitude or incidence of these costs. It is argued that the benefits derived from responsibility accounting would be reduced and incorrect or sub-optimal judgements made if uncontrollables are not eliminated from the manager's responsibility centre.

Advantages of applying the controllability principle

- From a motivation point of view it can be demoralising for a manager to feel that his performance is based on something over which he has no influence.

- It is also important from a control point of view in that reports should ensure that information on costs is reported to the manager who is able to take action to control them.

Disadvantages of the controllability principle

- An alternative view argues that holding managers responsible for costs even when they have no control over them can have beneficial effects in two ways.

- It stops managers from viewing some costs as "free services" and thus discourages overuse.

- Holding managers responsible for costs outside their control may encourage them to become more involved with these costs and as result contribute to their reduction or to the more efficient provision of these services.

- It is not always clear cut which costs are controllable or uncontrollable and therefore, following very closely the controllability principle may exclude partially controllable costs from the decision making process.

(f) Transfer pricing is used when divisions of an organisation need to charge other divisions of the same organisations for goods and services they provide. The basic object of transfer pricing is the relevant divisions within an organisation are evaluated effectively ant ht e transfer price does not distort divisional performance evaluation.

The level at which a transfer price should be set, however is not a straightforward decision for organisations. The situation is even less clear cut for organisations operating in a number of countries, when even more factors need to be taken into consideration. Some of these factors and their impact on the transfer price are set out below. Moreover, the manipulation of profits through the use of transfer pricing is a common area of confrontation between multinational organisations and host country governments.

- **Exchange rate fluctuation**

  The value of a transfer of goods between profit centres in different countries could depend on fluctuations in the currency exchange rate.

- **Taxation in different countries**

  If taxation on profits is 20% of profits in Country A and 50% of profits in Country B, a company will presumably try to 'manipulate' profits (by means of raising or lowering transfer prices or by invoicing the subsidiary in the high-tax country for 'services' provided by the subsidiary in the low-tax country) so that profits are maximised for a subsidiary in Country A, by reducing profits for a subsidiary in Country B.

  Artificial attempts at reducing tax liabilities could, however, upset a country's tax officials if they discover it and may lead to some form of penalty. Many tax authorities have the power to modify transfer prices in computing tariffs or taxes on profit, although a genuine arms-length market price should be accepted.

- **Import tariffs/customs duties**

  Suppose that Country A imposes an import tariff of 20% on the value of goods imported. A multi-national company has a subsidiary in Country A which imports goods from a subsidiary in Country B. In such a situation, the company would minimise costs by keeping the transfer price to a minimum value.

- **Exchange controls**

  If a country imposes restrictions on the transfer of profits from domestic subsidiaries to foreign multinationals, the restrictions on the transfer can be overcome if head office provides some goods or services to the subsidiary and charges exorbitantly high prices, disguising the 'profits' as sales revenue, and transferring them from one country to the other. The ethics of such an approach should, of course, be questioned.

- **Anti-dumping legislation**

  Governments may take action to protect home industries by preventing companies from transferring goods cheaply into their countries. They may do this, for example, by insisting on the use of a fair market value for the transfer price.

- **Competitive pressures**

  Transfer pricing can be used to enable profit centres to match or undercut local competitors.

- **Repatriation of funds**

  By inflating transfer prices for goods sold to subsidiaries in countries where inflation is high, the subsidiaries' profits are reduced and funds repatriated, thereby saving their value.

- **Minority shareholders**

  Transfer prices can be used to reduce the amount of profit paid to minority shareholders by artificially depressing a subsidiary's profit.

Question 3

(a) Summary statement for six months to 30 September 2003

	Budget for the period	Actual budget for the period	Total variance	Price/ spending variance	Efficiency/ usage variance
	£	£	£	£	£
Production	30,000 (1)	29,600			
Costs	£	£	£	£	£
Materials	1,184,400 (2)	1,207,100 (6)	(23,100)	(1,100)	(22,000)
Labour	976,800 (3)	846,129 (7)	130,671	130,671	0
Variable overheads	444,000 (4)	455,000 (8)	(11,000)	(11,000)	0
Fixed overheads	710,400 (5)	738,000 (9)	(27,600)	(18,000)	(9,600)
Total cost	3,315,200	3,246,229	68,971	100,571	(31,600)

() = Adverse variance

The summary statements can be presented in a number of different ways.

WORKINGS

Budget

(1) The cumulative budget for the period is based in the monthly production budget of 5,000 for each of the six months.

(2) The budgeted materials cost based on actual production

∴ 29,600 × £40 = £1,184,000

(3) The budgeted labour cost based in actual production

29,600 × £33 = £976,000

(4) The budgeted variable overhead based on actual production

29,600 × £15 = £444,000

(5) The budgeted fixed overheads based on actual production

29,600 × £24 = £710,400

Actual

(6) Materials

Budgeted cost + Adverse price and usage variance

= £1,184,000 + £1,100 + £22,000 = £1,207,100

(7)   Labour

      Budgeted cost – Favourable rate and efficiency variance

      = £976,800 – £130,671 = £846,129

(8)   Variable overheads

      Budgeted cost + Adverse spending variance

      = £444,000 + £11,000 = £455,000

(9)   Fixed overhead

      Budgeted cost + Adverse volume and variance

      £710,400 + £27,600 = £738,000

(b)   Report to the operations director of Marshall Limited.

Performance of services department

Service output

The service output is slightly lower than budget by about 1.5%. Although this may not appear very significant overall, the month by month variation over the period is significant and should be investigated.

In the first month budgeted production is achieved and in the second and third budgeted production is exceeded by 4% and 8% respectively. In the last three months output is going down and this appears to be on a downward path.

This could be due to a number of factors and it should be investigated.

- Is there seasonal variation in the business?
- Is the reduction due to increased competition?
- Is the reduction due to customer dissatisfaction?
- If this is a trend can it be reversed?

Materials

Price

Materials prices are on a general upward trend during the six month period. Is this because of a materials shortage. Can the business look for alternative suppliers offering better prices?

Usage

Materials usage is not in line with budget. Given every service is very similar, using standard materials and parts we would not expect this to happen.

There is a significant adverse variance every month except in month 2 which shows a favourable variance. Month 4 in particular gives cause for concerns with an adverse variance of 12,000.

Labour

Labour rate variances are out of line with the budget giving rise to large favourable variances. The variance is more than 13% of budget and must be investigated.

- Is this because lower pay than expected had been negotiated?
- Is it because a different grade/mix of labour was required?
- Could it be that the lower than budgeted labour costs are leading to low performance and the low efficiency from month 4 onwards?

- Could this also explain the very inefficient material usage variance at its worse in month 4?

Labour efficiency

Labour efficiency although favourable in the first three months, seriously worsens in month 4 and continues to be adverse for the next period.

Month 4 is significantly out of line with other months, showing significant adverse variances in materials usage, labour efficiency and variable overhead efficiency.

- Has something happened in month 4? Has there been a labour dispute, perhaps over pay?

- Are what appear to be unusual circumstances in month 4 linked with the downward path in output?

- Total variable overhead variance reveals a worsening position after the unusual circumstances in month 4.

- Fixed overhead spending appears to be under control in months 5 and 6, showing a favourable variance. In line with the rest of the departmental costs, there appears to be a major problem in month 4 as well.

- The fixed overhead volume variance represents the difference between planned and actual production.

- Overall costs are 2% below budget. Although this appears to be a satisfactory position there is considerable variation which needs to be investigated, particularly the circumstances relating to month 4.

Answer to Question Four

(a)

Process 2 account

	Litres	£		Litres	£
Opening work in progress	1,200	7,640	Normal waste	920	nil
XP1	5,000	15,679	By-product Z	460	920
P2A	1,200	6,000	XP2	7,850	51,450
P2B	3,000	4,500			
Conversion cost		22,800			
Abnormal gain	280	1,753	Closing work in process	1,450	6,002
	10,680	58,372		10,680	58,372

WORKINGS

Equivalent Units

	Process 1 and materials added	Conversion
Output:		
Started & completed in this period	6,650	6,650
Completion of opening work in progress	Nil	720
Abnormal gain	(280)	(280)
Closing work in progress	1,450	435
	7,820	7,525
	£	£
Period values	26,179	22,800
By-product Z at resale value (Note)	(920)	
	25,259	22,800
Cost per equivalent unit	£3.25	£3.03

(b)   Valuation statement

			£
Finished output:			
Started and finished	6,650 litres ×(£3.25 + £3.03)	=	41,629
Opening work in progress			
	Cost bought forward	=	7,640
	Cost of completion 720 litres× £3.03	=	2,181
			51,450
Abnormal gain			
28 litres × (£3.23 + £3.03)		=	£1,753
Closing work in progress			
1,450 litres × £3.23		=	£4,684
(1450 × 30%) being 435 litres × £3.03		=	£1,318
			£6,002

Note

By-product Z at resale value

5% of new input of XP1, P2A and P2B

= 5% × (5,000 + 1,200 + 3,000) = 460 litres

460 litres × £2 per litre = £920

List of key terms and index

Note: **Key Terms** and their references are given in **bold**

Interpolation, 316
Interpreting variances, 251
Interrelationship of variances, 240
Investment centre, 388
Investment centre, 391
Investment centres, 386
Islands of automation (IAs), 92

Jobbing industries, 89
Joint cost, 66
Joint product valuation, 66
Joint products, 65
Joint variance, 251
Just-in-time (JIT), 97
Just-in-time production, 97
Just-in-time purchasing, 97
Just-in-time systems, 97

Kanban, 98
Key budget factor, 271
Key metrics, 286

Labour budget, 274
Labour mix variance, 217
Labour yield variance, 217
Lean approach, 95
Least squares technique, 313
Limiting budget factor, 271
Line of best fit, 313, 317
Linear regression analysis, 313
Linear relationships, 310
Logistical transactions, 142
Long-range planning, 268
Long-term planning, 268
Losses in process, 37

Machine cells, 98
Managed cost, 298
Management by exception, 158
Management reporting, 339
Managerial performance, 368
Manufacturing resource planning (MRPI), 93
Manufacturing resource planning (MRPII), 94
Marginal cost, 4
Marginal costing principles, 4
Marginal costing, 4
Mass production, 90
Master budget, 286
Material purchases budget, 277
Material requirements planning (MRPI), 93
Materials mix variance, 210

Materials yield variance, 210
McDonaldization, 165
Mix variance, 210
Model, 334
Modern business environment, 88
Motivation, 362
Moving averages, 327
Multiplicative model, 332
Mutually exclusive packages, 293

Negative correlation, 320
Negative feedback, 359
Negotiated budget, 367
Negotiated transfer prices, 427
Non value-added activities, 99
Non-conformance, 108
Non-controllable costs, 167, 356
Non-linear, 320
Non-production cost variances, 195
Non-value-added costs, 99
Normal idle time, 184
Normal loss, 38, 81

Operating statement, 200
Operating variance, 221
Operation planning, 268
Opportunity cost and transfer prices, 413
Optimal transfer price, 426
Optimised production technology (OPT), 95

Participation in the standard-setting process, 167
Participation, 364
Participative budgeting, 366
Participative/bottom-up budgeting, 366
Pay, 364
Pearsonian coefficient of correlation, 321
Percentage variance charts, 243
Perfect correlation, 319
Performance evaluation, 367
Performance standard, 161
Periodic budget, 299
Planning variance, 221
Planning variances, 221
Planning, 268
Policy cost, 298
Positive correl, 320
Positive feedback, 359
Practical capacity, 164
Prevention costs, 108
Principal budget factor, 271
Principal budget factor, 271

Review Form & Free Prize Draw – Paper P1 Management Accounting Performance Evaluation

All original review forms from the entire BPP range, completed with genuine comments, will be entered into one of two draws on 31 January 2005 and 31 July 2005. The names on the first four forms picked out on each occasion will be sent a cheque for £50.

Name: _____   Address: _____

_____

_____

How have you used this Study Text?
(Tick one box only)

☐ Home study (book only)

☐ On a course: college _____

☐ With 'correspondence' package

☐ Other _____

Why did you decide to purchase this Study Text? *(Tick one box only)*

☐ Have used BPP Texts in the past

☐ Recommendation by friend/colleague

☐ Recommendation by a lecturer at college

☐ Saw advertising

☐ Other _____

During the past six months do you recall seeing/receiving any of the following?
(Tick as many boxes as are relevant)

☐ Our advertisement in *CIMA Insider*

☐ Our advertisement in *Financial Management*

☐ Our advertisement in *Pass*

☐ Our advertisement in *PQ*

☐ Our brochure with a letter through the post

☐ Our website www.bpp.com

Which (if any) aspects of our advertising do you find useful?
(Tick as many boxes as are relevant)

☐ Prices and publication dates of new editions

☐ Information on Text content

☐ Facility to order books off-the-page

☐ None of the above

Which BPP products have you used?

Text	☑	MCQ cards	☐	i-Learn	☐
Kit	☐	CD/Tape	☐	i-Pass	☐
Passcard	☐	Big Picture Poster	☐	Virtual Campus	☐

Your ratings, comments and suggestions would be appreciated on the following areas.

	Very useful	Useful	Not useful
Introductory section (Key study steps, personal study)	☐	☐	☐
Chapter introductions	☐	☐	☐
Key terms	☐	☐	☐
Quality of explanations	☐	☐	☐
Case studies and other examples	☐	☐	☐
Questions and answers in each chapter	☐	☐	☐
Fast forwards and chapter roundups	☐	☐	☐
Quick quizzes	☐	☐	☐
Exam focus points	☐	☐	☐
Question bank	☐	☐	☐
Answer Bank	☐	☐	☐
OTQ bank	☐	☐	☐
Index	☐	☐	☐

Overall opinion of this Study Text   Excellent ☐   Good ☐   Adequate ☐   Poor ☐

Do you intend to continue using BPP products?   Yes ☐   No ☐

On the reverse of this page are noted particular areas of the text about which we would welcome your feedback. The BPP author of this edition can be e-mailed at: stelladinenis@bpp.com

Please return this form to: Nick Weller, CIMA Range Manager, BPP Professional Education, FREEPOST, London, W12 8BR

Review Form & Free Prize Draw (continued)

TELL US WHAT YOU THINK

Because the text contains new material under the new syllabus your comments are particularly welcome. Please note any comments and suggestions/errors below

Free Prize Draw Rules

1   Closing date for 31 January 2005 draw is 31 December 2004. Closing date for 31 July 2005 draw is 30 June 2005.

2   Restricted to entries with UK and Eire addresses only. BPP employees, their families and business associates are excluded.

3   No purchase necessary. Entry forms are available upon request from BPP Professional Education. No more than one entry per title, per person. Draw restricted to persons aged 16 and over.

4   Winners will be notified by post and receive their cheques not later than 6 weeks after the relevant draw date.

5   The decision of the promoter in all matters is final and binding. No correspondence will be entered into.

See overleaf for information on other
BPP products and how to order

CIMA Order

To BPP Professional Education, Aldine Place, London W12 8AW
Tel: 020 8740 2211 Fax: 020 8740 1184
email: publishing@bpp.com
Order online www.bpp.com website: www.bpp.com

Mr/Mrs/Ms (Full name) _____

Daytime delivery address _____

Postcode _____

Daytime Tel _____ Email _____

Date of exam (month/year) _____

Occasionally we may wish to email you relevant offers and information about courses and products. Please tick to opt into this service. ☐

CERTIFICATE / FOUNDATION*	6/04 Texts £24.95	1/04 Kits £10.95	1/04 Passcards £6.95	Big Picture Posters £6.95	Success CDs £14.95	Virtual Campus £50	8/04 i-Pass £24.95	10/04 i-Learn	11/04 MCQ cards
C1 Management Accounting Fundamentals (Foundation 2)	☐ £24.95	☐ £10.95	☐ £6.95	☐ £6.95	☐ £14.95	☐ £50	☐ £24.95		
C2 Financial Accounting Fundamentals (Foundation 1)	☐ £24.95	☐ £10.95	☐ £6.95	☐ £6.95	☐ £14.95	☐ £50	☐ £24.95		
C3 Business Mathematics (Foundation 3c)	☐ £24.95	☐ £10.95	☐ £6.95	☐ £6.95	☐ £14.95	☐ £50	☐ £24.95		
C4 Economics for Business (Foundation 3a)	☐ £24.95	☐ £10.95	☐ £6.95	☐ £6.95	☐ £14.95	☐ £50	☐ £24.95		
C5 Business Law (Foundation 3b)	☐ £24.95	☐ £10.95	☐ £6.95	☐ £6.95	☐ £14.95	☐ £50	☐ £24.95		

MANAGERIAL	7/04 Texts £24.95	1/05 Kits £12.95	1/05 Passcards £9.95	Big Picture Posters £6.95	Success CDs £14.95	Virtual Campus £90	9/04 i-Pass £24.95	10/04 i-Learn £34.95	11/04 MCQ cards £9.95
P1 Management Accounting - Performance Evaluation	☐ £24.95	☐ £12.95	☐ £9.95	☐ £6.95	☐ £14.95	☐ £90	☐ £24.95	☐ £34.95	☐ £9.95
P2 Management Accounting - Decision Management	☐ £24.95	☐ £12.95	☐ £9.95	☐ £6.95	☐ £14.95	☐ £90	☐ £24.95	☐ £34.95	☐ £9.95
P4 Organisational Management and Information Systems	☐ £24.95	☐ £12.95	☐ £9.95	☐ £6.95	☐ £14.95	☐ £90	☐ £24.95	☐ £34.95	☐ £9.95
P5 Integrated Management	☐ £24.95	☐ £12.95	☐ £9.95	☐ £6.95	☐ £14.95	☐ £90	☐ £24.95	☐ £34.95	☐ £9.95
P7 Financial Accounting and Tax Principles	☐ £24.95	☐ £12.95	☐ £9.95	☐ £6.95	☐ £14.95	☐ £90	☐ £24.95	☐ £34.95	☐ £9.95
P8 Financial Analysis	☐ £24.95	☐ £12.95	☐ £9.95	☐ £6.95	☐ £14.95	☐ £90	☐ £24.95	☐ £34.95	☐ £9.95

STRATEGIC	Texts £24.95	Kits £12.95	Passcards £9.95	Posters £6.95	CDs £14.95		i-Pass £24.95		
P3 Management Accounting - Risk and Control Strategy	☐ £24.95	☐ £12.95	☐ £9.95	☐ £6.95	☐ £14.95		☐ £24.95		
P6 Management Accounting - Business Strategy	☐ £24.95	☐ £12.95	☐ £9.95	☐ £6.95	☐ £14.95		☐ £24.95		
P9 Management Accounting - Financial Strategy	☐ £24.95	☐ £12.95	☐ £9.95	☐ £6.95	☐ £14.95		☐ £24.95		
P10 Test of Professional Competence in Management Accounting (TOPCIMA)	☐ £24.95		☐ £14.95 (For 5/05: available 3/05)						

Toolkit ☐ £24.95
Learning to Learn Accountancy (7/02) ☐ £9.95

Total ☐

*For material published before May 2004, Certificate assessments were known as Foundation assessments and numbered as shown. The syllabuses for these assessments are unchanged.

POSTAGE & PACKING

Study Texts and Kits

	First	Each extra	Online
UK	£5.00	£2.00	£2.00
Europe*	£6.00	£4.00	£4.00
Rest of world	£20.00	£10.00	£10.00

Passcards/Success Tapes/MCQ Cards/CDs/Posters

	First	Each extra	Online
UK	£2.00	£1.00	£1.00
Europe*	£3.00	£2.00	£2.00
Rest of world	£8.00	£8.00	£8.00

Grand Total (incl. Postage) £ ☐

I enclose a cheque for (Cheques to BPP Professional Education)
Or charge to Visa/Mastercard/Switch
Card Number
Expiry date   Start Date
Issue Number (Switch Only)
Signature

We aim to deliver to all UK addresses inside 5 working days. A signature will be required. Orders to all EU addresses should be delivered within 6 working days. All other orders to overseas addresses should be delivered